CADOGAN
guides

W9-CAS-284
Frank Kusy & Rupert Isaacson

SOUTH INDIA

Cadogan Books plc
London House, Parkgate Road,
London SW11 4NQ, UK

Distributed in North America by
The Globe Pequot Press
6 Business Park Road, PO Box 833,
Old Saybrook, Connecticut 06475–0833

Book and cover design by Animage
Cover illustrations by Jenny Robinson
Maps © Cadogan Guides, drawn by Map Creation Ltd

Series Editors: Rachel Fielding and Vicki Ingle

Editors: Vicki Ingle and Dominique Shead
Copyediting: Toby Bourne and Dominique Shead
Proofreading: Julie Shaw
Indexing: Dorothy Frame
Production: Rupert Wheeler Book Production Services

A catalogue record for this book is available from the British Library
ISBN 1–86011–070–3

Printed and bound in Finland by Werner Söderström Oy

About the Authors

Frank Kusy is a professional travel writer. The son of Polish-Hungarian immigrants, he first travelled abroad at the age of four, and has been wandering ever since. Born in England, he left Cardiff University for a career in journalism and worked for a while with the *Financial Times*. India is his first love, the only country he knows which improves on repeated viewings. He now visits for pleasure and on business, for at least three months every year.

Rupert Isaacson has travelled extensively, feature-writing on Eastern Europe, North America, Africa and now India, where he spent months gaining access to the remote regions mentioned in this book. He is the author of the Cadogan Guides to South Africa and Goa.

His mother, Polly Loxton, illustrated the guide.

Acknowledgements

Frank: There are many without whom this guide would not have been possible. Special thanks go to Maggi Nixon and Oberoi Hotels and Pleasureseekers Lkd, Steve Pettitt, Nigel Berry and Pettitts India, Surendra Singh and Pushkar Hotel, Dr S. Dandapani and the Government of India Tourist Office. I would also like to thank the many travellers, hoteliers, restaurateurs, tourist officers and local Indian people who have contributed information, experiences and anecdotes over the years. A final mention goes to my parents, for putting up with blaring Indian music and a humming word processor for over three years.

Rupert: First of all, thanks to Ranjan Abraham and Varkey Kurian for putting up with me, for their endless patience in securing the permission to enter the tribal areas and for proving such excellent trekking companions. Thanks also to Roma Satara for fixing my first itinerary, for looking after me long-distance in bad old Bombay and for sorting out my endless money hassles.

To Keith at Jungle Hut—thanks for showing me the trekking route up into the Nilgiris; to Mr and Mrs Kothavala at Bamboo Banks—many thanks for the Christmas dinner and good conversation; to Mahesh at Monarch Safari Camp—thank you, thank you for letting me ride your superb horses; to Yvonne and Ken Neale, thank you for the lift from Jungle Trails and for the tea that hot afternoon during Holi. And to Sini at Ooty—without you I would never have stayed with the Todas.

Dr Javarlial Rodrigues—thanks for mending me in Goa, despite my stupidity in falling off the ravine, and also to the Mallya Hospital in Bangalore for dealing with my subsequent complications at such short notice.

On the home front, thanks to Vicki for commissioning me and for all her hard work, to Justine for her superhuman ability to pull me out of the poo despite intervening oceans and time zones. To Dom and Toby thanks for pulling the book into order, to Polly, my mum, once again your pictures surpass any expectations I may have had. Vikram—I must owe you about 5000 pints, not to mention the Loony Tunes and incisive history comments. And Rachel—as always full of wisdom, sympathy and support.

Lastly Kristin, thank God you said 'yes' to Bangalore.

Contents

Contents　　v

There is a period on Indian buses that I call the hell-wait. To secure a seat, you have to get on half an hour before the bus is due to leave, and for that time, with the temperatures hitting 40°C, you must grit it out, the sweat running inside your shirt and from your hair into your eyes. Children selling fruit climb onto the bus and thrust their wares at you. Beggars proffer their sores and stumps, but you cannot speak or even think beyond the next breath. Your

Introduction

every nerve is focused on the moment when the driver will climb into his metal cage at the front and kick the old engine into life; then, with a great grinding of gears, the bus will move and the breeze will come through the open window. You can live again.

The bus lumbers through the crowds: auto-rickshaws and pony carts swing dangerously close, and the driver seems not to notice them, nor the sluggish cows in the road, nor the furiously pedalling bicycle with three passengers precariously balanced on the cross-bar. Yet neither does he hit them. And suddenly, you are out of the sweating, heaving town. Away on either side of the banyan-shaded road stretch the green paddies. Bullock carts, piled high with rushes to be used as thatch, roll ponderously along the middle of the road. The driver leans on his horn for a full thirteen seconds, bearing down on them without braking or swerving, but somehow manages to miss them, and the next cart, and the tiny old man with the bow legs and coquettishly short *lunghi* who carries an impossibly large cloth-wrapped bundle on his head. The man sitting next to you, hair neatly oiled and moustache clipped 'military style', distracts you from the green parakeets flying past the window to ask, 'Your native place?'

In the high Nilgiris, we trekked over sunbaked pastures where buffalo share the grazing with herds of wild ibex. We had arranged to stay with the Toda tribe, animist buffalo herders whose women still practise quiet polyandry, despite the state laws forbidding the practice. Staying in their curved longhouse that night, the women traded songs with us, singing in a high nasal chant unlike anything else we had heard in India. We asked our interpreter to translate. 'Oh', he said vaguely, nearly asleep in his bedroll at the far end of the smoky hut. 'It is very complicated; their uncle who was a buffalo priest died last year at the festival in Pykara and they are remembering the prayers he used to sing. But the women are asking you a question. They want to know what is your idea of God?'

In the dry forest below the Toda country we had heard that wild elephants were common. The lodge owner had built a *machan*, or viewing platform, into a giant mango tree by a waterhole. 'But be careful you don't run into any elephants,' he said. 'Last year a Canadian tourist got killed, the year before that it was a German.' As we came out of the scrub by the waterhole, there he was, huge and grey, with short tusks and a small, beady eye looking right at us. With the river bank between him and us we turned and ran back to the verandah. Later that night, under the moon, the elephants came into the clearing. We watched them from our bedroom window, massive but silent as ghosts, tearing idly at the bamboo stands that fringed the clearing.

At Gokarn the mountains tumble into the Arabian Sea. It is sunset and a lone girl is silhouetted against the waves. On the backwaters of Kerala, wheeling above your slow-moving boat, are white-headed brahmini kites. Villages appear amid the coconut palms and the water is cloaked with blue-flowering water hyacinths. You know that if time stopped here you would be content. Crowds of ragged children pestered you mercilessly at the gate, but once inside the silent ruins of the Golconda fortress near Hyderabad the sense of fallen grandeur over-whelms you. Looking up above the ruined fountain court, an owl, out in broad daylight, stares back at you from the shattered filigree work of the limestone wall. In the seething, stinking town of Madurai you were kept awake by the squeals and thumps from next door's room—your lodge doubles as a brothel. In the great Menakshi temple, you start at the nightmarish wail and boom of the weird instruments resounding down of the gloomy corridor. Out of the incense smoke shuffles a caparisoned elephant, a near-hysterical crowd of pilgrims dancing around him. Someone is pulling your arm. 'My brother, he has a shop outside. Very good view of the temple. Very good prices. No obligation, only for looking.' In the hellishly hot medieval lanes of Bijapur a man, stripped to his waist, rolls pink twists of molten enamel over a fire to make bangles. Next to him, crouched on the floor, another man is inlaying them with silver.

These are just glimpses. In India, the calmer you are, the smoother things will go. So when you find yourself waiting in the heat for the bus to move, chafing, sweating and wondering why you came, think on this south Indian prayer:

> *Peace be in the higher worlds:*
> *Peace be in the firmament:*
> *Peace be on earth.*
> *May the waters flow peacefully;*
> *May the herbs and shrubs grow;*
> *May all the divine powers bring us peace.*
> *Brahman, the supreme, is peace.*
> *May all be in peace, in peace and only peace*
> *And may that peace*
> *Come to me.*
> *OM*
> *Peace Peace Peace.*

Travel

By Air

Try to book your flight to India three months or so before departure, so that you can take advantage of any cheap flights and get a firm reservation with the airline of your choice.

The price of air tickets to India varies according to three major factors: whether you pay a full fare or a discount fare; when you go and how long you're planning to stay. If you contact an airline direct they will usually give you full fare prices, which tend to be much the same no matter what the airline. Standard fares are cheapest when you book an *excursion fare*, which requires that you to stay in India for a minimum of 2 weeks and no more than 3–4 months.

Ticket prices for excursion fares vary according to whether it is high season (July–August and December–January) or low season (anytime outside the above dates). The exact dates for high and low season vary according to the air carrier. If you want to stay in India for longer than a few months, you can get what is known as a *one-year open-ended return*, which allows you to stay in India up to one year and be flexible about what date you want to return (fares usually do not vary according to season). These tickets can be surprisingly cheap, if you ring around the 'bucket shops' or discount airline specialists.

Discounted fares of up to 50% are often available from bucket shops. Major airlines sell these travel agencies a certain number of tickets at greatly reduced rates, so it is always worthwhile taking your time and finding the best deal (*see* below). Discounted fares often have restrictions on cancelling or changing your ticket, so make sure you know all the relevant details before you commit yourself.

From the UK

standard carriers

The standard round-trip excursion fare from London (low season, economy class, 4-month stay) is £700 to Bombay and £778 to Madras. In high season the fares go up to £770 for Bombay and £856 for Madras. A one-year open-ended return costs £995 to Bombay and £1190 to Madras. Airlines providing good, regular and reliable services from the UK to India include **Air India, British Airways, Air France, Cathay Pacific, Emirates, Gulf Air, KLM, JAL, Lufthansa, Thai International, Alitalia, Swissair**, and **Singapore Airlines**. Students under 26 should enquire about the generous student discounts offered by some of these airlines, notably Thai International and Singapore Airlines.

discount air travel

Shopping around for discount fares can save you a lot of money. Many cheap bargains are advertised in magazines like *Time Out, LAM, TNT* and *Australasian Express*, and there are many cut-price travel agencies around Earl's Court, London. For example, a discounted 4-month excursion fare on Lufthansa from London to Bombay costs £385 in low season and £462 in high season, and £407 in low season, £473 in high season to Madras. Gulf Air usually offers very cheap fares to India (you cannot buy directly from Gulf Air but must go through a travel agent). Their tickets are valid for one year and cost £468 in low season and £590 in high season to Bombay and £489 in low season, £704 in high season to Madras. Contact the following travel agencies for good deals on flights:

Flamingo Travel, 24 Wardour St, London WC1, ✆ (0171) 287 0402
Flightbookers, 118 Tottenham Court Rd, London WC1, ✆ (0171) 757 2000
GSA Hindustan Travel, 30 Poland St, London WC1, ✆ (0171) 439 9801
STA Travel, 117 Euston Rd, London NW1, ✆ (0171) 937 9962
Trailfinders, 42–50 Earls Court Rd, London W8, ✆ (0171) 938 3366

From Mainland Europe

From **France**: full fare from Paris to Bombay on Air France (3-month maximum stay, no high or low season) is FFr10,595. A one-year ticket is FFr16,000. Air France will also directly sell you a non-refundable reduced fare ticket, costing FFr8270 (3-month maximum stay, no high or low season).

From **Germany**: full fare from Frankfurt to Bombay on Lufthansa (3-month maximum stay) costs DM1572 in low season, DM1722 in high season and DM4773 for a one-year ticket. Frankfurt to Madras is DM1772 in low season, DM1922 in high season and DM5368 for a one-year ticket.

From **Holland**: full fare from Amsterdam to Bombay on KLM (economy class, 2-month maximum stay) is DFL2175 for low season, and DFL2440 for high season. One-year tickets cost DFL5752.

Call your local travel agent to find out about discounted fares.

From North America

From the **USA**: full fare from New York to Bombay on Air India (4-month maximum stay) costs US$1433 in low season, US$1601 in high season, and US$2722 for a one-year ticket. New York to Madras is US$1540 in low season, US$1712 in high season, and US$2882 for a one-year ticket.

For discounted tickets, try calling STA Travel in New York, ✆ (212) 477 7348, or San Francisco, ✆ (415) 391 8407, or look in the Sunday travel section of your nearest big city newspaper. To save money and to get the best flight availability, many American travellers fly into New York on cheap internal flights from various other parts of the country. Those flying from the west coast may also save money by flying west via Bangkok, as certain airlines— Singapore, United, Korean and Northwest Orient—offer discounted rates in this direction.

While discounts can be found in the US if you're prepared to shop around, it is sometimes easier to get decent fare concessions in the UK. Many American visitors travel to India by booking a flight to London, where cheap flight deals are readily available, then making another booking from London to India (call the travel agencies listed in the UK section to pre-book the connecting flight from the UK to India).

From Australia and New Zealand

From **Australia**: full fare from Sydney to Bombay on Cathay Pacific (3-month maximum stay) costs A$1868 in low season, A$2322 in high season and A$4956 for a one-year ticket.

From **New Zealand**: full fare from Auckland to Bombay on Cathay Pacific (3 month maximum stay) costs NZ$2150 in low season, NZ$2350 in high season and NZ$5596 for a one-year ticket. Note that this flight requires an overnight stay in Hong Kong.

Many Australian and New Zealand travellers save money by getting cheap tickets to Singapore or Bangkok and flying on to India from there. **Jetset**, 99 Walker Street, North Sydney, N.S.W., ✆ (02) 956 9333, offers attractive flight discounts, or try the **STA Travel** chain in both Australia and New Zealand. Possibly the cheapest Australia/New Zealand–India option of all is a flight hop to Bali, followed by an overland trek up through Southeast Asia.

Returning from India

Instead of buying a round-trip ticket to India, you may choose to buy a one-way ticket and book your departing flight once there. This option will be attractive to those who want to continue travelling after visiting India but don't know where their next stop will be. Full one-way fares originating from India are even more expensive than full fares originating from abroad, so buying a discount ticket through a travel agent is your best option. It will be much easier to find an inexpensive fare leaving from Bombay than Madras, though travel agents in Bangalore, Madras, or Trivandrum can certainly book your tickets for you. Be persistent in tracking down cheap tickets. Some travel agents will tell you that no reduced fares exist and that you must pay the full published fares. Don't believe it. Discount fares from Bombay to major cities in Europe cost from Rs10,000 to 15,000, and Bombay to the US from Rs15,000 to 20,000. Carriers like Kuwait Airways or TAROM (Romanian Airlines) offer good deals, and are worth investigating.

Note: if you intend to stay in India for more than 180 days, you are supposed to obtain an income tax clearance certificate (*see* p.32) Most airlines mark their discounted tickets 'subject to income tax clearance', though in actuality airport officials very rarely ask anyone to produce this certificate.

By Sea and Overland

Sea travel is an expensive (often around £40–50 per day) but interesting way to travel if you have the time and if you fancy visiting foreign ports along the way.

From the UK and Mainland Europe

by sea

You can pick up a cargo ship from Felixstowe, Antwerp, Rotterdam, Hamburg or Le Havre and reach Bombay in about 25 days, with stops at various ports en route. Agents include: **N.S.B Frachtstchiff-Touristik**, Violenst. 22 D–28195, Bremen, Germany, ✆ (0421) 32 16 68, ✆ (0421) 32 40 89; **Strand Cruise and Travel Centre**, Charing Cross Shopping Concourse, The Strand, London WC2N 4HZ, UK, ✆ (0171) 836 6363, ✆ (0171) 497 0078.

by overland truck

Both **Encounter Overland**, 267 Old Brompton Road, London SW5 9JA, ✆ (0171) 370 6951, ✆ (0171) 244 9737, and **Dragoman**, 63 Camp Green, Debenham, Stowmarket, IP14 6LA, ✆ (01728) 861 133 or ✆ (0171) 370 1930, ✆ (01728) 861127, offer overland trips from London to India.

From North America

by sea

Try the **Cruise and Freighter Travel Association**, Dept V5, P.O. Box 218, Flushing, NY 11358, USA, ✆ (800) 872 8584; **Anytime Anywhere Travel** 91 North Bedford Road,

Chappaqua, NY 10514, USA, ✆ (914) 238 8800; **CDP Travel** 5 Third Street, Suite 820, San Francisco, California 94103, USA, ✆ (415) 882 4490; **Pearl's Travel Tips** 9903 Oaks Lane, Seminole, Florida 34642, USA, ✆ (813) 393 2919, ✉ 392 2580; or **The Cruise People** 1252 Lawrence Avenue East no.202, Don Milss, Ontario, Canada, M3A 1C3, ✆ (416) 444 2410, ✉ 447 2628.

Entry Formalities

Passports and Visas

All foreign visitors to India must obtain a **visa** in advance from the Indian embassy or consulate of their home country. Make sure you have a full, up-to-date passport. Visa fees and requirements change frequently, so use the following information as a general guide only and check with your nearest Indian tourist office or consulate for exact information.

The **standard tourist visa** is valid for either 90 or 180 days, and entitles the holder to multiple entries into India within that period. Visas can be applied for from any Indian consular office or High Commission. In the UK, a multiple entry visa costs £13.00 for 90 days, or £26.00 for 180 days (prices vary in other nations). Once in India, visa extensions can be obtained from various Foreigners' Registration Offices. Special long-term visas are available for business, education, the study of yoga, dance, traditional medicine, or other specific projects. Applications for these visas must be submitted well in advance.

Apply for visas in the **UK** to the High Commission of India, Consular Dept., India House, Aldwych, London WC2B 4NA, ✆ (0171) 836 8484/0990, 9.30am to 5.30pm. Application forms are available from the Commission office, and also from the Government of India Tourist Office, 7 Cork Street, London W1, ✆ (0171) 437 3677, ✉ (0171) 494 1048. You can apply either by post, which can take up to four weeks to process (send passport, three passport photos and postal order to 'High Commission of India'); or in person, which takes just 24 hours. Arrive with your passport, three passport-size photos and an application form at the High Commission building, 9am latest, to avoid the queues. It's open 9.30am to 1.00pm weekdays, and you'll have to return the next working day to collect your passport and visa between 4.30 and 5.30pm.

Trailfinders, Thomas Cook and American Express have quick, efficient visa services for travellers, and for a small charge will do all the waiting and queuing for you.

Travellers from other nations should apply to the Indian embassy, consulate or high commission nearest them.

Australia: 3–5 Moonah Place, Yarralumla, ACT 2600, ✆ 062 733 999

Canada: 10 Springfield Road, Ottawa, K1M 1C9, ✆ 613 744 3751

France: 15 Rue Alfred Dehodencq, 75016 Paris, ✆ 1 40 50 70 70

Germany: Adenaverallee 262, 5300 Bonn, ✆ 228 540 50

Ireland: 6 Lesson Park, Dublin 6, ✆ 1 4970843

New Zealand: 180 Molesworth St, Princess Towers, Wellington, ✆ 4 73 6390

UK: India House, Aldwych, London WC2B 4NA, ✆ 0171 836 8484; 82 New Street, Birmingham B2 4BA, ✆ 0121 212 2782

USA: 2107 Massachusetts Avenue NW, Washington, DC 20008, ✆ 202 939 7000; 3 East 64th Street, New York, NY 10021, ✆ 212 879 7888; 540 Arguello Boulevard, San Francisco, CA 94118, ✆ 415 668 0662

If you want to **extend your visa**, the Foreigners' Regional Registration Offices are based in **Bombay**: Annexe 2, Police Headquarters, Near Crawford Market, 400 001, ✆ 261 1169 and **Madras**: 9 Village Road, Nungambakkam, 600 034, ✆ 47 7036. Elsewhere the Superintendents of Police in all District Headquarters also function as Foreigners' Registration Officers.

customs formalities and regulations

Visitors are required to make an oral baggage declaration upon arrival, and should also fill in the Disembarkation Card given to them by the airlines during the course of their flight to India. Personal effects such as jewellery, cameras or cassette players are allowed duty free into the country. Up to 200 cigarettes and 1 litre of alcohol are also allowed duty free. It is prohibited to bring weapons, live plants and gold or silver bullion into the country.

Upon leaving India, an Embarkation Card should be filled out. There are restrictions on the export of antiquities and art objects more than 100 years old and it is forbidden to take articles made from indigenous wild animals, such as skins, ivory, or rhino horns, out of the country.

foreign travel tax

All visitors are required to pay a Foreign Travel Tax of Rs300 upon departure (Rs150 if travelling on to Afghanistan, Bangladesh, Bhutan, Burma, Nepal, Pakistan, Sri Lanka, the Andamans, Lakshadweeps or the Maldives). If flying, you pay the tax at a special desk located in all international airports, which usually accepts foreign currency if you've spent all your rupees. If travelling to islands offshore, your travel agent will levy the tax in his or her tariff.

Main Agents and Special-interest Holidays

With so many different cultures, languages and customs, the variety of things to do and see in India is endless. For general tours or private itineraries look under the main agents section below. If you are after something more specific, go straight to the special-interest holidays section further down. However, for special-interest holidays it can be better to book direct with a good Indian agent. By far the best in the south for **trekking, riding, wildlife viewing** or **cultural activities** is **Clipper Holidays**, Suite 406, Regency Enclave, 4 Magrath Road, Bangalore 560 025, ✆/✉ (080) 5599032/34/5599833, tlx 0845-3095. Travellers wanting to hook up with special interest activities in the north should contact **Distant Frontiers**, B2/1, Safdarjung Enclave, New Delhi 110029, ✆ (011) 685 8857, ✉ 687 5553.

Main Agents and Operators

These offer general south India travel itineraries only. The companies in the first paragraphs of the UK and US sections are expensive, the ones in the second paragraphs moderate.

in the UK

Abercrombie and Kent, Sloane Square House, Holbein Place, London SW1 8NS, ✆ (0171) 730 9600, ✉ (0171) 730 9376. A&K offer expensive set tours or private itineraries, as well as specialist sporting holidays (*see* below). **Cox and Kings**, St James' Court, Buckingham Gate, London SW1E 6AF, ✆ (0171) 873 5000, ✉ (0171) 873 5008. **Global Link Ltd**, Colette House, 52–55 Piccadilly, London W1V 9AA, ✆ (0171) 409 7766, ✉ (0171) 409 0545.

Petitts India, 14 Lonsdale Gardens, Tunbridge Wells, Kent, TN1 1NV, ✆ (01892) 515966, 🖷 (01892) 515951.

Bales Tours, Bale House, Junction Road, Dorking, Surrey, RH4 3EJ, ✆ (01306) 885 991, 🖷 (01306) 740 048. **Cape Travel Agency**, 28 High Street, Teddington, Middlesex, TW11 8EW, ✆ (0181) 943 4067, 🖷 (0181) 943 4086. **Elite Vacations Ltd**, Elite House, 98–100 Besborough Road, Harrow, Middlesex, HA1 3DT, ✆ (0181) 864 4431, 🖷 (0181) 426 9178. **Inspirations Holidays**, Victoria House, Victoria Road, Horley, Surrey, RH6 7AD, ✆ (01293) 822244, 🖷 (01293) 821732. **Jasmine Tours Ltd**, High Street, Cookham, Maidenhead, Berks, SL6 6SQ, ✆ (016285) 31121, 🖷 (016285) 29444. **Manos Holidays** (Kerala only), 168–172 Old Street, London EC1V 9BP, ✆ (0171) 216 8000, 🖷 (0171) 216 8099. **Mysteries of India** (beach holidays only), 92 The Green, Southall, Middlesex, UB2 4BG, ✆ (0181) 574 2727, 🖷 571 (0181) 0707. **NADFAS Tours**, Hermes House, 80–98 Beckenham Road, Beckenham, Kent, BR3 4RH, ✆ (0181) 658 2308, 🖷 (0181) 658 4478. **Puma Menon Tours**, 564 Kingsbury Road, London NW9 9HJ, ✆ (0181) 204 9905, 🖷 (0181) 206 0818. **Somak Holidays**, Somak House, Wembley Hill Road, Wembley, Middlesex, HA9 8BU, ✆ (0181) 903 8166, 🖷 (0181) 903 9464. **Ultimate Holidays Ltd**, Twyford Business Centre, London Road, Bishop's Stortford, Herts, CM23 3YT, ✆ (01279) 508034, 🖷 (01279) 655603.

in the USA

Abercrombie & Kent, 1520 Kensington Road, Oak Brook, IL 60521–2141, ✆ (708) 954 2944, 🖷 (708) 954 3324. **Cox & Kings**, 511 Lexington Avenue, New York, NY 10017, ✆ (212) 9353935, 🖷 (212) 751 4091. **Sita World Travel Inc.**, G.M. Plaza, 767 Fifth Avenue, New York, NY 10153, ✆ (212) 759 8979, 🖷 (212) 759 0814. **Lotus Travel**, 475 Fifth Avenue, No.1112, New York, NY 10017, ✆ (800) 998 6116.

South India Travel Agency Ltd, 352 Seventh Avenue, New York, NY 10001, ✆ (212) 631 7520, 🖷 (212) 265 3770. **Rama Tours**, 8 South Michigan Avenue, No.20003, Chicago, IL60603, ✆ (312) 853 3330, 🖷 (312) 853 0225. **World Wide Travel**, 1815 H. Street NW, Suite 10001, Washington DC 20006, ✆ (202) 659 6430, 🖷 (202) 659 1111. **Absolute Asia**, 155 W. 68th Street, Suite 525, New York, NY 10023, ✆ (800) 736 8187. **Asia Pacific Travel Ltd**, P.O. Box 350, Kenilworth, IL 60043, ✆ (800) 262 6420. **India Tours**, 230 N. Michigan Avenue, Chicago, IL 60601, ✆ (312) 726 6091, 🖷 (312) 726 6121. **Geeta Tours and Travels**, 1245 W. Jarvis Avenue, Chicago, IL 60626, ✆ (312) 262 4978, 🖷 (312) 262 4978.

Specialist Operators in the UK

sporting holidays

Wildlife viewing: David Sayers Travel, 10 Barley Mow Passage, London W4 4PH, ✆ (0181) 995 3642; **Discover India Tours**, 29 Fairview Crescent, Rayners Lane, Harrow, Middlesex, HA2 9UB, ✆ (0181) 429 3300, 🖷 (0181) 248 4249; **Explorasia Ltd**, 13 Chapter Street, London SW1P 4NY, ✆ (0171) 630 7102, 🖷 (0171) 630 0355; **Peregrine Holidays Ltd**, 41 South Parade, Summertown, Oxford, OX2 7JP, ✆ (01865) 511 642, 🖷 (01865) 512 583; **The Imaginative Traveller**, 14 Barley Mow Passage, Chiswick, London W4 4PH, ✆ (0181) 742 3113, 🖷 (0181) 743 3045, **Twickers World**, 22 Church Street, Twickenham, Middlesex, TW1 3NW, ✆ (0181) 892 7606, 🖷 (0181) 892 8061.

Trekking: Capricorn Adventure, Pen-y-Crueddyn Apple Farm, Glanwydden, nr. Llandudno, Gwynedd, North Wales, LL31 9JL, ✆ (01492) 549733; **Discover India Tours**, 29 Fairview Crescent, Rayners Lane, Harrow, Middlesex, HA2 9UB, ✆ (0181) 429 3300, 📧 (0181) 248 4249; High Places, **The Globeworks**, Penistone Road, Sheffield, S6 3AE, ✆ (0114) 275 3870; **India Link**, Weaners Cottage, Westgate, Lapford, Crediton, Devon, EX17 6QF, ✆ (01363) 83487; **Maxwell Scott Agency**, Foss House, Sutton Road, Strensall, York, Y03 5TU, ✆ (01347) 878 566, 📧 (01347) 878 493; **The Imaginative Traveller**, 14 Barley Mow Passage, Chiswick, London W4 4PH, ✆ (0181) 742 3113, 📧 (0181) 743 3045; **Exodus**, 9 Weir Road, London SW12 OLT, ✆ (0181) 675 5550; **Trans Indus Travel Ltd**, Northumberland House, 11 The Pavement, Popes Lane, London W5 4NG, ✆ (0181) 566 2729, 📧 (0181) 840 5327.

Riding: Indian Encounters, Creech Barrow, East Creech, Dorset BH20 5AP, ✆/📧 (01929) 480 548; **Abercrombie and Kent**, Sloane Square House, Holbein Place, London SW1 8NS, ✆ (0171) 730 9600, 📧 (0171) 730 9376.

Railways: Butterfield's Indian Railway Tours, Burton Flemming, Driffield, East Yorkshire, Y025 OPQ, ✆ (01262) 470 230.

Cycling: World Expeditions, 7 North Road, Maidenhead, Berkshire, SL6 1PE, ✆ (01628) 74174, 📧 (01628) 74312.

Fishing: Maxwell Scott Agency, Foss House, Sutton Road, Strensall, York, Y03 5TU, ✆ (01347) 878 566, 📧 (01347) 878 493; **Abercrombie and Kent**, Sloane Square House, Holbein Place, London SW1 8NS, ✆ (0171) 730 9600, 📧 (0171) 730 9376.

Botanical tours: Coromandel, Andrew Brock Travel, 54 High Street East, Uppingham, Rutland, Leicestershire, LE15 9PZ, ✆ (01572) 821 330, 📧 (01572) 821 072, offer tailor-made botanical tours anywhere in India.

cultural holidays

Temple tours: Discover India Tours, 29 Fairview Crescent, Rayners Lane, Harrow, Middlesex, HA2 9UB, ✆ (0181) 429 3300, 📧 (0181) 248 4249; **Maxwell Scott Agency**, Foss House, Sutton Road, Strensall, York, Y03 5TU, ✆ (01347) 878 566, 📧 (01347) 878 493.

Historic towns: Swan Hellenic, 77 New Oxford Street, London WC1A 1PP, ✆ (0171) 831 1515, 📧 (0171) 831 1280.

Battlefields: Holt's Battlefield Tours, 15 Market Street, Sandwich, Kent, CT13 9DA, ✆ (01304) 612 248, 📧 (01304) 614 930.

Craft and painting: Indian Encounters, Creech Barrow, East Creech, Dorset BH20 5AP, ✆/📧 (01929) 480 548.

Festivals and dance: Maxwell Scott Agency, Foss House, Sutton Road, Strensall, York Y03 5TU, ✆ (01347) 878 566, 📧 (01347) 878 493

Specialist Operators in the USA

sporting holidays

Wildlife viewing: American Museum of Natural History Museum Discovery Tours, Central Park West, 79th Street, New York, NY 10024, ✆ (800) 462 8687; **Abercrombie and Kent**, 1520 Kensington Road, Oak Brook, Illinois 60521–2141, ✆ (708) 954 2944,

✈ (708) 954 3324; **Big Five Tours and Expeditions**, 110 Route 110, Suite 200, Huntington, NY 11746, ✆ (800) 445 7002; **Micato Safaris**, 11th Floor, 15 West 26th Street, New York, NY 10010, ✆ (212) 545 7111, ✈ (212) 545 8297; **Photo Adventure Tours**, 2035 Park Avenue, Atlantic Beach, NY 11509–1236, ✆ (516) 371 0067, ✈ (516) 371 1352.

Riding: Abercrombie and Kent, 1520 Kensington Road, Oak Brook, Illinois 60521–2141, ✆ (708) 954 2944, ✈ (708) 954 3324.

Bird-watching: Wonderbird Tours, P.O. Box 2015, New York, NY 14851, ✆ (800) BIRDTUR.

Fishing: Abercrombie and Kent, 1520 Kensington Road, Oak Brook, Illinois 60521–2141, ✆ (708) 954 2944, ✈ (708) 954 3324.

cultural holidays

Temple towns and historic towns: Abercrombie and Kent, 1520 Kensington Road, Oak Brook, Illinois 60521–2141, ✆ (708) 954 2944, ✈ (708) 954 3324; **Distant Horizons**, 619 Tremont Street, Boston, MA 02118, ✆ (800) 333 1240.

Craft, festivals and dance: Craft World Tours, 6776 Warboys Road, Byron, NY 14422, ✆ (716) 574 2667.

Getting Around

Unless you are flying, and thus missing all the scenery between your destinations, travel in India is slow. For overland travel, whether by bus or train, you should reckon on an average of 20–25 miles per hour in flat country and 12–18 miles per hour in mountains. Even the trunk roads are seldom more than two lanes wide, and are always clogged with bullock carts, trucks, cyclists, walkers or people sitting inexplicably in the path of the traffic. Trains are more comfortable but no faster. This naturally limits the amount of ground you can cover during your trip and those who want to pack everything in are soon reduced to quivering wrecks of frustration. Allow yourself more time in a few places, rather than trying to hurry between a score of different ones, and you will come home with memories of those places, rather than of an endless succession of sweaty, crowded bus and train rides.

To make things easier for yourself, you should always book your onward bus or train ticket as soon as you arrive at a place: if you decide to stay longer then losing your reservation doesn't matter, but leaving your departure to the last minute always seems to coincide with a miraculous drying-up of available tickets.

By Air

transport to and from the airports

Once you've arrived at an airport, you normally have three options for getting into town: taxi, auto-rickshaw and bus (unless you're staying at a luxury hotel which offers a courtesy van). Auto-rickshaws are not comfortable for very long journeys, although they are certainly less expensive than taxis. Taking a bus into town is the cheapest option, but buses often stop running by 10pm—no use if your flight has arrived in the early hours (as international flights often do). If arriving late at night, the most convenient way to get into town is by pre-paid taxi (look for the pre-paid taxi counters inside the airport).

A word of warning: The jet-lagged traveller to India arriving for the first time, late at night, is a perfect target for crooks. One fairly common scam actually operates in collusion with the airport pre-paid taxis. Here is one woman's account of how it happened to her:

'I arrived in India at 3am, after an exhausting 30-hour plane flight and hired a pre-paid taxi to my hotel, where I had a reservation. Somewhere en route I was asked to get out of the taxi and into an auto-rickshaw, on the pretence that the rickshaw driver knew the directions and the taxi driver did not. I was then driven to my hotel, but the night guard there—no doubt working with the others—stated that he did not have my reservation and refused to let me into the hotel. He then told me that rioting had broken out in the city and the streets were unsafe. I asked the rickshaw driver to take me to another hotel quickly, and he started telling me that all the hotels in town cost between US$200–300. I knew these prices were grossly inflated, and was extremely frightened, especially as someone on the street had tried to grab my bag out of the open-sided rickshaw (this stunt perhaps being part of the scam). I was taken to a small dreary hotel and told it would cost US$70 for a room. Tired, scared, and alone, I felt I had little choice but to pay what was demanded. I went straight to the room, locked the door, and stayed there until dawn broke.' To avoid being a victim of scams such as these, some words of advice. First, single travellers, especially women, should probably avoid travelling late at night from the airport to the city at all. Wait in the airport until daylight. If you must get to your hotel, call ahead from the airport to confirm your reservation. If you do get into trouble, make a scene and demand to be taken to the nearest police station. Indians often respond to forcefulness, even from women (*see* 'Women Travellers', p.41).

Most of the air traffic inside the Indian subcontinent is handled by **Indian Airlines**, although they are increasingly being given competition by smaller, private airlines.

booking

Book internal air flights well in advance, as demand normally exceeds availability. Go to a travel agent to buy your ticket, as they will find you the best price and not charge any commission.

discounts

Domestic flights are surprisingly good value. Youth and student discounts from 25% to 50% are often available, so make sure you ask your travel agent if you qualify. If you have booked your flights from home, you'll need to reconfirm your entire itinerary immediately to be sure of keeping your reservations.

Indian Airlines offers a 25% youth discount for those between 12 and 30 years of age. Children between 2 and 12 get a 50% discount, and infants under 2 travel at 10% of the adult fare. Students between 12 and 26 years of age get a 50% student discount, though certain formalities prior to booking student tickets are required. Check with your travel agent for details.

Indian Airlines also offers air packages which function similarly to rail passes. They're not bad value if you're planning to make a lot of flights. The 'Discover India' package buys 21 days of unlimited economy class air travel anywhere in India for US$400. The 'India Wonderfares' package gets you 7 days unlimited economy class travel within one region of India (north, south, east, or west) for US$200.

Indian Airlines tickets are refundable up to one hour before scheduled flight departure, minus a Rs100 fee. No refunds are applicable for lost tickets. If your flight is delayed for over one hour, a full refund is also allowed.

Indian Airlines Offices

Bangalore: Housing Board Building, Kempe Gowda Road, ✆ 211211, airport, ✆ 566233.
Bombay: Air India Building, Ist Floor, Madam Cama Road, Nariman Point, ✆ 2876161,
airport, ✆ 6114433—you can call the airport line 24 hours a day.
Cochin: Durbar Hall Road, Ernakulam, ✆ 353901, airport, ✆ 364433.
Goa (Dabolim): Dempo House, Cample, Panjim, ✆ 4067, airport, ✆ 2568.
Hyderabad: Saifabad, near Legislative Assembly Building, ✆ 243333, airport, ✆ 844433.
Madras: 19 Marshalls Road, ✆ 8251677, airport, ✆ 2344433.
Trivandrum: Near Mascot Hotel, Museum Road, ✆ 62288, airport, ✆ 72740.

domestic flight timetable

Below is a schedule of regular flights offered by major carriers within India. The fares quoted below are Indian Airlines' one-way, full adult fares; the private airlines flying the same routes usually offer very similar ones. Check all available flights with your travel agent before planning an itinerary, as scheduled flight days and fares may have changed since the time of writing.

Code: Damania Airways = DA; East West Airlines = EWA; Indian Airlines = IA; Jet Airways = JA; Modiluft = ML; NEPC Airlines = NA.

Flights available	Fare (Rs)	Airlines
Bangalore to:		
Bombay (daily)	2347	IA, DA, JA, EWA
Calicut (daily ex Mon)	1157	IA
Cochin (daily)	1306	IA, NA
Coimbatore (daily ex Wed/Fri)	944	IA, EWA
Goa (Tues/Thurs/Sat)	1657	IA
Hyderabad (daily)	1674	IA
Madras (daily)	1128	IA, NA
Mangalore (Mon/Thurs/Sat)	1197	IA
Trivandrum (Mon/Tues/Thurs/Sat)	1841	IA
Bombay to:		
Bangalore (daily)	2347	IA, DA, JA, EWA
Calicut (daily)	2721	IA, EWA, JA
Cochin (daily)	2985	IA, EWA, JA
Coimbatore (daily)	2640	IA, EWA, JA
Goa (daily)	1352	IA, DA, JA, EWA, ML
Hyderabad (daily)	1962	IA, EWA, JA
Madras (daily)	2876	IA, DA, JA, EWA
Madurai (daily)	3325	IA, EWA
Mangalore (daily)	2140	IA, EWA, JA
Trivandrum (daily)	3440	IA, EWA
Calicut to:		
Bangalore (daily ex Tues)	1157	IA
Bombay (daily)	2721	IA, JA, EWA
Madras (daily ex Sun)	1582	IA

Cochin to:

Bombay (daily)	2985	IA, JA, EWA, ML
Goa (daily ex Sun)	2019	IA
Madras (daily)	1973	IA, NA
Trivandrum (daily ex Sun)	829	IA

Coimbatore to:

Bangalore (Tues/Thurs/Sat/Sun)	944	IA
Bombay (daily)	2640	IA, JA, EWA
Madras (daily)	1542	IA, NA
Madurai (Wed/Fri/Sun)	864	IA

Goa to:

Bangalore (Tues/Thurs/Sat)	1657	IA
Bombay (daily)	1352	IA, DA, JA, EWA, ML
Cochin (daily ex Sun)	2019	IA
Madras (Tues/Thurs/Sat)	2313	IA
Trivandrum (daily ex Sun)	2428	IA

Hyderabad to:

Bangalore (daily)	1674	IA
Bombay (daily)	1962	IA, JA, EWA
Madras (daily)	1646	IA

Madras to:

Bangalore (daily)	1128	IA, NA
Bombay (daily)	2876	IA, DA, JA, EWA
Cochin (daily)	1973	IA, NA
Coimbatore (daily)	1542	IA, NA
Goa (Tues/Thurs/Sat)	2313	IA
Hyderabad (daily)	1646	IA, ML
Madurai (daily)	1467	IA, NA
Mangalore (Mon/Thurs/Sat)	1657	IA
Tiruchipalli/Trichy (Tues/Thurs/Sat)	1197	IA
Trivandrum (daily)	1922	IA, NA
Vishakapatnam (daily ex Thurs/Sun)	1887	IA, NA

Madurai to:

Bombay (daily)	3325	IA, EWA
Madras (daily)	1467	IA, NA

Mangalore to:

Bangalore (Mon/Thurs/Sat)	1197	IA
Bombay (daily)	2140	IA, JA, EWA
Madras (Mon/Thurs/Sat)	1657	IA

Tiruchipalli/Trichy to:

Madras (Tues/Thurs/Sat)	1197	IA
Madurai (Tues/Thurs/Sat)	611	IA

Trivandrum to:

Bangalore (Mon/Tues/Thurs/Sat)	1841	IA
Bombay (daily)	3440	IA, EWA
Cochin (daily ex Sun)	829	IA
Goa (daily ex Sun)	2428	IA
Madras (daily)	1922	IA

Vishakapatnam to:

Madras (Mon/Wed/Fri)	1887	IA

By Boat

The most famous south Indian boat journeys are the catamaran trip from Bombay to Goa, and the many small-boat trips through the backwaters of Kerala. The Bombay–Goa catamaran takes 8 hours and costs about US$40 for foreigners, but you get a wonderful view of the mountainous Malabar Coast, and schools of dolphins play across the bows (*see* p.101 for full details). The Keralan backwater boats are like slow buses moving through a watery paradise, and are as useful as buses for getting about, but much more relaxing. For full details, *see* p.212.

By Rail

Since the days when it was developed to link the commercial and military centres of the Indian Empire, the Indian Railways system has expanded considerably. By the close of the 19th century, there were 40,000 miles of track, stretching to the remotest parts of the country. Today, Indian Railways is the largest system in Asia, and the second largest in the world. Each day, over 11 million people travel to and from a total of 7021 railway stations.

Rail travel is a leisurely way of taking in the varied scenery—mountains, lakes, rivers, fields, forests, dense jungles and hill terrains. It also offers the opportunity to meet a great many people who are eager to share food and conversation with you. Whenever the train pulls into a station, platforms are an explosion of noise and colour: cries of '*chai-ya!*' and '*samo-sa!*' float invitingly over the general hubbub. Here you can buy fresh(ish) fruit and vegetables, *idli* or *pakora* for next to nothing. Or you can wait until the daily shipment of *thali* suppers is loaded onto the train and dine in a more civilized fashion later on. Train food is cheap (around RS20–30), though rather bland. If on a marathon journey, it's a good idea to bring along supplies of your own water, chocolate, biscuits and oranges. Hot drinks are never a problem. At the larger stations, a boy with an aluminium teapot will invariably be beetling up and down the aisles doling out tea or coffee.

India's rail network is extremely extensive, always a madhouse and yet amazingly efficient (though few trains leave on time). If you're going to be spending much time on trains in India, buy a copy of *Trains at a Glance*. Sold cheaply at most large rail stations, this booklet provides a complete timetable of the rail services in India.

There are five basic classes of passenger rail travel: 1st class air-conditioned sleeper (operates on certain trains and routes only); 2nd class air-conditioned sleeper; 2nd class air-conditioned chair-car; 1st class non air-conditioned and 2nd class non air-conditioned. For over-night journeys, the nicest way to travel is via 2nd class air-conditioned sleeper (costing half of the overrated 1st class air-conditioned sleeper fare, far more private and comfortable). However, if the weather's not too hot, a 2nd class non air-conditioned sleeper is relatively clean and comfortable and is very inexpensive. For day trips, air-conditioned chair-cars are cool, spacious, and relaxed, whereas 2nd class is often hectic and crowded. However, if you want an adventure, 2nd class certainly allows you to meet and interact with a broader and more interesting range of local people.

Always choose the quicker mail, express or superfast trains, as local passenger trains take ages. A sleeper berth on an overnight train is a smart way to travel since you don't have to pay for a night's hotel accommodation and time passes more quickly while you're unconscious! Better yet, a berth offers privacy and room to stretch out during the daytime portion of your trip.

You should always travel with a reservation for long train journeys, this being absolutely essential for air-conditioned and sleeper classes. Popular routes often fill up weeks in advance so the sooner you book your ticket the better. For short hops you can usually buy your ticket the same day. Just make sure you get to the platform 30 to 60 minutes early to buy your ticket, and push your way on to the train aggressively when it arrives to ensure you get a seat. If all the seats are taken, just stand or sit in the aisle-way. Eventually some seated passengers will get off the train and they tend to offer their seats to Westerners.

Train reservations are made at a separate reservation office normally adjacent to the station. Sometimes, you'll get a doleful shake of the head from the reservation clerk and the apologetic words, 'So sorry, all full'. This means you'll have to apply for the **tourist quota** of tickets, usually issued by the District Commercial Superintendent of the railway department. His office is sometimes miles away from the station, but you'll be surprised how easily he'll supply you with a ticket. Other 'quotas' are hidden away in all sorts of subterranean places in and out of the station complex. If you are really stuck, ask the nearest tourist office if there's a 'tourist quota' on the train you want. Or approach the stationmaster and try and break into his **VIP quota**. If nothing works, it's worth paying a few rupees *baksheesh* to a station porter to get a seat in an unreserved compartment.

Once you have your tickets sorted out and are ready to get on the train, it's sometimes difficult to find the right platform. At the larger stations there will usually be an electronic board that lists the relevant out-going train information. If not, there should be an inquiry desk which can help you and, if this fails, ask a porter, but avoid spurious 'guides' who will see you to the train and then try to extort as much money as possible out of you. Your train ticket will have your carriage and seat number printed on it and there will also be a 'reservation sheet' posted on the sides of each carriage which will have your name and berth number printed on it (assuming you've bought a reserved ticket).

Hiring a porter to carry your bags is a luxury that is easily affordable in India. The going rate is about 5 or 10 rupees per bag (depending on how far the bags need to be carried), although the porter will start out asking for something five times as high. Just hold firm to your price and he'll eventually relent (grumpily).

Indian railway stations often have good waiting-rooms and a decent restaurant. Tourists can use both 1st and 2nd class waiting-rooms, and even sleep free in them, provided they have a valid train ticket. Most stations also have a **left-luggage** room where you can leave your bags for just a few rupees per day—very useful if you're only spending a few hours in a town and don't want to book into a hotel.

Indian rail fares (Rs)

Note that railway tickets can be cancelled and your money fully refunded (minus a Rs10–30 cancellation fee) if you cancel more than one day in advance. You pay a 25% cancellation charge if your ticket is cancelled one day in advance up to 6 hours before scheduled departure and 50% if cancelled within 6 hours before scheduled departure and up to 3 hours after the actual departure of the train.

The following table lists railway fares on routes originating from Bombay and Madras only. For a complete listing of routes and fares in India, buy a *Trains at a Glance* booklet, or inquire about your desired journey at any Indian railway station reservation office.

Station	Miles	1st a/c	2nd a/c	1st	a/c chair	2nd class
Bombay to:						
Bangalore	750	1725	961	757	420	239
Cochin	1148	2286	1216	1001	543	289
Madras	793	1725	961	757	420	239
Secunderabad	496	1252	706	552	311	180
Trivandrum	1278	2475	1291	1081	581	302
Vasco da Gama	477	1234	698	541	310	179
Madras to:						
Bangalore	222	668	400	296	178	99
Bombay	793	1725	961	757	420	239
Cochin	440	1154	668	507	291	169
Coimbatore	306	865	487	382	227	128
Hyderabad	322	896	537	394	238	132
Madurai	345	944	554	415	249	139
Mangalore	558	1313	730	575	325	193
Tiruchipalli/Trichy	209	636	377	282	170	95
Tirunelvelli	402	1073	617	473	274	158
Tirupati	79	312	203	131	86	62
Trivandrum	571	1356	755	593	335	202
Tuticorn	444	1154	668	507	291	169
Vijayawada	268	797	461	352	216	118

Indrail Passes

If you're going to be doing a lot of rail travel, the Indrail Pass can be very good value. Valid for one year from purchase date, it gives unlimited travel on Indian trains for specified lengths of time (e.g. 7 days, 60 days) and allows you to go where and when you like without ever (if travelling unreserved) having to join a ticket queue. If you do want a reservation, you'll still have to queue but the Indrail Pass carries a bit of weight and often produces quotas denied to other ordinary rail travellers. It is also very useful for gaining access to 1st class station waiting-rooms and retiring-rooms. To make the best use of your Indrail Pass, pick up a free copy of *Indrail India Rail Rovers* booklet from the agent which issues your pass. It lists all trains, discusses all rail travel options, and generally helps you plan your itinerary.

Outside India, Indrail Passes can only be bought through authorized agents. In the UK, you can buy the Indrail Pass from S.D. Enterprises Limited, 103 Wembley Park Drive, Wembley, Middlesex, HA9 8HG; in France, from Carrefour, 15 Rue des Ecoles, Paris; in the USA, from Hari World Travels, 30 Rockefeller Plaza, Shop No.21, Mezzanine North, New York; and in Australia, from Penthouse Travel, Suite 5, Level 13, Commercial Union House, 109 Pitt St, Sydney. Contact your local Government of India Tourist Office to find out the agent in countries not listed.

In India, Indrail Passes are sold by many travel agents or Central Reservations Offices at major railway stations such as Bangalore, Bombay, and Madras.

Indrail passes are sold only to foreign nationals and Indians residing abroad holding valid passports. Payment is accepted only in US Dollars and Pounds Sterling. A tourist travelling on the Indrail Pass is exempt from paying reservation fees, sleeper charges and other supplementary charges levied in the case of ordinary tickets. Children aged between 5 and 12 years are charged half the adult Indrail Pass fare.

Indrail Pass Costs (US$)

Validity	1st a/c	2nd a/c, 1st, a/c chair	2nd class
7 days	270	135	70
15 days	330	165	80
21 days	400	200	110
30 days	500	250	135
60 days	720	360	165
90 days	960	480	210

By Car

This is a mode of transport that tends to be more hassle than it is worth—Indian roads being sheer hell for anyone unused to them. Car hire in India is relatively new and even Hertz, Budget and EuropCar offer both self-drive cars and ones with drivers. Mad streams of crazy traffic, aimless herds of sacred cows, nippier pigs and goats and deep pot-holes make Indian driving something of an endurance test. If you want to travel by car, use taxis or hire a car *and* driver. This will secure you a chauffeur-driven Hindustan Ambassador (an unashamed replica of the mid-50s British Morris Oxford). Prices are quite reasonable considering the freedom and flexibility it gives your itinerary. The driver often doubles up as a trained guide, as well as useful interpreter and watchman.

bringing your own vehicle

Some people drive their own cars, vans or motorbikes into the country. If you choose this option, you'll need to: a) fill out a customs declaration form (called a carnet) requiring you to bring the vehicle out again at the end of your stay; b) be in possession of an International Driving Licence. It is much better to save yourself the bother of importing and simply buy your vehicle out there. This is especially true of motorbikes. In 1989, a Swiss couple who'd bought an Enfield motorbike in Delhi for Rs16,000, motored all round India on it, and sold it in Srinagar for Rs13,000. They had no problems.

You can get just about anywhere by bus, and it's cheap. India has a very extensive and comprehensive bus system. Each state offers its own service—usually a combination of local, deluxe, super-deluxe and video buses—and tickets are usually purchased direct from the state bus stands. Buses are often cheaper and more exciting than the trains, and go to several places not linked by rail. They can also be a lot quicker. Most buses in India, whether local, state, or privately run, roar to their destinations with reckless verve and daring. Their drivers seem to have a particular grudge against 'public carrier' trucks, which often carry provocative slogans like 'Owner is God—God is Grate'. All bus drivers have a little box containing their personal gods above their seat. From time to time, often when stopped by the police for not paying a speeding fine, they will pray to these. At other times, they will pull up at a roadside Hindu shrine and pay a priest to ring a bell to summon the major deities; this is often to give thanks for avoiding a major collision.

Every bus journey is an experience in itself, especially the ones which wind round an escalating series of hairpin bends on their way up to remote hill stations. And when the interior is full your only option is to sit on the roof. But there are always entertaining road-signs to keep your mind off the perilous drive. These signs are the creation of Public Works Department (PWD) poets, who are notoriously sexist. 'When you approach a corner, get horny', is one of their classics. 'Don't gossip—let him drive' is another. 'Family awaits—please oblige', a direct appeal to the paternal instinct, is the only thing likely to make him slow down at tight corners.

Buses often stop at spots of great natural beauty, which makes a pleasant change from the hurly-burly of railway platforms. Another good thing about buses is that they leave so frequently, often every hour or half-hour and they are much less trouble to book and board than trains. Buying a reservation slip often gets you onto buses where seats are likely to be at a premium, but you will need to turn up at the bus station at least 40 minutes in advance to be sure of getting one.

Local buses are incredibly cheap and will often run you from one end of a state to another for less than Rs50, but they are also crowded, occasionally smelly and usually uncomfortable. Air-conditioned 'deluxe' buses are slightly less so. Video bus journeys are a nightmare: constant disco music and blaring video shows can grind you down, especially when sharing a two-seater built for one. It's almost impossible to hear yourself think, let alone read, but Indian travellers adore the video bus, and the more distorted the sound, the more they like it.

Whenever leaving a bus to go to the toilet or to eat, leave a newspaper or something on your seat. This will reserve it. Take any other hand luggage off the bus with you. Backpacks and large cases are usually strapped under tarpaulin on the bus roof, or stored in the hold-all. If you're looking after them under your seat, make sure they are securely zipped and locked (padlocking to a bolted seat is best) before vacating the bus.

Bus stops can be either very short or very long (driver wanders off to visit his family). Passengers have been known to be left holding full cups of tea or squatting in ditches while the bus roars off without them. The only way of tracking its movements is to keep one eye constantly on the driver. As soon as he's back in his seat, you've got approximately 5 seconds to get back in yours.

Bus travel is best over short distances, for long journeys take the train. Indian roads are badly surfaced, full of yawning potholes, and always seem liable to collapse. So are the back axles of the overloaded buses. The hard, cramped seating, the draughty, rattling windows, the screaming children, the infrequent toilet stops and the constant blare of the air-horn as the bus ploughs inexorably towards its destination, may leave you blinded, shell-shocked and with your nerves (and your backside) shot to pieces. But the network is extensive, and you can always reduce your discomfort by a) inserting earplugs; b) sitting on a soft pillow or sweater; c) jamming a sleeping bag into window gaps; d) wearing a hat and scarf (or crash helmet).

prices

A seat on a deluxe bus is approximately 2 to 3 times the price of one on an ordinary bus—but some large Europeans literally cannot *fit* into the space offered in the latter. Prices vary, but it is almost always the case that they will be a fraction lower than the fare for a 2nd class rail ticket along the same route. The longer the journey, the lower the rate per mile.

To anticipate a very approximate fare on a deluxe bus, divide the distance you wish to travel, in miles, by 2—and that will give you a rough idea of your fare in rupees. Sample inter-state bus fares:

Bombay to Vasco da Gama: 477 miles; about Rs260
Madras to Bangalore: 222 miles; about Rs120
Trivandrum to Madras: 571 miles; about Rs306.

by tour bus or coach

As a quick, cheap and comfortable introduction to larger Indian centres, sightseeing coach tours operated by government and state tourist offices are unbeatable value. Costing around Rs45 for a half-day, Rs80 for a full day, they work out far less expensive than sightseeing by taxi or rick-shaw, and of course you see more in less time. Their main advantage is their rapid orientation of foreign visitors to large, sprawling cities. There are rather too many stops at obscure temples and holy shrines for most Western passengers, and the deluxe buses themselves are sometimes draughty and dilapidated but you'll cover an incredible amount of ground in just a day and other forms of in-town transport can be even less comfortable. Sightseeing buses can also be a great way of meeting people because you'll often be the only foreign tourist on board and it's common to be adopted for the day by friendly home tourists and fed large quantities of Indian picnic lunches. When booking your tour, ask for a seat at the front of the bus; it's far less bumpy, quicker to get to the toilets, and you'll hear more of the guide's talk.

By Taxi and Auto-rickshaw

These are the two most common forms of in-town transport, most popular for short-distance hops to and from bus and rail stations when loaded down with luggage, or for solo sightseeing in smaller towns where tour buses aren't such good value. Taxis are usually black, with yellow tops, cost around Rs6–7 per mile with a minimum fare of Rs5.60, and are quite comfortable. Auto-rickshaws are three-wheeled scooters (a two-stroke motorcycle engine with two-seater canopy strapped behind it), which are noisy, less comfortable, but very nippy. They cost anything between Rs4 and Rs5 per mile.

Taxis and rickshaws are usually metered but the meters are often not working. As soon as you walk off in search of another taxi, they suddenly begin working again. But even when the meter's returned from the dead, you're wise to fix the cost of your journey before setting off. A succession of recent fuel price increases has left taxi meter-readings way out of date. You'll often be handed a fare adjustment card indicating a far higher fare than that shown on the meter. In Bombay, where taxi meters haven't been recalibrated in ages, surcharges of 400–500% can come as a real shock to the penny-wise traveller.

If overcharged—if you've agreed a fair rate for the journey in advance and the driver wants more at the end of it—don't get angry. Just write down the taxi number and announce in a calm, determined voice that you're going to the police. There are stiff fines for extorting money from tourists and your driver will usually 'remember' the correct fare instantly.

Another popular scam used by taxis and auto-rickshaws alike is to drive you miles out of your way, in order to collect a decent fare. Take a good city map with you and as soon as it's apparent that you're being taken miles out of the way, tell the driver firmly 'wrong way!' and manually reset his meter back to zero. But don't be too hasty to jump to conclusions, sometimes he will genuinely lose his way, or won't be able to understand where you want to go. Again, a city map is useful because you'll be able to point out your exact destination. In case you're totally lost in a big city, and need to get back to your hotel, always keep a hotel card handy. Drivers will usually take one look at the card, and take you straight home.

If hiring a taxi or auto-rickshaw between 11pm and 5am, be prepared to pay an additional 15% (up to 25% in the big cities) on top of the usual daytime fare.

Some major airports, including Bombay, Bangalore and Madras, have introduced a system of 'pre-paid taxis'. Before leaving the arrival terminal, go to the police-manned taxi booth and purchase a ticket to the area of town you need to reach. There is a small charge of a few rupees but this service ensures new arrivals are not going to be over-charged and that they generally reach their destination without detours.

However, some first-time travellers arriving in the small hours have been the victim of scams (*see* p.10) in which they are taken to their hotel, only to be told by the guard that there is 'no reservation', that the streets are dangerous and that they must go somewhere much more expensive. If this happens, be prepared to make a scene, refuse to leave the cab and demand to be driven to a police station. The guard will probably remember your reservation.

By Cycle-rickshaw

Unless you love an argument, it is best to avoid this mode of transport. These rather antiquated vehicles can be found only in certain places, usually in smaller towns. Cycle-rickshaws are cheap—usually just Rs4 per mile (again, always fix a total rate for your journey in advance), but their drivers are notorious for trying to overcharge, often very forcefully. This is often because they are unable to afford their own vehicles and are just hiring them out for a few rupees a day from someone else. Cycle-rickshaws are often ridden by some loquacious old pirate who hasn't the slightest idea of where he's going. It's accepted custom to get off and give him a push up steep hills. You'll probably also have to give him lots of directions and prompts—especially when he wants to stop for tea or for a chat with his mates halfway through your journey.

By Bicycle and On Foot

by bike

In the quieter towns, such as Goa's resorts, Hampi, Mysore, Pondicherry and the hill stations, bike hire is a good option for getting around. The usual daily tariff is about Rs30 (though you may have to bargain for this) and you can get a list of hiring centres from the local tourist information office. You should *always* test the brakes, wheels (for true running and healthy spokes), look at the tyres and try the seat before you hire. Most places will let you take a trial run around the block. If they refuse, don't hire from them. Don't bother with bikes in the big cities unless you have some experience with Indian traffic—it simply isn't worth the risk. The one thing your bike *must* have is a bell. In dense traffic you'll be ringing this continually (like everybody else) to avoid being mown down. If you get a puncture, you'll have no difficulty finding a repair man, they're all over the place—but you may well be hanging around for an hour while he spends overlong fixing it. You can usually speed him up by offering twice the correct Rs2 repair charge. Women in India travel side-saddle on cycles, so there is a great shortage of ladies' bikes. To snap up the few there are, be at the cycle-hire shop first thing in the morning.

on foot

Bear in mind that the real sights of Indian cities are out on the streets, not confined to monuments, palaces, parks and museums. Wandering off on foot or by cycle down small, narrow backstreets can turn up all sorts of delights—tiny local temples, quaint pavement shrines, colourful markets and bazaars, and out-of-the-way curio shops. Off the beaten track is usually where you'll find the real India—small, yet lively communities of local people working, eating, resting, playing and praying, who are invariably interested in, and keen to meet, foreign tourists.

Guided Tours

English speaking **guides** are available at all important tourist centres. You will usually have to haggle over a price, even though licensed tour guides are supposed to offer fixed rates. Make sure that if you do hire a guide, he/she speaks English well and has a personality you can live with. Some guides are very knowledgeable and enthusiastic, adding greatly to your appreciation of the site. Others leave you more confused and annoyed than enlightened.

Travelling Alone

Even if you've agreed to tour in company, do spend a few days travelling on your own. India is very much a country for the individualist, which quickly brings out all your hidden resources. For a start, there is no room for doubt, indecision or complacency. Without the insulation of a boon companion (a permanent reminder of home) you'll feel compelled to attune to the country, its people and its customs, at top speed. It's also an excellent spur to making new friends. There should be no worry about feeling alone. In India, nobody's alone for very long. The beauty of travelling by yourself is that you can go exactly when and where you please, with a growing sense of freedom and confidence. The perfect place for a modern-day walkabout, India rewards the solo traveller with a rich variety of intense experiences—some good, some bad, none dull—and brings him or her to a deeper understanding of the country. The reason so much more happens on your own is simple—you have to make it happen.

Practical A–Z

The climate in south India varies greatly, depending on season and location. India's three major seasons are winter, summer and the monsoon. Winter lasts from November to March and brings pleasant, sunny days. The summer months of April, May and June can get uncomfortably hot, and escaping to hill towns such as Ootacamund or Kodaikanal during this time is not a bad idea. India has two major monsoons. The southwest monsoon usually arrives during June along the west coast (arriving a bit later elsewhere) and slowly wends its way northwards; the northeast monsoon takes place between October and December. Monsoon season can actually be a pleasant time to go to India. In between the sudden, short downpours of rain are periods of clear, brilliant sunshine and all the foliage and flowers burst into colour. Trekking is not possible during the monsoon, however, because of leeches, and the heavy rains also put a dampener on beach going. Bombay and Goa are best from November to February. Thereafter, they are hot and humid until the monsoons in early June. The rest of south India is coolest from November to April, and starts getting the rains as early as late May.

Weather Chart

T = Temperature in °C (°F)   R = Rainfall in inches

City	Jan	Feb	Mar	Apr	May	Jun	July	Aug	Sept	Oct	Nov	Dec
Bangalore												
T max.	28(82)	31(88)	33(91)	34(93)	33(91)	30(86)	28(82)	29(84)	28(82)	28(82)	27(81)	27(81)
min.	15(59)	16(61)	19(66)	21(70)	21(70)	20(68)	19(66)	19(66)	19(66)	19(66)	17(63)	15(59)
R avg.	0.2	0.5	0.2	1.5	4.7	2.0	3.7	3.7	5.1	7.7	1.8	0.6
Bombay												
T max.	31(88)	32(90)	33(91)	33(91)	33(91)	32(90)	30(86)	29(84)	30(86)	32(90	33(91)	32(90)
min.	16(61)	17(63)	20(68)	24(75)	26(79)	26(79)	25(77)	24(75)	24(75)	23(73)	20(68)	18(64)
R avg.	0.0	0.0	0.0	0.0	0.8	25.5	37.2	26.0	12.2	4.6	0.3	0.0
Cochin												
T max.	31(88)	31(88)	31(88)	31(88)	31(88)	29(84)	28(82)	28(82)	28(82)	29(84)	30(86)	30(86)
min.	23(73)	24(75)	26(79)	26(79)	26(79)	24(75)	24(75)	24(75)	24(75	24(75)	24(75)	23(73)
R avg.	0.3	1.3	2.0	5.5	14.3	29.8	22.5	15.2	9.2	13.1	7.2	1.5
Hyderabad												
T max.	29(84)	31(88)	35(95)	37(99)	39(102)	34(93)	30(86)	29(84	30(86)	30(86)	29(84)	28(82)
min.	15(59)	17(63)	20(68)	24(75)	26(79)	24(75)	22(72)	22(72)	22(72)	20(68)	16(61)	13(55)
R avg.	0.1	0.4	0.5	0.9	1.2	4.2	6.5	5.8	6.4	2.8	1.0	0.2
Madras												
T max.	29(84)	31(88)	33(91)	35(95)	38(100)	37(99)	35(95)	35(95)	34(93)	32(90)	29(84)	28(82)
min.	20(68)	21(70)	23(73)	26(79)	28(82)	28(82)	26(79)	26(79)	25(77)	24(75)	23(73)	21(70)
R avg.	0.9	0.3	0.6	1.0	2.0	2.1	3.3	4.9	4.6	10.5	12.2	5.5
Madurai												
T max.	30(86)	32(90)	35(95)	36(97)	37(99)	37(99)	36(97)	35(95)	35(95)	33(91)	31(88)	30(86)
min.	21(70)	22(72)	23(73)	25(77)	26(79)	26(79)	26(79)	25(77)	25(77)	24(73)	24(73)	22(72)
R avg.	1.0	0.6	0.8	3.2	2.3	1.2	1.9	4.6	4.8	7.1	6.3	1.7
Panjim (Goa)												
T max.	31(88)	32(90)	32(90)	33(91)	33(91)	31(88)	29(84)	29(84)	29(84)	31(88)	33(91)	33(91)
min.	19(66)	20(68)	23(73)	25(77)	27(81)	25(77)	24(75)	24(75)	24(75)	23(73)	22(72)	21(70)
R avg.	0.1	0.0	0.2	0.7	0.7	22.8	35.1	13.4	10.9	4.8	0.8	1.5

Trivandrum

T	max.	31(88)	32(90)	33(91)	32(90)	31(88)	29(84)	29(84)	29(84)	30(86)	30(86)	30(86)	31(88)
	min.	22(72)	23(73)	24(75)	25(77)	25(77)	25(77)	24(75)	23(73)	23(73)	23(73)	23(73)	23(73)
R	avg.	0.8	0.8	1.7	4.8	9.8	13.0	8.5	6.4	4.8	10.7	8.1	2.9

Most foreign tourists visit India in season, to enjoy the best weather and facilities, and to meet other travellers. Christmas is a popular time to go to Goa, for instance, especially for those into the rave scene. A cunning minority of travellers go off season—usually a week or two before everybody else—to take advantage of the 30–50% accommodation discounts usually offered. Travelling off season also means fewer crowds, more seats on buses, and no long queues for train tickets.

Communications

Post offices in India provide a good, reliable service, and are open from 10am to 5pm on weekdays, until midday on Saturday. The cost of postage for letters sent within India is Rs1, and for international mail the cost is Rs11 for a letter, Rs6.50 for an aerogramme, and Rs6 for a postcard. Mail sent to Europe, North America, Australia or New Zealand usually takes 10 to 14 days to reach its destination. Most of the larger post offices now offer a Speed Post service which links over 60 towns in India and delivers to most countries worldwide. For sending documents, this service is a bit slower than a private courier company, but costs about half as much. For example, a speed posted letter sent from India will reach the UK in 4 to 5 days and costs Rs400. Private courier companies such as Blue Dart (the Indian company linked up with Federal Express) can deliver a letter in 2 to 3 days, but it will cost you Rs900.

A word of warning: enterprising postal staff have been known to remove unfranked (uncancelled) stamps from letters and postcards, which then go precisely nowhere. Either have your mail franked before your very eyes in a post office, or (better) buy a stack of pre-stamped aerogrammes, which can't be interfered with.

Postes restantes are usually located in main post offices. These provide a good service, and your expected mail is nearly always waiting for you when you call. If it isn't, check not only under the initial of your surname, but under that of your christian name (misfiling is common). When collecting mail from a *poste restante*, you'll need some proof of identity (e.g. a passport) to claim it. And if you don't claim it within a month, it's often returned to the sender. Have all letters and cards addressed to you in the following manner: Bloggs, J., *Poste Restante*, Bangalore 560001, India.

If you want your mail from home to be redirected to a different *poste restante* than the one you originally specified, visit the specified post office and fill out an instruction slip forwarding the mail to the new location. This procedure takes only a minute and will save you from having to write home to your loved ones to tell them you've moved.

Posting parcels home can be difficult. If possible, get someone to do it for you at a postal packing service. Otherwise, allow a whole morning to: a) take the parcel to a local tailor, ask him to stitch a linen bag for it, with the seams sealed with wax. This service is sometimes also available from people sitting outside major post offices in big cities, and will cost around Rs50; b) fill out two customs declarations forms at a post office, stick one to the parcel with glue, write your passport number and 'bona fide tourist' somewhere on the forms, describe the parcel contents as a 'gift', and its value as not more than Rs1000 (to avoid more paperwork hassle); c) have the parcel weighed, and establish the cost (air mail is a lot more expensive than sea mail, but gets home in a few weeks as opposed to a few months); d) buy the appropriate stamps, and glue them on; e) give the package in to the parcel counter and ask for a receipt.

Books or printed matter can be sent by bookpost at greatly reduced rates. These packages can't be sealed because their contents need to be inspected later on, so simply wrap the package in brown paper and tie it with some string.

Don't count on any parcels sent from home making it to you, especially if they have interesting contents like cassette tapes.

Telephones tend to be rather unreliable; the quality of the line often depends on the weather. The system is improving but many exchanges are overloaded and this leads to numerous problems. With local calls, you'll either get through immediately, not at all, or get connected to a number other than the one you dialled! If you don't get straight through to someone on a local call, hail a rickshaw and visit them personally, it could be much quicker. Luckily, there seems to be far fewer problems with long-distance calling.

To make a long-distance call (or a local call for that matter), you can go to any number of STDs (Subscriber Trunk Dialling). These are privately run companies that offer international or inter-state calling at government authorized rates. International calls cost you Rs80 per minute, with interstate rates varying depending on distance and time of day (rates go down after 9pm). Some STDs are high-tech communications centres, complete with fax machines, whereas others consist merely of a booth in a xerox shop, or perhaps a phone on a shelf at a roadside food stall. It's easy to spot these centres by their large posted signs reading STD/ISD. Making calls at STDs is easy and efficient—simply make your call and a digital readout let's you know how much cash you owe to the shopkeeper. STDs are everywhere, so are extremely handy. One drawback of the service is that you often have to make your call in the midst of a room full of people, which makes for lots of noise and little privacy. If you look around, however, you can often find a quieter shop with a private calling booth.

Fax services are available in most of the larger cities. You can usually send a fax at a luxury hotel, though their rates are often exorbitant, or at some of the nicer STDs (about Rs150 per page). The best option, however, may be to use the fax service at the government's local Central Telegraph Office. With private companies, you have to pay for faxes that don't transmit properly as long as a phone connection is made. At the government office, rates are cheaper to begin with (about Rs100), and the clerk will often try several times to get your fax through, without recharging you each time.

Telex messages can be sent from luxury hotels (again subject to a hefty service charge) or from main post offices, which are relatively cheap. The advantage of the telex is that it gives you a record of any hotel bookings or airline confirmations made—a wise precaution in a country notorious for double-booking suites and seats.

The government has established a few 24-hour communications centres with both phone and fax services, run by V.S.N. Ltd. In Bombay the centre is located at Mahatma Gandhi Road, ✆ 204 2728; in Madras at Swami Sivananda Salai, ✆ 56 6740.

Disabled Travellers

India is not a country which is easy to travel around if you have limited mobility, despite (and possibly because of) the fact that so many of her own population are disabled. Airlines and some major hotels are often helpful, but you can never rely on special facilities being available. For example, wheelchair ramps do not exist and access to bathrooms, restaurants and even hotel bedrooms is often impossible for those who cannot use stairs or pass through narrow doorways and passages. It may be possible to overcome these problems with the help of a companion.

The following organizations will be able to help you:

In the UK

Mobility International, 8 Borough High Street, London SE1 1JX, ✆ (0171) 403 5688, can offer some direct advice and runs seminars.

RADAR (The Royal Association for Disability and Rehabilitation), 25 Mortimer Street, London W1N 8AB, ✆ (0171) 637 5400, has a wide range of travel information.

In the USA

American Foundation for the Blind, 15 West 16th Street, New York, NY10011, ✆ (212) 620 2000; toll free ✆ 1-800 232 5463l, the best source of information in the USA for visually impaired travellers.

SATD (Society for the Advancement of Travel for the Disabled), Suite 610, 347 5th Avenue, New York, NY10016, ✆ (212) 447 7284, offers advice on all aspects of travel for the disabled, on an *ad hoc* basis for a $3 charge, or unlimited to members (membership costs $45, concessions $25).

Electricity

The electric current used in India is 220 volts AC, 50Hz. Sockets have two large round-pin holes. Current failures and power cuts are common all over India, and you should expect the power to go out about once a day. It's a good idea to always carry candles or a torch with you in case of blackouts.

Embassies and Consulates

Most of the larger cities have consulates (listed in the telephone directory), but any major problems have to be resolved at the regional offices in Bombay and Madras:

UK: (Bombay) 2nd Floor, Hong Kong Bank Building, M.G. Road, ✆ 274874; (Madras) 24 Anderson Road, Nunganbakkam, ✆ 473040.

USA: (Bombay) Lincoln House, 78 Bhulabhai Desai Road, ✆ 8223611; (Madras) 220 Mount Road, ✆ 473040.

Australia: (Bombay) Maker Towers, B Block, 41 Cuffe Parade, ✆ 218071; no office in Madras.

The Indian calendar is an ongoing procession of thousands of festivals each year. Nearly everywhere you go, some sort of temple celebration, religious pageant, or colourful arts festival will have just started or just ended. They are always worth going out of your way to see, most being highly spectacular and great fun. All Indian festivals have a strong cultural, artistic and religious theme and flavour, and the major ones attract some of the best exponents of music, dance and theatre in the country. There are also vast crowds of hysterical devotees, so be careful.

There are no fixed dates for many of these festivals. Their timing is determined by the Indian lunar calendar, and is calculable only during the previous year. Around October, your nearest Government of India tourist office should have the full list of festivals and dates for the forthcoming year. There are, however, a few national holidays when shops, banks and government offices are closed. Republic Day on **26 January**, Independence Day on **15 August** and Mahatma Gandhi's birthday on **2 October** are three days when everything is closed.

Some interesting and worthwhile festivals and fairs, together with their approximate dates, are listed below.

mid Jan	**Makar Sankranti/Pongal**. A major harvest festival, best seen in Tamil Nadu and Karnataka, involves lively processions, bullfights, and much decorating of sacred cows. *Pongal* is a sweet rice preparation prepared from freshly harvested paddy.
17–20 Jan	**The Great Elephant March**, Kerala. Elephant rides, dances, and boat races celebrate Kerala's cultural heritage.
26 Jan	**Republic Day**. A national holiday celebrated all over the country, marking India's adoption of their constitution.
Jan/early Feb	**Float Festival**. This festival in Madurai commemorates the birth of Thirumalai Nayak, the city's 17th-century ruler.
mid Feb	**Carnival**. Held in Goa, this non-religious celebration is similar to Mardi Gras, complete with feasting, drink, and costumed revellers dancing in the street.
mid March	**Id-ul-Fitr**. The end of Ramsan, the Muslim month of fasting, is celebrated with feasting and rejoicing.
late March	**Holi**. This rowdy celebration of the advent of spring is quite an eyeful—everybody pelts everyone else with coloured water and powder, and hapless tourists are fair game.
mid April	**Ramnavami**. The birthday of Lord Rama is celebrated by reciting the epic Ramayana in homes and temples throughout India.
April/May	**Meenakshi Kalyanam**, Madurai. Spectacular annual solemnization of Meenakshi's marriage to Shiva, held at the end of a 10-day non-stop festival in and around the famous Meenakshi temple. Excellent music.
mid July	**Teej**. To welcome the monsoons, women decorate swings with flowers.

15 Aug	**Independence Day**. The anniversary of India's independence from Britain is observed all over India.
mid Aug	**Onam**. The harvest festival of Kerala is marked by various cultural programmes, and the decoration of homes with flowers and swings. Snake-boat races, featuring the 100-oared boats once used by warring princes, are also held.
Aug/Sept	**Ganesh Chaturthi**, Bombay. The Elephant God Ganesh is celebrated with 11 days of music, dance, and drama.
Sept/Oct	**Dussehra**. A 10-day festival of national importance, celebrated every where. Most colourful and entertaining in Mysore, where the city palace is brilliantly illuminated and cultural programmes are held each evening. On the last day of the festival, the Prince of Mysore rides grandly through town on an elephant.
2 Oct	**Gandhi Jayanti**. This national holiday marks the birth of Mahatma Gandhi.
Oct/Nov	**Diwali**. The liveliest and noisiest of all Indian festivals, a night-long revel of firecrackers and general pageantry celebrates Laxmi, the goddess of wealth and prosperity. Houses of the rich and poor glow beautifully with light of special *diya* candles.
Nov/Sept	**International Sea Food Festival**. This fair in Panjim, Goa, lets you sample the local sea food, as well as displaying Goan folk arts and crafts.
25 Dec	**Christmas Day**. Celebrated all over India with music and dance festivals, but best in Goa.
mid-Dec–early Jan	**Madras Dance and Arts Festival**. Held in Madras, top dancers from all over the country perform nightly.

Be warned: Indian festivals are wonderful, exciting occasions most of the time, but occasionally they get out of control on the open streets. Excited crowds can be frightening, and at such times police find it difficult to keep public order. Watch events from the periphery and keep away from the centre of the crowds.

Food and Drink

South Indian Cuisine

South Indian food tends to be very spicy and also relies heavily on coconut. The base of almost every traditional meal is rice, rice, and then more rice. When you order a 'meal' in a south Indian restaurant, you will invariably be given a huge portion of rice with various things to put on it: *sambar*, a thin, mild, vegetable and lentil soup spiced with tamarind; *rasam*, a hot and savoury thin soup; a vegetable mixture of some sort, for instance green beans with coconut; and curd. You will also be served *poori*, a small fried bread to help scoop up your rice. Most 'meals' include unlimited portions, and you may have to put your hand firmly over your plate to refuse second or third helpings. You can also get a variety of prepared rice dishes such as *pulao*, made with tamarind and ground nuts, or *pulav*, made with chopped vegetables.

Some of the best south Indian food is not what we would call the main dishes, but the snacks, which are normally filling enough in themselves. A dish that is particularly associated with the south is *dosa*, a thin, fried pancake made from rice and lentils. When filled with spicy potato and vegetable curry, it is called a *masala dosa*, when prepared with onions and hot chillies, it is called an *onion dosa*, prepared as a thicker and chewier pancake it is a *set dosa*, and made with fermented dough, it becomes a *rava dosa*. A *dosa* will normally be served with a delicious coconut-based chutney and sometimes a spicy vegetable mixture as well. Try the different varieties to see which you like best. *Dosa* is incredibly cheap, around Rs10, and very filling. Also famous in the south are *idli*, delicate and subtle-tasting mounds of sticky rice flour, served with *sambar*. *Chaat* is the name given to a variety of spicy and savoury snacks served in the south which can be combined to make a wonderful meal. Look for *bhel puri*, a spicy, sweet and sour puffed rice mixture, *masala puri*, a green spicy sauce with peas, yogurt, and bits of fried pastry, *pani puri*, fried round pastry shells filled with onions, tomatoes, and coriander, or *sev dahi potato puri*, fried round pastry shells filled with potato and topped with a savoury sauce. Most *chaat* items only cost between Rs5 and Rs10, so just try anything on the menu that looks intriguing and see what appears!

Most of the nicer restaurants in the south also offer north Indian food, which is more familiar to westerners. Here you'll find the usual *naan* bread; *chapati*, a flat pan-cooked bread; *tandoori* oven-baked lamb and chicken; and curry dishes such as *palak paneer*, cheese cubes in a spinach sauce, and *aloo gobi*, potatoes and cauliflower. You can eat excellent seafood, notably in Goa and Kerala, near Mangalore in Karnataka and at other coastal resorts, where lobster, prawn, crayfish, crab and shark are often served fresh off the beach.

Indian desserts or sweetmeats are very sweet—often seeming to be little more than coloured sugar cubes. *Gulub jamun*, a fried doughnut in syrup, is good but amazingly rich. Some people love traditional Indian desserts like *barfi*, a sweet coconut mixure, *jalebi* (small snail-shaped pancakes, dripping with syrup) and milk/curd-based sweetmeats like *rasgulla* and *sandesh*, whereas others would rather eat an old shoe. If you're hard up for a sweet, you can always buy a chocolate bar, though the quality of the chocolate leaves much to be desired. The wonderful-looking cakes sold at every bakery are usually disappointingly dry and bland, with the notable exception of honey cake. The best Indian sweet, however, at least according to some addicts, is *chikki*. Similar to peanut brittle, but with a higher peanut-to-brittle ratio, this wonderful sweet can keep you going for days. The quality of *chikki* varies, but good *chikki* should be crisp and not stick to your teeth.

Fresh fruit is one of the best things about India. Mangoes, pineapples, bananas (five or six different varieties), melons, coconuts and tangerines are widely sold in markets or by street vendors. And it's all ridiculously cheap. It's often a bad idea to buy fruit and vegetables (e.g. cucumbers) cut into segments and sold on the street because they attract too many flies. Always buy complete fruits, and peel them yourself, or have the vendor cut open a new fruit for you. You'll soon get used to the luxury of never having to go more than a few paces to buy a piece of fruit. And the more fruit you eat the better, as your body seems to crave the vitamins after the strain of constantly moving about.

Drinks

The most popular beverage by far in India is *chai* or tea. Brewed up on every street corner, for Rs1 or Rs2 a shot, it usually appears as a glass of strong, filmy, dark brown liquid. *Chai* is commonly made with boiled buffalo milk, and is loaded with sugar. You come to crave the stuff after a while, even if you normally take your tea black at home, because it gives you an undeniable energy boost. You can order black tea at restaurants, however, if desired. Some travellers give up on tea completely and switch to coffee. This is often very good in the south and is available from Indian coffee-houses in most towns and cities.

One of the best drinks to have when you're hot and thirsty is a tender coconut. Sold everywhere at little stalls, these large green coconuts are filled with an unbelievable amount of cool, delicately flavoured coconut milk. Tender coconuts cost about Rs5, and the flesh on the inside of the shell can also be eaten (the vendor will usually split the coconut in half for you, and give you a sliver of the husk with which to scoop out the flesh). The skill of the machete-wielding vendors as they cut a perfectly round hole into the top of the coconut is quite impressive. Indian doctors swear by tender coconuts as a general health aid, and they are supposed to be especially good for those with stomach problems. Excellent natural fruit juices and curd-based *lassi* are widely available in India, as are a vast selection of carbonated bottled drinks. These go under names like Gold Spot (sickly-sweet orange), Citra, Limca, 7-Up or Teem (lemon), Campa Cola and Thums Up (cola). Pepsi and Coca Cola are also plentiful. To really replace all the fluids you sweat out in the heat, however, you should drink lots of bottled water. Numerous street kiosks sell litre bottles of mineral water for Rs10–15. Drinking bottled water will also help ensure that the water you drink is safe—just make sure the seal on the bottle is intact.

Alcoholic drinks can be relatively expensive, and imported liquor is only available at luxury hotels for outrageous prices. Indian brands are generally of a lower quality, but are passable. Beer is popular and widely available, and a large bottle of chilled, gassy, bland lager sells for around Rs30, though in Goa and a few other states the price is lower. Popular brand names include Golden Eagle, Black Label and Kingfisher. In Bangalore and Bombay, draught beer is readily available. Bangalore and Goa are two of the only places you can buy real wine (not the sweet stuff). The quality is not very good and it's very expensive at around Rs300 per bottle, but if you crave a glass of red it does the trick.

The only south Indian state where drinking is a problem is Andhra Pradesh, which was declared officially 'dry' in 1995. Foreigners can drink at big hotels only, and must buy a Rs200 alcohol licence at reception. A beer will then cost about Rs100.

Indians are very much into whisky, which sells in 'wine' shops (an ironic name since most 'wine' shops do not sell wine). It's very raw and hasn't got much of a bouquet, but at around Rs80 per half-bottle it's very cheap. Indian rum is generally of a high standard and locally made gin and vodka are in most cases good. In Goa you can find coconut or cashew nut *feni*, which is pretty good and laughably cheap—about Rs5–10 for a healthy-sized shot. Try mixing coconut *feni* with Teem or Limca.

Eating Out

It's a cliché, but true, that the best food you will eat in India is in private homes. And it is likely, given the enormously hospitable nature of the country, that you will be given the opportunity to discover this for yourself.

Food in south Indian restaurants tends to be fairly basic, although a number of excellent speciality restaurants have sprung up in Bombay and Bangalore over the past 10 years. As a general rule of thumb, always eat Indian instead of Western food. It's cheaper, tastier and more interesting. Go ahead and get your burger or pizza fix once in a while, but prices will be relatively high and the quality nowhere near what you'd expect at home.

If you are a confirmed carnivore travelling in the south, you'll have to look for restaurants advertising non-vegetarian food. Most restaurants are vegetarian unless otherwise specified (giving you insight into what vegetarians go through in the West). Indian vegetarian food is often better tasting and safer than the meat dishes, so you won't be missing much. In fact, many people return from India as dedicated vegetarians. If vegetarianism is something you've been meaning to try for years, this is just the place to do it.

South Indian fare may be very simple, but what there is of it is good, and consistently so. It's also very cheap and widely available. It has been said that the Indians invented the concept of fast food. Their ability to feed a whole busload of people at a roadside stall in under 10 minutes is quite remarkable. Simple, good and filling 'meals' (somtimes called *thali*) are served in small canteens for as little as Rs15, and will be served minutes after you order. Although the fried snacks sold at roadside stands are enticing and delicious, it is probably wise to steer clear of roadside food for the first few months until your stomach has had a chance to acclimatize.

At a high-class restaurant, particularly in the large international hotels, you can expect to pay anything beween Rs150–400 for a meal which outside would probably cost a quarter of that. Smart hotel restaurants also levy a 20% expenditure tax, and the food is rarely worth it. If you look around, you can often find less expensive, better quality restaurants aimed at tourists and middle-class Indians which will certainly offer better fare than hotel food.

In the south, Indians eat their food with their hands. This looks strange at first, especially since soupy rice forms the base of most meals, but Indians swear that food tastes better eaten this way and that spices can't be mixed properly into rice with a utensil. Although waiters will usually give you a spoon if you request it, try eating with your hands a few times. Where else will you get the opportunity to do so in public? All restaurants provide an easily accessible wash basin to wash your hands both before and after eating (napkins are only offered in more expensive restaurants). When eating out, you'll also notice that locals do all their eating with their right hand only (the left is used for something else). As a foreigner you can probably get away with using both hands without being laughed at, but learning how to tear a *poori* (a fried bread) with one hand gives a certain satisfaction.

restaurant categories

Restaurants in the guide are grouped according to cuisine, and then listed in descending order of price. All food in India is comparatively cheap for the foreign visitor, and it is true to say that excellent food need not be expensive. In fact, above the most basic restaurants, you tend to pay for the décor; this is especially true of restaurants in hotels.

Restaurants often wonderfully misspelt menus. Items like 'Sour and Acrid', 'Scream Bled Eggs' and 'Lemon Sod' will keep you entertained while you are waiting for your food.

After a meal at a restaurant, your bill normally comes in a dish of caraway seeds, eaten to cleanse your mouth after meals. Sometimes, so is a wad of *paan* (a mixture of spices, lime paste, and mildly addictive areca nut wrapped in a betel leaf), another popular aid to digestion.

You will need a course of vaccinations and a supply of malaria tablets for India. They are not essential requirements for entering the country but are very strongly recommended. A Yellow Fever Vaccination Certificate is required however if coming from a country recently infected with this disease. While sanitation and hygiene in India remain at their current levels, it's wise to take every possible precaution against ill-health.

Vaccinations

You'll need protection against typhoid, tetanus, polio, and hepatitis. The cholera vaccine is now considered ineffective against the strains prevalent in India. Diseases like malaria and hepatitis, which are both very easily contracted, can not only make your life a misery while you are abroad, but may also remain with you for the rest of your life.

In the UK, you can either make an appointment to see your local GP or use a local vaccinating centre. Your GP is likely to be the cheapest option, but make sure you leave yourself enough time. London has several quick and efficient drop-in centres: **West London Vaccinating Centre** at 53 Great Cumberland Place, London W1H 7LH, ✆ (0171) 262 6456, open from 9am to 4.45pm; the **London Hospital for Tropical Diseases**, 4 St Pancras Way, London NW1 0PE, ✆ (0891) 600350; **Trailfinders**, 194 Kensington High Street, London W8 7RG, ✆ (0171) 938 3939; **British Airways Travel Clinic**, 156 Regent Street, London W1P 0LX ✆ (0171) 637 9899, open daily from 9am to 4.15pm, 10am to 12.30pm and 2pm to 4pm on Saturdays. Expect to pay up to £50 for a full course of injections at a commercial travel clinic.

Vaccinations are best administered about two weeks before departure. This gives them time to take full effect (typhoid immunity takes 10 days to settle in properly), and allows you to get over any unpleasant side-effects before you travel. The commonly used vaccine against hepatitis A, gamma globulin, remains at peak strength for only a few weeks, so take it as close to departure as possible. If you are intending to stay in India for 6 months or longer, you might want to consider the newer, more expensive vaccine, which affords protection for up to a year. For frequent travellers, there is now a course which immunizes you for life. You can also get a rabies vaccination but this must be done 3 months before you travel since you need to have a booster six weeks to two months after the first.

Malaria Tablets

You will need both the daily and weekly varieties of tablets. Start taking them 10 days before you leave for India. This gives you a chance to change them if the ones prescribed by the clinic or your GP don't agree with you; and it also allows your body to start building up some immunity before you arrive. Continue taking them for 6 weeks after returning home. Malarial parasites are extraordinarily resilient and many varieties are now found in India. Unfortunately, resistance to the currently available drugs is now widespread but this does not mean that you should not bother taking them; rather, equip yourself with a mosquito net (if you intend to spend a great deal of time out of doors), some coils (to burn in hotel rooms) and a good repellent such as **Jungle Formula**, to give you double protection.

Once you've seen the doctor, see your **dentist**. Ask for spare caps, plus glue kit, for any teeth presently capped. While dental treatment in the major cities is of a high standard and not expensive, facilities outside the major cities are often more basic.

Contact-lens wearers should consider switching to specs for India, because of dust, heat, intense glare, etc. **Spectacle wearers** should note down their prescription. Opticians in India are cheap, and the cost of prescription lenses and frames is often a fraction of the UK equivalent.

AIDS

AIDS in India is much more prevalent than is officially accepted. The problem is not confined to the 'red-light' areas of the major towns but is possibly spread throughout the country. Anyone seeking a working or student visa for more than one year must take an AIDS test and submit a copy of the certificate verifying a negative result along with the visa application.

Travel and Medical Insurance

You don't have to believe everything you hear about theft and illness in India, but you can't afford to ignore it either. Good travel insurance is essential for your peace of mind, and has saved many travellers a lot of heartache. Take great care when choosing your policy, and always read the small print. A good travel insurance should give full cover for your possessions and health. In case of illness, it should provide for all medical costs, hospital benefits, permanent disabilities and the flight home. In case of theft or loss, it should recompense you for lost luggage, money and valuables, also for travel delay and personal liability. Most important (and this could be a life-saver) it should provide you with a 24-hour contact number in the event of medical emergencies.

If your own bank or insurance company hasn't an adequate travel insurance scheme (they usually have), then try the comprehensive, but expensive, schemes offered by **Trailfinders**, ✆ (0171) 938 3939, or **Jardine's**, ✆ (0161) 228 3742, or the Centurion Assistance policy (linked to Europ Assistance) offered by **American Express**, ✆ (01444) 239900. Travel companies often include insurance in the cost of a luxury tour but this is not always adequate. Whichever insurance you buy, take a copy of the policy with you to India. Most important, keep a separate note of the 24-hour emergency number and keep it on you at all times.

Should anything be stolen a copy of the police report or FIR (First Information Report) should be asked for and retained. A copy of the police report may be required by your insurance company when making a claim.

Money

Visitors are normally asked to declare the amount of foreign currency in their possession upon arrival in India. Those having more than US$10,000 in the form of travellers' cheques or bank notes are required to obtain a **Currency Declaration Form** before leaving Customs. This will ensure that you can reconvert any excess rupees upon departure. You will also need encashment certificates for the reconversion (*see* below).

Remember that you *cannot take rupees into or out of India*; you have to exchange them within the country. It is wise to bring most of your money in travellers' cheques as they can be refunded if lost or stolen, but a small amount of cash (about US$100) is useful in emergencies. You should always change your money into rupees at authorized money changers or banks. It is illegal to exchange money through unauthorized channels and sometimes people offering to change money on the street are actually police informers. Moreover, the street rate of exchange is often lower than the official bank rate.

Save the **encashment certificates** which official money changers issue for all transactions. These are needed to reconvert rupees into your original currency before leaving the country. Rupees cannot be reconverted once outside of India.

Note that if you stay in India for 180 days or more, you are supposed to obtain an **income tax clearance certificate**, for which encashment certificates are also required. This clearance is needed to show that you have been living off you own money (i.e. not working illegally) during your stay in India. The Foreign Section of the Income Tax Offices in Bombay and Madras issue these certificates on sight of passport, airline ticket, visa and encashment certificates. You are then supposed to show this document to officials at the airport when you leave the country, but in truth it is very rarely requested of anyone.

It is recommended you buy American Express or Thomas Cook travellers' cheques because they have many offices around India, and have good reputations for swift, efficient refunding in the event of loss. Other companies do not always refund losses immediately.

American Express has offices/agents in Bangalore (P.L. Worldways Limited, 26/1 Lavelle Road, ✆ 201 579); Bombay (276 Dr Dadabhai Naoroji Road, Majithia Chambers, ✆ 204 8291/8295); and Madras (Binny Limited, Ground Floor, L.I.C. Building, 102, Anna Salai, ✆ 840803/847024).

Thomas Cook has offices in Bangalore (55 M.G. Road, ✆ 5586742); Bombay (Dr Dadabhai Naoroji Road, ✆ 2048556/8); Cochin (Palal Towers, 1st floor, Right Wing, ✆ 369829); Hyderabad (Nasir Arcade, 6-1-57 Saifabad, ✆ 231988); Madras (112 Nungambakkam High Road, ✆ 8274941 and 20 Rajaji Road, ✆ 5340976); and Panjim (8 Alcon Chambers, Dayanand Bandodkar Marg, ✆ 221312).

Make sure that the travellers' cheque company you do choose gives you (in writing) the addresses of their refunding agents in India. Sign your travellers' cheques immediately on receipt and make a separate note of the cheque numbers. Store these numbers separately from the cheques and mark down which cheques you cash as you go along. In case your cheques are stolen, you will then be able to get them replaced with minimum hassle.

Budgeting Your Trip

If you're on a shoestring, Rs250–300 per day will cover basic accommodation, food, bus or 2nd class rail travel, and even leave enough for a beer at the end of the day.

If you want to shop, eat well and stay in air-conditioned accommodation as well as travel by luxury coach or 2nd class air-conditioned train, allow for Rs1000 per day.

If you want to use 5-star hotels, hotel restaurants and private cars, allow for a minimum of Rs3000–5000 per day.

Price ranges are often misleading: you don't need to spend a lot of money to ensure cleanliness and comfort. There is often little difference (except in price!) between 5-star hotels and more moderate accommodaton. Similarly, the most expensive restaurants are often the most bland. Explore the hotels and restaurants in the 'moderate' and 'inexpensive' categories of this guide and you will have a more interesting trip, stay healthy and save money.

Credit Cards

In India the American Express card justifies its additional expense by enabling you to raise cash readily from Amex offices, gets you into hotels if you've just lost all your money, and lets you use their mail-receiving facilities. Visa cards are also useful—airlines and big hotels accept it, as do most travel agents. Some banks will give you a **cash advance** on Visa cards—among them State Bank of Andhra and Grindlays Bank. Making purchases on your credit card is not a bad idea, as most credit card companies offer a competitive exchange rate and do not charge you any commission on the transaction.

Running Out of Money

This is another good reason to bring credit cards, as getting money wired over through the banks is slow and painful. It's not completely unknown for banks to keep the money in their system for up to three weeks before admitting that it has arrived. A good travel agent may advance you money if you put up your passport as security—but only if they know you. Always keep US$100 cash stashed away somewhere safe in the event of losing the bulk of your money. If you find yourself really desititute, head for the nearest Sikh temple. These have a law of hospitality similar to some Christian monasteries, and you will be fed and sheltered until rescue arrives.

Museums and Opening Hours

Most Indian museums are government-run and have a standard entrance fee of Rs2–5. Camera fees are charged separately ands cost Rs10–15.

Museum opening hours vary. To avoid confusion, the opening times of each individual museum are given in the guide. The only thing to remember is that *all* museums close for lunch, usually between 1 and 3pm.

As for **business opening hours**, there are no rules: shopkeepers stay open as long as they can to make the most of the trade, shutting only on religious holidays. Even on public holidays you will find some shops open.

The same cannot be said of **government offices**, which open from 9 to 5 only and shut at weekends. The only exceptions are the **central telegraph offices** in the larger towns, which stay open until midnight, allowing you to take advantage of cheap rates for long-distance telephone calls. However, all government offices shut for religious and public holidays.

As for **pubs**, these only exist in Bangalore and Mysore and close at 10.30pm sharp. After that you'll have to drink in your hotel. Bombay and Goa's **bars** stay open until the small hours, as do Bombay's **nightclubs** (*see* p.96).

Packing

South India's warm climate requires a minimum of clothing. The wisest travellers take only one change of clothes and buy whatever else they need out there: India's **handwoven cotton textiles** are dirt cheap, beautifully made, and let the skin breathe much better than their European counterparts. The same applies to Indian **leather sandals**. To kit yourself out on arrival, head straight for Crawford Market, if landing in Bombay (*see* p.89), Anjuna or Mapusa

Market, if arriving in Goa (see p.106) Russell Market, if arriving in Bangalore, or to the Ratten Bazaar if arriving in Madras.

Backpackers should definitely have a **water-bottle, water-purification tablets,** a good **pen-knife** and a light **mosquito net.** A free-hanging net is a hassle if there is no ceiling hook to hang it from and doesn't protect you from whatever bitey things might be living in the mattress. The best option is to buy a lightweight mosquito tent from a good outdoor store before you go. These are quite expensive but are worth the money—they give perfect protection in both hotel rooms and jungles and keep out everything from fleas to snakes. You should also take good **insect repellent,** though if you forget, you can buy a decent brand in India called Odomos.

If you plan to go **hiking** or **trekking,** don't take your heavy hiking boots: India manufactures excellent light canvas jungle boots with firm rubber grips and ankle support. These are called 'duckbacks' and sell for about Rs150–250 in the hill stations (you might not find them in lowland cities).

Buy all your **medical supplies** before you go: although India's many pharmacies carry large stocks, you may not be able to find exactly what you want (for instance malaria tablets) at the time when you most need it. Your first-aid kit should include antiseptic spray to both dry and disinfect wounds at the same time, gauze and medical tape for dressings, your own hyperdermic needles, several tubes of antihistamine cream to stop you gouging itchy bites into open sores, a healthy supply of aspirin, lip balm, and aloe vera gel to stop you peeling after getting sunburnt, as well as diarrhoea tablets and rehydration packs.

High-potency **sunblock** is a necessity. Make sure you buy more than you will need before you go, as it can be hard to find in India. Those who value their hair should also take a good **conditioner** with them, as your hair tends to dry out in the heat and break off like straw after washing.

If you are going into any wild area, take a small pair of **binoculars** with you for bird and game spotting—binoculars are also useful in large temples with intricate carvings on the high *gopurams* (towers). You should also buy all your **camera film** before your go, as Indian brands sometimes give a greenish tinge to their prints and occasionally don't come out at all.

Security

Theft is a fairly common problem in India, but you can minimize the risk by observing a few simple precautions. If you are backpacking, invest in some small padlocks for your pocket zippers and never, but never, leave your pack unattended, even for a minute. When booking into cheap lodges, check that your door has a padlock and make sure your windows are shut when you go out, even if they have bars—where people may not be able to get in, monkeys often can!

Personal security is not really a problem in peaceable south India, except in some areas of the large towns after dark, or when sleeping on the beaches in Goa or Karnataka—if you do either of these things, stay in a group and you'll be fine. In slums and villages, dogs and monkeys are more likely to attack you than people. In these areas carry a big stick: this will drive off most mammalian assailants if you hold your ground.

India is one of the great markets of the world. You can find a remarkable range of fabulous produce, including silk, cotton, leather, jewellery, carving and handicrafts at real bargain prices, sometimes four or five times cheaper than abroad. The quality of craftsmanship is often excellent, and even if what you want is not in stock it can invariably be made up for you—either on the spot or sent on later. Tailors can run up clothes overnight, and they will copy any design you provide to perfection, and it's worth bringing along a favourite piece of clothing for that purpose. Bulky purchases, such as carpets and large ornaments, can be shipped home for you. Expensive jewellery buys can be verified for you at gem-testing laboratories.

Always try to start your shopping tour with a visit to a government or state emporium. These stock the full range of local produce and handicrafts, sometimes with a selection of goods from neighbouring states. Because all prices are fixed, you are able to establish exactly what is available, and how much it should cost. This knowledge can be invaluable when it comes to buying things in less scrupulous high street shops, markets or bazaars.

The best all-round places to shop in the south are the huge Central Cottage Industries emporia in Bombay, Madras, Hyderabad and Bangalore. These are convenient for doing all your shopping in one place—very popular with people making last-minute purchases before flying home.

On the streets, you'll have to bargain hard. The big thing to bear in mind is that there is an Indian price and a tourist price for everything. Offer half the asking price and work from there. There are certain techniques you can try: the 'walk away' technique sometimes work, but many Indians have got wise to this, and you may end up walking away from something you really want, and never being called back. It is often far more effective to pretend interest in something you don't want, haggle over it a bit, affect to lose interest, then pick up the article you do want almost as an afterthought. To make some sort of sale, the vendor will often give a half-decent price immediately. It is also helpful to have asked a local Indian the correct price of the item even before entering the shop.

Bargaining can be great fun. Once you've got the hang of it, it's possible to buy things in markets and bazaars even cheaper than in fixed-price emporia. But beware, travellers do get carried away by success and it's not uncommon to meet someone stuck with £2000 worth of useless carpets, the result of being sweet-talked into visiting some street-tout's 'uncle's shop' or 'brother's silk emporium'. With big buys, you really do have to know what you're talking about. Don't let anyone take you anywhere you can't afford to go. In any shopping situation, as soon as you've lost the initiative, you're halfway to buying something you don't even want. Even worse, you may have to lug it round India with you until you find some way of sending it home.

Most decent shops and emporia give you a certificate of origin with major purchases and a receipt (essential when the article hits customs as it becomes very expensive if you can't produce it) and can arrange for the item(s) bought to be shipped home for you. In case a completely different article turns up at your front door, it can be a good idea to photograph or mark the item at the time of actually purchasing it.

Unless you have to, don't make all purchases in one place. Different areas of India are famous for different things. You'll always get a better choice and quality when you buy at source, rather than from a central government emporium.

In the south, go to Mysore for incense, silks and sandalwood, to Hyderabad for silver inlay, for pearls, and for cotton textiles, to Goa for colourful mirror-embroidery, silver and lapis lazuli jewellery and for Tibetan handicrafts, and to Ooty for woollen shawls and home-made chocolate.

If you want to know more about these products, their manufacturing processes, general prices and how to tell the real McCoy from cheap tourist tat, read the appropriate shopping sections in the main body of the text. If this only whets your appetite, there are ample opportunities in many handicraft centres to visit local crafts factories and see carpets, miniature paintings, tapestries, carvings and even incense being made. There is no obligation to buy at these places—just a lot of friendly pressure.

Sports and Activities

Outdoor Activities

The mountain forests offer some of the best **wildlife viewing** in Asia, (*see* p.70 for a full list of wildlife species), whether by vehicle, foot or horse. The mountains also offer some of India's most remote **trekking**, in jungles that have seen almost no other Western travellers, and where you can stay in tribal settlements: the 'Mountain' section of each state chapter lists the trekking possibilities where appropriate. For those who like **riding**, the Moyar River area of Tamil Nadu has lodges from where you can take guided treks into the forests. Otherwise you are restricted to the amateur rider's clubs at the racecourse in the main cities. The horses on offer at these clubs are worth riding though, and you can arrange to practise dressage, jumping or polo. **Horse racing**—probably the country's most popular sport for its chances of winning money—gives an insight into Indian urban recreation. The racing season runs through the winter and a day at the races in Bangalore, Bombay or Madras offers a chance to mix with an Indian crowd at its most boisterous.

Good **swimming** can be found at any of the beaches (and also in the high dams of the Nilgiri Hills of Tamil Nadu) listed in the guide. The big resort hotels offer **windsurfing**, while **scuba diving** can be found in the Lakshadweep islands off Kerala (*see* p.225).

Other outdoor sports include **trout fishing** in the rivers and dams around Ooty in Tamil Nadu (*see* p.308), although you will need to bring your own tackle; and **canoeing** in the Cauvery River near Mysore in Karnataka (*see* p.172). For the real specialist, the Indian **martial art** of Kalaripayat can be studied at the C.V.N. School in Trivandrum, Kerala (*see* p.203).

Cultural Activities

For sheer spectacle, the most exciting **festivals** to attend are the elephant temple festivals of Kerala (*see* p.198) and the summer **snake-boat races**, also in Kerala (*see* p.198). There is an annual **dance festival** at Manabalipuram in Tamil Nadu, just south of Madras (*see* p.258). Other places to find regular displays of **classical dance** are Cochin (*see* p.222), Trivandrum (*see* pp.203–4) and Bombay (*see* p.95). Mysore has a world famous **yoga** school that gives courses (minumum one month) in the dynamic Asthangya yoga (*see* p.174), while at Neyyar, in the Cardamom Hills east of Trivandrum, there is a less formal yoga *ashram*. For **ayurvedic medicine and massage**, head for the coast south of Trivandrum and speak to Raju at the Surya Samudra Beach Garden (*see* p.209).

Time

There are no time differences within India. Time differences between India and some major international cities are: Auckland +06:30; Berlin –04:30; London –05:30; Los Angeles –13:30; New York –10:30; Paris –04:30; Sydney +02:30; Toronto –09:00.

Tourist Information

There are national and state tourist offices in most of the larger Indian cities, which vary considerably in their degree of efficiency. Many state tourist offices run tourist bungalows which usually offer extremely good-value accommodation. Addresses for tourist offices located in more major cities can be found in the appropriate sections of this book. There is also an organization known as the Indian Tourism Development Corporation (ITDC) which often runs the city tour buses and a chain of hotels under the Ashok name. Most of the better hotels will be able to give you tourist information, as well as booking sightseeing tours.

Where to Stay

This book lists price categories for accommodation, per room, per night, as follows:

luxury:	over Rs1500 in small towns, beaches and the countryside over Rs3000 in the major cities
expensive:	Rs750–1500
moderate:	Rs350–750
inexpensive:	Rs100–350
cheap:	under Rs100

Note: these prices were valid at the time of publication. Expect a 10–20 per cent rise in tariffs for each subsequent year.

Hotels

As a general rule the further south you go in India, the cheaper accommodation becomes. In Goa, Kovalam and Ooty, prices rise by 25 per cent in the holiday, or 'high' season, from November to February, but outside these months, you will be able to bargain for up to half the advertised rates.

Officially, foreign guests in all hotels in India are charged in dollars, but in practice, most hotels below the luxury category only have a rupee tariff. Even in 5-star hotels, you can often pay in rupees against an encashment certificate—the hotel staff may be unwilling to allow this, but if faced with no choice, they are not going to refuse your money in whatever form it comes.

The 'luxury' hotels in the big cities charge prices on a par with the West. Thus, in Bombay, a night in a top hotel can cost as much as Rs5000 (about £100 or US$160)—for this you can expect a smart air-conditioned double suite (probably with private balcony and view), access to a good swimming pool, and a number of useful facilities like a shopping arcade, travel agency, bank, two or three restaurants, in-house entertainments, car park, beauty parlour and health club. Car hire and sightseeing tours are also often arranged, as are a selection of sports and activities. Out of the main cities and resort beaches, the standard of luxury hotels varies markedly, but the prices are far lower—averaging about Rs1500 per room per night in 1995/6.

Hotels in the 'expensive' category vary tremendously—the price is seldom an indication of quality. Often a town's best hotel will fall into a lower price bracket than this, and you should choose your accommodation according to the comments in each 'Where to Stay' section of the the guide (or from other travellers), rather than expecting automatic value for money.

A double room in a decent 'moderate' category hotel, will often buy the same facilities as an expensive one—air-conditioning, attached restaurant, some sort of room service and (occasionally) a lift and room telephone. Equally good but usually lacking in air-conditioning, are the 'inexpensive' hotels—often the best value, but occasionally appalling.

Until you're used to searching out the better places, it's generally advisable to stay at the state-run Tourist Bungalows. Most towns and cities have them, and though often drab and uninspiring, they are usually clean and well run, with good attached restaurants and a tourist information office. Tourist Bungalows often have cheap dormitories which are ideal for meeting people and swapping experiences (and books). A typical double room in a Tourist Bungalow will cost between Rs200 and Rs350, though a dormitory berth can cost as little as Rs40.

Before you take a room in a 'cheap' hotel, give it a thorough once-over for cleanliness and for facilities. In economy places, you can perhaps overlook the chipped basins, the peeling plaster and old coffee stains on walls. However, do not overlook the following check list: dirty bed linen; bedbugs under mattresses; cockroaches in bathrooms and waste bins; overhead fans that don't work or which have only one speed (turbo or snail); dead electric lights; no hot water (or no water at all) in showers; no lock on the door or no latches on windows and broken toilets.

In practice, a lot of travellers put up with basic, even unfriendly, accommodation and rarely give rooms a proper check. This is often because they arrive in towns too tired to really care, or too late to have much choice in the matter. Others put up with really awful dives on the basis that they're going to be out and about all day, and will only need a room to sleep in. A good way to make any room habitable is to buy a lightweight tropical mosquito-netting pop-tent before you go to India (*see* 'Packing', p.34). These excellent cocoons will protect you from all creeping, biting things, but will also allow the airflow to pass freely over you, so that you can lie naked and unbitten in the most bug-infested hole.

As a general rule, if you're just staying in a town for one or two nights, you're not going to have time or energy to traipse around looking for a decent hotel. If the recommended ones are full or unsatisfactory, you may have to take the first adequate place that comes along. This often means hiring a local hotel tout. There is no problem finding them—they find you. Bear in mind that they get a tidy commission for placing you, so don't pay them more than a couple of rupees.

hotel scams

A common scam worked by hotel touts, rickshaw and taxi-drivers, all seeking commissions from their hotels, is to deny that the hotel you want has any vacancies. 'Oh no, sahib', they will say, 'all full up'. But they're often not full up at all. And even if they are, you can probably find something else much better without their help. If the popular places have no room, take the time to wander round a few streets directly adjoining them. Remember, a lot of new hotels are opening all the time, and they're often just off the main tourist areas.

Having booked into a cheap hotel, you may also find yourself being constantly asked for tips for no service at all. Don't respond, only tip in return for a genuine service: Rs5 is ample.

Wildlife Sanctuaries, National Parks and Reserved Forests

Wildlife Sanctuaries

The Indian Tourist Board has traditionally promoted only its northern wildlife sanctuaries to foreign agents. Consequently, few western travellers have any idea of the richness and diversity of the southern wildernesses. And because of their lack of publicity, many of these sanctuaries are blessedly free from tourists. This guide carries a comprehensive listing of the south's wildlife sanctuaries. Browse through them to decide what kind of wildlife and landscape you would like to see, before planning your itinerary. For a full list of south India's flora and fauna, *see* **Topics**, p.69.

staying in wildlife sanctuaries

Most sanctuaries have **accommodation** in Forest or Wildlife Department resthouses, at an average tariff of Rs100 per person per night. You supply your own food. Resthouses usually have to be booked in advance through the Wildlife Department Office in the town nearest to the sanctuary. These are listed where appropriate in the guide.

wildlife viewing

The larger sanctuaries, such as Mudumalai, Bandipur, Nagarhole and Nagarjunasagar provide vehicles and sometimes elephants (or boats at Lake Periyar Sanctuary) for tourists to view wildlife. These go out for an hour, morning and evening, from the main reception office at the park entrance. Unfortunately, a tour in one of these vehicles is often spoiled by noisy Indian tourists who tend to scare the game off with their excited clamour. If you are a serious wildlifer, avoid the big sanctuaries and head for the Moyar River Wilderness Area in Tamil Nadu (*see* Reserved Forests, below), where a number of small lodges offer quiet viewing over waterholes in tree platforms. These lodges cater to all budgets, but if money is no object, you should head for the US$100 per night Kabini River Lodge at Karapura near Nagarhole Sanctuary, where trained naturalists take groups of four people into the forest in open-topped, quiet jeeps. Your other option is to **trek**.

trekking in wildlife sanctuaries

This is the most rewarding way to see both the forests and their wildlife. Trekking with a trained guide can be arranged at most of south India's sanctuaries, whether by the day, staying in the same resthouse by night, or over several days with accommodation in caves.

Officially, treks have to be arranged in advance at Wildlife Department offices in town near to sanctuaries. In practise, you can often arrange them by turning up and chatting to the sanctuary's chief conservator. This is not a foolproof method, however. To be absolutely safe, your best bet is to put your arrangements into the hands of a competent local travel agent used to dealing with trekkers. The best company for this is **Clipper Holidays**, Suite 406, Regency Enclave, 4 Magrath Road, Bangalore 560 025, ✆/✉ (080) 5599032/34/5599833, tlx 0845-3095.

National Parks

South India has very few national parks: sanctuaries designated to preserve a particularly rare ecosystem. With the exception of Nagarhole (*see* above), whose status was raised from a widlife sanctuary to a national park a few years ago, foreign entry to national parks is restricted to scientific study groups. However, Rajamalai/Eravikulam National Park near Munnar in Kerala, has now allowed tourists into a narrow 4-mile strip along its southern border, where you can see a large herd of Nilgiri *tahr*—a rare species of ibex found only in the south's Western Ghat mountains. The most difficult park to gain entry to is Silent Valley, also in Kerala, near Sultan's Battery, which preserves a virgin rainforest full of rare orchids and primitive hunter-gatherer tribes.

Reserved Forests

Like national parks, these areas tend to be difficult for foreigners to enter. Often backing onto wildlife sanctuaries, reserved forests act as buffer-zones between the sanctuaries and settled countryside. They also often protect tribal peoples and wildlife that wanders freely from reserved forest to wildlife sanctuary with no regard for the bureaucratic boundaries between them.

Trekking in reserved forest area is very rewarding if you can organize it: you can find tribal guides who will lead between forest settlements, staying overnight in their guest huts, and your chances of seeing wildlife are just as good as in a wildlife sanctuary. The south's most accessible reserved forests are Moyar River, in Tamil Nadu (*see* p.312), which has several wildlife-viewing lodges open to foreigners; the forest above Avalanchi in the Nilgiris (also in Tamil Nadu, *see* p.310) and the reserved forest below Munnar in Kerala (*see* p.234), though this is the most problematic of the three, as the forest's local Munnuvan tribespeople want to limit the amount of visitors to their territory.

As with trekking in many of the wildlife sanctuaries, the amount of paperwork you have to wade through before you get permission can be daunting: get Ranjan Abraham at **Clipper Holidays**, to help you (for address *see* above).

Women Travellers

India is one of the world's safest countries to travel in, and few women experience any serious danger here, unless out on their own after dark, when Indian men become drunker and bolder. However, 'eve-teasing', as the Indians call sexual harassment of women, can be a common sport among groups of Indian men. This is almost always confined to stares and rude remarks, but women may find themselves groped in crowds. If this happens, don't be afraid to make a scene, or even strike your molester—public opinion will certainly be on your side.

Ways to avoid unwanted attention are: don't smoke in public—this is a sign of a 'loose woman'; don't wear short shorts or leave the whole arm uncovered when out in public; don't respond to persistent questioning—learn to be rude, everyone else in India is. If you go topless on the beaches in Goa or Kerala, you just have to expect crowds of men to gather—bare breasts are almost never seen in India, and the sight of a pair will stop a whole street.

Culture

South India comprises a wide-ranging amalgam of races, religions and cultures. The main Dravidian Hindu culture of Tamil Nadu, Andhra Pradesh and southern Karnataka is offset by all manner of Aryan, European, Arab and Semite permutations along the western coast. There are Syrian Orthodox Christians in Kerala, Portuguese-creole Catholics in Goa, devout Muslims in every Malabar port and on the Deccan Plateau, tribes descended from Alexander the Great's troops in the Nilgiri Hills of Tamil Nadu, and even southeast Asian and negroid aboriginals in some of the Kerala forests.

The welding of so many different cultures into one nation unity has been achieved in the face of a dramatic population explosion. The current national figure of around 900 million increases at a rate of 18 million a year—that's the size of the population of Australia, or the size of the work-force on Indian Railways. Following the unfortunate experiment of enforced sterilization in the mid-70s, subsequent Indian governments have adopted a very low profile on population control. It is probable that by the end of the century, there will be one billion Indians.

The unexpected (to Western prophets of doom) national unity of India following Independence was largely due to the age-old moral and spiritual unity of the people. The essential beliefs and social institutions which marked Indians as a self-contained people originated long before the time of Buddha: some *vedas* (domestic rituals and ceremonials) were inscribed as early as 2000 BC; the *Mahabharata* (book of sacred myth) was written around 900 BC; and their legal system was codified two millennia ago. Little wonder, therefore, that Indian society, morals and laws resisted and often absorbed the civilizations of numerous foreign invaders, or that they formed the strong, solid basis on which to unite modern, free India.

Hindu society, from the earliest times, was distinguished by three characteristics: the caste system, the joint family, and the codified system of law.

Caste

The caste system is highly complex, dividing the whole of society (in theory at least) into four castes—**Brahmins** (priests, men of learning and general arbiters of morals); **Kshatriyas** (soldiers and administrators); **Vaisyas** (traders, men of commerce); and **Sudras** (farmers, peasants and the great mass of the working people). Below these are the 'untouchables' who perform all menial jobs. Grindingly poor, they represent one of the worlds most neglected groups. In practice, with social evolution these basic four divisions have fragmented into hundreds of sub-castes, and the original definitions have lost their meaning. Only the Brahmin class, by virtue of its exclusiveness, can be said to have clung, more or less, to its original function. This is perhaps appropriate, since it was the Brahmins—doubtless to preserve their privileged rights and position in society—who seem to have developed the caste system in the first place. The more romantic explanation is that the four castes sprang from the mouth (Brahmins), arms (Kshatriyas), thighs (Vaisyas) and feet (Sudras) of the creator, Brahma.

Society still tends to determine every facet of an Indian's life: the kind of work he can do, the woman he will marry, the people he will (and won't) mix with and the type of religious observances he will perform. This gives him a strong social identity, a certain sense of 'belonging' and a definite role in life. All these things contribute to the great openness, lack of social inhibition (no neuroses here!) and personal confidence of the Indian people. Yet caste, despite its great social value, can be a severe restriction on individual growth and national progress. Many well-qualified and professional Indians, for example, find caste a real block to incentive, and prefer to work abroad. It is still possible that a man might wait 10 years for promotion, working in the same low-paid job and then when his superior leaves or dies he finds that someone of a higher caste but less experience has been promoted over his head.

On a wider level, the lack of social mobility created by caste is 'free' India's most complex challenge. Whether or not it is productive of widespread apathy among the people is open to debate, but it is certainly no spur to individual incentive.

Cracks in the armour of caste have started to appear. Curiously, these are less the result of legislation than of the powerful stimulus of the West. The new Indian middle class which arose in the 19th century was formed as a result of Western education and industrialization with its attendant economic changes. The powerful Indian business class that had gained power over centuries became concentrated in the big capitals of Bombay, Calcutta and Delhi during the rapid industrial growth after Independence. The critical factor, though, was the legacy of the British Raj. When the English moved out in 1947, they left behind the elitist and influential traditions of the armed services, the civil service, the judiciary, the universities, the press and the political structures. This new Indian elite was brought up with alien concepts of Western clothes, ideas, food and social customs. For the previous century at least, this created a market and a dumping ground for all sorts of Western produce. Even India's street lamps were imported from Britain. It is in the continuing tradition of English education that the Raj continues to influence every level of Indian life. Those who can afford an English education for their children are the 'haves', while those who can't are the 'have nots'. All sorts of doors— social, political and economic—open to people with the right (English) education, especially in the British heritage of clubs and societies. This breed of snobbishness, a direct hangover from the Raj, is Britain's own contribution to Indian class and caste. In effect, the Raj created a completely new caste, one that was particularly relevant to modern industrial India—of the privileged, British-educated ruling elite.

Small wonder, then, that Indians are so keen to communicate with English-speaking visitors. For English is the chosen lingua franca of India's upper classes. It has status value, it is a passport to senior jobs, it is the language of central government, of the higher law courts, of business and of the professional classes. Most important of all, it is a language of opportunity, unfettered by traditional caste and social restrictions, to which anyone with enough enterprise and money can aspire. Not that this is a desirable situation. Advancement, restricted to the urban middle classes on which the Raj pinned their hopes, is still denied to the great mass of poorer people who flock to the great towns and cities of British India, notably Bombay and Calcutta, in search of food and work.

Rich and Poor

Another thorn in the side of social progress is the unequal distribution of wealth in the country. As one young Brahmin remarked: 'For many ages past, the rich have been lazy and the higher castes spoilt, leaving the lower castes to work all day long for practically nothing.' At present, about 2 per cent of India's population are rich, with some 25 per cent salaried; the remainder are the homeless, jobless and often landless poor, who live mainly in the villages. Indians of education and vision point out that the same state of affairs existed in England and the USA a century ago, when similar socio-economic inequalities existed, yet were quickly harmonized after the triumph of democracy. The more optimistic of them predict the same rapid improvements in India. But others, more realistically, fear that India will make the same mistakes as the West and that society will lose its cohesiveness.

Joint Family

The joint family was a system under which property was held in common and brothers and sons lived together under one roof: lacking in privacy, yes, but also productive of great community spirit and strength, as can be seen in many of the village areas of India today. A less satisfactory consequence of the joint family arrangement, however, was that all property was inherited not by succession to the eldest son, but divided equally between all sons. In the long term, this led to wide and disparate fragmentation of the land, each successive generation inheriting less property than the last.

Law

The system of law was a complicated batch of rights and obligations based on ancient texts and local customs. Eventually associated with Hindu religion, it was archaic in the extreme, particularly where women were concerned. An independent life for women had never been contemplated under Hindu law, and their economic dependence on men (including only limited right to property) was at all times heavily emphasized.

Then came the social revolution. At Independence, the new constitution set itself the task of bringing India up-to-date with the rest of the modern world. It followed on in the footsteps of Gandh's attempt to help the lowest caste—he changed their name from 'untouchable' to 'harijan', meaning 'chosen by God'. The new government abolished 'untouchability' altogether (at least officially), redesignating the harijans as a 'scheduled caste' with full democratic and human rights; it offered a secular law for all Indian citizens to opt for while allowing all communities to retain their own traditions; it broke down the joint family system with new inheritance laws, giving daughters equal rights to inherit with sons; it offered a unified marriage law all over India, not only permitting marriages between different castes and religions but allowing women the right of remarriage and divorce (*see* below).

In theory, modern India is no longer a socially backward country, dominated by caste and anachronistic customs, denying millions of people social rights. It has promised itself a major revolution, and would like to think of itself as moving rapidly towards it. In practice, however, India has always been slow to change. To understand why this is so, one has to appreciate the great social emphasis of the country. Far more than in the West, Indian life is governed at all levels by the extended family, a system of favours and obligations, of communal identity and sharing, by age-old social ethics and morality.

Marriage Act

The 1952 Marriage Act gave women the right of remarriage but very few young widows, even today, take advantage of it. The customs of thousands of years that have proved for some reason beneficial to society are very difficult to break, and even if these women were to declare themselves available, few Indian men would have them. Arranged marriages are still the general rule, and 'love matches' the notable exception. Marriage in India always was, and still is, a social phenomenon first, and a matter of personal preference second. In most cases, parents and relatives continue to select the bride from a similar background with some political, financial and social benefit. In some southern states (notably rural Karnataka and Andhra Pradesh) child marriages still go on, despite being strictly illegal; and it is still rare today for the bridegroom to be left alone with his betrothed before the marriage ceremony. The pertinent traditional argument in favour of arranged marriages (and a major stumbling block to social liberation in the Western sense) is that the bride and groom have to make the alliance work. Both parties are responsible not so much to each other but to society, for a successful married life. To fail in marriage is to fail in society and the divorce rate is consequently low. Because Indians can't think simply of their own needs, but must also take into account their wider responsibility to society, they generally make far greater efforts than Westerners to make marriages work.

But when marriages do break down, it can be very tough on women. To leave a marriage is, effectively, to step right out of society. Disownment by the family, loss of caste and social identity, and, in the absence of any social security arrangement, financial deprivation, are all problems faced by women seeking divorce in India today. And modern Indian marriages are by no means as stable as before. The tradition of dowries—whereby the prospective bride's father practically gives the shirt off his back—persists despite being against the law. Today, the average dowry demanded by middle-class parents for their often overpriced boys can be anything from Rs10,000 to Rs1,000,000, which often puts the bride's

family into debt for the rest of their lives. The scale peaks for boys living and working abroad, with those holding US green cards fetching the best price. IAS officers (the senior cadre of civil servants), doctors and lawyers receive higher bids than idealistic teachers or publishers. Worse, 'kitchen accidents' still occur: young wives who disappoint greedy in-laws are doused in kerosene and incinerated in locked kitchens. This leaves the husband free to remarry and collect another handsome dowry. Such practices reflect the temptations generated by an increasingly consumer-orientated society.

History

As late as 1920, it was believed that civilization in India dated back only to the time of Alexander's invasion in the 4th century BC. The problem was that the Hindu people, unlike the Greeks, the Europeans, the Chinese and the Arabs, never developed the art of historical writing. India did have a considerable historical tradition, embodied in both its literature and its semi-religious works known as the Puranas, but until the early 1800s little was known of the history of the Hindu people before the Muslim invasions of the 11th century AD.

Ancient India (*c.* 5000–31 BC)

The Dravidians of the Indus Valley

Some time in the mid-19th century, British engineers laying a rail track between Karachi and the Punjab stumbled across a vast quantity of ancient sun-baked bricks, which were being used by locals to provide solid foundations for the track. It was later found that these bricks were over 5000 years old. Intrigued, archaeologists visited the area in the 1920s and presently came up with two buried cities—Mohenjodaro (mound of the dead) along the Indus, and Harappa on the Ravi. A rapid series of other discoveries, in the Punjab and in Gujarat, confirmed that an ancient civilization with well-planned cities, large-scale commerce, skilled craftsmen, knowledge of mathematics and script, and sophisticated social structure existed in India as long ago as 3000 BC. This was a timely discovery. To know that they belonged to one of the earliest areas of civilization in the world, contemporary with ancient Egypt and Sumer, provided the modern Indian people with just the kind of national pride and feeling they needed to achieve unity, and with it Independence.

Aryans, Persians and Greeks

The Indus civilization of cities, farms and sacred megaliths was created by the 'original' Dravidian Indians, whose descendants still inhabit the south today. This civilization then spread to northern and western India while the original cities fell into disuse. Around 1500 BC the Aryan tribes came from the north, mounted on horses and riding in chariots. They were a Caucasian people who brought a rich language tradition to India, later to result in the Sanskrit literary classics of the *Puranas*. Around 800 BC they learned how to make iron tools and weapons, and then pushed further east and southwards to the Gangetic plain, where they founded villages, tribal republics and powerful states.

From roughly this period onward, the respective histories of south and north India diverged. The Indus Valley and much of the northwest was overrun first by Cyrus of Persia, then by his son Darius (521–485 BC). Alexander overthrew Darius III in 331 BC, advanced as far as the Beas River in 326 BC, conquered King Porus and his elephants, but was then compelled to return home by his mutinous troops, who could see no end to the conquest and feared being cut off from Greece forever. Alexander left behind a series of non-mutinous garrisons and administrators to keep the trade links open with west Asia and the consequent exchange of ideas and art.

The Mauryan Period

Taking advantage of these upheavals among the Aryan states, the tribes of Magadha (present-day Bihar) rose under King Chandragupta and cut out an extensive swathe of territory from Bengal in the east right across the north, founding the powerful Maurya dynasty. By this time the religious legacy of the first Aryans, Brahmanical Hinduism, had laid down firm roots and the 6th-century BC protest movements of Buddhism and Jainism were also well-established. The caste system, interestingly, was starting to splinter—by Chandragupta's time, the original four castes had given way to at least seven definite classes of Indian society: priests and scholars, graziers and hunters, artisans and traders, tillers, police and bureaucrats.

The Mauryan empire reached its zenith under Ashoka (268–31 BC), who consolidated the north, conquered Andhra Pradesh and fought battles as far south as Mysore, then drove east to Orissa. His fateful battle here, at Kalinga, caused him to renounce warfare forever (so appalled was he by the carnage that he had wrought) and to espouse Buddhism. He had messages of peace inscribed on rocks and pillars all over his domain. He also sent his son Mahendra over to Sri Lanka (armed with a sapling of the Bodhi Tree) to spread the message of Buddhism.

Mauryan power collapsed within a century of Ashoka's death. In its heyday though, this empire probably ruled over more of India than any other until the time of the British. As it rolled back from the south, a number of different dynasties sprang up in its place—the Samadhavan and Ikshavaku Telugus of the Deccan plateau, the Cholas in modern Tamil Nadu's eastern plains, the Cheras in modern Kerala, and Pandyas in the far south of modern Tamil Nadu.

While the Tamils busied themselves in exporting Hinduism, Buddhism, Jainism, Indian philosophy, art and medicine to Ceylon, Cambodia, Java, Rome and the Far East (by invasion or trade), the Telugus—self-styled 'Lords of the Deccan'—were mainly engaged in building Buddhist *stupas* (burial mounds). The hilltop of their great 2nd-century city at Nagarjunakonda is now an island in a vast dam on the Krishna River and is a World Heritage Site. During their rule Hinayana Buddhism, in which the Buddha was represented by *stupas*, footprints, elephants and trees, flourished. This form of Buddhism continued to around AD 400, but had been effectively supplanted by the Mahayana form at least a couple of centuries earlier.

The Early Medieval Period (31 BC–c. AD 700)

Invasions

Through the first few centuries AD, northern India suffered countless invasions from the Middle East and Asia. Some say it was simply born to be invaded, and its geography certainly points that way. The northernmost zone of the country—the soaring Himalayan range of mountains—gave Indians the illusion of being guarded by an impassable wall. But there was always a series of accessible passes—the Khyber, the Bolan and the Khurram in the northwest, and others linking India to Tibet—and these were the routes which for three millennia at least brought invader and trader across the Afghan-Punjab saddle. Marauders poured in from western China, from Scythia (around the Caspian Sea) (around 130 BC), from Parthia (modern Iraq), and central Asia.

In spite of these continual invasions, during this period the north managed to produce India's greatest Hindu dynasty—the Imperial Guptas. This empire was founded by Chandragupta II in AD 319, and for the ensuing three centuries (ending in AD 647) ruled an expanding domain which eventually extended down to modern Karnataka and northern Andhra Pradesh.

During this era of peace and stability, art and literature flourished (polished Sanskrit replacing Pali script) and extremely fine painting and sculpture was executed at Buddhist centres like Ajanta, Nagarjunakonda and Vijayawada.

The end of the Gupta period—around the 6th–8th century AD—saw Buddhism wane and the star of Hinduism rise once again. The break-up of the Gupta Empire meant the general splintering of north India into a number of separate Hindu kingdoms.

The High Medieval Period (AD 700–1565)

This was an age of high culture for the Dravidian south: a series of inter-related dynasties raised the great temple cities that still stand on the coastal plains and Deccan Plateau and established Vedic and Sanskrit colleges throughout their separate kingdoms. Although different areas of the south were prominent at different times in these early centuries AD, they shared a common religious and architectural culture, each borrowing from the other to develop highly urbanized states of great wealth.

The first dynasties to rise to prominence were: the **Andhras** of Vijayawada and the northern Coromandel Coast, whose cities grew rich on trade with Rome; the **Pandyas** of the southern Coromandel Coast (also great traders with Rome) and their more powerful neighbours the **Pallavas** of southern Andhra Pradesh and northern Tamil Nadu, a dynasty that traced its origins from the early Scythian invaders of the north. All these dynasties were energetic builders, but it was the Pallavas who first began to build the Tamil temple cities that still stand today, such as Madurai and Tiruchipalli, as well as the great temple at Kanchipuram and the cave and shore temples at Mahabalipuram. The Pallavas gradually reduced the Pandyas to client kings and ruled the southern Coromandel plains from the 4th to the 8th century.

In the later centuries of their era, the Pallavas came into increasing conflict with their northern neighbours, the **Chalukyans** of Badami on the Karnatic Deccan, whose rule lasted from AD 543–755. Impressed by the Pallavan temple towns they saw on their southward campaigns, the Chalukyan kings hired Pallavan architects and brought them north to create a more ornate style of temple building. Their temple cities of Aihole and Pattadkal in northwest Karnataka were sacked by later Muslim invaders, but even ruined they are so magnificent that both cities are now protected as World Heritage sites.

The Pallavas declined quickly during the early 9th century and power in the Tamil plains shifted to the **Chola** dynasty. They carried on the tradition of temple building, particularly under their 11th-century warrior-king Raja Raja, who raised the temple complexes at Thanjavur and conquered both the Panya cities of the southern Coromandel and the **Chera** dynasty of coastal Kerala. Over the next 200 years, the Cholas waged war right up into central Andhra Pradesh, annexed Sri Lanka and overran much of Karnataka. But so much conquest overtaxed their resources and the Cholas began to lose control of the southern Coromandel coast in the late 12th century, and the wealthy territory broke away under a second dynasty of **Pandya** kings.

The 13th and 14th centuries saw the emergence of two new powers in the Karnatic Deccan Plateau; the **Hoysalas** of Halebid and Belur, west of modern Bangalore, and the **Vijayanagars** of northern Karnataka. Once again, these dynasties kept up the tradition of building temple cities. However, the south's equally strong tradition of dynastic warfare meant that the area was caught completely off-guard when the first Muslim invaders swept down from the north.

Enter the Muslims

The Muslim conquest of India had far-reaching effects on the political, social and cultural life of the whole country. Between AD 1001 and 1027, the infamous Mahmud of Ghazni mounted 17 separate attacks, eliminating northern Hindu armies (notably at the great battle of Somnath), ransacking temples and sacking cities on each occasion. Mahmud also picked up the nasty habit of collecting severed Hindu fingers, one for each chieftain vanquished.

But Mahmud was never anything more than a glorified bandit, who returned home to Ghazni in Afghanistan after each individual raid. The real conqueror-founder of Indian Islam was Mohammed of Ghor, who mounted the first wholesale invasion of the country in 1192 and brought Muslim power to stay. The northern Hindu kingdoms of the Gangetic Valley fell within a single decade. One of Mohammed's generals, Mohammed Khilji, swept through Bihar in 1193 and effectively destroyed Buddhism overnight, razing all the monasteries and massacring all the monks. Another general, Qu'tb-ud-din, became Mohammed of Ghori's direct successor, and in 1206 became the first Sultan of Delhi. From this point on, no Hindu monarch was ever to sit in power at Delhi.

In 1296, Qu'tb-ud-din's dynasty fell to a set of Turkish kings called the Tughlaqs, who consolidated the Muslim conquest of the north between 1296 and turned their eyes on the rich Hindu kingdoms of the south—notably the Vijayanagars and Hoysalas. The first Muslim armies came marching over the southern Deccan from Delhi in 1323 and one by one the Hindu Deccan cities fell. Warangal in northern Andhra Pradesh, and Bidar in Karnataka, once in Muslim hands, became the first strongholds for Islam's slow annexation of the rest of the south.

The Rise of the Deccan Sultans

Being so far away from Delhi, the Muslim generals who had overrun the Deccan in the 14th century were tempted to carve out kingdoms for themselves. The most successful of these privateers was Ala-ud-din Hasan Bahman Shah, who governed Bidar in northwest Karnataka. In 1347, he risked an open rebellion against Delhi, which had been attacked by tartar invaders and was to be kept busy fighting in the north throughout the rest of the medieval period. Ala-ud-din Hasan founded his own dynasty, the Bahmanis. From Bidar, he set up a new fortified capital at Gulbarga in Karnataka. For the next 100 years the Bahmanis consolidated their rule of northwest Karnataka and western Andhra Pradesh, fighting off other warlords and holding at bay the Hindu Vijayanagar armies of Hampi in central Karnataka—the last powerful Hindu kingdom left on the Deccan.

By the 1470s, the Bahmani Sultans were maintaining a standing army of over 100,000 men which, supplemented by feudal levies in times of war, meant that medieval warfare on the Deccan Plateau was being fought on a scale seen nowhere else in the world at the time. Mercenaries from the Middle East flocked to the Bahmani cities and, by the end of the 15th century, each stronghold had a private army of its own. Inevitably, the Bahmani empire, which by now extended as far west as the Goan coast and south to Tamil Nadu, began to break up as different warlords and sons of the royal house tried to assert themselves as rulers. Various minor wars were fought, and the beginning of the 16th century saw the Bahmani empire fragment into several separate sultanates: notably Bidar, Bijapur and Golconda, near modern Hyderabad.

This fragmentation left the Hindu Vijayanagars of the southern Deccan in a perfect position to expand. Their capital at Hampi was the most fabulous city that the south had ever seen (its ruins are still one of the most impressive sights in India). During the early 16th century, their rajahs successfully exploited the divisions within the Bahmani royal house, lending troops for one side to fight another and ensuring their own safety in the process. However, the various sultans soon began to feel insulted by this obvious manipulation and finally in 1565 managed to bury their differences and launch a combined attack on Hampi. Five Muslim armies converged on the city, wiped out its army in one bloody battle and sacked the place so throroughly that it has never been inhabited since.

The bickering sultans could not keep their alliance going long enough to completely finish off the Vijayanagars, who retreated to their southern cities and ruled from around Mysore for another 200 years but all Hindu power had now vanished from the Deccan. Golconda and its Qu'tb Shah dynasty emerged as the most powerful sultanate of the Deccan and spent the following 100 years fending off the Mughals of Delhi and fighting with and finally conquering Bijapur. However, in the final decades of the 17th century, the Mughal emperor Aurangzeb repeatedly attacked Golconda and finally invested the citadel. The Qu'tb Shahs prepared to fight it out with Delhi once and for all, but both they and the Moghuls found themselves distracted, at the end of the 17th century, by a new set of invaders—this time from Europe over the Western seas.

The Early Modern Period (1565–1803)

The Europeans

While the Vijayanagars and the Deccan sultanates wrestled for power through the late medieval period, the deep south had taken its own course. In the Tamil plains a multitude of petty princes set themselves up in the palaces of the ancient Chola and Pallava temple cities and, between minor wars among themselves, prospered indirectly from the trade with Arabia coming through the port cities of the Malabar Coast of Kerala.

As early as the late 14th century coastal Kerala had divided itself up into separate city states ruled by Travancore Hindus in the south near Trivandrum and by Christians in the north. The northern port towns were the most prosperous, especially Calicut, but all the cities vyed for control of the sea trade with Arabia. In 1498, a ship full of Portuguese under Vasco da Gama arrived in Calicut and promised foreign aid to the *Nizam* (ruler) there in return for a trading site on the Kerala coast. The Nizam gave them Cochin, hoping to use these powerful allies to establish complete mastery over the Arabian Sea. But he was quickly disillusioned. The piratical Portuguese began competing directly with Calicut as soon as they had established a safe harbour at Cochin and, though a series of wars in the 16th century disrupted trade, took control of the inland trade with the Vijayanagar kings and sent the deep south into a steady economic decline.

Still taken up with their own power struggles, the Deccan warlords failed to take advantage of the south's weakness and the Portuguese gradually established control of the whole Malabar Coast, founding a major stronghold in the old Bahmani ports at Goa.

Soon other Europeans, attracted by the Portuguese successes, were descending on both the Malabar and Coromandel coasts. The Dutch arrived in the early 1600s and in turn offered their services to Calicut. They managed to drive the Portuguese out of Kerala but did nothing for the Calicut *Nizams*. Iinstead they followed the Portuguese example, both poached the Arabian trade and raided Keralan ships. In 1620, trading posts were set up by the Danes and by the **British East India Company**—a government-sponsored commercial body that had its own troops—on the Tamil Nadu coast, who set up trading posts with Sri Lanka and the Far East. The British soon got the upper hand in the Coromandel trade, founding a large fort at Madras in 1639. British power held and began to creep inland, despite the arrival of the French, who set up rival trading posts at Pondicherry in Tamil Nadu and at various points of the Andhra Pradesh coast in the 1670s.

Thus, when the Delhi Mughals and Qu'tb Shahs of Golconda prepared for a final showdown for mastery of the Deccan in the late 17th century, the balance of power in the south had shifted away from the Deccan and back to the plains of Tamil Nadu and the Keralan coast, and was being controlled by European traders with superior weaponry and unchallenged maritime supremacy. After the Mughal emperor Aurangzeb's death in 1707, a series of weak-minded successors prevented the dynasty from making good its victories in the south. The Qu'tb Shahs realized the importance of getting in on the wealth being generated by the European trade on the Coromandel coasts, and set aside their long-cherished ambition to conquer the whole south.

Meanwhile, using the armies of the southern princes, the French and the English began to fight it out in the plains of Tamil Nadu and in naval battles offshore, while the Dutch and Portuguese quietly prospered on the Malabar side. For a while the French seemed to be gaining the upper hand. They seized Madras in 1746, occupied Arcot, the Muslim principality of northern Tamil Nadu, and made plans for a conquest of the Deccan, including Hyderabad (as Golconda was now called).

However, the British rallied under Clive; they campaigned in the north against a combined French and Mughal army, finally winning a decisive victory at Plassey in Bengal in 1757. They followed up their success by invading Arcot in southern Andhra and by the early 1760s had regained Madras and control of the southeast. In 1763, a treaty was made with France in which she gave up her ambitions for an Indian empire in return for some trading posts—at Pondicherry and at a few places on the Andhran and Orissan coasts.

Their loss of the south did not stop the French from doing their best to sabotage British power there. In 1761, a Muslim warlord called Hyder Ali had usurped the Hindu prince of Mysore and began his own conquest (helped by French money and troops) in direct competition with the British, defeating an allied army of redcoats and troops from Hyderabad.

The French, though officially out of the game, kept supplying money to Hyder Ali over the following two decades and involved Britain in an expensive quagmire of inconclusive campaigns. When Hyder Ali died in 1781, his son and chief general Tipu Sultan proved just as aggressive and, again with French money, he succeeded in conquering almost the whole of the Deccan and deep south, including the ports of Kerala. However, following the Anglo–French treaty of Versailles in 1783, the French withdrew their support and the British began to make headway against Tipu Sultan, gradually whittling down his armies in battle after battle. Kerala was taken by the British in 1792 and Tipu Sultan besieged in his fortified capital of Sriringapatnam, just north of Mysore. The campaigning went on for the rest of the decade, but in an ever decreasing radius of Mysore. Sringapatnam was finally sacked in 1799 and Tipu Sultan died in the fighting. The British were the unchallenged masters of the south.

The Madras governor at this time was Colonel Arthur Wellesly, later the Duke of Wellington, and he wisely allowed Hyderabad and Mysore to remain as self-governing states, but ruled the

Tipu's tiger: a carved and painted wooden effigy which simulates the growls of the tiger and the cries of his victim. Presented to the Sultan of Mysore in the 1790s and seized by the British after his death at the seige of Sriringapatnam in 1799. It is now on display in the Victoria and Albert Museum, London.

rest of the south directly from Madras. It was from here, via trading posts in Andhra Pradesh, Orissa and finally Bengal, that the British Raj of all India began.

There was resistance on the Deccan from the powerful Marathas—Hindu warlords who had gradually been annexing the old Mughal and Qu'tb Shah territories while the Europeans and the southern princes fought it out in Bengal and Tamil Nadu—but Wellesly defeated them at Assaye in 1803 and the East India Company became the effective sovereign of all India.

Modern India (1803–Present)
The Raj

The princelings of the south, despite having been delivered from Hyder Ali and Tipu Sultan, resented being subject to yet another set of outside rulers. This resentment was especially strong among the Travancore princes of Trivandrum and the new Maharajah of Mysore, a puppet king whose Wadeyar dynasty, originally usurped by Hyder Ali, had been restored by the British. Mysore rose in 1831 but the Maharajah was quickly defeated and exiled, and the city was ruled by a governor until 1880, when the Wadeyars were restored for a second time, and the state was allowed semi-autonomy. The redcoats' quick and brutal subjugation of Mysore kept the Travancore princes quiet, especially as the British allowed self-government for the rulers of Hyderabad in return for military aid from the Deccan should the need arise.

The last southern state to come under the Raj was the tiny country of Coorg, which lies in the mountainswest of Mysore on the border with Kerala. The British annexation of Coorg in 1853 was virtually bloodless, the Company having been actually invited by the state's ministers to remove their monster of a Rajah (*see* p.144). Coorg was also allowed self-government.

The south escaped most of the horrors of the Indian Mutiny of 1857; the Indian troops in the southern garrisons were watched over by Coorg and Hyderabadi guards, and remained peaceful through the latter part of the 19th and early 20th centuries. During this time, the region had something of a Golden Age, especially the state of Mysore, whose last Maharajahs created a philanthropic government that Gandhi described as 'near perfect'.

Towards Independence

After 1880, the histories of south and north India can be seen to converge, becoming one national history. The British happily exploited India's natural wealth—in the south developing large-scale tea production in the Keralan and Tamil Nadu mountains, coffee-growing in Coorg, and cotton growing on the plains. To facilitate this exploitation the Brits constructed an extensive system of railways, massive irrigation and agricultural programmes, and (some say most importantly) a code of civil law. In fact, it was far from democratic since the conquerors always held the privileged positions, but it did ensure an element of equality among the Indians themselves. And this was in a country where Hindu law had previously differentiated strictly between Brahmin and non-Brahmin, and where Islamic law had one set of codes for Muslims and quite another for *kafirs* or infidels. The British also instituted the bureaucracy of the civil service and—while keeping the Indians at a comfortable distance from any real power within it—set about creating an Indian middle class with an increasing responsibility for it. Ultimately, knowledge of ideas and institutions brought an intense desire for self-government.

The Indian Mutiny, though it had been crushed, had kindled a spirit of rebellion that slowly began to grow. During the closing years of the 19th century, resistance was centralized in a sudden, wholesale reform of Hinduism itself. Previous attempts to rally Indians round the banner of the Hindu religion had always foundered on the rocks of caste—the exclusiveness of the Brahmins gave them no feel for the mass popular pulse. But a few determined vision-aries—Ram Mohun Roy, Ramakrishna, Swami Vivekananda, Dayananda and even the European Mrs Annie Besant—led a series of important reforms designed to revive Hinduism as a truly modern religion, and thus totally to reorganize (and standardize) Hindu society. The movement for social reform ran alongside a parallel movement for national identity and freedom. The latter was fed by a number of timely developments in the early 20th century, including the discovery of India's antiquity (excavation of the Indus Valley civilization, *see* p.48); the revival of Sanskrit and renewed appreciation of its classics like the *Bhagavad Gita*; and the repatriation of Buddhism, with the coming to light of its long-lost literary, artistic and philosophical achievements. Hindu history and heritage was refound, largely through the researches (ironically) of Western scholars, and this contributed significantly to the evolving national self-image of India as a whole. Other groups, such as the Muslims, also began to develop a sense of national pride and seek self-determination.

The Indian National Congress, founded in 1885, was destined to give the British their most prolonged opposition. It began by trying to unite all the communities in India under one banner but this was not always possible. The Muslims, in particular, still regarded themselves as a race apart, with their traditions rooted outside India, and were alarmed by the growth of Indian nationalism and its demands for political freedom. Faced by the prospect of a Hindu-dominated free India, they founded the Muslim League in 1906 and began making demands for a separate communal electorate for themselves. The Anglo-Muslim alliance of 1906 was a decisive development: it split India into two nations and Hindus and Muslims were embarked on two entirely different courses. In 1909, perhaps the greatest mistake the British ever made, the Morley-Minto reforms initiated the creation of separate Muslim electorates which directly paved the way for the partition of the Indian Empire.

Gandhi and Independence

The cry for independence, which had become nationwide by the turn of the century, was muted by the arrival of the First World War. Then it burst forth again—this time as an insistent roar—under the charismatic leadership of Mohandas Karamchand Gandhi. Soon to be styled the *Mahatma* (Great Soul) of the nation, Gandhi arrived in India in 1915, following a long period of fighting on behalf of human rights in South Africa. Gandhi fervently believed in Hindu-Muslim unity: at no time did he contemplate India as an exclusively Hindu state. His life and thoughts were a direct reflection of the 'Karma Yogin' (saint in action). His campaign for the abolition of untouchability, his famous fasts compelling Hindus and Muslims to live together in harmony, his ideals of *ahimsa* (non-violence) and *satyagraha* (passive resistance), and his own life of extreme austerity were all in strict accordance with Hindu traditions. He focused on the movement for independence after the disgraceful massacre of peaceful protesters by armed British troops at Amritsar in 1919 and turned the movement from an ineffective middle-class one to a village-based one of irresistible power.

Gandhi was also a wily politican. He knew that if the extremists and terrorists were very active, the British would be more likely to accept Gandhi as the 'acceptable' face of the freedom movement. Gandhi never really tried to stop the extemists as he tried to stop communal violence. Rather, he relied on the extremists to produce situations for which his *ahimsa* politics could be seen as the antidote.

As the clamour for independence reached its peak, Gandhi was forced to fight a rearguard action against the revived Muslim League under Mohammed Ali Jinnah. After 1936 a demand began for the creation of an independent homeland for Islam and the fight was on for a partitioned India. The Second World War brought matters to a head. When in 1942 the Mahatma launched his last great struggle, two things became clear: first, that full independence was the only settlement that Indian nationalists were willing to consider; second, that partition was inevitable. Jinnah out-manoeuvred both the British and the Indian Congress. When, on 9 August 1942, Gandhi uttered the words in every Hindu's heart and told the British to 'Quit India', Jinnah followed with the demand to 'Divide and Quit'. Against their better judgement, the British were forced to do just this. It was a simple case of partition or civil war. As bloody clashes between Muslims and Hindus mounted in frequency and intensity, even the Congress—after a few months' experience of coalition government (1946–47)—realized that partition was inevitable. As the new British Viceroy, Lord Louis Mountbatten, issued the date for Independence—14 August 1947—the old Indian spokesman, Mahatma Gandhi, left the political scene, darkly predicting chaos.

It was worse than chaos. In 1947, the Indian subcontinent had its eastern and western extremes sliced off to form the two wings of Pakistan, one of which is present-day Bangladesh. But at the time of partition, the new India contained over 35 million Muslims, while the new Pakistan housed vast numbers of Hindus. The problem was worst in the new border states of Bengal and the Punjab, which had very mixed populations and a long history of intercommunal antagonism, and which were both neatly chopped in two by partition. The situation was explosive, and when, during the weeks following Independence, the mass exodus of Hindus and Muslims, uprooting homes in now 'alien' states and travelling to their new homelands, began, it was the signal for bloody and prolonged carnage on an unimaginable scale. Trainloads of Hindu and Sikh emigrants going east were stopped and butchered by Muslims, while parties of Muslims fighting their way west suffered the same fate from Hindus and Sikhs. Around 10 million people were 'exchanged' following Independence; some 500,000 perished en route.

Such was the extent of the holocaust that Jawarhalal Nehru, Gandhi's political disciple and the first Prime Minister of India, made an unexpected plea for help to the ex-British Viceroy, Mountbatten. 'Ours is the politics of agitation, not of government!' he declared. 'Please come back and help us out till we find our feet!' Mountbatten returned and the crisis was soon overcome. Only in Kashmir was a satisfactory long-term solution not found. The region was claimed by both Pakistan and India, and since neither would give way over it, the UN was forced to step in and divide it with a demarcation line. But Kashmir continues to be a strong bone of contention, neither side having ever agreed to an official state border.

On 30 January 1948, in the last act in the bitter-sweet drama of Independence, Gandhi was assassinated. Shot three times by a Hindu fanatic, he died a disappointed man—his dream of an undivided, free India never realized.

Since Independence

Fortunately for India, Nehru was a capable successor. Following Independence, he steered the country on a balanced course which made the initial transition to self-government both quick and painless. His favourite word may have been 'dynamic', but his political, economic and social outlook was basically conservative (even static, some say). 'The developing countries need peace for their development,' he stated. 'They need at least two decades of uninterrupted peace.' To ensure this, he adopted a strict policy of non-alignment with other world powers. For the first nine years of his premiership, it worked. But at heart Nehru was a convinced socialist, more than somewhat influenced by Marxism, and he tended to lean markedly in favour of the communist world rather than the democracies. For a non-aligned country to rely heavily on one side put India at a disadvantage, and lost her both friends and influence over the years. In 1956 Russia invaded Hungary, and Nehru was forced to show his hand. India was the only non-aligned country to support the USSR's move, and henceforth nobody took his non-alignment seriously. The final humiliation took place in 1962, when Sino-Indian border clashes led to the threat of a Chinese invasion. Nehru made pleas for military aid to both East and West, but while Britain and the US promised immediate help, the USSR stood on the fence of 'non-alignment' and simply advised restraint.

Domestically, Nehru's record was far better. He used a charismatic persona and an unchallenged majority to build up a strong, cohesive central government and thus to consolidate the nascent unity of India. He also made important, progressive social changes, especially with regard to the liberalization of policies for women. Despite criticism, he also retained good relations with the British ex-colonizers and encouraged both a free press and an independent judiciary.

He was succeeded by Lal Bahadur Shastri (for just 20 months), a meek but (when the occasion called for it) surprisingly strong-willed leader. His premiership was overshadowed by Pakistan's twin attack on India—in the Rann of Kutch and in Kashmir—in 1965. Shastri, who had never felt that Nehru was militant enough, abandoned India's long-standing policy of peaceful neutrality and retaliated with force. But he was essentially a man of moderate views, and his untimely death—shortly after the Pakistan armies had withdrawn—spelt the advance of extremism in the country.

A feature of Indian politics is its emphasis on 'personality' leaders. A second has been the failure of these leaders to surround themselves with strong, capable lieutenants. Mahatma Gandhi was an exception. He had begun grooming Nehru for power as early as 1929, realizing perhaps the truth of the old Buddhist precept, that a master's prime duty is to create a disciple even stronger than himself. But Nehru himself failed to do this and the vacuum of younger generation leaders in the Congress following his death left it seriously out of touch with the masses. Inevitably, the old and the new had to fall out, and Congress was doomed to split.

Into the political breach created by Shastri's death stepped Indira Gandhi, Nehru's only daughter. She was elected Prime Minister in 1966. Her landslide victory at the polls was partly due to her extravagant promises of bread for the masses, but doubtless owed more to the magic of the name 'Gandhi' (though no relation to the Mahatma), coupled with the right amount of forceful 'personality'. Subsequent re-election in 1971, swept in on a tidal wave of war-fever created by Pakistan's treatment of East Pakistan and the subsequent creation of an independent Bangladesh, confirmed her in a dangerous situation of unchallenged power. By 1975, as attempts to suppress the free press and to muzzle the judiciary gave way to more openly fascist policies, serious opposition to her rule surfaced. She retaliated with the so-called state of emergency, freeing herself of regular parliamentary restraints and functioning virtually as an unchallenged ruler. This enabled her to push through a number of positive economic reforms and generally improve efficiency. On the other hand, the imprisonment of protesting elements and the disastrous sterilization and 'people's car' programmes initiated by her son,

Sanjay, set the nation against her. (The idea behind this was to produce a car made in India costing Rs10,000, but the programme failed and the enterprise was nationalized in 1978. Suzuki now own 50 per cent of the factory.) Under the illusion that the people would support her whatever she did, she unwisely went to the polls in 1977 and lost.

In the place of Indira and the Congress Party came the conservative Morarji Desai and his uncohesive Janata 'People's Party'. Not equal to the task of government, unable to stop inflation spiralling, Janata broke apart in 1979 and Indira Gandhi returned triumphant in 1980. She tried and failed to deal with escalating social problems including rife corruption, police brutality, persecution of untouchables and Hindu/Muslim/Sikh intercommunal unrest. Her drastic solution to Sikh unrest in the Punjab, culminating in the armed occupation of the Golden Temple in Amritsar, eventually cost her her life. She was shot by an assassin's bullet in October 1984.

The circumstances of her death ensured her son, Rajiv Gandhi, an unprecedented victory at the polls in December 1984. In early 1985, everyone was confidently predicting great things of the young Rajiv. 'If the man is not assassinated first,' joked one prominent official, 'he will challenge caste, remove poverty and rid us of corruption.' Within three years Rajiv Gandhi was under attack in his own country. People were sceptical of his promise to usher India into the 21st century by means of a technological revolution—many Indians see technology as a threat to jobs—and it was almost with glee that Delhi newspapers announced, in 1987, that two defence scandals had surfaced: the Swedish Bofors company admitted paying millions of pounds in 'commission', and a 7 per cent 'agent's fee' had been involved on a German submarine deal. Members of Rajiv Gandhi's own family were implicated, and his own image as 'Mr Clean' was tarnished beyond repair. To make things worse, he embroiled himself in several regional conflicts, starting with Tamil Nadu (where his peacekeeping force sent to Sri Lanka was nicknamed 'Indian people-killing force' by resentful Tamils), and later with Pakistan, West Bengal, Kashmir and the Punjab, where his soft approach brought forth a growing voice of disapproval. Rajiv Gandhi lost the next general election in 1990.

For the second time since Independence the Congress Party found themselves in opposition. A coalition government led by V.P. Singh, who had earlier been Finance Minister and Defence Minister under Rajiv Gandhi, tried to form a united government and weather the storm created by Congress rule. Failing miserably this National Front government was replaced by an interim minority government under Chandra Shekhar. This led to fresh elections in May 1991. Congress, under Rajiv Gandhi, were confident of winning because the National Front government had been unable to govern and many of its policies were thought to have divided the country; Congress saw themselves as a party of unification. What the result would have been under normal circumstances will never be known, for Rajiv Gandhi was assassinated on 21 May 1991. Congress was returned to power as the largest party in Parliament but was without a majority. P.V. Narasimha Rao, an elderly, experienced Congress politician, became the next Prime Minister and has had to face the effects of years of misrule.

Today India is still struggling towards a clear, solid identity, with unity as its prime objective. No amount of self-criticism, however, can disguise some truly remarkable achievements since Independence in 1947. India is presently one of the top industrial powers in the world: her government and her legal, educational, and military institutions are strong, she is agriculturally self-sufficient, and making rapid strides in space-age technology (in Delhi, computer technology now helps the railways make 45,000 seat reservations a day).

Westerners have difficulty understanding the importance of religion to the average Indian. It governs his every thought, regulates his every action, and gives him his strong sense of identity—his *dharma*, or personal course in life. Religion is everything in India, and there are just as many different faiths to be found here—Hinduism and Buddhism, Jainism and Sikhism, Christianity, Zoroastrianism and Islam—as there are different peoples, tongues and cultures.

Some 80 per cent of Indians are Hindus; another 10 per cent follow the Muslim faith; Sikhs and Christians, combined, make up a further 5 per cent. All the others—Jains, Parsis, Buddhists, Bahai, etc.—comprise the remainder. Social traditions differ among the Muslim, tribal, Christian, Sikh, Parsi and other communities that constitute more than 20 per cent of India's population today. Each of these communities is governed by its own social mores and traditions.

Hinduism

An ancient repository of Indian spiritual consciousness, Hinduism is the oldest surviving religion in the world, and has more adherents than any other religion in Asia. Hinduism went through various periods of prosperity and decline, but demonstrated the most amazing capacity for absorbing and assimilating all competing faiths, and was never down for long. One of its earliest scriptures, the *Upanishads* (400–200 BC), stated 'The Great God is One, and the learned call Him by different names'—and it was this aphorism which encapsulated the unique talent for Hindu religious tolerance. It never destroyed other beliefs, just synthesised them into its own philosophical system.

Although all forms of worship are acceptable to Hinduism, there are a few basic beliefs which tie the various creeds together. The main three are Samsara, Karma and Dharma. Samsara is the eternity of life, in which the soul is believed to pass through a cycle of births and deaths on its way to perfection, and to union with the Supreme Being (Brahma). Karma, or the law of cause and effect, is where every thought, word and deed produces a consequent reaction (good or bad) in this or in a subsequent incarnation. Dharma, the code of living, is where every person has a specific role or set of moral duties to perform in life, through which he can break the cycle of rebirth and attain nirvana (heaven).

There are many thousands of gods in the Hindu pantheon. The Aryans were a nomadic people, worshippers of the natural elements. They had a Supreme Being, a central figure who controlled everything in life, but they also had gods to represent all forms of natural energy (sun, moon, wind, water, etc.) and all facets of human life and endeavour (courage, faith, luck, beauty, etc.). The total number of gods was calculated from the estimated population of the known world round the time of the mythical Mahabharata. This was the classic battle between good and evil in which five good brothers, aided by the god Krishna, defeated 100 wicked cousins. It was written down between 200 BC and AD 500, and Indian literature is full of references to it. Over the centuries, many stories and legends grew up round the various gods and goddesses. The main group—the Puranas (AD 500–1500)—became the base of all art in India. Most sculptures and paintings told a 'purana' story, and through such legends and parables, Hindu morals, customs, manners and traditions slowly became crystallized. It was the only way in which the common people received any social education, for the Brahmin priest caste had exclusive access to the ancient Vedic scriptures and holy books, and never transferred this knowledge to the masses, except in such symbolic form.

The one supreme God of Hinduism, Parabrahma, has three physical manifestations—Brahma the Creator, Vishnu the Preserver, and Shiva the Destroyer. Representing the three basic processes in human life (birth, life and death), this main trinity rules over all the lesser gods. All three deities are normally depicted with four arms, but Brahma also has four heads to show his omniscient wisdom. Unlike the other two, however, he has had very few temples built for him.

Each god has a 'carrier', an animal or bird who transports him about. Vishnu is often seen sitting on an eagle with human features called a *Garuda*. He has visited earth in nine incarnations (avatars), and is due to pay one last visit, as the horse-headed Kalki. He has already appeared as a fish, a tortoise, a boar, a half-man, a beggar-dwarf, and in human form carrying an axe. On his seventh call, he came as Rama with an impossible mission to destroy the demon king Ravana of Lanka (Ceylon). The dramatic story of his success, aided and abetted by the faithful monkey-god Hanuman became one of the world's greatest epics, the *Ramayana*. Vishnu made his eighth appearance as Krishna, the dark-skinned boy of the Mathura milkmaids, whom he married *en masse* after releasing them from the demon king Naraka. A good start for any religious debate with a Hindu is to ask him what he makes of Krishna having 16,000 girlfriends. The ninth incarnation of Vishnu, an imaginative ploy to reabsorb Buddhism back into the Hindu religion, is supposed to have been the Buddha himself.

Shiva's main symbol is the cobra, the virulent snake of death and destruction, though he generally rides out on the bull Nandi. His creative/sexual function is symbolized by the stone lingam. He is often shown with a third eye (sometimes used as a death-ray), and is believed to spend a lot of time in his Himalayan mountain home smoking the holy weed (cannabis). When roused, Shiva has a very nasty temper. First he chopped off Brahma's fifth head, and had to wander round as a beggar until the severed skull unstuck itself from his palm. Then he lopped off the head of his younger son, Ganesh, for refusing to let him visit his wife Parvati while she was having a bath. Repenting of his error, Shiva looked round for a new head for his offspring, and came up with one of an elephant. Thus, 'lucky' Ganesh, god of good fortune (and divine remover of obstacles) was born. His animal vehicle is the bandicoot, or rat.

Each of the Hindu trinity has a consort, representing the feminine side of their energy. Brahma is married to Saraswati, the goddess of learning, and her vehicle is the swan. Vishnu's consort is the beautiful Lakshmi (Laxmi), goddess of wealth and prosperity. Shiva started out with Sati (who burnt herself to death—the original 'sati' victim), then acquired Parvati, symbol of cosmic energy in the form of Shakti, the World Mother. She is also the symbol (in her dark aspect) of destruction in the form of either Kali, wearing a wreath of skulls, or Durga the terrible, riding a tiger and waving weapons from 10 hands. In addition to

Ganesh, Parvati had one other son by Shiva, the six-headed God of War, Kartikkeya (Murugan in south India or Subramanhya).

The good-humoured, indulgent, even playful attitude of many Hindus to their gods is something that mystifies many Westerners, used to religion as rather a solemn business. But while Hinduism is a strict faith, with many rituals, ceremonies and practices geared towards keeping the individual on the general straight and narrow, it has a great inbuilt sense of fun and spectacle. This is especially true on a social level, where births, marriages and even deaths are all an occasion for colourful, noisy bands and processions, complete with caparisoned elephants, performing monkeys, lots of firecrackers and entertainments, and (of course) plentiful free food. It's all a perfect reflection of, and a tribute to a pantheon of gods who may be gaudy, boisterous and flamboyant, but never dull.

Jainism

Jainism was the first major sect to break away from Hinduism, and was founded around 500 BC by Vardhamana Mahavira. He was the last of the 24 Jain saints or Tirthankars, and was an older contemporary of the Buddha. The schism from Hinduism came from his belief that there was no Supreme Creator of the universe, but that it was infinite and eternal. The Jains did believe in reincarnation (like the Hindus), but their method of achieving salvation was much more extreme. Mahavira preached the total subjugation of the senses as the most direct path to the world of the spirit, and Jain monks became noted for their great asceticism. They wandered about in a loin cloth, with just an alms bowl and a stave as possessions. In this, they resembled the Shaivite Hindu ascetics called *sadhus*, but their strict doctrine of *ahimsa* (non-violence to any living creature) caused them to go even further—thus, they also carried a broom to sweep the ground before them clear of any insects, and wore a muslin mask to prevent them swallowing any flying parasites. The Jains found little problem finding a sanctuary in India—for the simple reason that the Hindus considered them even better Hindus than they were.

Around the 1st century AD, the Jains split into two sects: the white-clad Shvetambaras and the sky-clad Digambaras. The latter were literally 'sky-clad', being so contemptuous of material possessions that they wore no clothing at all. Jain temples are often quite beautiful, with highly ornate carvings on columns and ceilings. The best of these can be seen in Rajasthan (Mount Abu and Ranakpur), Gujarat (Palitana and Junagadh) and Bombay, the main Jain centres. Jainism is particularly strong in Rajasthan, for it is believed that the Tirthankars were also Rajput princes. The Jains themselves are today few in number but have great commercial and business influence. Many of them are successful traders, bankers and philanthropists.

Buddhism

The Buddhist religion was the second reformist offshoot of Hinduism, and presented it with a far greater threat. Founded by Siddhartha (Shakyamuni) Gautama (during the 5th century BC) in northern India, it was a dynamic force which thrived for 1700 years before slowly being won back to the Hindu fold by the revivalist movement started by Sankara in the 8th century AD.

Buddha was a Kshatriya prince who, preoccupied by the human problems of old age, sickness and death, forsook riches to embark on a long quest for the Truth. After several years of rigorous ascetic practice, he attained his enlightenment at Bodhgaya and spent the final 45 years of his life teaching his new philosophy. This incorporated Hindu elements, like the doctrines of karma and reincarnation, but reinterpreted them in a far more dynamic form. As far as Buddha was concerned, karma had nothing to do with fate or predestination. It was a strict causal law of dynamic action. He taught that every living being (not just priests or ascetics) could aspire to enlightenment in this lifetime, without passively awaiting better circumstances in a future incarnation. His central doctrine, whereby enlightenment could be achieved and the cycle of rebirth extinguished, was the eightfold path of the 'middle way'. This put the case for moderation in all things, and rejected as harmful the rules, regulations and general extremism of Hinduism and Jainism (Buddha had tried ascetic starvation, and found it more likely to lead to death than enlightenment). It was a simple, optimistic message, but the Hindus rejected Buddhism as a religion of compromise. With the 'middle way' discarded, India became progressively a land of extremes and stark contrasts.

Buddhism took its big leap forward in India when adopted by the great emperor Ashoka (3rd century BC). It was carried outwards to every part of his extensive empire, and spread in time to Burma, Thailand, Sri Lanka, Korea, China, Vietnam, Nepal, Tibet, Central Asia and Japan. But in India, it quickly experienced a schism, leading to two main schools. The Hinayana or 'lesser vehicle' held that enlightenment was an individual pursuit; the Mahayana or 'greater vehicle' held that it was a collective one, with the ultimate aim of bringing all humanity to salvation. After Buddhism's collapse in India, the centre of Mahayana transferred to Japan, where the essence of Gautama's final teaching (the Lotus Sutra, or Myoho Renge Kyo) was revealed by the 13th-century monk Nichiren. Unlike the Hinayana sect, who always referred to the Buddha in terms of external symbols (the lotus for his birth, the tree for his enlightenment, the wheel of law for his first sermon, and the *stupa* for his final nirvana or salvation), the growing realization of the Mahayana sect was to seek Buddha nowhere else but in themselves, and in every living thing.

Islam

There are more Muslims in India (around 100 million) than any other religious minority group. The most recent and successful Asian religion, it was founded by the prophet Mohammed in the early 7th century AD. The Muslim canon, the Koran, is a collection of apocalyptic messages delivered to Mohammed by Allah (God). A keynote of the faith was its militancy, its evangelical zeal to spread the good word—by the sword, if necessary. Starting in Arabia, Islam extended its influence east for several centuries, and was eventually firmly established in three continents. Conversion was easy—to become a Muslim required only saying the words, 'There is no God but Allah and Mohammed is his prophet'. It was especially easy in India, where the Muslims arrived in the 11th century AD, for there were a great many low-caste Hindus seeking escape from the discriminations of Brahmanical Hinduism. They could no longer turn to Buddhism (there were no Buddhists left), so their only recourse was Islam. But in the long term Hinduism was too strong to be dislodged.

There are two types of Muslim, resulting from an early schism. These are the Sunnis (the majority), whose allegiance is to the succession from Mohammed's direct successor, the Caliph; and the Shias or Shi'ites who follow the descendants of the prophet's son-in-law, Ali. For both, the main objective is to make the pilgrimage to Mecca (Mohammed's birthplace in AD 570) and become a *haji*. Muslims may have come to north India first as ruthless, iconoclastic conquerors, but their contribution to Indian civilization is still prevalent in art, architecture and culture.

Sikhism

Though rare in the south, Sikhism has become an important factor in modern India's political life, and a religion chapter would be incomplete without a section on Sikhs. The Sikh religion is comparatively new, having broken away from Hinduism as late as the 15th century. It was born of the frictions between Hindus and Muslims in the Punjab, and was founded by Guru Nanak (1494–1538). Originally a pacifist movement, aimed at synthesizing the best of the Hindu and Islamic religions, it turned into a militant brotherhood under the 10th Guru of the line, Guru Gobind Singh, in the 17th century. This was a reaction to the extreme persecution which the Sikhs of those times were suffering and all of them thereafter bore the surname Singh or 'Lion'.

The Sikh Bible is called Granth Sahib. It is opposed to several Hindu tenets, including the caste system and the dominance of the Brahmins. It differs from other Hindu-based faiths in its unique rejection of non-violence and it condones the killing of animals for food. The Sikhs believe in one god, have temples known as *gurdwaras*, and have had a total of 10 Gurus whose collected writings (plus various Hindu and Muslim scripts) form the Granth Sahib.

Sikhs are instantly distinguishable by their five symbols or *kakka*, introduced by Guru Gobind Singh: *kesa* or unshorn hair (normally wrapped under a turban); *kachcha* or short trousers; the steel bracelet or *kara*; the wooden or ivory comb called *kangha*; and the *kirpan* or sword.

Although just 2 per cent of the Indian population follows the Sikh religion, Sikhs dominate the army and the transport and light engineering industries. They have a well-earned reputation for a no-nonsense attitude, a capacity for hard work, and skill in mechanical matters—they are said to be the best car mechanics in the world.

In the early 1980s a section of Sikh extremists took up the call for a separate country, called Khalistan. This led to the political and economic decline of the Punjab, the most prosperous state in India. The terrorists converted the Golden Temple, the most venerated Sikh shrine, into their headquarters and this led to army action in 1984. This further alienated Sikhs from the rest of the country and ultimately resulted in the assassination of Indira Gandhi by her Sikh bodyguards. The subsequent riots, during which several thousand innocent Sikhs were massacred, led to an even greater rift. At the time of writing, the political situation has yet to be resolved, but personal relationships between Sikhs and other members of the Indian community remain relatively unscathed.

Zoroastrianism

The tiny community of Zoroastrians, commonly known as Parsis, are concentrated in Bombay. Theirs is one of the oldest religions known, founded by the prophet Zoroaster (Zarathustra) in

Persia, around 800 BC. Forced to flee their native country by a Muslim invasion of Persia, they were given sanctuary in India. Their scripture, the Zend-Avesta, describes the ongoing battle between good and evil, and their god is Ahura Mazda who is symbolized by fire. Parsis revere the elements of nature, but are not fire-worshippers: they keep the sacred flame burning in all their temples only as a symbol of their god. To preserve the purity of the elements they do not defile fire, earth, water or air by burying or cremating their dead. Instead, they leave the bodies atop the 'Towers of Silence' (Bombay) to be devoured by vultures.

As a community, the Parsis are distinctive and enterprising, contributing much to modern India. They have an extraordinary talent for commerce, and the Tatas, a highly respected Parsi business group, has wide-ranging and extremely profitable interests in the oil, steel, automobile, computing and tea industries, amongst others. The Taj Group of Hotels is run by Tatas, and Air India was a Tata enterprise which was later nationalized. Parsis are also renowned for their philanthropy, and run a range of trusts to look after the interests of their own community.

Only if the father is Parsi can the children be Parsi, and you cannot join Parsi ranks through conversion. This, combined perhaps with the apparent reluctance of well-educated and increasingly independent Parsi women to settle down, has resulted in a marked decline in numbers of the Parsi community.

Christianity and Judaism

There have been Christians in India since St Thomas, one of Christ's disciples, arrived in Kerala in AD 54. The Syrian Church he founded here is the second oldest Christian Church in the world, after that in ancient Palestine. During the mid-4th and 8th centuries, two waves of Christian immigrants arrived from the Middle East, and a substantial community of 'Syrian Christians' grew up in Kerala.

Later still, in the 16th century, Catholic and Protestant missionaries made a number of converts from various Portuguese, Dutch and English settlements. In the Indian community, they concentrated mainly on areas where large numbers of labourers were gathered, such as tea gardens and oil fields, and on the tribal areas of Bihar and north-east India, where they experienced considerable success. The lower castes were naturally more susceptible to conversion, as a means of escape from their unchangeably low status in the Hindu caste system.

However only in Goa, where the Portuguese left a sizeable Christian community of relatively influential men, were the efforts of the missionaries longlasting; though the Syrian Orthodox Church in Kerala is still fairly strong. Amongst the disaffected Hindus of the lower castes, the religion could not find the power it needed to become widespread. Nevertheless Christians in India have made their mark in social, medical, educational and philanthropic fields.

In Kerala once more, the Jews of Cochin deserve a special mention—their ancestry goes back to the 6th century BC. They were a highly influential community in their time and the Cochin synagogue is the oldest in the Commonwealth, but at present there are only about 28 Cochin Jews remaining, most of whom are in their seventies.

A larger, more ancient and more significant Jewish community called the Bene Israel exists in and around Bombay. It is estimated that there are about 4000 Jews in the whole country but, like the Parsis, their community is declining.

Topics

Ayurvedic Medicine and Massage

The people of southern India, particularly Kerala, practise what is probably the oldest system of alternative medicine in Asia. Ayurveda, as set out in the Sanskrit text of *Ashtanga Hrudaya*, recommends the daily ingestion of certain herbs combined with massage based on a system of acupressure as the way to good health. In the south ayurvedic treatments are as commonly sought as Western ones (though many people hedge their bets and take both), there are clinics and hospitals in most of the large towns, and chemists in every shopping district.

Travellers who fall prey to Indian ailments and consult ayurvedic doctors are usually pleasantly surprised by the results, which appear to be particularly good for the treatment of parasitic complaints such as amoebic dysentery. And ayurvedic massage is an experience worth chasing even if you are in the best of health. The only problem, especially for women, is finding a masseur who is neither a creep nor a charlatan. Trivandrum and the Keralan coast seem to have the best practitioners (*see* pp.207 and 209).

Martial Arts and Dance

Kalaripayat fighting and Kathakali dramatic dance are Keralan traditions. Kalaripayat, which evolved in the 2nd and 3rd centuries AD, is designed to be used in conjunction with ayurvedic medicine; the martial arts master is trained at the same time as a physician who can heal wounds. Thus most Kalaripayat schools, such as the C.V.N. Institute in Trivandrum, also double as ayurvedic clinics for the general public (*see* p.203).

Training of boys and girls begins at eight years old. Various weapons are introduced over the years, starting with wooden staffs of varying lengths, progressing through daggers, several sword and shield techniques, spears, axes and flails, and finally to a fearsome six-foot long flexible sword, a kind of razor-wire whip. Students trained in the use of this weapon are incredibly dextrous: one exercise involves a man lying on the ground using his flexible sword to parry the attacks of four others using the same weapon.

Kathakali, by contrast, is the peaceful art of story-telling through dance. While the content of the stories (mostly episodes from the *Ramayana* and *Mahabharata*) is often very warlike, the rigidly formalized systems of movement are performed with beauty, rather than with aggression in mind. Heavily made up so that their faces resemble brightly coloured masks, the dancers (all male) cloak their bodies in ponderously heavy upper costumes while leaving the ir legs relatively free for the various stamps and postures, which, combined with a system of exaggerated facial expressions and gestures of the hand, constitute both narrative and script. A small orchestra provides constant musical accompaniment.

Beautiful, but somewhat slow as a spectacle, Kathakali performances can only be followed if you already know the extraordinarily complex 'language' of the movements, or if you have an interpreter. The best introduction to the art is to visit one of the three centres in Cochin that hold regular shows. You can then see the act from start to finish, watching the dancers make themselves up before the performance, then have the story explained. For full details, *see* p.222.

The south holds the heart of India's Hindu culture, its great temple towns having upheld the religion and its way of life for more than a millennium. Yet in the forests and mountains of the Western Ghats there are cultures that predate even Hinduism. In Kerala, the Munnuvans of the rainforests near Chinnar cultivate wild spices and worship an elephant god, while the Cholakainals near Wynad still live as semi-nomadic cave-dwellers, hunting small animals with fire-hardened bamboo spears and gathering forest fruits. Up in the Nilgiri Hills of Tamil Nadu the Todas herd buffalos on the high grasslands, worship a buffalo goddess and retain a matriarchal culture. Their neighbours, the Kotas, fashion musical instruments for ritual use and, although they practise Hinduism, keep themselves apart from the local farmers. Back in the Moyar River forests below the Nilgiris, the Kurumbas pray to the gods of wood and water in return for milk and grain from those outside the forest.

Some parts of the Deccan plateau also have strong tribal cultures, notably those around Hospet and Hubli in Karnataka, where members of the Lambadi tribe make the brightly coloured, mirrored clothing that tourists love to buy. Many Lambadi women, dressed in their bright clothes and with heavy silver ingots hung in their hair, make an annual trek to Goa. Here they stay for the whole season and hawk their wares up and down the beach.

This involvement with modern market culture does not seem to have interfered with the Lambadi's habitual way of life, and the same can be said for the Todas, who sell buffalo milk, eucalyptus oil and wild honey at local markets, yet continue to live traditionally. However, some tribes like the Munnuvans and Cholakainals hold themselves almost completely apart, seldom leave the forest and do not welcome strangers unless accompanied by a guide known to them.

Other tribes, like the Kurumbas, *have* suffered a degeneration of their culture, having had parts of their forests cut down by the government and sandalwood smugglers. Many have sought agricultural work outside the forest and are entering the rural mainstream. Some Cholakainal settlements on the forest fringes have disintegrated under the effects of alcohol. The government's forest department, which 'administers' the jungle tribes, is now anxious to preserve the remaining cultures and to keep outsiders away from the forests. As a result, travellers must have government permission before entering many of the deep forest areas. This can be a tricky process, as officials are suspicious of outsiders and unwilling to assume responsibility for foreigners. However, if you persevere, permission can be obtained and local guides hired, and you can trek into the forests and stay in some of the tribal settlements (*see* pp.234 and p.310 for details).

You will see many beggars, mainly around temples, holy places and railway stations. The Indian people themselves respect their beggars and few of them will enter a temple without a handful of small change to give to the less fortunate. To give to the poor is considered necessary for the accumulation of good karma for a decent reincarnation in the next life.

This unofficial form of social security ensures that at least some apparently desperate beggars are better off than they appear. A few are experienced professionals, who shed their grime and rags for new, clean clothes when 'off duty'. Unfortunately for the foreign tourist, faced by armies of apparently identical skinny women toting dirty babies and old men wearing doleful expressions, there is no way of knowing who really needs help and who doesn't.

Giving money to beggars is a very personal matter. Some travellers, stricken by conscience, give away all their money and possessions hours after arriving in the country. Others go to the opposite extreme and treat the haves and the have-nots with equal indifference.

The Indian way is to give nothing to a man who is able-bodied, because he can make more money from begging than from working, nor to children as it may encourage them to leave school. Many give small change or food to the elderly, sick or disabled. If you feel strongly about this issue there are, of course, many charities in India which will always be grateful for anything you are able to donate.

The Hippy Techno Trail

South India's resident hippy scene has changed in recent years, particularly with regard to music. It is Indians who now listen to Bob Dylan, the Doors, Hendrix, Jefferson Airplane and Cream—almost all the Europeans are now heavily into techno. While the old hippy uniform of long hair and loose, brightly patterned clothes is still in evidence, it is rapidly being replaced by the New Age Traveller look of shaved heads or dreadlocks (there are even skinny dogs on the beaches to adopt).

The mellow hippy attitude has changed along with the music and the clothes. The all-night techno parties at Goa's Anjuna and Vagator beaches, and now even at Kovalam, are about ecstasy, acid and money first, and peace, love and dope second.

Those who love New Age hippiedom and its 'smart' techno fashions will find heaven in north Goa and even the unconverted should find the parties fun—who wouldn't want to dance all night on a warm tropical beach, whether they liked loud, incessant techno or not? If you want to find the Goan parties (the Kovalam ones are on Lighthouse Beach), head straight for the Shore Bar at Anjuna or the Primrose at Vagator, and you will be told when the next party is (probably that night).

There is still no cover charge for parties, but once you have paid for your transport there and back by motorcycle taxi, a few beers, and some *chai* and cake between dances, you will find it hard to drop less than Rs200 for the night. If you buy drugs, it will cost you considerably more.

This is where a word of warning is needed. Many people now visiting Goa and Kovalam are tourists rather than travellers—preferring to party away their holiday on the beach without travelling inland at all. This is fine, but the lack of experience with India leaves them vulnerable, particularly with regard to drugs. The general attitude of *laissez-faire* on the beaches is misleading. If you look the part, it is not uncommon to be spot-searched by police. For some years now, the Goan and Kovalam police have been making money out of spot-fines and even planting drugs on suspects. If you are caught with any drug, it's off to jail. You'll generally be given a straight choice: 10 years, or a Rs10,000–20,000 fine. If you are caught with heroin or its local derivative, 'brown sugar', you may not even be given the choice.

The older, slower hippy scene has fled to the far northern beaches of Goa, to the mountains at Kodaikanal, and is still gamely resisting the techno invasion in Kovalam. It has also colonized some new beaches (since the late 60s, hippies have found all the best beaches), where the facilities are too basic and the life too mellow to attract ravers. The best of these are Varkala and Bekal in Kerala, and Gokarn and Ankola in Karnataka, where the impact of travellers is still very light and techno has not yet crept in to obliterate the sigh of moonlit ocean.

Temple Towns

There are temples all over India. Every street and backstreet in town, city or village has at least one. But the south, particularly the plains of Tamil Nadu, has a profusion of great temple cities that attract hundreds of thousands of pilgrims from all over the country to huge shrines that have been pilgrimage centres for over a thousand years. Built mostly under the early medieval Pandya, Pallava and Chola dynasties of the south (see p.50), these vast temple complexes constitute some of the most imposing Dravidian architecture in India, and many now have great sprawling cities and towns around them. Many travellers to south India do little else but travel from temple town to temple town: to Kanchipuram, with its thousand-pillared hall; to Srirangam, enclosed by 16 miles of curtain walls; to Thanjavur, whose 200 foot-high temple is surmounted by a vast granite dome carved from a single piece of rock; to Madurai, with its cavernous halls and temple elephants.

Elephants are an integral part of the Keralan temple towns, especially at Trichur, where the bi-annual elephant festivals are among the most wondrous spectacles to be seen in India (a full list of elephant festivals is given on p.227). The Deccan also has some great temple towns, notably at Tiumallai in southern Andhra Pradesh, where the temple claims to receive the largest number of pilgrims of anywhere in India outside Varanasi, and where visitors often offer their hair to the gods when asking for special favours. Many of the other Deccan temple towns were destroyed by Muslim armies in the 16th century, but their ruins are often magnificent, especially at Hampi, Aihole and Pattadkal in Karnataka and Lepakshi in Andhra Pradesh. There, instead of the rush and babble of the working temples, with their beggars, touts, pickpockets, merchants and shuffling crowds, you wander the great buildings in the silence of a wide, dry landscape, sharing them only with the lizards that bask on the carvings and the birds who nest in the eaves.

Fauna and Flora

Mammals

South India has some of the country's more remote wildlife sanctuaries and national parks, mostly in the Western Ghats near the Malabar Coast. Many of these forest reserves are huge, covering more than 200 square miles, and are home to a fabulous range of exotic fauna. Largest of these is the wild elephant, present throughout the Western Ghats, but with large concentrations in Mudumalai Wildlife Sanctuary, the adjacent Moyar River Reserved Forest, Anamalai Sanctuary (all in Tamil Nadu); and in Periyar Wildlife Sanctuary, Kerala.

Less dangerous to man is the tiger, again present throughout the Western Ghats, but most concentrated in Nagarjunasagar Reserve in Andhra, Nagarhole National Park, Bandipur Wildlife Sanctuary and Bhadra Sanctuary (all in Karnataka); Mudanthurai Sanctuary in Tamil Nadu and Chinnar Sanctuary in Kerala.

Unique to the Western Ghats is the Nilgiri *tahr*, a short-horned ibex or mountain goat that lives only at the highest altitudes. The largest herd is protected by Erivakulam/Rajamalai National Park in Kerala, but you should also spot them at Mukurthi Peak National Park in Tamil Nadu and in the Coorg region of Karnataka.

wild elephant

The Western Ghats' other mammal species are fairly common and include leopard, sloth bear, striped hyena, *dhole* (wild dog), jackal, jungle cat, *gaur* (bison), wild boar, *sambar*, *chital*, muntjac and mouse deer (the latter is little bigger than a rabbit), the *chousingha* or four-horned antelope (another tiny one), giant squirrel, flying squirrel, otter, civet and genet cats, various mongoose species, *pangolin*, porcupine, slow *loris*, fruit bat and monkeys such as bonnet macaques, lion-headed, Nilgiri and common langur.

gaur

Extending eastward from the Western Ghats across the Tamil Nadu–Karnataka border are the Biligiri Hills, which extend northeastwards into Andhra Pradesh to become the Eastern Ghats. In these dryer forests, the wildlife sanctuaries harbour similar game to those of the Western Ghats (though there is seldom elephant), but with a few central Indian additions. These include wolf, *chinkara* (the Indian gazelle) and *nilgai* (also known as 'blue bull'—a very large, short-horned antelope). The most rewarding sanctuaries to visit in this zone are Karnataka's Bannerghatta National Park, Biligiri Temple Sanctuary and Andhra's Nagarjunasagar Tiger Reserve (the largest in the country), Kawal Sanctuary, Ethurnaganam Sanctuary, Papikonda Sanctuary and Pakhal Sanctuary. In the remote Kinnersani Sanctuary in the north of Andhra Pradesh, you can see India's southernmost wild buffalo population—huge beasts prone to attack with little provocation.

Even the dry Deccan Plateau has a few sanctuaries worth visiting, particularly for seeing blackbuck antelope. Try the huge Rannebennur Sanctuary in northern Karnataka and Pocharam Sanctuary in Karnataka. Wolf, leopard, *chinkara* and some deer species are also present in these Deccan reserves.

blackbuck

Birds

Sub-tropical countries always have a wealth of exotic birds and south India has about 1750 indigenous species, including many brightly coloured songbirds, large raptors and some spectacular waterfowl.

In the forest zones look out for the russet or white paradise flycatcher, with its flamboyant tail, the jet-black but equally dressy racket-tailed drongo, the golden flash of black-headed orioles, the iridescent green and yellow of common kingfishers and bee-eaters, multicoloured magpie robins, tree-pies, rollers, green pigeon, hoepoes, chattering mynas and black woodpeckers, jewel-like sunbirds, handsome parakeets, silvered jungle-fowl (much more elegant than its cousin the domestic chicken) and the brown and black coucal, or crow-pheasant. In the northern forests of Karnataka and Goa, you should see flocks of hornbills.

pariah kite

Hunting above the canopy will be the large serpent eagle and various kites, including the water-loving brahmini kite, whose handsome brown body and white head makes him look like a fish eagle, and the ever-present paraiah kite, as common in cities as in the wild.

The south has some huge sanctuaries for waterbirds, the largest being Point Calimere Sanctuary in Tamil Nadu, as well as Pulicat Sanctuary and Kolleru Sanctuary in Andhra Pradesh, all three on river deltas. From November to February you can see large flocks of flamingos on these protected marshes. You may also see ospreys and the white-bellied sea eagle as well as numerous brahmini kites, various plovers, egrets and herons, including the shy night heron. The painted stork ranges from the coastal sanctuaries to inland lakes, as does the pied kingfisher and spoonbill.

The birdlife of the dry Deccan also has a few surprises, notably vultures, goshawks, spotted eagles, sandgrouse and the great Indian bustard of northern Karnataka and central Andhra. Anywhere with water, even a village tank, will attract flocks of paddy birds and white cattle egrets, both small varieties of heron.

great Indian bustard

Reptiles

India is famous for two snakes: the king cobra, which can grow to over 16 feet long and the reticulated python, which can grow considerably longer. These are both deep-forest dwellers and are seldom encountered.

India's most dangerous snakes are the Indian cobra, present everywhere, but particularly in long grass and rocks, the small krait—a blue-black species of pit viper with narrow white crosses that can strike in the dark using scent as a guide, the chain-patterned Russel's Viper and the triangular-headed saw-scaled viper, which can be accidentally stepped on along forest and mountain paths. Almost all the 10,000 snakebite deaths that occur in India every year are caused by these four snakes, but even local hospitals should carry anti-venom serum. General precautions are: don't wander about in wooded areas at night unless you are wearing good boots, and swish a stick through long grass as you walk to give the snakes a chance to move out of the way—they'd rather do this than be stepped on.

cobra

rat snake

Far more common are India's many harmless snakes, including the large rat-snake (often seen swimming in lakes and rivers), tree snakes and even flying snakes. Forest areas are the best for seeing snakes. Killing them is supposed to be bad luck, as they are sacred to the old gods or *nagars* who came before the present pantheon.

Crocodiles are common in the protected river and marsh areas: muggers, or marsh crocodiles, which though large don't often attack people, and gharials, slender-snouted crocodilians which also grow to over six feet but whose jaws are too narrow to take anything but fish. More dangerous are the salt-water crocodiles of the mangroves on the eastern coast. However, as it is unlikely that you will be swimming in these brackish, muddy waterways, there is little to fear.

Lizards, including some brightly coloured skink species, are seen everywhere on land, as are freshwater turtles in any stretch of water. Look out for the giant monitor lizard, which can grow to six feet, in forest areas and lakes. All travellers will see geckos in their hotel rooms. These small, near-transparent lizards make a distinctive chittering sound, hang upside-down from the ceiling and eat all the nasty creepy-crawlies, so don't chase them out.

mugger

Trees

Sacred to all Hindus is the great banyan tree, symbol of life, which sends down roots from its own branches, constantly renewing itself and creating a mini-forest of its own. A species of wild fig, banyans can spread to cover several acres and live for up to 2000 years. They start their lives as parasite stranglers on host trees, whose trunks they gradually engulf and who die disintegrating under the weight of their foster-child. Banyans grow even in the dry Deccan Plateau and are often used as shade trees in villages and along roads, as well as marking the site of most rural Shiva temples.

banyan tree

In the forests of the Western ghats, the different climatic zones (evergreen rainforest on the western slopes, deciduous trees on the drier eastern side), have spawned a profusion of valuable deciduous species, notably teak, rosewood, frankincense, camphor, mahogany, ebony and sandalwood. All grow to become forest giants if allowed, but unfortunately timber smuggling is common and the forestry and wildlife departments are having increasing difficulties in preserving the ancient stands. However, to the traveller's eye the vast stretches of forest seem untouched and there is little evidence of clear-cutting.

Equally valuable are some of the creepers and shrubs, which include spices such as pepper and cardamom, with lemon-grass growing in-between. Flowering trees sometimes break the pattern of greens, notably the red-blossoming 'flame of the forest', a feather-leaved variety of acacia.

Flowers

Like its forests, south India's wildflowers could fill a book in themselves. The traveller will notice flowers everywhere except on the Deccan plateau—bougainvillaea and wild jasmine on city walls and hanging from trees in the countryside, blue and purple water hyacinths carpeting the surface of the Keralan backwaters, yellow lotuses on the temple tanks, orchids in the western rainforests and the rare *strobilanthus*, which once every twelve years covers the grasslands of the Nilgiris in a carpet of sky-blue flowers.

Bombay

The hall was full of them shouting their wares, haggling, arguing, a continual searoar background, punctuated by an occasional shout or call raised above the din... all packed to overflowing with a mighty stuffing of sound...

Ranga Rao, *Fowl Filcher*

Bombay is a dynamic, go-ahead city of heaving crowds, poverty and desperation, but also of hope. Above the clutter ride tycoons, skyscrapers, film studios and big business—the chance to climb from the gutter to the sky, the nearest thing to the West in the East. In just 40 years it has mushroomed from a small, though thriving, coastal port-town of 500,000 inhabitants to a crowded industrial metropolis of 13 million and rising. A futuristic vision of India, with gleaming luxury hotels, high-rise business houses and air-conditioned shopping centres, it rises from a sea of street squalor, an irresistible land of opportunity for masses of homeless, jobless poor and refugees that flood in at an average rate of 6000 new families per day. They come in search of work or glamour or money and most of them end up sleeping on the streets. The result is severe overcrowding and an appalling shortage of housing—a second city of ragged, squalid slum dwellings has grown up alongside the modern business capital of gleaming plate-glass buildings. Bombay is, like Calcutta, a city of powerful contrasts, though it's not just all the problems of modern India that are highlighted here, but all her potential and brighter prospects too. Here there is hope, optimism and great prosperity, for Bombay handles half the country's foreign trade, manufactures the same percentage of her textiles and pays a third of her income tax. The affluent rich, a hardworking cosmopolitan mixture of Hindus and Parsis, Jews and Jains, Arabs and Sikhs, divert surplus revenue to the philanthropic construction of hospitals, schools, museums and rest houses. But it is Bombay's 'action' that draws everybody here—this is a city bursting with life, colour, noise and vitality. And you can almost smell the money.

All this has happened since the Second World War, since the rise of India's new business class in the wake of Independence. Until the 18th century, Bombay was just a marshy, diseased quag of seven islands, inhabited by a simple fisherfolk called the Kolis. Their name for the place was Mumbai or Bombaim, after their patron goddess Mumba Aai (Mother Mumba). This was later corrupted into Bom Bahia ('good bay') by the Portuguese. Ptolemy mentioned the islands as Heptanesia in the 2nd century AD, after which they faded from historical sight until occupied in the 13th century by the Hindu king, Bhimdev. The Sultans of Gujarat held the site briefly before the Portuguese arrived (1534). The first flush of Portuguese enthusiasm wore off— they saw its potential as a port, but the malarial swamps dissuaded them from developing it as a trading-post—and they offloaded it on the British, as part of Catherine of Braganza's dowry when she married Charles II in 1661. Charles didn't see its possibilities either and leased Bom Bahia, port and islands both, to the British East India Company for a nominal £10 per year in gold (1668).

The Company's President, Gerald Aungier, became the founder father of modern Bombay, bringing in the influential Parsi merchant class and a host of assorted artisans and builders, to make possible the conversion of the port from pestilential swampland to thriving trading-centre. By his death, it was well on the way to becoming the centre of all the west-coast trade in India. But it was in the mid 19th century that development suddenly became rapid—the railway arrived, as did the first textile mills and Bartle Frere's stately Victorian buildings. A series of large-scale land-reclamation projects took place in 1862 when the seven isolated mud-flat islands were joined into a single land mass and Bombay's future success was assured.

Today the city is a single, long peninsula island, a dynamic commercial and industrial centre, and a major international port and city. For the foreign visitor, it is probably the easiest place, after Goa, to acclimatize to India. Westerners tend to like its bright, brash quality (it certainly has more character than colourless Delhi), also its fine international facilities—quality restaurants, shops, bars and luxury hotels.

Despite the intense poverty existing cheek-by-jowl with the wealth, Bombay has little in the way of street crime and travellers should not be paranoid about personal safety. Here and in the rest of south India, violent crime against foreigners is almost unknown and while theft and rip-offs are problems, mugging is so rare as to be almost non-existent. Also, Bombay sees so many other foreign visitors, that you just don't get the same hassle, stares or curiosity as in many places elsewhere in the country. What you do get is a lot of noisy traffic, smells and rubbish. As one Indian journalist warned: 'Whichever way you enter the city, you are face-to-face with streets pockmarked with rotting garbage dumps, pavements in ruins, and general confusion and chaos'.

Past the initial shock, however, Bombay is a fabulous place to be. Despite the chronic overcrowding and teeming traffic, the city boasts some fine parks, a cricket stadium, a couple of nice beaches and a long sweep of seafront. It's always possible to escape from the madhouse inner city into quiet environs, and many wise newcomers do just that: heading straight for the peaceful, elegant surrounds of **Colaba** at the southern tip of the peninsula, to settle into India the civilized way—over a cocktail or a light meal at the famous Taj Mahal Hotel near the Gateway. After that, it's in with the earplugs, on with the smile and the money belt—Bombay is a pickpockets' paradise—and out into some of the most vibrant, teeming street-life in the world.

Climate and When to Go

The best season is from **October to February**. It's very hot from **March** onwards (if possible, stay in the Colaba district near the sea, to avoid boiling over), and the **monsoon** is from **July to September**. For a good festival, come in the post-monsoon celebration of **Ganpati**, held in honour of Bombay's favourite god, money-lucky Ganesh. Ganpat also has a historical association, as it became a symbol of Indian nationalist spirit during the struggle for independence in the 1930s and 40s. The **February/March Holi** festival is not a good time to visit— over-excited and occasionally hostile crowds, lashings of red paint, and hapless tourists diving for cover all over the place.

Getting To and From Bombay
by air

Bombay has two airports: Sahar International, ✆ 6366700, is 16 miles from the city centre, and is used by all international airlines including **Air India**. It also has **Indian Airlines** flights to Karachi (Pakistan) and Colombo (Sri Lanka). The international carriers connect Bombay with Africa, the Gulf region, most of Europe, New York, Southeast Asia, Japan and Australia. The domestic airport is at Santa Cruz, ✆ 6126343, and is used by **Indian Airlines**, ✆ 6114433, **Vayudoot**, ✆ 6146583, **EastWest Airlines**, **Damania**, **Moduluft** and other internal operators (*see* p.79 for telephone numbers). There are two terminals. The newer one handles **Indian Airlines Airbus** flights while the other, original terminal handles all other domestic traffic.

Airport–City Transport

EATS coach service runs hourly, on the hour, from Sahar airport into city between 2am and 11pm; runs hourly, on the half-hour, from Santa Cruz into city between 2.30am and 11.30pm; returns hourly, on the hour, from Air India building, Nariman Point, to both airports all day, except 2 to 4am; journey time can be anything from 1 hour to 3 or even 4 hours in rush-hour chaos. If flying out from Bombay, aim for a night flight: traffic out to the airport is much lighter in the evenings.

Suburban train (take an auto-rickshaw from Sahar to Andheri station, from Santa Cruz to Vile Parle station, for cheap 1st-class, 2nd-class trip to Churchgate/Victoria Terminus stations in the heart of the city; best return trains to airports leave

Churchgate station every 4 minutes, from platforms 1 and 2). Quick and comfortable, trains are much more reliable than buses: airport/city journeys by rail rarely take more than 45 minutes.

Airport taxi service (Sahar has a well-controlled meter-taxi booth open round the clock that provides pre-paid taxi services on the basis of fixed fares—an average Ambassador car ride to, say, Nariman Point, would be around Rs140). Having stated your destination, you purchase a coupon for the correct fare and amount of baggage you are carrying—this is handed over to the driver on reaching your destination. Alternatively, walk to the auto-rickshaw stand just outside Sahar airport concourse, and bargain a ride into town—officially auto-rickshaws are not allowed further into town than Mahim but are ideal if going to Bandra or Juhu. Travelling by airport coach, taxi or rickshaw, prepare yourself for horrendous traffic, grim slums and ripe garbage dumps lining the highway all the way into the city.

leaving Bombay by air

Make sure you have the right airport. An alarming number of people miss flights by sitting dreamily in Sahar lounge waiting for a domestic flight (which never comes) or in Santa Cruz coffee shop waiting for an international flight (likewise). Discovering your error at the last minute can be horrendous—the two airports are 3 miles apart, and you'll have to forget about the leisurely EATS coach connection in favour of a frantic taxi-dash.

Late arrivals at airports can lose their reservations. For domestic flights, be at Santa Cruz a good hour ahead of check-in. For international flights, allow 2 hours and have your Rs300 *departure tax* ready. You must pay this *before* checking-in your luggage.

Note: For Indian Airlines/Air India reservations, confirmations or cancellations in Bombay, avoid the Air India building in Nariman Point (open Monday to Saturday 8am to 6.45pm, Sunday 8am to 5pm—but the queues never move). Instead, either pay a travel agent to handle bookings for you, or wait until you reach a quieter centre (e.g. Goa, Cochin, Trivandrum) where you can do them quickly yourself.

by rail

Bombay's two separate railway systems handle a staggering 4 million people every day and cover all major tourist destinations outside the city. **Central Railway** services the east and the south—Calcutta, Aurangabad, Goa, Gujarat, etc.—and a few places in the north. Reservations are from the special **tourist booth** opposite platform 9, Victoria Terminus (this is also the place to buy your Indrail Pass, if required). **Western Railway** services the north and west, including Delhi and Rajasthan, and has booking offices at both Churchgate (next to Government of India Tourist Office) for 1st class, and at Bombay Central for 2nd class. The Victoria Terminus booking office has a Railway Tourist Guide, who handles a limited tourist quota of 1st and 2nd class tickets for all routes—he should be your very first option. In high season (October to February), it's essential to advance-book all rail tickets a few days ahead.

Some useful trains are the *Rajdhani Express* and the equally fast *AC Express* to Delhi from Bombay Central (17 hours, air-conditioned seats and 1st class only); the *Calcutta Mail* (35 hours) from Victoria Terminus; and the *Dadar Madras Express* (24 hours), leaving Dadar station—seven stops up the main line from Victoria Terminus—at 2.45pm daily.

The State Transport Bus Depot, opposite Bombay Central station, is the place to book long-distance buses. Places covered by road—MTDC luxury coaches are best—include Aurangabad, Panjim (Goa), Hyderabad, Bangalore, Madras, Delhi and Calcutta. MTDC also have booking desks at the Government of India Tourist Office, and at the Air India building, Nariman Point. For destinations like Udaipur, Mount Abu and Ahmedabad, you may have to check out the private bus companies at 9th and 11th Lane, Khetwadi.

by catamaran

A daily catamaran service between Bombay and Panjim, in Goa, opened in 1994. The trip down the Maharashtra coast takes approximately 8 hours and is often booked up weeks in advance. The only reliable way to book a seat is via a good travel agent (try Garha Tours, Green Street, Fort District, Bombay, ✆ 226 1186, or try for a cancellation by going down to the catamaran jetty at Ferry Wharf, 2 miles south of the city centre (take a taxi).

Getting Around

For a major capital, Bombay is quite easy to negotiate. This is because most tourist facilities are concentrated in one place: a narrow 2-mile strip running down from Churchgate to the bottom end of the island (Bombay is connected to the mainland by a series of bridges). This strip is bounded to the southeast by the Taj Hotel, Colaba, and to the southwest by the Oberoi Hotel, Nariman Point. The former hotel is in the area of most of the budget hotels, the latter is in the 'classy' end of town, where you'll find many of the airline offices, banks and upmarket hotels and restaurants.

For transport around town, you're best off with (black and yellow) taxis. They normally know where they're going, and many carry electronic tamper-proof meters. Taxi rates in Bombay are revised every time there is a petrol price rise or devaluation in the value of the rupee. Consequently, while a meter may indicate a Rs2 fare the tariff card displayed in the taxi will show Rs10. Also, the meter clocks up time, not distance, so traffic jams can be expensive. As a general guide, a clear one mile run from Colaba to Nariman Point (from the Taj to the Oberoi Hotels) should cost about Rs10. Auto-rickshaws are on a similar metering system and are usually restricted to airport/suburb routes. Horse-drawn carriages or 'Victorias' can be found at the Gateway of India for an evening promenade up Marine Drive, also at Bombay Central and Chowpatty. Catching local buses is pot-luck: drivers tear across town like men possessed, passengers tumble off like D-Day landing forces hitting the beaches, but it's all great fun, and very cheap. There's only one problem: how do you find the right bus and bus stop when the numbers on both are so often in Hindi? For what it's worth, **BEST bus depot** in Colaba (next to Electric House) sell a decent local bus timetable.

Tourist Information

The **Government of India Tourist Office**, 123 M. Karve Road, Churchgate, ✆ 293 144, is open 8.30 to 5.30 Monday to Friday, 8.30 to 12.30 Saturday, closed Sunday.

Sadly understaffed, but helpful. They have good handout information, including an excellent monthly city-guide called *Bombay Calling*, which is also available from any bookstore. Book your **MTDC city tour** here (they run twice daily except Monday, from 9am to 1pm and then from 2 to 6.30pm; tickets Rs35) and get your city map. There are Government of India tourist counters (24-hour service) at both airports.

The **Government of Maharashtra Tourist Office**, is at Madame Cama Road, ✆ 2026713. The **Government of Goa Tourist Office**, is in Bombay Central Station, ✆ 396288, and is useful if you're planning to follow the Goa–Diu routes in this book. The **Government of Gujarat Tourist Office** is on Dhanraj Mahal, Ch. Shivaji Road, Apollo Bunder, ✆ 243886.

The **Foreigners' Registration Department** is at Annexe 2, Office of the Commissioner of Police, Dadabhai Naoroji Road, near Crawford Market, ✆ 268111.

The **Post Office** is on Nagar Chowk, near V.T. station. Open from 8am to 8pm (*poste restante* 8am to 6pm) Monday to Saturday, and from 10am to 5.30 pm on Sunday. For Colaba residents, there's a useful little sub-post office in Mandlik Road, just behind the Taj Hotel. The **Central Telegraph Office** is located at Flora Fountain.

The **State Bank of India** has several branches (there's one behind the Government of India Tourist Office, Churchgate) and facilities at the airport are surprisingly efficient.

Good **bookshops** include Nalanda in the Taj Mahal Hotel, Strand (just off Sir P.M. Road) and Wheeler's (branches at all three rail stations). A readable introduction to Bombay is Gillian Tindall's *City of Gold, the Biography of Bombay* (Penguin, 1992).

airlines and flights

Note: The airport telephone number (listed below as 'apt') is usually only answered a few hours before and after a scheduled arrival/departure.

Domestic airlines: Indian Airlines, ✆ 2023031/2048282, apt 6144433/6114433/ 6112850/611142/611143, **Vayudoot**, ✆ 2048585, **EastWest**, ✆ 6431630/ 6441880/ 6436678, apt 6112090/6112143/6117952, **Jet**, ✆ 2875091/2855789, apt 6140140, **Damania**, ✆ 6102525/6102546/6102547/6102548, **Modiluft**, ✆ 3631921/3635085/3635380/3635087/3635859/3635960, apt 6103806/ 6103807/6101121.

International airlines: Air India, ✆ 2024143/2023747, apt 8329090/8329092/ 8322768/8326767, and **Singapore Airlines**, ✆ 2023365, 2023316, apt 6327024, 6327861, are in the Air India building, Nariman Point. **Cathay Pacific**, ✆ 202 9112/3 apt 6321965/6, **Delta**, ✆ 2024024, 2029020, apt 6324769, 6349890, and **Air France**, ✆ 2025021, 2024818, apt 6328070, are located in the Taj Hotel, Apollo Bunder. **Aeroflot**, ✆ 221743, apt 6320178, and **Swiss Air**, ✆ 222402, 222559 apt 6326084, are both on Veer Nariman Road. **Lufthansa**, ✆ 2020887, 2023430, apt 6321485, is in Express Towers, Nariman Point, and **British Airways**, ✆ 220888, apt 6329061/4) is in Vulcan Insurance Building, Churchgate. **Emirates**, ✆ 2871648, apt 6365730/1) Mittal Chambers, Nariman Point.

For **cheap flights**, visa assistance, student travel service etc., contact **Space Travels**, Nanabhay Mansion, 4th floor, Sir P.M. Road, ✆ 2864773, open from 10 to 5 Monday to Friday, 10.30 to 3 Saturday. Spaceway also has agencies at Panjim and Calangute,

Bombay

Arabian Sea

Nehru Planetarium

●Amateur Riders' Club

Chinchpokli

Cotton Green

Mahalaxmi Racecourse

Haji Ali Tomb

Mahalaxmi

N M JOSHI MARG

MESSANT ROAD

HAY BUNDER ROAD

BARRISTER NATH PAI MARG

Reay Road

MAULANA AZAD ROAD

Byculla

Breach Candy Swimming Club

Bombay Central

BOMBAY CENTRAL

JEHANGIR BOMAN BEHRAM MARG

Dockyard Road

KAMATIPURA

Grant Road

MAULANA SHAUKATALI RD

Sandhurst Road

KHARA TALAO

KHETWADI

SARDAR VALLABHBHAI PATEL ROAD

D. MELIO ROAD

Hanging Gardens

Jain Temple

BHULESHWAR

PYDHUNI

All Saints' Church

Kamala Nehru Park

GIRGAUM

Masjid

MALABAR HILL

Chowpatty Beach

Charni Road

WALKESHWAR RD

Taraporevala Aquarium

Walkeshwar Temple

Marine Lines

Back Bay

Marine Drive

MAHAPALIKA MARG

MAHATMA GANDHI RD

VITHALBHAI PATEL RD

VEER NARIMAN RD

Cross Maidan

Victoria Terminal

10 H 4

BANK ST.

Churchgate

FORT

Bombay Natural History Society

11

University of Bombay

MADAME CAMA RD

M GANDHI RD

SHAHID BHAGAT SINGH ROAD

Prince of Wales Museum

Nariman Point

H

S. MAHARAJ MARJ

To Elephanta Island

Gateway of India

ORMINSTON RD

6

9 5 1

7 8

COLABA

BHUSHAP MARG

A. BUNDER RD.

MERRIWEATHER RD

SHAHID BHAGAT SINGH BUNDER ROAD

CUFFE PARADE

H 3

St John's (Afghan) Church

Colaba Point

Hotels :
1. Taj Mahal Hotel
2. Oberoi Hotel
3. Taj President Hotel
4. Windsor Hotel
5. Rex Stiffles Hotel
6. Salvation Army Hostel
7. Garden Hotel

Bars :
8. Crown and Anchor Bar
9. Leopold's

Banks :
10. Canara Bank
11. State Bank of India

Main nightlife areas

N

2 km

1 mile

in Goa. Discounted tickets are also offered by touts outside the American Express building, and from budget hotels around Merriweather Road.

travel agents

The better ones are **Garha Tours and Travels**, Elve Chambers, Green Street, Fort, ✆ 2661186/2665160, and **SITA World Travel**, 8 Atlanta Building, Nariman Point, ✆ 2233155; **Mercury Travel**, 70 V.B. Gandhi Marg, ✆ 203663 with a desk at Oberoi Hotel; **Cox and Kings**, 270/2 Dr D. Naoroji Road, ✆ 2043065; **Thomas Cook**, Cooks Building, Dadabhai Naoroji Road, ✆ 2048556. **American Express** is at Majithia Chamber, Dadabhai Naoroji Road, ✆ 2046349.

consulates

Among the many countries represented in Bombay (listed in telephone directory) are:
UK: 2nd floor, HongKong Bank Building, M.G. Road, ✆ 274874.
USA: Lincoln House, 78 Bhulabhai Desai Road, ✆ 8223611.
Australia: Maker Towers, B Block, 41 Cuffe Parade, ✆ 218071.

credit card offices

American Express have their main office, 276 Dr D.N. Road, **Visa** are at ANZ Grindlay's Bank, 90 M.G. Road, and **Mastercard** at the Bank of America, Express Towers, Nariman Point.

hospitals

To call an ambulance, dial 102, but be aware that this is India and the vehicle could take anything from 2 minutes to two weeks to arrive. More convenient, and less risky is to jump into a taxi and head to Beach Candy Hospital on Jagmohandas Marg, across the road (on the west side) from the Hanging Gardens. If staying in a larger hotel of the luxury/expensive standard, they generally have a house doctor on permanent call who can treat you in your room if you feel too sick to move.

The City

Bombay's few conspicuous 'sights' are very spread out. To see everything in the two days most visitors allow requires a lot of stamina and a very energetic, knowledgeable guide. The alternative, as usual with a large Indian city, is to cover the main points of interest on a conducted bus tour, and then mop up the rest at leisure later on.

Alternatively, if money is no object, hire a private guide through the Tourist Office at 123 M. Carve Road, Churchgate, ✆ 293144/5, 296854/292932, who will take you around by car. Tours round the city or out to the Elephanta and Kanheri caves are more rewarding this way, as you get the benefit of a local's personal knowledge and anecdotes, as well as detailed explanations of religion, mythology and other cultural points that a group guide will gloss over. All guides provided by the Tourist Office are qualified and are, in general, very charming. Mala Banguera is a mine of information on culture and general Bombay know-how. If possible, ask for her by name when booking a guide through the Tourist Office.

Whichever way you do it, allow a full day to see any set of sights, or tours degenerate into a hot, uncomfortable rush.

City Tour

tour bus, 4 hours

Gateway of India–Aquarium–Mani Bhavan–Jain Temple–
Hanging Gardens–Kamla Nehru Park–Prince of Wales Museum

For a good introduction to Bombay, and to avoid the crowds, take the MTDC morning tour. Buses are comfortable, guides are good, and you are given some background history on the city. This said, insufficient time is allowed for each stop and you may well wish to backtrack to one or two places later.

At **Colaba**, named after the Koli, Bombay's original fisherfolk who still live in shanties set along the Cuffe Parade Road, you'll see **Apollo Bunder**—the traditional reception point for dignitaries visiting India in the days of sea travel. In 1911 King George V stepped ashore here, accompanied by Queen Mary. To mark the occasion (it was the first time a reigning monarch had made a state visit to India), a hasty decorative arch of white plaster was erected on the edge of Bunder pier. Sixteen years later, a proper monument—the present **Gateway of India**—was built to commemorate the historic occasion. Designed by a government architect, George Wittet, it is now Bombay's principal landmark. Built of local yellow-basalt, the 85 feet (26 metre) high gateway is an architectural oddity: designed in the Gujarat style of the 16th century, yet incorporating traditional Hindu and Muslim features, notably minarets and *jalis* (the trellis stonework in the side-hall arches which eliminate tropical sun-glare yet allow cool sea breezes in). Return to the Gateway in the evening—it's a popular after-work promenade spot for Bombayites and a relaxing place to end your day, though the crowds can press in a little, and you should watch your pockets. The ebony-black equestrian statue you see facing onto the gate depicts the mighty Maratha emperor, Chatrapati Shivaji, who became the bane of the Mughal Aurangzeb. It was set up soon after Bombay became capital of Maharashtra state in 1961.

From Colaba, the tour moves into the city via **Flora Fountain**. Situated at the top of Mahatma Gandhi Road, this is the heart of downtown Bombay, home to most of the city's major banks and offices. Nearby is the imposing Gothic structure of **Victoria Terminus** (or 'V.T.'), the largest railway station in the East, as well as the Cathedral of St Thomas, begun in 1672 by Gerald Aungier, yet only opened in 1718. Then to the seafront, for a beautiful trip up **Marine Drive** (uninspiringly renamed Netaji Subhash Road) built on reclaimed marshland in 1920. It sweeps up in a long elegant arc from Nariman Point to Chowpatty at the top of Back Bay, and is another favourite promenade spot.

Below Chowpatty, the tour makes a stop at **Taraporewala Aquarium** (*open daily, 11–8, except Mon; the admission is money well spent*). One of India's finest, the aquarium was opened in 1951 and houses a wide selection of interesting marine life—giant lobster, batfish, shark, sea-turtle, stingray and turbot—supplied with fresh sea water via an underground pipeline.

At **August Kranti Gardens** (*open daily, 9.30–6, except Sun and Mon afternoons*), a mile above Chowpatty, you'll find one of Bombay's most important buildings—**Mani Bhavan**, 19 Laburnum Road. This was Mahatma Gandhi's residence during his visits to Bombay between 1917 and 1934. From here, he launched both his *satyagraha* (non-violence) and civil disobedience campaigns (1919 and 1934 respectively) and you can see within an exact reconstruction of the room he lived in—his simple pallet-bed, spinning-wheel, walking-stick, sandals and quaint old telephone, kept just as they were during his life, along with his few religious texts:

the Koran, Bible and Gita. On the floor, there's a beautifully crafted tableau of 28 model panels depicting key events in the great man's history. If you want to see and learn more about Gandhi, return later to browse through the extensive library or to see one of the regular film-shows held in the auditorium.

Next stop, at the top of Back Bay, is the **Jain Temple** on Bal Gangadhar Kher Marg. Take time out at this colourful shrine to study the marvelously intricate carvings on its exterior walls. Then climb to the upper storey and watch the monks (their faces masked to avoid swallowing insects) tracing complicated *mandalas* (sacred patterns) in powder and ash before the image of the god.

On the heights of nearby **Malabar Hill** are the famous **Hanging Gardens**. They are not as exotic as they sound, being simply a terraced garden landscaped in 1881 over three reservoirs supplying water to Bombay city but they compensate with a truly bizarre topiary of trimmed animal-shape hedges. The popular flower-clock in the garden is near the privet 'elephant'. Hidden behind a wall beside the Hanging Gardens is the **Towers of Silence** (visitors not allowed), where the Parsis (popularly regarded as Bombay's wealthiest clan, though some say that this title is held by the Jains) leave out their dead to be consumed by crows and kites. Locals claim that the odd morsel of Parsi is sometimes dropped by these birds on a window-sill or balcony of the surrounding apartment blocks. This may or may not be true, but certainly the reservoirs that lie beneath the Hanging Gardens' lawns were covered over with the turf you now see because the local authorities feared contamination of the city's water supply by rotting body parts. Across the road from the gardens, there's the pleasant **Kamala Nehru Park**. Laid out in 1952 in memory of Pandit Nehru's wife, it is a colourful, touristy place with a children's playground and a giant Old Woman's Shoe. Ignore the jibes and climb it, for spectacular views down over Marine Drive and Chowpatty Beach—especially good around sunset.

The tour ends at the **Prince of Wales Museum** (*open daily, 10–5.30, except Mon; adm free on Tues*), off Willingdon Circle in Colaba. This beautiful Gothic structure—designed by Wittet in the Indo-Saracenic style, with imposing dome in the 15th/16th-century Western Indian style—was built in 1905 to commemorate the first visit of George V (then Prince of Wales) to India. It stands in oriental splendour in spacious palm-decorated gardens and reminds many visitors of Monte Carlo. Within, you'll find one of the finest collections of art, archaeology and natural history in the country. Start off in the 'key gallery' just inside the entrance. This introduces all the other galleries in the museum, and exhibits the choicest specimens from each one. If your time is short (and it will be if you want to rejoin the tour bus: it stops here for only 35 minutes), use this gallery to choose a couple of selected areas. Better still, leave the tour and do the whole museum properly. On the ground floor, you'll find sculpture and stonework, much of it Buddhist (Gandharan) and some huge ceiling slabs from Chalukyan temples in northern Karnataka, dating back to the 6th century AD. Also on the ground floor is the Indus Valley Civilization gallery, displaying exhibits from India's earliest known towns (c. 3500 BC). Contemporary with the Sumerian cities of the Tigris/Euphrates region of Mesopotamia which was thought to be the 'mother culture' of civilized Europe—and remark-ably similiar in artistic style, as well as in customs such as architecture and burial rituals, the Indus Valley artefacts display the common ancestry of the first Indian and European cultures.

On the first floor, there are some excellent ceramics, pottery and necklaces. Also on the first floor is one of the jewels of this marvellous museum—the manuscript gallery with illustrations of Hindu texts, Mughal miniatures, including the magnificent portraits of Jahangir and Dara Shikoh and the collection of later Pahari school paintings from the hill states of Punjab and Himachal. Look closely at the subtle detail of the colours, each one painted on with a brush whose tip ended in a single strand of squirrel hair. Of all the colours used in these exquisite pictures, the yellows are often the most vibrant. There is a reason for this. The colour was extracted from camel's urine—a strongly coloured liquid even before refining. To achieve a golden tinge, some unlucky camels were apparently infected with jaundiced urine (using the diseased excretions of a goat or donkey in the camel's feed), proving that even animals suffer for art. On the third floor, is the unmissable Purshottam Vishram Mawji collection of art, a worthwhile Tibetan/Nepalese gallery, and good exhibitions of Continental pottery and Victorian glassware.

Elephanta Island Tour

excursion boat, 4 hours

This is a good way to occupy a Monday (when most sights are closed), a Sunday (when the rest of Bombay is closed) or any day when you need a break from the city. What you're going to see are four rock-cut **cave temples**, dating from AD 450–750, situated on the densely forested Elephanta Island some 6½ miles northeast of Apollo Bunder. To get there, you've a choice of a 'Big Boat' (Rs40) or a 'Little Boat' (Rs25), tickets for which are sold from the small office oppo-site the Gateway of India from where the boats leave. Take a 'Big Boat'—they have good guides (all archaeology graduates) who'll teach you a lot about Hindu religion, art and philosophy. Boats leave every hour, between 9am and 2pm, and take an hour to reach the island.

Elephanta has the longest historical pedigree of any of Bombay's seven islands. While the others were still boggy marshes, Elephanta was being developed between the 7th and mid 8th centuries. The extent and quality of the rock-cut architecture and monumental sculpture is well worth the trip over. Much later, the Portuguese landed on the rear side of the island, found a massive stone elephant there (presently housed in Bombay's Victoria Gardens) and renamed it Elephanta. Later, as disenchantment set in, bored Portuguese gunners spent long, hot monsoon months using its beautiful cave temples for target practice.

The caves themselves are a testimony to the faith of those who excavated them. Some contain 25-foot (7.7-metre) high friezes of astonishing workmanship and figurative detail. The quality, despite cannon-damage and loss of much of the original, beautiful paintwork, is quite as fine as that of the more popular caves at Ellora.

Arriving at the island, it's a gentle climb up 125 sloping steps to the main cave, dedicated to Shiva. On the ascent, keep an eye out for acquisitive monkeys (don't display any food or bright jewellery, and don't tease them, as you may see the Indian tourists doing—the monkeys bite). There are *palanquins* available for those who don't like exercise. At the top, pay your admission and follow the guide directly into the caves for the excellent half-hour lecture.

Away from the caves, there are three fishing villages whose inhabitants now draw their livings almost entirely from tourism, selling cheap jewellery, crafts and photos of themselves in traditional dress along the steps leading from the jetty to the caves.

The main cave, carved out of the hard, durable blackstone around the middle of the 7th century AD, comprises a pillared hall and a small shrine (this has four entrance doors, flanked by *dvarapala* guardians). The architectural style is a combination of Chalukyan (cushion capitals and graceful sculptures) and Gupta (mountain, cloud, nature imagery) influences. The cave itself features a series of large sculptured panels, the finest of which, the 19 foot (5.8 metre) high *Trimurti* monolith, depicts Shiva in a rare role as creator, protector and destroyer combined—a sacred grouping known as the *Mahesamurti*, or portrayal of the Hindu Trinity. He is shown first as a young man/Brahma/creator, holding lotus blossom (gentle, feminine face on right), then as a middle-aged man/Vishnu/preserver (wise, mature central face, wearing enigmatic smile comparable to that of the Mona Lisa), and finally as a wizened, ferocious old man (left panel), representing Shiva himself as destroyer, holding a skull. It's an exquisitely balanced piece of work, and the only one that escaped being shot at by the Portuguese, probably owing to its resemblance to the Christian idea of the Holy Trinity.

Nearby is one of the finest sculptures in India—Ravana lifting Mount Kailash. This tells the epic story of the Lankan (demon) king, Ravana—often shown with 10 heads to denote superior intelligence (though not supreme intelligence, as the demon was to find out)—who took advantage of Shiva's deep slumber to try to displace his mountain home. But then Shiva woke up and, with just the gentle pressure of his toe, pressed the teetering peak back into place again, burying the demon king beneath it for 10,000 years. Such is the skill of the sculptor here, that you can actually see the strain on Ravana's rippling shoulder and back muscles.

To the left of the Trimurti is another masterstroke—Shiva as *Ardhanarisvara*, or half-man half-woman. This is a representation of the twin force of masculine spirit and feminine creativity. Viewed from the centre, the bisexuality of the figure's form and features appears quite harmonious: a remarkable achievement. The 'female' face is looking into the mirror of *maya* or illusion. Another important tableau shows Shiva playing chess with Parvati on Mount Kailash, surrounded by awed domestic servants. In the legend, Parvati loses the game, becomes angry and throws a tantrum at Shiva, who soothes her by saying that life is a game and that she, though married to the crerator himself, is still a mere creation of his and should be content to merely participate in the game. Some would call this sexist, but brahmins see this as an allegory of the unity and interdependence of the created (and thus human) and universal soul. In the same panel, Shiva is seen performing the earth-shaking Tandava dance (*Nataraja*); and demonstrating the discipline of yoga (*Yogisvara*).

Surrounding the caves is dense forest. A wide trail leads on through the trees, away from the main caves to various sets of smaller carved caves and wide views out over the blue, winking, Indian ocean.

Sights Round-up

by sightseeing bus or taxi, full day

*Kanheri Caves–Juhu Beach–St John's Church–Chowpatty Beach–
Cross Maidan–Falkland Road Red Light District*

If you enjoyed Elephanta, there's a second state-conducted tour out to **Kanheri Caves** 26½ miles away. This is one of the largest groups of Buddhist caves (109 in all) in western India. Set high on a hill in extensive wild forest, the caves are at the edge of the Borivali National Park, a wilderness that, despite having Bombay right on its doorstep, supports such wildlife as *sambar* deer, leopard and a host of monkeys. Dating from around the 2nd to 9th centuries AD, the earlier *Hinayana* caves have been excavated from a huge circular rock. Most of them are simple monks' cells of limited interest, but caves 1, 2 and 3 are noteworthy for their massive pillars, sculptures and *stupas*. Cave 3 is the famous **Chaitya Cave** whose icons and long, pillared colonnade were carved from the solid mountain rock. It is worth being a little bit naughty and wandering away from the main group to explore the dozens of rock-hewn stairways that wind away over the basalt outcrops to over one hundred smaller caves, and finally into the great forest itself. You will be called back by your guide before you have gone very far. Those who think they might like to explore more extensively should pay a little extra and hire a guide and private car through the Tourist Office on Churchgate (*see* above). The caves are too fascinating to be seen in a rush, and the green woodlands are so peaceful that the thought of returning to the dusty roar and heat of Bombay is not attractive.

On the regular tour, the next stop is **Juhu Beach**. This is a 3-mile long beach fringed with palms and coconut trees: a popular week-round picnic spot, with good beach entertainments at weekends. Juhu has lots of big hotels but is highly insanitary and therefore has lousy swimming.

Back in Colaba, **Sassoon Dock**, a mile down Shahid Bhagat Singh Road from the Bunder, is a great place to watch all the fishing boats unloading their catch around dawn. While you're in the area, walk 10 minutes further south to Colaba's most significant monument: the elegant **St John's (Afghan) Church**, built in 1857 in memory of British soldiers who died in the first Afghan War. Its tall spire has become a familiar landmark for sailors far out at sea.

For a good evening out, start with a high-rise cocktail at the Oberoi's rooftop restaurant, the **Malabar** and watch the sun set gloriously over Back Bay. Then cruise the 2½ miles up to **Chowpatty Beach** by cab. This is where tired Bombay businessmen come, with friends and families, to wind down after a hard day making money. After tucking into typical Bombay snacks like *bhel puri* (spicy mix of puffed rice, peanuts, onions, potatoes and chutneys) and *chaat* (fruit and veg tossed in a banana leaf) they enjoy a relaxing evening massage. The beach is lined with expert masseurs. One end of the beach is a regular meeting area for Bombay's gay community. Come to Chowpatty for authentic local atmosphere and for the popular view of Malabar Hill, beautifully lit after dusk. This is the renowned 'Queen's Necklace' around the 'throat' of Back Bay. Swimming, by the way, is not possible here.

On the way back into the city centre, ask to stop at the **Dhobi Ghats**, or laundry quarter, where the *dhobi wallahs* (laundry men) and their families thump and slap the ingrained dirt of Bombay from the clothes of the middle classes. Each family rents two small concrete tanks (one for washing, one for rinsing) and a lean-to shanty in the same compound, creating a self-contained world of relentless activity that can be viewed from a traffic bridge—ask your driver for it and he'll know where to stop. Many of the clothes are laid out to dry on the smutty streets nearby, where no one seems to steal or mischievously soil them. Despite Bombay's pervasive grime, the *dhobi* wallahs somehow manage to end up with linens whiter than anything in a Western detergent advert. The job is inherited, as is the rented tub and drying spot, so competition is fierce between families to get enough business to keep up with the rent and ensure their livelihood—several generations of each family can be seen at work in the *dhobi ghats*. Think about this as you peer over the bridge's parapet, and you will get an insight into the desperate race to scrape a living that consumes Bombay.

Finish your tour at **Cross Maidan**, in the heart of the city. These urban gardens are overlooked by **Bombay University** (a wonderful Gothic horror, dominated by the 260-foot (80-metre) high **Rajabai Clock Tower**) and surrounding **High Court** buildings topped by the figures of Justice and Mercy. In contrast to this colonial austerity, the Maidan itself is a popular evening exhibition centre of twinkling lights and general jollification. There's nearly always something going on here. Perhaps an inflatable Taj Mahal at the entrance and a novelty funfair going on inside: stoical Brahmin families traipsing unamusedly through the 'Baby Diamond Laughing House', films about lion-taming playing to packed houses in the 'Family Planning Video Booth', and hordes of ticketless local youths clambering over the scaffolding of the '32 foot-height (*sic*) Ropeway'.

Off the Tourist Trail

Not included on any official tours, but definitely worth seeing, is the Falkland Road, or **Red Light District**. Jump into a cab and ask for either Grant Road or Falkland Road, and you will eventually be deposited at the bottom of a busy street, both sides of which are lined with prostitutes offering their services from narrow doorways—usually for pitifully small amounts of money. These streets bring home the extent of sexual exploitation and the sadness of the general plight of rural women in India; most of the girls are only just teenagers, sold into the trade by poor peasant families in the provinces, who cannot afford the necessary dowries to marry them off. Even very poor families are expected to provide quite excessive dowries if they want to see their daughters hitched, and so surplus daughters are often sold in this way. Tragically, the incidence of AIDS among Bombay's prostitutes has recently been estimated at 80 per cent or higher, so that even those who manage to escape the effective slavery of the brothels (some girls are chained to their beds at night) may not live long on the outside.

From a safety point of view, the Red Light District is generally fine by day, but is obviously dodgy by night. If exploring on foot, search the skyline for the weird semi Islamic-style 1960s skyscraper built for Muslim pilgrims stopping in Bombay on their way to Mecca. If you head in that direction through the crowded street bazaars of the Muslim market quarter, you will emerge after half an hour or so near Crawford Market and the Victoria train terminus. However, if night is coming on or the prospect of the walk through the crowds is too daunting, head back to Falkland Road and take a cab.

Sports and Activities

Bombay is rather exclusive when it comes to sports. For the best facilities, you'll either have to pay out for an expensive hotel (the Taj and the President for **tennis, golf** and **swimming**; the Oberoi for the best swimming pool) or hover round in hope of an introduction to the two best social clubs—the **Bombay Gymkhana**, Mahatma Gandhi Road, ✆ 204101 and the **Willingdon Sports Club**, K. Khadye Marg, ✆ 391754.

Swimming in the sea round Bombay is not really on, the water is badly polluted. If you want a swim, go up to **Breach Candy Club** on Bhulabhai Desai Road, a mile north of Hanging Gardens. This has a large, fun **swimming pool** in the shape of India before Partition—'Ceylon' is the kiddies' pool. Breach Candy has several other good recreation facilities too, but only lets foreign guests in on production of their passport.

Any good hotel should be able to arrange a game of golf at **Presidency Golf Club**, ✆ 5513670, about an hour's drive out of town and worth it. The Taj and Oberoi hotels can arrange **sailing, horse-riding, racquet games** and **buggy-rides** around town—but only for their guests. **Fishing** is easier: apply to the Secretary of Maharastra State Angling Association, ✆ 571641 for temporary membership. Good *katla, rahu, mirgil, bekti* and *gorami* fishing at Powai Lake, 14 miles by rail to Andheri and then 5km (3½ miles) further by road. A day's angling will cost you around Rs500, inclusive of boat-hire, tackle and bait.

Riding can be had on well-schooled horses at the **Bombay Amateur Riders' Club**, ✆ 3090509/3071445, next door to the Mahalaxmi racecourse (*see* below). The club has a stable of thoroughbreds and smaller, crescent-eared Rajasthani horses. A temporary membership costs Rs8,200 and every ride thereafter Rs100 per half-hour. However, you may be able to persuade the secretary to waive the temporary membership fee if you stress that you are only in town for a day or two. This might get you a cheap hack around the racetrack. However, you will certainly have to buy the temporary membership if you want to practise any other equestrian activities, such as dressage, jumping, or the old cavalry sport of tent-pegging, in which you try to spear a wooden peg from the ground at full gallop and keep it on the end of your lance. Summer riding times are from 6 to 8am and 5.15 to 6.45pm, while winter rides go from 6.15 to 8.15am and from 4.45 to 6.15pm. Rides are paid for by the half-hour.

Horse Racing at the Mahalaxmi racecourse, opposite Haji Ali Mosque, takes place every Sunday and public holiday between November and March. The big meetings are in February and March and the cream of Bombay society turns out to be seen.

Trekking and wildlife viewing in the wild areas and sanctuaries of central and southern India can be arranged through the **Bombay Natural History Society**, Hornbill House, Brabhat Singh Road, ✆ 243421/243869, situated on the big traffic island between Colaba and Fort. The society's regular outings are usually 2–5-day trips, often offering access to areas where tourism is seriously restricted. A foreign membership of the society costs £12 or US$30 and you should expect to pay about Rs400 per trip thereafter inclusive of transport and/or equipment and accommodation, but not food. Apart from getting you into wild places that most tourists never see, the society's trips also have the benefit of qualified guides who know the flora and fauna intimately and can tell you in detail what you are seeing. Those interested should pop down to the headquarters at Hornbill house and pick up a prospectus of the season's upcoming trips.

Shopping

Here, as in Delhi, you can buy practically anything, and often a lot cheaper than anywhere else in India.

Bombay's shops are generally open daily from 10am–7pm although many bazaars and most shops in the Oberoi arcade stay open till 9pm, exc. Fri.

crafts

For an idea of what's available and how much it should cost, start at the **Central Cottage Industries Emporium**, 34 Chatrapati Shivaji Maharaj Marg, just up the road from the Taj Mahal Hotel, ℃ 202 2491. Although not as good as the main branch in Delhi, this fixed-price place stocks a wide range of regional crafts: silks from Kanchipuram, carpets from Kashmir, *saris* from Varanasi, marblework and jewellery from Agra and Jaipur. Probably the best general buy is top-quality Bangalore silk—either as material or in *sari* form (from Rs500 to 20,000.). Opening hours are 10 to 6.30 Monday to Saturday (closed Sunday). To compare prices and quality, there's another good government emporium, **Khadi and Village Industries Emporium**, at 286 Dadabhai Naoroji Road. **Gujarat Government Handicrafts Emporium**, Khetan Bhavan, J.N. Tata Road, ℃ 296292, has the best reputation for high-quality crafts— mainly silk, cotton, bright appliqué-work, brass and wood. Finally, before launching yourself into the high- street shops and markets, visit the shopping arcades at the Taj and Oberoi hotels. The Oberoi arcade is especially good for leather shoes and bags.

markets

The old **Crawford Market** (1867), now renamed **Mahatma Phule Market**, is one of India's best. Raw, bloody, vital and colourful. Travelling in by taxi, keep your window wound up. Once there, resist the attentions of persistent 'guides', and be on your guard against pickpockets. Crawford Market is essentially a fruit, flower, vegetable, meat and fish market, but you can find many other things too, ranging from toy dogs and screeching parakeets to heaps of old machinery bits. The favourite anecdote in nearby **Chor Bazaar** ('Thieves Market') is that you can be sold spare parts from your own car.

Visit Crawford Market around 6 to 7pm, when crowds are thinner and shopping more civilized. Inside the covered warehouse, you'll find **Hakimi Stores**, which does a complete range of spices and curry powders: all the ingredients you need to reproduce good Indian cooking back home. Alternatively (and these make good little presents), you can buy small packs of ready-made curry powders.

silk and scent

Just outside the covered market, **Gulf Silk Centre**, 406 Shaikh Memon Street, is a friendly shop—very useful indeed for picking up small, attractive last-minute presents before flying home. Choose from a wide range of silk/cotton *saris*, shawls and bedcovers, and from a marvelous selection of aromatic perfumes and spices. Men can pick up cool, practical 'Congress' outfits here (*kurta*/pant sets), which double up as jazzy pyjamas. Across the road at **Chinubhai B. Shah**, 346 Abdul Rehman Street, you can buy the Congress hat to go with them. For making fabric buys into pants, suits, saris etc., try **Mod Tailor** at 408 Shaikh Memon Street. This place also has some nice outfits for ladies—traditional three-part suits (*kameez* tops, *churidhar* trousers, plus *dupata* scarves) at reasonable rates. Again, very cool and practical.

cottons

Buy cotton clothes and materials at **M.G. Market**, just right of Crawford Market.

metalwork and leather

Visit **Zaveri Bazaar** off Mumbadevi Road; for brass and copper, the adjoining **Brass Bazaar**; and for smuggled goods, leather and curios, the aforementioned Chor Bazaar.

bookshops

Bombay has some very good bookshops, both new and second-hand, where you can stock up on good literature by Western and Indian authors at very cheap prices. For new books, the best deals are offered by a small shop called **Smoker's Corner Books** on Sir Phirolshah Mehta Road, in the Fort District. Good **second-hand bookstands** can be found lining the railings on either side of Verenariman Road between the Fort District and Churchgate, outside the Main Post Office.

Bombay ℗ (022–)   ### Where to Stay

Living in Bombay is very expensive and good rooms are hard to come by. With housing such a problem, decent hotels are often fully booked, and the few habitable budget lodges packed out. In the former instance, make advance reservations; in the latter, arrive very early in the morning to snap up any rooms going. The most difficult time is the January/February high season.

Prices listed below do not include luxury tax, currently at 20%. In Bombay, guests at 5-star hotels are generally required to pay in US dollars.

luxury

The top hotels are all central. More an institution than a hotel is the **Taj Mahal**, with its new addition the **Taj Mahal Intercontinental**, Apollo Bunder, ℗ 2023366, ℗ 2872711. The old building is one of Bombay's major landmarks: opened in 1903 and accorded (with its new skyscraper relative) the accolade of being one of the world's 12 best hotels. It is a major focal point of all visitors to Bombay. Rooms are US$155 for standard rooms and up to US$700 for a suite, and (if you have the choice) are best at the top of the new building, with views overlooking the sea, or in one of the large sea-facing rooms in the 'old Taj'. Guests also get the fine swimming pool, the famous health centre, an excellent discothèque and the resident astrologer. Food is superb. What the London *Times* wrote in 1903 still applies, the Taj is '...the finest caravanserai in the East.'

Over at Nariman Point, the soaring **Oberoi Towers**, ✆ 2024343, ✉ 2043282/ 2041505, is the tallest building in India, with 35 storeys. Efficient and personal, it has an opulent reception lounge and is superbly located for shopping centres and the airport. Overlooking the Arabian Sea on all sides, it offers elegantly furnished rooms (meticulously colour-matched) at US$155 single, US$170 double. For stunning views over Marine Drive and Back Bay, get one as high up as possible. Facilities include six speciality restaurants, massive swimming-pool, high-rise landscaped garden and vast shopping arcade. Only one other hotel comes close to this one and it's next door. Unmatched facilities and designer elegance are the keynotes of **The Oberoi Bombay**, Nariman Point, ✆ 2025757, ✉ 2043282/2041505. This new structure (opened 1987) features an imposing 11-storey atrium, a high-level pool with cascading water-fall, a string quartet in the polished granite lobby and a futuristic 'environmental unit' in the health club (lie back and computer-control your sauna, steam-bath, jacuzzi, sun-tan, even tropical shower). Geared to the top corporate business traveller, the décor may lack personality but all standards are very high. There's a 24-hour business centre, an exclusive Supper Club, and every conceivable five-star amenity. In addition to three select restaurants and a rooftop bar, guests arriving in the dead of night are greeted by an immaculately turned-out butler bearing gifts. His first question will be: 'Does sir/madam prefer the juice or the champagne?' Rooms are priced at US$200 single, US$215 double. They are all beautifully furnished and command prime views of the metropolis and the sea.

Fourth down the list and probably more in the range of the general traveller, is Taj Group's **Hotel President**, 90 Cuffe Parade, Colaba, ✆ 4150808, ✉ 2151201. This hotel remains one of the warmest, most pleasant upmarket hotels in India—a refreshing contrast to large businessman's hotels like The Oberoi. Many couples and families stay at the President: they like its informal atmosphere and relaxing pool, its famous service and food, and its cosy, stylish rooms—more reasonable at US$125 single, US$140 double.

Other luxury and five-star hotels are located in the suburbs and toward the airport. At Juhu Beach, 15½ miles from the city centre but only 5 miles from the airport are a range of properties. The **Centaur Hotel Juhu Beach**, ✆ 6113040, ✉ 6116343, has every conceivable facility and rooms from US$95. The **Holiday Inn**, ✆ 6204444, ✉ 6204452, has rooms from US$100. The **Ramada Inn Palm Grove**, ✆ 6112323, ✉ 6142105, has rooms from US$95. Nearer town is the **Welcomgroup Searock Sheraton**, at Land's End, Bandra, ✆ 6425454, ✉ 6408046. The Searock has good restaurants and for those who over indulge, an excellent health club. Rooms are from US$120.

One of India's best hotels is located next to the international airport at Sahar. The **Leela Kempinski Bombay**, ✆ 8363636, ✉ 6360606, 6341865, has excellent service, good rooms from US$150, good restaurants and a health club.

expensive

The **Ambassador**, Veer Nariman Road, Churchgate, ✆ 2041131, ✉ 2040004, has a good central location, popular rooftop revolving restaurant, useful facilities, and attractive single/double rooms from US$75. A less expensive hotel on Marine Drive is **Hotel Nataraj**, ✆ 2044161, ✉ 2043864, with rooms from Rs1200. Its advantage is the classiest disco in town—**R.G.'s**—but otherwise lacks charm. At Santa Cruz (domestic airport) the **Centaur Hotel** has 24-hour check-in/check-out facilities and is only walking distance from the domestic airport, ✆ 6116660, ✉ 6113535. Rooms are from US$80. A Colaba option is **Fariyas**, 25 Arthur Street, ✆ 2042911, ✉ 2834992 with good restaurants, including a roof garden, and rooms from Rs1200.

moderate

Top prices in this category are charged by the comfortable **Garden Hotel**, on Garden Road, Colaba, ✆ 2834823/2841476/2841706. A 2-star hotel with clean, air-conditioned rooms and attached marble bathrooms. Next door is the **Hotel Godwin**, ✆ 2872050, offering similar quality and comfort, with some good views out over the city and the bay. Also in Colaba is the **Hotel Apollo**, Lansdowne Road, behind Regal Cinema, Colaba, ✆ 2873312, well known for style and comfort. It has a nice restaurant, attentive service, and pleasant air-conditioned rooms. Ask for one with a sea view. Even better is **Hotel Diplomat**, 24–6 Merriwether Road, ✆ 2021661, located just behind the Taj Hotel. It's in serious need of renovation, but travellers still love it. Friendly staff, quiet location, homely atmosphere and cosy rooms with TV and balcony. For good views of the Arabian Sea, try **Sea Green Hotel**, ✆ 221662, at 145 Marine Drive. Staff can be po-faced but the rooms are good value. Don't be fobbed off with one with (depressing) rear views of the cricket stadium. Another option is **Shelly's Hotel**, 30 P.J. Ramchandani Marg, ✆ 240229, 240270, still very friendly after years spent servicing Western travellers.

Moving up to the city, there's **Chateau Windsor Guest House**, 86 Veer Nariman Road, next to the Ambassador Hotel (✆ 204 3376), a very friendly place with great roof views, useful facilities, and smart rooms, disinfected daily, though smaller ones can be windowless and poky. A reasonable fallback is **Hotel Oasis**, 276 Shahid Bhagat Singh Road, near the post office. This is a quiet, clean place with a good central location.

inexpensive

Most budget travellers stay in the Colaba area, a number of 'cheapies' being situated just behind the Taj Hotel. Space and hygiene are at a premium. For maximum comfort, stay at **Whalley's Guest House**, 41 Merriweather Road, ✆ 221 802. Renovated, this old favourite offers huge rooms, complete with verandahs and Victorian tub-baths on pedestals, at low rates and breakfast is included. Ask for a top-floor room with balcony overlooking the street. If you're feeling more extravagant, splash out on one of the new air-conditioned double rooms with tiled bathrooms; they're the perfect antidote to hot, steamy Bombay. Needless to say, the average backpacker still makes a beeline for popular **Rex/Stiffles**, round the corner from the Taj Hotel. Just like its more fêted neighbour, this place has become an institution. Despite its many drawbacks travellers love it, for the warm family atmosphere and the grim-faced security guards, keeping Colaba's relentless touts at bay. Try also the **Carlton Hotel**, on the first floor of 12 Merriweather Street, opposite the big grey back of the Taj Hotel, ✆ 2020642. The Carlton has a few air-conditioned rooms. The cheaper ones are still clean, if basic, and have fans, but share bathrooms. The hotel's verandah looks across at the the open windows of a busy brothel, whose inmates sit and preen and lean out to invite passing men up to join them. Also in Colaba are two hotels in much the same quality and price range, carrying the same name of **Apollo Guest House**. The first is on the Causeway, opposite the Electricity Board's headquarters, Electric House, *✆* 2041302, while the second is round the corner on Garden Road, *✆* 240121. Both offer clean, if cramped, non air-conditioned rooms, but with fans.

The **Samson Guest House**, 2 minutes' walk from the Taj, is a useful alternative. This place is run with efficiency by a tolerant ex-police officer, and has clean, comfy double rooms (with common bathroom). The nearby **Shilton Hotel** is tricky to find (look for the 'Sex and Alcohol Clinic' next to the movie theatre, by the circle) but is a real bargain with tiny, but spotless air-conditioned double rooms. Equally good value is provided by **Seashore Hotel** at 1–49 Kamal Mansion, Arthur Bunder Road, *✆* 287 4237. Nice people and lovely large sea-view rooms.

In Bandra and many of the mid-town areas small guest-houses have recently become very popular. The tourist office also keeps a list of paying guest accommodation but before going down for their computer print-out, try **Mrs Olga Nobre** at Nobre Villa, Bandra, *✆* 6497929, whose three available rooms cost about Rs200 per day for non air-conditioned and Rs300 air-conditioned (both with meals) and **Mrs Rinku Bhattachrya**, 36 Carter Road, Bandra, *✆* 402431, who offers rooms at Rs350 non air-conditioned and Rs450 air-conditioned.

cheap

Much cheaper is the Salvation Army's **Red Shield Guest House**, just across the road from Rex. It's the obvious shoestring fallback, occupying three storeys of cheap dormitory beds at Rs75, or Rs120 inclusive of three meals (you have to get up for breakfast: a booming gong sounds at an unearthly hour in the morning until all guests are at table). It's a great place for meeting fellow travellers, but has poor luggage security.

Given the difficulty of finding rooms in Colaba at high season, you might do well to stay in the city instead. There are a few good places here, very well-located for the post office, tourist office, V.T. station and the better cinemas. Try first **City Lodge**, 121 City Terrace, W.H. Marg, opposite Victoria Terminus station, *✆* 265515, which is also a tailor's and cloth merchant's shop. Ask for either of the Rs150 rooftop doubles (rooms 5 and 6), which have first-rate city views. This place is run by a very pleasant family. Alternatively, there's **Rupam Lodge**, 239 P. D'Mello Road, just past the post office, *✆* 2616225, with 24-hour room service, telephones in rooms and, a real rarity, thick mattresses on beds. It's rather run-down nowadays, but rooms are still cheap and it's often full. For a few rupees more, you can enjoy a much comfier stay at **Lord Hotel**, just off P. D'Mello Road, at 301 Mangalore Street. This has friendly staff, popular beer bar, and really nice rooms. With all the above hotels, don't forget the golden rule: the early bird gets the vacant room!

If really down to your last rupees, there are two truly awful guesthouses on Merriweather Street in Colaba, offering cramped dorm beds, complete with fleas and worse for Rs50 per night. These are the **Seaview** (ho ho!) and **Jones Guesthouses**, both on the seaward side of Merriweather about 200 yards down from the Taj. Please bear in mind that these are last resorts only.

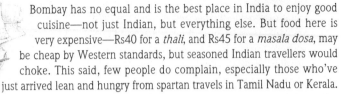

Bombay has no equal and is the best place in India to enjoy good cuisine—not just Indian, but everything else. But food here is very expensive—Rs40 for a *thali,* and Rs45 for a *masala dosa,* may be cheap by Western standards, but seasoned Indian travellers would choke. This said, few people do complain, especially those who've just arrived lean and hungry from spartan travels in Tamil Nadu or Kerala.

expensive

The Taj Hotel is often the first place people head for when they want good food. It has a nice choice of air-conditioned restaurants, starting with the mid-range **Shamiana** coffee-shop with an all-you-can-eat buffet breakfast for Rs175 and buffet lunch for Rs250, working up to the sophisticated **Tanjore** (*biriani* or *thali* suppers from Rs400, tying in with cultural dance entertainment programmes at 7.45pm, 9.45pm and 10.45pm), and hitting the heights up at the **Rooftop Rendezvous**, which has superb Continental dishes, notably French, from Rs500. The **Menage à Trois** restaurant, also at the rooftop, offers designer dining from an exciting lunchtime menu created by London's well known chef and restaurateur, Anthony Worrall-Thompson. Well-presented, well-priced food from Rs500 and superb views from the 21st floor.

But it's the Oberoi Towers, Nariman Point, that has the prestige restaurant in Bombay. This is the **Café Royal**, a very select Parisian-style eatery where every item of food is specially flown in from France. Start with *escargots* or smoked salmon, move on to lobster, king prawn or steak for a main course and conclude with *crêpes suzettes.* To wash it all down, you've a wide choice of vintage wines, or the speciality 'fruit punch'. Next door at the new Oberoi Bombay hotel, the French **Rôtisserie** restaurant offers an Executive Lunch for Rs400, while the downstairs **Kandahar** serves authentic North West Frontier food (huge portions) from about Rs500. It's a toss-up between the Kandahar and Oberoi Towers' **Mughal Room** (famous *tandoori* cuisine) for the best Indian restaurant in a Bombay hotel. The Towers also has a Polynesian restaurant, the **Outrigger**, which has a good-value lunchtime buffet for Rs350 and is certainly popular. Meanwhile, the famous **Samarkhand**—a 24-hour coffee shop overlooking busy Marine Drive—continues to enchant visitors and residents alike. It's one of the 'places to be seen' in Bombay.

moderate

A better value restaurant is the Taj-run **Rangoli**, at the NCPA, Nariman Point, ℂ 234678. Open every day with a good buffet lunch for Rs220, it's popular with local offices staff—reservations are needed at lunchtime and at weekends.

Nearly all Bombay's restaurants are more interesting than those of Delhi. This is because city residents eat out far more—their prime concern is making money and they have little time for cooking. Bombay is not unlike New York in that people go out to be seen and because most accommodation is so cramped they prefer the space of restaurants. If Bombayites choose a hotel restaurant, it's usually for something of value (like the buffet lunch at Taj Hotel's **Crystal Room**) or something fancy (like pizzas, home-made ice cream, and serenading violinists at President Hotel's delightful **Trattoria**). But in the main, they stick to local restaurants like the renowned **Shalimar** in Bhendi

Bazaar. This place serves cheap, delicious north Indian specialities (a whole leg of lamb for Rs150) and has a real family atmosphere. For fast food, they favour **Open House** opposite Churchgate station (pricey, but good) or the nearby **Ahyadri** restaurant (not only burgers and hot dogs, but excellent Punjabi cuisine too). South Indian fare 'local-style' is nowhere better than at **Sanmans** (behind the Government of India tourist office) or **Sadkar** (opposite Churchgate station) restaurants.

If you like seafood, try the excellent **Excellensea** at 317 Arun Chambers, Mint Road, Fort, ✆ 2618991, which offers shellfish in air-conditioned comfort for Rs50–200 per head. Round the corner is the **Round Table** at 287 Shahid Bhagat Singh Road, ✆ 2611859/2665831, which offers Indian and Western dishes in a similar price range.

Many travellers prefer to stick to tried-and-tested favourites. Places like **Talk of the Town**, 143 Marine Drive (top of Veer Nariman Road), with its popular lunchtime buffets (Rs200) and breezy open-air section, overlooking the seafront. Or for the best Chinese food in town the **China Garden**, at Kemp's Corner, 131 August Kranti Marg, ✆ 8280842, offering hot 'n' spicy Szechwan cuisine for about Rs325 per head in a beautiful setting of cultured trees, greenery and marble. It's the place for spotting Bombay's glitterati and reservations are recommended. Or (for cheaper Chinese fare) **Kamling** in Veer Nariman Road and the ever popular **Nanking**, ✆ 2025940, near the Taj—opposite Cottage Industries.

cheap

Colaba has the best cheap restaurants. At lunchtime, people still pack into friendly **Martin's** for Goan specialities like grilled fish and fiery pork *vindaloos*. Diplomat Hotel's **Silver Plate** has a good reputation for cheap, reliable vegetarian food—continental and Indian—and is well-patronized by locals. **Dipty's Juice Bar** opposite Rex Hotel has delicious *lassis*, juices, ice creams and snacks. There's a line of popular eateries running up Shahid Bhagat Singh Road, starting with **Food Inn** (a 'Catch and Carry' fast-food place, serving cheap north Indian, Hyderabadi, Chinese and Japanese fare); moving up to **Leopold's** on Colaba Causeway, which serves English breakfasts (though lay off the bacon), chilled beer and an Art Deco interior open to the street. This is the place to meet other travellers, Bombay media people and general party goers. You can get a good chicken *biriani* here for about Rs65. **Laxmi Vilas** down the alley past Leopold's serves good-value *thalis*; **Kamat**, opposite Leopold's, has good ice cream and vegetarian snacks. **Delhi Durbar**, also on the Colaba Causeway, is the best mid-range Indian restaurant in Colaba, specializing in tandoor dishes and Indian sweets. A surprising number of backpackers turn up in Taj Hotel's **Shamiana** lounge—word's got around that you can have unlimited coffee here.

Entertainment and Nightlife

For an evening's entertainment, choose from Bombay's good selection of **classical music**, **dance** and **drama** shows. Start by visiting the Government of India Tourist Office for the list of current cultural events, listed in the *This Fortnight for You* handout. For classical dance recitals (including Bharatnatyam, Kathakali, and Odissi styles), pop along to Taj Mahal Hotel's **Tanjore** restaurant (performances at 6.15pm most nights, adm Rs90). For drama (Marathi, Gujarati and Hindi styles), there's the

Sahitya Sangh Mandir, Patkar Hall and **Tata Theatre** (named after the supremely wealthy Parsi family called Tata, whose name adorns many of Inida's automobiles, phone books and countless other manufactured products) at the National Centre for the Performing Arts (NCPA) at Nariman Point. The last two places also hold occasional music recitals. Performances start at 6.30 or 7pm.

Regular **art exhibitions** are held at **Jehangir Art Gallery**, adjoining Prince of Wales Museum and at the **Taj Gallery** in the Taj Mahal Hotel. The **Nehru Planetarium**, 5 miles north of city centre, above the racecourse, has daily star-gazing shows in English at 3pm and 6pm (except Mondays).

Going to the **cinema** in Bombay is a must—it's not only the film capital of India, it also produces more movies than any other city in the world, Hollywood included. There are literally hundreds of cinema houses here (although the advent of the video has resulted in some having to close), most are air-conditioned and very comfortable. To tune in to Bombay movie-madness, buy any of the 'juicy screen gossip' mags peddled on the streets (*Star and Style* is a good one), then buy a newspaper to see what's on. Just head down the street opposite V.T. station, where three good cinemas—Excelsior, Empire and Sterling—show current epics (English, Hindi and Marathi) at 3, 6 and 9pm daily, with a few extra matinees thrown in. Outside, there's a couple of good ice cream parlours and fast-food places—handy for inter-film refreshments. Later, ask the tourist office to arrange a visit to one of the film studios, where you can have a chat with the stars and watch them playing three different parts in three different movies at the same time. Meet them again later in **Studio 29** discothèque (the place to be seen) in Bombay International Hotel, junction of D. Vacha Road and Marine Drive or **R.G.'s** at the Nataraj Hotel on Marine Drive. Temporary membership at both places for foreigners is generally possible.

Bombay is one of the few Indian cities that has a genuine **nightlife**. It's not cheap though, at least if you want to go dancing. Start off with a drink at one of two interesting bars: **Leopold's**, a handsome, Art Deco bar on Colaba Causeway (*see* above) or the **Crown and Anchor**, just around the corner on Merriweather and Tulloch. Leopold's has good conversation, a mixed clientèle of travellers, students and local professionals and celebrities, and is open to the street, while the hot and sweaty Crown and Anchor is a simple pick-up joint for prostitutes, with deafening *bhangra*. The girls don't sit on your lap, Bangkok style, but pass by with a raised eyebrow and a swish of the sari. Occasionally, one will get up to dance in front of the band, swaying to and fro with great sensuality. Oddly enough, the bar is not an exclusively male hang-out, partying couples on their way to other places quite often drop by to soak up the sleazy, charged atmosphere.

Nightclubs are ridiculously overpriced and play a predictable mixture of Top 40 Western dance music and techno. **Upstairs at Leopold's**, on Colaba Causeway, the dance floor is cramped and packed and the average dancer about 18 years old. More sophisticated is the **Cellar**, at the Oberoi Towers Hotel on Nariman Point, whose stiff entry fee (currently Rs350) buys a packed but fun night of exaggeratedly energetic Travolta-style dancing from Bombay's young and wealthy. Alternatively, the **Ghetto**, on the seafront, near the Ambassador Hotel, offers free entry, but very expensive drinks.

Konkani fishermen: Baga beach

Goa

Once the jewel of Portugal's eastern empire, Goa still retains many of the ways of the old Portuguese colony and is an increasingly popular tourist favourite. Lush and green after the summer monsoons, golden-brown through the drier 'winter', this narrow coastal territory of coconut palms and quiet villages nestles between forested mountains and mile upon mile of beautiful beaches. The emphasis here is very much on fun and relaxation: with good food, strong wine, song, dance and general merriment, it's just the place for winding down and enjoying life. There's a beach here to suit every taste and pocket: from high-class Aguada and Bogmalo, to busy package-holiday Calangute and Colva; from the party-going hippy beaches of Anjuna and Arambol, to peaceful palm-fringed coves with not a soul in sight.

It can be easy to forget, therefore, that Goa is not simply beaches. Within striking distance of the capital, Panjim, one of India's prettiest cities, is a variety of historic temples, churches, lakes and parks, market towns and old Portuguese villas. A short drive away, there's the impressive ghost city of Catholic cathedrals, Old Goa. Up in the mountains, the wild forests are home to leopard, *gaur* (bison), bear, and even the occasional tiger or elephant.

The main industries are mining, fishing and tourism, but most of the state's million or so inhabitants make their living from agriculture, growing mainly rice, coconut and cashew. The population is divided pretty evenly between Catholics and Hindus, coexisting in a state of pleasant harmony. The Goans are a devout people, happiest when celebrating the feasts of their saints or deities. They love anyone who loves a good party. Not surprisingly, therefore, many travellers end up staying a lot longer than they originally planned.

History

Hindus believe that Goa was reclaimed from the sea by the sixth *avatar* (incarnation) of Vishnu. Historically, it can be dated back to the 3rd century BC, when it formed part of the Mauryan Empire. Through the early centuries AD the coast changed hands between various local dynasties until its potential wealth came to the attention of the powerful Hindu dynasties of the Karnatic Deccan Plateau. Goa was conquered in turn by the Chalukyan kings of Badami (580–750), by the Kadambas (credited with first settling the site of Old Goa in the mid 11th century), and by the Vijayanagars of Hampi in the early 14th century. In 1469 it was seized from the Vijayanagar kings by the Bahmani Muslims of Bijapur in Karnataka, but the Muslims lost it in turn to the Portuguese in 1510, who had drifted up the coast from Kerala after several years of inconclusive warfare with the rulers of Calicut, vying for control of the trade routes of the southern Arabian Sea.

With its natural harbours and broad rivers, Goa made the ideal base for the trading, seafaring, evangelical Portuguese, bent equally on spreading Catholicism and exploiting the eastern spice route. They named it Goa Doirada, or 'Golden Goa', and began a systematic programme of building churches and destroying Hindu temples. Behind the conquistadors came Jesuit and Franciscan missionaries, who achieved spectacular success in converting most Goans from Hinduism to Roman Catholicism, largely an achievement of the Inquisition, which arrived in 1560. The Jesuits also introduced the first cashew saplings to Goa and

Goa

Terekol Fort
Naibaga
Corgao
Paliem
Pernem
Chandel

MAHARASHTRA

Hermal Beach
Harmal
Arambol Beach
Mandrem

Latombarcem

Tivim
Assonora
Mulgao

Chapora Fort
Vagator Beach
Mapusa
Assagao
Bicholim
Sanquelim

Anjuna Beach
Baga Beach
Arpora
Mayem Lake
Calangute Beach

Arvalem Water Falls
Valpoi

Candolim Beach

Sinquerim Beach

Aguada Fort
Miramar Beach
Panjim
Old Goa
Bambolim

BONDLA WILDLIFE SANCTUARY

Dona Paula Beach
Gangem

Marmagao
Agassaim

Vasco da Gama
Ponda
Sancordem

Bogmalo Beach

Molem
BHAGWAN MAHAVIR WILDLIFE SANCTUARY

Dudhsagar Water Falls

Majorda Beach
Codli

Arabian

Colva Beach
Margao
Benaulim Beach
Benaulim

Varca Beach
Carmona
Quepem

Sea
Cavelossim Beach
Mabor Beach
Rivona

Betul Beach
Colomba

Western Ghats

Netorli (Netravali)

Quisconda
Nundem
Mamai Devi Temple

Goundongrem
Canacona
COTIGAO WILDLIFE SANCTUARY
Salginim

N

Palolem Beach
Rajabag Beach
Butpal

KARNATAKA

20 km

10 miles

Kerala—the most lucrative commercial crop of the two regions—and developed the art of cultivating coconut trees, whose tall trunks and tossing fronds shade the coastal villages from Goa's fearsome summer sun.

Portuguese control began in Old Goa and gradually extended to include most of the territory, displacing a succession of disgruntled local Hindu rulers in the process. Old Goa remained the colonial capital until a terrible outbreak of plague in 1738 prompted a gradual move to Panjim. Portugal's power then began to fade in Europe in the late 18th century, and Goa was briefly occupied by the British during the Napoleonic Wars. However, Britain honoured Portugal's claim under the later British Raj and all three pockets of Portuguese power in India—Goa, Daman and Diu—remained essentially intact right up to December 1961, when they finally returned to Indian control.

During the past 30 years, Goa's Indo-Portuguese character has remained essentially unchanged; the Portuguese themselves have gone, but they left behind a new ruling class of Indo-Portuguese landowners. In fact, being part of India has brought Goa considerable benefits. The Portuguese did little for the territory: until 1961 there were no bridges, no roads (just bullock tracks), and no electricity. The Indians built bridges over Goa's principal rivers, the Mandovi and the Zuari, and Panjim was at last connected up with north and south Goa. They also developed Pilar Harbour, a vast natural harbour backing onto a coastal mountain rich in seams of iron ore, and Goa became wealthy practically overnight.

Finally, having constructed paved roads, modern buildings, hotels, and proper communications, the Indian government prepared Goa for tourism. The potential was always there—the charming little villages with their sunny piazzas, the unbroken miles of wide sandy beaches, the pretty whitewashed churches and chapels, and the exotic combination of the Latin and Indian. But it was only in the 1960s, with the arrival of the hippies, that its vast tourist market was at last recognized.

Tourism

The Goan people have mixed feelings about tourism: some have made fortunes but others consider it to be a threat to their culture and traditions. 'Tourism brings degradation', is a typical comment. 'Drugs, pimping, gambling, touting—all these things come around. Police are doing something now, but it is too little and too late.' But the fiercest local reaction is against 'Indian big business', the hotel chains and corporations who are trying to gain control of the state's tourism, ousting the local villagers who now rely on the beach tourists for income.

This local feeling has grown especially strong since Goa finally gained her own identity, on 31 May 1987, and became the 25th state in the Union of India. As one aggrieved local remarked, 'The Indians are coming and taking all our land. Over the past ten years, our population has doubled—it's getting all crowded, not only with tourists but with financial sharks from elsewhere in the country buying up all our land. It's not good for the Goan people, you know. We'll be submerged as a minority. Even our culture is being wiped out. After twenty years, you'll find nothing of it.' The only thing that made this man smile was the news that police had just arrested some Western girls for topless sunbathing on Colva and Anjuna beaches.

Climate and When to Go

The climate in Goa is most pleasant from **November to February**. It is less crowded but hot from **March to April**. Be sure to avoid **May**, the month of Indian annual holidays, when some beaches are packed with camera-clicking voyeurs. The monsoon season is from **June to October**. Temperatures usually range from 21° to 32°C (but it can get much hotter, of course...).

Getting There

by air

Indian Airlines have at least two flights daily between Bombay and Goa, as do **Damania, EastWest** and **Modiluft**; during the peak winter months of December and January a third and occasionally a fourth daily flight are introduced. There are regular flights to Delhi, Cochin, Bangalore, Madras and Trivandrum. At Goa's Dabolim airport, outside the state's one industrial town of Vasco da Gama, the major hotels have set up reception counters and many operate free transfers by coach for prospective guests. Otherwise, it's an airport bus or a Rs200, 7-mile taxi-ride along twisting country roads into the capital, Panjim.

There are now direct charter flights to Goa from Germany (Condor), the United Kingdom (British Caledonian, Monarch and Air Europe), Finland (Emere) and Denmark (Time Air). Flights from Portugal, France, Sweden and Austria are also being negotiated.

by catamaran

In 1995 the long disused Bombay–Goa shipping service was re-opened by Damania, replacing the old boat journey of several days with a new high-speed catamaran that takes only 8 hours. Unfortunately the catamaran service costs much the same as a flight to Bombay (in 1995 approx US$40), so there is no saving, only the fun of rushing down the coastward waters of the Malabar Coast with the hazy blue line of the Western Ghats marching forever to the east. Another problem is the potential for delays and cancellations due to poor weather conditions.

The catamaran leaves Bombay from New Ferry Wharf, Mallet Bunder. Reservations from MTDC, Madame Cama Road, Nariman Point, ✆ 2026713, 10 to 3 daily except Monday. Return reservations from Bombay can be made from the Indian Tourist Office. In Goa you can make them from V.S. Dempo and Co., Custom Wharf, ✆ 3842, direct from the Damania office opposite the steamer jetty in Panjim; or from the Government of India Tourist Office in Margao.

by train

A narrow-gauge line links Goa with Miraj from where broad-gauge trains will soon run to Bangalore, Bombay and Pune (line re-opens in 1996). Trains between Bombay and Vasco da Gama (for Bogmalo beach) and Margao or 'Madgaon' (get off here for buses to Panjim) take a long 20–22 hours and are generally on hard wooden seats, but are still more comfortable than the bus.

Rail bookings can be made in Panjim at the KTC Terminal, ✆ 45620, at Margao Station, ✆ 22252, and Vasco Station, ✆ 2396.

by bus

Several luxury buses, both state and private, link Bombay and Goa daily, journey time is 16–18 hours. Most of them are of the dreaded 'video' variety. The least unpleasant, by all accounts, are those operated by Maharastra State Transport Development Corporation. There's a particularly good MRSTDC bus leaving Bombay for Panjim at 3pm daily. If returning from Goa to catch a plane in Bombay, then the bus driver can deposit you at the closest point to the airport to save going all the way into Bombay centre, only to have to trek out again.

Where to Stay and Eating Out

All **hotels** in Goa offer generous discounts between April and May (semi-season), and very generous discounts between June and October (low season). All rates quoted for hotels in this chapter are the maximum prices only—for the high season months of November to March.

A delicious mixture of Asian and Western cooking, **Goan cuisine** is a popular escape from the usual south Indian diet of *thali*, *masala dosa* and curry. Long-term travellers flock here for the continental-style beach restaurants, with their pancakes, spaghetti, baked beans on toast, and chips. New arrivals, unaware of the local pigs' diet of human faeces, tend to favour the traditional Goan pork sausages (*chourisso*) or classic pork dishes like *vindaloo* (marinated in toddy vinegar, and very spicy) and *sorpatel* (pig's liver pickled in hot savoury sauce). *Xacuti* is a biting-hot coconut/*masala* preparation of chicken or mutton, and the rich, layered *bebinca* is a traditional, very filling Goan sweet made of coconut and jaggery. The other main fare is, of course, seafood. The Arabian Sea lapping Goa's coastline yields a variety of delicately flavoured fish and shellfish, including crab, oysters, king prawns, massive shark steaks and snapping-fresh lobsters.

Goa has the cheapest **beer** in India as well as the famous *feni*, a smooth, potent brew (usually distilled just once) made from either the cashew apple or the coconut palm and sold for next to nothing. The local Goan **wines** are also popular and cheap, this being one of the few places in India where 'wine' shops actually sell wine, not just whisky.

Goa's Coast

Goa's long, narrow 62 mile stretch of coastline runs between the Arabian Sea and the Western Ghats. It has some of the best beaches in the world and is India's favourite winter resort. The Mediterranean feel of the place adds to its charm and many travellers come here for a break from India proper. Inland from the beaches the landscape is gently rural, dotted with picturesque forts and churches, temples and small market towns. On the eastern horizon rise hills and mountains.

Getting Around

Coastal Goa has four main towns: **Panjim** in the centre (with its 'local' beaches of Miramar and Dona Paula); **Mapusa**, above the Mandovi River, near the northern beaches of Vagator/Chapora, Anjuna/Baga, Calangute and Aguada; **Margao**, below the River Zuari, which connects to the southern beaches of Majorda, Colva/Benaulim, Betelbatim and Betul; and **Vasco da Gama**, near the Dabolim airport, the gateway to the exclusive luxury beach of Bogmalo. Some useful distances are: Panjim to Vasco (18½ miles), Panjim to Calangute (10 miles), Panjim to Vagator

(20 miles), Panjim to Tiracol (26 miles), Margao to Dabolim (18 miles), Vasco to Dabolim (2 miles) and Vasco to Margao (18½ miles).

For short hops between these towns, there are either **local buses** (Rs1–5) which begin and end their journeys in Panjim's scruffy, stinky Kodamba bus terminal, near Patto Bridge, or **shared taxis**, which can work out almost as cheap. **Motorbike 'taxis'** pick up from the bus stand and from the post office, offering cheap rides up to sites around Altino Hill. Panjim, a convenient base for exploring Goa, is just 20 minutes (7½ miles) from Mapusa, and 1 hour (20 miles via Courtillim) from Margao, for the northern and southern beaches respectively. To tour the beaches themselves, there are motorbikes for hire at Calangute and Anjuna, though these are expensive (in 1995, about Rs150 per day), and rather dangerous if you are not used to Indian road hazards, like cows, pigs and maniacal fellow drivers.

Panjim

Until it replaced Old Goa as capital of Portuguese India in 1843, Panjim or Panaji ('Land which does not get Flooded') was only a small fishing village. Today, it is one of India's smallest and most pleasant capital towns, and also one of the least 'Indian'. Its Portuguese heritage lingers on in the whitewashed, red-tiled houses and narrow, winding avenues dotted with cafés, bars and tavernas of its 'old town', up on the hill above the Mandovi river estuary.

Panjim is the obvious base from which to discover the rest of Goa, not simply because most tourist facilities (Indian Airlines, banks, the post office and jetty) are concentrated here, but also for the two Goa sightseeing tours running from Panjim's tourist office—useful both for checking out the major beaches and viewing the better inland sights.

Tourist Information

The **Goan Tourist Office** is at the Tourist Home, Patto Bridge, below Panjim bus stand, ✆ 225715, open from 9.30 to 1.15 and from 2 to 5.45, Monday to Friday. Excellent information and helpful staff and a trained guide service for about Rs350 per day. They have regular launch cruises with a cultural programme (departures daily at 6pm and 7.15pm, a 1-hour trip costs Rs50). Tourist taxis and luxury mini-coaches are also for hire. The **Goa Tourism Development Corporation—GTDC**, Trionora Apartments, ✆ 226515, run various tours which are available from the Tourist Hostel.

There are Government of India tourist information counters at the Municipal Building, Church Square, ✆ 223412, Panjim bus stand, ✆ 225620, and at Dabolim airport.

The **State Bank of India**, just up from the Tourist Hostel, is open from 10 to 2 Monday to Friday, and from 10 to 12noon Saturday, closed Sunday. The **Foreigners' Registration Office** is at the Police Headquarters in Panjim, ✆ 45360. Note that most shops are closed on Sundays.

The **post office** is midway between Tourist Hostel and Patto Bridge.

Indian Airlines, at Dempo House, D. Bandodkar Marg, ✆ 223826, lays on regular Rs30 buses to the airport. Other domestic airlines are handled by **Jet Air**, ✆ 223891 and the **National Travel Service**, ✆ 223324. **Air India** is at Hotel Fidalgo, 18th June Road, ✆ 224081.

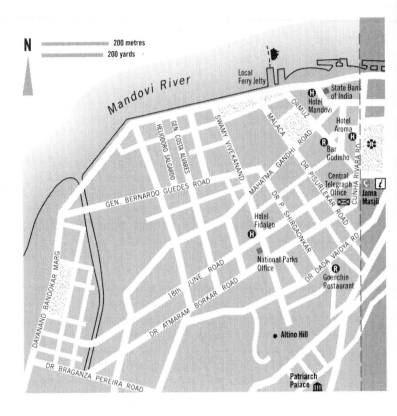

The City

Panjim is a place for gentle, relaxing evening promenades and cosy evening drinks in jolly tavernas. You can visit its few sights in a couple of hours on foot or by auto-rickshaw. Start in the main thoroughfare, Dayanand Bandodkar Road, at the **Tourist Hostel**. Opposite, you'll see the busy little **steamer wharf**, which services the Bombay catamaran and runs evening river cruises. Strolling right, you'll pass the small sub-post office (with its distinctive striped postbox), then the extraordinary statue of **Abbe Faria**, an 18th-century Goan churchman, believed to be father of hypnotism, who has been carved, looming demonically (or lecherously?) over a woman who, it seems, he has just knocked to the ground with his crucifix and transfixed with his hypnotic stare. Opposite this the **Idalcao Palace** or **Secretariat building** (originally built by the Adil Shah of Bijapur and until 1759 the residence of the Portuguese viceroys).

Turning left here, you'll soon find yourself in scruffy Church Square (Communicada Street), with its beautiful white **Church of the Immaculate Conception**, built in 1600, sitting on the hill above. A short walk behind this is the 18th-century **Jama Masjid** mosque and the

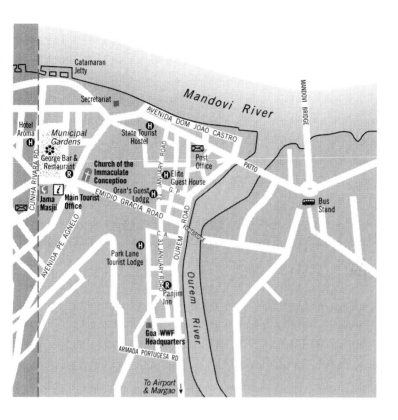

The following labels appear on the map:

Catamaran Jetty

Secretariat

Mandovi River

MANDOVI BRIDGE

Hotel Aroma

Municipal Gardens

State Tourist Hostel

AVENIDA DOM JOAO CASTRO

George Bar & Restaurant

Church of the Immaculate Conceptioo

Post Office

PATTO

Elite Guest House

Oran's Guest Lodge

G. P.

Jama Masjii

Main Tourist Office

EMIDIO GRACIA ROAD

31 JANUARY ROAD

C. A

Bus Stand

CUNHA RIVARA RD.

AVENIDA PE AGNELO

Park Lane Tourist Lodge

OUREM ROAD

FOOTBRIDGE

31 JANUARY ROAD

Panjim Inn

Ourem River

Goa WWF Headquarters

ARMADA PORTUGESA RD

To Airport & Margao

Mahalakshmi Temple, an interesting Hindu shrine. Next, make the 20-minute ascent up to **Altino Hill**, with its stately **Patriarch Palace** (where the Pope stayed during his 1986 Goan tour) and panoramic views over Panjim's red-tiled roofs and tree-shaded squares, with the glittering Mandovi spilling over into the Arabian Sea beyond. On the walk down, note Altino's bungalows and colonnaded houses, with their flower-decked windows, overhanging balconies and verandahs. This is the oldest, most Latin, quarter of town, and runs from the terraced hillock of Altino down to 31 January Street, where the town's cheaper tourist lodges are.

Government of India Tours from Panjim

These are worthwhile for orientating yourself before a long stay—getting an idea of how Goa is laid out and which place appeals to you most.

While the north Goa tour is worthwhile, if you're short on time or impatient to get to the beaches make the south Goa tour your priority: that one visits Old Goa, the main inland attraction. Both tours use buses so you'll need a front seat to hear a word the guide's saying but the sights and glorious scenery speak for themselves. Sufficient time is allowed at the beach spots to check out the current accommodation situation.

North Goa Tour

by tour bus, full day

Altino Hill–Mayem Lake–Bicholim–Mapusa–Northern Beaches

The north Goa tour winds up to **Altino Hill**, Panjim, for the spectacular view of the city, then proceeds inland through acres of paddy fields and palms to the natural lake resort of **Mayem**, a popular picnic spot with lovely gardens of bougainvillaea, crimson *cana* orchids, and china roses, together with peaceful lake views. Mayem is a wide basin lake encircled by green hills and dense palm groves. From here you'll move on to **Bicholim** to see a couple of **Hindu temples**, before arriving at **Mapusa** for lunch.

Mapusa is the crossroads of northern Goa and its main market centre. If possible, return to Mapusa for its **Friday market**. People from all over Bardez (the local region) pour in to do their weekly shopping here, and you can buy anything from glass bangles to water buffalo. Open from around 8am to 6pm, Mapusa's bazaars are the cheapest and best place to shop in Goa. After the market, hang around for live music, folk dances and buffet at the **Haystack** (Friday nights from 8.30pm to very late).

If staying in Mapusa, try the pleasant **Tourist Hotel**, ✆ 262694 (rooms priced in the 'inexpensive' category) with a nice attached rooftop bar/restaurant. If full, one-night fall-backs are the **Hotel Bardez** ('inexpensive') on Coscar Corner, ✆ 262607, or the **Hotel Satya Heera** ('moderate') near the bus stand, ✆ 262849/262949.

Eat out either at **Sanbhaya** restaurant (superb seafood and Goan curry) or at the **Haystack**. Mapusa's useful little tourist office is housed in the Tourist Hostel.

In the afternoon, the tour covers the northern beaches—first **Vagator**, then the 'freak beach' of **Anjuna** (though the real hippies have long since moved to beaches further north), before heading back south for the (now spoilt) 'Queen Beach' of **Calangute** and the exclusive **Aguada** resort, marked by its 17th-century fort (now converted into a jail). There's just time at each place for a quick dip.

South Goa Tour

by tour bus, full day

Miramar–Dona Paula–Old Goa–Mangesh Temple–Margao–
Colva–Marmagao

First stop on this tour is **Miramar Beach**, popular for its wide golden sands and lovely sunset views. Located just 2 miles out of Panjim, it's the ideal place to come for a swim, if staying in the capital. Unfortunately, everyone else in town has the same idea. **Dona Paula**, a further 3 miles up the road, is much quieter. A sheltered palm-fronted cove, with enchanting views of Marmagao Harbour and the Zuari river estuary, this is another beautiful sunset spot (though new hotels are going up all the time). The sophisticated **O'Pescador** restaurant and exclusive **Hotel Cidade de Goa** are both located here (*see* 'Where to Stay', p.110).

From here, the bus drives on to the Goa's oldest colonial town. **Old Goa** (5½ miles from Panjim), is described by many as a cathedral 'ghost town'. This is misleading: true, the huge basilicas (which rival anything in Europe for size and splendour), now stand alone amid tended lawns, but in fact houses still dot the palm forest behind, and Old Goa still 'lives', despite having been abandoned by the Portuguese early last century after a succession of plagues.

In the High Renaissance heyday of Goa's prosperity, the priests of Rome were the real rulers, not the Portuguese conquistadors, and the religious arrogance of the 17th-century Catholic Church is reflected in the grandiose complex of churches, monasteries and convents. The Portuguese arrived here in 1510, bearing a sword in one hand, a crucifix in the other and within 150 years, Goa Velha, as Old Goa was then called, became a city of great splendour and power, dominated by the huge ecclesiastical buildings which replaced the old mosques and temples of former Muslim and Hindu rulers. But with the buildings came great plagues (1543, 1635 and 1735), which decimated 80 per cent of the population. In 1835 Old Goa was abandoned and the administrative capital transferred to Panjim. Today, only the hulks of the huge convents and churches (some half-ruined) and the tourists that beetle between them over the sparkling lawns, testify to Old Goa's past splendour.

At present, only six of the town's original 14 churches remain in good condition, their red laterite structures eroded by centuries of wind and rain. They're a complete contrast to Hindu temples and shrines, though some find these haughty Catholic structures uncomfortably unlike India, much more reminiscent of Lisbon or Rome. If returning for a longer look, come in by local bus from either Panjim (20 minutes) or Margao (40 minutes). Old Goa really should be appreciated at leisure—one can spend hours wandering round the vast, deserted cloisters and corridors of these decaying old buildings. The Archaeological Survey of India has published an excellent 52-page guide, *Old Goa*, which is available locally and at their New Delhi office.

On tour, you'll first visit the **Basilica of Bom Jesus** (*open daily, 9–6.30; Mass at 7am and 8am weekdays, 8am and 9.15am Sunday; no photography allowed*), Goa's most popular and famous church (now a World Heritage Site). Built between 1594 and 1604, the rather dim interior is enlivened by the gilded baroque high altar, with elaborate screens and spiral columns, and by the huge, gaudy statue of Ignatius Loyola, the founder of the Jesuit order. To the right of the altar is the Basilica's big attraction—the silver casket enshrining the mummi-fied **remains of St Francis Xavier**, Goa's patron saint, who spent his life spreading Christianity among the Portuguese colonies. Murals of events from the saint's life run round the walls of the Italian-marble sarcophagus enclosing the casket. One of the most well-travelled corpses in history, Xavier was taken all over the place after his death in China in 1552 and only came to rest here in 1613. During his posthumous travels, one of his toes was bitten off in 1554 by a Portuguese hunter of holy relics, who apparently kept the member hidden in his mouth until his return to Europe. Later, as the grisly process of dismemberment continued, he lost a hand to the Japanese Jesuits (1619), had various sections of intestine removed, and suffered a broken neck after being stuffed in an undersized grave. Today, what's left of his corpse is remarkably well preserved. If you don't believe it, you can peer at Xavier's bald, mottled head—illuminated within the casket by a naked bulb—or, for a donation, view his silver-encased toes. Every 10 years, the shrivelled cadaver is given a public veneration (the next occasion will be 2004) and the town becomes a stadium of hysterical devotees. The same thing happens, to a lesser extent, at the annual celebration on 3 December of the saint's death. Behind the casket, steps lead up to a small museum housing various portraits and relics attributed to Xavier, his life and times, as well as a collection of truly awful modern religious paintings, ham-fistedly executed after the style of Salvador Dali.

Across the road is the huge **Se Cathedral** (1562–1652). Dedicated to St Catherine of Alexandria, a pagan girl who embraced Christianity and was beheaded on the same date (25 November) that the Portuguese took Old Goa from the Muslims, it is one of Asia's largest churches, having 15 altars. The harmony of its façade was destroyed in 1776, when lightning demolished one of its twin bell towers. The remaining tower houses the famous 'Golden Bell' which would ring the death knell of burning heretics during the Inquisition, and now sounds over a deserted city (*three times a day: 5.30am, 12.30pm, 6.30pm*) to be heard up to 6½ miles away. Walking up the crumbling staircase to view it is highly unsafe. The grand Renaissance cathedral is built in the Portuguese-Gothic style—its Corinthian interior a baroque riot of gilded carvings, with a vast barrel-vault ceiling and a glittering, gilded main altar (featuring painted scenes from the short life of St Catherine) which is the finest in India. Look at the 'miraculous' stone cross in one of the 14 side-chapels. According to the guide, it 'grew' so high over the centuries that the ceiling had to be raised. Nowadays it's protected by a sturdy wooden support to stop relic hunters chipping away souvenirs. Undeterred, they chip away at the wood surround instead.

The nearby **Convent and Church of St Francis of Assisi**, notable for its two-storey façade crowned with twin octagonal towers, is one of Old Goa's most fascinating buildings. Originally a small Franciscan chapel (commenced in 1517), the present structure was constructed in 1661. It is notable for its richly carved woodwork, Renaissance frescoes and flooring of 16th-century gravestones, their heraldic devices announcing the deaths of well-born Portuguese. The **Archaeological Museum** to the rear (*open daily, 10–5, except Fri*) has a poorly lit model Portuguese caravelle, while upstairs is an entertaining gallery of ex-Portuguese viceroys—possibly the worst portraits ever painted, each viceroy looking suitably corrupt and thuggish. More beautiful are the sculptures downstairs, recovered from the Hindu temples over which the great basilicas were built (great Christendom crushing the heathens etc. etc.).

If you want to make a day of it at Old Goa, leave the tour at this point. There's no problem getting back to Panjim: buses make the 15–20-minute journey about three times an hour. Make sure you wander up to the tall ruin of the **St Augustine Tower**, where the nave of what was once a great church now lies open to the sky, under whose broken arches local tribeswomen gather and talk. After that head down to Old Goa's boat jetty, walking downhill towards it under the old Portuguese 'Gateway to India' arch. A ferry plies across the estuary to **Diwar Island**, from where a connecting bus takes you into the wonderful little demi-paradise of the island's interior—empty beaches, shady palm bowers, and rustic old Portuguese houses. A short, strenuous climb takes you up to the hilltop at the centre of the island, with memorable views from the church. Return down for a relaxing afternoon on the beach before gettting the ferry back to Old Goa. Don't forget to bring a packed lunch.

If you decide to stay the night in Old Goa, you can find **accommodation** in the excellently named **Our Own Den Hotel** at Bella Vista, Corlim, © 86194/86292, or at the **Hotel Juliet**, also in Corlim, © 86311/2. Both are in the 'cheap' price range. Take an auto-rickshaw from the bus stand to Corlim for about Rs7–10.

Staying on the official tour, you'll continue on to the **Ponda** district, to see the 18th-century **Shri Mangesh Temple**, one of the few Hindu shrines in Goa to survive Muslim and Portuguese iconoclasm. Attractively situated on a hillock surrounded by green hills, it's a simple, elegant structure dedicated to Shiva. The temple musicians here are astonishingly good. Set in an open courtyard, the shrine is notable for its glass chandeliers and blue-china murals. At nearby Mardol, you'll see the **Shri Mahalsa Temple**, one of Goa's oldest temples, dedicated to Vishnu and shifted here from its original site when Muslim persecution threatened its survival. You may also see the **Shanta Durga Temple** at Kavlem, with its impressive idol of the Goddess of Peace (Shanta Durga) flanked by Vishnu and Shiva.

At **Margao**, the tour stops for lunch. This is Goa's southern urban centre and a thriving commercial metropolis. It has parks, modern buildings and a very Latin flavour. Here are some of the area's most beautiful old Portuguese mansions, with balconies, patios, terraces and red-tiled sloping roofs—some still lived in by descendants of the families who built them 400 years ago.

There is not much for the tourist in Margao—most folk just pass through on their way to Colva and Benaulim beaches (20 minutes by rickshaw or shared taxi). But if you get stuck here (on your way in from the south by train, perhaps) stay at the cheap and pleasant **Tourist Hostel** (✆ 221966/220470) at the top of the main square, with rooms from Rs100. It has a clean, adequate restaurant. Another hotel is the **Goa Woodlands**, ✆ 221121, opposite the bus stand on Miguel Loyola Furtado Road. **Casa Menino** and **Longhino's**, opposite the Municipality building are both excellent for Goan food. **Gaylin**, by the Garden View Building on Valde Valankilar Road is one of Goa's best Chinese restaurants. You can get clothes made up in on of the many shops along the Cloth Market.

Margao's **tourist office** is in the Municipal Building. To get here from the airport, get a bus to Vasco, then another into Margao (total journey time 1–1½hrs). To make any travel arrangements in Margao, head straight for **Paramount Travels**, ✆ 221 150, ✉ 732 572, opposite the Tourist Office. Paramount are models of efficiency and are very good at getting you the cheapest deal, especially on domestic flights.

Regular **buses** run to Benaulim 3 miles and Colva 6½ miles from Margao.

A pleasant hour at **Colva Beach** is followed by a visit to **Marmagao**, one of India's finest natural harbours. Here you can see mountains of iron ore (crushed from the cliff directly over the harbour), and fleets of tankers loading up 1000 tons of crude oil per hour. Located close to busy, modern **Vasco da Gama** (the airport gateway to Goa), tourists are shown Marmagao's massive refinery and shipping port, ostensibly for its fine views over the surrounding coastline, but more (one suspects) to demonstrate the new-found industrial muscle of this previously poor, agricultural territory.

If you're not into such propaganda, leave the tour at Colva and spend an altogether more enjoyable afternoon on the beach.

Sports and Activities

River cruises: these are run by the **Goa Tourism Development Corporation (GTDC)** and **Goa Sea Travels Agency** at the jetty. The Full Moon Cruise is best, 7.30–9.30pm, with lively Portuguese folk dances on deck, meals provided, and an unforgettable moon rising above the night horizon like a giant tarnished penny.

Cinema: For English-language films, look in the Tourist Hostel lobby.

Swimming: you can find safe clean water at Panjim's two local beaches, Miramar (2 miles away) and Dona Paula (5 miles away), both well connected by a regular local bus service.

Football: the Portuguese left their passion for soccer in Goa, just as the British left theirs for cricket in the rest of the country. Panjim's big local sport can be seen at the stadium every Sunday afternoon (4pm kick-off).

Panjim ☎ (0832–)

Where to Stay

expensive

The only luxury-style option is the **Cicade de Goa**, ☎ 2233228/ 221301/6/7/8, ✉ 243303, a resort at Dona Paula with attractive rooms, marvellous water sports and superior Goan/Mughlai cuisine. A popular place for family holidays is the **Prainha Cottages by the Sea** at Dona Paula, ☎ 224162/225917, ✉ 223433/80218, with fully air-conditioned rooms.

In Panjim itself, the top place is **Hotel Fidalgo**, 18th June Road, ☎ 226291/9 or 223330/2, ✉ 225061, with fawning flunkeys, central air-conditioning and a swimming pool. Rather more relaxing is **Hotel Mandovi**, D.B. Bandodkar Road, ☎ 226270/4 or 224405/9, ✉ 225451 offering nice air-conditioned rooms with river views and staff who leave you alone when you want to be left. The 2-star **Hotel Nova Goa**, Dr Atmaram Borkar Road, ☎ 226 231/9, has air-conditioning, restaurant and snack bar.

moderate

One of Goa's most stylish hotels is the **Panjim Inn**, on 31 January Street, ☎ 226523, ✉228136. An old understated Portuguese villa, it has a beautiful verandah and rooms with grand old mahogany beds, some of them four-posters, hung with mosquito netting. The owner is a bit of an art connoisseur and has hung the old halls with abstracts. These sit eclectically next to trophy heads of *sambar* deer shot in the mountains. The food is very good traditional Goan fare and there is a free airport pick-up service for guests.

inexpensive

The **Hotel Aroma**, on Cunha Rivara Road, ☎ 223984, is a well-located place with clean rooms and pleasant air-conditioned restaurant opposite the Municipal Gardens. The state-run **Tourist Hostel**, ☎ 225715/227972, faces the river near the Secretariat. It is exceedingly popular (often booked out weeks ahead), has a good open-air restaurant, useful shopping complex and spacious rooms, some with balconies and good river views. If the hostel is full, Panjim has some other decent options: try the **Mayfair Hotel**, Dr Dada Vaidya Road, ☎ 225772, 226174/5, 225952 or 225773; the **Hotel Neptune** on Malaca Road, ☎ 222601; the **Hotel Samrat**, also on Dada Vaidya Road, ☎ 223318/9 or 224546/7/8; or the **Hotel Sunrise**, ☎ 223960, opposite the Sheela Building on 18th June Road.

cheap

Anything in this category is bound to be rough: Panjim's hotel owners are used to the idea that tourists have money and seldom offer good value for cheap rooms. You should certainly have your own mosquito net and sheet. However, on 31 January Street you can find several cheap lodges that aren't too awful. The best is the **Hotel Venite**, ☎ 225537/227455. If that's full, walk along the street and try the **Poonam**

Lodge, Orav's Guest House, Lilia Dias Guest House, Elite Lodge or **Delux Lodge** (although the last two are both pretty ropey).

Other options in town include the **Safari Hotel** opposite the Municipal Gardens on Cunha Reveira Road, ✆ 226475/226054, the **Mandovi Guest House**, ✆ 226852/223928, behind the Tourist Hostel, overlooking the boat jetty and **Frank's Inn** on the second floor of the Orion Building on the Rua Menezes Braganza.

Eating Out

Avanti, near Patto Bridge, is probably Panjim's favourite eating spot, with a popular air-conditioned lounge. Get your spicy Goan sausage, prawn curry and rice here; no dish is more than Rs25. Don't show up between 1 and 2pm, when it's packed with local diners. The **Panjim Inn** on 31 January Street serves traditional Goan dishes like spicy chicken and sole in wine—not cheap but good value and served on the verandah of an old Portuguese villa.

Despite rather risky food, **O'Coqueiro** is still the nearest thing to non-hippy nightlife in Goa, according to many locals. Despite poor service, **Hotel Mandovi** is still capable of producing excellent Goan and Portuguese cuisine, and there's often a live band. Of Panjim's numerous bars, try **Casa Olympia**, opposite the gardens in Communicada Square. It's owned by a real old pirate, and is a great place to meet the local people.

Other typically Goan eating places are **Bar Godinho**, the main backpackers' hangout near the National Theatre in Cinema Square, **Bar George** on Communicada Square and the slightly more expensive **City Bar and Restaurant**.

For lighter food, cross the street from Godinho's and go round the corner to the **Hanuman Cold Drink House**, which serves excellent shakes, ices and *lassis*. Nearby **Kamat Hotel**, at the top of Municipal Gardens, does delicious and cheap vegetarian food, while **Chit-Chat** at the Tourist Hostel has 'ravishing tandooris', and is a pleasant place to sit out in the evenings.

Panjim has a superb, but expensive, Chinese restaurant with a relaxed atmosphere: **The Riverdeck**, near the jetty and on the waterfront. The **Mandan** vegetarian restaurant, attached to the Hotel Rajdhani on Dr Atmaran Barker Road is air-conditioned and serves excellent Indian and Chinese food in spotless surroundings.

Goa's Beaches

Goa's beaches are world famous—long idyllic sweeps of silvery sand overlooked by undulating palms and the calm blue Arabian Sea. The hippies discovered them in the early 1960s, domestic tourists flocked to them in the 1980s (mainly to see the hippies), and two or three of them (notably Colva, Baga and Arambol) deserve the description of being the best beaches in India. Despite creeping development, there are still miles of unspoilt strands where you can exist in shacks for next-to-nothing, as well as some first-class resorts. You can also find everything in between: hotels that exist solely for package tourists (always demanding inflated prices), quiet guest lodges, complete solitude, horrible crowds. The trick is to be independent, to know what to avoid.

taking it easy on the northern beaches

Because there's so much choice, the 'sneak previews' provided by the Panjim tours can be a real help in selecting the best beaches to visit. But if you're determined to hit the beaches first thing, here are a few tips. Owing to rapid development, Goa's beaches are constantly changing, but the following guide should hold true for a while. The three luxury beaches of **Majorda**, **Aguada** and **Bogmalo** may have the best facilities, but are short on social life and laughs; the north-central beaches of **Baga**, **Vagator** and **Anjuna** (strung close together, easily negotiated by foot) are ideal for those who bore easily—they have the best parties, cheap accommodation, and the worst reputation for drugs despite regular police searches. Goa's best-known beach, **Colva**, is rapidly becoming over-developed, but just to the south **Benaulim**, **Betul** and **Palolem** have a more equal balance of tourists and locals. Those in search of complete peace and quiet should either go to the far north, to **Arambol** and **Terekol**, or to **Rajabag** in the far south. In these places, you can walk or swim all day long without seeing a soul.

Beach Preparations

The Indian sun is strong, and you should be prepared—high-factor sun block, flip flops, sunglasses, etc. (all things people later regret not bringing)—and have the right attitude—relaxed, yet not too switched-off (theft, sunburn and drugs are all risks). Good sun cream and sunglasses are not readily available in Goa (although RayBans are now made in India for those wanting to emulate Tom Cruise). Some of the oil sold on the beach will be local concoctions in discarded bottles. Sleeping on the beach is not a good idea. If you are on a really tight budget, local families let out rooms in the far north or south for a few rupees a night.

Fort Aguada

This jet-set resort, notable for its 16th-century fort (*open Mon–Fri, 4–5.30 only*) and apparently endless expanse of white sand, has the best water sports, the best coastal views and the most famous beach hotel in India. This is the Taj group's **Fort Aguada Beach Resort**, ✆ (0832) 276201/276210. Rooms here start at US$60 single in the off season (July, August and September) rising to US$145 during the Christmas and New Year period. The best ones, with excellent views from large terraces, are in the main block. Good facilities for waterskiing, windsurfing, parasailing, fishing and scuba-diving. Right next door is the equally fine **Taj Holiday Village**, ✆ (0832) 7515, which offers charming beach cottages designed like Goan homes, in a private, romantic setting. Prices start at US$45 in the low season, for a non air-conditioned room in a cottage, and reach US$130 in the high season for air-conditioned rooms. Single-bedroom cottages, two-room villas and family units are also available. The high level of service, the excellent facilities and special areas for children make the Holiday Village one of Goa's best options.

The state's most exclusive and ridiculously overpriced resort is at Aguada. The Taj's 20-villa **Aguada Hermitage**, ✆ (0832) 276 201/276 210, was built for the Commonwealth Heads of Government conference in 1982 and is situated on the hillside above the beach resort overlooking the sea. There are four types of villa with rates ranging from US$135 in the low season to US$475 during the Christmas–New Year period.

Candolim

Candolim is a beach that most independent travellers avoid, it has the long palm-fringed sands, but is known for wind and lacks the social life of the northern beaches. It also gets crowded with Indian tourists at weekends.

There is a variety of accommodation here, however.

Candolim ✆ (0832–)

Where to Stay

luxury

The **Taj Holiday Village** in Candolim, ✆ 27047/7733, is a large, self-contained resort with a stretch of private beach and watersport facilities. Very comfortable but a little bland. In the same price range is the **Whispering Palm Resort** on Waddi Candolim Beach, ✆ 886140/1/2. Here, rooms can be bargained down to about Rs500 in the off season.

expensive

The **Holiday Beach Resort**, ✆ 2762335/276088, has little character, but is small, with just 20 rooms and, again, you can negotiate much lower prices out of season. You can also arrange water sports and local day trips through the resort.

moderate

Right on the beach is the **Palm Spring Beach Resort**, but this is often full. If so, the following all offer decent rooms near the beach: the **Alexandra Tourist Centre** on

Murrad Vaddo, ✆ 276097/276250, ✆ 276250; the **Marbellla Guest House**, 77 Sinquerim (no phone); the **Altrude Villa** on Murod Vaddo, (no phone); and the **Sea Shell Inn**, ✆ 276131.

inexpensive

There a several reasonable places within this category, but unfortunately none of them have telephones as yet. You have to turn up on the doorstep and negotiate for a room. However, they are all fairly close together, so you can walk or take an auto-rickshaw beteen them without difficulty. Try the **Ave Maria Guest House** on Camotim Vaddo, the **Coqueirial Holiday Home** on Camtomim Vaddo, or the B&B run by **Innocencia de Souza** on Camtomim Vaddo.

cheap

Again, there are no telephone numbers for places to stay in this category. Try the **Pinto Beach Cottages** on the beach, house no. 81–9, the brilliantly named **Pretty Petal Guest House** at 824 Camtomim Vaddo or the **Manuel Guest House** on the same street. A number of families rent rooms: Isabel Fernandes, who lives at 73a Candolim Beach; Josephin Fernandes at 74–9 Escrivao Vaddo; Jacinta Cardoz, 71B/9 Escrivao Vaddo; Deodita Rodrigues, 1067 Escrivao Vaddo and Milagrina de Souza, Velina VIIla, 23/A/10 Simer. If these particular people cannot accommodate you, they will know someone who can.

Calangute

The old 'Queen Beach' of Goa, where coconut palms once shaded a mile-wide stretch of tranquil orange sands, has sadly been overdeveloped and ruined by unsightly tourist hostels, souvenir stands and noisy, busy traffic. Bus loads of Indian voyeurs turn up here daily, hoping to photograph Western women unclad on the beaches. Calangute is now a fully fledged Indian holiday resort with popcorn stands, iced beer stalls, and shifty businessmen, and is both dirty and commercial. Most travellers head straight on to Baga or Vagator, but a few hang around for the 'action'. This includes a trio of useful travel agencies offering cheap international flights near the tourist office and various stalls selling cheap-and-nasty Indian crafts and good but pricey Tibetan/Rajasthani items. Also, some good eating places like **Souza Lobo Restaurant** (lovely setting, superb seafood and Indian wine), **Wilson's** (on the beach), **Alex Cold Drink House** (by the statue, with good sounds), **Modern Tavern** (cheap drinks) and **Dinky Bar & Restaurant** (nice Goan food). For travellers, Calangute's main function these days is as a shopping/communications/bank centre for those staying up in Baga, Vagator, Anjuna and the northernmost beaches. There are several STD/ISD places on Calangute's main road, as well as a branch of the Wall Street Finance Company, where you can change travellers' cheques.

Calangute ✆ (083288–)   *Where to Stay*

If you get stuck in Calangute en route for Baga and the northern beaches, here are some pointers.

expensive

The most expensive place in Calagute is the **Hotel Goan Heritage** on Gaura Vaddo, ✆ 276120/253/254/027, ✆ 276120. A large complex built around an old Portuguese house it offers good food, but little atmosphere.

moderate

The best place to stay in Calangute is the charming **Varma's Beach Resort**, ✆ 276077, behind the bus stand, with lovely gardens and homely air-conditioned rooms with verandahs. The **Concha Beach Resort**, ✆ 276056/078 at Umtawaddo (on the beach) has a good restaurant, decent rooms and all services.

inexpensive

Towards the bottom end of this price range, the clean, comfortable **Tourist Hostel**, ✆ 6024, is good value, but often full and noisy. If it is full, try to get in at either the **Hotel Mira** on Umtavaddo (no phone), or the **Golden Eye** on Gaura Vaddo, which has clean, basic cottages.

cheap

If the various cheapies (mostly unsatisfactory) that you will undoubtedly hear about on the travellers' grapevine don't appeal, stay in a family house behind the beach. Here are some names to try: Annie Fernandes, 15 Gaura Vaddo; Agostino de Souza, E6/1 Cobra Vaddo; Antonio De Souza, 5/226 Umta Vaddo; Anthony de Souza, 189 Umta Vaddo; Cecilia Lobo, 1985 Cobra Vaddo; or Bethe Andrade, 2231 Sauntavaddo. Families often meet travellers off the bus, and offer clean, simple, double rooms. These are recommended but have your mosquito net handy.

Baga

As you head north, the beaches become better and better. Baga, overlooked by a high promontory, is a fine example. Just 1½ miles north of touristy Calangute, it is far more secluded and pleasant, at least at its northern end near the forested headland that separates Baga from Anjuna Beach. A small river meets the sea at the base of this headland.

For relative quiet plus good facilities (it even has a small windsurfing school), Baga is still the best of Goa's northern beaches. If you want peace and quiet, stay in the wooded end north of the river, from where you can reach all the beach-shack bars and restaurants, but go home to a quiet haven under the coconut palms. To get a motorcycle over the river, cross via the concrete bridge, a mile's detour to the east.

Getting There

by bus

Only one service, at 5pm, goes from Panjim all the way to Baga. However, regular half-hourly services run from Panjim to Calangute, from where you can either walk along the pleasant beach or busy road, or hire a motorbike taxi to take you and your gear the rest of the way.

by motorbike and bicycle

If staying in Baga, it's a good idea to hire a motorbike, scooter or bicycle for trips to Panjim. Ride as far as Calangute, then take the bus—the police run a racket of waving down Westerners on motorcycles near Panjim and demanding on-the-spot 'fines'.

Where to Stay

moderate

The **Hotel Baia Do Sol**, ✆ 6084, offers superb recreation (river cruises, water-skiing, yachting and fishing), good entertainment (traditional folk dances and music), great food (at the renowned **Seafood Restaurant**) and lovely riverside cottages on the seafront.

inexpensive

The **Riverside Hotel**, ✆ 6062, at the north end of Baga near the turn-off for the concrete bridge, has a superb riverside location, a charming lady owner, delicious home cooking, and roomy two-person cottages. Failing this, try the **Sunshine Beach Resort** (no phone), a self-contained place with a pool built around its own courtyard behind the beach on the Baga–Calangute road.

cheap

Nani's and Rani's is a guest house on the north side of the river, owned by a friendly Indo-Portuguese family. They rent out small, self-contained chalets set in a garden around their own old Portuguese villa, from which they run a very good restaurant and STD/ISD service.

If you cannot find a place at Nani's and Rani's, walk on 50 yards past their villa, then take the footpath's right-hand fork up through a grove palm trees. A number of small farmsteads are scattered on the wooded hill at the end of the palm grove, and most have rooms for rent for very little. Often they can rent you a scooter or motorcycle as well, and will provide morning tea, do the laundry and arrange taxis to and from the airport for an extra charge. Just walk up to the first house and ask, and you will soon be directed to soemone who has a room free.

Eating Out

The **Casa Portuguesa** at the Baga end of the Baga–Calangute road is the most expensive place in town, but also one of the best in Goa for traditional local cuisine. You can eat on the verandah or in one of the spacious colonial dining rooms and even get the owner to sing some bad but passionate *fada* for you on his guitar. The restaurant occupies his grandmother's house and is about as traditional a place as you are likely to find on the tourist trail.

To be avoided for food is **Tito's**, Baga's most popular bar—a big American-style bar/restaurant full of package tourists and Indian boys from Bombay loudly on holiday. Everything at Tito's is grossly overpriced, but it serves as a good orientation point, as it sits at the top of a narrow road connecting the south end of Baga beach with the main Calangute road. It is also a good place to find out where the next all-night techno party is happening.

Much cheaper is the **Ancona**, a small Tibetan restaurant on the road between Tito's and the Calangute road. Run by a group of cousins, Ancona serves great *momos* (veg and meat), cornbread and hearty soups, as well as superb cakes. Two standard cheapies popular with backpackers are **Vicky's**, a seafood place/bar on the beach about halfway between Tito's and the river, and **Britos**, at the north end of the Calangute road, which serves good Indian food (try the *sag paneer*) as well as slightly overpriced Western dishes.

For excellent value on the north side of the river, try **Nani's and Ranis**. The breakfasts here are particularly good; sit out on their verandah and eat stuffed pancakes and fresh juices. A little further along the headland footpath is the **Sunset Restaurant**, which does good, standard seafood under a palm-thatch awning that looks out over the Arabian sea.

Anjuna

Just 10 minutes' walk further north (cross the river at the top of Baga, walk round the headland past the chapel) is the 'freak beach' of Anjuna. A marvellous place for meeting people, illegal nude bathing, just hanging out, it has big pros and cons. It's famous for its beach parties, where everyone flips out on heavy techno music and goes skinny-dipping. Also for its superb **Flea Market**, which takes place at the southern end of the beach every Wednesday between 2 and 7pm. This is a great place to sell your unwanted jeans, watch, camera or Walkman, or shop around for Tibetan/Kashmiri jewellery, Rajasthani handicrafts, stylish cotton clothing and funky hippie handicrafts. The atmosphere is great. The whole of Goa seems to turn up, also loads of Arabs, Chinese and Indians, either to buy Western luxury items or just to 'see the hippies'. Anjuna itself is a small, attractive cove, backing onto swaying palms. The sea is very

suitable for swimming, except in the afternoon, when it is swept by strong onshore breezes. At this time of day, walk round to the quiet, protected coves between Anjuna and Baga which are beautifully secluded. In the town is the splendid 1920s **Albuquerque Mansion** (*open weekdays, 10–5*), a massive Portuguese villa, still partly inhabited, which operates as a kind of living museum.

Note: between November and February, when all accommodation is booked weeks ahead, don't turn up on spec unless you're prepared to sleep on the beach for a few days.

Also, beware of smoking marijuana openly: police informers often spy out smokers, then plant large amounts of drugs in their bags, in advance of an out-of-the-blue 'official search', after which you will be 'fined' as much as the policeman in charge thinks you can pay.

Getting There

The most common approach to Anjuna is via local bus or shared cab from Mapusa (Rs7–10). But some travellers hire motorcycles from Calangute and bike up. These can be hired at Anjuna too, for about Rs1000 per fortnight, and are a popular, if injury-fraught, method of beach-hopping.

Sports and Activities

Healthier than raving is **parascending**. There is a school which operates on the cliffs above Anjuna throughout the Christmas season (as well as up at Arambol). To sign up for a course, ask at the **Shore Bar**.

Anjuna © (083226–)

Where to Stay

inexpensive

There are just two proper lodges: **Bougainvillaea**, with over-priced, basic rooms, but a lovely garden and good food; and the **Tamarind Lodge**, a collection of stone cottages (some with air-conditioning) on Kumar Vaddo about 2 miles from the beach, and a well-known seafood restaurant. It's only worth staying here if you have your own transport.

cheap

The choice of lodges is very limited: try the **Poonam Guest House** near the flea market (though rooms here will be over Rs100 during the season), or **Grandpa's Inn**, © 26250, out on the Mapusa Road. Otherwise, you have to find a room with a local family. If you intend to stay a long time, you can negotiate very cheap rooms back off the beach. Ask at the **Shore Bar** at the south end of the beach, and the owners there will put you in touch with someone.

Eating Out

Anjuna has some very good eating places: try **Tamarind Lodge** on Kumar Vaddo, about 2 miles from the beach, for traditional Goan dishes. Cheaper is **Poonam's**, or the **Rose Garden Restaurant** on the beach. In the town is **O'Coqueiro**, © 7271, at Porvorim with excellent Goan food. For tasty snacks, try the **German Bakery** near the flea market which serves good lasagne and tofu-oriented veggie food as well as breads and biscuits. If you want to make a night of it, ride your bike or take a motorbike taxi 4 miles towards Mapusa to **The Haystack**, where you can hear live music and eat traditional Goan food and drink cheap, cheap local wine. Wherever you eat, be aware that service at all Anjuna's restaurants is notoriously slow.

Most young travellers come to Goa for the **all-night techno parties**. These are grand affairs; outdoor raves, often right by the sea, held among luxuriant sub-tropical vegetation. Almost all the parties are held around Anjuna, Vagator and Arambol. The exact location tends to be kept secret until a few hours before, but all the motorbike taxi men get tipped off on the day. The **Shore Bar** on Anjuna beach, or the **Primrose** on the road to Vagator also good for finding out where parties are.

If you turn up around midnight, when the local Indian men in search of a female tourist have got drunk and gone home, the parties can be magical, with local tribeswomen turning out with *chai* and cakes for sale, spreading mats on the ground for you to sit on, and makeshift bars with beers illegally for sale. The parties are famed for having any amount of marijuana, acid and ecstasy.

A word of warning though, if you intend to 'trip', try not to wander too far afield, as the coastal country is incised with small ravines that are very easy to fall into. The local doctors make a good living from patching up people who have hurt themselves at parties, taken the wrong drug, or crashed their motorbike. If you need **medical attention** at one of these parties, get a motorbike taxi immediately to **Dr Henriques Jawarharlal**, whose clinic is on **Rodrigues Vaddo**, Siolim, near Vagator.

Chapora/Vagator

A 7-mile bus ride from Mapusa, these beaches are beautifully secluded. If you tire of Anjuna, they are just a 1¾-mile stroll up along the headland. Vagator is strikingly beautiful, a small cove of rich orange sands embraced by green-gold coconut palms. (But avoid the picturesque rocky promontery at the centre of the beach: the locals use it as an outdoor loo.) The small sandy coves of Chapora adjoining it to the north are overlooked by the old **Portuguese Fort** (built 1717, now in ruins but worth a visit for the fine views from the ramparts), and back onto a charming little village.

Vagator ℂ (083226–)   **Where to Stay**

moderate

The upmarket place to stay is **Vagator Beach Resort**, ℂ 3276, with friendly atmosphere, good restaurant and lovely red-tiled beach-view cottages in the garden.

inexpensive

The **Royal Resort**, ℂ 3260, near the Vagator Resort, has some air-conditioned rooms, a decent restaurant and its own pool.

cheap

Dr Lobo's or **Noble Nest** are friendly and clean, but basic. Otherwise here are some places to try for family rooms: Acacia Fernandes, 562 (1), Vagator; Agosthino Tinoco, 564 Vagator; the Anita Lodge, 511, Vagator; Apolin Fernandes, 526 Vagator; Carmina Morais, 581 Vagator; or Benvilla 594 Vagator. If none of these have room, they will soon put you in touch with somebody who does.

Eat at the big **Vagator Resort** hotel, at **Lobo's** on the beach (not at the lodge of the same name in the village) or at the **Laxmi** on the beach. The **Primrose**, on the road between Vagator and Anjuna, serves cakes and desserts as well as the usual fish & chips-style beach food, and is a good place to find out where the parties are being held (sometimes they are held right there).

Arambol/Terekol

These two northernmost beaches are the final retreat of the hippies and the place to really get away from it all. Bring a sleeping bag, just in case you have to sleep on the beach, but be careful not to let your belongings out of sight. Arambol has a beautiful freshwater lake (a little muddy, but pure and ideal for washing-off after swims in the salty sea), lovely sands, free camping, also beach huts, and great expanses of empty beach. The friendly village close to the main beach has restaurants with reasonable food.

There are plans to build a huge 5-star hotel compex, complete with golf course at Arambol. The locals all oppose it, as they rely on the budget travellers for a living, and would make no money from rich tourists stayng behind a high wall in the hotel compound. They also fear that their wells will be made dry by the golf course's tapping of the water table. However, until the hotel is actually built, Arambol remains a paradise. A final ferry ride north of Arambol, **Terekol** beach marks the northern boundary of Goa's coast, and has a fine Maratha fort, captured by the Portuguese in 1776, with a small church and good views.

Arambol is 3 hours by **bus** from Mapusa, or 4 hours from Panjim. A long trip, involving a **ferry** crossing at Siolim, and then leaving the bus and taking a **shared taxi**, but well worth it. Terekol involves another ferry crossing at Keri, from which you need to take another shared taxi on to the fort. To call Arambol, phone the operator and ask for Redi followed by the number.

Try **Lizzy's Guest House**, Shri Benedict Fernandes house number 686, Arambol, or the **Hotel Miramar**, in Pednem, near the beach, for cheap, cleanish rooms. Otherwise, it's rented rooms in family houses again. Walk from the beach to the small village of Waddo and ask for any of the following: Alex Fernandes, 660 (B) Khalcha Vadda, Bella Fernandes, 676 Socoilo Vaddo; Maria Rodrigues on Socoilo Vaddo, Paul de Souza, 665 Socoilo Vaddo; Sulochana Naik, 701 Khalcha Vaddo; Shreepad Mayekar, 688-A Arambol; or Uttam Kochrekar, at the Yellow House, 685 Khalcha Vaddo.

Terekol is the place to get away from things, and you can stay at the fort, which has now been converted to the **Terekol Fort Tourist Rest Home**, book via Panjim or Margoa tourist offices. Priced at between Rs100–350 per room per night, the fort offers accommodation in separate cottages. Otherwise, you have to stay in Arambol and walk up.

Bogmalo

This is one of Goa's best beaches, a secluded crescent-shaped cove with calm waters for swimming (a contrast to the powerful breakers of the more open beaches) and a friendly fishing village. Behind the beach rises the small upland of the Marmagao peninsula. But Bogmalo is an exclusive beach, presided over (as at Fort Aguada) by a single luxury hotel: the **Oberoi Bogmalo Beach**, © (0834) 513291/311, ✆ 243303. If you can afford it, at only 5 minutes' drive from the Diabolim airport, this is an excellent holiday option with marvellous water sports, freshwater swimming pool, quality multi-cuisine restaurants, breezy open-air barbecues, and elegantly furnished rooms, each one with a private balcony overlooking the sea. Few budget travellers make it out here: transport is too awkward (1 hour minimum by bus from Panjim, with a change at the 'Aerodrome' stop 2 miles before Vasco) and there's nowhere cheap to stay. Oberoi lays on free transport from the airport for residents.

South of Bogmalo are the Velsao and Majorda beaches. Both remain fairly quiet, and again, there is a single luxury hotel, the **Majorda Beach Resort**, © (08342) 220025/6 or 220164, ✆ 220212, set slightly back from the beach with all facilities.

Colva

Goa's longest beach is 12 unbroken miles of virgin white sand. Like Calangute to the north, Colva has been spoiled by progress—crowds of Indian men hassle western women, there are inflated hotel and food prices, as well as aggressive hawkers. Now a money-making town receiving thousands of package tourists every year, Colva is no longer for the backpacker. However you need only walk a mile or two south of the main tourist drag to have the beach almost to yourself. The waters are warm and calm, and the only people you'll see are local fishermen.

Getting There

Colva is a half-hour **bus** journey from Margao, or a cheap **shared taxi** ride—pick one up from the taxi rank behind the Karmat Magdoot Restaurant on the right hand side of the Municpal Gardens.

Shopping

At the Colva bus stand there are a few pleasant shops, including **Damodar**, the place to buy or sell second-hand books. Reading is the main occupation on the beaches, so stock up. **Navneeta Handicrafts** is the place to buy cool, practical beach clothes. Other good purchases on the beach are beautiful lacquer boxes, eggs and painted shells. Buy cheap, attractive jewellery at Colva's Full Moon parties which some say are better than Anjuna (they are certainly more mainstream) with an illuminated marquee: great music and dancing, and lots of atmosphere.

expensive

The **Penthouse Beach Resort**, ☎ 721975, has no penthouses, being laid out in separate cottages (some with air-conditioning) around a swimming pool and garden. Many travellers recommend this place for its relaxed atmosphere and friendly, helpful staff. Since renovation, prices of rooms at the air-conditioned **Hotel Silver Sands**, ☎ 721645, ✆ 737749, have soared to the top of this price category in the high season. Still, you get all the luxury facilities, including swimming pool, health club, windsurfing, travel office and free airport transfer.

moderate

There are several smaller resort hotels in this category, the **Colva Beach Resort**, ☎ 221975, the **Sukhsagar Resort**, ☎ 221888 the **William Beach Resort**, ☎ 221077 and the **Longuinhos Beach Resort**. Of the three, the Longuinhos is the favourite, being right by the beach, some rooms having balconies and a good restaurant. The others all have clean, comfortable rooms, with a few air-conditioned (though you don't really need it so near the sea), and facilities for arranging watersports, day trips, etc.

inexpensive

The **Colmar**, ☎ 721253, is at the top end of this price range and offers either small cottages set in gardens, or a cheaper dorm for backpackers. The restaurant is cheaper then the other resort hotels but is just as good. Try also the **Whitesands Hotel**, ☎ 721253. Right on the beach, it is good value with clean, non air-conditioned rooms and good food.

At the lower end of the range, avoid the state-run **Tourist Hostel**, often full and much-frequented by Indian tourists and head for the **Sea View Cottages** opposite the Silver Sands Hotel instead. If full, try in some of the guest houses: **Glowin's Abode** and the **Vailankanni** are both on the street behind the beach (4th Ward), and are popular with travellers for their friendly owners and clean rooms. You might also try **Hotel Vincy**, ☎ 722276, above Vincy's Bar. This used to be very popular with independent travellers, but has apparently fallen off a little lately, perhaps owing to the vast choice of more upmarket accommodation now available. A short bicycle ride from the beach are the **Garden Cottages** near the popular Johnny's Restaurant.

cheap

Many people are quite happy to put up at one of the many cheap lodges near the beach—after all, all you really need here is a bed for the night. A couple of goodies are **Fisherman's Cottage** (200 yards from the bus station with friendly people) and the nearby **Rose Cottages**. Also try **Maria's Guest House, Rodson's Cottages** or **Bruno's** on the 4th Ward, or the **Tourist Nest**, 2 miles inland, which also has bicycles to hire.

During the high season, when beach accommodation is very thin on the ground, try family houses like **Sabfran Tourist Cottages**, about two-thirds of a mile before Colva beach (ask the bus driver to drop you off) which charge less than Rs1500 per *month* for clean, habitable double rooms. Many of the houses on the 4th Ward rent cheap rooms and just wandering down the street with your backpack should be enough to bring out offers. Bargain down to just over half the asking price.

Eating Out

 Most Colva residents eat at one of the ramshackle (but good) beach restaurants situated right on the shoreline. Regular favourites—all serving excellent seafood in addition to the usual pancakes, chips and omelettes—are **Sunset**, **Lucky Star** and **La Mir**. This is where people come to enjoy tasty fish dishes, spaghetti 'sizzlers', and a *feni* nightcap, after a hard day's sunbathing. In the morning, they pile over to **Umita Corner Restaurant and Bar** (away from the beach, near Tourist Nest) for breakfast. Recommended, and less than a mile from the beach, is **Sucorina**, which is good for seafood.

There's always a small gathering around the kiosks by the roundabout at 9 each morning, when hot doughnuts arrive.

Benaulim

If mainstream Colva is too busy for you, stroll a mile down the sands to quiet, secluded Benaulim beach—far cheaper and more pleasant than Colva.

Benaulim has a pretty fishing village behind the beach, full of quaint, sleepy old Portuguese houses and buildings. The noise and 'tourist business' hustle of Colva fall away and you are back in quiet, rural Goa. There are a variety of places to stay and eat, both on the beach and in the village, but the village has the more sheltered accommodation—the beach can be shadeless and windswept. Hire a bicycle, which most lodges rent out for Rs20–30 per day, for getting to and from the beach.

Getting There

Direct **buses** run almost every half-hour from Margao, and a **shared taxi** can be picked up from behind the Karmat Magdoot restaurant on the east side of the Municipal Gardens in Margao. An **auto-rickshaw** costs between Rs30–45 depending on how much of hurry you are in and how good you are at bargaining. Journey time is approximately 30 minutes.

Benaulim © *(0834–)*   **Where to Stay**

On the Beach

moderate

 The **Carina Beach Resort** has very clean rooms, some with air-conditioning, and a good restaurant. However, it's more fun to eat at one of the beach shacks.

inexpensive

L'Amour Beach Resort, © 223720/6, is right on the beach, with nice clean rooms, some with a bath, but disappointing overpriced food. You can also try the **O'Palmar Beach Cottages**, © 223278, where the rooms have showers, but whose hotel compound is a little windswept.

In Benaulim Village

Brito Tourist Corner at the village crossroads, offers large rooms with balconies, as does **Rosarios's** on Vasvaddo, which also hires bikes and arranges transport to and from the airport. Vasvaddo has some other good cheapies, like the **Palm Grove, More Cottages**, the **Bamboo Grove Cottages, Jack Joana Tourist Home, Fern Cottages**, the **Anita Tourist House, Amal Guest House** and the **Alfa Tourist Live-Inn**. All offer decent double rooms with attached bathrooms and Indian or European-style loos.

Eating Out

On the beach, eat at the **Splash Restaurant**, which has good service and nice seafood, but steer clear of the pork sausages which, like sausages everywhere in Goa, come from pigs whose diet is principally one of human faeces. **Xavier's** has superlative fish dishes, and reasonable sounds. **Pedro's** has gone into steep decline, but **Johncy's**, always packed and popular, though not always serving the best food, still has jolly beach parties.

Cavelossim, Varca and Mabor

These adjacent stetches of sand are really just extensions of Benaulim's long, lonely southward sweep of sand that heads down towards Betul.

There are a few over-priced isolated package-style hotels here, full of people looking a little bored and wondering where the famous zest of Goa can have disappeared to. However, in the off-season, these hotels can be bargained down to about a third of their asking price, and by staying in them, you can guarantee some isolation.

For orientation, the beaches run like this: Varca in the north, Cavelossim in the middle and Mabor in the south. Varca village is a mile behind the beach, Cavelossim village is 2 miles inland from Cavelossim beach and Mabor is right on the beach.

Getting There

Several **buses** run out to these villages from Margao each day, but you have little chance of finding anyone to share a taxi with, as few travellers head here. An auto-rickshaw will cost near to Rs50. Journey time is approx 40 minutes.

Cavelossim, Varca, Mabor © (0834–)   **Where to Stay**

luxury

The **Goa Renaissance Resort** at Varca Village, © 245200/ 245218, ✆ 245225 offers the usual Goan style of luxury— air-conditioned rooms overlooking the sea, watersports, good food and a private stretch of beach to enjoy. The hotel, supposedly designed by Hawaiian architects, has a 6-hole golf course, a series of swimming pools and direct access to the beach.

Another 5-star property is **The Leela Beach** at Mabor, ℂ 246363/73, ℮ 246352, with rooms in villas, 'pavilions' or private suites.

expensive

The **Holiday Inn Resort** at Mabor, ℂ 246304/5/6, ℮ 246333 and the **Old Anchor Resort**, ℂ 23005, with watersports facilities.

inexpensive

The **Gaffino Beach Resort** between Cavelossim beach and village, ℂ 246 315/9, is considerably cheaper than the other resorts, largely because it cannot offer air-conditioned rooms. A small place, it can make a nice out-of-season hideaway.

Betul

This lovely beach, located on the estuary of the river leading off from the bottom of Benaulim's 6-mile long swathe of sand, is serviced by direct buses from Margao. Almost untouched by tourism, Betul offers seclusion, magical beaches, and unspoilt scenery. At present, there is just one decent place to stay—a small lodge-cum-restaurant, run by a friendly Goan, right next door to an ancestral summer-house. This is a very well-run establishment with rooms with a balcony overlooking the river from Rs100. It is tricky to find. If coming in by bus, you still have to walk across the river via the bridge. Another problem is lack of direct access from the lodge to the beaches. You either have a half-hour walk over the hills to a secluded, idyllic beach, or you take a ferry across to the main beach, which runs down from Colva. Betul represents, for the time being at least, the perfect little getaway for the peace-loving beachcomber.

Palolem

A little more developed than Betul, Palolem is still one of the cheapest and quietest of Goa's beach enclaves. Its small village is strung out under the palms, and has two beaches. The main one, a 2-mile golden crescent complete with fishing boats and beach shack restaurants, runs between two forested headlands. The smaller beach, south of the southern headland, can be yours all day with almost no disturbance.

Getting There

Palolem is the southernmost tourist spot in Goa, reached by a 2-mile sideroad from the town of Canacona. **Buses** run to Palolem from Margao every hour (as well as down the Karnataka coast to Gokarn and Mangalore), but to get out to Palolem you have to take either an **auto-rickshaw** (don't pay more than Rs25) or a **motorbike taxi** (about Rs10).

Palolem ℂ (0834–)

Where to Stay

inexpensive

Palolem's one resort hotel, the imaginatively named **Palolem Resort** has self-contained chalet-style rooms with attached bathrooms or very comfortable cheaper safari tents with a shared ablution block, set in a small garden right on the beach. There is a smaller resort of palm-thatch huts next door, but it is booked through the Indian Tourist Office in Bombay and is always full.

cheap

There are several places where you can rent family rooms two-thirds of a mile into the coconut groves, behind the beach. The best place to start looking is at **Jackson's**, a shabby bar/general store 50 yards south of the turn-off for the beach along the Canacona road. The owner can be a little brusque and charges inflated prices for his rooms but if you stick to about half what he asks (he asks about Rs80, you offer Rs40–50), he will show you to someone who can rent at that price.

Rajabag

The southernmost beach in Goa has no development at all. The only place to stay is a lonely hotel, often all-but empty, 1½ miles behind the beach, involving a walk through sand-scrub and cashew bushes. The hotel is reached from Canacona by auto-rickshaw or motorbike taxi (same prices as for Palolem), or from Palolem by walking 3 miles to the south and staying parallel with the coast where the road forks off to Canacona. A very pleasant walk in the morning or evening, Rajabag makes a good day trip from Palolem.

Rajabag ℂ (0834–)

Where to Stay

inexpensive

 If you decide that you like the solitude of Rajabag, the **Molyma Hotel**, ℂ 643 082, ✉ 643 081, is a mile away, sitting south of the junction of the footpath to the beach and the road from Canacona. Unfortunately the building itself is rather bland and modern, but its pleasant little garden and tennis court make up for that and you cannot help feeling sad for the owners who cannot have recouped their investment. The food is quite good, as long as you stick to Indian items and avoid the prawns, which are of the disappointing, small, packaged variety.

Goa's Mountains

Few travellers to Goa manage to prise themselves from the beaches and explore the nearby mountains. But those who do will discover an accessible wilderness of dry deciduous forests, small rainforests, waterfalls, river gorges and wildlife sanctuaries. There is good **trekking** in the sanctuaries, most of which are within two hours of the beach, and the forests are still well populated with wildlife.

The Worldwide Fund for Nature (WWF) is particularly active in Goa and the conservation movement here has more influence with the government than in many other Indian states. The Goan branch of the WWF is based in Panjim and offers guided treks into the mountains. Although you can travel independently into most of the wild areas, going with a guide will increase your chances of seeing animals. The guide will also explain the local ecosystem and can usually identify the flora. For more information contact the **WWF Goan Divisional Office**, Hillside Apartments, Block B, B-2, Ground Floor, Fontainas (off 31 January Street), Panjim, Goa 403001, ℂ 226020.

Lambadi tribal woman

Bondla Wildlife Sanctuary

This is Goa's smallest sanctuary at only 3 square miles, and is 30 miles east of Panjim at Ponda Takula. You can reach it by bus from Panjim (2 hours) via Ponda, and there are regular hourly services between the city and the sanctuary.

Bondla is more of a zoological park than a wild reserve—although the surrounding conserved forest is very wild, and it is possible to **trek** into the wilderness via the WWF in Panjim (*see* above). Indigenous wildlife is kept in large, open-air fenced areas. Of particular note are the semi-domesticated herds of *gaur* (bison), who come very close to the fence and offer superb possibilities for photography. In the surrounding forest, the largest animals are a migratary herd of wild elephant who come in from Karnataka during the dry season (February–August). Trekking during these months can thus be dangerous and should not be attempted without a guide. Other local wildlife includes, leopard, sloth bear, *sambar* and *chital* (spotted) deer, wild boar and common *langur* monkey. A few hundred yards into the forest from the reception office is a waterhole overlooked by a large *machan* or viewing platform, built into a tree. Again, this offers good chances for photography, but it can also make a good place to spend the night if you can persuade the local Wildlife Department officials. You will need a mosquito net for protection against insects and snakes.

There is more comfortable accommodation in a Forest Department resthouse but this is usually booked up by school groups. If you want to stay overnight, bring a tent or mosquito net and ask the people at the reception office to let you pitch it somewhere quiet—they are usually amenable.

Bird species at Bondla include paradise flycatcher, racket-tail drongo, grey hornbill and peacock.

Bhagwan Mahavir Wildlife Sanctuary

About 35 miles east of Panjim near the village of Sanguem Taluka, this is a much larger sanctuary than nearby Bondla (about 90 square miles). The dense forest harbours similar game species to Bondla, and there is **trekking** down to the **Dudhsagar Waterfalls** and to the deep **Devil's Canyon**. You can reach the sanctuary by bus from Panjim (journey time about three hours, services run every 1½ hours).

The waterfalls can also be reached by a light-guage **railway** that runs from Margao (journey time about four hours, services three times daily) and can be treated as a day trip from the southern beaches.

Accommodation at Bhagwan Mahavir is in two Forest Department resthouses. There is generally room if you *insist* on staying, although the wildlife department officials at the reception office often claim that the resthouses are full. As with most of the Goan sanctuaries, your best bet of getting in is via a WWF trip (*see* above).

Birds are also the same as for Bondla, with the addition of Malabar trogon, great pied hornbill, ruby-throated yellow bulbul (wow!) and the magnificent crested serpent eagle.

chital

Cotigao Wildlife Sanctuary

This is another large conservation area—about 40 square miles—but in the far south of the state. The easiest way to reach Cotigao is by bus from Canacona, near Palolem (services every hour, journey time about an hour) and there is accommodation in one small resthouse. However, it is very difficult to get permission to stay here. If you want to get into Cotigao, you are more or less on your own. You will need a tent and a good compass, as no maps or guides are available. Camping in the forest is safe as there are no elephants or tigers but getting lost is a real problem. The dense undergrowth has innumerable narrow paths snaking through it, trodden by local tribals gathering wood and these form an immense labyrinth. Again, unless you are a very experienced hiker, and have all your own food, it is best to arrange a trip through the WWF in Panjim (*see* above).

Again, the fauna is the same as for Bondla and Bhagwan Mandavir sanctuaries. Bird-watchers should look out for the white-eyed buzzard eagle, rufous woodpecker, the Malabar crested lark and rosy minivet.

Other Conserved Areas of Goa

Goa has about 5000 acres of mangrove swamp around its river estuaries. The largest areas are along the Zuari river delta, the Mandovi river delta, along the Cumbarjua canal and at a few spots near Chapora and Terekol in the northern beaches. There has even been some re-planting of destroyed mangroves. About four million seedlings have been planted since 1985, but the success rate has been low (under 50 per cent). For the most part, it is impossible to explore these swamps—not only are they physically difficult to enter without a boat, but permission for entry is officially denied, as the government wants the areas left undisturbed.

However, there are two bird sanctuaries where tourists can see the swamps. Two miles outside Panjim on the road to Old Goa is the **Chorao Bird Sanctuary** which covers about 500 acres. Its mangrove-fringed mud flats attract thousands of migratory birds and provide excellent bird-watching, especially from November to March. Among the migrants that fly in during these months are huge flocks of sandpipers, stilts and snipe, pin-tail ducks, shoveler ducks, purple moorhens, several species of tern, adjutant storks, teal and garganey.

Seven miles from Panjim at Carambolim is another sanctuary, **Karmali Lake**. At about 140 acres, Karmali also has a November–February season. The migratory bird species are the same as for Chorao sanctuary but with the addition of lesser whistling teal, whitenecked storks and *nakta* (combduck). Year-round residents include dabchicks, night and reef herons, bitterns, brahmini duck, glossy ibis, openbill stork, kites and marsh harrier. There are regular buses from Panjim to Carambolim but from there you will have to take an auto-rickshaw or taxi.

whitenecked storks

The Maharajah's palace, Mysore

Karnataka

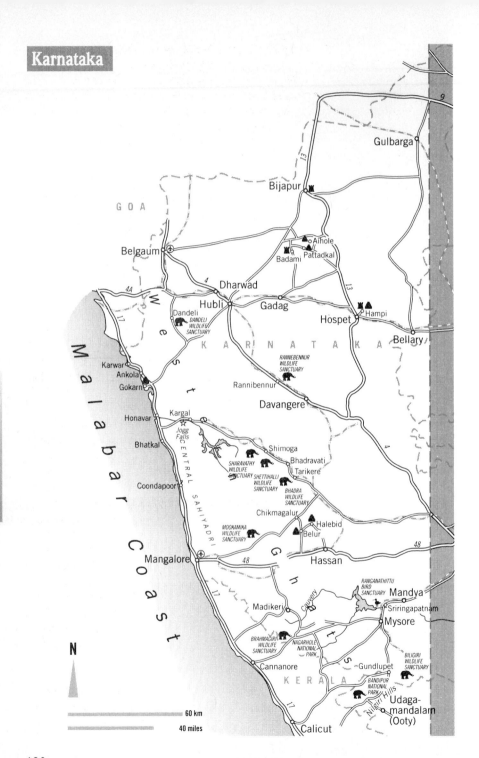

Karnataka

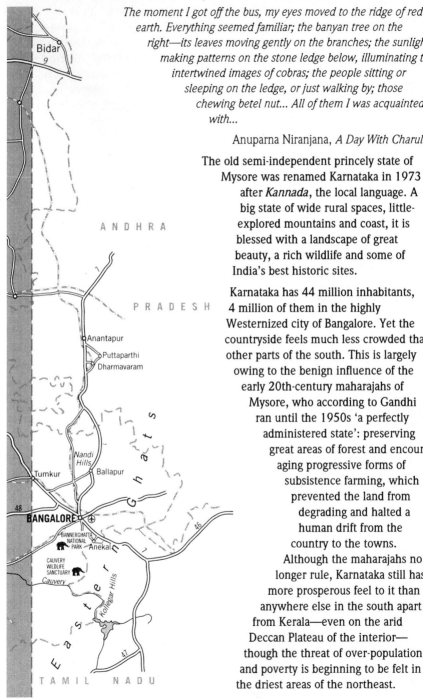

The moment I got off the bus, my eyes moved to the ridge of red earth. Everything seemed familiar; the banyan tree on the right—its leaves moving gently on the branches; the sunlight making patterns on the stone ledge below, illuminating the intertwined images of cobras; the people sitting or sleeping on the ledge, or just walking by; those chewing betel nut... All of them I was acquainted with...

Anuparna Niranjana, *A Day With Charulata*

The old semi-independent princely state of Mysore was renamed Karnataka in 1973 after *Kannada*, the local language. A big state of wide rural spaces, little-explored mountains and coast, it is blessed with a landscape of great beauty, a rich wildlife and some of India's best historic sites.

Karnataka has 44 million inhabitants, 4 million of them in the highly Westernized city of Bangalore. Yet the countryside feels much less crowded than other parts of the south. This is largely owing to the benign influence of the early 20th-century maharajahs of Mysore, who according to Gandhi ran until the 1950s 'a perfectly administered state': preserving great areas of forest and encouraging progressive forms of subsistence farming, which prevented the land from degrading and halted a human drift from the country to the towns. Although the maharajahs no longer rule, Karnataka still has a more prosperous feel to it than anywhere else in the south apart from Kerala—even on the arid Deccan Plateau of the interior—though the threat of over-population and poverty is beginning to be felt in the driest areas of the northeast.

131

Karnataka's architectural heritage is rich too, inherited from the various Hindu and Muslim rulers who fought over the region from the early medieval period to the early 19th century. Some very handsome towns have survived, including 19th-century Mysore, the 17th-century coastal temple town of Gokarn and medieval, walled Bijapur; in these places the traditional architecture has escaped the onslaught of raw concrete that has afflicted so much of urban India in recent years. Karnataka also has some fabulously romantic ruined cities, most notably at Hampi, the old capital of the high medieval Vijayanager empire; and at Pattadkal, northern capital of the early medieval Chalukyan kings. Both ruins are World Heritage Sites.

Karnataka's stretch of the Malabar Coast is the most beautiful in south India, as in many places the foothills of the Western Ghats come right down to the sea, and the beaches are still largely undiscovered. Up in the higher mountains, trekking can be had in dense hardwood forests still populated by tiger and elephant. On the eastern slopes, near the Kerala border, the tiny sub-state of Coorg has forest temples that will feed and accommodate travellers, set in a landscape so beautiful that the travel writer Dervla Murphy was moved to write 'I am beginning to feel vaguely guilty about having fallen so deeply in love with Coorg. I set out, after all, to tour south India.'

Allow time for Karnataka. Try and spend at least a week trekking or wildlife viewing in one of the vast mountain sanctuaries, at least a week on the undeveloped beaches near Gokarn, at least a week in the dreaming ruins at Hampi, and a few days in sedate Mysore and in the pubs at Bangalore. But if you have to rush through, then spend all your time in Coorg.

Karnataka's Coast

With the quietest, least developed beaches on the southern Malabar Coast, this 200-mile stretch is the most beautiful in south India. Curved beaches nestle between mangrove-lined estuaries and the forested spurs of the Western Ghats. Even the towns and villages are charming, with red-tiled, carved wooden Brahmin houses giving way to fishermen's palm-thatch huts on the coconut palm-fringed shore. Inland, the paddy fields are overlooked by the sharply-rising tiers of the Western Ghats. On the beaches themselves long, dark fishing boats sit in rows, as if keeping watch between the gentle breakers and the jewelled green countryside behind.

Karnataka's coast is known to only a minority of independent travellers and only a few places cater in any way for tourists. Even in the relatively populated beach spots the volume of travellers is very low, with only basic facilities, and the local people still regard Westerners as amusing eccentrics rather than mere walking dollar signs. Those travellers who do make it to the Karnatic beaches glaze over and smile silly smiles when asked to describe the place.

Change will inevitably come, but fortunately Karnataka's coast does not lend itself to quick development. Due to the mountainous nature of the coast, most of the beaches can only be reached by rocky paths, sometimes of a few miles in length. You have to carry your gear—something most package tourists will never do. There are few actual towns, and to stay in the smaller villages you need to master the local language and take all your own supplies.

A railway is currently being built from Mangalore in the south, right up the Karnataka coast to Goa, but it will be some years before it is completed and at the moment there is only one road along the coast. Away from this narrow stretch of tarmac the 20th century has only a tenuous hold: there are no crowds, no aggressive hawkers, no blaring radios, buzzing scooters and noisy trucks; only the waving of windblown palms above the endless sigh of the Arabian sea.

Mangalore

Getting Around

by air

Indian Airways and **Jet** fly into Bajpe airport, about 20 miles from the town centre. Indian Airways flights go to Bangalore and Madras 4 times a week and twice-daily to Bombay. Jet flies daily to Bombay.

by train

It really is worth making the train journey from Bangalore via the Deccan Plateau near Hassan and over the forested Western Ghats. There are also direct connections with all points on the coast of Kerala and with Madras when travelling via Bangalore. A railway, due to open 1997/8 is being constructed north up the coast to Goa.

by bus

The bus stand is 2 miles north of the town centre, so allow for this when catching buses. Direct daily services go to all points on the Karnataka Coast and to Goa (13 hours)—the best one being the 11am bus. From Goa, you can take a connection on to Bombay if you are a real masochist. Bangalore and Mysore are also serviced every half-hour, each ride taking about 10 hours. Madras and Madurai have express buses too, but it is far nicer to go by train.

Tourist Information

The **Tourist Information** office is on Station Road, by the Railway Station. The complex housing the **G.P.O.** and **Telegraph Office** is on Dr. U.P. Mallya Road downhill from the mosque. The **State Bank of India** is on K.S. Rao Road, as are most of the hotels and restaurants.

The City

You won't find the natural splendours of the Karnatic coast in Mangalore, the coast's only large town. This humid, smelly port town has the usual modern Indian semi-industrial ugliness on its fringes and crowded, motor-horn honking stress at its centre.

You should use Mangalore only as a brief rest-stop before going on up the coast to discover the beauty of the region. But while in Mangalore it is worth exploring the small part of town that centres around the old port or **Bund**—still a working labyrinth of 100-year-old 'go-downs' (warehouses), their piles of merchandise piled in cool shade away from the glaring sun. The port is run partly by Indo-Portuguese Christians, (Mangalore was one of the few points of the Karnatic coast developed by the Portuguese traders) and partly by white-robed Muslims (this is the Arabian Sea after all); it would be hard to say which community is the most prosperous.

The Bund is therefore a strange architectural mish-mash of old Catholic churches, carved wooden Mosques in the Keralan style, wizened labourers bent double and straining under huge loads of coffee—the Bund handles 75 per cent of Karnataka's annual harvest—*coir*, spices, forest hardwoods, cotton, cashews, or fish. Poor Hindu prostitutes hover in the side alleys, and the town's original fishing tribe are crowded into a stinking slum of dusty palm-thatch lean-tos on the dockside, their ragged children assailing any traveller walking there with demands for money.

To get to the Bund, head for the centre of town, whose big landmark is **Malagres Church**, then due west (downhill) along Bibi Alabibi Road and you will come into the Bund. The Bund itself is bisected by the large Jammu Masjid Road, which becomes Goods Shed Road south of the wharves, before curving back up into the small old Portuguese residential quarter, from which the astonishingly named Old Kent Road (who was the cockney explorer here?) takes you back to Malagres Church. Walk around the streets that run parallel with Jammu Masjid and Good Shed, and the alleys that connect them, to pick up on the atmosphere (and take a camera). One word of warning: at night the Bund can be as rough as any other dockside, so after dark it is best to be in a group.

Despite its heat and general unattractiveness, upper Mangalore has a few surprises. The 19th-century **St Aloysious Chapel** on Lighthouse Hill Road has a ceiling covered with frescoes painted by a Jesuit named Moshcheni. The official tourist literature has dubbed St Aloysious the 'Sistine Chapel of India'. While the paintings are not the work of a Michaelangelo, they are nonetheless very beautiful.

If you take an auto-rickshaw up Old Lighthouse Road (Rs10), you come to a hill with gardens and ornamental lakes, on which stands an **18th-century lighthouse**, supposedly built by the Karnatic Muslim warlord Hyder Ali, though this is now disputed by historians. Also in the gardens is the 10th-century **Managaladevi Temple**, a superb piece of Keralan wooden temple architecture; also the small **Kadri Caves**, ancient hermits' cells next to which is the 11th-century **Sri Manjunatha Temple**.

Back in the main town, if the heat hasn't knocked you over, you can visit the **Mahatma Gandhi Museum** in the grounds of the Canara High School (*open Mon–Fri, 9.30–12.30 and 2–5.30*), a small, dusty place with rather neglected displays of stuffed local fauna and some good bronze sculpture. Alternatively, stroll down Dr U.P. Mallya Road, past the big mosque and the G.P.O. and Telegraph Office to the 19th-century **Santa Rosario Cathedral** and its attached Catholic school. You cannot guarantee that the cathedral will be open but if you wander around the elegant but decaying school grounds, you will be kept company by scores of charming, playful schoolchildren, eager for a game of tag.

Suratkal Beach

About 10 miles north of the town centre and overlooked by the town's new lighthouse and a small temple is this quiet sweep of golden beach with good swimming, although it is by no means as idyllic as the beaches further up the Karnataka coast. Visit only in the week—at weekends it gets very crowded with townspeople.

Mangalore ✆ (0824–)

Where to Stay

expensive

The Taj-group **Manjuran** on Old Port Road, ✆ 420420, ✆ 420585 has a swimming pool (relief in this fetid town). Just above the old port, it is convenient for exploring the Bund. Other facilities include a bar, two restaurants and a bookshop.

moderate

Try the **Moti Mahal**, on Falnir Road, ✆ 2221. It also has a pool, and a more faded, old-fashioned feel. More brash are the modern **Srinavas Hotel** on Ganapathi Road, ✆ 2238, and the **Poonja International** on K.S. Rao Road, ✆ 440171.

Out of town is the **Summer Sands Beach Resort**, ✆ 6400, a good option for a couple of day's relaxing before heading up the coast. With its own private beach (which attracts hawkers), the six miles from Mangalore makes it a world away from the hot bustle of the town. To get there, take a taxi out to the town of Choltamangalore/Ullal.

inexpensive

Two hotels on K.S. Rao Road are worth giving a go: the **Navaratha Palace**, ✆ 441104, and the **Manorama**. Both are clean and friendly, with decent restaurants and foreign exchange.

cheap

Mangalore's cheap hotels are run-down at best and mosquitoes are a continual problem. However, the state-run **Mayura Netravati**, 2 miles north of the town centre is clean and conveniently placed for the bus stand. Cheap rooms can also be found at the rather dingy **Panchami** opposite the bus stand and at the **Vasanth Mahal** on K.S. Rao Road, which is more central but with tiny, flea-ridden rooms.

Eating Out

Try the Taj Manjuran's two restaurants (Western and very good Indian, catering for both vegetarians and non-vegetarians). Otherwise there is reasonable vegetarian food (and some fish) at the other main hotels, or cheap *thali* houses.

Bhatkal

Heading north from Mangalore, you pass the large town of Udupi, and the smaller village of Malpe, off which is the island where Vasco da Gama made his first East Indies landfall in the late 1490s. The road then continues past the largish port town of Coondapoor, but the first point worth stopping at is **Bhatkal**. Of mostly historical interest, this small Muslim port was developed in the 16th century to service Hampi, the fabulous but now ruined capital of the Vijayanagar kings on the Deccan Plateau (*see* p.180). The small town is a dusty treasure-trove of wooden Keralan and Karnatic architecture, boasting several small temples and a 17th-century Jain *basti* (small shrine) Bhatkal is also the most convenient point on the coast from which to travel up to the spectacular **Jog Falls** (2–3 hours by bus, four services daily) and the vast wildlife sanctuaries of Karnataka's Shimoga region (*see* p.139).

The town is on the main north–south coastal highway between Mangalore and Goa, a 5-hour bus ride from Mangalore. Several services run daily.

Where to Stay

Bhatkal is not a tourist town, and has only the most basic (meaning dirty) lodges. A selection of these are clustered near the bus stand. They are very cheap at about Rs35 per room, but you will not want to spend more than one night in them.

Gokarn

Getting Around

Gokarn is 6–7 hours by **bus** from Mangalore and there are several daily services. Direct buses also go up to Margao in Goa (via Palolem), a 4–5 hour journey, and to Hubli, 4 hours over the mountains, from where an express connection can be made for Hospet and the ruins at Hampi (another 4 hours). Margao and Hubli services run several times daily.

Gokarn is a jewel—an unspoilt town of old Keralan-style houses with wooden-slatted balconies rising to several stories. The streets radiate out from an ancient sanskrit school and college for brahmins. There are several medieval temples, and two huge temple cars stand in the main street, which is lined with stalls selling religious accoutrements for trainee priests—images of gods, incense holders, brass bells, pestle and mortars and holy pictures. The brahmins, heads shaven but for the top-knot that signifies their office, bustle to and fro in white lungis, caste cords lying diagonally across their bare chests. The young brahmins are wiry, underfed and obsequious; their seniors often quite obscenly fat. All are full of quiet disdain for scruffy Westerner backpackers.

Despite the architectural beauty of the town, it is Gokarn's wonderful scimitar-shaped **beaches** that most attracts the traveller. You should allow at least a week to enjoy them properly; once you have made the trip over the rocky path down to the sea, you will discover sublime tranquility, and you will not want to get back on a loud, sweaty bus for some time.

Gokarn's Beaches

Avoid Gokarn's town beach (except for a walk when you first arrive) and check into one of the lodges for the night. Take the small alley that leads away between small houses to the left of the big temple car shed as you walk down from the bus stand. The alley soon emerges from the houses and becomes a path that snakes uphill over black and pink volcanic rocks to **Kudle Beach**, the closest piece of paradise to the town. This walk takes about half an hour and should be done at early morning or evening, before or after the main heat of the day. You can leave the bulk of your gear under lock and key at one of the lodges in Gokarn and just take the bare necessities over to the beaches (the first two beaches also have safe places to leave clothes and money). If the sun does get too hot on your walk, you can stop halfway at a small *chai*-shop, appropriately called the **Halfway House**, and drink sodas in the shade until the sun loses its ferocity.

Kudle Beach is, like all the beaches of Gokarn, a long, curved strip of white and gold sand set between two forested headlands. A strip of paddies and coconut palms occupies a narrow flat strip inland from the beach. After this the ground rises steeply to the first foothills of the Western Ghats, which tumble almost to the sea on this part of the Malabar Coast. Because Kudle Beach is the closest to town, it is the most 'developed', but this only means it has three timber-and-thatch tea-houses serving food and drink. For next-to-nothing, these places will rent you a palm-thatch or *adobe* hut to stash your gear in while you swim in the warm, lapping ocean, drink *chai*, eat fish or *thalis*, and sleep on the beach by night.

A half-hour's walk on from Kudle, over the headland, is **Om Beach**. Smaller than Kudle, the water here is calmer and offers some of Gokarn's best swimming. Tranquil, and a good place to see dolphins, the beach gets its name not from stoned hippies chanting on its sands, but from the locals, who say that its shape resembles that of the sacred Om if seen from the hills above. The beach has one tea-house serving food, but no organized place to stay. A couple of palm-thatch beach shelters serve as wind-breaks if you want to sleep here. The locals are prone to stealing anything left unguarded, however, so keep your valuables within sight at all times.

One more half-hour walk southward over the next headland takes you to **Half-Moon Beach**. Here there is not a single tea-house, and it makes a great place to camp. But food and water are problems: there is no natural spring as at Kudle and Om, and so you'll have to go back to Om for your sustenance unless you have the foresight to bring your own supplies.

A final half-hour's southward hike over a last wooded headland and you are on **Paradise Beach**, so called for its near-inaccessibility and complete peace—nothing but the sea, the sky, the sand and you. Unfortunately, there is no freshwater supply here either, but this does not stop people from hiking in and losing themselves for weeks.

One word of warning: recently reports of night-time muggings have come in from people staying out at Half-Moon and Paradise Beaches. The classic scenario seems to be local toughs either demanding money from women walking alone on one of the headlands, or attacking lone travellers and couples sleeping on the beach. The best way to avoid this is to get together with some others when sleeping. If this is not possible, head back to Kudle or Om before dark, where there will always be a few other travellers, and sleep there.

Where to Stay

Gokarn Town ✆ (08386–)

Gokarn's most expensive hotel, **Om Lodge**, ✆ 4644/4645/46244, is not the best place to stay, but it has the most modern-style rooms (some with air-conditioning). It tends to fill up with large groups of Indian tourists come to worship at the town's temples and its food is not of the highest standard. Rooms are clean, however (inexpensive).

Gokarn has several very cheap guest lodges, all clustered together about half a mile from the bus stand on the main street. Walk up the way the bus is pointing, then turn left at the T-junction and keep walking for about 3 minutes and you will come to a few lodges. However, only one warrants recommendation, the **Vaibhav Nivas Lodge**, ✆ 46289 (cheap) set back a little from the road. Run by a family of Brahmins, this has double rooms with shower and (Indian) toilet attached, or cheaper ones with shared bathrooms. The lodge occupies an old Karnatik house, and there are pet birds (and two white rats) in cages, reasonable food, and beer for sale. The Vaibhav will look after your belongings for Rs5 per day while you are at the beaches.

Beaches

The only place resembling an organized lodge is the *chai*-shop at the foot of the head-land path as it comes down to Kudle beach. Here you can eat and rent a secure *adobe* hut (with padlock) to sleep in or stash your rucksacks. There is a 'shower' consisting of a hose attached to the local freshwater spring. If this place is full, which is unlikely, the owners will point you to one or two other places on the beach where you can sleep and leave your gear, but in slightly less secure palm-thatch huts.

On the other beaches, you have to camp in the open.

Eating Out

Gokarn Town

You can eat at the cheap restaurant in the **Om Lodge** and drink beer with the local drunks. To do the same, but with other travellers, try the **Vaibhav Nivas Lodge** (*see* above). On the same road as the cheap lodges you can find some very good, cheap *thali*-houses.

Beaches

Kudle Beach has two places to eat: a sort of guest lodge at the foot of the headland path leading back to town, which serves indifferent *thalis* and fish, or the really good but unnamed restaurant set among some kept gardens just back from the centre of the beach, and owned by a Spanish lady who came to stay for a while and ended up marrying a local. Her restaurant serves home-made garlicky pasta (oh joy!) and fish. She also has a charming dalmation dog. Prices are very cheap.

At Om Beach, there is another *chai*-shop serving *thalis*, *parathas* and some Western food (cheese on toast, omelettes, etc). Again, prices are very cheap.

Ankola

North of Gokarn, the coast road winds on for about 20 miles to another small town, also known for superb beaches. **Ankola** is less interesting as a town than Gokarn, but its ruined 15th-century Vijayanagar fort is worth seeing and on the main street stand two massive temple chariots housed in a kind of wooden hangar.

There are a few bottom-end lodges in Ankola, all pretty awful. Most visitors prefer to camp by the beach for a couple of days before moving on. Take food and water.

Karwar

Karwar lies north of Ankola, just before the Goan border. An ugly town, it is larger than both Gokarn and Ankola and has useful facilities such as banks—all the long-stay travellers from

Gokarn come up here to change money. You can find quiet, little-used beaches 20 minutes' walk from town; not quite as picturesque as those at Gokarn, but then there are fewer travellers and, as yet, no facilities beyond *chai*-shops, so you have to camp.

The town has several cheap lodges where you can leave your belongings before heading for the beaches. Try the **Anand Bhavan,** which has doubles for under Rs100 with attached bucket bathroom and Indian toilet. If the Anand is full, the **Hotel Ashok,** by the bus station, or the **Govardhan** are good value and reasonably clean, but you will need a mosquito net.

Connections to Goa

North of Karwar, the road continues for another 20 miles before crossing the border into Goa. Buses run directly from Karwar up to Palolem, Margao and Panjim.

Karnataka's Mountains

Then Kala Nag reached the crest of the ascent and stopped for a minute, and Little Toomai could see the tops of the trees lying all speckled and furry under the moonlight for miles and miles, and the blue-white mist over the river in the hollow. Toomai leaned forward and looked, and he felt that the forest was awake below him—awake and alive and crowded. A big brown fruit-eating bat brushed past his ear; a porcupine's quills rattled in the thicket; and in the darkness between the tree stems he heard a hog-bear digging hard in the moist, warm earth, and snuffing as it digged.

Rudyard Kipling, *Toomai of the Elephants*

Karnataka's mountains are the wildest and least touristy in the whole of south India. While they lack the tribal diversity of Kerala and Tamil Nadu, the forests are far less disturbed and the plentiful wildlife can move more freely through the different climatic zones.

Karnataka encompasses both western and eastern zones of the Western Ghats: unlike Kerala, whose mountain territory extends for the most part only up the western slopes on the Western Ghats, and Tamil Nadu, whose mountain territory mostly comprises the eastern slopes. Thus in Karnataka you can visit both the deciduous dry forest (east side) and evergreen rainforest (west side) without leaving the state, and often staying inside the same reserved forest area or wildlife sanctuary.

The same game species occur in Karnataka as in the rest of the south: elephant, *gaur* (bison), tiger, leopard, sloth bear, *dhole* (wild dog), striped hyena, *sambar* and *chital* (spotted deer), muntjac (barking) deer, wild boar and monkeys such as Nilgiri, lion-tailed and common *langur* and bonnet macaque are fairly common. There are also some north Indian mammals in the state, including the tiny four-horned antelope in the evergreen forests, blackbuck antelope on the dry (Deccan Plateau) side of the mountains, and wolf in some parts of the hills that run east–west below Mysore and Bangalore.

For **wildlife viewing,** try to make sure you spend a few days in **Nagarhole National Park** in the south of the Coorg region, inland from Mangalore. Further north, the **Bhadra Wildlife Sanctuary** in Shimoga district gives access to deep, deep forest and is convenient for the spectacular **Jog Falls** and its surrounding spray-forest, near the mountain town of Sagar. In the far north, the vast dry-forest sanctuary of **Rannebennur**, near Dharwad, has few visitors, and you are likely to have the whole place to yourself.

Another scarcely-visited region is the Biligiri range that runs along Karnataka's southern border with Tamil Nadu, and which connects the Western Ghats with the Eastern Ghats of Andhra Pradesh. There are several big sanctuaries which have been declared in this region: **Biligiri Wildlife Sanctuary**, south of Mysore, the **Cauvery Wildlife Sanctuary** east of Mandya, and the **Bannerghatta National Park**, just south of Bangalore.

The only reserve to *avoid* if you are short of time is Bandipur, in the far south, which gets mass tourism and therefore has shyer game.

For **trekking**, many of the wildlife sanctuaries have huts and will supply guides where appropriate (details listed in the following section). No mountain walker should miss the **Coorg District**, where hiking trails run from paddy fields and lowland jungle up through coffee plantations shaded by indigenous jungle trees and finally through wild forest onto high ridges of natural grassland. You sleep and eat in forest temples and have to finish walking before the elephants come out at dusk.

Bandipur National Park

Bandipur is part of what is now called the Nilgiri Biosphere—a vast conserved wild area that includes Mudumalai National Park in Tamil Nadu, Wynad in Kerala and Nagarhole and Bandipur in Karnataka. The southernmost nature reserve in Karnataka, Bandipur is also one of its largest. Alas, it is also the most crowded, being within easy reach of Mysore. There are direct **bus** services connecting Bandipur's entrance office with Mysore, running roughly every hour between 7.30am and 3.30pm.

While there is no trekking, there is good game viewing from *machans* (raised platforms) hidden near some water holes. Unfortunately these get booked up far in advance so for most visitors game viewing is limited to big, rattling government vehicles (some jeeps, some minibuses) on a few shortish roads, and to even shorter elephant rides near the main office.

As most of the wildlife stays in the 'core' region of the park, where tourists are not allowed, serious wildlifers will find the place a bit frustrating, knowing that there are rare species like tiger, leopard and sloth bear in the forest. If you get lucky and see anything other than spotted deer, distant bison or perhaps elephant, the animal will quickly run away as the occupants of your vehicle shout and exclaim excitedly.

If you do visit Bandipur, do so between November and February, after the rains and before the hot season. In the summer (February–August), the deciduous forest (mainly teak, rosewood, and silk-cotton) loses its leaves. Most of the game then migrates over to the eastern slopes of the Western Ghats. You will certainly need a few days to have any chance of spotting something, so it is worth booking accommodation inside the park, if it's not full.

Where to Stay
inexpensive/cheap

Bandipur has cheap dormitory accommodation near the park office at the main reception area, as well as several slightly more expensive lodges and cottages. If you can, book the one called **Venuvihar Lodge** up in the Gopalaswamy Hills, deep in the forest. It is hard to get accommodation in Bandipur and it must all be booked in advance, either directly through the Field Director of Project Tiger, Mysore, ✆ 20901, or through a travel agency specializing in wildlife areas. Try **Clipper Holidays** in Bangalore, ✆ (080) 5599032/34. Avoid visiting at weekends if you want to be sure of getting somewhere to stay in the park.

Nagarhole National Park

To the west of Bandipur, wild forest reaches up into the foothills of the Western Ghats. It follows the course of the Nagarhole ('snake-river') into the higher country via a large dam whose shore makes for good game viewing in the dry season (February to August).

Getting There

Those wanting to stay at the luxury-priced Kabini River Lodge (*see* p.142) in the south have to go by **private car** (2 hours) or **bus** (3 hours) to Karapur, 3 miles from the southern entrance to the park. The rest of us enter at the northern gate via the town of Munsur, 3 hours by **bus** from Mysore, or 6 hours from Bangalore.

Another Project Tiger Reserve, Nagarhole is less visited than Bandipur, and thus offers a better chance of seeing big cats, especially if you are prepared to fork out for the exclusive Kabini River Lodge near the south of the park, which sends its guests into the forest in jeeps of no more than five people accompanied by a trained naturalist. You can also take an elephant ride and a short excursion onto the sanctuary's huge dam by coracle—a traditional round boat made of tarred leather which is indigenous to the region. Budget travellers have to stay in the north of the park and take government vehicles for their game drives. However, even in these noisier vehicles, the chances of game-spotting are better than at Bandipur, because of the comparative lack of tourists.

It is also possible to arrange accompanied **trekking** in Nagarhole, despite the presence of dangerous game, but you have to apply at least a month in advance to ensure a place. If you do go to the trouble, ask to be guided into one of the forest's Kurumba tribal settlements. This tribe, completely hunter-gatherer until the 1960s, still retains a 'primitive' culture in that they live by collecting forest fruits and roots (also honey), and worship forest deities rather than a strictly Hindu pantheon.

Although the Nagarhole forest trees lose their leaves during the dry season, the sanctuary's closer proximity to the moist forests of the high Ghats and its thick stands of bamboo provide sufficient food for most of the game to remain in the forest year-round. The dry season can therefore be a good time to visit, as the animals congregate on the banks of the big dam, morning and evening, to drink. As the water level drops, so the strip of exposed shoreline increases, creating a no-cover zone in where game-spotting is easy. Large herds of elephant are often seen at this time, as well as tiger, leopard, sloth bear and *dhole* (wild dog).

Where to Stay
luxury

The state-run **Kabini River Lodge** (book via Karnataka Jungle Lodges in Bangalore, ✆ (080) 5587195/5597021/5, or ✆ 558 6163, occupies what used to be the Maharajah of Mysore's old hunting lodge just outside the village of Hunsur in southern Nagarhole. Although overpriced, the facilities are excellent. Kabini's rooms and cottages are built by the huge dam that runs into the forest itself, and there is interesting wildlife inside the compound; white paradise flycatchers are a speciality. There is a colony of several hundred fruit bats (flying foxes) living in one of the big trees. Kabini is run by a hunter-turned-conservationist, now in his eighties, who runs the whole place with military precision and great concern for the wildlife. Best of all are the twice-daily game drives in small quiet jeeps that give a good chance of spotting rare game, and the presence of trained naturalists who know the trees and plants.

inexpensive

If you cannot afford Kabini, the northern section of the park has two lodges, **Gangotri Lodge** and **Cauvery**, pleasant old forest resthouses with 2 bedrooms and a cook. As with Bandipur, accommodation here can be booked long in advance, so allow a month before you go. Apply directly to the Wildlife Office, Aranya Bhavan, Mysore, ✆ (0821) 21159, or indirectly (but with better results) through **Clipper Holidays** in Bangalore, ✆ (080) 5599032/34.

Elephants at Nagarhole

The Coorg Region

We woke to an Irish morning; thin, drifting cloud was draped over Mercara's mountains and the air felt cool and moist. 'A fine soft day, thank God!'

Dervla Murphy, *On a Shoestring to Coorg*

Centred around the small market town of **Madikeri**, north of Nagarhole, this semi-wild region of coffee plantations, montane forest, paddies and lowland jungle is one of the most beautiful in India. Away from the region's few roads, the only way to travel is on foot—along old sunken lanes between towering trees, crossing wooden stiles into open paddies and pastures, and finally heading up through coffee and cardamom into the mountain forest. Wilderness and rural landscape blend effortlessly. There are very few tourists, and the locals (prosperous descendants of the original *Coorgi* or *Kodagu* tribespeople), though friendly, have their own language and distance themselves from the rest of Karnataka.

The hills of Coorg are also a pilgrimage destination for Hindus all over southern India: the sacred Cauvery River, known as the Ganges of the South, rises in Coorg before flowing down across the broad plains of Tamil Nadu and watering the large temple towns there. A small mountain temple has been built around the Cauvery's source and pilgrims trek or take buses up the steep mountain road to bathe in the tank and wash away their sins.

History

The Coorgis have never been conquered. Their mountain region has always been remote and is still largely inaccessible during the monsoons. But from the early medieval period the little kingdom of Coorg began to prosper from the salt trade that came through its mountains from the Kerala coast to the great cities of the Deccan Plateau. Coorg's relative wealth attracted several would-be invaders including the Vijayanagars and the late medieval Deccan sultanates but the fierce mountain tribesmen repulsed all of them.

The Coorgis have always been great lovers of freedom—orthodox Hinduism only took over from the indigenous animist cults in the early 18th century, and the caste system never penetrated to the hills. Even the kings, though Hindus, deferred to a council of ministers and were much more accountable than was usual for Maharajahs.

In their desire to keep their freedom, the Coorgis even beat off invasions from Hyder Ali and his son, Tipu Sultan—the great Muslim warlords who conquered almost the entire southern

third of India in the 18th century. Even these all but invincible warrior-sultans found it impossible to campaign among Coorg's tactically valuable mountain routes to the coast. The Rajahs of Coorg and the local headmen deliberately kept the hill country devoid of roads, allowing only the narrowest of jungle trails between settlements, thus making the uplands impregnable against anyone unfamiliar with the territory.

However, this security eventually resulted in the late 18th-century and early 19th-century rajahs becoming corrupt, petty despots, who finally alienated their freedom-loving people. During the reign of King Chikaveera Rajendra in the 1830s, Coorg suddenly relinquished its long-coveted independence—giving it up voluntarily to the British!

The conditions that brought this about were complex but resulted in one of the most unusual and romantic episodes of south Indian 19th-century history.

King Chikaveera Rajendra (better known by his shortened name of Veeraraja) had inherited a predilection for sexual perversity from his father. But where the Coorgis had tolerated the old man, who only used poor girls, often bringing them in from outside the state, Veeraraja began to abduct high-ranking Coorgi women and flouted them openly in front of the queen, who was popular with the public and pitied by the ministers.

Veeraraja was also suicidally profligate with the state treasury and his rapacious spending on luxuries threatened to ruin the merchants of Madikeri, who supplied goods and lent money to the palace. By the time Veeraraja had been on the throne a few years, he had plunged the proud, cohesive little state into a turmoil of insolvency, political instability and moral outrage. Veeraraja became paranoid about assassination. He imprisoned his sister, keeping her as a hostage against her husband, whom he thought might attempt a usurpation, and began to order summary excecutions of anyone who defied him or showed displeasure—usually by impaling or crucifixion, leaving the condemned to be eaten alive by vultures.

The king had one great ally in his criminal rule, his chief minister Basava, who had risen from the palace kennels under the old king's reign to public office by befriending the young king while they were adolescents. Basava, crippled in one leg, was unpopular with the more noble ministers for his low birth and his devotion to the delinquent king. One minister in particular, the aristocratic Bopana, publicly began to accuse Basava of exerting a corrupting influence over the king.

The other ministers and the merchants of Coorg wanted to depose Veeraraja and elect Bopana as the new king, but he refused, saying this would be dishonourable. The ministers then began writing in secret to the British Resident of neighbouring Mysore state, which had been annexed a few years before on the pretext of removing a similarly abusive raja. The ministers and the British had to bide their time until Veeraraja performed some outrage so awful that even the Coorgi people would not mind seeing a foreign force come in and liberate them from their oppressor.

Meanwhile, other forces began to play for the throne: Veeraraja's old satyric father had sired several other sons by his mistresses, most of which he had put to death or sent out of the kingdom as babies. Rumours began to circulate that such a son had returned and was biding his time in the Madikeri Bazaar, plotting a coup. At the same time, an old woman priest took up residence in an abandoned temple in the forest near Madikeri and began proclaiming that Veeraraja was not, in fact, the legitimate ruler and that a son of the old king would come and claim the throne.

Such was the public desire for a usurpation that even the cripple Basava tried to persuade the king, bloated and weakened with alcohol and venereal disease, to moderate his behaviour, and rode out in secret to the woman priest to beg her to stop her proclamations, lest civil war overtake the state. To the surprise of Basava and his guard, as soon as he entered the temple, the old priestess threw her arms around him and kissed him.

Meanwhile, Bopana and the other ministers had suggested to the British governor at Madras that he send an ultimatum to the king demanding that he release his sister from her unlawful imprisonment. Veeraraja persistently refused, and the British waited for an excuse to invade. It did not take long. One night, in a drunken rage, Veeraraja killed his sister's baby son and would have killed his sister too had he not been restrained by Basava and the queen. When news of this had been circulated, Bopana and the other ministers finally felt it safe to invite the British in.

A small force of redcoats arrived on the frontier and were met as allies by the usually fierce Kodagu border guards, who escorted the British soldiers to Madikeri. The raja and Basava fled to the small royal summer palace in the foothills of the Western Ghats, where after an afternoon-long siege, they surrendered. But as the king and the chief minister were led out, Veeraraja suddenly rounded on Basava, unjustly accused him of treachery, pulled a pistol from his robes and shot the minister dead.

When Basava's death became known, the old priestess came in from the forest and produced documents proving that she had been a palace woman seduced by Veeraraja's father, and had had a son by him, but that once the old king had tired of her, he had taken up with another concubine, and sired a son by her. This new woman had apparently demanded that the old king make her son the heir and he, in a fit of cruelty, drove out his former lover after having seized her infant son, broken his leg, so as to make the child a cripple, and sent him down to live among the servants. This cripple was the same Basava who had become Veeraraja' confidant and ally. Veeraraja himself had been the son of the second concubine. Thus, he had murdered his brother, who all the time had been the rightful heir.

The British declared Coorg to be a protected state of the empire and asked the Coorgis to choose a governor from among their own people. The council of ministers elected Bopana, the minister who had openly defied both Basava and the king, and when this was cried around the kingdom, none of the headmen and nobles raised any objection. From 1834 onwards, Bopana and after him his descendants, administered Coorg. In return for their co-operation, the British allowed the state to retain a nominal independence. The rule of the Raj was thus never directly applied in Coorg and even today the place has a separatist movement and a cultural flavour distinct from the rest of Karnataka, the Coorgis having never been conquered, even by the British.

Getting Around

Regular **bus** services (several daily) run from Mysore (3–4 hours) and Bangalore (6 hours) every 30 minutes. The most painless way to go is to take one of the overnight express buses from either city, which leave around midnight and arrive just before dawn.

Several daily services also run to Mangalore (6 hours) and twice-weekly services run to Madurai and Ooty in Tamil Nadu. There are plans to run more services to these towns, so it is worth asking at the bus station.

Tourist Information

The **Karnataka Tourism Office** is on Munnar Road and has a small guesthouse attached which is usually full. You can get information on trekking here, but only of the sketchiest nature. The office is more efficient for booking bus tickets and finding out about local festivals in the hill temples. The **post office** is behind the bus station, and you can find **foreign exchange** at the **Bank of India** on College Road or **Canara Bank** on Main Road.

The old capital of Coorg is a small market town set among cool hills. Although it has some hand-some old buildings, modern Madikeri (also confusingly known as Mercara) is rather run-down and should be used only as a jumping-off point for exploring the region's beautiful countryside.

There are no museums here but it is worth stopping at the **Omkareshwara Temple**, a comparatively modern edifice (built 1820) dedicated to Siva and Vishnu and constructed in the old Keralan carved wooden style. Above the town is the old **fortress** of the kings of Coorg where the turbulent events surrounding the reign of the last king Veeraraja, took place in the 1830s. It is quite an impressive stronghold, made of solid stone, with posterns and barbicans guarding the entrance.

The stone elephants flanking the steps into the royal residence were put there after Veeraraja had had both his favourite palace elephants and their *mahouts* put to death after he had been awakened one night by trumpeting from the elephant stables. He was said to have later regretted the loss of such valuable animals.

The Coorgi Rajas are buried just north of town (take a rickshaw and don't pay more than Rs20) where you can see the old tyrant Veeraraja's stone monument. He died in exile in Britain but his remains were shipped home to Coorg.

Madikeri comes alive every Friday, when the Coorgis from the hills come to the **market** near the bus station. It's a good place to buy really good, cheap coffee and cashews, as well as wild spices.

Madikeri ✆ (08272–)

Where to Stay

moderate

The modern **Coorg International**, ✆ 27390, a mile uphill from the bus stand, offers the standard comfort and service of a well-run expensive hotel. The owner knows the local trekking routes very well and the restaurant serves good local dishes such as pork curry and rice *paratha*. For more traditional accommodation try the **Capitol Village**, a small resort about 4 miles from town (Rs40–50 by auto-rickshaw) built in the old Keralan carved wooden style. The resort is in fact an old estate house, and the coffee, cardamom and spice plantation is open for guests to wander in. You have to book via Hotel Cauvery in Madikeri, ✆ 26292.

inexpensive/cheap

The **Hotel Cauvery**, on School Road, ✆ 26292, the **Coorg Side** on Daswal Road, ✆ 26789 and the **East End** on Thimaya Road, ✆ 26496 all offer clean, basic comfort within a mile of the bus station. All also have good, cheap vegetarian food.

On the hills above town, known as Rajah's Seat, is the state-run **Mayura Valley View**, ✆ 26387. It's worth trying to get a room here, as the views out over the hill forests are superb and the rooms are well kept and clean.

In all the above hotels, you may be able to bargain a cheaper rate, as Madikeri seldom overflows with tourists.

The Coorg Hill Country

Forest temples that shelter wayfarers, elephants feeding among coffee plantations, high meadows where half-wild cattle fall prey to tigers by night, clean water in the *sholas* (woodlands) and the plaintive cry of hawks wheeling on the wind below the peaks. This is one of the south's best **trekking** areas.

Getting Around

Although local **buses** run out to many of the villages from which you can begin trekking, these are very slow and crowded. By far the most convenient way to travel is to hire a local phenomenon known as a **jeep taxi** (all taxis in the region have to be 4-wheel-drive to cope with the tough hill roads). Prices for these correspond with taxis elsewhere (about Rs6 per mile), and you can generally find someone to share with you and split the cost. Go to one of the lodges listed above to call a jeep taxi.

For the few **excursions** local to Madikeri (*see* below), a bus or rickshaw will do.

Short Excursions from Madikeri

The 40-minute rickshaw ride out to **Abbi Falls** (Rs80–90 return trip) is a pleasant drive through a countryside of paddies, eucalyptus plantations and coffee shaded by tall forest trees. The falls themselves have been spoilt by graffiti painted on the rocks and dumped garbage. More interesting, and on the way to the trekking routes, is the temple at **Bhagamandala** (25 miles by bus or jeep from Madikeri), where the Cauvery, Kanike and Suiyothi Rivers join, although all three are mere streams at this point. A path lined by beggars leads down to the bathing *ghat*, where pilgrims wash away their sins, from the main road outside the temple. The temple itself is a handsome example of Keralan

red-tile and carved wood building. From Bhagamandala, the road climbs a further 6 miles up into the steep ghats to the **Cauvery Source Temple**, another pilgrim site, with steps set into the high hill behind, which rewards the climber with sweeping views of the Coorg ranges.

You should spend no more than an afternoon on these day trips, as Coorg's real beauty lies in its wilder mountain reaches.

Trekking in the Coorg Hills

The best place to base yourself from is the old ruined summer palace of the Coorgi kings, known as **Malkavad Palace**—the very place where the last king surrendered to the British in 1834, after shooting dead his chief minister Basava, whom he wrongly believed had betrayed him to the redcoats. A small place with a central courtyard and temple, the old palace sits below the house where the minister Bopana lived (Bopana was the minister who opposed the old tyrant king openly and who ruled for the British after the monarch's fall—*see* pp.144–5), and where his descendants live still, their houses approached by a garden path lined with old cannon balls. The family takes care of the palace and charges a small fee to those staying there.

From the palace you can take **guided day treks** up into the hills; whether to climb the 5700 foot **Tadiandamole peak** behind, or to trek via forest and rice fields to the temple of **Igutappa Padi** (another old red-tile and carved-wood affair) for lunch. You can make this second hike an overnight one by then trekking up and over a high ridge, the **Igutappa Kundu,** which reaches 5400 feet, then down through jungle and coffee plantations to the **Igutappa Nelgi Temple.** About 250 years old, this temple is dedicated to Siva and will shelter and feed trekkers. From here you either hike back to the palace the following day or take a local bus or jeep (by prior arrangement at the palace) via the village of Kakhabe. A night spent in this old temple courtyard under the clear stars, surrounded by the sounds of the forest, will be one of the most magical of your stay in India.

Other guided treks available from the palace are into the montane rainforest, good for seeing elephant and possibly sloth bear, from Talacauvery to Mundrotu (3–4 days) and up to the mountain village of Srimangala to the Iruppu temple (2–3 days), another forest temple set under a 40 foot high waterfall. Legend has it that the cleft through which the water springs was punctured by an arrow shot by Lakshmana, brother to Rama, after Rama and his wife Sita had begged the archer to quench their thirst while journeying through the mountains.

A much wilder trek into the vast forest of the **Mookamika Wildlife Sanctuary** (3–4 days) requires government permission, but it's worth the effort. You stand a good chance of seeing elephant, sloth bear, perhaps a tiger and certainly spotted deer (*chital*). Applications should be made via an agent (*see* below).

Arranging Treks in Coorg

As always, the problem facing the would-be trekker in southern India is the lack of maps and the need for a local guide. Although you can find both by journeying to the Nalaknadu Palace guesthouse by bus from Madikeri and talking with the owner, it is less risky to book it all before you go. Treks can cost as little as Rs150 per person per day, including food and guide, if you take your own sleeping sheet and are prepared to rough it on the temple/palace floors. If you need more comfort, the prices go up, but not extortionately. You can book through

Clipper Holidays, Suite 406, Regency Enclave, 4 Magrath Road, Bangalore 560 025, ✆ (080) 5599032/34, who cater for low or high budget travellers, and have the necessary experience to process applications for entry into wild areas. Otherwise accommodation is scarce. The house above the palace now operates as a **guest lodge**.

The Shimoga Region

North of Coorg the Western Ghats become even less accessible, except via a few wildlife sanctuaries near the foothill towns of **Shimoga** (175 miles northwest of Bangalore by bus/train via Hassan and Belur) and **Sagar** (50 miles futher west of Shimoga).

Near Shimoga, the vast **Bhadra Sanctuary** comprises a moist deciduous forest set around the Bhadra reservoir. All the big game species can be found here, and forest resthouses are available for stays of several days. You may be able to organize trekking with the chief conservator, but the usual way to get around the sanctuary is by jeeps driven by a forest guide. You pick these up at the small village of Muthodi, 12 miles by bus from Shimoga, or from the station at Tarikere (8 miles).

The Karnataka government was planning to set up **elephant safaris** of several days into the forests at Bhadra for 1996, moving between permanent tented camps, with excellent opportunities for game viewing and photography.

Reserve your accommodation, at Bhadra in advance via the Deputy Conservator of Forests: Wildlife Preservation, Jayanagar 1st Cross, Shimoga, ✆ 2983, or through the main **Karnataka Tourism Office**, Bangalore, ✆ (080) 5585917, on Church Street.

Also in the Shimoga area are **Shettihalli Wildlife Sanctuary** and **Sharavathi Wildlife Sanctuary**. Again, these forests harbour the full range of south Indian jungle wildlife, including all the big species. For accommodation, both sanctuaries have four resthouses open to **trekkers**, reserve in advance through Wildlife Preservation in Shimoga, ✆ 2983, or the tourist office in Bangalore, ✆ 558 5917.

Access for Shettihalli is easy, being only 2 miles from Shimoga. Sharavathi is a bit more difficult, a full day's bus journey through the twisting mountain roads from Shimoga to Sagar and then by local bus to the small town of Kagal, from where you can walk to the sanctuary's entrance office.

Jog Falls

The magnificent **Jog Falls** and their surrounding spray forests are 20 miles west of Sagar, and can be reached by either train or bus from Shimoga in the mountains or Karwar and Honavar on the coast.

Situated at the western end of the 30-mile long Hirehasgar reservoir on the Sharavathi River, the actual fall of water at Jog is now controlled by a large hydro-electrical plant, which opens the locks for the falls only on the second Sunday of the month, so that the rest of the time the four sets of falls are only running at a small percentage of its natural volume. However, they are a spectacular sight at any time—the longest actual fall being about 850 feet.

Walking through the forest to the viewpoints can be unpleasant, despite the scenery, because of leeches. Although these usually disappear from the forests of the Western Ghats during the dry season (November–May), the spray around Jog Falls makes it nicely moist for them all year. Wear a long shirt and trousers and carry a box of matches to burn off any leeches that get through your defences.

Accommodation at Jog Falls is quite easy to secure and should cost less than Rs100 per room per night. The cleanest and best-run places are the **Inspection Bungalows**—there are two of them, one at the falls and one at the small hydro-company village nearby. The only problem with these is that they are often full of government officials. Try the **Jog Falls Guest House** or **Tunga Tourist Home** if you have no luck at the bungalows. Also, several unofficial, rather basic guesthouses have opened near the falls.

Trekking Around Jog Falls

It is possible to go trekking into various **tribal regions** in the forest near Jog Falls. Apply for information either at the Inspection Bungalows or in Bangalore, at the main Karnataka Tourist Office on Church Street, ℂ 5585917.

The railway ends at Jog Falls but the road continues over the mountains to the coast at Honavar.

Rannebennur National Park

North again of the Shimoga/Sagar district is the huge **Rannebennur Wildlife Sanctuary**, near the town of Rannibennur, is 200 miles (8 hours) northwest of Bangalore and is accessible by direct train or bus services from the city. This sanctuary lies in the scrubby eastern foothills

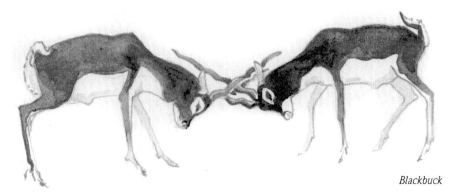

Blackbuck

of the Western Ghats (dry deciduous forest) and spills down onto the arid Deccan Plateau. Because of this, its wildlife includes some semi-desert and grassland animals as well as forest species (though no tiger or elephant), notably blackbuck antelope and wolf. Dry-country birds occur here too: look out for sandgrouse, hoopoes, vultures and the great Indian bustard. Crocodiles swim in the river that runs through the sanctuary and there are some large stretches of open ground, good for game viewing. Unlike the mountains, which are inaccessible from May to October because of the monsoons, Rannebennur can be visited all year (though after May it is blisteringly hot). The reserve has two **resthouses** and you can book them on site at the entrance office via the Range Forest Officer.

Dandeli and the Far North

Back in the higher mountains again, and even further north along the Bangalore–Belgaum rail and highway, is **Dandeli Wildlife Sanctuary**, 100 miles west of the Deccan town of Dharwad and reached by local bus from the town of Dandeli. Another tiger reserve, Dandeli has sloth bear, leopard, elephant, *dhole*, *sambar*, muntjac and spotted deer, *gaur* and various *langur* monkeys. The occasional wolf also passes through. Accommodation is in six resthouses and jeeps with forest guides can be hired from the entrance office. Make advance reservations via the Government of India Tourist Office, 48 Church Street, Bangalore, ✆ 579517.

North of Dandeli, the Western Ghats, though wild, have no more sanctuaries or trekking sites until you cross the western border into Goa or the northern border into the Maharashtra mountains. However, heading back to the far south of Karnataka again you come to a range of hills that juts eastward from the coastal ghats at Bandipur Wildlife Sanctuary and marches across to the Eastern Ghats of Andhra Pradesh.

The Biligiri Hills

The forests of this range are drier than those of the Western Ghats. They harbour the same range of game species, and for **trekkers** there is a far longer season, because the hills remain accessible during and immediately after the monsoons. Where the fast-flowing Cauvery River runs through them, the Biligiris have several large wildlife sanctuaries with opportunities for **game-fishing**, **canoeing** and **white-water rafting**. Travellers can choose between the most basic trekking, sleeping in forest resthouses or shelling out for luxury tented safari camps.

B.R.T. Wildlife Sanctuary and Surrounding Forests

The first sanctuary east of Bandipur, where the Biligiris begin, is the **Biligiri Rangaswamy Temple Wildife Sanctuary** (B.R.T. Sanctuary), 75 miles southeast of Mysore. It has all the of southern Indian game species, both big and small and you can arrange guided trekking from B.R.T., with accommodation in 2 forest resthouses, through the ACF Wildlife Preservation, Mysore, ✆ 21159. Access is by bus, via the town of Chamarajanagar.

In the reserved (protected) forest just east of B.R.T. Sanctuary is the state-run luxury **Karnataka Jungle Lodges Tented Camp**, a champagne safari camp in the African tradition. Guest are taken on game drives into the forest morning and evening, whether in jeeps or on elephant back. Prices are very high, at around US$100 per person per night (all inclusive) for foreigners but if you can afford it the tented camp guarantees a more comfortable forest stay than the regular resthouses. Food is good (Western and Indian) and the game drives accompanied by naturalists offer a better chance of sighting animals than you could expect from trekking in the regular sanctuary. Book via Karnataka Jungle Lodges, Bangalore, ℰ (080) 5587195 or 559 7021/5

Cauvery Fishing Camp

Slightly closer to Mysore (55 miles), in the Biligiri foothills is the Cauvery Fishing Camp, another state-run luxury lodge that caters almost exclusively for game fishermen seeking to catch the mighty *mahseer*, a game fish that some anglers rate higher than salmon for fighting ability and difficulty to hook. The weather conditions have to be just right, with high water and a certain amount of humidity in the air before these huge fish (30lbs is not uncommon) will take the lure. The camp supplies gillies, food, permits and the fishing beats, but guests bring their own tackle. Once caught, the *mahseer* are weighed, photographed and released. Book through Karnataka Jungle Lodges, Bangalore, ℰ (080) 5686163/5597021/5.

The Cauvery River also has **canoeing** and **white-water rafting** trips that leave from Sriringapatnam near Mysore and end up at the fishing camp (*see* 'Activities', p.172).

Mekadatu and Goat's Leap Falls

If you have a car, it's worth making a day trip about 3 miles north of the fishing camp, to the point where the Arkavati River joins the Cauvery. A Wildlife Department resthouse has been built here, and its lawns make a good spot to take a picnic. After eating, take the footpath along the southern bank of the Cauvery for about ½ mile to **Mekadatu**, where the Cauvery roars through a short, narrow gorge. The word 'Mekadatu' means 'goat's leap' and the place is so named because at one point the lips of the gorge are sufficiently close for a goat to leap across (though it looks too wide for a human).

Those interested in Indian history will find it rewarding to drive on to the village of **Malvalli**, the battlefield where the British finally defeated the ferocious Deccan warlord Tipu Sultan in 1799, forcing him to retreat back to his walled city of Sriringapatnam , on the banks of the Cauvery just north of Mysore (*see* p.172). About 7 miles on from Malvalli are a beautiful set of waterfalls, known as **Sivasamudram**, which cascade down a drop of 350 feet.

Cauvery Wildlife Sanctuary

Further towards Bangalore, at the eastern end of the Biligiris, is the Cauvery Wildlife Sanctuary. Like the B.R.T. sanctuary, Cauvery comprises thick stands of dry deciduous forest—mostly teak and rosewood, with some sandalwood. Elephant are quite common here, as are sloth bear, leopard, wild boar and all the deer species. Forest resthouses are available, as are guided **trekking** routes. Book in advance via the chief Wildlife Warden, Aranya Bhavan, Bangalore, ℰ 341993. Access is by bus or car from Bangalore via the town of Mandya, a total distance of about 40 miles.

Sloth bear

'Herding in India is one of the laziest things in the world....The sun makes the rocks dance in the heat, and the herd children...sleep and wake and sleep again, and weave little baskets of dried grass and put grasshoppers in them; or catch two praying mantises and make them fight...or watch a lizard basking on a rock, or a snake hunting a frog near the wallows...and perhaps they make a mud castle with mud figures of men and horses and buffaloes, and put reeds in the men's hands and pretend they are kings and the figures their armies, or gods to be worshipped...

Rudyard Kipling, *The Jungle Book*

East of the mountains stretches southern India's central plain, a wide semi-arid plateau of yellow grass, dry-stone walls, low thorn trees and arable fields of broken earth, red from the plough. An almost Mediterranean landscape, the Deccan's ochres and reds betray a long dry season, but not a land beset by drought. After the August rains, all turns a vivid sparkling green and the dry river beds run with brown water. Indeed, some parts of the Deccan, particularly around Mysore and Bangalore, stay green all year, a patchwork of paddies and palms with occasional high outcrops of bare rock, often topped by a medieval fortress.

In the 16th and 17th centuries this dry but fertile land fell to ferocious invading Mughal armies, who smashed the decadent kingdom of the Hindu Vijayanagar kings and sacked their fabulous temple city at Hampi. The Muslim invaders carved new sultanates from the ruins. Today, many of these castles and walled towns still stand—strongholds that have survived three centuries of warfare between rival sultans. The British conquered the Deccan's two greatest warlords, Hyder Ali and his son Tipu Sultan in the late 18th century and restored the southern plains to the old Hindu princes. But the greater part of the warlike Deccan was wisely left to govern itself under the Raj.

Despite its succession of aggressively Muslim rulers, most of the rural Deccan Plateau stayed Hindu: the ancient, and often magnificent temple complexes that still dot the landscape were largely left alone. Many of these were built on old megalithic sites and you can sometimes see dolmens and menhirs from the Neolithic era standing close to the medieval temples, showing a continuity of worship that has lasted for thousands of years. Travelling across the Deccan, you also see rural life at its most timeless, the women standing in front of their thatched huts winnowing grain by hand, like prospectors looking for gold. Round and round a central pole walk the oxen, their hooves crushing the grain from the wheat, from the rice and from the barley.

By contrast with this age-old rural cycle, Karnataka's Deccan cities have developed into the most sophisticated and liberal in southern India. Mysore is one of the handsomest towns in the country, with wide avenues radiating from its sumptuous palace and progressive university. In bustling Bangalore, the silicon industry has taken off with a vengeance and the 5 million or so inhabitants have embraced Western culture, spawning a nightlife of pubs and dance clubs where Indian women may actually be seen out for the night—without men.

Bangalore

Capital of Karnataka state, Bangalore is fairly clean—at least by Indian standards—and is a spacious, well-planned city. It has beautiful parks, some magnificent Raj buildings and long boulevards now sadly choked with traffic. One of Asia's fastest-growing cities, it has now lost many of the trees, private gardens and quaint bungalows that gained it the soubriquet 'Garden City of India'. But despite this it still remains the nation's tidiest and greenest capital. A busy commercial and cosmopolitan centre, Bangalore is rapidly advancing towards Nehru's vision of it as India's 'City of the Future', yet retains its old summer-resort charm and sophistication. It is an ideal base from which to discover the south of India.

This 'town of boiled beans' (the derivation of its name) began as a small mud fort, built in 1537 by a feudal chieftain called Kempe Gowda (1513–69). He predicted a great future for his new town, and built four watchtowers at four elevated points around it to demarcate what he envisaged to be its future boundaries. These have now been far exceeded. The small fort was ruled by various dynasties over successive centuries, before being enlarged and rebuilt in stone by Hyder Ali in the late 18th century. Significant improvements to the new structure were made by his son, Tipu Sultan. The arrival of the British (1809) spelt further changes, and a spacious cantonment town, with parks and gardens, museums and churches, Gothic bungalows and colleges sprang up. Encouraged by the enlightened Maharajahs of Mysore, Bangalore swiftly became a leading educational and industrial centre and eventually replaced Mysore as the state capital.

Now, Bangalore is a city of the '90s. Many hi-tech industries have been developed here; India's huge computer software industry operates from Bangalore, jet fighters and helicopters for the air force are made here and some of the country's largest garment exporters have made the city their manufacturing base. Yet, 'beautiful Bangalore' still has a wealth of colourful vegetation; notably its two lungs of Cubbon Park and Lal Bagh, and is one of India's most physically attractive cities. And despite the crowds, there's a refreshing sense of space. Bangalore's inhabitants have an air of orderly sophistication about them—a well-educated, invariably polite people, who even form queues outside cinemas. And Bangalore has an awful lot of cinemas.

Climate and When to Go

Situated on a high, cool plateau above the plains, Bangalore has an all-year tourist season but is most pleasant in **October to November** and **February to May**. To see the gardens, parks and flowers at their best, come in **January** or **August**.

Getting There
by air

International travellers can now fly to Bangalore from London Heathrow, changing planes at Bombay but not going through immigration until they reach Bangalore—a great bonus as it cuts out the long queues at Bombay airport. For domestic travellers, **Indian Airlines**, **Modiluft**, **Jet** and **EastWest** all offer daily flights between Bangalore and Bombay, Calcutta, Cochin, Coimbatore, Delhi, Goa, Hyderabad, Madras, Pune, and Trichy. There are less frequent flights to centres like Madurai and

Trivandrum. Bangalore airport is 8 miles from the city centre and is connected by taxi or auto-rickshaw (approx Rs50).

by train

There are several trains daily to and from Madras (6–7 hours) and to Mysore (about 3 hours). From Madras the two best trains are the *Brindhavan Express* and *Bangalore Mail* from Madras Central Station (7 hours). The *Hyderabad Express* leaves Bangalore at 5.15pm daily, arriving Hyderabad around 8am the next day. The *Hampi Express* leaves at 9.40pm daily, getting in to Hospet at around 6am the following morning. The *Bangalore–Trivandrum Express* leaves daily at 6.15pm (journey time 18 hours) and the fast *Karnataka Express* goes daily (journey time 38 hours) to Delhi. At the time of writing, a faster *Shatabdi Express* was due between Delhi and Bangalore and it is worth asking at the station or tourist office whether it has opened for business. There are various express trains to Bombay (24–27 hours), some of them requiring a change of train at Miraj. The station is on Bhashyam Road.

by bus

Bangalore's efficient central bus station, directly opposite the city rail station, offers superb connections to Mysore (express buses every 15 minutes from 6am to 9.30pm; 3½ hours), to Madras (many departures throughout the day; 9 hours), to Bombay, via Belgaum (buses at 8am and 2pm; 24 hours), to Ernakulam and to Hospet (plus two buses direct to Hampi; journey time 8–9 hours). There's also at least one bus daily to Ootacamund/Ooty and to Panjim in Goa.

Tourist Information

KSTDC Tourist Office, 10/4 Kasturba Road, opposite the Aquarium, ℂ 221 2901/2/3, gives information in slow motion (essential to visit with precise questions) but is generally helpful. It's open daily from 10am to 5.30pm, except Sunday. A second KSTDC office, on the 1st Floor, F Block Cauvery Bhavan on K.G. Road, ℂ 221 5489, sells the useful Bangalore city tour (7.30am–1.30pm, 2–7.30pm daily), the comprehensive day tour to Mysore, Sriringapatnam and Brindhavan (7.15am–10.45pm daily), and the over-ambitious tour out to the famous temple spots of Belur and Halebid (7.15am–10.30pm daily). To find out anything about **trekking** and **wildlife** in Karnataka, go to the **Government of India Tourist Office** in the K.F.C. Building on Church Street (1st Floor), ℂ 558 5417.

If you would like to book any of the prestigious state-run jungle lodges in Nagarhole National Park, Biligiri Temple Wildlife Sanctuary or Cauvery Fishing Camp, contact **Jungle Lodges and Resorts** in the Shrungar Shopping Centre, M.G. Road, ℂ 5586163/559 7021/5.

The **post office** is at Vidhana Vidhi (but the *poste restante* is at the old G.P.O. by Bangalore International Hotel, Crescent Road), while **foreign exchange** can be had at the **State Bank of India** on St Mark's Road, or **Thomas Cook** on M.G. Road near the junction with Brigade Road. The **Indian Airlines** office is at M.G. Road (ℂ 2211211/ 2211914, airport, 566233) and Cauvery Bhavan complex, District Office Road (ℂ 572605).

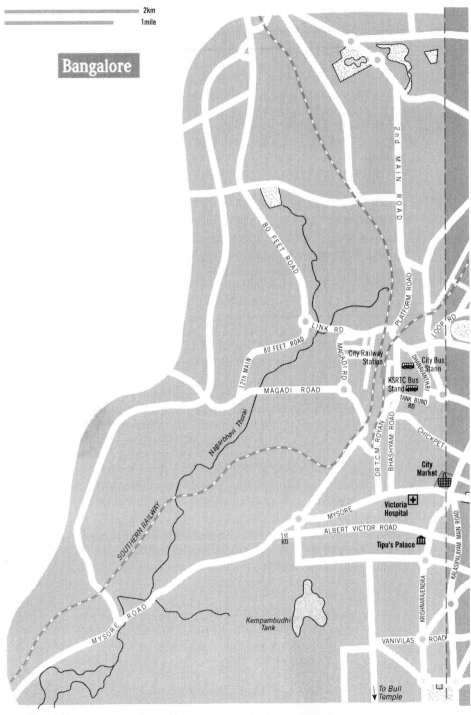

Bangalore

2km
1mile

2nd MAIN ROAD

80 FEET ROAD

PLATFORM ROAD

LOOP RD

LINK RD

80 FEET ROAD

12th MAIN

MAGADI RD

City Railway
Station

City Bus
Stann

DHANWANTHRI

KSRTC Bus
Stand

TANK BUND
RD

MAGADI ROAD

Nagarbhavi Thorai

DR T.C.M. ROYAN

BHASHYAM ROAD

CHICKPET

City
Market

SOUTHERN RAILWAY

MYSORE

Victoria
Hospital

ALBERT VICTOR ROAD

1st
RD

Tipu's Palace

KALASIPALAYAM MAIN ROAD

KRISHNARAJENDRA

MYSORE ROAD

Kempambudhi
Tank

VANIVILAS ROAD

To Bull
Temple

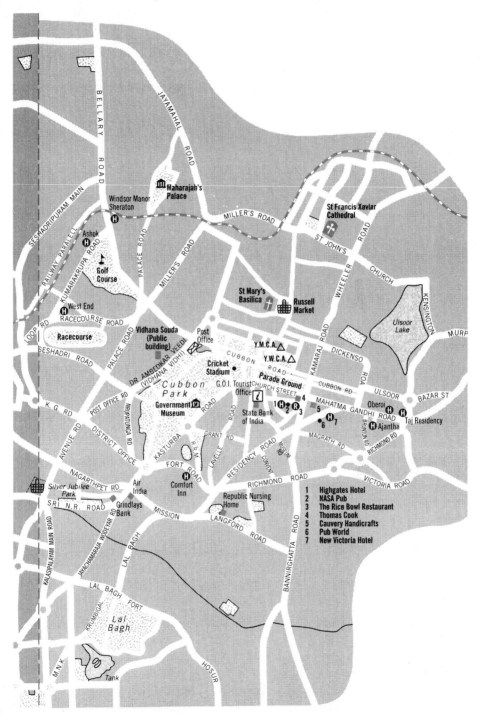

Maharajah's Palace

Windsor Manor
Sheraton

St Francis Xaviar
Cathedral

Ashok

Golf
Course

St Mary's
Basilica

Russell
Market

West End

RACECOURSE ROAD

Ulsoor
Lake

Racecourse

Vidhana Souda
(Public
building)

Post
Office

Y.M.C.A.

Y.W.C.A.

SESHADRI ROAD

CUBBON

Cricket
Stadium

Parade Ground

Cubbon
Park

G.O.I. Tourist
Office

CHURCH STREET

CUBBON RD

ULSOOR

BAZAR ST

K. G. RD

Government
Museum

State Bank
of India

MAHATMA GANDHI ROAD

Oberoi

Taj Residency

Ajantha

MAGRATH RD

Silver Jubilee
Park

Air
India

Comfort
Inn

Republic Nursing
Home

1   Highgates Hotel
2   NASA Pub
3   The Rice Bowl Restaurant
4   Thomas Cook
5   Cauvery Handicrafts
6   Pub World
7   New Victoria Hotel

Grindlays
Bank

Lal
Bagh

Tank

157

If you have any health problems, Bangalore's private **hospitals** are among the best in India and well within most people's budget (for example, an operation to remove glass from the author's infected hand cost Rs350 in 1995). Best is the **Mallya Hospital**, ✆ 2217979 on Vittal Mallya Road. The Mallya used to be called the Apollo Hospital, and some rickshaw drivers still know it by the old name. If the Mallya cannot deal with you, try the **Republic Nursing Home**, ✆ 2213310, on Longford Gardens near Richmond Circle. Women with gynaecological problems should ring Dr Shetty's private clinic (Dr Shetty is a woman), ✆ 3342233.

The City

Because Bangalore has few sights of its own, and these widely dispersed, travellers tend to spend just a couple of days here, resting up and cooling off before heading off to other destinations. But if there are few museums and monuments in the city itself, there are some marvellous ones within easy reach. A number of good tours run out to Hampi and Ooty, to Belur/Halebid, to Bandipur Tiger Reserve and Nagarhole National Park or the wildlife sanctuaries of the Biligiris and (best of all) to Mysore, Sriringapatnam and Brindhavan Gardens.

For orientation in Bangalore itself, use taxis or auto-rickshaws. The latter are about Rs5 per mile—though you might have to insist that they use the meter. If the driver refuses, just push down the meter yourself: once it's ticking he's bound to take you. Trying to get around on foot is a disheartening experience: this is a big city, with very long roads, few of them well-signposted and many of them with broken pavements that can be difficult to negotiate. All the interesting spots are miles away from each other. The 'budget' sector, with the cheaper hotels and restaurants, is around the bus and railway stations on the east of town, and is perhaps the easiest area in which to acclimatize to the busy city. The best time for independent sightseeing is the afternoon, when Bangalore goes into siesta. For a quick, comprehensive overview of the city take a conducted tour. Follow this with a day of shopping (excellent here) or discover the beautiful parks. Out-of-town excursions are optional extras.

Bangalore City Tour

by sightseeing bus, half day

Government Museum/Art Gallery–Tipu Sultan's Palace–
Bull Temple–Lal Bagh–Ulsoor Lake–Vidanha Vidhi–Vidhana Souda

A short tour of the palatial buildings round Cubbon Park brings you to the three museums in **Jayachamarajendra Park**. Best of these is **Government Museum**, one of the oldest museums in India (established 1866). It has 18 sections, housing fine collections of miniatures, inscriptions, coins and sculptures recovered from the Neolithic-period Chandraval excavation. The **Venkatappa Art Gallery** (*open daily, 10–5 except Wed*), forms one wing of this museum, and has well-presented exhibitions of water colours, plaster-of-Paris sculptures, bronze antiquities and various contemporary works of art (by the famous artist Venkatappa and other court painters). There are regular modern art exhibitions on the third floor. The adjoining **Technological Museum** is generally unexciting. Just down the road, opposite Queen Victoria's statue, is the **Aquarium** (*open daily, 10–7.30 except Mon*), not covered by the tour, but worth returning to. South of town (½ mile from City Market), you'll visit **Kempe Gowda Fort**, Hyder Ali's stone stronghold built in 1761 on the site of the original mud fort. While the fort interior is closed to the public, you can enter the first two courtyards and pass through an impressive gateway. The exterior view of the lovely 16th-century **Ganpati Temple** within the walls merely whets the appetite. Much more satisfying is **Tipu Sultan's Palace** (*open daily, 8–6*), started by Hyder Ali in 1781, completed by Tipu in 1789. One of three summer palaces built by the two Mysore rulers, it is (like the others) made entirely of wood, except for the internal pillar-supports. Within are gloriously painted walls, ceilings, balconies and soaring pillars of green, red, black and gold; also elaborate arches, surrounded by minarets and family paintings. The palace here has a small museum, illustrating the life and times of Tipu Sultan, who presented the British with their most stubborn resistance in the south.

Near the palace you'll see the **Venkataramanaswamy Temple**, built by the Wodeyars in the 17th century. An attractive example of Dravidian-style architecture, it was restored for the use of the Wodeyar kings who recovered their throne after Tipu's death in 1799.

From the palace, it's a one-mile drive south to the **Bull Temple** up on Bugle Hill. Here you'll find the fourth-largest Nandi bull in India, made of black granite and measuring 20 feet across by 15 feet high (6.3 metres by 4.6 metres). Credited with miraculous 'growing' power, the Nandi is chiefly notable for being so much larger than its 'master', Shiva. You'll find Shiva's tiny image in the small temple at the foot of the hill. Also here is the strange **Ganesh Temple**, with its large elephant made of 240lbs of strong-smelling butter. Donated by wealthy devotees, the butter is broken up every four years and distributed to pilgrims. Local philanthropists are then 'buttered up' to donate a fresh coating.

The beautiful botanical gardens of **Lal Bagh**, 1¼ miles southeast of the City Market, were laid out by Hyder Ali in 1760, and substantially added to by Tipu Sultan. Smaller than Cubbon Park (*see* p.160), they are in every way superior—240 acres of trees and plants (1000 tropical and sub-tropical varieties, many of them rare), 19th-century pavilions and lamps, landscaped gardens and avenues, fountains and flower-beds, even an elegant glasshouse modelled on London's Crystal Palace! The best time to see the dahlias, marigolds, and rose gardens as well as many other varieties of flowers here is either January or August. Just up from the entrance, overlooked by Kempe Gowda's statue, is the flower-bordered **Lawn Clock** (completed 1983), accurate to three seconds each month. Just right

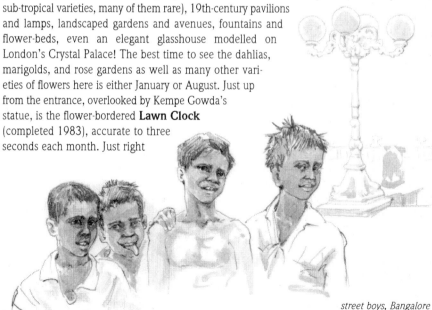

street boys, Bangalore

of this is the area where visiting dignitaries/state leaders are invited to 'dedicate a tree' (in olden days, they had expensive monuments erected to them, now they get a shrub).

Ulsoor Lake last stop of the day, is on the eastern edge of town two miles from the bus station. A pleasant boating lake with white-headed brahmini kites wheeling on the air above, wooded islands and rose-pink water lilies. It has a small **Boat Club** (*open daily, 9.30–5.30*), with rowing boats for hire at Rs30 per hour and a peaceful set of lawns called Kensington Gardens.

Around sunset, take an enjoyable promenade down **Vidhana Vidhi** (Bangalore's finest avenue) and admire its attractive selection of Greco-colonial style buildings. Start with the palatial post office (India's grandest) and walk down the tree-lined boulevard to **Attara Kacheri** ('18 Courts'), the stately red-brick structure housing the High Court. Recently saved from development and now restored to its original splendour.

Opposite this is the magnificent post-Independence **Vidhana Souda**, housing the Secretariat and the Legislature. Built in 1954, this four-storey ornamental structure of solid granite was designed in the neo-Dravidian style.

Apparently the building was conceived following the visit of a Russian delegation to the city in the 1950s. As the Indian officials were proudly showing off Bangalore's old government buildings, one of the leading members of the Russian group remarked that this was all very well, but that the buildings the citizens were the most proud of had been built by the British, and were no more than legacies of outdated imperial oppression. Why were there no grand Indian public buildings, asked the Russian? Embarrassed to the core, the Bangaloreans immediately set about remedying the situation, with the result that the grand Secretariat and Legislature were built just a couple of years folllowing the Russians' departure. It is notable for its soaring columns, charming frescoes and excellent carvings. Visitors are only allowed inside between 3.30 and 5.30pm, and must get permission from the public relations officer in the entrance lobby.

If you're around on a Sunday evening, between 7 and 9pm, you can see Vidhana Souda beautifully illuminated. Just down the road, at the bottom of Vidhana Vidhi, **Cubbon Park** has nightly illuminations and features a popular 'Fairy Fountain'.

Sports and Activities
riding

Bangalore's **Amateur Rider's Club** (*open daily except Monday*) is at the racecourse in the centre of town. Admission is Rs170, and you buy a coupon book for Rs250 which entitles you to 10 rides. The club has some well schooled Rajasthani horses (the ones with the crescent-shaped ears) and various thoroughbreds retired from the track. You can either hack out around the racecourse or school for dressage or jumping. Riding times are early morning and evening. Rides are for half an hour.

horse racing

There are regular meetings at Bangalore's beautiful racecourse in the centre of town (November–March, mid-April–July).

Coarse fishing is allowed at Hesaraghatta Lake or Chamarjasagar Reservoir (enquire at the tourist office). If you are a game fisherman, you can go after the mighty *mahseer* at the exclusive Cauvery River Camp 60 miles to the south (*see* p.152). For all places you need your own tackle.

golf

There is an 18-hole course in the city centre (nearby Windsor Manor or West End hotels arrange games for visitors).

Shopping

Next to Madras, Bangalore is the prime shopping centre of the south. It is famous for its fine silk, particularly traditional Mysore silk *saris*. Other good buys include rosewood, sandalwood, lacquerware, *bidri*ware and wooden-inlay items.

general crafts

A good place to see the range is the **Cottage Industries Emporium** on Mahatma Gandhi (M.G.) Road, alternatively the **Cauvery Arts & Crafts Emporium**, 26 M.G. Road. The latter is particularly good for hand-crafted rosewood furniture and sandalwood carvings. Prices tend to be just a little above normal in these shops, though.

silks

For quality silks, try **Janardhana Silk House**, located in the main general shopping complex of **Unity Buildings**, Jaya Chamaraja Road. For cheaper silks and textiles and amazing atmosphere, there's the **City Market** in Chickpet, or the big shopping centre in M.G. Road.

jewellery

The best gold and silver jewellery shops are on Commercial Street.

bookshops

Higginbotham's bookshop on M.G. Road and inside the rail station, does a good range of city/state guidebooks. Another bookshop on M.G. Road is **Gangarams** who have the widest selection of both books and magazines.

kitsch

Bangalore is home to one of the world's kitschest shops, inexplicably called **Big Kid's Kemp**. A budget-style department store at the far end of M.G. Road (opposite the Taj Residency), it sells everything from *saris* to radio-controlled aeroplanes and stays open until late at night. There is nearly always some kind of cheesy promotion stunt going on outside the front doors, usually people in cartoon animal suits dancing to Michael Jackson tunes. Above them a huge neon sign announces that 'You Are A Star Customer'.

Bangalore has hotels belonging to all India's major chains. The oldest hotel in Bangalore, the Taj Group's magnificent **West End Hotel** in Racecourse Road, ✆ 2269281, ✉ 2200010, is set amid 20 sweeping acres of landscaped gardens, splendid trees and bird life. Rooms prices vary depending on their layout and location. Welcomgroup's **Windsor Manor**, 25 Sankey Road, ✆ 2269898/2296322, ✉ 2264941, is a first-rate hotel, with exquisite decor, immaculate service, nice restaurants, and well-furnished rooms and old-fashioned courtesy. The **Taj Residency**, 14 M.G. Road, ✆ 5584444, ✉ 5844748, caters more to business than to general travellers, but has a good pool, a gym and a decent, if overpriced, Chinese restaurant. The new **Oberoi Hotel**, M.G. Road, ✆ 5585858, ✉ 5585860, opened in August 1992 and has very expensive rooms, superb gardens surrounding a pool and outside restaurant. The mosquitoes can be bad in the gardens though. The **Ashok Hotel**, High Grounds, ✆ 226 9462, ✉ 226 0033, is the cheapest within the luxury range.

expensive

Perhaps the best value of any hotel in India is the Taj Group's **Gateway Hotel on Residency Road**, 66 Residency Road, ✆ 5544545, ✉ 5544030, a luxury-style hotel that falls within the expensive category, but offers the same comfort as the more expensive hotels. The **Comfort Inn Ramanashree**, 16 Raja Ram Mohun Roy Road, ✆ 223 5250, ✉ 221214, has very comfortable rooms and includes breakfast in the tariff.

moderate

A little run-down, but cheaper and with much more atmosphere than the expensive hotels is the late-19th century **Victoria Hotel** at 47 Residency Road, ✆ 5584077/5585028, ✉ 5584945, whose rooms still have their old (but basic) hardwood fittings. Built around a courtyard restaurant and bar with famously inefficient service, the Victoria is walled off from the crazy crowds and traffic of Residency Road, and is something of a quiet haven. Another travellers' favourite is the **Highlands** at 33 Church Street, ✆ 5589989, ✉ 260174. Much more modern than the Victoria with some air-conditioned rooms, this hotel offers efficient, friendly service. If you don't mind being above a shop, try the **Nilgiris Nest** at 171 Brigade Road, ✆ 588401. This a very comfortable hotel with big rooms for the price.

The **Cauvery Continental**, 11/37 Cunningham Road, ✆ 2266966, is a favourite spot for Sai Baba devotees, with cosy rooms and a cheap vegetarian restaurant ('Executive Lunch—limited *thali*' for Rs50).

inexpensive

Budget hotels are mainly in the city market area. **Hotel Luciya International**, 6 O.T.C. Road, ✆ 224148, has a popular restaurant, tourist bus service and smart rooms. The **Hotel Ajantha**, ✆ 558432, further into the town centre on M.G. Road (in fact it's opposite the Oberoi but down a side street marked by a big sign) offers basic but clean and comfortable rooms with good room service and a cheap vegetarian, restaurant. The **Hotel Geo** on Devganga Hostel Road (near Richmond Circle),

$\mathcal{C}$ 2221583, is not quite such good value, charging slightly inflated prices for nothing special. But the surrounding neighbourhood is one of Bangalore's friendliest and it is fun to wander around after dark, taking in a cheap meal or a fresh fruit juice from one of the street kiosks. The **Hotel Gautam** on Museum Road, $\mathcal{C}$ 557461, offers similar rates as the Geo, but in a more central location.

cheap

The cheap-rate accommodation in Bangalore is heavily over subscribed, and you may be forced to take a hotel in a more expensive price range than you wanted, just to find a room. It really is worth trying to book cheap and inexpensive hotels a few days in advance rather than on arrival. Try **Sudha Lodge**, 6 Cottonpet Main Road, $\mathcal{C}$ 660 5420, with a central situation, good information, hot and cold running water, and clean rooms. It's a great meeting-place but often full. The next-door **Hari Priya** restaurant does the cheapest Indian breakfast (Rs6 for *masala dosa* and coffee). **Sudarshan Hotel**, near the bus station, $\mathcal{C}$ 72702, is a friendly place with cheap rooms. The **Tourist Hotel** on Racecourse Road has many rooms but is often packed out with local tourists. You could try the **Jarnardhana** instead, $\mathcal{C}$ 2264444, near the railway station (Kumara Krupa High Grounds), but be aware that this is also likely to be full.

Eating Out

Food in Bangalore is excellent and it is one of the few cities, Bombay is another, where there is a wide range of cuisine available outside major hotels. In order to compete, the hotels themselves have good restaurants.

Indian

Among the Indian restaurants, the **Coconut Grove** on Church Street, and the **Karavati** at the Gateway Hotel both serve excellent Malabar, Konkan and Coorg food from Rs100 per head. The **Windsor Manor Hotel** has the best northwest frontier food. A traditional Keralan restaurant, set in an old 1930s Raj Art Deco building, is **Koshy's Restaurant** on St Mark's Road, $\mathcal{C}$ 221 3793, where you can go for either a beer and a snack (Rs35–50) or a full meal (Rs50–75). Cheaper Indian restauarants include the excellent **Ullas Refreshment Rooms** on M.G. Road—a 1st floor restaurant in a modern complex with an outdoor terrace serving *chaat* and vegetarian dishes for about Rs20 each; the **Chalukma** vegetarian restaurant on Racecourse Road, near the West End Hotel and the **Plantain Leaf Brigades** on Church Street (serving traditional *thalis*), also with individual dishes at Rs20–35.

continental

For continental food there are excellent non-hotel restaurants, for example the exclusive **Prince's Restaurant**, 9 Brigade Road, $\mathcal{C}$ 558 0087 (it's wise to book), with amazing steaks, popular Indian food (around Rs100 per head), lovely décor, great service, and attached 'Knock Out Disco' (free to restaurant customers Tuesday to Thursday, otherwise Rs125 per couple). The **Peacock** in Residency Road has top-notch Indian/Western cuisine at Rs150-plus per head); **MTR Restaurant**, by the main entrance of Lal Bagh, has a famous bar and a solid reputation for good mid-bracket food (roughly Rs75–150 per head). It's open from 7 to 11am and from 4 to 7pm.

Chinese

For Chinese food, try the **Rice Bowl**, 215 Brigade Road or **Memories of China** in the Taj Residency Hotel where a meal would cost Rs150. The **Paradise Island** at the West End Hotel serves Thai food and a multi-cuisine buffet at lunch time for Rs135 per head.

light meals

Most restaurants in Bangalore serve draft beer and there are numerous pub lunches throughout the city. Tasty snacks for under Rs50 are served at **Excel Restaurant** in Tank Bund Road, behind the bus station. This place also has a well-stocked bar, and lots of 'local' character. On Gandhi Nagar in Kempe Gowda, travellers favour **Hotel Blue Star** (opposite Tribhuvan cinema) for its 'well-experienced cook' and tasty chicken dishes at around Rs45–60. Nearby **Sukhsagar Food Complex** (opposite Majestic Theatre) has Gujarati/Punjabi food on the 3rd floor, south Indian meals on the 1st floor, and mouthwatering ice creams, sweets and juices on the ground floor (average price around Rs50 per head).

Finally, there's **Chit-Chat** on M.G. Road, one of the ritziest ice cream parlours in India. It has chandeliers, musical fountains, and toffee-nosed waiters who won't serve you unless you sit on the ground-floor and look very rich. More friendly is **Baskin-Robbins American Ice Cream** on Residency Road near the junction with Brigade Road. Expect to spend between Rs60 and 120 in either place.

A useful general listing for the towns services and entertainment is *Bangalore This Fortnight*, available from most hotels and bookshops.

Bangalore is one of the few Indian cities with any real claim to nightlife. **Pubs** (with real beer on tap) in particular, have really taken off in recent years and the city centre seems to crawl, or rather stagger, with them. The most friendly is definitely **Pub World** on Residency Road which, despite terrible piped music (Bryan Adams a speciality), is a good place to meet and chat with locals. Amusing for its décor is the **Nasa** on Church Street, done up inside to resemble a space-ship. The **Downtown Pub** (also on Residency Road almost opposite Pub World) has three full-size snooker tables. The **Guzzler's Inn** on Brigade Road is a more low-key place where people relax after work.

The only place to really *avoid* is **Black Cadillac** on Residency Road (further towards the train/bus station than Pub World or Downtown). Black Cadillac has pretensions to be a sharp cocktail bar, but this only means more expensive drinks and surly staff. New pubs are opening up all the time, so it is also worth just following your nose and going into whatever looks good. Licensing hours are as ridiculous as in Britain—pubs close at 11pm. A regular draught beer is normally about Rs15.

Bangalore also has a number of places for **dancing**, usually to a mixture of bhangra, raga, hip-hop and old disco. Young couples dressed in Western designer gear gaze intently at each other and gyrate pelvises longingly. Some clubs, like the **Underground** pub's dance floor, have overpriced admission charges (Rs250–350 per person), while others are far more reasonable at around Rs50–150. Try the **Blue Fox** club on M.G. Road, **Time and Again** on Brigade Road or **19 Church Street**, just off Brigade Road.

Otherwise try one of the 100 or so **cinemas** here; Bangalore is a film-making capital. A few theatres along M.G. and Brigade Roads show recent English-speaking releases, though these are usually pretty terrible films that died quickly in the West, and are shown for their bare breast and violence content.

Cultural entertainments are best in March and April, when regular shows of Karnataka dance and music are held at **Chowdiah Memorial Hall**, Sankey Road and **Bharatiya Vidya Bhavan**. For details of current programmes and events (there's something going on most evenings), buy a *Deccan Herald* or *Indian Express* newspaper. The cultural shows held at **State Youth Centre**, Nrupathunga Road, are supposed to be especially good.

Bangalore has something of a **music scene** and it's worth keeping an eye out for band posters around town. Concert venues often turn out to be in big hotels, which are short on atmosphere but it is fun to see how Bangalore rocks, even if there is no biting off of bat's heads, on-stage nudity nor drug-crazed guitar-smashing. Bands that were big at the time of writing included Warden (heavy metal), Millennium (also heavy metal) and Pulse (funky fusion of raga and rock).

If you get sick of the smog and noise of Bangalore, head out to **Bannerghatta National Park**, a short 15-mile bus ride southeast of town. Around the sanctuary's entrance office is a safari-park, or open-style zoo (*open daily, 9–12noon, 2–5, except Tues*) with Asiatic lion, tiger, elephant, *gaur* (bison) and a few other indigenous species. Beyond the park, you enter a wild forest that's home to a small elephant herd, *chital*, wild boar and a few shy leopard. The bird-watching is good; colourful species such as bee-eaters, tree pies, green parakeets and hoopoes are common, and you may spot *coucal* (crow-pheasant) and crested or serpent eagles in the high canopy. There are jeeps driven by guides.

The **Nandi Hills** jut suddenly from the Deccan Plateau about 35 miles north of Bangalore. The small massif of just over 3000 feet commands wide views of the surrounding plains and it is not surprising that both Hyder Ali and Tipu Sultan used them to protect the northern boundaries of their Deccan kingdom. The main stronghold was at **Nandidurg**, now a minor hill station for day-trippers from Bangalore during the summer hot weather. The ruins of Tipu Sultan's massive fortifications still stand on the west side of Nandidurg, and there is a small Hindu temple (approximately 10th century AD). Accommodation is at the state-run **Mayura Pine Top**, ✆ (08156) 8624, a well-run comfortable but basic place with rooms for around Rs200 per night. Around Nandidurg are a number of short hikes that cling to the cliff-sides and scrub woodland of the massif, with some superb viewpoints out over the plateau. Buses run up to Nandidurg from Bangalore every few hours. Nandidurg is 50 miles from the city on the road north to Puttaparthi, a 3 hour ride.

Kokrebellur Bird Sanctuary is about 60 miles west of Bangalore between Channapatna and Maddur on the Mysore road. One of the Deccan Plateau's occasional marshlands, this sanctuary comprises riverine and swamp woodland and is a good place for seeing pelicans and painted storks. There is no accommodation, but you can make the trip there and back in a day from Bangalore, with several bus services daily.

A little kitsch, but interesting nonetheless is the **Nrityagram Dance Village**, a strange concept stuck out in the countryside 20 miles from Bangalore. Designed by a French architect as a school and performance centre for various forms of Indian Classical dance, the village won an award for its design. Conducted tours are offered with rather glib explanations of the philosophy and culture but on the other hand the tours include some absolutely beautiful displays of classical dance, and include a vegetarian lunch made from produce grown in the village. A day's tour is quite expensive (about Rs300 per head), but rewarding for those genuinely interested in dance. Contact **Clipper Holidays**, ✆/✉ 5599032/34/5599833 to book.

Mysore

The golden age of maharajahs and princes may be over but Mysore remains a splendid city of palatial buildings, beautiful gardens and handsome, tree-lined boulevards. There are 17 palaces here in all, and even the most common public buildings are adorned with domes, turrets, pavilions and vaulted archways. Many of the buildings are now in disrepair, and Mysore may have a noisy crowded centre like any other, but it nevertheless retains something of its old charm. There is a stately atmosphere to the town: the Maharajah still lives in a wing of the city's main palace and still keeps elephants, camels and horses in his stables. The university campus, founded by the British and built in grand Indo-Saracenic style sprawls elegantly over its lawns, even if the lawns are now yellowed and ill-kempt and the buildings in need of some paint. Mysore's fame as the 'Sandalwood City' of the south remains undiminished—both carving and reducing the chippings to oil is a major industry here, the trees coming from the dense forests to the south and west. A major centre for the manufacture of incense, the air in its markets and bazaars is fragrant and sweet with the perfume of musk and jasmine, sandalwood and rose.

Mysore derives its name from *Mahishasura*, the demon who wreaked havoc among the people in this area until destroyed by the goddess Chamunda, who seems to have liked the place, for it was the only state in the Deccan Plateau that managed to stay Hindu for almost all of its history. By the high Middle Ages, *Mahishuru*, town of Mahishasura, had become 'Mysore', the cradle of many great dynasties in the south. During the rule of the Hoysalas, from the 12th to 14th centuries, art and architecture came to their peak resulting in the five famous sculptured temples of nearby Halebid, Belur and Somnathpur. Then, later in the 14th century, Mysore became the permanent capital of the Wodeyar Maharajahs. They lost it just once; to Hyder Ali in 1759 but regained it from the British after the death of Ali's son, Tipu Sultan, in 1799. Under the protection of the Raj, the Maharajahs had nothing left to fear and went into palace-building in a big way. Yet the coming of Independence in 1947 spelt the end of their power and of their many opulent palaces, the finest, Amber Vilas, was turned into a museum, another into an art gallery, and three more into luxury hotels. The tourist revenue coming in from these establishments is sufficient to guarantee the present Maharajah just as rich a lifestyle as that of his predecessors.

Climate and When to Go

Like Bangalore, Mysore is at a fairly high altitude (2500 feet, 770 metres), giving it a pleasant climate throughout the year. It is most most temperate from **September to January**, but travellers drift in right up to May. The best two months are **September** and **October** when the city is a post-monsoon spectacle of lush greenery and the 10-day festival of **Dussehra** takes place. This is the spectacular 'Festival of Nine Lights', when many of the top musicians, dancers, and artists of Karnataka state turn up to give exhibitions and shows. It's best to arrive on the last (10th) day of the festivities, when a victory procession of caparisoned elephants, jingling cavalry and (real) gold and silver coaches, accompanied by bands, floats and parading soldiers (all supplied by the present Maharajah), celebrate Chamundi's defeat of Mahishasura. Throughout **October**, the Maharajah's Palace is illuminated nightly.

Getting Around
by train

Mysore has regular services to Bangalore (6–7 daily, 3½ hours), to Goa (one train daily, changing at Londa Junction—from here, rather than wait many hours for a rail connection, proceed to Goa by bus), and to Bombay, Delhi and Calcutta.

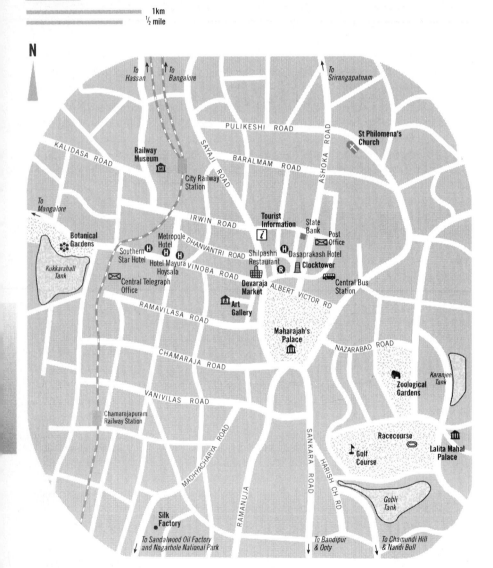

Mysore

1km
½ mile

N

To Hassan
To Bangalore
To Srirangapatnam

PULIKESHI ROAD

ASHOKA ROAD

St Philomena's Church

KALIDASA ROAD

Railway Museum

SAYAJI ROAD

BARALMAM ROAD

City Railway Station

To Mangalore

IRWIN ROAD

Tourist Information
State Bank
Post Office

Botanical Gardens

Metropole Hotel

DHANVANTRI ROAD

Southern Star Hotel

Hotel Mayura Hoysala

VINOBA ROAD

Shilpashri Restaurant
Dasaprakash Hotel

Clocktower

Kukkarahall Tank

Central Telegraph Office

Devaraja Market
ALBERT VICTOR RD

Central Bus Station

RAMAVILASA ROAD

Art Gallery

Maharajah's Palace

NAZARABAD ROAD

CHAMARAJA ROAD

Zoological Gardens
Karanjee Tank

VANIVILAS ROAD

Chamarajapuram Railway Station

MADHYACHARYA ROAD

RAMANUJA ROAD

SANKARA ROAD

HARISH CH. RD

Racecourse
Golf Course
Lalita Mahal Palace

Gobli Tank

Silk Factory

To Sandalwood Oil Factory and Nagarhole National Park
To Bandipur & Ooty
To Chamundi Hill & Nandi Bull

by bus

The new central bus stand in Irwin Road (north of Hotel Ritz) offers non-stop express buses to Bangalore (every 15 minutes; 3 hours) and Interstate buses to Ooty (scenic ride; 5½ hours), to Cochin (one night bus, departing 9.30pm; no advance-booking so arrive early to grab seats) and to Coimbatore (14 hours) for Trivandrum (another 4 hours, by train). There's a useful cloakroom at the bus stand where you can leave your bags if you're only visiting Mysore for the day.

Tourist Information

KSTDC's **tourist office**, ✆ 22096 is open daily from 10am to 5.30pm, in the Old Exhibition Building, Irwin Road; waffly but helpful staff, poor handouts, but good information (hotels, tours) posted on various boards.

KSTDC's **tourist reception centre**, ✆ 2365, is in Hotel Mayura Hoysala, open daily 6.30–8.30. It sells the Mysore city sightseeing tour which includes Somnathpur (Rs100, 7.30 am–8.30pm) and the over-ambitious tour to Belur, Halebid and Sravanbelagola on Fridays and Sundays (Rs100, 7.30am–8.30pm).

Indian Airlines, ✆ 25349, is also in Hotel Mayura Hoysala complex, open daily 10–5.15 except Sundays.

For **foreign exchange**, the **State Bank of India** is in St Mark's Road. Some of the local **Canara Bank** branches also change traveller's cheques, as will the managers at the **Southern Star**, if asked politely.

The central **post office** is in Ashoka Road.

The **Basapa Memorial Hospital** on Vinoba Road about 1½ miles west of the Southern Star, and the huge colonial pile of the **Mary Holdsworth Hospital** on Sajaki Road in the town centre are recommended.

The City

Mysore is a compact town easily negotiable on foot. There is a lot to see and do in the centre, and some worthwhile excursion spots (Sriringapatnam, Chamundi, Somnathpur, Brindhavan, etc.) just outside it. Orientation is easy; you can walk from one end of the town to the other in about 30 minutes. Auto-rickshaws cost Rs5 per mile, and because journeys are so short, you should never have to pay more than Rs10–15 anywhere, though you'll have to haggle and, if necessary, push down the rickshaw meter yourself. Local buses are useful for out-of-town destinations like Brindhavan, Chamundi, Sriringapatnam, Government Silk Weaving Factory etc., and leave from the bus stand near New Statue Square.

For a comprehensive viewing of the many sights, take one of the (good) city conducted tours, then allow a second day's sightseeing to return to certain places you want to see more of.

Mysore City Tour, Including Chamundi Hill

conducted tour bus, full day

St Philomena's Church–Art Gallery–Zoo–Maharajah's Palace–
Chamundi Hill–Sriringapatnam–Brindhavan Gardens

The first call is generally **St Philomena's Church**, at the north of town. This is one of the largest neo-Gothic style churches in India. Though built in 1931, its lofty grandeur and stained-glass interior are more suggestive of medieval than modern origin. Tour buses rarely stop long here and few of your Indian co-passengers will be Catholics. When and if you return, go down into the crypt, where a rather romantic life-size plaster image of the saint reclines in a glass case. In a side alcove lies an almost alarmingly life-like image of the dead Christ, taken down from the cross and laid to rest.

The **Sri Chamarajendra Art Gallery** (*open daily, 8–5, no photography allowed*), just off New Statue Square, is of more general interest. It is housed within Jaganmohan Palace, and contains treasures of rare musical instruments (though mostly broken), exotic wall decorations, original paintings of Ravi Varma, a couple of beautiful mother-of-pearl inlay sofas, and a marvellous French musical clock (each second marked by a drum beat, toy soldiers march out on parade every hour). Other treasures include a life-size lobster made from carved ivory and grains of rice with microscopic pictures painted upon them. Some of the landscape paintings are worth seeing—painted during the Art Nouveau period, they display an Indo-European version of that style that makes them more successful than most other 20th-century Indian paintings. By contrast, the late Victorian life-size panels of scenes from the *Ramayana* are chocolate-boxy and overly sentimental.

Mysore's **Zoological Gardens** (*open daily, 8.30–5.30*), have their entrance gate on Lalitha Palace Road, ½ mile east of the central bus stand. With the exception of the zoological gardens in Hyderabad, these are the best in India. Over 1500 varieties of animals and birds live here, in near-natural surrounds. The brief tour stop is insufficient to see half what's available. Return on a separate occasion for a comprehensive visit (come early, when the big cats are awake).

Dominating the town centre is the huge Indo-Saracenic **Maharajah's Palace** (*open daily, 10–5.30; free tours run every hour from 10am*), Mysore's main attraction. Entrance is by the South Gate only. Built over a period of 15 years (1897–1912) after the old wooden palace was razed by fire, this imposing structure, a gleaming profusion of domes, turrets, archways and colonnades, was designed by the English architect Henry Irwin, with workmanship by local artists (the Hoysala-style wall decorations are especially fine). An immense structure, it measures 244 feet long, 144 feet high and 155 feet wide (74.5 by 44 by 47.5 metres). The interior is a Pandora's box of treasures: a Durbar Hall with jewel-studded throne, mosaic

marble floors, crystal furniture, stained-glass domed ceiling (a miracle of art and design), hammered silver doors opening onto sumptuously furnished apartments, mirror-spangled pleasure rooms and a lovely portrait gallery. Hugely extravagant, but great fun. Cameras and shoes must be left at the entrance, unless you get permission from the Museum Director (office near ticket desk) to take photos. If you're in town on a Sunday evening between 7 and 9pm, return to the Palace to see it brilliantly illuminated with thousands of tiny bulbs. The atmosphere is amazing: teeming crowds of picnicking tourists, balloons, toys, snacks and food, fruit and sweetmeats, Indian music wailing out of loudspeakers and of course the glittering backdrop of the fairytale palace.

After shuffling around the huge building between the ropes designed to keep the crowds from soiling the attractions, take a walk around the back of the palace to the stables, where the Maharajah still breeds thoroughbred horses. For a small *baksheesh*, the grooms will be happy to show you around.

Chamundi Hill, 2½ miles out of Mysore, at an altitude of 3512 feet (1072 metres), is a popular beauty spot with panoramic views. Once a royal summer resort, the hill is now a major pilgrimage and tourist centre. At the top, visit the 12th-century **Sri Chamundeswari Temple** (*open daily, 9–12noon and 5–9*), built in the southern Dravidian style with a distinctive *gopuram*. Inside there's an interesting pillar with silver panels depicting Ganesh, Nandi, and Shiva's trident, facing into the solid-gold Chamunda figure. In the open courtyard below it, you'll find the **Mahishasura Statue** (a giant technicolor pirate) erected in memory of Chamunda's slain demon. Behind it is the small **Godly Museum**, a sort of advertisement for a poly-religious cult that would very much like you to donate some money. It's worth going inside for the displays that explain how all the gods of each religion are in fact cousins, with each relationship shown on a chart.

To escape from the heat, aggressive incense, flower vendors, beggars and general touristiness of the main temple complex, walk a third of the way down Chamundi Hill (about 600 yards) to the huge black granite monolith **Nandi Bull**—at 160 feet (49 metres) high the third-largest in India—taking in the views out over Mysore and the Deccan Plateau. Around the bull, the atmosphere is a little more relaxed. The Nandi itself is always decorated with garlands of flowers and painted with sacred designs in sandal paste, and at the base, a brahmin will offer you the chance to do *puja*, though without the usual pushiness of priests at popular pilgrimage sites. There are generally a couple of fruit and vegetable sellers offering cool chunks of pineapple and cucumber.

If you're not on the official tour, rather than climb all the way back up to the bus stop, take the easier, shaded walk from the bull back down to the rickshaw stand at the foot of Chamundi Hill. You should not have to pay more than Rs15 for the ride back to town, but you'll have to bargain like hell because the rickshaw drivers are used to tourists paying over the odds. The ride is only about a mile though, so stick to your guns.

Out at **Somnathpur**, 28 miles from Mysore, there's one of the finest temples in the south (*open daily, 9–5*). Built in 1268, and dedicated to Keshava, it is one of the three great **Hoysala Temples** of Karnataka. Covered with exquisite carvings portraying various scenes from the *Ramayana* and other epics, also numerous fascinating depictions of Hoysalan life and times—the temple is especially notable for the six horizontal friezes running round its base-line. The Rs1 admission includes a free guide service and there's a tourist canteen-cum-resthouse in Somnathpur, should you wish to stay overnight.

The next stop on the official tour is the ruined town of **Sriringapatnam**, 10 miles out of Mysore. From this small island fortress-town straddling the river Cauvery came the two brilliant Muslim leaders Hyder Ali and his son Tipu Sultan, who ruled a powerful empire comprising much of southern India for 40 years. Tipu Sultan, the 'Tiger of Mysore', became the most dreaded foe of the British in the south, and inflicted two punishing defeats on the forces of the East India Company before at last being overcome in 1799. Tipu was killed and his town razed, but his elegant **Summer Palace**, or Daria Daulat Bagh (*open daily 9–5*), remains intact: the British kept it for their own use—Arthur Wellesly, later Duke of Wellington, lived here for a spell while serving as governor of Mysore.

The official tour visit here is a little rushed; visit Sriringapatnam independently to really see the sights. Take a bus or train (services every half hour) out to the town, then a rickshaw or pony cart 1½ miles out to the Summer Palace (about Rs10 round trip) from Mysore. Set in beautiful gardens and approached via an avenue of clipped cypresses, the stylish little palace presents open sides to the world, but you can't see in, so effectively was it designed for shade. Built in 1784, the palace is mainly constructed of wood, its interior beautifully painted in black, red and gold and hung with portraits of Tipu's contemporaries. Amongst the murals depicting battle scenes, there is one commemorating Tipu and Hyder Ali's victory at Polilur, the plaque beneath mocking the opposing Deccan forces who arrived too late to help the British, with the taunt that 'they came like a boar and fled like a cow'. The superb little museum upstairs has a fascinating collection of engravings, family ink drawings, coins and prints illustrating Tipu's life and times, plus a number of his belongings. From the palace, take one of the waiting rickshaws 2 miles further on to the **Gumbaz**, burial place of Tipu and Hyder Ali.

To get back to Sriringapatnam itself, grab a rickshaw from outside the Gumbaz (Rs10) and have it set you down at the bus stand. Then walk in under the ruined gatehouse to the extensive Fort ruins, noting the small plaque, on your right, which marks the spot where Tipu Sultan died in combat (or rather, where the British found him lying under a pile of redcoats he had killed). Nearby stands Tipu Sultan's mosque, the large and imposing **Jami Masjid**, notable for its tall minarets. Sriringapatnam still feels like a 19th-century town, even though it gets a lot of tourists, with old Karnatik houses, cows in the streets and the atmosphere of village, rather than a tourist site. There are quite a few cheap *chai*-houses to rest in as you walk down the main street to the **Sri Ranganathaswamy Temple**, one of the oldest Dravidian temples in Karnataka, built in AD 894. A prominent white blockstone structure, supported by hundreds of monolithic pillars, it houses a massive Vishnu reclining on a serpent and a soaring brass prayer column. Outside the temple are the town's *dhobi* ghats, stone steps leading down to the Cauvery River, which flows fast over the shallow rocks and rapids. The local kids here have a good eye for unwatched articles, so keep cameras or any other belongings close to hand.

The Cauvery River at Sriringapatnam

Karnataka Tourism has started to run **canoeing** and **white-water rafting** trips from Sriringapatnam down to the Cauvery Fishing Camp near the Biligiri Hills. The trips run during the high-water season after the August rains. There is also a very good bird sanctuary about 1½ miles southwest of Sriringapatnam (Rs20 by rickshaw—round trip). Set in thick woods by the river, the **Ranganathittu Sanctuary** is home to vast numbers of herons, ibis, storks, spoonbills, terns and other waterfowl and forest species. Boat rides are provided at a small extra charge to take you around the waterways. Crocodiles lurk by the marshy banks and you may spot an otter. The sanctuary has three riverside cottages, each with two double rooms, but these are usually full. Bear in mind, if on a day trip that the foreigner's entry fee for the sanctuary is Rs100 per person. If you wish to stay at Sringapatnam , there are cheap riverside cottages for rent at the **Hotel Mayura River View**, ✆ 114.

Brindhavan Gardens

The ride back from Sriringapatnam to Mysore is very picturesque, a continuous vista of palm-groves, paddy fields and sugar-cane plantations. For this journey alone, the bus tour is worthwhile. Last stop of the day is at the fabulous **Brindhavan Gardens**. Twelve miles north of Mysore, these are among the best known of Karnataka's attractions. Beautifully terraced below the recent (1937) Krishnarajasagar Dam, Brindhavan's ornamental gardens take their name from an original series in Mathura, south of Delhi. Taking as their theme the pastoral frolics of Krishna with his 16,000 *gopis* (handmaidens), they are of enormous popularity among young Indian couples. In high season (April–May) up to 400 tour buses per day swarm up here. Weekends are also excessively busy. Arriving here around dusk, you'll have time to view the landscaped lawns, rose gardens, flower bowers and conifers in the vast southern section before the mass exodus starts via the central boating lake (Rs3 boat trips) to see the pretty musical 'dancing fountains' (*illuminated weekdays 7–8pm, weekends 7–9pm*). The gardens are also transformed into a colourful fairyland of cascading fountains and twinkling lights. The walk back to the tour bus is delightful.

For overnight stays, choose between the ex-palace **Krishnaraj Sagar Hotel**, ✆ Beluga 22, with rooms from Rs550 single, Rs700 double or the cheaper **KSTDC Tourist Home**, ✆ Beluga 52, with single and double rooms at Rs125 and Rs170. Both offer fine views, but are often full.

The Railway Museum

One sight rarely seen in Mysore is the marvellous **Rail Museum** (*open daily 9–5, except Mon*) in Krishnarajasagar Road, just above the railway station itself. Almost as good as the one in Delhi, it houses antique engines, rolling stock, the Maharani's coach and a joyride mini-train.

Sports and Activities
horse racing

There's a good racecourse below Chamundi Hill, with popular meetings on Wednesdays and at weekends during a three month season between September and November.

canoeing

Karnataka Tourism offers 2–3 day trips down the Cauvery, starting at Sriringapatnam and ending up at the Cauvery Fishing Camp south of Mysore. For details contact Mysore's tourist office, ✆ 22096.

yoga

Mysore has one of India's best yoga schools in the Lakshmi Puram neighbourhood, run by an 80-year old master who looks no more than 50. His particular brand of yoga, known as Asthanga Yoga, is much more physically demanding than the more traditional forms, as testified to by the superb bodies of the long-term yoga students who come from all over the world and pay in excess of US$300 a month for the daily tuition (Indians pay far less). Casual students are not allowed to take classes, only those staying for a month or more.

swimming

You can escape the heat by visiting the pool at the Southern Star—a regular meeting point for tourists and long-stayers, like the yoga students. It costs Rs150 per day though.

white-water rafting

Also on the Cauvery, starting from Sriringapatnam; ring ✆ 22906 for details.

Shopping

Mysore is famous for its incense and sandalwood, and these are the best buys. Other popular purchases are silk *saris*, printed silk, inlay work and jewellery.

general handicrafts

To see the full range, visit **Kaveri Arts and Crafts Emporium**, (✆ 21258), Sayaji Rao Road (closed Thursday), but avoid badly joined furniture and overpriced sandalwood. The best buys here are incense (*agarbathi*), rosewood (inlaid with deerbone, not ivory) and silk.

silk

For quality silks, catch a no.4 or 5 bus out to the **Government Silk Weaving Factory** and **Karnataka Silk Industries Corporation Workshop**, both on Mananthody Road.

sandalwood and rosewood

For pure sandalwood; carvings, powder, paste, dust, oil, incense and even soap visit the small row of shops opposite the Zoo on Dhanvantri Road, round the corner from the Kaveri Emporium. These are a group of shops specializing in sandalwood and rosewood carvings; the town's best selection is probably to be found here. Compare prices from store to store before you begin bargaining.

If bargaining is too much of a hassle, head for the **Handicraft Sales Emporium**, ✆ 23669, where you can buy small sandalwood Buddhas or Indian deities from Rs200–300, bigger ones for Rs600–1200; sandalwood oil by the vial or bottle and sandalwood paste and powder by the ounce. The upstairs section does a fine line in gems and jewellery.

jewellery

Apart from Jaipur, Mysore is the best place to buy semi-precious stones and precious gems. The rubies, garnets and lapis lazuli are of particularly high quality. But take care when buying a 'line' stone; the orientation is all-important. With moonstones, sapphires and rubies alike, the line *must* be central.

cotton textiles

For *batiks* and good quality cotton *sulwars* (punjabi suits) try **Sarong** on Devaraj Urs Road. You can find good *khadi* fabric (handwoven cotton that breathes in the heat and keeps in the warmth) in the shops opposite the palace bus stand on Sayaji Road. If you buy some and want to get it made up, go to **Krishna**, a tailor specializing in Western-style clothes, whose shop is oppsite the entrance to the Shilpshri hotel and rooftop bar on Gandhi Square.

markets

Mysore's **Devaraja Market** is probably the best fruit and vegetable market in India. It's certainly one of the largest, running all the way down Sayaji Rao Road from Dhanvantri Road to New Statue Square. There's one section devoted exclusively to bananas and their many varieties. You can wander round here all day, and not get bored. Nobody returns empty-handed. Good purchases here include colourful bangles, lacquerwork and crafted silver jewellery. Marvellous little souvenirs are the packs of 10 assorted incenses, sold for around Rs30. Be sure to pack these carefully.

bookshops

Gita Book House, New State Square (near the bus stand), is possibly the only place in town which sells a decent Mysore map.

Mysore ✆ (0821–)   *Where to Stay*

luxury

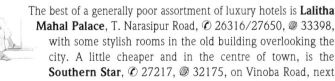

The best of a generally poor assortment of luxury hotels is **Lalitha Mahal Palace**, T. Narasipur Road, ✆ 26316/27650, ✉ 33398, with some stylish rooms in the old building overlooking the city. A little cheaper and in the centre of town, is the **Southern Star**, ✆ 27217, ✉ 32175, on Vinoba Road, next door to the much better Hotel Metropole (*see* below). The Southern Star has a decent restaurant—really good if you like big buffet breakfasts but the rooms are bland. It does have a pool though, which is open to non-guests at Rs150 per day. It is also worth letting the hotel's resident magician who hassles you as you go in and out of the front door) show you his tricks—they're better than you'd think. There's also a rickshaw and pony-cart rank outside the gates. One of the carts has a very smart (and properly fed, for once) little skewbald Rajasthani stallion in the shafts, and it is a pleasure to be driven around town behind his trotting hooves.

Out in the Chamundi Hills, about half-an-hour by taxi from Mysore's centre is the **Rajendra Vilas Palace**, ✆ 20690, a big Edwardian wedding-cake of a building. Recently done-up from its rather run-down state of a few years ago, it really is luxurious now and commands panoramic views of the city and the plain beyond.

expensive

Mysore's most stylish hotel is the **Metropole**, ✆ 208681, 🖂 31869, on the corner of Jhansi Lakshmibai Road and Vinoba Road. A colonial set-piece, its vast airy dining room is still presided over by the stuffed head of the largest tiger to be shot by the last Maharajah. In its small, shady bar, the waiter will bring you your bill in a little sandalwood box and the rooms are still furnished with Victoriana.

Hotel Dasaprakash Paradise, 105 Vivekananda Road, Yadavagiri, ✆ 26666/25555, is in the suburbs, about a mile north of the railway station, but is the town's best Indian-style hotel, with a very good restaurant and a pool. If you cannot get in at the Metropole or Dasaprakash, try the slightly bland but perfectly good air-conditioned comfort of **King's Kourt**, ✆ 25250, 🖂 32684, on Jhansi Lakshmibai Road opposite the Metropole.

moderate

Mysore has two interesting hotels in this price category. The hotel **Park Lane**, ✆ 30400, opposite Curzon Park on Sri Harsha Road has clean but basic rooms still decorated Raj-style, as well as one of the town's best open-air restaurants. If this is full, try the **Lokranjan Mahal Palace**, ✆ 21868, on the appropriately named Lokranjan Mahal Road. It's very good value for the price, with run-down colonial rooms (some air-conditioned), plenty of atmosphere and a pool.

inexpensive

An enjoyable Indian-style hotel is the **Siddhartha**, 73 Guesthouse Road, Nazarbad, ✆ 26869. Well-located and quiet, with large carpeted rooms, tiled bathrooms and free newspapers. Otherwise, KTDC's **Hotel Mayura Hoysala**, 2 Jhansi Lakshmi Bai Road, ✆ 25349, is very much a case of pot luck but is generally clean.

cheap

As a travellers' centre, Mysore has any number of budget guesthouses, most of them clustered around the bus station and Gandhi Square. However, two of the best on Dhanvantri Road are **New Gayathri Bhavan** and **Hotel Indra Bhavan**, with clean rooms (bathrooms attached). Over at Gandhi Square, **Hotel Durbar**, ✆ 20029, has okay rooms and two very popular restaurants, including a rooftop bar. The nearby **Srikanth Hotel**, ✆ 22951, is also worth checking out for its clean rooms with bath. Try also the **Govardhan**, a friendly place with one of the best cheap vegetarian restaurants in town, on Sri Harsha Road, about a block towards the palace from the Park Lane Hotel and the **Cauvery** on Ashok Road, where many of the long-term yoga students stay.

Eating Out

The **Hotel Metropole** is the place to dine in style: a stately, palatial restaurant offering well-priced Indian, Chinese and continental cuisine and elegant service. After your Rs150 per head meal, relax in the air-conditioned bar. Cheaper but equally stylish is the **Park Lane Hotel** where you sit in a tree-shaded coutryard, listen to live Indian classical music and eat for about Rs100 per head. Above your table hangs a little red light bulb which, if you pull the cord, illuminates and attracts (immediately) a waiter supressing a kind of desperate irritation at being so summoned. Evidently these red lights are the bane of their life—nobody explains their use to new customers, who all pull them out of curiosity—and the waiters have no choice but to respond. Only pull the cord if you want something specific. The Lalitha Mahal Palace has very good Indian food, though rather indifferent Western dishes. The dining room is grand but the service is rather poor.

At the **Southern Star**, next door to the Metropole, the main restaurant has extensive buffet lunches for Rs125 and a 24-hour coffee shop. Over at the **Hotel Dasaprakash**, there's a good cheap vegetarian restaurant, with meals from Rs80–120 per head and a memorable ice cream parlour.

Two popular rooftop bar/restaurants in Gandhi Square are **Shilpashri** (consistently good vegetarian and non-vegetarian fare, nice bar, but expect to queue) and **Hotel Durbar** (cheap Chinese, Mughlai and Indian food, tinny taped music). Both will cost you around Rs100 including beer.

Indra's Fast Food on Devaraja Urs Road is very cheap and serves the best *chaat* (south Indian snack dishes) in Mysore. It's also a hang-out for students, most of whom are anxious to try out their English on you. You can eat for under Rs50 including a juice. **Samrhat** on Dhavantri Road serves good north and south Indian *thalis* for about Rs30–60 including *nan* and a drink, as does **Paras Café** on Sayaji Road.

Entertainment and Nightlife

Though far more sedate than buzzing Bangalore, Mysore is quite sophisticated and offers much more in the way of nightlife than most Indian towns, with some reasonable bars and dance clubs as well as the more traditional forms of entertainment.

cinema

Two cinemas, the **Woodlands** and the **Ritz**, show English films as matinées. Others, like the **Shalimar** and **Sterling**, show English films all day.

classical music

Nightly *sitar* and *tabla* recitals are given to diners at the outdoor Park Lane Restaurant on Sri Harsha Road, just opposite Curzon Park, and at the Lalitha Mahal's restaurant.

classical dance

Regular performances are given at the theatre inside the **Chamarajendra Art Gallery** in the old Jagamohan Palace. Dates are advertised in the *Deccan Herald*.

bars

Away from the big hotels, Mysore has two lovely rooftop bars, the upmarket(ish) **Shilpashri,** and the slightly more run-down **Durbar,** both opposite each other on Gandhi Square.

dance clubs

The Royal Legacy Pub has a dance floor—downstairs is dark and depressing and full of Indian men on the pull. But upstairs, the dance club plays too-loud music that ranges from awful (Bryan Adams) to reasonable (reggae and funk), with some popped-up bhangra in between. The atmosphere is very relaxed—sometimes the owner's friends come by with their little kids. A few young Indian couples come here, though often chaperoned by their families, but the crowd is mostly composed of Western tourists.

live rock and pop

Bands are sometimes brought in from Bangalore to play at the Southern Star Hotel (*see* below). Whoever books them must regard Western music as all one thing: when the author was in town he stayed in the Southern Star and was surprised to find a heavy metal band providing the evening's entertainment in the dining room—the lead singer yelling into the mike, and the lead guitarist doing the axe-hero bit among the bemused, deafened diners. The little girls of 8 years old or so, all in pink and yellow frou-frou dresses, danced like demons while their families grit it out with Indian stoicism.

Temple Towns of the Central Deccan Plateau

Of the many temple towns of the central Deccan, the best is the fabulous ruined city of **Hampi,** the Vijayanagar capital that was sacked in the 15th century and lies abandoned in a landscape of huge, scattered boulders. If you are short of time, head straight for Hampi. But if you have some time to spare, take in the 8th-century temple complexes at **Belur** and **Halebid** on the way.

Belur and Halebid

These twin temple towns lie about 100 miles northwest of Bangalore and Mysore via the small town of **Hassan** on the Mangalore Highway. Hassan itself can be reached by bus or train from either city (approximately 4 hours) and has a variety of accommodation from which to base your excursions out to the temples.

Getting There

by train

The nearest access point is Hassan. Several daily services connect Hassan with Bangalore (4 hours), Mysore (3 hours) and Mangalore (8 hours over the mountains). The train station is a mile east of town on the Bangalore road.

by bus

Buses run between Hassan and Bangalore (every half hour) and Mysore (every hour). Several services daily to Mangalore, Hampi, and Goa.

Local buses run from Hassan to the temple complexes at Belur and Halebid every half hour. The bus station is by Maharaja Park in the centre of town.

Hassan ✆ (08172–)

Where to Stay

expensive

The **Hassan Ashok**, ✆ 68731, is a well-run place with a good vegetarian restaurant and air-conditioned rooms. You can arrange for transport out to the temples by taxi from here (round trip approx Rs250) and also check out the hotel's resident magician, begs you to watch his performance as you go in and out of the entrance. His tricks include apparently swallowing a live coal and sending a live cobra down his throat to retrieve it, as well as regurgitating several pounds of old rusty nails. If you have a few minutes, it's worth watching him go through his repertoire.

moderate

Hassan has only one hotel in this category. The **Ambilee Palika**, on Racecourse Road, ✆ 67145, is just as comfortable as the Ashok but has no magician. It does have foreign exchange though, and a bar.

inexpensive

Try the **Vaishnavi Guest Lodge** on Church Road, ✆ 67413, or the **Satyaprakash Lodge** on Bus Stand Road, which has rooms from below Rs100.

Halebid

An hour's bus ride from Hassan through the Deccan countryside leads to Halebid, the 11-century capital of the (Hindu) Hoysala Empire. The Hoysalas are long gone—their city razed by the Northern Mugals in the 14th century—but the main **Hoysalasvara temple** still stands amid well-kept lawns. A small Nandi bull and a 30 foot (9 metre) Jain statue of Lord Gomateshvara stand outside. The temple entrance is flanked by carved friezes from the *Ramayana* while inside, squat rounded pillars, their capitals carved into various Gods, rise from a marble floor polished smooth by centuries of feet. There are no *gopurams* at Halebid, whose flat-roofed design has a more homely feel to it than is usual to the flamboyant Dravidian temple architecture.

A mile south of the main temple is a small Jain temple from an earlier period— the Hoysalas had converted to Jainism during the 10th century but abandoned it for Hinduism by the middle of the 11th. However, they did not raze their Jain monuments, but tolerated the practice of the religion despite the withdrawal of royal patronage. There are seldom any visitors at Halebid's Jain temple, unlike the Hoysalavara temple where would-be guides assail you. The entrance to the Jain temple is guarded by two low stone elephants and there is a free-standing tower inside the compound with a beautiful carving of a prancing horse at eye level.

Belur

The original capital of the Hoysala empire, Belur was abandoned for Halebid during the 11th century. This loss of status proved fortuitous; while only the temples at Halebid were left after the city was destroyed by the invading Mughals in the 14th-century, Belur, no longer of any importance, survived and remains a town to this day. Still a market centre for the surrounding Deccan villages, Belur sits beside the Yagachi river and has the superb **Chennakesava Temple**, built in 1116 and dedicated to Krishna in commemoration of a great victory of the Hoysalas over the Cholas.

The temple does not look anything special from the outside, until you go up close and see the rows of friezes: processional elephants, dancing girls and musicians border scenes from the great Hindu epics, runnning all the way around the sides of the temple in a delicate tracery of stone. Inside is a central pillar, known as the Narasimha pillar, covered in almost microscopically intricate carvings of temple dancers. Apparently the pillar could once be rotated, but it now stands rooted to the floor.

A smaller temple complex, the **Viranarayana temple**, stands just a little to the west of the Chennakesava temple.

Belur ℭ (08172–)

Where to Stay
inexpensive

The **Mayura Velapuri** is a state-run guesthouse on Main Road, with clean but basic comfort.

cheap

There's a number of pretty awful guesthouses on Main Road, but they'll do for a night if you can't face getting back on a bus to Hassan.

Hampi (Vijayanagar)

It was a question of light, of entering the cave at a time when the rays of the sun, pouring through the irregular fissure in the roof, fell transversely across the rock chamber, illuminating the whole main wall...upon this wall, lovingly sculpted in frieze upon frieze, were Valmiki's gods and godesses.

Karmala Markandaya, *Obsesssion*

Up in the Central Deccan Plateau, about 115 miles east of Belgaum and 200 miles north of Bangalore lie the ruins of Hampi, once the greatest of all medieval Hindu capitals. Founded in 1336 by two local princes, Hari Hara and Bukka, it became the seat of the mighty Vijayanagar empire, which held sway over south India for more than two centuries. By the reign of Krishnadeva Raya (1509–29), generally considered the golden period of the empire, its rule extended from the Arabian Sea east to the Bay of Bengal, and from the Deccan plateau south to the tip of the peninsula. The Vijayanagar kings built up Hampi as a showpiece of imperial magnificence, and a definitive Vijayanagar style of architecture emerged, typified by lofty *gopurams*, stylized sculptures (often depicting scenes from the *Puranas* and the *Ramayana*), intricately carved columns, and separate shrines for goddesses.

The city itself had, and still has, a spectacular natural setting, enclosed on three sides by the Tungabhadra river and by rocky gorges, with huge boulders strewn across the landscape as if thrown there like pebbles from the hands of giants. The addition of seven concentric rings of massive fortifications made it almost invulnerable to attack. Hampi had a series of enlightened rulers who patronized the arts and education, cultivating it as a centre of learning and culture,

Hampi

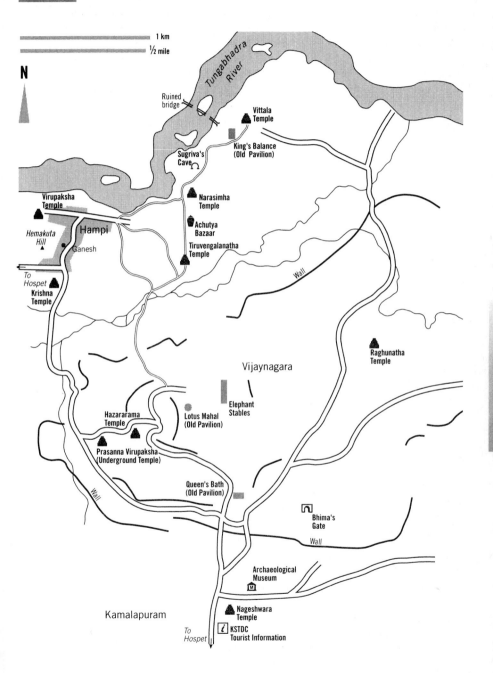

1 km
½ mile

N

Tungabhadra River

Ruined bridge

Vittala Temple

King's Balance (Old Pavilion)

Sugriva's Cave

Virupaksha Temple

Narasimha Temple

Hemakuta Hill

Hampi

Achutya Bazaar

Ganesh

Tiruvengalanatha Temple

To Hospet

Krishna Temple

Wall

Raghunatha Temple

Vijaynagara

Elephant Stables

Hazararama Temple

Lotus Mahal (Old Pavilion)

Prasanna Virupaksha (Underground Temple)

Queen's Bath (Old Pavilion)

Wall

Bhima's Gate

Wall

Archaeological Museum

Kamalapuram

Nageshwara Temple

To Hospet

KSTDC Tourist Information

as well as of the erotic arts, as many of the temple carvings illustrate. Meanwhile, a growing trade in spices turned its busy, colourful bazaars into an international centre of commerce. In its heyday, the city had a population of half a million, bolstered by a powerful mercenary army of an incredible one million soldiers. Such a large force was required to defend the supremacy of Vijayanagar against rival Muslim sultans and Hindu kings. In 1565, however, it was finally overcome by five allied Deccan sultans in the disastrous battle of Talikota. The king fled southwards, and the invaders spent six long months systematically sacking and looting the abandoned city, burning and pillaging without mercy. The empire lingered on for another century, but Hampi itself was never occupied again.

To miss Hampi is to miss one of the principal treasures of India. Now a World Heritage site, the ruins are well worth the 24-hour haul from Bangalore, Goa or Hyderabad, and you should allow at least three days here to get around the whole place and soak up the atmosphere. Many people stay for weeks, but as yet there has been no real tourist development at Hampi, so most of the visitors are hippies and independent travellers.

So well preserved is this fantastical abandoned city, and so vividly does it reflect a vanished glory, that Hampi has been termed 'The Pompeii of India'. Spread over a vast area of 6400 acres, including temples, pavilions, whole bazaars, bath complexes and palaces, the ruins are on a very grand scale. High *gopurams* rear to the sky, and some of the sculptures alone have been hewn from single blocks of granite up to 24 feet (7 metres) high. You can really sense a mighty civilization at work here. With only the slightest effort of imagination, you can easily visualize it. At present, the Government of Karnataka and the Archaeological Survey of India are trying to restore the capital to something of its past glory. An ambitious project perhaps, but not impossible. A great many of the ruins are in surprisingly good condition.

Climate and When to Go

Hampi has a very dry, exposed location and is best visited in the cool months of **December to February**. Travellers do trickle in as early as **August** and **September**, when the river is swollen by the monsoon and the surrounding countryside a rich lush green, and as late as **March**, but after that it's too hot for comfort.

Tourist Information

The **KSTDC tourist office**, behind Hospet bus stand, is open daily from 10 to 1 and from 2 to 5. It's fairly helpful and has a free map of the site, but **Malligi Tourist Home** has the better information.

There are **post offices** at Hospet, Hampi and Kamalapuram.

For **foreign exchange**, the **State Bank of Mysore** is next to Hospet tourist office.

warning to travellers

The police in Hampi are not well-disposed towards the hippy type of traveller and sometimes come looking for trouble. The commonest trick is to summarily arrest young men for not wearing shirts in the main bazaar, pulling them out of the restaurants and *chai*-shops with a great deal of shouting and some rough handling and hustling them off to the station. Although many of the local Indians walk around shirtless, this does not exempt Westerners. If so caught, expect a Rs100–300 fine, whether on the spot or in court at Hospet the following day. Obviously, if you are carrying any hashish (and Hampi is a smoker's mecca), the fine will be much more expensive. In two days, the author saw five young male travellers arrested and fined with the policemen doing their best to humiliate them in front of the local populace.

Getting Around

Hampi lies outside the town of Hospet, which can be reached within a day from both Bangalore and Hyderabad, or a day and half from Panjim in Goa.

by train

From Bangalore and Hyderabad there is one overnight train daily taking 8 and 13 hours respectively. From Bangalore the *Hampi Express* overnight train leaves at 9.30pm and reaches Hospet at 6.20am the following morning. The return departs Hospet at 9pm and reaches Bangalore at 8am. From Hyderabad you have to change trains at Guntakal. At present, Goa only has bus services (10 hours travel plus the time between changes), but there are plans to re-open the railway line that used to run over the mountains to Hospet, once it has been built up to broad gauge—the projected opening date being some time in 1996/7.

by bus

There are 10 express buses daily from Bangalore (9 hours) and two from and to Hyderabad (11–12 hours). Two buses a day to Mysore (10½ hours), and a few morning buses to Hubli, for Goa (4–5 hours). Hubli has one express bus to Panjim (departing at 11am, arriving 3pm), four slow buses to Panjim (7 hours), and one slow bus to Vasco da Gama (7–8 hours). There are also two trains (departing at 7am and 11pm) from Hubli to Goa. Gokarn, the jewel on Karnataka's coast, is 8 hours away by bus via Hubli, with several services daily.

A regular local bus service covers the 13 miles between Hospet and Hampi. Otherwise, hire an auto-rickshaw or taxi (approx Rs75 round trip), or a bicycle (*see* below).

Touring the Ruins

If you're touring on foot, bear in mind that the complete round-trip (from Hospet to Hampi, round the ruins, and back) is 30 miles. Some people stay in Hospet, taking a bus to **Hampi Bazaar**, then walking up to the **Vittala Temple** complex, returning to the bazaar, striking south to **Kamalapuram** (via the Palace complex), and finally plopping, exhausted into a mid-afternoon bus from Kamalapuram back to Hospet. They then try to mop up the remaining sights on a second day's forced march. However, there is no longer any need for this for although the accommodation in Hampi itself is basic, it is far better to stay there and see the ruins at leisure.

Opinion differs as to whether it is better to see the ruins by foot or bike. On foot you spend no money, you are free to scramble up to all the little rock temples, and you do not have to worry about your bike being stolen. But a bike covers more ground. You can hire bicycles by the Vittala Temple, then pedal up to Hampi Bazaar (via the Palace complex), walk along the river to the Vittala Temple (leaving bikes at the bazaar), and finish off with a ride back to Kamalapuram, via **Ugranasimha** and **Sister Stone**. Either way, if you start out at 6.30–7am (the best light for photos), you can be back at your lodge by midday before it gets too hot.

Alternatively, you hire an auto-rickshaw (Rs60–70 for up to 3 persons) or a taxi (Rs200–250) from Malligi Tourist Home in Hospet. This is the most comfortable option, but it lacks the romance of wandering the fantastic, boulder-strewn landscape, and coming upon the ruins naturally. Also, only the largest temples and palaces are actually accessible by car. For the most part, you still have to get out and walk.

However you decide to see the ruins, the best place to start from is Hampi Bazaar bus stand, at the **Virupaksha Temple**, the only sacred complex in Hampi still 'living' (still in worship). Dedicated to Virupaksha, an aspect of Shiva, it has two main courts, each entered by a towered gateway or *gopuram*. The larger *gopuram* is over 160 feet (50 metres) high, and looks incredibly new and gets a fresh coat of whitewash every year, at **Shivratri**. Inside the temple, look out for finely carved columns with rearing animals, and for the semi-erotic reliefs of temple maidens. Also watch out for hordes of acquisitive monkeys. If you're here around 7am, you can watch Shiva and other resident deities being woken up by the priests.

Walking up along the river, you'll soon come to **Sule Bazaar**, a long, ruined arcade of arched pillars, where fruit, gems and spices were once sold. Past this, up a low rise, is the **King's Balance**. In ancient times, the king established the wealth of his kingdom by sitting in one scale, while his rich vassals poured cash and jewellery into the other. The proceeds went to the temple brahmins. Enjoy the views here, then walk down to **Vittala Temple**, the finest achievement of Vijayanagar art. Constructed in the 16th century and currently being restored by the archaeological department, this is a delightful complex of structures set within a rectangular courtyard. The main temple is famous for its rearing animals and for its 'musical' columns. Each series of 16 columns is hewn from a single granite block, and each one plays a different scale of musical notes or phrases when struck. There are 250 pillars either side of a central path, which leads up to the Marriage Hall. Again, there are some erotic reliefs on the pillars—though you have to look for them—some of which feature scarcely believable acts involving horses.

East of this hall is an exquisite, though huge **temple car** carved in stone. A faithful reproduction of a real temple chariot (as used in festivals), it is said to symbolize the ancient University of Gulbarga, 200 miles from Hospet. The miniature car houses Vishnu's vehicle, the *garuda*, and is drawn by a pair of stone elephants. Traces of the original bright paintwork still cling to the wheels. Out of the temple, walk down to **Purandaradasa Hall**, a low-ceilinged temple down by the riverside. According to legend, a famous 16th-century musician, Purandara, was turned to stone here, for singing a particularly divine song. A tiny figurine of him playing his mandolin is propped against one of the pillars. Opposite, there's a spectral group of stone pylons spanning the river. These once supported the old stone bridge which linked the two banks. You can cross Tungabhadra River in traditional 'coracle' boats (Rs5 per person).

On the other side of the river, a few scattered temples soon give way to a much wilder landscape. If you are camping, this is the place to pitch tent and wander among the boulders by night.

Back at Hampi Bazaar, a short walk south takes you up onto Hemakuta Hill. Best views are from the **Kadalaikullu Ganesa Temple**, notable for its unusually tall columns and huge image of the elephant god. Nearby, another Ganesh image stands with an open hall known as **Mustered Ganesh**. Off the hill, **Badavi Lingam** is a massive monolithic Shivalinga within a chamber, fed with water from a narrow roadside stream. Next to it is the famous figure of **Narasimha**, half man, half lion *avatar* of Vishnu, carved out of a single boulder.

Driving south, keep an eye out for **Sister Stone**, two huge boulders propped against each other like a pair of Siamese twins. They are apparently two of Shiva's sisters, whom he petrified after a family squabble. Down at the **Royal Palace Complex**, you'll find state archaeologists busily at work restoring the ruins. Walk inside the palace walls to find a large raised dais from which the king observed festival rites, various columned structures (for officers and guards), a roofless subterranean chamber (possibly the state treasury) and various civic buildings and watchtowers. Past these is **Lotus Mahal**, a beautiful two-storey pavilion with distinctive arches. It was built for the ladies of the court, in a skilful blend of Hindu and Islamic architectural styles. Nearby, there's a large step-well, extremely well-preserved, which served as a royal bath. Behind this is the **Queen's Bath**, a square water basin surrounded by a vaulted corridor. It was originally covered by a large canopy, supported by four pillars. This is now gone, and the walls are defaced by graffiti. But there's nice stucco work, and the remains of a narrow moat.

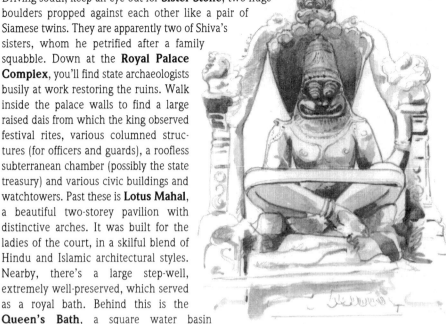

Also look out for the fine carvings, mainly of monkey figures, on the ceilings of the corridor. The tiny niches in the ceilings were for candles which illuminated the baths at night. Just outside the enclosure, to the east, look out for the largest **elephant stables** in the world. A row of 10 chambers with high vaulted roofs, they are symmetrically disposed around a central two-storey pavilion.

If you have bicycles, a rickshaw or taxi, it is worth making a side-trip from here to **Kamalapuram**. Built as a fort with circular bastions, this small town has an interesting **Archaeological Museum** (*open daily 10–5, except Fri*) with many fine recoveries from the Hampi site. It has a good scale model of the ruins which is useful for orientation, if you're starting out from Kamalapuram by bike. The museum also sells the useful ASI booklet on Hampi.

Sports and Activities
tubing on the river

No stay in Hampi is complete without a trip down the river on an inner tube. Although there are signs up warning of whirlpools and drownings, the river is only dangerous at high water (August–October), after which the level drops to a safe, steady flow. You can hire tubes for about Rs25 per day from the Rao Guest House, or anywhere else on the bazaar that has put up a sign. Once you have your tube, walk up to the big temple, bear right and follow the path parallel with the river bank, just past a sign pointing to a shack called the 'Mango Tree Restaurant'—a *chai*-house set under a big wild mango tree. The path then leads down to the river through a short section of paddy fields. Sit inside and go. You can drift down for well over an hour. When you have had enough, paddle to the shore and walk home. Make sure you take sun-screen, and some money in a plastic bag to have a drink at one of the *chai*-shops on the riverbank as you return.

swimming

The safest swimming spot is reached by taking the side street off the main bazaar past the Ashok Restuarant and Guest House and down to the river—you will see where the local boys are splashing about. The river is deep and calm enough here to allow a decent swim, but try not to swallow the water: though fast flowing and not officially used as a human toilet, the local buffalo know no rules when it comes to water hygiene.

Shopping

Hampi has no indigenous crafts, but there is always a stall outside the big temple gate in the main bazaar selling overpriced 'antique' bronzes (bargain down to at least half the asking price). The **Aspiration Store** in Hampi Bazaar has a wide range of produce from Sri Aurobindo *ashram* in Pondicherry; marble, silk fabrics, hand-made paper, postcards, even herbal bath powder. Good books to buy here are R. Sewell's *Forgotten Empire* and Longhurst's *Hampi Ruins*. Though most people get by with Michell and Fritz's *Hampi*, issued free at the tourist office.

Where to Stay

Hampi

cheap

Hampi has some good, but very basic guesthouses, with rooms still under Rs100 per night. The most popular are the **Rao Guest House**, just around the corner from the bazaar bus stand and the **Shanthi Lodge**, built around a central courtyard, and reached by turning right by the big temple at the top of the main bazaar and following the road for about a minute—the Shanthi is on the right. Partiers stay at the **Ashok**, the only place in town that serves beer (illegally). You can bargain for really cheap rates here. Both the Ashok and the Rao have cheap restaurants, and the Shanthi sells home-made banana bread.

In all the lodges, you will need a mosquito net at night.

If you want more comfortable, or air-conditioned accommodation, you'll have to stay in Hospet.

Hospet

moderate

Hospet has the new KSTDC **Hotel Mayura Vijayanagar**, ✆ (08394) 8270, which has the best facilities and rooms—there is no air-conditioning but the rooms have good fans and mosquito nets are provided. There is a second KSTDC unit at **Tunga-bhadra Dam**, 4 miles away.

inexpensive/cheap

The **Malligi Tourist Home**, 6/143 Jambunatha Road, ✆ (08394) 8101, is a short rickshaw ride from the bus stand and good value. Friendly and comfortable, it has two air-conditioned doubles at the top end of its range, a good restaurant, bakery and ice-cream parlour, running hot water till 10am, laundry and money-changing facilities, small library and bookshop, TV lounge and cool gardens. Malligi can arrange all local sightseeing and pre-book all onward travel. As a fallback, try **Hotel Sudarshan**, ✆ (08394) 8574, on Station Road. Service is poor, but rooms are reasonably priced from under Rs100 (single, no bath) to more expensive clean doubles, with bath.

Eating Out

Hampi

The main bazaar has India's best restaurant—a simple outdoor (but shaded) affair called the **Krishna** which does great pancakes, watermelon juice, home-made pasta (yes, really) and, best of all, has a pet bull who comes in every morning and walks confidently between the tables to the counter where he is given a banana by the owner. Having eaten it meditavely, the great, stately beast then turns politely around in the narrow space, careful not to knock over any tables and chairs, and walks out. You can eat at the Krishna for under Rs40 per head, including drinks (no beer though).

If you want a beer with your meal, go to the **Ashok** down a side-street towards the river on the opposite side of the bazaar from the Krishna. The service is terrible and the food pretty poor, but the beer is cold.

Travellers also rate the restaurant at the **Rao Guest House**, which serves decent Western dishes and *thalis* under a shady tree for about Rs25–30 per head.

Hospet

Malligi Tourist Home has two good restaurants. The indoor **Nirmal** does cheap vegetarian fare, including tasty standard *thalis*. The garden restaurant, the **Eagle**, is the perfect spot to cool off after a hot, dusty day in the ruins. It serves a range of tasty non-vegetarian meals, and has a bar with ice-cold beers.

The Hotel Mayura has a restaurant and the **Shanbag Hotel**, next to the bus stand in Station Road, is famous for its vegetarian food, and is always crowded. Another **Shanbag,**, on the way to College Road, offers north Indian cuisine in comfortable and more relaxed surroundings.

In general you can eat out in Hospet for between Rs25 and Rs50 per head, going up to Rs100 if you have beer.

Northwest Karnataka

Discomfort is now forgotten—my total attention focused dead ahead on a...treeless skyline out of which, as we climb, grows something which at first appears as a mere blip, and then gradually becomes a dark dome...in another kilometre we top the rise, where the entire dome is visible along with many other minarets, cupolas and battlements...

Robin Brown, *Deccan Tamasha*

North of Hampi stretches the far Deccan—a region of fortress cities that suffered continual warfare from the Middle Ages to the 19th century. Even today, the plains of northern Karnataka still feel closer to the ancient and medieval world than to the modern. Various Hindu and Muslim dynasties had their strongholds here. There are some spectacular ruined Chalukyan cities at Aihole and Pattadkal; and Mughal walled towns, like Bijapur and Bidar, that have hardly changed in centuries. In the countryside, siege-battered castles sit grumpily on the the granite hilltops and Neolithic megaliths dot the outskirts of villages that seldom see a traveller. Away on all sides stretches the vast, dry Deccan, its scrubby red hills silent under the heat. By night the stars blaze like living jewels.

History

The first warlords to hold this wide, dusty territory were the Andhras, who held the region from about 100 BC to 200 AD. After them came the Chalukyans, Dravidian Hindu kings who flourished in northern Karnataka from the 4th to the 8th centuries, building the great fortress towns of Badami and Aihole. In the 12th century power passed to the Vijayanagar dynasty of Hampi, but they were heavily defeated in the mid 14th century by the Bahmani sultans of the north (modern Maharashtra), who then ruled from the towns of Gulbarga and Bidar. The Bahmanis and the Vijayanagars fought up and down the northwest Deccan until the mid 15th century, when the Hindu armies abandoned the region. Flushed with their success, the Bahmanis expanded their territory as far south as Hampi and westward over the mountains to Goa and, for a time, became the major trading power in the Arabian seas, despite their fortress capitals being so far inland.

In the 16th century, the Bahmanis decided to finish off the Vijayanagars once and for all and allied with the other Deccan sultanates of Golconda (now Hyderabad) and Bijapur to sack Hampi and drive the Hindus south. All went as planned until after the ruin of Hampi, when powerful Golconda, now attracted to the fertile Deccan, turned its armies upon the Bahmanis, whose power declined from this point. Through the 17th and 18th centuries Golconda dominated the area and seized most of the fortress towns, treating the Bahmani sultans as local governors, and exacting tribute from them. Also, from the 1650s Maratha raiders began sweeping down from the north, and it was not until the arrival of the British in the early 19th century that an uneasy peace was forced on the northwest Deccan.

Since then, the northwest Deccan has remained a deeply rural backwater, its strongholds and capitals almost untouched by modern development and preserved by the dry climate, making them set-pieces of southern Indian medieval temple and castle architecture.

Badami

The most convenient jumping-off point for the great ruins of Aihole and Pattadkal, Badami is a small town lying below two great fortified bluffs. Although not as spectacular as the nearby ruined cities, Badami is also an ancient site worth seeing. Built as a capital by the Chalukyans between the 6th and 8th centuries, the town fell to just about every other set of invaders that followed.

Its two strategic walled hills have historic sites from most of the important Deccan periods. The **South Fort** has a set of three Hindu and one Jain **cave temples**, carved out by hand during the 5th and 6th centuries. Visit the first cave, reached by a stone stair, for its superb dancing Siva and the third cave for its magnificent sculptured panels showing various episodes from the Ramayana and traces of 6th-century frescoes. Under the **North Fort**, a cluster of small 7th-century temples surround a large tank that served as the town's water supply in times of siege. In a man-made cave by the water's edge is an early **Buddhist temple** (2nd–4th century), and further along, several smaller Hindu caves sacred to Siva. On the townward shore stands the big **Jambulinga Temple** (7th century) and the 10th-century **Virupaksha Temple**. Sculptures collected from the various temples of Badami and the surrounding district are on display at the **Medieval Sculpture Gallery** (*open daily 10–5 except Fri*).

Getting There

Daily **train** services run from the station three miles north of town to Hubli, Hospet, Bombay, Madras and Bijapur, most of which involve changes from the local narrow guage to the inter-state broad gauge lines.

There are direct **bus** services to Hospet, Hubli, Bijapur, Pattadkal and the other towns in the northwest Deccan, which run several times daily.

Where to Stay
inexpensive

The **Chalukya Lodge** and **Mahakuteswara Lodge** on Station Road, just north of the main town are clean and basic, as is the state-run **Mayura Chalukya**, 800 yards west of town in the PED complex on Ramdurg Road.

Pattadkal and Aihole

Pattadkal

A convenient day trip from Badami (about 12 miles south), Pattadkal was a later Chalukyan capital, but seems to have been in existence long before that. Some very grand temple building went on here during the 7th and 8th centuries, notably under the powerful king Vikramaditya who ruled between 734 and 745. The mish-mash of various temple styles—both Dravidian and northern—demonstrate the cosmopolitan outlook of the Chalukyan rajahs. What makes the temples doubly unusual is that almost all are Jain, despite their carvings of Hindu deities—the Chalukyans having been converted during the 9th and 10th centuries—a stangely pacifist move for such a warlike dynasty.

Scattered among the temples are various megaliths from the 6th–3rd centuries BC. Tumbled down low dolmens and menhirs prove that the settlement has never been erased, despite centuries of warfare and new building. The official tourist literature claims that Pattadkal was written about by the Greek historian Ptolemy during the 1st century AD in one of his gazetteers of the great towns of the orient.

Now a World Heritage Site, Pattadkal has several temples of major archaeological importance. Most impressive are the three-storyed **Virupaksha** temple and the great **Mallikarjuna** temple (both mid 8th century), built to commemorate a great victory by the Chalukyan rajah Vikramaditya over the rival Pallavas of the south. Vikramaditya had been so impressed with the Pallava temples seen during his southward campaigns that he commissioned architects from the region to come and build the victory temples, and to carve out intricate friezes of the *Ramayana* on the inner pillars. Every January, the two big temples are host to an annual **Classical Dance Festival**, the *Nrutytsava*, and have their own **temple car festivals** in March and April.

Aihole

Getting Around

Direct **buses** from Badami, Pattadkal, Bijapur and Bidar connect sleepy Aihole with the outside world.

Another Chalukyan capital (6th century), Aihole has about 150 early temples and is regarded by many architectural historians and archaeologists as the place where high Dravidian temple architecture began. A 12-mile bus ride on from Pattadkal, Aihole's ruined temple city lies inside a ruined defensive wall. Eager guides cluster round the bus stand from Pattadkal and you really do need some kind of steering around the temples of this vast, rambling site; some are Buddhist, some Jain, some Hindu. All have superb carvings, and some rise to more than two storeys. The last temples built on the site date from the 12th century and amazingly, none were destroyed by the region's later Muslim invaders.

Of particular interest are the **Konti temples** in the middle of the bazaar and the **Durga temple**, the most elaborately carved building of the lot. It's a Viaishavite temple, built as a long hall (blessedly cool on a Deccan afternoon) with a high, platformed altar at the far end. Also try and make time for the **Hucchapayya Math** (7th–9th century), which forms a cluster of four buildings with some good examples of early erotic (more like pornographic) sculpture. Drier and more earnest is the **Archaeological Museum** (*open daily 10–5 except Fri*), which displays some of the best of the smaller sculptures excavated from the area.

Where to Stay

Pattadkal

Pattadkal is not a developed town and the only clean lodges in the area are 12 miles north at Badami.

Aihole

There is a state-run **Tourist Home**, © Aminagad 41, with clean, basic rooms, next to the entrance to the main temple complex near the bus stand with rooms from Rs100–350.

Bijapur

One hundred miles north of Badami and the Chalukyan temple towns, **Bijapur** is a walled stronghold of domed palaces, mosques and bazaars built round a hill on which sits a strong, but decaying, citadel. Roads into Bijapur still pass under the curtain wall's seven great gate-houses, structures that withstood uncounted sieges throughout the turbulent history of the Deccan Plateau.

Badami fell only four times in 600 years: to the Vijayanagars who ousted its Chalukyan founders in the 12th century; to the Northern Mughals of Delhi in the early 14th century, who ousted the Vijayanagars; to the Bahmani sultans in the late 15th century, who rebelled against the Delhi Mughals; and finally, after a civil war against the Bahmanis, its new local rulers (the Abdil Shah dynasty), ousted the Bahmani garrison in 1686. Throughout the 16th and 17th centuries, both the Bahmanis and the Abdil Shahs fought inconclusive wars with the rival sultanate of Golconda, but by the time the British arrived in the late 18th-century, the city had become a prosperous backwater. Under the British, the Abdil Shahs ruled semi-independently, but Bijapur has been in decline ever since the dynasty died out in the early 19th-century.

Tourist Information

The **tourist office** is in the Mayura Adil Shahi Hotel at the foot of the Citadel, open daily from 10.30 to 1.30 and from 2.15 to 5.30 except Sundays.

For **foreign exchange** try the **State Bank** in the Citadel.

Getting Around

by train

Bijapur has a direct service to Badami (3–4 hours) and indirect services to Bombay and Hyderabad (change at Solapur). Trains also run daily to Hospet with a change at Gadag. The train station is west of the walled city, just outside the Gulbarga Gate.

by bus

Direct daily services run to Bidar, Belgaum, Hospet, Hubli, Bangalore and Hyderabad.

Bijapur has had its day, and the old walls monuments are beginning to tumble down in places, but the medieval buildings are still strong. Of several large mosques, the **Jama Masjid** is the largest and lies southeast of the citadel near the walls. Built from 1557–9, the mosque is in the grandest style, with a huge entrance hall and room for over 2000 worshippers. It is still packed every day for morning and evening prayer. Further towards the citadel along Jama Masjid Road is a small palace, the **Mehtar Mahal**, a fine piece of Islamic whimsy with carved filigree work and fairytale minarets built as a pleasure palace for the later queens of Bijapur. By contrast, the **Citadel** itself is mostly ruined—largely because the later rulers of Bijapur were disdainful of living in such a dour place and moved out to the grander city palaces. However, the Durbar Hall is still intact as is **Jal Manzil**, a pleasure pavilion built round a set of ornamental pools (now dry).

Bijapur has two superbly ornate Islamic tombs. The early 17th-century **Ibrahim Rauza** which lies just outside the city's western (Zohrapur) gate, houses the remains of Ibrahim Abdil Shah, a prominent sultan of Bijapur who originally had it built for his wife, but died before her, so she put him in it instead. At the opposite end of the walled town, just inside the walls and south of the eastern (Gulbarga) gate, is the late 17th-century **Gol Gumbaz**, where the greatest Bijapur sultan Abdil Shah, the man who wrested power from the Bahmanis, lies buried with his family.

Gol Gumbaz

According to the official tourist literature, this tomb boasts the world's second largest free-standing dome (after St Peter's in the Vatican City). Its concave, airy space certainly is vast. A **Whispering Gallery** runs around the base of the dome, midway between floor and ceiling. It would be interesting to find out if there was any connection between Sir Christopher Wren's building and this one, seeing as they were constructed within decades of each other. The sheer scale of the Gol Gumbaz illustrates clearly how powerful Bijapur was before the British conquest reduced its rulers to mere client kings.

In the gatehouse of the Gol Gumbaz is the **Nakkar Khana**, a small museum whose display comprises a brief history of the Bijapur sultans.

The **Bara Kamam** on Jama Masjid Road, is the first storey of a never-completed artillery tower that Abdil Shah designed to command the entire surrounding plain. It still houses a huge cannon known as the *Ruler of the Plains*, whose bronze barrel exceeds 12 feet in length, and was a prize piece of booty brought home from Abdil Shah's wars with Golconda. Inside the lions jaws of the cannon's mouth, an elephant is being swallowed. Although the Bara Kamam never reached its intended height of over 196 feet (60 metres), a slimmer 80 foot (24 metre) high watchtower stands on a raised mound next door, and points lighter cannon out at the surrounding plains. The door is open and you can climb up for the view.

Three miles east of town is the **Asar Mahal**, a small palace believed by some to contain relics of the Prophet Mohammed. Built in 1646 it has some very beautiful frescoes in the Mughal style. Unfortunately no women are allowed inside.

Where to Stay
inexpensive

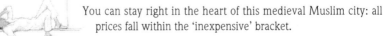

You can stay right in the heart of this medieval Muslim city: all prices fall within the 'inexpensive' bracket.

The best place is the **Mayura Adil Shahi Hotel**, at the southern foot of the Citadel (Anandamahal Road), ✆ 20934. Run by the state tourist board, its rooms are built around a central courtyard and have Indian-style bathrooms.

attached. If this is full, try the clean but basic **Sanman** on Station Road, near the Gol Gumbaz, ✆ 21866, the **Samrat**, also on Station Road, ✆ 21620, or the **Hotel Lalitha Mahal**, opposite the bus stand.

If these places are full try the **Hotel Prasad**, on Azad Road, or the **Hotel Tourist** on Main Road, ✆ 20655. These two are not so clean as the other lodges, but they'll do for a night or two.

Bidar

Far off the tourist track on the northeast border with Andhra Pradesh is Bidar, another Muslim fortress town that started life as a Chalukyan stronghold. Reached via the old 14th–15th century Bahmani capital of Gulbarga (now a scruffy modern town with a broken-down fort) Bidar, like Bijapur, still has its medieval walls. A mere northern outpost of the Bahmani empire until the late 15th century, it rose to prominence after the Bahmani sultans, feeling cramped in Gulbarga's small fort, moved their capital here in the 1420s. A 200-year period of palace and mosque building followed until 1619, when the Bahmanis were defeated by their local rivals, the Abdil Shahs of Bijapur. Bidar fell a third time to the northern Maratha sultans of Auranzgeb in 1686, and remained a Maratha stronghold against Golconda until the British conquest.

Getting Around
by train

Bidar only has a narrow gauge line and the only direct connection is with Hyderabad. The railway station is situated next to the bus station on Ugdir Road, west of the old town via thge Shah Ganj Dharwaza gate.

by bus

Daily services run from Bijapur via Gulbarga (6–7 hours), Hospet via Bijapur (12 hours) and Hyderabad via Zahirabad (4–5 hours). The bus station is on Ugdir Road west of the old town.

Bidar's **Old Fort** was originally built by the Chalukyans in the 10th century but was added to by just about every other Deccan dynasty over the following centuries. The present walls were built by the Bahmani kings in the 15th century, who also dug the triple moat, each bank connected by a narrow causeway and protected by a massive postern.

Inside the old fort is the modest royal residence, the **Rangin Mahal** or 'Coloured Palace'. Built in 1487 it was lavishly decorated inside with painted tiles and mother-of-pearl inlay, some of which survives but most of which is now in disrepair. The front door may be locked but you can ask for the key at the adjacent museum (*see* below). Outside stretch the vast palace kitchens and bathhouse, now housing a small **Archaeological Museum** (*open daily 8–5 except Sun*) displaying medieval weaponry and Neolithic artefacts dug up during excavations inside the fort.

Behind the museum is the **Tarkash Mahal** or old harem, and the ruins of its fountained garden, the **Lal Bagh**. From here, a small mosque and a path lead to the **Gagan Mahal**, a covered arena for watching gladiatorial combats and fights between wild beasts. Other ruined buildings in the fort include the **Takht Mahal**, which had its own swimming pool and underground passageways out of the fort, the **Powder Magazine** and the fort commander's house.

These are now filled with bat colonies and are dangerous due to snakes and falling masonry.

After exploring the old fort (allow a good couple of hours for this) head back over the triple moat (keeping an eye out for possible cannon fire from the Naubat Khana) to the old town, which also lies within its own curtain wall. Turn right as you pass under the final postern and walk for a block down Multani Badshah Road, then turn left into Hospital Road and after about three minutes you come to the **Madrassa of Mahmud Gawan**, built in 1472.

Jami Masjid, Bidar

Mahmud Gawan was an exiled Persian merchant who enlisted with the Bahmanis in 1453 after political indiscretions at home and by 1461 had risen to become Bidar's military commander. His career did not stop here: by 1466 he had been appointed deputy ruler of the kingdom. His notable military achievement was the conquest of Goa in 1470. The Madrassa was built upon Gawan's retirement, as a college of military and philosophical arts. Apparently its library was once one of the best in India, but sadly it was burned down during the Maratha's 17th century storming of the town.

Continue down Hospital Road, take the first right, then first left and you reach a tall watch-tower, the **Chaubara**, which stands about 80 feet (25 metres) high and commands the whole city. Just to the southwest stands the **Jami Masjid** (built in 1430), Bidar's largest mosque.

Bidar's various sultans still lie buried in grand **mausolea** outside the city walls. To the south-west, via the gatehouse on New Arch Road, are the **Barid Shahi Tombs**, a 20-minute auto-rickshaw ride from the town centre. The largest tomb, that of Sultan Ali Barid who died in the early 16th century, has a dome 80 feet (25 metres) high decorated with coloured tiles. Even more spectacular are the **Bahmani Tombs**, another 20 minutes east of town on the Ashtur Road. Carved in the Persian style with stylized animals, birds and swirling floral patterns, the highest dome rises 114 feet (35 metres) above the tomb of Sultan Ahmad Shah, the Bahmani ruler who moved the capital to Bidar from Gulbarga in the 1420s. There are seven other tombs, all beautifully decorated, though somewhat battered by time.

Where to Stay
inexpensive

The state-run **Mayura Barid Shahi**, ✆ 20571, is good value. On Ugdir Road, near the bus station, it has clean, basic rooms, a decent vegetarian restaurant and a shabby bar. Apart from this, there is the overpriced **Bidar International**, also on Ugdir Road, or a number of very cheap but flea-ridden guest lodges in the old town.

Kerala backwaters

Kerala

Then the revered Agastya drew near to Rama and taught him...'Do thou worship the Sun, lord of the world in whom dwells the spirit of all the gods. Hail, Hail! Oh Thousand-Rayed, Thou Wakener of the Lotus, Thou Source of Life and Death... Do thou worship with this hymn the lord of the universe and thou shalt conquer Ravana today.

Then Rama hymned the Sun, and purified himself with water sippings and was glad; and he turned to deal with Ravana, for the demon king had come to himself again, and was eager for the battle.

The Ramayana

Ah, Kerala. Warm breeze on palm-fringed beaches; winding, wooded inland waterways slowly plied by long, hardwood boats with curious, carved prows; dazzling sunlight on the great, brass headdresses of temple elephants at festival time; and everywhere a green riot of vegetation.

A narrow sliver of territory between the Western Ghats and the Arabian sea, Kerala is one of India's calmest and most prosperous states. Blessed with 340 miles of tropical coastline, ample freshwater and rich soil, the state is characterized by vast expanses of waving coconut palms shading quiet villages and a well-kept patchwork of cultivated land. It has India's densest population—more than 29 million people spread over just 15,000 square miles (that's an area roughly twice the size of Wales)—but there are still large areas of virgin rainforest in the mountains, wildlife sanctuaries harbouring big game, and jungle tribespeople who live in caves and have never left the forest.

The word 'Kerala' derives from 'Chera', the name of the region's ruling dynasty in the 1st and 2nd centuries AD. The Cheras were great traders, and ships from all over the civilized world including Rome put in at the Chera ports (Ptolemy mentions their splendid cities.) It was a Roman ship that brought St Thomas and Christianity to Kerala in AD 52. The religion spread through the early medieval period, along with the wealth of the coastal cities, which traded with Arabia after the fall of Rome.

Such dazzling riches attracted frequent invaders: the Chola kings of Tamil Nadu between the 10th and 15th centuries; the Portuguese (who founded Cochin) from 1498 until 1640 when the better armed Dutch arrived; the Muslim warlords Hyder Ali and Tipu Sultan in the 18th century; and finally the British, who took power away from Calicut and Cochin and ruled through the

Kalaripayat

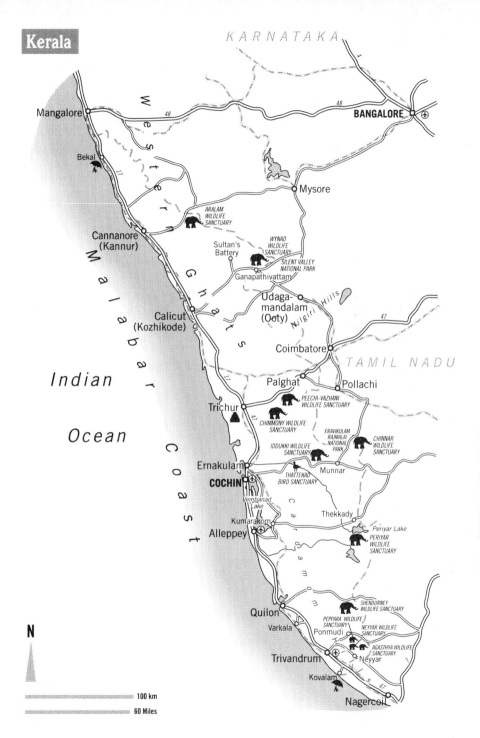

Kerala

KARNATAKA

Mangalore

BANGALORE

Bekal

Mysore

ARALAM
WILDLIFE
SANCTUARY

Cannanore
(Kannur)

Sultan's
Battery

WYNAD
WILDLIFE
SANCTUARY

SILENT VALLEY
NATIONAL PARK

Ganapathivattam

Udaga-
mandalam
(Ooty)

Nilgiri Hills

Calicut
(Kozhikode)

Coimbatore

TAMIL NADU

Indian

Palghat

Pollachi

PEECHI-VAZHANI
WILDLIFE SANCTUARY

Trichur

CHIMMONY WILDLIFE
SANCTUARY

Ocean

ERAVIKULAM
RAJMALAI
NATIONAL
PARK

CHINNAR
WILDLIFE
SANCTUARY

IDDUKKI WILDLIFE
SANCTUARY

Ernakulam

Munnar

COCHIN

THATTEKAD
BIRD SANCTUARY

Vembanad
Lake

Kumarakom

Thekkady

Periyar Lake

Alleppey

PERIYAR
WILDLIFE
SANCTUARY

SHENDURNEY
WILDLIFE SANCTUARY

Quilon

PEPPARA WILDLIFE
SANCTUARY

Varkala

Ponmudi

NEYYAR WILDLIFE
SANCTUARY

N

AGASTHYA WILDLIFE
SANCTUARY

Trivandrum

Neyyar

Kovalam

Nagercoil

100 km

60 Miles

Hindu princes of Travancore , at Trivandrum. Today, in Kerala's highly politi-cized society, her fine old warring spirit is reduced to a babble of competing politicians endlessly blaring slogans from car megaphones and stage platforms, whether there is an election on or not.

Kerala has one of India's most educated, as well as most politicized popula-tions: it's the only state that can boast a literacy rate of almost 100 per cent, and its language, Malayallam, is believed by some linguists to be the fastest-spoken in the world, in terms of syllables per second. Listen to two stallholders arguing in the market place and you'll appreciate this.

But not all Kerala's traditions are so noisy. The art of Ayurvedic medicine began here and still thrives, along with disciplined Kalaripayat—the old martial art of the warring city armies—and the studied poise of Kathakali classical dance. Despite occasional explosions into life for elephant festivals or boat races, the pace of life seems slower here then in many other parts of the country, the Indian struggle for survival slowed to a leisurely cycle of fishing, rice farming and trade in hardwoods, coconut oil and *coir*.

Kerala's Coast

It was just about noon, and far away, high above even the tallest trees, a fish-hawk called its shrill, long cry. Trilling down the lonely paths of the blue sky, radiant with the midday brilliance of the autumn sun, it was like the voice of a goddess.

Bhibhutibushan Banerji, *Pather Panchali,* or *The Song of the Road*

For a long time the haunt only of hippies and travellers looking for a quiet backwater away from the teeming bustle of Northern India, Kerala's coast has now been officially 'discovered', and the old hippy beaches of **Kovalam** and **Varkala** are fast becoming developed for mass tourism. But as ever in traveller's India, the demise of one place's tranquility coincides with the discovery of somewhere new: in this case, the (as yet) undeveloped cove at **Bekal** on Kerala's northern coast, where the only accommodation is in an old fort, and the visitor can share the beach with local fishermen and few others.

Inland, village life moves slowly in the tropical heat, each settlement hidden under the tall shade of coconut palms and cooled by a labyrinthine system of **backwaters**—pure heaven to travel by boat. Yet the calm explodes every August, when the larger backwater towns such as **Alleppey** and **Kottayam** hold **snake-boat races**—dramatic events involving frenzied teams of straining paddlers, who brave the heavy monsoon heat and churn up the waters to the approving roar of the crowds on the banks. Throughout the year, temple towns such as **Trichur**, **Perandur** and **Thiruvallam** (as well as the main cities of Ernakulam and Trivandrum and a host of other places), hold **elephant festivals**, during which caparisoned temple tuskers are paraded to the accompaniment of wailing medieval music, for the glorifica-tion of various gods. For sheer spectacle, the snake-boat races and elephant festivals are hard to beat, even in India.

It is best to use the big cities of **Trivandrum**, **Ernakulam** and **Calicut** only as jumping-off points for quieter destinations, for the intense, often humid heat of Kerala's coast becomes

compounded by crowds and bumper-to-bumper traffic. However, the exception to this is **Cochin**, India's first Portuguese settlement in the islands off Ernakulam harbour. Cochin's 18th-century Jewish quarter, 17th-century palaces and great 16th-century Catholic church (founded by Vasco da Gama, the first European to colonize India) front a shoreline of Chinese fishing nets—huge wooden contraptions controlled by weights and pulleys, that hang above the water like giant, skeletal hands, supporting nets that can gather several hundredweight of fish.

On the coastal plain, the coconut groves and backwaters give way to managed teak and rosewood forests, plantations of rubber trees and cashew groves, before the land rises sharply towards the planatations, forests and wild grasslands of the Western Ghats.

Climate and When to Go

The best (coolest) season is from **November to April**. From then on the heat builds steadily to the **June monsoons** which last until **October**. The cool season temperature averages about 21–28°C but in summer they can soar well above 35°C.

Trivandrum

Most travellers begin their exploration of Kerala from Trivandrum on the coast, heading for the nearby beach resorts of Kovalam and Varkala, before starting to explore the backwaters and the mountains.

Hot, bustling Trivandrum is Kerala's state capital and has been so since the British ended the region's 500 years of warfare and made the local Travancore dynasty into regents in 1789. Yet despite a few surviving monuments and palaces, Trivandrum doesn't look or feel like a state capital at all, having more the air of a large town than of a city.

But Trivandrum is the centre of Keralan culture: Kathakali dance, Kalaripayat martial art, Ayurvedic yoga, medicine and massage evolved here during the early Middle Ages. Many travellers stay in Trivandrum for weeks on end studying one or other of these ancient arts and sciences.

Built over seven hills, Trivandrum derives its name from *Thiru-Anantha-Puram* ('Home of the Serpent'), and is believed to be the home of Anantha, the sacred snake on which Vishnu reclines. Its official name, Thiruvananthapuram, is never used.

Getting Around

by air

From Trivandrum airport (4 miles from the city centre, Rs1 by no.14 local bus) there are daily flights to and from Bombay, Cochin and Goa. There are less frequent services which fly to Bangalore, Hyderabad and Madras.

Trivandrum is also an international airport with **Air India** flights to Gulf cities including Dubai and Muscat. Some of these flights continue on to Europe and New York and there are plans to expand the airport to take more European air traffic over the next few years. **Indian Airlines** operates flights to Male in the Maldives and Colombo in Sri Lanka. **Air Lanka** also operates to and from Colombo. **Gulf Air** operates from and to Abu Dhabi, Bahrain, Doha and Muscat with onward connections to Europe.

by train

From Trivandrum railway station (opposite the bus station), there are a number of trains daily to Ernakulam (Cochin), via Quilon. The fastest train is the 6.15am *Pareswarum Day Express*, which gets to Quilon, 45 miles away, in 1½ hours, and to Ernakulam in just 3 hours. It's a wonderfully scenic ride, cutting right through the eight creeks of Ashtamudi Lake. Best of all, you don't even need to pre-book: just hop on, and pay for your 2nd-class air-conditioned seat on the train.

The best train for Goa leaves Trivandrum at 11pm, arriving in Mangalore at 10am the next morning. Proceed immediately by auto-rickshaw to Mangalore's government (not private) bus stand, in order to catch the 11am express bus (10 hours) to Panjim. Don't miss this early bus as the next one bound for Goa is in the evening.

by bus

Trivandrum has two bus stands. Buses for Kovalam leave from the Fort bus stand. Buses for all other destinations leave from the city bus stand, opposite the railway station. Destinations include Madurai (many buses from 4.30 to 10am and from 5 to 11pm; 7 hours), Kanyakumari (9am, 3pm, and 10.15pm; 2½ hours), Coimbatore (6.30pm; 12 hours), Madras (12.30pm and 7pm; 17 hours) and Kumilly (8 hours). For all these long-haul destinations, you'll have to advance-book tickets: a real pain, in view of the long queues. Try to find a boy to queue up for you for Rs8–10 while you go sightseeing.

Fortunately, there's normally no need for advance reservations on the hourly buses to Ernakulam (4 hours) which run from 5am to midnight, calling at Quilon (2 hours) and Alleppey (3 hours). Just toss your bags in the window and pay on the bus.

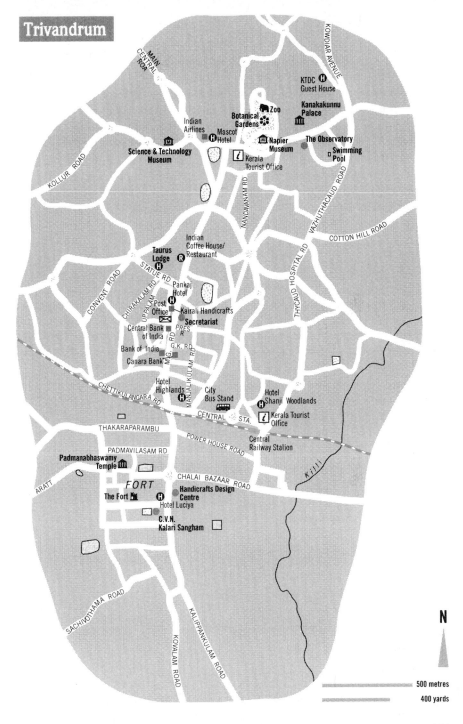

Trivandrum

KOWDIAR AVENUE

MAIN CENTRAL ROAD

KTDC **●** Guest House

Kanakakunnu Palace 🏛

Zoo **🐘**

Botanical Gardens

Indian Airlines

Mascot **🏨** Hotel

The Observatory

Napier Museum 🏛

Swimming Pool □

Science & Technology Museum 🏛

i Kerala Tourist Office

KOLLUR ROAD

NANDAVANAM RD

VAZHUTHACAUD ROAD

COTTON HILL ROAD

Indian Coffee House/ Restaurant **®**

Taurus Lodge ●

STATUE RD

CONVENT ROAD

CHIRAKALAM RD

UPPLAM RD

Pankaj **🏨** Hotel

● Post Office ✉ **Kairali Handicrafts**

Central Bank of India ■ ■ **Secretariat**

PRESR

Bank of India ■

G.K. RD

M.G. RD

MANJALIKULAM RD

Canara Bank ■

THYCAUD HOSPITAL RD

CHETTIKULANGARA RD

Hotel Highlands **●**

City Bus Stand 🚌

Hotel **●** Shanji Woodlands

i Kerala Tourist Office

CENTRAL STA.

THAKARAPARAMBU

PADMAVILASAM RD

POWER HOUSE ROAD

Central Railway Station

KILLI

Padmanabhaswamy Temple 🏛

ARATT

FORT

CHALAI BAZAAR ROAD

The Fort 🏯 **●** **Handicrafts Design Centre**

Hotel Luciya

C.V.N. Kalari Sangham □

SACHIVOTHAMA ROAD

KOVALAM ROAD

KALIPPANKULAM ROAD

N

500 metres

400 yards

201

Tourist Information

The **KSTDC Tourist Office**, ✆ 451085 is at Parkview, opposite the museum complex. It has very friendly, helpful staff and excellent published information, including a useful festival list for Kerala.

The **KSTDC Reception Centre**, ✆ 75031, is near the bus stand in Station Road opposite the railway station exit, open 6am–10pm. Also very helpful, it offers a number of tours: Trivandrum city sightseeing, Rs85; Kanyakumari; Thekkady (Periyar), Rs225. There is also an information counter at the **airport**, ✆ 71085.

The **GPO** is just off M.G. Road, between the bus and railway stations and the Secretariat. **Indian Airlines**, ✆ 66370, is at Mascot Junction. **Air India**, ✆ 64837, is at Vellyambalam. **Gulf Air** use Jet Air, Saran Chambers, Diamond Hill, ✆ 68003/67514.

A good travel agent is **Sheriff Travel**, Patan Palace Junction.

The City Centre

Trivandrum city is bisected by a single long thoroughfare, M.G. Road. Getting to the museum, zoo, art gallery, main tourist office and Indian Airlines (all at the top of M.G. Road) from Padmanabhaswamy Temple, or the Kovalam bus stand (opposite each other, at the bottom of M.G. Road) is a long 15 minute ride by auto-rickshaw (Rs10–15) or taxi (Rs20). It is a good half-hour walk, or a Rs10 rickshaw ride from the main bus stand and rail station, opposite each other in Station Road, to the Secretariat and Statue Junction at the centre of M.G. Road.

The city's main landmark is the **Padmanabhaswamy Temple**, a fine example of south Indian architecture, constructed in the Dravidian style by a Maharajah of Travancore in 1733 and dedicated to Lord Vishnu, the presiding deity of Trivandrum. Its magnificent seven-storeyed *gopuram* is reflected in the placid temple pool, and the interior is decorated with intricate carvings and murals.

Unfortunately it is off-limits to non-Hindus. That said, some travellers have sought and gained permission to enter from the Ramakrishna Centre, near the temple. You must dress traditionally inside, in *dhotis* or *saris*. Even if you can't get in, the exterior view is fine, and there are many interesting old houses in the surrounding backstreets. At 4pm Vishnu is taken on his daily procession round the temple grounds.

Proceeding north up M.G. Road by rickshaw, look

out for the white-stuccoed **Secretariat** on your right. It's an impressive building, fully reflecting the pomp of the British Raj. Much more impressive is the vast, landscaped museum complex to the north of town. Here are the spacious **Botanical Gardens** (*open daily 10–5, except Mon; adm Rs5, plus a further Rs3 to visit the art gallery. Camera fees are Rs5 extra*), 80 acres of beautifully laid-out lawns, lakes and woodlands. Practically every known variety of tropical tree can be found here. Within the grounds is the dingy and rather depressing **Zoo** (though it has to be said that the animals are in goodish nick, and it makes a good place to learn your Indian wildlife), the magnificent, Indo-Saracenic red-tiled **Napier Museum** housing a famous collection of bronzes and **Sri Chitra Art Gallery** with a modest display of Indian and far-Eastern paintings. The complex is a good place to bring a packed lunch, and spend a relaxing day.

Back on the south end of M.G. road is the **C.V.N. Kalari Sangham** in the East Fort area. This is Trivandrum's oldest existing institute for both the Kalaripayat martial art, and for Ayurvedic medicine and massage. It operates partly as a clinic for the paying public, partly as a fighting school, and will take foreign pupils for courses of several months. Built of stone, its Kalaripayat training arena allows visitors in (6.30–8am) to see the warriors (who begin as young as 8 years old) perform their limbering exercises and fighting with the fourteen different weapons. You can also get a superb massage there and consult one of the doctors about any health problems. The institute's rather strange name derives from the late Sri C.V. Narayanan Nair, a fighting champion from the early part of this century who laid down a single system for Kalaripayat from the many then practised, and founded several schools across Kerala. To make an appointment or find out about training programmes call, ✆ 74182.

Sports and Activities

Classical dance: Two troupes, **Kathakali Club** and **Drisyavedi**, give displays of traditional Kathakali 'story-play' dance twice monthly, usually at the **Karthikathirunal Theatre**, near to Padmanabhaswamy temple. Both outfits draw their players from the Margi School of Kathakali, near the West Fort, and if you turn up at the Fort High School behind Padmanabhaswamy temple in the early morning, you can make an appointment to watch classes the following day.

Yoga and Ayurvedic massage: Instruction is given by Dr Pillai at the **Yoga Therapy Hospital** in Bazhuthacaud Junction. The doctor prefers you to take the full 3-month course, but if you've only a week to spare, he may decide he can do something for you.

Shopping

Popular buys in Trivandrum are carvings and curios, bell-metal lamps, screw-pine items, handloom fabrics, and Kathakali masks and dolls in *papier mâché* or wood. The two (good) government emporia are **Kairali**, ✆ 60127 at Statue Junction, and **SMSM Institute**, behind the Secretariat. Both are fixed-price establishments, offering the full range of local produce. Although some shops still offer ivory items, the sale and export of ivory is banned by both Indian and international law.

Where to Stay

expensive

For modern, clean comfort, try the KTDC **Mascot Hotel**, ✆ 68990/68475, well situated at the top of M.G. Road, near the museum complex, with a pool and sauna. If you prefer something a little more eccentric, the new **Hotel Luciya Continental**, East Fort, ✆ 73443, ✆ 73347, offers air-conditioned rooms and suites done up in a variety of styles, including Chinese and a ham-fisted half-timbered attempt at Olde English style. The **Madison Fort Manor**, Power House Junction, ✆ 70002, is centrally located, has a good travel desk and clean, airy rooms.

moderate

Least expensive in the range is the central **Highlands**, on Manjalikulam Road in Thampanoor suburb, ✆ 78440/78466, which has air-conditioned rooms and a good restaurant. The modern, state-run **Chaitram** on Station Road, Thampanoor, ✆ 75777, is very near to the railway and bus stations. Again, air-conditioned rooms here are very good value—almost at the bottom of the price range. A little more expensive is **Hotel Pankaj**, opposite the Secretariat on M.G. Road, ✆ 76667. The least 'Indian' of Trivandrum's big hotels, it can be snobby (*very* reluctant to show backpackers rooms) and food is pricey, but there's good service, stylish rooms and a nice rooftop restaurant.

inexpensive

The **Highlands Hotel** (*see* above) has non air-conditioned rooms. Also good is the **Hotel Poorna**, ✆ 331315/331729, on M.G. Road south of the Secretariat. Within the price category are the **Hotel Safari**, ✆ 77202/72778, opposite the S.M.V. school on M.G. Road, the **Hotel Samrat** on Thakaraparampu Road, ✆ 463314 and the **Highness Inn** on Airport Road, Peruntanni, ✆ 450983.

cheap

Try the **Taurus Lodge**, located down Statue Road. It's run by 'George', one of those polite, informative lodge-owners who help make travel in India a joy, rather than a continual struggle. Rooms are clean and quiet and the best ones (nos.21, 24 and 25) are spacious, with good views. Whatever you want to know about Trivandrum, its culture, transport, entertainments or shopping, ask George. In the same price bracket is the small, clean **Omkar Lodge** on M.G. Road, ✆ 78503.

Eating Out

The best upmarket restaurants are at **Hotel Shanti Woodlands** (Thycaud) and **Hotel Pankaj**. Both offer mid-priced quality fare in air-conditioned comfort. For great grills (burgers etc.) and Indian food, try **Kalabara Restaurant** near Taurus Lodge. The **Mayfair Hotel** opposite has a good bar. Two other popular restaurants with more local food are **Ananda Bhavan** and **Athul Jyoti**, both on M.G. Road, just along from the Secretariat.

Kovalam

Kovalam, 7 miles from Trivandrum, was once the Arabian Sea beach resort of the court of the Rajahs of Travancore. Today, its two scimitar-sweeps of sand comprise the most popular tourist draw in southern Kerala. The place used only to cater for hippy backpackers but now matches Goa for restaurants, hotels and shopping. However, despite a massive increase in visitors, Kovalam still has its soft yellow-white sands, warm, clear waters, and wide views of the ocean horizon. Small beach restaurants provide the laid-back tourist community with fresh seafood and slightly overpriced Western-style cuisine. Fishermen still put out to sea in their catamarans each morning and most visitors find it very difficult to leave. The coolest and best months to come are between December and March. In April the heatwave arrives, driving many people north. The result (if you don't mind sunburn and a few pre-monsoon showers) is empty beaches and cheap accommodation.

Getting Around
by bus

Bus no.9D (every half-hour, from 6am to 10pm) from the city bus stand at East Fort (40-minute journey, Rs4 fare). Sometimes, auto-rickshaws offer cheap 'share' rides (Rs25 per head) from the bus stand. The normal point-to-point rickshaw fare is nearer Rs60. Taxis and hire cars regularly ply this route.

Tourist Information

The nearest **tourist office** is in Trivandrum. So is **Indian Airlines, State Bank of India**, and the **post office**. To **change money**, use the bank at **Kovalam Ashok Beach Resort**. To post letters, buy aerogrammes and the like, use the small **sub post office** in Kovalam Village (a 20-minute climb up the back of the beach, near the top of the headland).

The Beaches

Kovalam has two popular beaches, separated by a large rock outcrop extending into the sea. The luxury beach, overlooked by the five-star Ashok Beach Resort Hotel, is just below the bus stand. The main beach, with all the budget accommodation and beach restaurants, is a 1-minute walk through shady palm groves from the bus stand. The end of this 'budget' beach is marked by the lighthouse up on the headland.

Popular beach activities at Kovalam include snorkelling (easy to hire equipment), water-skiing (contact the Ashok Hotel), and body-surfing the big waves about 200 yards off the shore. Swimming is very pleasant in the shallows, which extend a long way out, but don't go much further as the currents become dangerously strong.

One problem that women will encounter is unwanted attention from the crowds of Indian tourists who come down at weekends to see bikinied or topless Western flesh. You will have to be firm, if not abusive in getting rid of such company, but also use common-sense and don't go topless—remember that in India a bare breast (let alone a pair!) is something worth travelling miles to see. In high season, you will also be assailed by hordes of grinning salesmen selling fruit, seashells, sarongs and soft drinks. For peace and quiet try the quieter cove directly behind the lighthouse, or wander up to the bay above the big Ashok hotel, which is often quite deserted.

Kovalam is also a pot-smoker's paradise, and as such provides occasional rich pickings for thieves and corrupt policemen. Don't let too much sun, sea and smoke make you careless. Doze off on the beach and you may wake up, badly sunburnt, to find all your belongings gone. Smoke drugs too openly and you may also find yourself in trouble: there are police informers all over the place and an on-the-spot fine may cost you everything you have.

If inertia or boredom set in, and you need a break from the beaches, it's time to get out and about. For many people, this just means a leisurely stroll up onto the headland, to visit the shops in Kovalam Town. For something more rewarding, try the following short excursion.

Fishing Village

by foot, a morning

This walk is a treat. Be down on the beach at 7am to watch the fishermen put out to sea, then take the high road running up from the lighthouse to the top of the headland. From here, it's a scenic 1½-mile stroll, offering beautiful views along the coastline, to the small decorative Muslim shrine perched on the cliff edge. There's a path here, which takes you down to the beach again. Keeping to your left, you'll shortly arrive at the fishing village. The beach is lined with the hulks of long, primitive wooden dugouts and the way to introduce yourself (they don't see a lot of tourists) is to lend a hand with a fishing rope, net or boat. At the back of the beach, you'll see the charming tiered Catholic shrine housing a red-faced Jesus and Mary, the community's patron saints. Climb the rise behind this for a cold drink and stunning coastline views. Then drop in on the village, an interesting collection of narrow, cobbled streets and thatched dwellings with wide courtyards for drying out the fish. Behind the village, back on the main road, you'll find the modern seaside town, with Portuguese-style bungalows, little knick-knack shops, a couple of cafés and lots of locals on holiday. From here, it's a leisurely 45-minute walk back up the headland to Kovalam Beach for a well-earned rest in the sun.

Massage

Kovalam is full of places offering Ayurvedic massage, but of course there are also many charlatans. Head straight for **Medicus Massage** opposite the Rockholm Hotel on the Lighthouse road, a small clinic run by a husband and wife team, Drs. K.R.C. and Lalitha Babu. The clinic is opposite the Rockholm hotel.

Shopping

The most common buys at Kovalam are suntan lotion, funky beach clothes and mosquito repellent. You can find all this stuff, plus cigarettes and confectionery, at the small general stores by the bus stand. Good tailor-made clothes can be made up by K. Surash's Fashion Tailoring Shop, a little place next door to the second-hand book exchange on the road leading down to the firt beach from Kovalam town. Suresh's prices are fair, but this cannot be said of the book exchange next door, which charges more than the new retail price for its second-hand stock. Seashells, sarongs and (fake) jewellery are hawked by children on the beach, but Kovalam just isn't a buyers' market. Like Goa, it's a place to sell things. Unload any unwanted film, cameras, Walkmans, and even snorkel equipment here. You'll have no problem swapping books either. Most people, remember, spend all day on the beach reading!

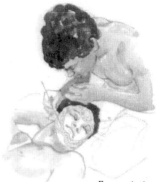

Face-painting

Kovalam ✆ (0471–)

Where to Stay

Note: In all of Kovalam's hotels you may be able to bargain discounts of up to 50% in the low season (any time apart from November to February).

luxury

The prestige place to stay is the five-star **Kovalam Ashok Beach Resort**, ✆ 68010/ 653236, ✆ 62522, with its superb location, water-sports, yoga and massage facilities, but the standard of service and food fluctuates. The beach cottages are pleasant, but as the air-conditioning rarely works, are not recommended in the hotter months. The large balcony rooms, which cost 25% higher between mid-December and the end of February, have the famous sunset view. A new wing opened in late 1992 and the old Palace guest house on the hill above the resort has four suites.

expensive

Try the well-appointed **Hotel Rockholm**, ✆ 584306 up on the lighthouse headland. This has some lovely, breezy rooms overlooking the cliffs, and an excellent restaurant with open-air patio. KTDC's pleasant **Hotel Samudra**, ✆ 62089 a 15-minute walk north of the luxury Ashok hotel, is a modern building, tastefully done, commanding a quiet stretch of beach. In season, it has a good restaurant on the roof. Some rooms have balconies and sea views. You can also try the **Hotel Aparna** on Lighthouse Road, ✆ 64129/74367, which has rooms, again with some overlooking the sea.

moderate/inexpensive

Two hotels have rooms that fall within both categories. Directly behind the Rockholm on Lighthouse Road, is **Syama Lodge** with huge, well-furnished rooms which drop to half-price in the low season. You can try for a big double room with a sea-view balcony at **Hotel Seaweed**, near the lighthouse, ✆ 480391.

cheap

There are now so many small, cheap, and generally comfortable lodges, either right on the beach, or set just back from it that recommending any one over another is a difficult exercise: they're changing all the time. Many have rooms from Rs100 per night and it is also possible to rent rooms with local families for Rs300 a week. Try the **Achuta Lodge Guest House**, the **Neptune Hotel** or **Holiday Home Guest House**—all on Lighthouse beach—or ask at any of the beach restaurants and you will soon find your way.

Eating Out

Kovalam has some excellent restaurants, although some of the old favourites on the beach have been closed down. Good Italian, French, Chinese and Malabar dishes plus the local seafood are all just a short, lazy stroll up the beach. Two popular beach restaurants are the **Black Cat** and **Coral**. The **Rockholm** (✆ 306) has excellent fish dishes, depending on what's available that morning in the market. While the menu includes some European dishes it is their seafood that excels. Lobster, crab and mackerel can be prepared to order. Meals cost anything from Rs60–250 a head depending on how many dishes of crab curry you can eat. The **Searock** restaurant has a menu of Indian and continental dishes and meals are from about Rs60. No restaurant is in a hurry to serve you in Kovalam.

South of Kovalam

A good day trip is to the Arabian Nights splendour of the ruined **Padmanabhapuram Palace**, built in the 16th century by the nationalistic Rajas of Travancore, who ousted the Dutch in 1740, fought Tipu Sultan's armies and were finally rewarded with power by the British in 1789. The best of Keralan architecture and crafts are displayed here—particularly apparent in the use of carved hardwoods for the palace interiors. The building is huge and it is best to hire a guide (they hang out at the main entrance), but don't pay more than Rs150 for the tour. There are 14 magnificent rooms, many with their carved furniture still intact. The highlight of the tour is in the armoury, which displays an iron cage in which those who had displeased the raja were hung alive, but unable to move, as kites and vultures tore at their flesh through the metal slats. Access to Padmanabhapuram is by bus from Trivandrum (several services daily) or Kovalam (two services only, check at the tourist office for times) or by auto-rickshaw (approximately Rs100 round trip).

For those who can afford it, there are several private beach resorts offering complete tranquility, a small number of guests at any time, and hassle-free beaches shared only with the fishermen

who go out at dawn and return at dusk. The closest to Kovalam (3 miles to the south) is **Lagoona Beach**, run by Kerala Tourism, ✆ 443738. Occupying the meeting of several palm-fringed backwaters with the sea, this long sweep of empty beach is a perfect place to relax. Backwater trips to quiet villages are offered. Prices start from about Rs600 per person per night.

Much more expensive and much more exclusive is the **Surya Samudra Beach Garden** at Pulinkudi, some 5 miles further south, ✆ 480413/481824/481825, ✉ 481124. Set in a sloping woodland of coconut palms, Surya Samudra (which means 'sun and sea' in Mallayalam) offers accommodation for just 24 people in antique, carved wood Keralan houses (imported from upcountry), two secluded beaches, a freshwater pool, one of the best restaurants in the state, and landscaped grounds filled with ancient sculpture. Klaus, the German owner, has gradually developed the place from a single original house that he used to use as a private getaway while working as a teacher in Madras. He does his best to employ as many locals as possible, spends large amounts on local conservation, and charges each guest a dollar a day for donation to the local villagers.

Best of all, Surya Samudra has Raju, one of Kerala's most gifted Ayurvedic doctors and masseurs. An hour and half under his hands leaves you about a year younger. Raju is also a Kalaripayat martial arts master, and his local school gives displays at the resort by request. Prices at Surya Samudra are very high: from Rs2000 per person per night.

A few mjiles south is the **Sometheeram Beach Resort**, ✆ 480600, ✉ 481600. Designed along the same lines as Surya Samudra, with antique Keralan houses, an Ayurvedic spa and day trips to local sights, it lacks the former's intimacy. Prices are slightly lower though.

The Coast North of Trivandrum

The prime attraction on this stretch of coastline is **Varkala**, a quieter beach haven than busy Kovalam. But before heading straight to the beach from Trivandrum as most travellers do, take in a side-trip on the way to the Tropical Botanic Garden and Research Institute.

The Tropical Botanic Garden and Research Institute

About an hour's bus ride north of Trivandrum, this 300 acre landscaped garden of wide lawns and well-spaced tropical shade trees has close ties with Kew Gardens in London (they're about the same size). The huge garden is surrounded by forests rich in birdlife, monkeys, deer and wild pig, and there are walking trails winding off into its cool interior. Longer guided hikes into the deeper forest where you may see elephant or bison, can be arranged at the Institute's main office. They don't get many casual visitors here, and the staff are usually happy to show you around if you are really interested. The institute is also a good place to pick up information on Kerala's mountain tribes. As many of the resident botanists use tribal guides and stay in tribal settlements while in the field.

To get there, take a bus from the City Bus Stand in the east Fort area of Trivandrum to Palode, then take an auto-rickshaw (approximately Rs20). Accommodation is offered in two Forestry Department guest houses, but these must be booked in advance via the Institute's office, ✆ 84236/226.

Varkala

Exactly 1 hour by train from Trivandrum (30 miles; several services daily from Trivandrum/ Quilon), this delightful unspoilt little seaside resort has a mineral-water spring, a Vishnu temple dedicated to Lord Janardhana with fascinating rituals, a beach that is empty except at weekends, good swimming and lovely country scenery. Apart from a minor problem with theft, the beach and its small village are mercifully free from the hassle of Kovalam—no groups of Indian tourists turning out to see European flesh, and few hawkers. Visit soon however, as Varkala's beauty has not gone unnoticed; the Taj hotel group is planning to build a huge resort hotel and golf course on the cliffs above the beach in the next few years.

Varkala has a few lodges, but ignore these and head a mile towards the smaller beach village.

Where to Stay

The more expensive places to stay are in the 'moderate' price category. They include the **Hill Top Beach Resort** and the **Varkala Marine Palace**—both with prices starting at Rs300 per person, but it is better to eschew these rather bland places and head for the cheaper, friendlier lodges nearer the beach. For Rs100 or less for a double, try the **Tourist Home**, the **Mamma Home** in an old Keralan house, and the ambitiously named but very basic **Beach Palace**. Long-stay travellers can find rooms in local houses for about Rs35 per night. Some travellers book into the cheap lodges in the town itself, mainly in the area of the Krishna temple: a famous saint called Sri Narayana used to live here and many followers have stayed on.

The Kerala Backwaters

Quilon

The gateway to Kerala's beautiful backwaters, Quilon (also called Kollam) is a rather ugly town situated on the edge of the more beautiful Ashtamudi Lake, 'lake of eight creeks', whose shore are fringed with luxuriant coconut groves and cashew plantations.

An ancient commercial centre, the site on which modern Quilon stands was used by the Phoenicians, Persians, Greeks, Romans, Arabs and the Chinese. Even today, you can see the Chinese fishing nets, more commonly associated with Cochin further north dotted round the lakes here. Quilon town, established in the 9th century, is associated with the origin of the Malayallam-era 'Kollavarsham', which began in AD 825. In more recent times, its commercial wealth made it a bone of contention between Portuguese, Dutch and English trading interests. Today, it is just a sleepy market town of divided into a picturesque quarter of red-tiled wooden houses and winding backstreets, and half usual scrubby Indian semi-industrial hellhole.

You need not linger here more than a day: the big attraction in these parts are the famous backwaters, best visited from December to February. By March, the heat and the mosquitoes are too oppressive. Budget travellers will need a mosquito net if sleeping in Quilon's cheap hotel rooms.

Tourist Information

There is a **tourist information desk** at the Government Guest House (✆ 76456). The **post office** and **Bank of India** are both at the top of Parameswar Nagar, two thirds of a mile above the bus stand. Boats can also be hired from the **Quilon Boat Club** (✆ 72519) or through the tourist office.

Arriving in Quilon, go straight to the boat jetty, a minute's walk below the bus stand, to check the departure time of the morning backwaters' boat. You'll need to arrive early to get a seat on this government-run, and therefore cheap, service. Private boat trips are more expensive at about Rs100–200, but can be booked through almost any hotel. Then use any free time in Quilon to stroll around the pretty part of town around the lakeshore, or to visit **Thangasseri Beach** for its sands, lighthouse and Portuguese/Dutch fort ruins 2 miles away. For a short while Thangasseri was a British trading outpost.

Quilon ✆ (0474–)

Where to Stay

Note: all hotels have a problem with mosquitoes, so bring lots of repellent.

moderate

The **Sudarshan** on Hospital Road near the boat jetty, ✆ 75322, has air-conditioned rooms (though only some) with attached, Western-style bathrooms and two restaurants. Private backwater trips to Alleppey cost about Rs100 and can be booked from here.

The **Government Guest House**, ✆ 76456, is a former British Residency with lovely gardens, good Keralan-style food and a useful jetty. Boat hire is available from 10am to 4pm daily.

cheap

The most popular among backpackers is the **Karthika** halfway up Main Street (also called Paika Road) from the station end, ✆ 76241. The Karthika has a reasonable-to-awful restaurant, a shop and, again, you can book a private backwater trip to Alleppey from reception. Also on Main Road, nearer to the bus station is the **Lakshami Tourist Home**, ✆ 70167, which is a little cheaper, though it has a few air-conditioned rooms. Try also the **Iswarya Lodge** on Main Road, but further east, ✆ 77801.

Eating Out

For good Indian, Chinese and continental food, try the **Hotel Sudarshan** (two restaurants, plus an air-conditioned bar); for cheaper vegetarian meals, visit the **Hotel Guru Prasad** on Main Road. For a big breakfast before the boat trip (you may not eat again all day) try **Mahalaxshmi Lodge** opposite the bus stand. The **Indian Coffee House** on Main Street is good for snacks and coffee.

The Backwaters

The **Kuttanadu Backwaters** between Quilon and Alleppey are unforgettable. The 8½-hour boat journey takes you from narrow canals canopied by dense foliage out into large inland lagoons framed by dense tropical palm groves. Fishermen stand waist-high in the waters and cast their nets. Families of river-dwellers pass by in narrow punted dugouts. Wooden vessels with primitive Chinese sails drift up the waterways, stately and silent. Children run down from Portuguese churches and schools to welcome your approach. In the lush season (February), the boat carves a plough through canals carpeted with blossoming water hyacinths. At sunset, you chug across a huge lake into Alleppey harbour, a corridor of gently swaying coconut palms, backing onto brilliant green meadows. The trip is a delight. Take plenty of camera film (the views cry out to be photographed) and lots of food, because there are only two stops, at about 1pm and 4pm, for *thalis* and coffee. Try to get a berth on the boat roof; you're generally allowed up, depending on the mood of the crew, a short while after departure from Quilon. A couple of rupees *baksheesh* may be in order, but it's well worth it. Make sure you have a hat and plenty of sunscreen.

If you take a private boat, try and get the pilot to stop for lunch at Mannarsala, where there is a famous Nagaraja, or **snake temple** (complete with live temple cobras), run by one of the few high priestesses in the country.

Naga temple carving

Mannarsala is the home of an *ashram* run by a woman guru credited with miraculous powers of healing. An increasing number of Westerners are coming here, and many of their stories are quite incredible. One Spanish traveller spoke of an incident involving his girlfriend, who had badly hurt her foot. Apparently the guru, known as *Amma*, or 'Mother' approached the girl, touched her foot and declared 'my pain is your pain'. Both the Spaniard and his girlfriend were amazed to see the wound disappear from the girl's foot and reappear on the guru's. An hour later, all trace of it had gone. 'When I get home there are maybe two people I can tell this to,' said the Spaniard. 'The rest will think me mad.'

Backwater Alternatives

The Backwaters between Quilon and Alleppey are not the only ones available for exploration. Smaller, quieter waterways wind from Alleppey out to Kottayam (which has a fantastic lagoon resort for those who can afford luxury accommodation), as well as up to Ernakulam (Cochin) and into various backwaters around that city. It is possible to make some of these trips by government boat (information available from the Tourist Office at the boat jetty in Alleppey) but it is far, far more pleasant to go by **private houseboat** for a few days. These old Keralan craft are made of dark hardwood with impressive carved prows, have cabins of woven palm-leaf and can accommodate several people. Prices are expensive—around Rs2000 per boat per day, but you can split this between about four people. Contact Varkey Kurian at **Clipper Holidays** in Cochin, ✆ 0484 364453.

Alleppey

Far more attractive than Quilon, Alleppey is a small market town, built around a curious maze of bridges and canals. These have earned it the title 'Venice of the East'—a trifle far fetched, owing to its small size, which gives it a pleasantly intimate feel. The canals are surprisingly filth-free, often green with water hyacinth and, if you look closely, you will often see schools of young fish feeding near the surface. Kingfishers fly by in flashes of iridescent azure, and along St George's Street, which flanks the main canal, merchants load and unload directly from the long hardwood trading boats that ply the backwaters with cargoes of mostly yarn, rope and mats—for Alleppey is the centre of Kerala's famous *coir* products. The town merchants in their old Keralan houses, heap their wares in open 'go-downs' (warehouses) at street level. Take a walk down St George's Road, which starts about 550 yards south of the boat jetty, to pick up the laid-back, yet prosperous atmosphere of the backwaters. Otherwise, especially if you stay in the tourist lodges near the jetty, you will never get a feeling of what this town is all about.

Once a year the town explodes into furious life for the spectacular **Nehru Cup Snake-Boat Race**, held on the second Saturday of August, when the 90 foot-long boats (paddled by 60 men) fly down the long backwater straights to the boom of drums and the roar of a crowd tens of thousands strong. Teams train and prepare throughout the year and up to 70 boats compete over a mile-long course. The Allepuzhans' enthusiasm and rivalry for the coveted trophy is similar to that of the Siennese of Italy for their famous *Palio* horse race and similar attempts by the different factions to undermine the boats and teams of the others' lend a euphoric ferocity to the whole proceeding.

The start: Nehru Cup

Alleppey © (0477–)

Where to Stay

moderate

Alleppey's only hotel in this range is the **Alleppey Prince**, © 3752. The Prince has flexible rates, so do not hesitate to bargain. Situated halfway down A.S. Road, a long mile from the town centre, it works hard for custom. Touts selling this hotel board your boat just as it drifts into Alleppey. The Prince has a swimming pool, a superb Keralan restaurant and a boat.

inexpensive

The **Komala**, opposite the jetty, © 3631, has clean rooms and a good restaurant. The old travellers' haunt, **St George's Lodge** in C.C.N.B. Road near the boat jetty, © 3373, is useful for its money exchange facilities, (as is the Canara Bank in St George's Buildings). However, the food is not good.

cheap

The **Karthika Guest House** on S.V.D. Road, © 5524, over the bridge, one block north of the boat jetty. Good value, with some air-conditioned rooms, the place has a reasonably good travel service and an Ayurvedic massage clinic. On the same side of the bridge is the **Kerala Hotel**, easily visible from the jetty, which has cleaner rooms with bathrooms attached.

Eating Out

Far and away the best place for food, drink and relaxation is the **Indian Coffee House**, a mile south of the boat jetty towards St George's Street, with Raj-style waiters and décor, cheap non-vegetarian food and excellent coffee. For good Rs10 *thalis*, you can try

Vijaya Restaurant in Jetty Road. Otherwise check out the inexpensive vegetarian places near the Raja Tourist Home. The vegetarian **Arun Restaurant** at the Komala Hotel is considered by some to be the best in Alleppey.

Backwater Routes from Alleppey

For travellers, Alleppey is simply a jumping-off point for another amazing trip up the Keralan waterways. Many find the shorter 2½-hour journey from here to Kottayam far more satisfactory than the preceding trip from Quilon: you don't tend to get jaded with the scenery.

Furthermore, being so near to the extensive Vembanad Lake stretching north to Cochin, Alleppey is a major centre of inland water transport, so there's a good deal more to see on the lakes. It's a very scenic run, with many country craft, laden with *coir* goods and cashews, gliding up the canals. And there are some lovely inland lagoons, fringed by thin green necklaces of vegetation. The narrower stretches of water are often covered with a purple-green blanket of blossoming water lilies. The final approach into Kottayam is down picturesque avenues of lush tropical trees.

There are a number of boats leaving for Kottayam daily. But for maximum comfort and superior scenery, an early morning or mid-afternoon departure is best.

Kottayam

About two hours by either train or backwater boat from Cochin and Alleppey, Kottayam is principally a springboard point for Periyar Wildlife Sanctuary in the mountains to the east, and for the expensive Coconut Lagoon backwaters resort. A prosperous commercial town (and thus now ugly and increasingly polluted at its centre), famous for its cash crops of rubber, tea, pepper and cardamom, it was developed as an educational centre by English missionaries. Indeed, Kottayam's Christian history extends back into antiquity: it was patronized by St Thomas (1st century AD), and the descendants of some of the wealthy Brahmins he converted later helped build some fine churches here, notably the 16th-century **Vallia Palli Church** some 3 miles northwest of the railway station. Mass is sung at 9am on Sundays. Vallia is notable for its Pahlavi inscriptions and for its Nestorian cross, which is said to have come from St Thomas' original church at Cranganore. Kottayam is an important centre for Syrian Christians in Kerala, as well as being the place where many of Kerala's leading newspapers are published.

Kumarakom

Much more pleasant then smelly old Kottayam, Kumarakom is the name for a thinly-spread set of fishing villages set around the massive Vembanad freshwater lagoon, about 7 miles from Kottayam. A superbly tranquil 'backwater' (pun intended), Kumarakom has a wooded, marshland **bird sanctuary**, through which you can walk, and has evolved a bizarre local method of fishing; the lagoon is no more than 4–5 feet deep in most places and a group of fishermen will wade in, two carrying a long rope, the others walking behind, dragging a small boat. The rope is dragged along the lake's glutinous floor, hitting the fish and causing them to burrow into the the mud for protection. The fishermen walking behind then dive down, feel around and grab the fish wherever they find them. These they then bring to the surface and chuck into the boat. It seems a time and energy-consuming way of catching fish but the fishermen are highly skilled and the local inhabitants are obviously well fed.

Kottayam ✆ (0481–)

Stay at either the 'moderate'/'inexpensive' category **Anjali Hotel**, K.K. Road, 2½ miles from the railway station, ✆ 563661, with clean, comfy air-conditioned rooms. In the same price range is the the **Hotel Greenpark**, Nagampadam, ✆ 563331.

In the 'cheap' category is the off-beat **Tourist Bungalow**, a tricky but rewarding 15-minute walk/climb from the boat jetty. It offers spacious double rooms (originally British officers' quarters) with period furnishings.

Kumarakom ✆ (048192–)

luxury

The recently established **Coconut Lagoon**, ✆ 668221, 🖹 668001, is a private resort of antique Keralan houses imported from various parts of the state and built around a minor labyrinth of waterways on the shores of the lake. An outdoor pool, superb Indian and continental restaurant, Ayurvedic spa (though the Ayurvedic massage here is not the best in Kerala) and ultra-efficient service make up the attractions. There is also superb birdlife—not just at the bird sanctuary on the opposite island (the management runs a boat over to the sanctuary every morning), but also in the complex itself: egrets, tree pies, black-headed orioles, bee-eaters, brahmini kites and a whole host of herons are just a few of the breeding species at Coconut Lagoon.

inexpensive

Fortunately, you don't have to be rich to stay on the lagoon. Almost equally idyllic, but costing a fraction of Coconut Lagoon is the KTDC **Kumarakom Tourist Complex**, ✆ 564866, an old building in extensive grounds. The woodland and lake attract many species of birds and rooms in the complex are airy and well ventilated.

Cochin/Ernakulam

Portugal's original trading station in the East Indies, Cochin is one of Kerala's most beautiful places; a town built around a saltwater lagoon of the Arabian Sea. Unfortunately, to get here you have to pass through one of Kerala's least beautiful places, the mainland city of **Ernakulam** (*see* below). Once there, Cochin seems to be a city from the past come to life. It comprises the southern peninsula of **Fort Cochin** and **Mattancherry**, and the islands of **Willingdon**, **Bolghatty**, **Gundu** and **Vypeen**, all connected by a network of bridges and ferries. The scenic setting of its natural harbour, away from Ernakulam, is famous— surrounded by palm groves, green fields, inland lakes and backwaters. All this beauty has earned Cochin the title 'Queen of the Arabian Sea'.

Cochin has a rich maritime history and still ships Kerala's *coir*, rubber, seafood and pepper products abroad. Influenced at various times by the Arabs, Chinese, Dutch, British and the Portuguese, it was Cochin's Jews who founded the first strong community here, over 1000 years ago, one of the only places that the dispossessed children of Israel found tolerant enough to allow them to prosper during their wanderings of the early medieval period. However, their

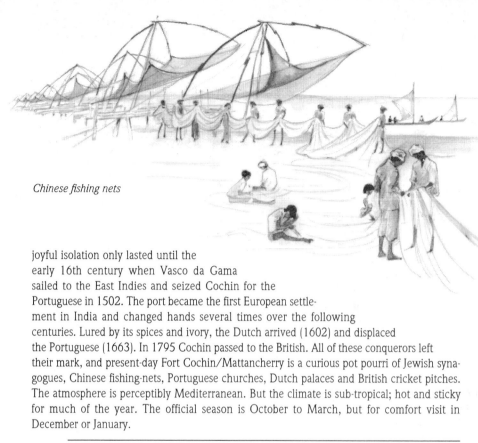

Chinese fishing nets

joyful isolation only lasted until the
early 16th century when Vasco da Gama
sailed to the East Indies and seized Cochin for the
Portuguese in 1502. The port became the first European settlement in India and changed hands several times over the following
centuries. Lured by its spices and ivory, the Dutch arrived (1602) and displaced
the Portuguese (1663). In 1795 Cochin passed to the British. All of these conquerors left
their mark, and present-day Fort Cochin/Mattancherry is a curious pot pourri of Jewish syna-
gogues, Chinese fishing-nets, Portuguese churches, Dutch palaces and British cricket pitches.
The atmosphere is perceptibly Mediterranean. But the climate is sub-tropical; hot and sticky
for much of the year. The official season is October to March, but for comfort visit in
December or January.

Getting There
by air

Although plans are afoot to build an international airport on the mainland (but then
such plans are always afoot in India), Cochin's present airport (Willingdon Island) is 4
miles from Ernakulam town centre, a Rs30 taxi ride, or Rs2.50 by bus to or from
Ernakulam's Kallor city bus stand, just above Ernakulam Town railway station.

Indian Airlines flies 3 times daily between Cochin and Bombay, and once daily to
Bangalore, Delhi, Dabolim in Goa, Madras and Trivandrum. **EastWest** Airlines operates a daily flight to and from Bombay. **Jet Airways** also flies twice a day to Bombay,
as does **Moduluft**, while **NEPC** flies to Bangalore and Madras.

by train

Ernakulam has two rail stations—Ernakulam Junction and Ernakulam Town—both
some 1½ miles from the main boat jetty. Ernakulam Junction is easier to deal with: the
Area Manager here (office open 10 to 5) may be able to get you tickets at short notice,
if you've failed to book in advance. There are daily trains to Alleppey, Kottayam,
Quilon, Trivandrum, Madurai, Trichy, Madras, Mangalore, Bangalore, Bombay and

New Delhi. For Ooty, take the daily 9.25am *Tea Garden Express* (via Mettapulayam/ Coimbatore). The final leg of this 15-hour journey, as the pretty blue steam train huffs and puffs its way up the mountainside on the narrow-gauge track, presents some memorable scenery. Get a window seat on the right-hand side of your carriage and have your camera ready.

by bus

Buses for Alleppey and Trivandrum (regular), Quilon (one express bus daily), Thekkady (6.30am and 8.15 am buses, 6 hours), Kottayam (regular, 2 hours), Bangalore (few Interstate express buses, 15 hours) and Madurai (regular, but 8.15am is best; 10 hours; superb scenery) all leave from the KSTDC bus stand in Ernakulam.

Getting Around

Fort Cochin and Mattancherry have the historical sites; modern Ernakulam has the bus and railway stations, the hotels, shops and restaurants as well as the filth, crowds and squalor. The real Cochin starts on Willingdon Island, the site of the airport, the two top hotels and the tourist office. Neighbouring Bolghatty island has its famous palace hotel, and Gundu its interesting *coir* factory. If peace and quiet are not your first priority, then stay in Ernakulam. It may be a busy, unrelaxing commercial centre, but it's certainly the most convenient base for sightseeing. All Cochin's islands are linked by a regular ferry service, operating from Ernakulam's three jetties. The main jetty charges a few rupees for trips over to Willingdon, Vypeen, Vallarpadam and Fort Cochin (either to Chinese Fishing Nets, or to Dutch Palace) islands. The High Court jetty, at the top of Shanmugham Road, has ferries to Bolghatty island. The Sealord jetty, near Sealord Hotel, is the venue for twice-daily KSTDC boat trips round all the islands (*see* 'Tourist Information' below). These excursions are an excellent way of covering Cochin's many sights in a single day.

To get around Ernakulam itself, you have a choice of **auto-rickshaws**, which don't use meters (establish your fare in advance) or **taxis**.

If staying out at Fort Cochin, which has limited but pleasant accommodation, the most enjoyable way of getting round is by cycle. There are several hire places, charging around Rs20 per day.

Tourist Information

The **Government of India Tourist Office**, is at Malabar Hotel, Willingdon Island, ✆ 340352, is open 9 to 5 weekdays, 9 to 12noon Saturday. It still enjoys the reputation of being the 'best tourist office in India'; hires out good approved guides (Rs50 half day, Rs80 full day) and the staff are invariably helpful. KTDC's **Tourist Reception Centre**, near Ernakulam jetty (Shanmugham Road, ✆ 353234) is open 8am–6pm daily, and sells the boat tours (9.30–1, or 1.30–5; Rs20) round Cochin and its islands. It also sells Jaico's monthly *Timetable*, an excellent little publication with up-to-date city information and local plane/train/bus timetables.

All other useful tourist addresses are in Ernakulam: **Indian Airlines** are at Durbar Hall Road, ✆ 353901/353826. For **EastWest Airlines**, call ✆ 361632/355342. The main **post office** is in Hospital Road (8 to 8, Monday to Saturday, 10 to 6 Sunday).

A useful travel agent for bus/train reservations, and any other travel arrangements is **Clipper Holidays**, Convent Road, ✆ 364453.

Cochin Islands Tour

conducted tour boat, half-day

Leaves from Sealord jetty, Shanmugam Road in front of Sealord Hotel

Mattancherry Palace–Jewish Synagogue–Chinese fishing nets–
St Francis Church–Santa Cruz Church–Bolghatty Palace–Gundu Island

Get a sun-deck seat aboard the 9.30am KTDC sightseeing boat leaving daily from Sealord jetty which is cooler than the 1.30pm departure. The tour passes by Willingdon Island, off which are moored giant cargo ships loaded with fertilizer, chemicals and palm oil, and makes its first stop at **Mattancherry Palace** in Fort Cochin. Presently administered by the Archaeological Survey of India, this large white, red-roofed structure has an interesting history. Built by the Portuguese *c.* 1555 and presented to Raja Veera Kerala Varma (1537–61) as a goodwill token in exchange for trading rights, it was later renovated by the Dutch in 1663 and gained the misnomer of the 'Dutch Palace' (*open daily 10–5, except Fri*). An interesting combination of Keralan and Dutch architectural styles, it stands in a walled garden enclosure fronted by a tank, backing onto mango groves and three Hindu temples. The palace is built on two floors and around a central quadrangle. Inside the palace, see the large central Durbar Hall, where the Cochin royal family held their coronation ceremonies. Here you'll find an assortment of their palanquins, weapons, dresses and turbans. The adjacent series of royal bedrooms and other chambers have some fine murals dating from the 17th century. The 45 murals depict scenes from the *Ramayana* epic, as well as the Puranic legends relating to Shiva, Vishnu, Krishna, Kumara and Durga. Vigorous, fresh and delightfully sensual; one can't help but notice Shiva's eight arms busily at work on eight grateful handmaidens. Unfortunately you cannot photograph them without permission from the Archaeological Survey of India, and there are no books or postcards for sale.

Just a few hundred yards south is the oldest **Jewish Synagogue** in the Commonwealth (*open daily, 10–12noon, 3–5, except Sat*). The present structure was built in 1568, destroyed by the Portuguese in 1662, rebuilt by the Dutch in 1664 and donated its distinctive clock tower by Ezekiel Rahabi, a wealthy Jewish trader, in the mid 18th century. He also provided its exquisite willow-pattern floor tiles, each hand-painted in a different design, brought from Canton in 1776. The synagogue interior is fascinating: 19th-century Belgian chandeliers, interlocking pews, a ladies' gallery, and a superbly crafted brass pulpit. The curator, Jacky Cohen, shows visitors around and gives full information. He can also sometimes be prevailed upon to show the synagogue's two most prized treasures: the Great Scrolls of the Old Testament, and the copperplate grants of privilege made by the Cochin Maharajahs (962–1020) to the Jewish merchant Joseph Rabban. Nowadays, the place has a rather empty feel: all but 27 of Cochin's Jews have left; many having migrated to Israel.

The tour boat proceeds to the northern tip of Fort Cochin, where huge, cantilevered fishing nets proclaiming the ancient trade connections with China are ranged along the water's edge like a string of filigree lace handkerchiefs. Probably introduced by traders from the court of Kublai Khan, these fascinating nets are still an efficient method of fishing. While not unique to

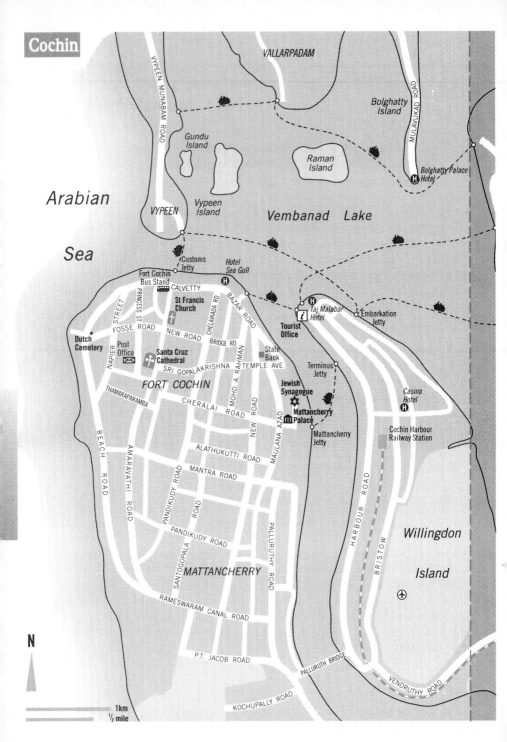

Cochin

VALLARPADAM

VYPEEN MUNABAM ROAD

MULAVUKAD ROAD

Bolghatty
Island

Gundu
Island

Raman
Island

Bolghatty Palace
Hotel

Arabian

VYPEEN

Vypeen
Island

Vembanad Lake

Sea

Customs
Jetty

Hotel
Sea Gull

Fort Cochin
Bus Stand

CALVETTY

St Francis
Church

PRINCESS ST

STREET

FOSSE ROAD

NEW ROAD

CHELAKADA RD

BAZAR ROAD

Taj Malabar
Hotel

Embarkation
Jetty

Tourist
Office

Dutch
Cemetery

NAPIER

Post
Office

BRIDGE RD

Santa Cruz
Cathedral

SRI GOPALAKRISHNA

MOHD. A. RAHMAN

TEMPLE AVE

State
Bank

Terminus
Jetty

THAMARAPARAMBA

FORT COCHIN

CHERALAI ROAD

NEW ROAD

MAULANA AZAD

Jewish
Synagogue

Mattancherry
Palace

Casino
Hotel

BEACH ROAD

AMARAVATHI ROAD

ALATHUKUTTI ROAD

MANTRA ROAD

Mattancherry
Jetty

Cochin Harbour
Railway Station

HARBOUR ROAD

BRISTOW ROAD

Willingdon

PANDIKUDY ROAD

ROAD

PANDIKUDY ROAD

SANTOGOPALA

PALLURUTHY ROAD

Island

MATTANCHERRY

RAMESWARAM CANAL ROAD

N

P.T. JACOB ROAD

PALLURUTH BRIDGE

VENDRUTHY ROAD

KOCHUPALLY ROAD

1km
½ mile

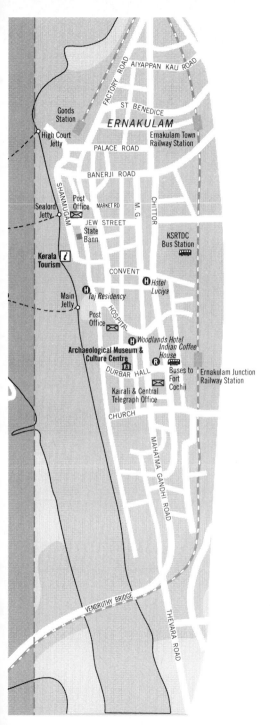

Cochin, the nets flanking the opening to the harbour are perhaps the best place in Kerala to see them at work.

A short walk below the nets is **St Francis Church**, believed to be the first European church to be built in India. The original structure built in 1503, presumably by Portuguese Franciscan friars, was of wood. Later, during the mid 16th century, it was rebuilt in stone. Over the years it has experienced a number of 'conversions' from Catholic Portuguese, to Protestant Dutch, to Anglican, before achieving its present status as the Church of South India. The exterior is notable for its impressive façade, and there's an array of interesting Portuguese and Dutch tombstones including that of Vasco da Gama, who died here in 1524 although his body was taken to Portugal 14 years later. Should you wish to leave the tour at this point, a short walk inland brings you to **Santa Cruz Church**. This is a Roman Catholic structure, built in 1557, with a brilliantly painted interior. Nearby, locals play polite games of cricket on the Surrey-style village green. Beyond this, walking up Calvetty Street, you'll find a medieval settlement of pastel houses, 16th-century Portuguese bastions and narrow alleys, and still more Catholic churches.

The tour continues on to **Bolghatty Island**, to visit the **Bolghatty Palace Hotel**. Set in 15 acres of lush green lawns, this palatial structure started life as a Dutch palace, built in 1744 and later became home of the British Resident to the Rajah of Cochin after 1799. Presently run as a hotel by the Kerala Tourism Development Corporation (KTDC), it has a golf course, a bar and a restaurant. From here, it's just a short chug across the harbour to **Gundu Island** (look out for leaping dolphins), for shopping at its small **Coir Factory**. Here a busy cooperative workers' society produce doormats handwoven from rough coconut fibre (*coir*) (Rs50–200). The weaving process is worth seeing.

Back in Ernakulam, off the boat, it's a short walk to Durbar Hall Road for **Parishath Thamburan Museum** in the old Durbar Hall (*open daily 9.30–12noon, 3–5.30, except Mon*). This has 19th-century paintings, copies of murals, old coins, delicate chandeliers, sculptures, musical instruments and lovely chinaware. The main attraction is the collection drawn from the Cochin royal family treasury.

Kathakali

No visit to Cochin is complete without seeing a performance of **Kathakali**, the famous dance-drama of Kerala. Kathakali started out some 2000 years ago as a temple art form, depicting themes from the *Ramayana* and *Mahabharata* epics. More an elaborate sequence of yogic exercises than a dance form, Kathakali may seem slow and stylized compared to say, Bharatnatyam, but it has a grace and a charm all of its own. A unique 'language' of 24 separate gestures has evolved over the centuries, any combination of which conveys a definite meaning. The eyes are especially important, suggesting an immense range of differing moods and emotions. The costumes, wigs and masks which are used are bright and flamboyant, all made from natural materials. Make-up is distinctive with several layers of paint being applied to the dancer's face to accentuate lips, eyebrows and eyelashes. The overall effect is highly dramatic.

At present, Cochin has three Kathakali dance companies. They are **Cochin Cultural Centre**, ✆ 353732, Durbar Hall Ground, D.H. Road; **See India Foundation**, ✆ 369471, Kalathiparambil Lane; and **Art Kerala** on Ravipuram Road. All three places charge the same (Rs50, pay at the door), and shows start at either 6.30pm (Cultural Centre) or 7pm (See India and Art Kerala). Turn up early to see the dancers applying make-up backstage which you can photograph, and bring mosquito coils to place under your chair. Of the three, the Cultural Centre has the best reputation, though Art Kerala puts on a wide range of Keralan dances (not just Kathakali), and See India gives the fullest, clearest explanations preceding each dance.

Sports and Activities

Other recreations include golf (9-hole course, Rs60 green fees include caddy, balls and clubs) and English films in air-conditioned comfort at the **Sridhar** cinema, near the KSTDC reception centre in Shanmugham Road.

The cool air-conditioned **Devi** cinema (Cochin's best) in Mahatma Gandhi Road, Ernakulam, is the ideal escape on hot, sticky afternoons. So is the swimming pool at the Malabar Hotel on Willingdon Island, open to non-residents (except Tuesday and Friday) for a daily charge of Rs60.

Shopping

Buy teas, spices (ginger, turmeric, cardamom, cumin and cloves) and cashew nuts along the roadside leading down to Ernakulam main market. Because these pavement vendors sell their produce in the open, they can't (unlike shops) adulterate them. Another good place to buy the famous Cochin spices at local prices is **Grand Bazaar** supermarket, at Abad Plaza Hotel in M.G. Road. For fabrics, rosewood, walnut, Kathakali props and masks, and assorted jewellery, try the various emporia and shops along M.G. and Broadway roads.

Cochin ☏ (048–)   ## Where to Stay

luxury

The two top hotels are on Willingdon Island near to the airport. The **Taj Malabar Hotel**, ☏ 340010, ☏ 69497, has an excellent location on the northwestern promontory of the island, overlooking Mattancherry and the Chinese fishing nets, with the Government of India tourist office on your doorstep. It has good first-floor balcony rooms in the original building and a nice swimming pool. The **Casino Hotel**, ☏ 340221, ☏ 34000, is slightly cheaper and has air-conditioned rooms throughout, a brand-new pool, informal (yet stylish) ambience, and two excellent restaurants. The Casino is also the only place from which foreigners may book tours of the Lakshadweep Islands (*see* below).

At the top of this price range is the spanking new **Taj Residency**, ☏ 682011, over the water in Ernakulam. Big, very comfortable, but rather bland, the Residency is close to the sea jetties on Shanmugam Road, and has fine views out over the bay.

expensive

Cochin is short of hotels that fall into this category. Try the **Hotel Presidency** on Paramara Road in Ernakulam, ☏ 363100, which has air-conditioned, bland comfort, but offers low prices for an expensive hotel.

moderate

One of Cohin's best hotels falls within this price range: over on Bolghatty Island, the KTDC **Bolghatty Palace**, ☏ 355003, is a rather run-down Raj-style hotel with large grounds, good recreational facilities, and lots of character. The massive old-wing rooms are not air-conditioned, while the newer air-conditioned rooms are not so attractive. The cottages down by the water's edge are often plagued by mosquitoes.

In Ernakulam, stay at air-conditioned **Sea Lord Hotel**, Shanmugham Road, ☏ 352682. The hotel has a good rooftop restaurant. The **Hotel Abad Plaza**, ☏ 361636, ☏ 0484-369729, on M.G. Road is clean and comfortable and is well-located with a nearby seafood restaurant and attached supermarket.

inexpensive

Top of this range is the **Woodlands Hotel** on M.G. Road, Ernakulam, ☏ 351372. It's a reasonably clean hotel, if tacky, with an air-conditioned vegetarian restaurant and ice cream parlour. In Fort Cochin, the **Hotel Sea Gull** in Calvetty Road, ✆ 352682, has a pleasant location between the two ferry stops, overlooking the harbour, and nice air-conditioned singles and doubles. The restaurant and bar are very popular.

cheap

Facing the Chinese fishing nets in Fort Cochin, there's KTDC's **Subala**, a nice friendly place with cheap restaurant, helpful staff and comfy rooms. It's very convenient for the boat jetty and bus stand. Other decent cheap lodgings are **P.W.D. Tourist Rest Home** near the beach (spacious but spartan rooms) and **Hotel Elite** near St Francis Church, with decent double rooms on the ground floor but cheaper, grimmer rooms upstairs.

In Ernakulam, many budget travellers enjoy **Biju's Tourist Home** in Market Road, opposite the main jetty, ✆ 369881, with a friendly and informative management and bright, spacious rooms. As a second string, try **Hotel Luciya** in Stadium Road, next to the bus stand, ✆ 354433, or the **Hotel Sea Rock** on M.G. Road, Palimukku (south of Shanmugham Road), ✆ 682016, or the **Hotel Yuvarani** at Jos Junction on M.G. Road in the same area, ✆ 681011.

Eating Out

The **Casino Hotel** on Willingdon Island has one of the most prestigious eateries in town, a seafood speciality restaurant called **Fort Cochin**. Service and food are excellent, and the lobsters unbelievably large. An average meal including dessert comes to around Rs300 per head. The Casino's other restaurant, the multi-cuisine **Tharavadu** features a daily lunch buffet for Rs175 and live music performances nightly. The Taj Malabar's **Rice Boat** prepares some excellent Malabar seafood from Rs350 per head.

There is good cheap food to be had in Fort Cochin. **Hotel Sea Gull** is good for non-vegetarian food, doughnuts and porridge, and KTDC's **Subala** has a nice breezy restaurant by the water, with cheap if rather unimaginative meals. The best treats are still at **Hotel Elite's** famous Parisian-style café with its choice of patisseries and refrigerated cheese.

Ernakulam has a wide choice of cheap eating places. The **Sealord Hotel** has a popular air-conditioned restaurant, with tasty Indian and continental food at around Rs40 per dish. For fast food and superb north Indian fare, try **Pandhal Restaurant** opposite Woodlands Hotel on M.G. Road. This is a relaxing air-conditioned place, with good lunchtime specials; *thalis* and Kerala-style curries from Rs20, 12noon to 3 daily, except Sundays. For seafood, try the Rs70 buffet lunch (12noon to 3) at **Abad Plaza Hotel**, which serves squid, lobster and prawns. At **Subhiksha**, the stylish vegetarian restaurant attached to B.T.H. Hotel in D.H. Road, you can enjoy amazing lunchtime *thalis* for about Rs40 and incredibly cheap south Indian food with most dishes only Rs8 in air-conditioned comfort. Next door, there's a popular little coffee shop. Ernakulam has two **Indian Coffee Houses**; one opposite the main jetty in Cannon Shed Road, the other below the rail station in M.G. Road, which do good cheap breakfasts for under Rs20. Two reliable Chinese restaurants are **Malaya** on Bannerjee Road and **Golden Dragon** opposite Park Hotel. Chinese food is also available at the Sealord's rooftop restaurant and The Hotel Presidency. Two good bakeries are **Cochin Bakery** opposite Woodlands Hotel, and **Ceylon Bake House** near the tourist office on the Broadway.

The Lakshadweep Islands

Until a few years ago these 36 coral islands in the Arabian Sea were off-limits to foreigners. However, non-Indians are now allowed to visit by boat on a paradisiacal tropical cruise, to snorkel or scuba dive over the brightly coloured reefs and their amazing marine life, and to explore a few of the islands. There is nothing remotely industrial out here, and the traveller will find the Lakshadweeps much as nature intended them. The people are Sunni Muslim and Mallayalam speakers who make their living from fishing the reefs and coconut cultivation. Trips are relatively expensive and are divided into three types: 3-day, 6-day or 7-day cruises. Contact the Lakshadweep Office, Harbour Road, Willingdon Island, Cochin, ✆ 69755/ 6374/6311.

Trichur

Also known as Thrissur, this large temple town about 45 miles north of Cochin/Ernakulam is unremarkable for most of the year, but very much worth visiting in mid-January and mid-April for its two great **elephant festivals**. January has the best—Kerala's largest elephant festival, known as the **Great Elephant March**. This involves about a hundred temple elephants (as well as some borrowed from local forestry camps to make up the numbers) parading in full caparisoned regalia—including brass headpieces with gold bosses; orange-robed mahouts sitting under brightly coloured sunshades; brahmins standing on the elephants' backs waving wide, circular fans known as lotus plumes and *kavadi* carriers—devotees and pilgrims bearing huge, multi-coloured structures made of painted bamboo on their heads to offer to the gods in return for special favours. The procession is led by white-robed women carrrying oil lamps.

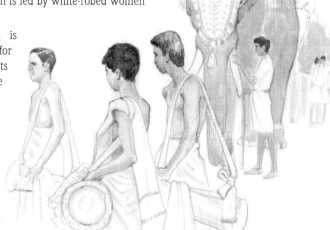

The whole shebang is repeated every day for four days, winding its way slowly from the town's central stadium up to a hillock where ancient tribal dances known as *theyyams*, thought to date from the Neolithic era, are performed to banish evil spirits.

The mid-April festival in Trichur is known as

the **Thrissur Pooram**, takes place at the town's **Vadakkamnathan Temple** and is dedicated to Siva. On the morning of the festivities, affiliates of two other temples in the town, the **Paramekavu** and the **Thiruvambadi** send a team of elephants to the Vadakkamnuthan site to compete for the crowd's approval. Each team of elephants, usually numbering 15 or so, is accompanied by a *panchavadayam* band of traditional musicians playing ancient curved horns, percussion and strange wind instruments, while the lotus fan-bearers on the elephants' backs twirl their plumes in a dance of hands and feathers. Around nightfall, once the crowd has indicated its choice of winning team, a thunderous display of fireworks is set off and non-Hindus are permitted to enter the Vadakkumnathan Temple, the only day of the year that this is possible, for *puja* (prayer), inside a particularly fine interior of medieval carved wood, heavily ornamented in the Keralan style.

Apart from its festivals, Trichur spends most of its time in sleepy torpor. There's a rather run-down **zoo** (*open 3–5.15*), which offers a collection of unhappy local and exotic inmates for inspection. The **State Museum** (*open 10–5 except Mondays*) has a gallery of the usual Chola bronzes and stone sculptures; and the town has an **Art Museum** with good medieval wood carvings and fine jewellery.

Twenty miles to the north is **Cheruthuruthy**, which has a famous school for **Kathakali Dance**. Training sessions last two hours and are open to the public. The first begins before dawn at 4.30am, the others at 8.30am and 3.30pm. The school is closed at weekends and on public holidays. You can stay at the Government Guest House, ✆ 498, for under Rs100 per room. Access from Trichur is by bus (1 hour) to Shornur, then by auto-rickshaw or taxi 2 miles to the school.

Getting There

There are several daily **train** services from Cochin and Calicut as well as over the mountains to Tamil Nadu's Coimbatore, Salem and Madras. **Buses** run daily from Cochin, Calicut, Madurai, Bangalore, Mysore and Madras.

Trichur ✆ *(0487–)*   **Where to Stay**

Trichur doesn't have a huge variety of accommodation. For between Rs200–600 there are air-conditioned rooms at the **Elite International** on Chembottil Lane near the town centre, ✆ 21033; and at the **Casino** on T.B. Road near the station, ✆ 24699.

Cheaper, at Rs80–200 per room, are the **Allukkas Lodge** by the railway station, ✆ 24067 (reckoned to be good value by backpackers); the state-run **Ramanaliyam Tourist Bungalow** on Palace Road, ✆ 20300, which has a rooftop restaurant; and the **Skylord Hotel** on Municipal Office Road, ✆ 24662.

Other Elephant Festivals in Kerala

Trichur has the state's biggest festivals but other, smaller ones (*Utsavams*) take place elsewhere throughout the year. There is even a Christian and a Muslim elephant festival. All festivals hold slightly different dates from year to year. The following is a rough timetable. Contact the tourist office at Cochin for this year's dates. All the above locations can be reached by bus from Cochin.

mid January	Trichur	Great Elephant March
early February	Ernakulam	Paramara Devi Temple Utsavam
end February/ first week March	Guruvayoor	Sree Krishna Utsavam (60 miles from Cochin)
mid March	Kottayam	Thirunakkara Mahadeva Utsavam
mid April	Trichur	Thrissur Pooram
mid May	Perandur	Sree Bhagavaty Utsavam (4 miles from Cochin)
mid August	Thiruvallam	Sree Parasurama Temple Bali (3½ miles from Trivandrum on the way to Kovalam)
early September	Thripinthura	Athachamayam Procession (6 miles from Cochin)
early October	Pazhanji, Kunnamkulam	St Mary's Church Feast (70 miles from Cochin)
early November	Trivandrum	Sree Padmanabhaswamy Utsavam
early December	Thripunithura	Sree Poornathrayeesa Utsavam (11 miles from Cochin)
end December	Changanacherry	Puthur Muslim Juma-at Chananakumam (12 miles from Kottayam).

Calicut

Also known as Kozhikode (pronounced 'cosycody'), this rather depressing coastal city 150 miles north of Cochin should only be used as a stopover on the way to Kerala's quiet northern coast or to the wild northern mountains.

However, Calicut has a fine history, having once been the capital of the medieval Zamorin kings, then the coastal capital of the sensual, hedonistic Vijayanagars of Hampi (*see* **Karnataka**), until it was seized by the effervescent Vasco da Gama in 1498. Over the following three centuries, the city passed from European to Indian hands and back again uncounted times, with the Dutch, Portuguese and local Hindu and Christian rulers all vying for possession. Finally Calicut was taken and sacked in 1766 by the Deccan Muslim warlord Hyder Ali, then by his son, the legendary Tipu Sultan in the 1780s, who looked set to conquer all Kerala and take Calicut as his base. However, the British stomped in and took Calicut in 1792, after having defeated and killed Tippu Sultan at his fort of Sriringapatnam on the Cauvery River near Mysore in modern Karnataka.

Under the British, Calicut became a textile centre (the official tourist literature still calls it the 'Manchester of the South'), and its imperial past has been obliterated by the pollution-spewing mill chimneys of its industrial present. This smog, combined with the humid heat of the Keralan coastal climate, makes modern Calicut insupportable for anything more than a day or two.

Getting Around
by air

There are daily **Indian Airlines** flights to and from Bombay, ✆ 55233, from the airport, 15 miles out of town.

by train

Several daily train services connect Calicut with Cochin, Mangalore and the north Kerala coast and there are other, but less regular, services to Madras, Coimbatore, Bangalore and Mysore.

by bus

Calicut is connected with all the Keralan coastal towns and cities by bus (several services daily), as well with Coimbatore, Mysore and Bangalore via the mountains (once-daily services).

Tourist Information

The **tourist office** is at KTDC Corner, ✆ 76101. For **foreign exchange** try the Kerala State Bank on the conveniently named Bank Road.

The Town

Calicut sounds a little like the old-fashioned English word 'calico', and guess why! The British used the port as a major cotton exporting centre through the 19th century. Today it thrives as much on timber, most of it felled only semi-legally in the rainforests of the Western Ghats, and if you go down to the docks, you will still see elephants moving the great timber loads around. The town itself has only two real tourist attractions.

Those interested in archaeology will find the **Pazhassiraja Museum** (*open Mon–Sat, 9.30–12.30, 2.30–5.30*) especially fascinating. Calicut sits at the edge of an area known for a proliferation of new Stone-Age megalithic sites (*see* below) and there is a good display here detailing what little is known about the culture of their builders, as well as where the sites can be found.

The town's second attraction is next door: the **Art Gallery** and attached museum (*both have same opening hours as the Pazhassiraja Museum*). The gallery has one of the few collections by Indian artists actually worth seeing, while the museum is good for antique wood carvings.

Calicut ✆ *(0495–)*

Where to Stay

moderate

Try the **Malabar Palace** on G.H. Road, ✆ 64974, for air-conditioned rooms and decent food. There is also the **Seaqueen** on Beach Road, ✆ 60201, which also has a good restaurant and a foreign exchange desk.

inexpensive

The state-run **Malabar Mansion** near the tourist office at Kerala Tourism Corner on S.M. Street, ✆ 76101, has clean rooms, as does the very pleasant **Hyson** on Bank Road, which has a garden and takes credit cards.

cheap

Try the **Alakapuri Guest House** on Jail Road—also known as Maulana Md Ali Road, ✆ 73361, and **Kalpaka Tourist Lodge** on Town Hall Road, ✆ 62371. Both are a bit dingy, but will do for a night.

The best places are the two *Indian Coffee Houses*, with their usual raj-costumed waiters and 'olde worlde' interiors on Kallai and Mavoor Roads. If that doesn't appeal, it's cheap *thalis* or bakeries. For the latter try **Royal Cakes** on Bank Road—a travellers' favourite.

Megalithic Sites Around Calicut

Before heading off up the coast to Bekal or into the mountains to Wynad and Silent Valley, it is worth making a foray about 6 miles east by bus or taxi into the lush countryside near the town of **Kunnamkulam,** to see the dolmens and menhirs standing in the woods and fields. These are particularly dense around the villages of **Chovannur** and **Porkalam**. Some of the megaliths are estimated to be about 3000 years old, parallel in date with the European Neolithic cultures that produced Stonehenge in Britain and Carnac in France. Like their European counterparts, the Keralan stones seem to have been used as sacred sites by later cultures— Dravidian equivalents of the Celtic Druids, perhaps—and, again as with the Western megaliths, archaeologists are still baffled as to how the stones were erected in the first place.

Bekal

If you have time to make this trip to the northern Keralan coast, you will come away a happy traveller, for Bekal is what Kovalam and Varkala were until a few years ago: secluded, visited by only a few 'real' travellers, dirt cheap, quiet, with clean beaches and good swimming. There is also an interesting fort to stay in. And, as yet Bekal does not seem to have attracted the inevitable droves of thieves and hawkers that attend the popular Indian coastal spots.

The fort at Bekal dates from the early medieval period and has some superb airy interiors, yet, having been taken over as a state-run guest house, it costs only about Rs100 per night to stay there (less if you bargain). Suffice to say that Bekal is one of the best places to go to in Kerala at the moment and really is worth making the long trip north from Cochin for (or a short trip down from the Karnataka coast). Its proximity to the wildlife sanctuaries and rainforests of northern Kerala's section of the Western Ghats is an added bonus.

Bekal can be reached by **bus** from the large town of Kannur (or Cannanore), north of Calicut, which has a good fort built by the Portuguese. It can also be reached from Mangalore in the north by local bus.

Kerala's Mountains

After the initial look of panic, the bull regains its composure. He stands there for what must be a minute—then with a toss of his head and a grunt of alarm he turns away from you. As if by magic the grass seems to explode as bison struggle to their feet. The bull leads them out of the glade into the jungle and soon they are gone.

Kunal Verma, *The Bison*

wild boar

Rising up about 35 miles east of the coast are the first steep foothills of Kerala's stretch of the Western Ghats. The roads from the plain wind up out of the coconut forest and paddies of the coastal plain, first to rubber and teak plantations that are protected from marauding cattle by high stone walls, then into natural evergreen forests. Great trees tower over the roads, villages become sparser and fast-running streams fall over shallow beds of rock and gravel. Away from the road, there are huge **wildlife sanctuaries** that are still home to tiger and elephant, leopard and bear, deer and wild boar.

In the very deep parts of the forest are **tribal people** who live outside the Hindu mainstream, worshipping their own forest gods and living off a mixture of gathering and shifting forest agriculture. Although it is difficult to get permission to visit Kerala's tribal areas, it is possible through a local guide if you are prepared for several days' hard trekking (*see* below).

Kerala's mountains comprise the seaward slopes of the Western Ghats. These catch the bulk of the monsoon rains, leaving enough year-round moisture to support great forests of vivid green. The exotic flora of these forests conjures tales from the *1001 Nights*—frankincense and camphor trees, wild cardamom and pepper vines, lemon grass scent blown in on the warm breeze, wild flowers growing by the streams.

At about 5000 feet, the treeline gives out onto upper slopes carpeted with the close-set shrubs of tea and cardomom plantations, trimmed to a uniform height and lending a comfortable, pillowed feel to the landscape. The air is fresh and cool. Then as you finally reach the peaks, natural grassland takes over, *shola* forests hang in the narrow ravines and the mountains return to the wild.

Trekking in Kerala's Mountain Forests

Gaining access to the best bits of Kerala's mountains involves some effort. Away from the two or three wildlife sanctuaries that allow anyone to trek (*see* below), access is limited by the government—partly to protect the tribal people, forests and wildlife from mass invasion by tourists but also partly to prevent foreigners from seeing to closely how things are run in the jungles. The Forest Department, Wildlife Department and police vie for control of the forests and are touchy about being too closely observed. That said, it is possible to arrange treks deep into the forest if you go through the official proceedure: apply for government permission from the central Wildlife Department Headquarters in Delhi via a reputable travel agency known to practise sound ecotourism policies. This means allowing at least a month for permission to come through. Those who take the trouble are well rewarded though—stepping back into a forest world where little has changed in several millennia.

As with Tamil Nadu and Karnataka's mountain areas, the most committed agents for Kerala, who care for both the environment and the tribal people by limiting visitor numbers, and who can arrange for tribal people to act as guides to the deep forest areas, are **Clipper Holidays** of Bangalore. To arrange treks in any of the areas that follow, contact their Cochin Office (c/o Mr Varkey Kurian) at 40/6531 Convent Road, Cochin 682035, ✆ 364453, but remember that you must, unless otherwise indicated in the text, allow a *minimum* of one month for the necessary permits to be obtained.

The Cardamom Hills

The southernmost part of Kerala's Western Ghats are named after the wild cardomon that grows in the forests. Two small hill stations in these 'hills' (in fact, small mountains) can be easily reached from Trivandrum, both being about 35 miles (3 hours by bus) from the town. The first, **Neyyar Dam** is an interesting settlement in its own right, with a **Yoga Ashram**, open to outside visitors, a small market where local forest tribals come to trade, a dam, with shoreline gardens decorated with garish scupture, where crocodiles swim, and a surrounding forest well populated with wildlife. Accommodation is cheap, both in the state-run **Agasthya House**, near which is a wildlife viewing tower, and which has a small bar/restaurant, or at **Neyyar Guest House**, ✆ 04725 4493.

Neyyar town lies in the foothills of the Ghats, but the nearby **Neyyar Wildlife Sanctuary** extends up into the high mountains. Around the entrance about 100 yards west of the dam, there is a park with animals in open cages, whose inmates include Asiatic lion. In the wild forest live elephant, tiger, leopard, sloth bear, bison, *sambar*, spotted deer. The reserve backs onto neighbouring **Mudanthurai Tiger Sanctuary** on the eastern slopes of the Ghats (officially in Tamil Nadu, *see* p.296), so the game can migrate freely from the wet to the dry zone forests.

One of Kerala's best trekking routes runs through Neyyar reserve—the three-day hike up **Agasthya Peak**, a 6122 feet high (1866 metres) mountain that was the mythological home of the sage Agasthya. The trip must be arranged via Clipper Holidays, Cochin (*see* p.219). For those not trekking, accommodation in Neyyar Wildlife Sanctuary is at a rest house at the entrance. Day walks can be arranged at the office.

On the north side of Neyyar Sanctuary is **Agasthya Vanam Biological Park**, overlooked by the great peak of that name, and which protects the **Kottur Reserved Rainforest**. As yet there is no general access to the reserve, but trekking routes are set to be opened in 1996/7.

Also neighbouring Neyyar Sanctuary is the **Peppara Wildlife Sanctuary**. A watershed area of river sources, highland meadows and evergreen rainforest surrounding the large Peppara Dam, this sanctuary is home to elephant, bison, tiger, leopard, wild boar, *sambar* and *chital*, nilgiri langur and a host of smaller game. There are also various tribal groups, of an African rather than strictly Asian cast of feature and hair. Their origins are uncertain; some anthropologists suggest they may be descended from negroid mariners from the Maldives. The tribals themselves are an independent bunch, still living partly by shifting forest agriculture (mostly slash-and-burn culti-vation of wild cardamom), gathering forest produce and a small amount of hunting.

Peppara has accommodation in a **Kerala Water Authority Guest House** by the dam. **Trekking** routes to Agasthya pass through the reserve. To arrange accommodation/trekking contact Clipper Holidays, Cochin (*see* p.219). Day visitors can take short guided walks into

lion-tailed macaque

the forest, or a boat ride on the lake. Access is by bus from Trivandrum to Peppara (4–5 hours).

At the northern end of the Cardamom Hills (also 3 hours by bus from Trivandrum) is the tiny hill station of **Ponmudi**. Set on a high peak above an area of alternate forest and tea planatation, Ponmudi is a superb centre from which to trek or look for wildlife—the full complement of south Indian wildlife lives in the forests and grasslands here. You do not need prior permission to walk in the surrounding ranges, and you can either venture into the forests alone or hire a guide through one of the two rest houses whose cottages and one main lodge comprise the entire settlement. Guides are about Rs100 per person per day, and you can trek into the surrounding forests for up to 8 days, sleeping in caves. You take your own food, but your guides will cook for you.

Ponmudi has accommodation in the state-run **Ponmudi Tourist Complex** (run-down but great views—rooms from about Rs40), up the hill from which there is a small restaurant/bar and the **Ponmudi Tourist Resort** which has a small collection of equally basic bungalows, starting at Rs8 per night. If you walk 1½ miles up the tar road from Ponmudi, you come to a fenced area of grassland, grazed by a resident herd of *sambar* (good photographic opportunities) and two lookout points that give spectacular views out over the neighbouring sections of the Western Ghats. One warning though, Ponmudi fills up at weekends with loud, drunken day-trippers from Trivandrum. Go in the week only, or make sure you are out in the forests by the weekend.

The **Shendurney Wildife Sanctuary** sits in a high forest valley about 35 miles north of Ponmudi (due east of Quilon/Kollam). Its sides are cut with steep ravines and overlooked by a set of frowning peaks; the tallest, Alvarakuruchi, rising to 5000 feet (1550 metres). During the 19th and early 20th centuries, much of the original forest was cleared for logging, but secondary growth has re-established the jungle, and a host of wildlife species now inhabit the sanctuary: elephant, gaur, *sambar*, muntjac deer, wild boar, lion-tailed macaque, flying squirrel and the Malabar giant squirrel are all common. Shendurney is open for **trekking** by prior permission. Apply via Clipper Holidays, Cochin (*see* p.219). The more casual visitor coming by bus from Quilon can take a day walk or a boat ride on the dam. Accommodation is in a forest rest house but ring first to make sure it is not full, call Kollam, ✆ 691308.

Munnar and the Annamudi Range

Kerala's highest mountains rear to the sky in a jagged line almost due east of Cochin. A tea-growing area of plantations almost entirely owned by the incredibly powerful, Parsi-run Tata Corporation (which seems to own and manufacture just about everything in India from cars to telephone directories), Munnar's climate is cool relief after Cochin's humid heat.

Munnar has access to the best **trekking** in Kerala, though into a tribal region that is very difficult to get permission for. There is also the superb **Rajamallai National Park** in the higher slopes near town, where India's largest herd of Nilgiri *tahr* (a species of ibex unique to the Western Ghats) is protected.

The Foothills Below Munnar

If coming to Munnar by bus or taxi from Cochin or Kottayam, try and stop for a day first at **Thattekad Bird Sanctuary**, about 35 miles east of the city. To cover the last leg of this journey, you and your vehicle have to cross the Periyar River, before arriving at the gates of the sanctuary, just outside a small village on the edge of thick forest. Although officially there to protect birds, Thattekad has other wildlife too: elephant have recently recolonized the forest, and tigers have been seen in the area for the past two years. Among the rare bird species found here are

pariah kite

the Malabar hornbill, Malabar Shama, the grey-headed fishing eagle, the beautifully named fairy bluebird, crimson-throated barbet, night heron and the iridescent-feathered, tiny sunbird. You can go **trekking** with a Wildlife Department guide (don't go into the deep woods alone, as the elephant round here are known to be aggressive) and there is a rest house for accommodation.

Also in the Munnar area is **Idukki Wildlife Sanctuary**, reachable by bus from Kottayam or Cochin (both about 75 miles). Set in the foothills west of Munnar, Idduki is undulating forest country, home to a very large elephant population, tiger, leopard, sloth bear, *dhole* (wild dog), *gaur* (bison), *sambar*, spotted *chital* and muntjac deer, wild boar and a host of bird species.

Idukki has a large dam, with boating facilities, and **trekking** is an option in the forests, with rest house accommodation. Trekking and the rest house must be booked in advance, ✆ Idukki 323/328. To get to Idukki, take a bus from Kottayam or Cochin to Cheruthony, Kattapana or Thodpuzha, and then go by local bus (about 1 hour) to the forest entrance.

From Thattekad or Idukki, the mountain road winds up a steep climb of several hours through cardamom and rubber plantations, until the high grasslands and tea estates announce that you are about to arrive in **Munnar** itself.

Munnar Town

Munnar is a strange little place—part olde worlde Raj survivor (it was developed by British tea planters in the 1920s, who left a church, some small but handsome government buildings made from stone and the tea estates), part truck-stop—for Munnar sits atop the commercial route between Coimbatore in Tamil Nadu and Cochin in Kerala, and there is a steady stream of lorries and buses going to and fro over the pass. The result is a scruffy little town centre on the banks of a mountain river choked with refuse, with, on the hills above, lovely winding lanes that lead to old British cottages, now the homes of Forestry and Wildlife department officers. To the northeast of town rises the great rock wall of Anamudi Peak, at 8828 feet (2695 metres) the highest in Kerala, while on every side green tea bushes march in neat close-set rows, pleasing to the eye, up towards the wilder hills where jungle and watershed grassland take over.

Several **buses** run daily from Cochin and Kottayam in Kerala (journey time is approximately 5 hours) and from Coimbatore in Tamil Nadu, with a change a Gundulpet (approximately 6 hours).

Munnar ✆ (04865–)

Where to Stay

Whether you take a day trip out to the national park (which has no accommodation of its own) or plan to get into the deep forest, you will have to stay in Munnar for a night or two.

moderate

If you can, stay at the **High Range Club** on the west end of town, ✆ 53—the old meeting point for the English planters that opened up the area. You are supposed to be a member but unless the place is full, you can generally swing it. The **Edassary East End**, in the centre of town is modern, ✆ 30451, but you'd never know it. Built in the style of a planters' bungalow, it has self-contained cottages and a good restaurant. More tranquil (about a mile out of town on the western side) is the **Hillview**, ✆ 30567, built by a river. Again, the hotel has a decent restaurant.

inexpensive

For about Rs100–150 per night, you can get a clean, basic room at the **S.N. Lodge**, also on the western edge of town, ✆ 212.

cheap

For Rs 50–80, try the **Krishna Lodge** next to the bus stand. It's a little noisy, but clean enough, and there are some cheap *thali* houses and bakeries nearby.

The Munnar Ranges

The main reasons to visit Munnar are the **Erivakulam/Rajmalai National Park**, 10 miles northeast of town, and the **trekking** in vast areas of **reserved forest** on the eastern side of the mountains. This deeply wild area, still home to a variety of wildlife and to the fiercely independent **Munnuvan** tribe, who have managed to hang on to their traditional way of life, despite various kinds of government interference over the years.

Getting into the Forest Areas

This is one of south India's most problematic regions to enter: the Forest and Wildlife Department both require permission and this has to be obtained via Delhi, which takes some time. However, those really interested in getting into the Munnuvan region should contact Varkey Kurian at Clipper Holidays in Cochin, ✆ (0484) 682 035. On no account try to hire a local guide yourself and go into the forest—when the author was 3-days' trek inside the Munnuvan tribal area, he and his group ran into a police raiding party looking for ganja plantations, which the Munnuvans allegedly cultivate in the jungle. Had we not had the necessary permissions, we would have ended up in jail and been heavily fined.

The Munnuvan Tribal Peoples

If you do manage to get permission for the Munnuvan region, it will be one of the most fascinating experiences you will ever have. The tribals will put up trekkers who come through a guide known to them, in their own villages, each of which has a guest house.

The Munnuvans worship an elephant god and live by planting wild cardamom under the towering forest trees and planting rice in small paddies in some of their hidden valleys. In the surrounding forests lives the full range of south Indian wildlife, and by night they echo to the whines of jackals and hyenas, and sometimes to the deep rumble of a tiger, the dark spaces between the trees a-dance with fireflies.

The Munnuvans themselves have an interesting society. Although male-dominated, the men help to look after small children—it's a common sight to see the elders walking around with babies strapped to their hips—and both male and female children are sent to live communally in school huts where they learn their roles and provide a task force for the old and sick people in the village. All trekkers are accommodated in the male school huts.

The National Park

The more casual visitor wanting to get into the hills should take a rickshaw or bus from town up to Erivakulam/Rajmalai National Park. Although this is a huge wild area, tourists are only allowed into a 4-mile strip on the southern edge, running along the tar road from the entrance to a police hut at the top of the pass leading over into the Munnuvan territory. However, you can see a lot of wildlife in this short section, notably small herds of Nilgiri *tahr*, the ibex species unique to the Western Ghats. On sunny days, these have a pleasing habit of posing majestically on rocks, horns silhouetted against the sky, just as you walk by with your camera. If it's drizzly, as it often is, the *tahr* tend to keep to the *shola* forests, so if you want to take wildlife photos, wait for a clear day.

Chinnar Wildlife Sanctuary

On the eastern side of the mountains, about 3–4 hours' bus ride from Munnar is **Chinnar Wildlife Sanctuary**, on the Kerala/Tamil Nadu border. This is a dry forest zone, so it is best to visit between November and January; after that most of the game migrates up to the wetter forests around Munnar. This is especially true of the tiger, leopard, elephant and *gaur*. *Sambar* and *chital*, *dhole*, wild boar and jackal may be spotted all year, and many people have reported good wildlife sightings from the reserve's **watchtower**, a few hundred yards from the

gaur

sanctuary entrance and forest checkpoint. The main road from Cochin to Coimbatore passes through the reserve, and all traffic is stopped at a barrier to make sure nobody is smuggling out forest products like sandalwood or skins. There is dormitory accommodation—often full, but if you insist on staying, they'll generally put you up in one of the other buildings, and you can take guided walks, morning and evening, into the bush.

Chinnar has a beautiful river flowing just below the forest checkpoint, and the woodland along its banks is alive with exotic birds. Paradise flycatchers, black-headed orioles, kingfishers, bee-eaters and bulbuls are all common. Look out also for the giant grizzled squirrel among the riverside trees, and when picnicking, beware of fleet, thieving monkeys (bonnet macaques).

Periyar (Thekkady)

Just outside the mountain town of Kumilly is the Periyar Wildlife Sanctuary (Tiger Reserve) at Thekkady. One of the main sanctuaries of southern India, it is also one of the largest in India. Comprising 300 square miles of lush, tropical forest, with a vast artificial lake in the centre, it is the natural habitat of an extensive range of wildlife. The huge Periyar Lake, measuring 10 square miles in area, was formed in 1895, with the completion of the Periyar Dam by the British government in Madras. Its original purpose was irrigation, but its conservation potential was soon recognized.

Getting Around

From Kottayam or Cochin (and over the mountains to Madurai) there are several daily **bus** services, that take about 4–6 hours. One direct service connects Kumilly with Kovalam and another with Kodaikanal in Tamil Nadu.

If staying in Kumilly, you can hire **bicycles** from most of the cheaper lodges to go in and out of the sanctuary (½ hour ride to the boat jetty).

Tourist Information

Kumilly **tourist office** is located at the top of the main street, opposite Lake Queen Hotel. When open, it dispenses boat-trip tickets, maps and walking/trekking permits. The **Wildlife Preservation Office**, ✆ 27, is at Periyar, overlooking the boat jetty.

The Sanctuary

The first game warden was appointed in 1923, the area was constituted a sanctuary in 1934, and it came under **Project Tiger** management in 1978. The rapid decrease in the population of tigers (from 40,000 at the turn of the century to just 1830 in 1972) led to the creation of Project Tiger, and the immediate management of 7 parks. Eighteen now come under the project, and the tiger population had increased to 4334 in 1989, 48 of them at Periyar.

Situated at a high altitude of between 3000 and 6000 feet (914 and 1828 metres) Periyar has a comfortably cool climate between November and January. But to see the wildlife at close quarters, it is best to come during the 'dry' months of February to June, when the animals, deprived of the forest water-holes, come to water down by the lake.

Periyar has a rich variety of wildlife, notably tiger, elephant, leopard, *gaur*, *dhole*, *sambar*, *chital*, wild boar, monkey, and a few Malabar flying squirrels, among many mammal species.

The extensive bird life to be seen includes heron, hornbill, jungle fowl, kingfisher and egret. The forests are dense jungles of creepers, spices and blossoming trees interspersed with some grassland.

sambar deer

To see the best of the wildlife, take the early 7am boat onto Periyar Lake (Rs20–30, tickets from the Wildlife Office, above jetty). Unless you are trekking, or are prepared to spend a couple of nights in one of the forest watchtowers, this is your best chance to see elephants, *gaur*, deer and, occasionally, tiger at close quarters; they come to water only very early in the morning, and in the late afternoon. You will not see many animals at any other time of day. At weekends, a motorboat full of tourists will send most animals on the banks scurrying for cover, so you may be better off hiring a private launch, from the Wildlife Office at about Rs80 per hour.

The boat tour lasts 1½ hours, and is a useful introduction to the sanctuary's flora and fauna. To follow up, it is necessary to explore the surrounding forests on foot. The Wildlife Office runs 3-hour **forest group treks** (Rs50 per person) which, if the group is small and disciplined, is worthwhile. These walks are often good for bird-watching. Some people, disregarding the injunction not to wander into the forest unescorted, report alarming experiences, returning with tales of unexpected eyeball encounters with bull elephants. If you want to get into the deep forest, the wisest course is to hire a private guide from the Wildlife Office (Rs100 per day) who'll take you to the best hides in complete safety, or for an **overnight trek** to one of the **forest rest houses** (an extra Rs100 per night, and you take your own food), enabling close sightings of elephants, bison, snakes, monkeys and a rich array of bird life.

Persuade the wildlife officer at Periyar that you're not a typical tourist, that you've come here specifically to study wildlife, and he may just let you stay alone at one of the **observation watchtowers**. These stand in the heart of the forest, on stilts, and elephants come to rest in their shade. To get to them, you take the tour boat out onto the lake, then walk a couple of miles into the jungle along with the park ranger. Since there are only two watchtowers available, it's worth booking 3–4 days in advance. A flashlight, blanket, food, drinking water and mosquito repellent are essential.

Kumilly ℂ (ring operator and ask for Kumilly) **Where to Stay**
expensive

If staying in the nearby village of Kumilly (a short bike or taxi ride from Thekkady, 2 miles from the lake), stay at **Spice Village**, a new resort with well-furnished cottages, bookable through the Casino Hotel, Cochin, ℂ 340221, ✉ 340001. The food is very good, wild spice trees grow on the lawns, and there is a pool.

The hotel can arrange all your transport into the sanctuary and can also put together treks, supply food etc.

moderate

The **Government Rest House** in the forest has three very comfortable rooms and they provide a servant to cook for you. Check availability with the tourist office in Kumilly. The plush **Lake Palace,** ✆ 24, is an island bungalow fairly deep within the sanctuary with nice gardens, a prime lake-shore situation, and pleasant rooms. Book through KDTC in Trivandrum, ✆ 61132.

inexpensive

Aranya Nivas Hotel, ✆ 23, is a fair fall-back with dodgy food, but good facilities. Rooms face the lake, and are reasonably priced. Pre-book through the KTDC office in Trivandrum, ✆ 61132. The **Ambadi,** at the checkpost, near the sanctuary entrance, ✆ 11, offers well-furnished, homely cottages.

cheap

Budget places include the **Lake Queen Tourist Home** opposite the tourist office, or **Hotel Vanarani,** ✆ 7, with excellent spacious rooms and a cheaper dormitory. The Lake Queen has some nice first-floor rooms with views of the hills, but guests complain of the alarming 6.30am 'breakfast calls'. The Vanarani arranges boating, sightseeing, trekking, and has a marvellous restaurant.

For dirt cheap accommodation, the **Forest Rest House** inside the sanctuary costs well under Rs100 per night, but with only 3 rooms it's generally full. In Kumilly try the **Holiday Home,** ✆ 22016 and **Rani Lodge,** both of which are basic.

Eating Out

The best eating places are in Kumilly. **Hotel Vanarani** offers a fine range of south Indian cuisine, very cheaply; **Hotel Paris** is the best for Western food, with quick service; and **Hotel Ambadi** often lays on displays of Kathakali dance in its popular open-air restaurant. All the hotel restaurants are open to non-residents.

Chimmony and Peechi-Vazhani Wildlife Sanctuaries

Just to the north of Periyar, set in the western foothills, is **Chimmony Wildlife Sanctuary,** 7 miles from Trichur (go by bus to the village of Ampalloor then Echippara). By contrast with busy Periyar, Chimmony is almost free of visitors, even between November and February, when the forest is full of game. Lying around a large reservoir dam, the sanctuary used to be the royal hunting forest of the King of Kochi. Under the British most of the big teak trees were felled, until by the 1940s most of the forest had gone. However, strict conservation measures since have allowed the trees to regenerate, and now elephant, leopard, sloth bear, *gaur, dhole, sambar* and muntjac deer are common again.

The sanctuary has several good **trekking paths** for day visitors and for once, it is not a hassle to get permission, though in India you never quite know for sure... Accommodation can be arranged at the Inspection Bungalow, ✆ (0487) 680347, or in cheap lodges at Ampalloor.

In the same area of foothills just east of Trichur is the **Peechi-Vazhani Wildlife Sanctuary**, a protected forest set around yet another reservoir, and backing onto Chimmony Sanctuary to the south. The same forest types and the same fauna as at Chimmony are found at Peechi-Vazhani, which has the additional attraction of tiger and a large *dhole* (wild dog) population. Over 50 species of orchid also grow in the forest.

Peechi-Vazhani is only 12 miles northeast of Trichur and is easily reached by bus. Day-treks into the forest can be arranged and there is accommodation at the Wildlife Division Rest House and Information Centre, both at the sanctuary entrance. Book in advance, ✆ Kannara 17, or just show up—at only 12 miles by bus from town, it's worth taking a chance.

Silent Valley and Wynad

North of Trichur's foothill forests stretches a vast wild area that sees almost no visitors: the combined **Silent Valley National Park** and the **Wynad Wildlife Sanctuary**. Lying on the western side of the Nilgiri Hills (the Western Ghats' highest range), these two reserves form the western part of the great **Nilgiri Biosphere**, which incorporates hundreds of square miles of forest and grassland, and includes the Project Tiger reserves of Mudumalai (Tamil Nadu), Nagerhole and Bandipur (Karnataka).

Silent Valley and Wynad both protect highly fragile evergreen rainforest. They are also the territory of some of India's most primitive tribal peoples, particularly the **Sholakainal tribe**, cave dwellers who still live by hunting and gathering and who shun contact with the outside world.

Of the two reserves, it is **Silent Valley** that has the most delicate ecosystem and entry is highly restricted—you need to apply through the Chief Wildlife Conservation office in Delhi, and you should have a recommendation from a wildlife body or research centre.

Because of its relative inaccessibility in the high Ghats, Silent Valley escaped exploitation under the Raj, so the primeval forest has survived intact. At present, however, there is a threat from gangs of sandalwood smugglers, who operate in the area and dragoon the local tribals into working for them. Because of this, it can be dangerous to go in alone and that is a secondary reason why the government restricts foreign visitors to scientific parties only. Perhaps this is a good thing: several new species of orchid have been discovered here in recent years and although forest plundering by the sandalwood smugglers damages a certain amount of the land every year, the plant life would suffer far more if unlimited tourists were allowed to tramp through.

Silent Valley has all the southern Indian big game and some spectacular birds too—including the great Indian hornbill, Malay bittern, rufous-bellied shortwing and the Nilgiri laughing thrush.

Although your chances of getting into Silent Valley are very slim, it is possible to visit the larger **Wynad Sanctuary**, though again, you should apply for

langur

239

permission first. **Clipper Holidays** in Cochin, ✆ (0484) 682035 should be able to sort this out for you, but you should allow at least a month for the paperwork to be processed.

Easily accessible by bus from the coast at Calicut, via the scrubby little hill town of **Sultan's Battery** (also called Sulthanbatheri), there are also direct connections with Ooty in Tamil Nadu and Mysore in Karnataka.

Wynad has elephant, tiger (of which there are frequent sightings), leopard (black panther is recorded here), sloth bear, *dhole, gaur, sambar* and *chital*, primates such as Nilgiri *langur*, lion-tailed macaque, flying squirrels, big monitor lizards and pythons, and good birdlife. Tribals also share the forest (*see* above), and the sanctuary is geared for **trekking** by prior permission, with accommodation in wooden lodges with game-viewing platforms; ✆ (048968) 454.

Should you be travelling up to Wynad and need to spend the night in Sultan's Battery before going into the sanctuary, you can find accommodation at the **Resort** (some air-conditioned, Rs300 per room) or at the much cheaper **Modern Tourist Home** (under Rs100 per room), before taking a bus to the Wynad Sanctuary entrance.

The Far North

In the mountains where Kerala and Karnataka meet, is the small **Aralam Wildlife Sanctuary**. Near the small town of Iritty, about 30 miles northeast of Kannur (Cannanore) on the coast, this is a tropical evergreen forest where elephant and *gaur* are commonly sighted while *sambar, chital*, wild boar, leopard, *dhole* and the smaller mammals are well represented. If you can make the trip it is worth trying to get into Aralam, as it sees almost no visitors at all and the game is thus less used to disturbance and more likely to be viewed, even in thick forest. You can ask to stay at the Wildlife Department Rest House but it's best to check before sweating up there by bus, ✆ (04869) 454.

Tamil Nadu

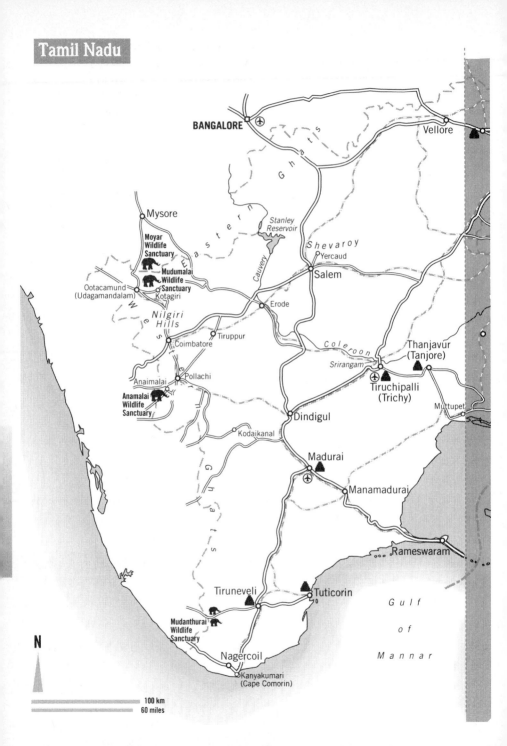

Tamil Nadu

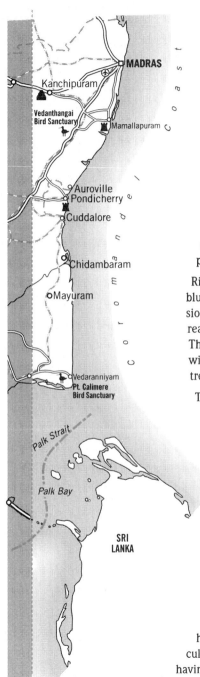

A green, fertile state at the extreme south-east of the subcontinent, bounded to the east by the tropical beaches of the Coromandel Coast, Tamil Nadu is roughly the size of England (about 81,250 square miles) and has a similar population (55.6 million at the last estimate).

Stretching inland is a flat plain of rice-growing farmlands, cut by wide rivers from whose banks rise the great temple cities of Madurai, Thanjavur and Tiruchipalli. Tens of thousands of Hindu pilgrims from all over India are continually on the move between the temples of the plain, built by the highly cultivated medieval dynasties ruling between the 6th and 14th centuries, and about 90 per cent of the state population are practising Hindus.

Rising abruptly to the west of the plain is the long blue mountain wall of the Western Ghats, a succession of connected ranges whose steep-sided peaks reach an elevation of 8000 feet at their highest point. Thickly forested, the ghats have some of India's best wildlife sanctuaries for elephant and tiger, and offer trekking into remote tribal regions.

The state capital is hellish-hot Madras, India's fourth-largest city with a population of 6 million at the last count. Founded by the British as a trading post in 1639, it became the headquarters for their conquest of south India during the 18th century and remained the centre of south Indian government until Independence in 1947. Now the main international gateway to south India, it receives direct flights from both Britain and continental Europe (*see* p.246).

Tamil Nadu became a state in 1956, its boundaries determined by those areas where Tamil was the main spoken language. Tamil literature, dance and sculpture are still widely practised here, and the Tamils often claim that their Dravidian culture is the 'purest' in India—its continuity never having been broken from antiquity to the present day.

The best time to visit is the warm, sunny 'winter' (average temperature 25°C) from **November to March**. From **April** to the monsoons of **October**, the heat can be unbearable—an average of about 33°C, but rising to a staggering 45–50°C in the crowded city centre. From **October** to the end of **December** the monsoon rains gradually cool the temperatures. Travel in the southeastern monsoon is not disrupted by rain, which comes in sudden showers of an hour or two between periods of bright sunshine.

Tamil Nadu's Coast and Plains

Child of the sun am I, and of the breezes, juicy as mangoes, that mythopoeically caress the Coast of Coromandel far away on the porphyry and lapis lazuli Indian shore where everything is bright and precise as lacquer.

Overture and Incidental Music for A Midsummer Nights' Dream,
Angela Carter

Tamil Nadu's flat coastal plain stretches 200 miles from the mountains of the Western Ghats to the the southern Bay of Bengal—the Coromandel Coast. Deeply rural in its rice-growing countryside, hellish hot and crowded in its fantastic temple cities, all-but-deserted along its palm-fringed storm-swept coast, this is the living heart of old India. The Dravidian cultures of the Hindu south resisted and survived the successive waves of invaders that ate up the north—Mughals, Deccan Sultans, British—all absorbed and digested by the ancient southern culture that peaked under the Chola kings of the 9th and 10th centuries, and left the great temples that still attract legions of black-lungied pilgrims from all over the sub-continent.

Make time to visit the shore temples and rock carvings at **Mamallapuram**; the thousand-pillared hall of the temple at **Kanchipuram**; the French colonial/New Age town of **Pondicherry**; and the surrounding countryside and wild beaches owned by the **Auroville** Community. About 200 miles inland are the temple towns: the great temple at **Madurai**, where elephants wander the ancient corridors and weird percussive instruments roar out of the gloom like monsters from childhood nightmares; the beautiful, towering *gopurams* at **Srirangam** and **Thanjavur**, also hot and crowded but rewarding for their ornate temple interiors.At the end of your tour, for a little peace, head back to the coast to the great swamp at **Point Calimere**, whose waters turn a mass of shifting pink when the flamingos arrive in warm November, and whose quiet woods are home to blackbuck antelope and spotted deer.

Madras

Capital of Tamil Nadu, Madras differs from India's other large cities in three major respects. First, it is the home of the ancient Dravidian civilization, hardly touched by the invasions from the north, and often claimed to be 'pure' Indian. Next, it is still unusually spacious, at least away from its main commercial centre: a wide, green and airy 31 square miles of parks and gardens, beaches and esplanades with very few built-up areas despite a population of about

6 million, although in the last few years land prices have soared and a number of new high-rise buildings have started to spring up. Lastly, it has managed to grow from rural village to modern metropolis in 350 years without losing much of its simple charm. All three factors have combined to give Madras, and the south in general, growing popularity as a tourist destination.

History

An important port, Madras has a long history of association with other cultures. The names of many of its streets—Armenian Street, China Bazaar Road, Portuguese Church Street and so on—reflect its early days of international trading importance. Even before the British arrived, its precious cargoes of handlooms, fabrics, silk and hides had attracted European interest, leading to the establishment of a small Portuguese settlement at San Thome.

Madras was also the first English settlement in India. The East India Company arrived here in 1639, and was granted by the Rajah of Chandragiri the small village of Chennapatnam (later the city of Madras), located between the ancient towns of Mylapore and Triplicane in the south and Tiruvottiyur in the north. On this site, in 1641, the Company constructed Fort St George and began exporting cloth back to England. To the north of the European fort arose a second town, called Madraspatnam or 'Black Town' for the Indian community, which later (following King George's visit in 1911) became the present Georgetown. Following its grant of a municipal charter in 1688 by James II making it the oldest Municipal Corporation in India, Madras became a battleground for competing French and British trading interests in 18th century, and was even occupied by the French for a brief spell (1746–9) before the young Clive removed them at the Battle of Arcot in 1751. Though replaced a short time later by Calcutta as the primary British settlement (1772), Madras continued to be one of the four major seats of British Imperial power in India throughout the 19th century. Under the Madras Presidency, the city expanded rapidly outwards, giving birth to a relaxed, open garden city of clubs, churches, parks and elegant Victorian monuments. Today, Madras is transforming its traditional textile-based economy in favour of rapid industrial and technological development, but it still remains a pleasant, semi-rural town, a unique blend of the old and the new.

Despite its heat (Madras has three seasons, hot, hotter and hottest), many feel Madras to be the most pleasant introduction to India: except at rush hour, it lacks the frenetic pressure of Bombay, and it is possible to adapt to the Asian way of life much more quickly. There is no cushioning effect here: you're face-to-face with 'real India' right from the start. Madras is a typical Indian city: one minute you'll be walking along an elegant main thoroughfare admiring well-to-do Madrassi women, sweet-smelling jasmine wound into their jet-black hair; the next, you'll turn into a dirty, crowded street full of thin men on the pavements in dusty sarongs, and even thinner mothers with ragged babies. But if the sights are contrasting, the people are uniform: dark-skinned, shock-haired; irrepressibly friendly and insatiably curious Tamils with an obsessive love of foreigners. Here, a casual enquiry for directions will cause a vast, swaying crowd of helpful locals to gather within seconds. They'll even follow you down the road afterwards, just in case you want something else.

Climate and When to Go

The one big drawback to selecting Madras as an arrival point in India is the heat. The climate is tropical and despite two monsoons a year (**June to August** and **September to November**) it is *always* very hot and very humid. Remember, they've named a

Itinerant fortune teller,
Pongol festival

curry after Madras. Some like the fetid atmosphere and slip easily into the calm, relaxed pace of life for which Tamil Nadu is famous; others simply melt, and regret not choosing a northern capital in which to adjust to Asian temperatures. The coolest time to go, but still rather warm, is between **December and February**, and it's worth turning up for the **Pongal** (Spring Harvest) festival of **mid January**. During this extravaganza, Madras paints itself and its sacred cows in bright colours, and goes singing, dancing and begging for a whole week. Though more sedate, the big **Dance and Arts Festival** of **mid December** is also a major attraction. Madras has any number of festivals, and each one is a near-riot.

Getting There

by air

Meenambakkam airport is connected by **Indian Airlines** to Bangalore (several daily), Bombay (several daily), Mangalore (Tue,Thur, Sat, Sun), Cochin (Wed, Fri, Sun), Goa (Tue, Thur, Sat), Hyderabad (two daily), Madurai (Tue, Thur, Sat), Tiruchipalli (Tue, Thur, Sat), Trivandrum (one daily) and Vizakhapatnam (Mon, Wed, Fri).

Vayudoot fly to Coimbatore, Madurai and Cochin. **EastWest Airlines** fly to Bombay. **Damania** fly to Bombay (once daily), Bangalore, Cochin, Coimbatore, Madurai, Trivandrum and Vishakhapatnam. **Jet** fly to Bombay (twice daily), and Cochin. **Modiluft** fly to Hyderabad daily except Sunday.

International flights are operated by **Air India** from Frankfurt, Jeddah and Kuala Lumpur; **Air Lanka** from Colombo; **British Airways** from London (Heathrow) via Abu Dhabi; **Indian Airlines** to Colombo and Singapore; **Malaysian Airlines** from Kuala Lumpur and **Singapore Airlines** from Singapore.

The airport has international and domestic terminals, linked by PTC buses, and is located 9 miles from the city. From the airport, you've a choice of Aviation Express private coach, PTC mini-coach, taxi (Rs120–200) or auto-rickshaw (Rs80–100) into town. It's a 40–60 minute journey.

by rail

Madras has two stations: **Egmore**, which serves the south (right down to Kanyakumari), and **Central**, which connects with the rest of India (notably Bangalore, Bombay and Cochin). Both stations are close to each other, off Poonamallee High Road, and you can use the suburban trains to get around Madras itself—say, up to Fort St George or to Madras Beach, or down to Guindy for the National Park. Railway seat

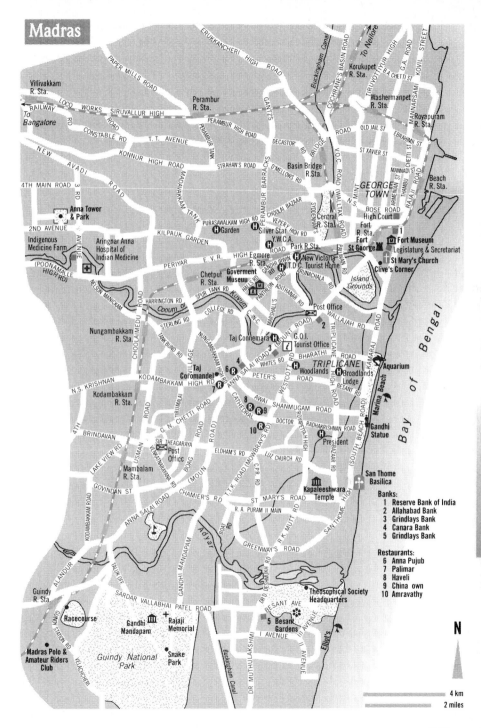

Madras

Villivakkam R. Sta.

To Bangalore

RAILWAY
LOCO WORKS
SIRUVALLUR HIGH
ROAD
NEW AVADI ROAD
3RD ROAD
CONSTABLE RD
T. T. AVENUE
KONNUR HIGH ROAD
PAPER MILLS ROAD
ERUKKANCHERI HIGH ROAD

Perambur R. Sta.

PERAMBUR HIGH ROAD
PERAMBUR TANK
STRAHAN'S ROAD
MADAVAKKAM TANK RD
DECASTOR'
D'MELLOWS RD
PURASAWALKAM HIGH
RD
GANTZ
BUCKINGHAM Canal
COCHRANE'S BASIN ROAD
TRIVUOTTTIYUR HIGH
B.A. CHETTI ST
C.A. ROAD
KOVIL STREET
To Nellore

Korukupet R. Sta.

Washermanpet R. Sta.

OLD JAIL ST
V.O.C. ROAD
BRIDGE
ST XAVIER ST
EBRAHIMJI ST
MANNARSAMI

Royapuram R. Sta.

MANNADI
ARMENIAN ST
THAMBU CHETTI ST
RAJAJI ROAD

Beach R. Sta.

GEORGE TOWN

4TH MAIN ROAD

Anna Tower & Park

2ND AVENUE

Indigenous Medicine Farm

Aringnar Anna Hospital of Indian Medicine

(POONAMALLE HIGH RD)

KILPAUK GARDEN

NELSON MANICKAM

HARRINGTON RD
STERLING RD
SPUR TANK RD
COLLEGE RD
Coovum or

PERIYAR E.V.R.

Chetput R. Sta.

Goverment Museum

CHOOLAI BAZAAR
VEPERY HIGH RD
PERAMBUR BARRACKS RD
WALTAX RD
N.S.
MINT
STOODS RD

Garden
Silver Star
Y.W.C.A.
HIGH Egmore
R. Sta.
Park R.Sta.
New Victoria
T.D.C. Tourist Home
ARUNACHALA
GANDHI IRWIN RD
PANNIARAM RD

Central R. Sta.
BOSE ROAD
High Court
Fort R. Sta.
Fort St George
St Mary's Church
Clive's Corner

Fort Museum
Legislature & Secretariat

Island Grounds

MARSHALL'S
PANTHEON ADITHANAR RD
KUTCHERI
Post Office
WALLAJAH RD
C.N.C.

Nungambakkam R. Sta.

STERLING RD
TANK BUND RD
NUNGAMBAKKAM HIGH ROAD
VILLAGE
KODAMBAKKAM HIGH ROAD

Taj Connemara

G.O.I.
Tourist Office

2

BHARATHI ROAD

WHITES RD

PETER'S ROAD

TRIPLICANE

Woodlands
Broadlands Lodge
BESANT RD
TRIPLICANE HIGH
KAMARAJ ROAD

Aquarium

Marina Beach

N.S. KRISHNAN

Kodambakkam R. Sta.

G.N. CHETTI ROAD
SIR THEAGARAYA
Post Office
BRINDAVAN
4TH
LAKE VIEW RD
USMAN RD
VENKATNARAYAN RD

Taj Coromandel

ANNA SALAI ROAD
AWAI
CATHEDRAL ROAD
DOCTOR
SHANMUGAM ROAD
RADHAKRISHNAN ROAD
ROYAPETTAH HIGH

President

Gandhi Statue

Bay of Bengal

Mambalam R. Sta.

GOVINDAN ST
KODAMBAKKAM ROAD
ANNA SALAI ROAD
BOAG RD
T.T.K. ROAD (MOWBRAY'S
CHAMIER'S RD
ELDHAM'S RD
LUZ CHURCH RD
R.A. PURAM II MAIN
ST MARY'S ROAD
R.K. MUTT RD
C.P.R.D.

Kapaleeshwara Temple

San Thome Basilica

Banks:
1 Reserve Bank of India
2 Allahabad Bank
3 Grindlays Bank
4 Canara Bank
5 Grindlays Bank

Restaurants:
6 Anna Pujub
7 Palimar
8 Haveli
9 China own
10 Amravathy

Guindy R. Sta.

Racecourse

Gandhi Mandapam

Rajaji Memorial

Madras Polo & Amateur Riders Club

Guindy National Park

Snake Park

SARDAR VALLABHAI PATEL ROAD
TALUK OFF
GANDHI MANDAPAM
Adyar
GREENWAY'S ROAD
DR DESHMUKH RD
BESANT AVE
VELACHHERI
DR MUTHULAKSHMI
Buckingham Canal
Elliot's
I AVENUE
II AVENUE

Theosophical Society Headquarters

Besant Gardens

5

N

4 km
2 miles

reservations are easy; to tap the tourist quota, go to the Indrail office, 2nd floor, inside Central station. It's open from 10am to 6pm and you don't need an Indrail Pass for reservations, just your passport.

by road

TTDC buses (for short-range destinations like Mammallapuram, Kanchipuram, Tirupati etc.) leave from Mofussil bus stand, off Esplanade Road. TTC buses go from the nearby Express bus stand at Parry's Corner, just behind the High Court building, and service long-haul venues like Hyderabad (15 hours), Bangalore, Kanchipuram (3 hours), Coimbatore, Madurai, Mysore (9 hours), and Trivandrum (16 hours). Inside the chaotic terminals, there are always kids eager to direct you to the right bus for a small tip. To avoid long queues for tickets, buy them at the TNTDC tourist office, and at the crowded bus stations. Tamil Nadu has one of the country's most efficient public transport systems and even the smallest district town is connected with Madras.

Getting Around

Madras divides into three main sections: busy, commercial **Georgetown** to the north (with G.P.O., American Express, bazaars, budget hotels, in and around Netaji Subhash Bose Road); **Egmore** in the city centre (for bus/rail terminals, airline offices, consulates, tourist offices and decent hotels/restaurants, in and around Anna Salai/Mount Road); and **Guindy/Adyar**, the quiet, semi-rural 'green belt' (with wildlife park, beaches and Theosophical Society) to the far south.

Getting around Madras presents you with two problems: first, all the streets were renamed following Independence, and the new names haven't stuck (everybody still calls Anna Salai, Madras's chief thoroughfare, by its old title of Mount Road); second, transport round town is hit-and-miss. The inner city is crowded with unemployed **auto-** and **cycle-rickshaws** who'll do anything, even mount the pavement, to get your business. But few of them speak English, and even fewer know where they are going. With rickshaws always fix the cost of the journey—around Rs3 per mile for auto-rickshaws, Rs2 per mile for cycle-rickshaws—in advance. Sometimes it's better to hire a **taxi** as they do tend to use meters, and have a better sense of direction. Most travellers see Madras by **bicycle**.

Tourist Information

Madras' **Government Tourist Office**, 143 Mount Road, © 830 390, open from 10 to 5 daily, and round the clock for tour bookings. It's still the most useful and helpful tourist office in India. Walk in to find culture-show videos playing, staff fighting to answer ringing phones, brochures and maps readily available, and everybody doing something. Here you can pick up a complimentary copy of *Hello Madras* (full of useful information), buy a decent city map (Rs5), advance-book TTDC accommodation throughout Tamil Nadu, and watch a film. Also come here to book your tours—for Madras city (8.30 to 1.30, or 2 to 6 daily; Rs45); or for Kanchipuram, Thirukalikundram and Mahabalipuram (7.30 to 6 daily).

TTDC also has an information counter open 6am to 9pm at Central railway station, while the more general **Government of India Tourist Office** is at 154 Mount Road, ✆ 88685/6, open 9 to 6 weekdays, 9–1 Saturdays).

banks

Banking hours are from 10 to 2 weekdays, Saturdays 10 to 12noon. You'll find the **State Bank of India** at 103 Mount Road, ✆ 840393. **ANZ Grindlays Bank**, Padmanabha Nagar, Adyar is open Sundays from 8.30 to 10.30am and closed Mondays. Both the above handle foreign exchange.

airline offices

Air India, ✆ 474477, and the domestic **Indian Airlines**, ✆ 477977 enquiries, 478333 reservations, are both at 19 Marshalls Road, Egmore; **Air France**, 769 Mount Road, ✆ 88377; **Air Lanka**, 758 Mount Road, ✆ 861777; **British Airways**, 26 Commander-in-Chief Road, ✆ 477388; **Delta Airways**, 163–4 Mount Road, ✆ 88493; **Lufthansa**, 171 Mount Road, ✆ 81483; **Malaysian Airlines**, 189 Mount Road, ✆ 868625; **Qantas**, 112 Nungambakkam High Road, ✆ 478680; and **Singapore Airlines**, 167 Mount Road, ✆ 862404.

Apart from Indian Airlines, other domestic airlines include **East West Airways**, with flights to most major destinations, ✆ 477007, 866669; **Modiluft** who also have a wide network, ✆ 826 9572 and **Jet**, who offers flights to Bombay only, check via the Government of India Tourist Office, ✆ 88685/6.

consulates

USA: 220 Mount Road, ✆ 473040.
UK: 24 Anderson Road, ✆ 473136.
Germany: 22 Commander-in-Chief Road, ✆ 471747.
France: 26 Cathedral Road, ✆ 476854.
Netherlands: 739 Mount Road, ✆ 811566.
Japan: 6 Spur Tank Road, Chetpet, ✆ 865594.

NB: all consulates are closed at weekends.

travel agents

The best is probably **Clipper Holidays**, Suite 405, Hotel Ganpat, 103 Nungumbakkam High Road, ✆ 8256787. Other good ones include **Trade Wings Ltd**, 752 Mount Road, ✆ 864961, **Sita World Travel (P) Ltd**, 26 Commander-in-Chief Road, ✆ 478861, and **Travel Corporation India (TCI)**, 734 Mount Road, ✆ 868813.

The Town

Madras is a big, sprawling city and its few sights are very spread out. Take a conducted tour bus for quick, cheap orientation, then go exploring by car or cycle. Madras has one of the longest beaches in Asia, and this is where to head when sightseeing is over. There's also loads of 'street action', and good cultural entertainments, thus little danger of running out of things to do. Travellers tend to stay in Madras a good deal longer than originally intended.

City Tour

by tour bus, 4 hours

Fort St George–St Mary's Church–Government Museum–National Art Gallery–Valluva Kottam–Guindy Snake Park–Kapaleeshwara Temple–San Thome Basilica

From the tourist office, it's a straight run up Anna Salai (Mount Road) to the birthplace of Madras, **Fort St George**. Still surrounded by cannon-proof walls (in whose guradhouses tailors and barbers have now set up shop), the fort was rebuilt several times between 1642 when its original bastions were completed and 1749 when the French left, it remains—moats and all—pretty much today as when first made the seat of empire. Declared a national monument in 1948, most of its buildings have been converted into government offices, notably the Legislature and Secretariat. At various times the fort was home of Robert Clive, Elihu Yale and Sir Arthur Wellesley (later Wellington). Within the fort, visit the sturdy little **St Mary's Church** (*open daily, 8.30–5.30*), the oldest Protestant church east of the Suez and the first Anglican one in India. Built in 1680 from voluntary contributions of the Fort's English inhabitants, it gained its spire in 1710 and was completely renovated in 1759. Designed by a British gunner and built to last, with walls 4 feet thick and a roof 2 feet thick, this church is noteworthy for its total stone composition: no wood is used anywhere. The three aisles, arched with brick and stone, have a bomb-proof vaulted roof. The gallery has a finely carved nave, with two curved outer staircases. On the walls, it's worth noting the fine memorials to the East India Company's 18th-century administrators and soldiers who died at Madras. Few seem to have made it past the age of 50, giving an insight into the pre-vaccination and malaria tablet conditions of the time. In the courtyard, you'll see some of the oldest British tombstones in India; some have been moved inside and are now beneath the altar. The Renaissance painting above the altar was painted by an unknown artist and brought here from Pondicherry in 1761. Famous people who married in St Mary's include Lord Cornwallis, Elihu Yale (early Governor of Madras, who later founded Yale University in the US) and Robert Clive. Clive House, behind the church, is another reminder of the great empire-builder who started out as a humble clerk within this fort.

The nearby **Fort Museum**, (*open daily, 9–5, except Fri, adm free*) now housed in the Fort's Exchange Office (1780–90). The museum has 10 galleries with many exhibits telling the story of the East India Company's activities in south India. The top floor has some good French porcelain, clocks and glass, and, of most interest, some rare 19th-century prints of Madras. The ground floor has East India Company memorabilia, including officers' medals, tea sets and cutlery. The weapons gallery has some good curiosities, including early 19th-century mines, mortars and chainshot—two iron balls linked by a chain, fired from a light cannon and designed to rip, literally, through massed ranks of soldiers. A collection of armour includes a helmet that looks uncomfortably like that of a Second World War German infantryman. Next door is an old palanquin used by the pre-Raj Nawabs, and a scale model of the fort. However, the museum's real treasure is back in the weapons gallery: a weird little iron cage in which a huge, whiskered officer called Captain Philip Anstruther spent a month after being captured by state guards in China in 1840 while on Company business. Anstruther was chained into the cage, with a split open head, and displayed for the derision of the local Chinese until he received a miraculous pardon and was set free. He asked to keep the cage. Local stories about the man are not confined to this incident. Apparently Anstruther was something of a character in his own right. One story reports that he once gave a beggar a gold sovereign in the street, exclaiming, '*Good God Man, you're the first man I've seen who's even uglier than me!*'

Just north of the fort is the magnificent **High Court** (built in 1861), reputed to be the finest example of Indo-Saracenic architecture in India. It's worth returning to later on (as you only get a fleeting glimpse from the bus) for a leisurely tour round its stately corridors, courts and staircases. There are several rare paintings here too, and a 'lighthouse' tower which was in use until 1977. You can climb to the top.

Returning to the city centre, the tour makes a worthwhile visit to the beautiful, if decaying **Government Museum** in Pantheon Road (*open daily 8–5, except Fri*). A Classical structure with faded red walls and a delightful internal labyrinth of staircases and interconnecting galleries, the museum is notable for its annexe, which houses an unequalled collection of **fine bronzes**, mainly from the early Pallava, Chalukya and Vijayanagar periods. Of particular beauty is a dancing, 8-armed Shiva (in the act of creation), which occupies the central position in the gallery. In the main museum, the largest exhibits are the panels from the *c.* 200 BC **Amaravati Stupa**, said to have been erected over Gautama Buddha's relics. The collection, which occupies a whole gallery, was discovered, and later excavated in 1816, by Colonel Colin Mackenzie who found the panels being used as building material. One warning: the museum staff may encourage you to take photographs of exhibits, and then immediately demand *baksheesh*. Although you do not have to pay up (the penalty for staff caught in the scam is supposed to be sacking), the resulting scene can be a bore, so it is best to say 'No' and pass on.

Attached to the museum is the **National Art Gallery**, a fine Indo-Saracenic building (which keeps the same hours and is covered by the same admission ticket). The gallery has a good collection of Mughal and Rajput miniatures, glass-paintings from Tanjore and assorted 11th–12th-century metalware. However, some of the paintings of early 19th-century rajahs and ranis are little more than sickly sweet caricatures of fat, baby-faced people, and there is a truly disturbing miniature of Jains being impaled during the 18th-century south Indian persecution of the sect.

Down in Nungambakkam, the Hollywood of south India, and full of film studios, there's an overlong stop at **Valluvar Kottam**, a memorial dedicated to the poet-saint Thiruvalluvar. Opened in 1976, its massive auditorium is one of Asia's largest, containing 4000 seats, and is an important culture centre. Inscribed on the polished granite are 1330 of the poet's verses from his classic *Thirukkural.* Outside, there's a 'temple chariot' in stone, a vast rectangular terrace and extensive gardens.

Guindy Snake Park (*open daily, 8.30–5.30*) is 4 miles further south, near Raj Bhavan (the Governor's House). It's a small, interesting reptilium of snakes, iguanas, crocodiles and spiders. Here you can go chameleon-spotting, investigate the curious 'Snake Worship Anthill', and watch the hourly (from 10am) demonstration of unfanged-cobras being handled. You are also allowed to handle the snakes. The Snake Park backs onto 300 acres of parkland supporting herds of blackbuck, many *chital* (spotted deer) and monkeys. For a pleasant day here, return via urban train, or by no.45 bus from Anna Square in the city centre.

Off R.K. Mutt Road, in the old Mylapore district, you'll come next to **Kapaleeshwara Temple**. Dedicated to Shiva, the temple's legend (Parvati as a peacock, praying to Shiva for deliverance after some domestic transgression) is portrayed in sculpture within. The tall, 130 feet (40 metre) high *gopuram* tower, festooned with richly coloured deities, is a distinctive feature of Dravidian temple architecture. You'll see more of these throughout Tamil Nadu. Their principal purpose was to guard the inner shrine from attack, either spiritual or temporal. Considering how few south Indian temples suffered damage over the centuries, they seem to have been remarkably effective. Here, as with other 'living' temples in Tamil Nadu, non-Hindus are not allowed into the inner shrine.

After a brief visit to **Elliot's Beach**, and just enough time for a paddle, the tour finishes off at **San Thome Basilica**, South Beach Road. This is a Gothic-style Catholic church said to house the remains of St Thomas, the 'Apostle of India', who died at nearby St Thomas Mount in AD 72. Despite being rather miffed at finding the Indian Christian Church (known as the Syrian Orthodox) alive and well and older than their own, the early 16th-century Portuguese missionaries quickly went about catholicizing St Thomas (he was an apostle after all) and built a church here in 1504. However, the Renaissance structure was sadly replaced by the present late Victorian edifice in 1893.

Triplicane

Busy, sprawling Madras lacks places to stroll and take in the real street life. The exception to this rule is the old residential quarter of Triplicane, reached by heading south along Anna Salai (Mount Road), a mile from the town centre. For easy orientation, jump into an auto-rickshaw and ask for Broadlands Lodge, an ex-Nawab's town residence (now a budget traveller's hang-out) in the heart of the quarter. Initially, you will wonder why you've come. The streets present the usual chaos of filth, livestock, beggars and people going hurriedly about their business, creating an atmosphere which, though full of busy charm, is little different from that of any other Indian town. However, look up above the shop fronts and you will notice many fine designs on the buildings, with balconies and rooftop terraces peeping over onto the squalid streets. This is the clue to the real Triplicane, for behind these fine, yet dirty fronts lie cool quiet courtyards with trees and gardens and a traditional south Indian town life that has remained unchanged for centuries. Visit Broadlands Lodge for a look at one of these interiors (*see* 'Where to Stay', p.256). Triplicane also has a plethora of cheap, clean eating houses, and is a good place to head for in the evening if you fancy a cool walk before supper, especially as the residents of the quarter are uniformly friendly.

Beach Excursion

by bicycle

Marina Beach–Theosophical Society–Elliot's Beach–Golden Beach

This is the ideal follow-up to the hot, sticky city tour—a cool, relaxing ride by bicycle down Madras's long seafront towards some of the nicest beaches of the south. Except in Georgetown, Madras is ideal for cycling, being largely on the flat and relatively free of traffic. Your hotel will usually know where to hire bikes.

From Anna Salai tourist office, a 15-minute ride down nearby Woods Road, (left into Bharathi Road) brings you out in the centre of **Marina Beach**, by the Aquarium. This long beach is a 7 mile strip of fine sandy shore known as the 'pride of Madras'. A favourite evening resort of Madras citizens, it is fronted by garden-fringed promenades dotted with statues and parks dedicated to prominent Tamil writers and educators.

Turn right down South Beach Road (the north part of the beach, round Georgetown, is too rough for safe swimming) until you come to **Gandhiji Statue** (1¼ miles). Just behind this is the new **Lighthouse**, where you can climb 150 feet for marvellous views of the coastline. If you want to go swimming here, the better stretches of Marina Beach are slightly further south.

Continuing on, it's a scenic half-hour journey via San Thome Basilica (turn off right here down San Thome High Road) into the quiet, rural Adyar precinct. Past the derelict **Ayappa Temple**, which appears on the left a mile inland, you'll turn left into Dr Durgabai Deshmukh Road, which takes you over the wide **Adyar Lake**. Over the bridge, turn left again into Besant Avenue Road for the **Theosophical Society** (*open Mon–Fri, 8–11am and 2–5pm; Sat 8–11am; closed Sun; gardens open sunrise–sunset*). The approach along pretty country lanes is the perfect introduction to the 270 acres of beautiful gardens within the Society's grounds. Established in New York in 1875 by Madame Blavatsky and Colonel Olcott, the Theosophical Society moved to Madras in 1882. It was formed to promote the study of comparative religions, philosophy and science. After its move to Madras the society was run by Annie Besant. The vast campus, spread over 1750 acres, houses a superb library with 17,000 manuscripts, has shrines to all faiths and also one of the world's largest banyan trees. Just 10 minutes ride past the Society, **Elliot's Beach** appears on your left. For a quick, quiet swim try the beach off V Avenue Road. Then return to the main road, continue down to IV Avenue Road for refreshments at the **Palace Tea and Coffee Centre**, which serves delicious samosas, ice cream and snacks. On the beach, be prepared for lots of local interest. Friendly fishermen take it in turns to 'guard' visitors and mind their clothes and belongings while they're in the sea. There's accommodation here at Elliot's Beach too; for a few thousand rupees per month, you can get a beach chalet for two. Ask around in the quiet residential road backing off the beach, or ring Mrs Savitri, © 479777/412134, for details of her furnished chalets and apartments in Besant Nagar.

Madras' best beach, **Golden Beach**, lies a further 6 miles south. If this is too much to handle by cycle (and it probably is), then you can get there by bus from Elliot's Beach, and return here to pick up your bike afterwards. Alternatively, be at **Kapaleeshwara Temple** for the sunset over Adyar River. To get there, go straight ahead at the end of Dr Durgabai Deshmukh Road, up R.K. Mutt Road for a mile. The evening lights over the small lake are beautiful, and so is the ceremony when the gods are brought out and shown the setting sun, to the accompaniment of bells, flutes, drums and invocations.

Sports and Activities

Golf: apply to the **Cosmopolitan Golf Club**, Mount Road, © 849946, to use the sandy but shaded 18-hole course.

Horse racing: The racecourse near Guindy rail station holds meetings most weekends from November to March.

Horse riding: The **Madras Riding Club** offers hacking and lessons on the Madras racecourse throughout the year with the exception of June, when it's too hot even in the early morning (apply to **Madras Race Club,** ✆ 431171, for temporary membership).

Boating: There's instant membership for guests at the **Boat Club.**

Swimming: You can find luxury pools at both at the **New Woodlands** (7.30 to 12noon and 2 to 4.30) and the nearby **Hotel Savera,** for a small charge. If you want to swim in the sea, the cleanest and safest stretch is at Mylapore Beach, near Mahatma Gandhi's statue on Beach Road, but avoid crowded Sundays.

Squash, tennis and **indoor games:** apply in writing to the Secretary of the **Madras Gymkhana,** ✆ 447863.

Shopping

Shops and stores in Madras are open daily, 9–8, except Sun.

For silk, the best buy, visit **Co-optex** just past the museum on N.S.R. Bose Road. It's a huge place, with a whole ground floor of quality silks and fabulous douth Indian handloom fabrics. All prices are fixed. There are other branches of Co-optex throughout Madras and most towns in Tamil Nadu. If you find some nice material here, then have it made up into a dress or suit by Chandron, one of Madras's excellent tailors. You'll find him in the **India Silk House (P) Ltd,** 846 Mount Road, ✆ 844930. India Silk House is one of many emporia on Mount Road that specialize in fabrics. Right next door, **Khadi Gramodyog Bhavan** has a fine range of hand-loom-cotton fabrics and furnishings at reasonable prices. For general handicrafts, try the interesting **Indian Art Museum,** 151 Mount Road, which does nice jewellery and sandalwood carvings. Otherwise have a look in the more exclusive **Cane and Bamboo,** 26 Commander-in-Chief Road, Egmore, which deals in high-quality rose-wood furniture, batiks and chess sets. Similar stuff, and rather cheaper, can be found at **Swallows Handicrafts Industrial Cooperative** (*open Mon–Sat 10–5.30*), which often has sales of high-quality clothes. A 10-minute bus ride (no.56M or 56N) from Triplicane, ask to be let off at 'Swallows Stop'. **Spencer's** offbeat department store on Mount Road is being rebuilt after a recent fire. Latest-design leather articles are available at the in-house arcades of the **Taj** and **Connemara hotels** and in shops along Mount Road. Madras is a major centre of the leather boom and the city is full of *haute couture* leather boutiques, offering good quality briefcases, handbags, jackets, coats and shoes at knock-down prices. For flashy, flamboyant stuff, try **Iguana Boutique,** at the WelcomGroup Adyar Park lobby. For soft leather in more subdued styles, go to **Fashion 'n' Gems** on Nungambakkam High Road. The best general market is the large **T. Mangaramteo** complex in Evening Bazaar, N.S. Bose Road, where you can buy practically anything and a good deal cheaper than in emporia. But bargain hard. If you've only got time for one shopping outing, head for **Victoria Technical Institute (V.T.I.),** 765 Mount Road. This has practically everything under one roof, and prices are fair.

For **bookshops,** try **Higginbothams** at 814 Mount Road, the **Oxford Bookhouse** in Cathedral Grounds, also off Mount Road, or the shop in the foyer of the **Taj Coromandel Hotel** at 17 Nungambakkam High Road.

As a 'Gateway City', accommodation in Madras is comparatively expensive. Yet, unlike in Goa, Bangalore or Bombay, it is possible to find good, mid-range comfort at comparatively low prices. Madras is also one of the few big cities that has cheap, good budget hotels.

luxury

The five-star hotels of Madras do very well, mainly because their tariffs are low compared to those of other big cities. They are particularly cheap in the summer months (May to July) when rates are discounted. Three top-bracket hotels are very well located, near to the city centre. **Taj Coromandel**, 17 Nungambakkam High Road, © 474849, ✆ 470070, is a typical Western-style hotel of glitzy Singaporean design, but the upper-storey rooms offer good views and the Indian restaurant is superb. The Taj group have recently renovated the **Connemara** in Binny Road, © 860123/8257351/8520203, ✆ 860193, which has considerable charm and large, quiet rooms at the rear of the old building. It used to be an ex-Nawab's town house. By contrast, the WelcomGroup's **Chola Sheraton**, 10 Cathedral Road, © 473347, ✆ 478779, has drab, overpriced rooms but scores on cheerful, personalized hospitality.

Oberoi's venture, the **Trident**, 1/24 G.S.T Road, © 2344747, ✆ 2346699, is a pleasant hotel a few miles out of town, making it slightly less convenient for sightseeing but, being only 2 miles from the airport, it is useful for an early morning flight departure. The new **Park Sheraton Hotel and Towers** is a totally renovated hotel in a quiet residential area at 132 T.T.K. Road, © 452525, ✆ 455913. Rooms are spacious but rather bland.

expensive

At the top end of this price range is the **Ambassador Pallava**, 23 Montieth Road, Egmore, © 862061, ✆ 868757, whose Chinese restaurant is a good place to meet the Madrassi upper classes, but which charges a little too much for the standard of room on offer. The **Savera**, 69 Dr Radha-krishnan Road, © 474700, ✆ 473475, is conveniently located, has a pool and rooms safely within the middle of the price range. The **Hotel Madras International**, 693 Mount Road, © 861811, ✆ 861520 has double rooms priced this category, but has single rooms that fall within the 'moderate' category. The Madras International has good Indian, Chinese and Continental cuisine, as well as a lively bar.

moderate

Two central, moderately priced hotels are **New Victoria**, 3 Kennet Lane, Egmore, © 8253638, near the station with air-conditioned rooms, a reliable travel desk and a good restaurant and the **New Woodlands Hotel**, 72–5 Dr Radhakrishnan Road, © 473111. This is very reasonable with spacious rooms, a swimming pool and an excellent restaurant. A slightly cheaper option within this price range is the **Hotel Kanchi**, 28 Commander-in-Chief Road, © 471100, which has a great vegetarian rooftop restaurant and a good travel desk.

inexpensive

Far and away the best 'inexpensive' bet is **Broadlands Lodge**, 16 Vallabha Agraham Street, opposite Star Cinema, Triplicane, ✆ 845573/848131. Like the Taj Connemara, this was one of the town residences of the old Nawab of Arcot in the 19th century but was acquired by the government after Independence. Unlike the Taj, the hotel has retained its period charm and is an Arabian Nights-style confusion of galleries, courtyards and rooftop terraces, with 44 rooms to choose from. Run by the genial Mr Kumar, it has all sorts of attractions: apart from the beautiful gardens and sun-roofs, there are swing-seats, filtered water, good information and noticeboard, even room service. Here you can hire out a cycle, use the library, and meet lots of people. Ask for the two prestige rooms: no.18, with the famous graffiti wall paintings, or no.44, the roof cottage. If Broadlands is full, and it often is, you can usually sleep on the roof until a room comes vacant. Bear in mind, however, that Broadlands is not for the politically correct, as it (for some reason) runs a policy of no Indians that even the management seems at a loss to explain, though they enforce it without a qualm.

Other good economy options are the **Tourist Hotel**, ✆ 416001, on Andhra Mahila Sabha (Adyar Bridge Road)—you might be lucky enough to get one of their air-conditioned rooms, the **Krishna** on St Peters Road, ✆ 868997, or the **Soornam International** on Stringer Street, ✆ 563063, worth staying in for its rooftop restaurant.

cheap

You might be hard put to find really cheap accommodation in Madras—most of it is confined to the YMCA's which are often full. However, it is worth trying the **YWCA Guest House and Camping Ground**, 1086 Poonamallee High Road, ✆ 39920, and the **YMCA** in Westcott Road, ✆ 811158, opposite Royapettah Hospital. Try also the **TTDC Youth Hostel**, on E.V.R. Road, near the Central Railway Station, ✆ 589132, or the **YMCA** on N.S. Bose Road, opposite the city bus stand, ✆ 58394.

Madras ✆ (044–)   **Eating Out**

Madras cuisine is essentially vegetarian and the food ranges in price from good value to extraordinarily cheap. The staple diet is the tray of assorted vegetables and spices, often served with a dollop of rice, called *thali* or 'meals'; also the folded pancake filled with spiced vegetables called *masala dosa*. Both are cheap (around Rs5) and although it takes a while to get used to them, extremely nourishing. There's also the famous south Indian coffee, generally served in two beakers. The idea here is to 'cool' the scalding brew by pouring it back and forth between the two utensils from increasingly high elevations until it's fit to drink. Losing half of it down your lap is an appalling loss of face and very painful!

Since *thalis* and *dosas* may be all you'll find elsewhere in Tamil Nadu, it's worth eating as well (and as much) as you can in Madras.

The Rs120 buffet lunches at the Taj Coromandel's **Pavilion** coffee shop (12.30 to 3pm daily) are ideal for budget travellers; arrive early, to be sure of a seat. For authentic *chettinad* south Indian cuisine (very hot and pungent, but it wakes up the jaded palate), try the Connemara's **Raintree** restaurant. It's an open-air establishment, set in 'sylvan surroundings', where a meal will start at Rs400 per head and local people love it. Slightly out of town, the Oberoi's **Trident** has fine Indian and Chinese restaurants. An upmarket option is Chola Sheraton's **Peshawri**—the only restaurant in the city serving meaty Northwest Frontier food: a last repast of tasty *tikkas, tandooris, birianis* or marinated meats before you plunge into the vegetarian heartland. Peshawri is open from 12.30 to 3pm and from 7.30 to midnight, and meals cost from Rs300 per head.

Cheaper 'kwality' fare is available at Spencer **Fiesta** restaurant, ☎ 810051. Local rich Indians come here to savour baked beans on toast and chilled glasses of filtered water. Westerners turn up for Indian/continental food, milk shakes and ice cream and to sit in the shade! They often move on to **Dasaprakash** ice cream parlour, 100 Poonamallee High Road, which is open until after midnight.

Of the many restaurants in Mount Road, the adjoining **Delhi Durbar** and **Sri Krishna Villas** (patronized respectively by Westerners and local Indians) are among the best places for cheap, reliable south Indian, continental and Chinese food. The former has a roof garden. The latter is famous for vegetarian cooking. Also worth a visit is the **Agra** near TTDC tourist office, another popular local eaterie, specializing in inexpensive south Indian food. **Chung-King Chinese Restaurant**, 67 Mount Road, ☎ 840134, is good for chicken, chips and springs rolls, for under Rs50 per head. The nearby **Southern Chinese Restaurant** at Whites Road junction is of similar quality.

Up in Triplicane, there are a couple of interesting eating places near to Broadlands Lodge. Best is **Hotel New Maharaja**, 307 Triplicane High Road (opposite Star Cinema), with a cool air-conditioned lounge and perhaps the cheapest and best vegetarian food in Madras. Ask for the 'limited meal' (served lunchtime only, and not on the menu), which is actually unlimited and costs less than Rs50. The Maharaja also offers good tandooris, ice cream and Indian sweets.

For really cheap eating, keep wandering the neighbourhood of **Triplicane** (*see* above) and check out one of the many clean, basic eateries there, where you can get full on *thalis* for under Rs25, including a soft drink.

Entertainment and Nightlife

Madras is the centre of *Bharatnatyam*, possibly the oldest classical dance form in India. Traditionally performed by young girls dedicated to south Indian temples (*devadasis*), it is today performed by women who describe not only passages from religious texts, but also the moods of a girl in love. Madras has a dozen good culture centres—notably **Kalakshetra Centre** at Thiruvanmiyur, **Music Academy**, T.T.K. Road, Alwarpet, and **Raja Annamalai Hall**, by the TTDC bus stand—and the day to go is Sunday. A great introduction to Tamil dance and music forms including *Bharatnatyam*, folk dances and shadow-puppet plays are the nightly cultural programmes (*performances from 6.30–7.30pm*) at **Sittrarangam** mini-theatre at Island Grounds, near the fort. TNTDC tourist office often lays on free transport there. To plan your entertainment programme—dance and culture shows, cinemas, drama and tourist fairs, temple celebrations, music exhibitions, craft presentations and even circuses, buy a Friday edition of the *Hindu* or the *Indian Express* newspapers which carry a full listing of upcoming events.

This is a small, quiet seaside resort with a unique 7th-century Shore Temple, a lovely beach, and some of the most beautiful rock-cut temples in the world. Situated on the shore of the Bay of Bengal, Mahabalipuram was already a famous seaport in the 1st century AD at about the time Tamil Nadu's recorded history begins. It was later adopted by the empire-building Pallava kings (AD 600–800), who turned it into a major trading port to service their nearby capital of Kanchipuram. They also used the town as a workshop for their temple-building schemes. The 7th century AD marking a move away from monolith rock-cut cave architecture to free-standing, structural temples. The seven 'rathas' or temple chariots, and the seven pagoda-style shore temples they built here at Mahabalipuram are the earliest known examples of Dravidian architecture, and were constructed in a single century-long burst of creative enthusiasm, starting in the reign of Narasimhavarman I (AD 630–68). For some reason, the large complex of caves, temples, bas-reliefs and friezes covering a huge hump-back hillock in the town centre was never finished. As at Ajanta and Ellora, the architects suddenly and inexplicably deserted the site, and its rich treasure of ancient art and sculpture lay lost and forgotten.

Now a small thriving township, Mamallapuram has innumerable stalls and workshops turning out good-quality religious sculpture in soapstone and granite, as well as a national College of Sculpture outside town on the road to busy Madras. The visitor's season lasts all year but it's still an ideal spot to wind down, switch off and relax, despite the slow and steady development of resort hotels and weird Disneyesque mini theme parks creeping south along the coast from Madras.

The Monuments

This is an ideal tourist situation, with lots to see, all of it interesting, and everything within walking distance. You can hire out auto-rickshaws, private cars (Rs5 per mile, from JRS Travels opposite the tourist office) and motorbikes (also from JRS, at about Rs75 per day), but few people bother. For sightseeing, allow a full day to wander round Mahabalipuram, then just flop on the beach. Doing it the other way round (relaxation first, sights second) is absolutely fatal— it'll take you a week to see anything.

Getting Around
by bus

Mamallapuram's bus stand is opposite the Mamalla Bhavan hotel. Daily services run to Kanchipuram from 5am to 7.30pm (2½ hours) and Madras at 6am, 12noon, 2.30pm, 3.45pm and 5.15pm (1½ hours). There are also buses daily to Bangalore (7–8 hours) and one bus to Madurai (10 hours). Several buses daily also run to Pondicherry (with one change) and Thanjavur. There's no need to advance-book tickets; you can buy them on the bus.

Tourist Information

The **TTDC** office, ✆ 232, on East Raja Street, near the post office, is friendly and helpful. The **Indian Overseas Bank** in the town centre, near the police station, will change most travellers cheques.

Temple and Cave Tour

by foot, one full day

Shore Temple–Krishna Mandapam–Descent of the Ganga–Cave Complex–Five Rathas

Time and tide have washed away all but one of Mahabalipuram's seven famous seashore temples. To see the single surviving example, take a 5-minute stroll down Beach Road (left out of the bus stand). Though built in the final phase of Pallava art by Rajasimha (700–28), the **Shore Temple** is the first thing most people head for. This, one suspects, is partly because nobody expects it to last much longer. It sits perched on the very edge of the angry sea, constantly battered by the pounding surf, and is almost certainly doomed. This, of course, only adds to its romantic charm.

A simple, elegant structure with layered pagoda roof, this shore temple is one of the oldest temples in south India. It's unusual in that it houses shrines for both Vishnu and Shiva. The Shiva temple faces east and opens out on the sea, allowing the first rays of the sun to enter the shrine each morning to pay homage to the god. The smaller shrine faces west. Between the two shrines is the Vishnu temple, without a *shikhara* tower. This is the oldest part of the temple.

For a proper appreciation of this spectacular monument, hire a guide at the entrance. They speak good English, and treat their subject with warmth. Bargain hard and try to knock at least a third off the asking price. Should you decide not to employ their services, one—or even several—will be sure to follow you anyway, and in the process of ignoring their incessant attempts to make you pay, you might spoil your visit. Hiring a guide can buy you peace of mind as well as information. Entering the temple enclosure, note the series of guardian bulls (Nandis) on the surrounding wall, and within the frontal shrine the bas-relief of Shiva, attended by Parvati (his wife), Brahma (as wisdom) and Vishnu (as eagle-god). Parvati's good-fortune son, Ganesh, is present, but not his brother Muruga (god of beauty and war). Left, in the second chamber (there's one on each side of the temple), you'll find the 8 foot (2.5 metre) monolith of Vishnu in the attitude of repose. The rear chamber has the ancient, much-prized lingam (*see* **Topics**, p.60), just a part of which now remains. Facing the lingam is the carving of a cow, representing a permanent sacrifice to the presiding deity. In the last chamber, you'll see the female symbol, a circular recess in the floor.

Walk down the beach to get the full effect of the shore temple; it is best viewed from a distance and in the subdued light of late afternoon. If going in for a swim, be careful—the waves are invigorating but the current very strong. Drying off, be prepared to entertain the 'lobster man', the 'coconut man' and a procession of hopeful youngsters hawking seashells (some very beautiful) and stone-carved images. To get some peace, stroll down the beach, either side of the temple, until you find a quiet stretch of sand.

Back at the top of Beach Road, bear left for Krishna Mandapam. Mahabalipuram has eight such mandapams (rock-cut cave temples), each one an exquisite study in bas-relief portraying various vivid episodes from Hindu legend or mythology. This one depicts Krishna using the umbrella of Mount Govardhan to shield his flocks of cows and shepherds from the rage of the rain god, Indra. It is noted for its realistic representation.

Nearby is the world's largest stone bas-relief, **The Descent of the Ganga**. This amazing piece of sculpture represents the earliest work of the Pallava sculptor, undertaken during the reign of

Narasimhavarman I after whom the town is also named (this king earned the title of Mamalla or 'The Great Wrestler'). The megalith itself is a massive whaleback-shaped rock, split down the middle with a fissure, the whole face of which is covered with relief sculptures. Measuring 88 feet long by 29½ feet high, this vast stone frieze faces out to the sea. It pictures over a thousand sculpted deities and animals, each one a work of art. Dominated by a procession of elephants, two of which are 16 feet (5 metres) long, it portrays a dynamic world of gods, demi-gods, angels, men, animals and birds, all apparently rushing towards the cleft in the rock's centre. It is said either to represent the *Mahabharata* fable in which Arjuna, the emaciated figure seen standing on one leg, did penance to Shiva after fighting alongside Krishna and killing many fellow human beings; or the 'descent of the Ganga' from Mount Kailash, the holy river seen flowing down from Shiva's matted locks. In this story Bhagiratha, a mythical hero, beseeched the gods to send down the celestial waters of the Ganga (the Ganges), to carry the ashes of his ancestors to *nirvana*. But he unleashed a mighty flood, only contained when Shiva mopped up the waters with his hair. Whatever the sculpture means, it's a masterpiece.

A huge granite hillock overlooks the *Descent of the Ganga*. The path up leads past a number of interesting rock-cut caves and peters out near **Krishna's Butter Ball**, an immense boulder delicately poised on the crest of the hill. Like the Shore Temple, you can't imagine it staying there much longer. Behind it, pause for the beautiful view over **Koneri Lake**, a pretty inland lagoon with one of the ancient *rathas* (chariots) situated on the far bank. Then proceed, via the colonnaded **Sthalasayana Perumal Temple**, to the high **Lighthouse**. You can climb to the top provided you arrive before noon, for a glorious view over the town and surrounds. Officially, photography is not permitted from the top. Below the lighthouse is the

Mahishasuramardhini cave

Mahishasuramardhini Cave, with a famous frieze of Durga (Kali) destroying the buffalo-headed demon Mahishasura. In the background, oblivious to all this activity, there's Vishnu in one of his famous 'cosmic sleeps'.

From the hillock, it's a mile walk down to the enclosure of the **Five Rathas**. These five mono-lithic 'temple cars' (four named after the Pancha Pandava hero brothers of the *Mahabharata* epic, the fifth after their wife, Draupadi) are the 7th-century prototypes of all Dravidian temples to come. Five differing monolith miniature temples, they display the familiar *gopurams* (gatehouse towers), *vimanas* (central shrines), *mandapams* (multi-pillared halls) and sculptured walls so characteristic of later temple architecture. The rathas themselves are simple, unadorned structures, each of a different style, but all are *viharas* (monastery buildings). They are either square or oblong in plan and pyramidal in elevation. Adorned with rampant lions, elegant pillars and sculpted divinities, they stand (unfinished) in lonely, isolated splendour, guarded by three life-size stone animals: a lion facing north, a central giant elephant looking south and a bull to the east.

End your tour with a visit to the pleasant open-air **museum** in town and be sure to return to the Shore Temple on a moonlit night.

Tirukkalikundram

by bus, taxi or motorbike, half-day

This semi-interesting little Shiva temple, situated atop Vedagiri Hill, is located 10 miles out of Mahabalipuram. It's covered on the one day tour to Mahabalipuram sold by TTDC in Madras, but is a worthwhile little excursion from Mahabalipuram itself.

Tirukkalikundram has a famous and popular 'eagle' sanctuary at the temple, where two white Egyptian vultures (apparently the reincarnations of two famous saints), rather than actual eagles, fly in around noon daily. Ostensibly this is for a rest on their holy flight between Varanasi and Rameshwaram, but in fact the vultures merely grab a free lunch issued by the temple priest. Before you make the wearisome climb up 565 steps to the hilltop sanctuary (in bare feet) check that the birds have actually made it. Other attractions at Tirukkalikundram include a large tank, to the southeast of town, with alleged curative powers, and a marvelous temple complex at the base of the hill.

Madras Crocodile Bank

Slightly easier to reach (a 9-mile bus or taxi ride north towards Madras), this sanctuary and breeding centre (*open daily 8.30–5.30*) for large reptiles was set up by an English herpetologist and eccentic called Romulus Whitaker, who, concerned for the survival of a shy, fish-eating and endangered giant lizard called the gharial (the same size as a crocodile but with a snout too thin to attack man or beast), decided to found a breeding centre for the reptiles and an educational centre for the local humans. The place was a great success and is now a principle tourist draw for the area, although it is seldom crowded. Whitaker's breeding programmes have since expanded to include snakes, crocodiles (Nile, Indian and Australasian), caimans and monitor lizards, and a fascinating hour can be spent under the Crocodile Bank's shady vegetation, regarding the great, unthinking creatures as they bask by their man-made pools.

Vedantangal Bird Sanctuary

Another worthwhile excursion, though it has to be done by motorbike or private car, is to this major waterfowl sanctuary 33 miles west of Mamallapuram. From November to February the wetland reserve throngs with migrants. To be seen at its best Vedantangal needs to be visited at dawn and dusk, so it's a good idea to spend the night in the forest rest house. But be warned, bookings must be made in advance, either through a travel agent (the best way), or independently (a hassle) via the Wildlife Warden, 50 Fourth Major Road, Ghandi Nagar, Adyar, Madras 20, ℰ 413947.

Sports and Activities

Boat Trips: During the day, you can hire out four-log fishing boats down by the Shore Temple. For around Rs50 per head, fishermen will take you about 1¾ miles out to sea—and then demand another Rs30 to take you home again.

Swimming: Mamallapuram's beach is clean and safe as long as you don't swim out further than about 30 yards, where rough waves and under-currents can get you into trouble.

Shopping

The town's stonemasons, drawing on the skill of centuries, produce some decent Indian images in marble and a lot of tourist tat in alabaster (which scratches, by the way). If you're going to do any shopping at all, save your money for **Poompuhar Government Emporium** on Shore Temple Road (and closed on Tuesdays). This has an interesting assortment of ceramics, handicrafts, perfumes, cut glass and dolls at more or less fixed prices. There is also a plethora of Kashmiri craft shops selling jewellery and textiles of good quality, but high prices. If you see something you like, try to bargain for half. The town is also a good place to buy sandals, but only from one place, a leather sandal maker whose stall sits on the left as you walk down the road from the bus station to the shore temple. He will make beautiful sandals to order for about Rs250, and which last (the author met several people wearing his handiwork in other parts of south India, and all were happy with his work).

Mamallapuram ℰ (04113–)

Where to Stay

luxury

The best hotel is 7½ miles to the north at Kovelong. The Taj Group's **Fisherman's Cove**, ℰ 44301/5, ☏ 44303, set in a beautiful cove has an excellent pool, wind-surfing, sailing and cottages in addition to rooms with views over the ocean. A stretch of private beach ensures clean uncrowded bathing but will not protect you from the local touts, who will appear miraculously as you go down to the water and try to sell you seashells (admittedly very beautiful ones) and stone carvings. The hotel occupies the site of a 17th century Dutch fort whose ruins jut from the lawns at the southeast end of the large garden, just before the grass gives way to beach.

At Mamallapuram the resort hotels include the **Shore Temple Bay Resort,** *✆* 235, 2 miles out of town, but ideal if you just want to snooze on a private beach. It has a good pool and restaurant, and large, bright rooms. There are also a few air-conditioned cottages. Nearer town, **Silversands,** *✆* 228 *✆* 280, in Kovelong Road is a simple, comfortable place with good facilities but excellent food. Single rooms here fall into the 'moderate' price category during the off season (May–July) and go up to about Rs1000 for a double in the high season (Dec–Jan).

The **Temple Bay Ashok,** *✆* 251, has cottages, some with attached kitchenettes, from Rs450 single and Rs850 double.

The **TTDC Youth Hostel and Cottages,** situated on the way to the Shore Temple, is another favourite. It's well-run, with clean rooms at Rs170 and a nice Rs30 dormitory.

Cheaper lodgings are fairly basic, but since most people spend all day on the beach and only go home to sleep, nobody appears to mind. The current travellers' favourite is the **Five Rathas Village,** a collection of huts and cottages with weekly rates of about Rs250 and nightly charges of about Rs75 per person. You find it by walking down the road leading to the Five Rathas monument, and turning right at the sign. If you get lost, ask any of the local sculptors for directions. **Mamalla Bhavan** by the bus stand, *✆* 250, has adequate double rooms for around Rs60. The best room—no.16—is light and airy, and has a lovely balcony. Downstairs is a great, cheap vegetarian restaurant. You could also try **Uma Lodge** (though the rooms here vary in cleanliness and quality, so ask to see first, remembering to turn up the mattress to look for bugs), which offers double rooms at around Rs75 per night, or **Khoteeswara Lodge,** which has double rooms, with bathrooms for Rs65 and without bathrooms for Rs50. For both, ask for directions at the bus station—they are less than a five minute walk.

Eating Out

Silversands still has the best, and priciest, food in town—Indian, Chinese and continental—with fresh grilled lobster the speciality. Seafood is very good in Mahabalipuram, as is the usual travellers' fare of pancakes, chips and *lassi*. The best-known establishment is the **Gazebo,** on the main street, just 75 yards north from the bus station on the west side, with meals for Rs75 per head. However, there are some equally good but cheaper seafood restaurants around the corner on the road to the Shore Temple. These, which include **La Vie en Rose** and **L'Auberge,** offer much the same menus as Gazebo but at about a third of the price, owing to their not having quite such a prime position. Their French names are a concession to the French government, which is very active further south in nearby Pondicherry and pays the restaurants a Rs500 subsidy per month provided they choose French names and include some French cuisine on the menu.

The **Sunrise** restaurant, also on the way down to the Shore Temple, has no Gallic pretentions and offers tasty grilled and boiled lobster with all the trimmings at Rs200, grilled jumbo prawns at Rs75 and a whole giant swordfish at Rs350. It's a popular meeting place. Nearby, the **Rose Garden** is popular for toasted sandwiches and chocolate milkshakes, while **Village Restaurant** offers fresh lobster from Rs50, Madras Chicken at Rs20 and Western breakfasts at Rs20. **Bamboo Hut**, near Sunrise, has a regular clientèle of laidback gourmands, though less patient diners head up to **Shore Temple Bay Resort** to get some food in under an hour.

Entertainment and Nightlife

In the evening, pop along to **Silversands** hotel classical dance performances and music concerts that are held here nightly from 9.30pm onwards. The admission charge of about Rs60 is steep, but it's the only show in town.

Kanchipuram

Kanchipuram is one of the oldest towns in India, famous for both its temples, many of them remarkably well preserved, and for its handwoven silks. Known as south India's 'Golden City of Temples', it is a major pilgrimage centre and the perfect introduction to anyone seeking a crash course in Hindu religion, mythology and architecture. Kanchipuram is one of the seven sacred cities of India (the others are Varanasi, Mathura, Ujjain, Hardwar, Dwarka and Ayodhya), and it is the only one associated with both Shiva and Vishnu.

It was the empire-building Pallavas (6th to 8th centuries AD) who turned the ancient holy town of Kacchi into the wealthy capital of 'Kanchi'. Under the artistic Mahendravarman I (600–630 AD), a sudden surge of cultural and building activity took place, starting the traditions of silk-weaving, temple building and Bharatnatyam dance for which Kanchipuram later became famous. In this period, Dravidian architecture developed from modest simplicity, as exemplified by the Mahabalipuram *rathas*, to wildly extravagant maturity. The development of the *gopuram* temple-towers into soaring stone leviathans dripping with tiny dancing deities was particularly dramatic. All this zealous religious activity attracted flocks of artists, educators and musicians to Kanchipuram, and it became a major centre of art and learning. But then, in the 9th century, the Pallava dynasty fell, and the city's power and influence rapidly faded. Under subsequent rulers—the Cholas, the Vijayanagar kings, the Muslims and eventually the British—it returned to being just a typical country town, enlivened by constant parades of devout pilgrims.

Kanchipuram today is a noisy, dusty place, with a definite shortage of good hotels and restaurants. But the temples are unmissable and the priests invariably friendly. The fever-pitch noise and bustle may come as a bit of a shock after tranquil Mahabalipuram but like Varanasi, the authentic spirituality of the place lies just beneath the surface.

There are around 1000 temples in and around Kanchipuram. About 200 of these are in the city itself and with one exception the best examples are all conveniently close to the bus stand. If you're short on time, hire an auto-rickshaw for a quick morning tour of the temples for around Rs45–50. If you've a full day to spare, do your sightseeing by cycle; there are many bike-hire places around, charging only Rs10 per day. Most of the temples worth noting are open only from sunrise to 12.30pm and from 4pm to sunset. At the temples, be firm in turning away uninvited guides and be prepared for the notorious temple beggars.

Climate and When to Go

The cool season to visit is **November to January**, but many brave the heat for the big **Car Festival** of **February to March**. Subsequent festivals in **April** and **May** are hot, crowded and uncomfortable.

Getting There

There are regular **buses** in and out of Kanchipuram from both Madras and Mahabalipuram. All are a mad scramble and you'll have to fight tooth-and-nail for a seat.

Tourist Information

The **tourist office** is at the Hotel Tamil Nadu. The Archaeological Survey of India office, opposite Kailasanathar Temple, is helpful, but often closed.

The **post office**, on Kossa Street, is just below the bus stand.

For **foreign exchange**, the **State Bank of India** is on Gandhi Road.

Temple Tour

by bicycle/rickshaw and bus, 4–6 hours

*Kailasanathar Temple–Ekambareshwara Temple–Kamakshiammon
Temple–Vaikuntha Perumal–Varatha Temple*

A short 15-minute cycle ride down Nellukkara and Putteri Streets takes you to the west of town and the 8th-century **Kailasanathar Temple**. This lies in a garden clearing and the giant Nandi bull in the grounds shows it's a Shiva temple. The structure itself is very early Dravidian architecture—with the exception of the front, which was added later by Mahendra Varman III. Delightfully simple and elegant, it has none of the decorative ostentation of the later Chola and Vijayanagar building styles. Built in sandstone, it has some beautiful carvings and sculptures (several of which are well-renovated) and remnants of bright frescoes still cling to a few of the 54 small shrines running round the inner courtyard, giving an idea of the temple's original magnificence.

Just to the left of Nellukkara and Putteri Street junction, you'll find **Ekambareshwara Temple**, marked by its towering 160 foot high *rajagopuram*. Inside, there's an extensive temple compound surrounded by a massive stone wall, added by Krishna Devaraja (a Vijayanagar king) in AD 1500. Ekambareshwara probably derives its name from 'Eka Amra Nathar'—Shiva, as 'Lord of the Mango Tree'. The ancient mango tree in one of its compounds which, according to local tradition, is over 2500 years old, is where Parvati is said to have done penance to Shiva, after misguidedly closing his eyes and plunging the whole universe into chaos. Pilgrims troop around the tree all day long, and will (after you've paid your camera fee) urgently insist that you join them. Actually, you are not allowed to see much more—Ekambareshwara is a living temple (the god still lives here, in the mango tree) and many of the other shrines are off limits to tourists. No matter, you can still climb the central *gopuram* for marvellous views down over the temple complex. Ask permission first from the temple curator found behind the **Thousand Pillar Temple** inside the compound. This particular temple does have a thousand pillars, a colourful display of temple chariots, and images of the various animal carriers who accompany the gods of the Hindu pantheon. Allow yourself a good hour at Ekambareshwara.

The most popular temple, **Kamakshiammon** (5 minutes left out of Ekambareshwara), is dedicated to Parvati and is the site of the February/March Car Festival. As one of the three holy places of Shakti (Parvati as bride of Shiva), it is considered particularly auspicious for marriage-blessings and up to 25,000 people show up at the larger festivals to supplicate the goddess for happy nuptials. Show up around 8pm on Tuesday or Friday evening for fireworks and music, caparisoned elephants and vast, swaying crowds—the Golden Chariot cruises slowly round the temple grounds, and the moaning hordes part like the Red Sea in the Cecil B. de Mille movie. It's a spectacle. By day, Kamakshiammon is surprisingly quiet and relaxed; a few visiting pilgrims stare appreciatively at the resident elephant, and you're free to wander around unmolested. In its present form, the structure is a 14th-century temple of *chola* construction, its central ghat overlooked by watchtower *gopurams*.

A short ride away, you'll come across **Vaikuntha Perumal**. This is one of the oldest temples in town, dedicated to Vishnu and built by Parameswar Varman in the 7th century AD. It is most notable for its cloisters within the outer wall which are prototypes of the 1000-pillared halls seen at later temples like Ekambareshwara. There's an interesting bas-relief circling the main shrine, which portrays battle scenes between the Pallavas and the Gangas/Chalukyas, as well as various depictions of Vishnu sitting, standing and lying down.

A rather alarming bus ride from the Nellukkara Street stand, just up from Raja's Lodge takes you 2½ miles across town to **Varatha Temple**. Recently renovated, this temple is in fine condition and features one of Kanchipuram's finest *gopurams*, and the views from the top are stunning. There's also an agreeable temple elephant contributed by the Elephant Shed Foundation, which will take you for a short ride round the grounds.

Pay your camera fee and head for the central 100-pillared **Marriage Hall**. The pillars are notable for fine base-carvings, of Vishnu (warrior-horses), Parvati, Ganesh, Brahma, Shiva and Buddha. The raised plinth within is the marriage platform, with seating space for wedding guests. In the corner lives the gloriously painted wooden chariot of Varatha (Vishnu). It is carried round town on festival days. Beyond the marriage hall is the large temple ghat and two small shrines. The small stone marquees dotted round the marriage hall are for pilgrims to relax under, tucking into popular temple sweets like lemon-rice *laddoo*.

Shopping

With a weaving tradition dating back to the Pallava era (when silk was the royal cloth, Kanchipuram is justly famous for its particularly fine silk saris, embellished with stunning patterns. There's no problem finding shops—over 5000 families are currently engaged in the weaving industry—but there is a problem finding ones which speak English or don't rip off tourists. Avoid expensive private emporia and stick to the cheap government cooperatives. Places like **Murudan** in Railway Road; **Srinivas and Co.**, 135 Thirukatchi Nambi Street; **Thiruvallur Cooperative Society** 207 Gandhi Road; or **Kamatchi Co-optex**, 182 Gandhi Road, have a good name. For shopping advice and to see top-quality Kanchi silk being produced on the looms, call in on the **Handlooms Weavers Service Centre** at 20 Railway Road, just up the road from the post office. Open on weekdays only from 9.15am to 5.45pm.

Kanchipuram is a typical temple town, with lots of pilgrim *dharamsalas* and hardly any tourist hotels.

inexpensive

The TTDC **Hotel Tamil Nadu**, 78 Kamatchiamman Sannathi Street, ✆ 2953/2954, is a pleasant place, with clean, comfortable rooms and a reasonable restaurant.

cheap

Try **Raja's Lodge** and **Rama's Lodge** which adjoin each other in Nellukkara Street, to be found close to the bus stand. Both have clean rooms with hard beds and boisterous Indian neighbours. The Rama is the better deal, with its pleasant sunroof and a vegetarian restaurant.

Eating Out

There is not a great choice: *Masala dosa* (the traditional south Indian snack of spiced vegetables within a thick pancake envelope), *thalis* and precious little else. For something slightly more thrilling, take a rickshaw over to **New Madras Hotel** or **Pandiyan Restaurant**. The latter is in Station Road, and attempts Chinese food. If you're happy with local food, try either **Hotel Tamil Nadu** or **Sri Rama Cafe** (opposite Raja's Lodge). The little restaurant next to Raja's has good value Rs5 *dosa* dinners and an air-conditioned lounge where you can practise 'cooling' coffee the Tamil way.

Pondicherry

Back on the coast, some sixty or so miles from Mamallapuram, everyone suddenly speaks French, the drinks get cheaper and the English colonial influence, so strong up in Madras, disappears from both the architecture and the ambience. Pondicherry, until the 1950s a far-flung outpost of the French maritime empire, is so different to the rest of Tamil Nadu that the traveller immediately feels that he or she has entered another country. This busy coastal town is divided roughly into two: the old White Town of elegant French houses, restaurants and old administrative buildings focused around the low, clipped hedges and disciplined lawns of the Government Square; and the Black Town west of the canal, where India takes over again. The offensive colonial/racist overtones of the names of these *quartiers* persist, but the (now largely Indian) residential community appears to have little problem with them.

Pondicherry's Factions

Pondicherry society is divided—interesting for the traveller and endlessly absorbing for the townsfolk, who seem to talk about nothing else. The old French colonial community (supplemented by a fair number of more recent French émigrés come to enjoy the sun and cheap cost of living) keeps its distance from the upper-class Franco-Indian families who also live in the White Town. Both groups are regarded askance by the devotees of a large, intellectually based *ashram*, the Sri Aurobindo Ashram, founded in 1920 and now a major property owner in the town, which itself became divided in the 1960s when several European devotees went off to found Auroville, an experimental rural community about 6 miles out of town. Meanwhile, many of the local Tamil townspeople, farmers and fishermen feel, with some justification, that their land is not their own.

To understand Pondicherry it is necessary to know about these factions but, having highlighted them, it should also be stressed that there is no open hostility, such as fighting or insulting behaviour, between the groups: Pondicherry is a peaceful, fairly prosperous place and the atmosphere is a happy one.

History

In the very distant past (around 1500 BC), the semi-mythological sage Agastya is thought to have set up his hermitage here, and a small village called Agastishwara is supposed to have grown up around it. One (brief) millenium later, a Roman trading centre is known (from archaeological excavation) to have operated nearby in the 1st century AD and through the subsequent centuries, the settlement graduated from fishing and trading town to become the site of a university under the high Dravidian culture of the 9th century. However, the place remained small until the French landed there in the 1670s and decided to base their southern Indian trade from this hot, windswept Coromandel shore. From then until the late 18th century, Pondicherry was the centre from which the French tried to oust British rule in India.

Throughout this period, the energetic French governor Dupleix tried valiantly to achieve the usurpation of British rule, forming alliances with the anti-British Nawabs and Maharajahs of southern India, including the great Tipu Sultan (*see* **History**) and fighting several campaigns at various locations in Tamil Nadu and Karnataka. Dupleix and his allies were eventually defeated, but following Tipu Sultan's death in battle in Karnataka and the gradual gathering of all south India under the Union Jack, the British were magnanimous enough to let the French keep Pondicherry. The little enclave subsequently outlived the British Raj, being voluntarily returned to India by the French in 1954.

Earlier this century, Pondicherry had achieved a limited international fame for reasons completely unconnected with empire. In 1908 an anti-British Hindu philosopher called Aurobindo Ghose came to Pondicherry after spending some 14 years studying in England. He chose Pondicherry because he wanted to follow in the antique footsteps of the sage Agastya and make the town his base. He founded an ashram whose teachings pioneered some of the ethics that were to flower, much later, into the Western Environmental Movement. Thinking of India, and thus the Earth, as a living entity ('the Mother' or *Shakti*, in ancient Hindu belief), Aurobindo attracted a wide circle of followers, many of them European, and taught a mixture of Hindu spiritualism and environmental ethics.

His most influential devotee was an aristocratic French woman called Mirra Alfassa, who later became known as 'the Mother' after Aurobindo's initial image of *Shakti*, and who helped from the 1920s onwards to bring Aurobindo's teachings to an international, though largely academic audience. She survived Sri Aurobindo, living until 1973 and helping to found, in the heady 1960s, the experimental agricultural community of Auroville, outside town, whose houses and central meditation centre were designed by a French architect and attracted many idealistic young European settlers (*see* pp.275–6).

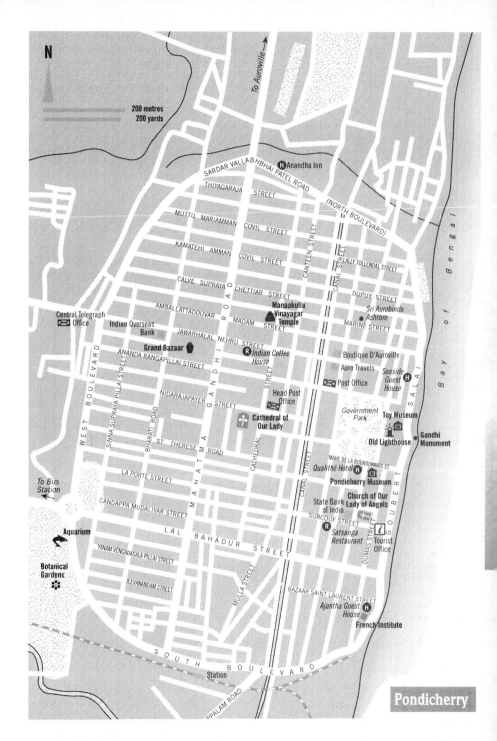

N

200 metres
200 yards

To Auroville

SARDAR VALLABHBHAI PATEL ROAD

Anandha Inn

THIYAGARAJA STREET

(NORTH BOULEVARD)

MUTTU MARIAMMAN COVIL STREET

CANTEEN STREET

KAMATEHI AMMAN COVIL STREET

CANAL STREET

LALLY TOLLENDAL STREET

CALVE SUPRAYA CHETTIAR STREET

DUPUY STREET

AMBALLATTADOUVAR

Central Telegraph
Office

Indian Overseas
Bank

MADAM STREET

**Manaakulla
Vinayagar
Temple**

*Sri Aurobindo
Ashram*

MARINE STREET

JAWARHALAL NEHRU STREET

GANDHI ROAD

Grand Bazaar

Boutique D'Auroville

ANANDA RANGAPILLAI STREET

**Indian Coffee
House**

Auro Travels

*Seaside
Guest
House*

WEST BOULEVARD

SINNA SUPRAYA PILLAI STREET

NIDARAJAPAYER STREET

BHARATI ROAD

STREET

Post Office

MAHATMA

ST. THERESE ROAD

CATHEDRAL STREET

Head Post
Office

**Cathedral of
Our Lady**

Government
Park

Toy Museum

Old Lighthouse

*Gandhi
Monument*

To Bus
Station

LA PORTE STREET

MAHE DE LA BOURDONNAIS ST

Qualithé Hotel

GOUBERT SALAI

CANDAPPA MUDALIYAR STREET

CANAL STREET

Pondicherry Museum

**Church of Our
Lady of Angels**

State Bank
of India

Aquarium

LAL BAHADUR STREET

SURCOUF STREET

*Satsanga
Restaurant*

YANAM VENGADASALA PILLAI STREET

MULLA STREET

DUMAS STREET

Tourist
Office

**Botanical
Gardens**

JEEVANANDAM STREET

BAZAAR SAINT LAURENT STREET

*Ajantha Guest
House*

French Institute

SOUTH BOULEVARD

Station

UPPALAM ROAD

Bay of Bengal

Pondicherry

Today the remains of both 'the Mother' and Sri Aurobindo are housed in the *ashram* in the old 'White Town', and both this and the now more-or-less autonomous Auroville community still attract a steady stream of visitors and pilgrims from all over the world.

Getting Around

by rail

A small narrow gauge line runs two services per day between Pondicherry and Villapuram, from where main line connections can be had to Madras, Trichy, Madurai, Trivandrum and other major centres in the south. The railway station is on Lal Bahadur Street at the far west end of the Black Town.

by bus

Pondicherry has two bus stands, one for long-distance travel and another for local hops, just 2 minutes' walk from each other on the north side of Lal Bahadur Street, near the train station at the far west end of town. Buses to Madras run all day, every half hour or so and there are daily direct services to other major towns in Tamil Nadu and Kerala, with a minumum of two buses per day. For the most efficient enquiries and bookings contact Auro travels, Karikar Building, Jawarhalal Nehru Street, ℰ 25128. Buses out to Auroville can be taken from the local bus stand on Lal Bahadur Street (the local bus stand is the one closest to town).

by bicycle

Walking is best in the White Town, but for excursions, you can hire bicycles at Jaypal on Gingee Salai (Canal Street) and at Supersnack on Jawahalal Nehru Street for around Rs35 per day. Motorbike hire can also be arranged at Supersnack, for around Rs65–70 per day. Take taxis or auto-rickshaws between the White and Black Towns (but insist on a meter).

Old Pondicherry: The White Town

Old Pondicherry is an excellent place for walking, its streets being neither dirty nor crowded (at least by Indian standards). The easiest place to start your exploration is **Government Park**, at the far east end of the White Town, just behind the seafront. Surrounded by quietly grand white stuccoed colonial buildings, the small park, with its low, cropped hedges and lawns, is in the Classical French style—planned as an octagon with short gravel walks radiating out from the centre. The measured calm of the place sets the tone for the whole atmosphere of the White Town, even at lunchtime, when the park becomes a meeting place for the town's office workers, who sprawl on the lawns, picnic and gossip.

On the south side of the park is the **Pondicherry Museum**, a real treasure house of dusty curiosities gathered from the ancient world, through the colonial period to the present day. The main room contains French 18th-century furniture and ornaments (all rather falling apart), including a big four-poster bed in which the French Governor Dupleix apparently slept. A faded early 19th-century oil painting of *La chasse à courre* ('Hunting to Hounds') hangs over the entrance doorway—calling to mind the later French governors' nostalgia for fresh autumn woods in Pondicherry's climate of feverish heat. At the east end of this main hall is a small sideroom where ceramic and stone artefacts (funerary urns, small carvings of the gods, ornamented oil lamps) from the nearby Roman trading settlement of Arikamedu gather dust in shabby glass cases stacked any old how. Some have been moved to make way for never-to-be-completed redecoration and are so jumbled as to make it impossible to see inside them without physically climbing over the others.

At the other end of the main hall, a small collection of French and Indian arms and armour includes, of all things, a boomerang which was used apparently on the battlefields of 18th-century India. Where and how this weapon developed is unclear: the piece is not of Antipodean workmanship and seems unique to Pondicherry. The arms and armour room gives onto another filled with indifferent wooden carvings, which in turn gives way to a small art gallery of paintings by local artists. With the exception of one or two fine landscapes, the work displayed is of a uniform garish awfulness—especialy the Dali-esque abstracts.

The Sea Front

Having seen the museum, you can either walk back into town along the Rue Mahe de la Bourdonnais, which runs along the south side of the park, or up to the hot windswept **Beach Road** (Goubert Salai). The word 'Beach' is misleading here as there is none at all: Pondicherry falls to the sea in a tumble of jagged rocks and even if there was a beach, the water just here is too polluted with the town's waste for swimming; the real beaches are out at Auroville—*see* p.276. However, it is fun to promenade along here in the morning or evening, when the sun is not too strong. The little **Pondicherry Café**, which sits right next to the **Gandhi Monument**, looks out to sea from the top of the short road leading back to Government Park. Have an ice cream or a coffee on the café's shaded (though windy) terrace with waves crashing on the rocks a few feet below. Just north of the café and memorial, by the **Old Lighthouse** on the landward side of the road is another eccentric museum, the **Jawamaz Toy Museum**, a one-room collection of painted dolls dressed in the various national costumes of India. Some of these seem indistinguishable from the others, but the dolls and their clothes are beautifully made. The little museum seems to have no connection with the town or region, or indeed to have any point at all, and this is somehow charming.

About 200 yards south along Goubert Salai (Beach Road) is the local **tourist information** office (one corner on the left after the junction with La Bourdonnais). A few minutes further on is the **Ajantha Guest House**, which has a shaded rooftop restaurant overlooking the ocean.

The French Residential Quarter & Aurobindo Ashram

Also south along the sea front 200 yards from the tourist information office, you eventually come to the Bazaar St Laurent, among whose fine colonial buildings is the **French Institute**. This is a good place to get local geographical or cultural information, as the institute, originally set up to study these subjects, has an extensive library. If you have the time, take a browse through its section on Indian mythology.

If you turn right into elegant Bazaar Street Laurent, and then turn right (back towards town), you pass the French 19th-century **École Français de l'Extrême Orient**, which has a renowned archaeology and Sanskrit school. Walk 2 minutes further on and you reach Canal Street (Gingee Salai), where another right turn takes you for a 5 hot minutes up to Pondicherry's main east–west drag **Jawarhalal Nehru Street**, where most of the useful shops and cheap eateries are. On the corner of Nehru and Canal Streets are a collection of good bookshops. If you turn right (east) up Jawarhalal Nehru Street, left on Manakula Vinayagar Street and right again on the Rue de la Marine, you will come to the **Sri Aurobindo Ashram**. Here, in the peaceful, tree-shaded courtyards, you can talk to various *ashram* members and ask to view the marble vaults that house the remains of Sri Aurobindo and 'the Mother' (*see* 'History'). Remove your shoes before entering the *ashram*, and don't arrive between 1 and 2 in the afternoon, when the buildings are closed to visitors. Those interested in more detailed information on the Ashram should visit the Auroshree shop, 2D Jawarhalal Nehru Street, or the Boutique D'Auroville at 12 Jawarhalal Nehru Street.

The Black Town

West of Canal Street is the 18th-century Indian quarter, among whose mostly Brahmin inhabitants the French Jesuits erected their high Baroque cathedral of **Notre Dame de la Conception**. The cathedral (built between 1691 and 1765) is on Saint Therese Road about five blocks southwest of the Sri Aurobindo Ashram. To ensure finding the cathedral open, go between 10 and 11am when morning Mass is being sung, or between 4 and 5 for evensong. St Theresa Street runs into Cathedral Street (also confusingly called Mission Street), where you can make international calls and faxes from the **Central Telegraph Office**. Another fine, but more recent, French colonial church is the **Église de Notre Dame des Anges** (built in 1855) on the corner of Surcouf Street and the Rue Roman Rolland, which runs south of Government Park. A number of late 19th-century religious paintings hang in the church, one donated to the colony by King Louis Napoléon III. The rest of the Black Town is Indian rather than colonial and has few sights beyond the usual colourful street of any Indian town, but is useful for shopping and cheap eating. Most of the shops and *thali* houses/cafés are located on the main commercial thoroughfare of Jawarhalal Nehru Street. Five minutes' walk to the west, in a large square between Jawarhalal Nehru and Nidarajapayer Streets (which both run east/west) and Mahatma Gandhi and Bharati Roads (which run north/south) is the **Grand Bazaar**. A hot, crowded general market, the bazaar's feverish activity makes a sharp contrast with the more measured (some would say sleepy) atmosphere of the rest of the town.

The Suburbs

Pondicherry's beautiful **Botanical Gardens** lie at the far western end of the Black Town, a ten-minute auto-rickshaw ride from the town centre via Lal Bahadur Street. The gardens, laid out in 1826 on the site of a fort that was razed by the British are designed according to the formal French style, with clipped trees, exotic flower beds, gravel walks and fountains. The old **Lieutenant Governor's Residence** sits amid the lawns and trees—a far nicer place to live than the old Governor's Residence on Government Park, which, despite the benefit of sea winds, has the heat of the town. Also in the Botanical Gardens is an **Aquarium**, where tanks display some of the more spectacular marine species from the Coromandel Coast and which has a small but rather dull museum on traditional fishing.

Fire-Walking Festivals

Despite being a largely Roman Catholic town, Pondicherry's Hindu residents observe several festivals throughout the year, mainly centred around the large **Manaakulla**

Vinayagar Temple on Cathedral Street The most important is *Masi Magam*, a moveable feast celebrated at full moon in the Tamil month of *Masi* (late February/early March). Images of the various gods are taken from the Manaakulla temple (and from several smaller ones) to the sea for a ritual immersion. Holy men walking on red-hot coals mark the highlight of the ceremony. If you miss the ones at *Masi Magam*, other fire-walking events take place at various times through the year. Contact the **Tourist Information Office** on Goubert Salai for firm dates.

Shopping

Pondicherry's Auroville *ashram* produces some high-quality goods. At the Boutique D'Auroville on Nehru Street, hand-made jewellery, Western-cut clothes, incense, pictures and books are sold at reasonable prices.

Pondicherry ℃ (0413–)   ### Where to Stay

expensive

The new **Anandha Inn** on S.V. Patel Road, ℃ 35456, ℮ 31241, is the only truly upmarket place in town. Although very comfortable, its location is slightly awkward, being a 10-minute walk, or a short auto-rickshaw ride, from the old White Town. However, it has two good restaurants, one northern Indian, one vegetarian, and the people on reception are very helpful with any travel arrangements you might need to make.

The **Pondicherry Ashok** on the coast at Chinakalpet, ℃ Kalapet 460 also has a rather inconvenient location for those wanting to explore old Pondicherry, being on a private beach slightly out of town. Points in its favour are its small size (20 rooms), and its small stretch of clean private coastline.

moderate

Back in town, the **Hotel Mass**, on Maraimalai Adigal Salai, ℃ 27221, while reasonably comfortable is overpriced and lacks character.

inexpensive

The most interesting hotels in Pondicherry fall into the 'inexpensive' category. Much cheaper, and with far more character than the expensive hotels, is the **Qualithé Hotel**, ℃ 24325, on the south side of Government Square. A fine piece of 19th-century colonial architecture, its rooms open onto a long verandah, and its beds—period pieces from the 1920s—come with optional mosquito nets. Run by a family of French-speaking Indians, the Qualithé has a restaurant, bar and an old function hall that, according to the owner, pre-dates the hotel building and served as a secret meeting chamber for the 18th-century French Governor Dupleix and Tipu Sultan during their many plottings against the British in Madras.

On the seafront (Goubert Salai) is the **Sea Side Guest Lodge**, ℃ 26494, also occupying an old building. Though very comfortable, because it is owned by the Sri Aurobindo Ashram, guests have to be back by 10.30pm, which can limit things—even though there is nothing beyond the town's restaurants to distract the visitor at night.

cheap

Pondicherry does not lack cheap, good places to stay. To get the sea breezes, try the **Ajantha Guest House** on Goubert Salai, ✆ 38927, which has clean, airy rooms, and a rooftop restaurant overlooking the wide ocean. Also on Goubert Salai is the **Park Guest House**, ✆ 24412, with basic but comfortable single and doubles and cheaper dormitory accommodation.

For dirt cheap but reasonably clean accommodation, try the **G.K. Lodge**, ✆ 23555, on Anna Salai in the Black Town, or the **Tourist Homes** on Uppalam Road, ✆ 26376, where you can pay extra for an air-conditioned room. The **Excursion Centre** next door has really cheap dormitory accommodation only. If you have a motorbike or are prepared to cycle half an hour, the **Youth Hostel**, ✆ 23495, north of town at Solaithandavan Kuppam, is a great place to kick back and relax in the middle of a traditional fishing village and right on the ocean.

ashram accommodation

Both the Sri Aurobindo Ashram in town and the Auroville community in the nearby countryside have guesthouses costing around Rs35–40 per night. The managements of both communities are not keen that just any old traveller should use their accommodation, but if you are genuinely interested in the *ashrams*, ask at one of their shops on Jawarhalal Nehru Street (*see* below) and you might be allowed to stay.

Eating Out

Pondicherry has one very good French restaurant, the **Satsanga** on Surcouf Street in the White Town, ✆ 605001, which occupies a grand building that served as a brothel in the 18th century. You eat on the beautiful verandah among a mainly French-speaking clientèle. Rs150–200 will buy three courses and decent wine. In the same price range is **Le Rendezvous**, around the corner on Sufferen Street, which also caters to the French crowd in an air-conditioned colonial hall.

Cheaper options proliferate in the White Town. Try the rooftop restaurant at the **Ajantha Hotel** on Goubert Salai for good seafood at about Rs75 per head. Also in Goubert Salai is the **Café Pondicherry**, right by the Gandhi Monument. Waves lap at the foot of the outdoor terrace, where you can eat good pastas and *birianis* for Rs50. Tibetan food can be had at the **Snow Lion**, 22 Rue St Louis and there is a good, if tiny **Vietnamese Restaurant** on Romain Rolland Street just south of the junction with Government Square. Prices for both the above Rs50–100.

Much cheaper, though only open until early evening, is the **Ashram Dining Room**. Another rooftop affair, this is run by the Sri Aurobindo Ashram on Canal Street (Gingee Salai). A Rs35 ticket will buy you a light vegetarian meal.

In the Black Town, cheap *thali* houses can be found on Jawarhalal Nehru Street and around the bus station on Lal Bahadur Shastri Street. All offer fresh, clean fare for around Rs20 per head.

Auroville

About 6 miles north of Pondicherry lies the utopian agricultural community of Auroville, an extended property of intensively farmed fields, blocks of forest and clean beaches whose 40 or 50 separate hamlets are populated by about 700 mostly middle-class Western families who have decided to give up the materialistic way of life, go back to the land and live a life of spiritual awareness and meditation. It sounds a little too good to be true and many locals will tell you of local conflicts between Auroville and its surrounding Tamil farming villages, as well as internal divisions within the community. But be that as it may, Auroville, founded by the Sri Aurobindo Ashram in 1968, has succeeded in many of its attempts at sustainable organic agriculture (helped by the fact that local farm labour is cheap to hire) and forestry and has survived its first generation intact.

The philosophy behind Auroville is a little confusing to the outsider. It seems that Sri Aurobindo's chief disciple and mouthpiece, the French woman Mirra Alfassa (generally known as 'the Mother') laid out plans for Auroville which complemented her idea of the human body—what she called 'cellular consciousness'. She believed that mankind was at an evolutionary crossroads, about to become a higher species, and that the old genetic programme of cells was becoming more harmonious. As a result, the human settlements of Auroville, centred around its huge, spherically shaped meditation centre (the Matrimandir, designed by the French architect, Roger Arger), reflect this idea of positive change, with names such as Gratitude, Transition and Grace.

Auroville is worth a visit whether or not you are interested in its philosophies, for the hamlets and farmlands are very beautiful, the beaches tranquil and clean, and there are several workshops turning out handicrafts of a very high standard.

Getting Around

Guided tours leave from the Boutique D'Auroville, 12 Jawarhalal Nehru Street, Pondicherry, about three times a week. However, if you do not want to hear the party line and want to move freely, then hire a motorbike or bicycle (*see* Pondicherry 'Getting There', above) and spend a day exploring.

The Ashram

The logical place to begin a tour of Auroville is at the Matrimandir, the metal, spherical building with a fountain, around which the first Aurovillites ceremoniously planted lumps of soil from their native countries in 1968. Most of the community members still come here every day to meditate and there is a sort of lecture hall-cum-theatre attached, called the Bharat Nivas. The main Auroville guest house is a few seconds' walk away, as is the main nursery, where the community's forestry seedlings and saplings are raised.

From Matrimandir, there are several roads leading off though the countryside to small villages: Forecomers, which concentrates on organic agriculture, Auroson, which has a nursery school, Udavi, which has an incense factory and Aspiration and Fraternity, which produce most of the textile handicrafts that are sold in Pondicherry.

If you get hot and tired (and you will) head for Aurobeach, a palm-fringed tropical delight of white sand and blue waves.

Ariyankuppam

This is the old Roman trading settlement, about 2 miles south of Pondicherry, situated on a wide riverbank next to a Tamil fishing village. Most of the site is now below ground but it was a flourishing port in the first and second centuries AD. It was excavated in the 1940s by the charismatic British archaeologist, Sir Mortimer Wheeler, who speculated that Ariyankuppam might have been the port of *Podouke* that Ptolemy mentions in his *Histories.* Most of the arte-facts found (coins, ceramic amphorae, funerary urns, clay figurines) are on display in the Pondicherry Museum (*see* above). To reach the site, take a bus from Lal Bahadur Shastri Road or an auto-rickshaw (don't pay more than Rs20 one way).

Vaitheeswarankoil

About sixty miles south along the coast from Pondicherry is the town of Chidambaram and an hour's bus ride further on towards Mayoram is the village of **Vaitheeswarankoil**. Few tourists have ever heard of this obscure little place but students of Sanskrit and astrologers know the place for its extraordinary temple collection of ancient palm-leaf manuscripts. Apparently (and rein in your disbelief), the lives of everybody who has ever lived and who will ever live *in the world*—their birth, death and the major compass points of the intervening life—are to be found written in brief code on these Sansrkrit palm-leaves. It seems impossible, of course but the author met a Dutch woman on a train who had just come from the village and had asked one of the Brahmins to look her up in the temple manuscripts and had found herself—birth, death and major events—as expected. A resident of an *ashram* in the north of India for over 10 years, she claimed to have been told of Vaitheeswarankoil while living up there and had been advised by her guru to visit it while on pilgrimage to the *ashrams* of the south.

Believe it or not as you wish but many Indians do: tens of thousands of Indians visit the village every year to consult the manuscripts. The author invites any interested traveller to visit Vaitheeswarankoil and look themselves up and write in to Cadogan guides with the results. The Dutch woman he spoke to advised that visitors should ignore the various transla-tors that will offer their services and go straight to the Arun Ganesham at 18 Milladi Street and there ask for a translator called Mr Shiva Guvunathan, © 436482. Apparently a reading costs about Rs150.

Where to Stay

You can stay overnight at one of the very good, very cheap guest houses but this must be arranged in advance via the Boutique D'Auroville in Pondicherry and you must convince the people there that your interest is sincere.

The Temple Cities and the Inland Plain

Inland Tamil Nadu presents the traveller with an endless succession of abrupt contrasts between the deep rural calm in its countryside and over-populated bedlam of its temple cities. Green paddy fields stretch to the horizon's edge. White cattle and egrets wade among the rice

plants, long beaks poised to spear the frogs that live in the shallow water and sing to the warm stars after sundown. There are arts piled high with rice straw, large, rumbling wheels pulled at the leisurely pace of a bullock's walk, the great, gentle beast itself groomed powder-white by its loving owner, horns painted blue and red, moving in and out of the shade of the banyan trees that line the road between the paddies. Blue with distance, the tall *gopuram* (towers) of temples a millenium old betray nothing of the rush and madness of the crowded city that sprawls around them.

A threshold decoration for a goddess

Tiruchipalli (Trichy)

One of the smaller temple towns of the Tamil Nadu plains, Tiruchipalli (usually known by its shortened name of Trichy) is regarded by many Tamils as their heartland town, the centre of their cultural region. Rising from the south bank of the sacred river Cauvery, Trichy is calm for a temple town. Unlike aggressive, bustling Madurai or stately Thanjavur, the temple complexes are still visited more by pilgrims than by foreign tourists. Although a city in size, Trichy has more the feel of a large town, its buildings cluster around a great rocky outcrop, some 250 feet high, on top of which sits an ancient Rock Fort Temple. The old town, whose narrow, crowded but surprisingly clean medieval streets centre around the rock fort, is lively, friendly and crowded with small shops. By contrast, the newer town, south of the Rock Fort Temple, is as dusty and traffic-cursed as any other Indian town. Unfortunately the new town has most of the accommodation, as well as the bus and train stations but it is possible to stay in the old town if you don't want anything too fancy and in this town it might be worth sacrificing a little comfort for atmosphere.

Getting There

by air

Despite its small size, Trichy has an airport with flights to and from Madras, Trivandrum and Colombo in Sri Lanka.

by bus

The bus stand is on Warners Road, just south of the junction with McDonald Road. Several times-daily services include buses to Madras (250 miles), Madurai (100 miles), Pondicherry (75 miles) and—for changes to Ooty and the mountains—Coimbatore (125 miles).

The railway station is Trichy Junction, on Junction Road. Regular services include Madurai, Thanjavur, Madras, Bangalore, Mangalore, Coimbatore, Tuticorin, Tiruneveli, Quilon and Cochin.

Tourist Information

The **Tamil Nadu Tourist Office**, ✆ 25336, is on McDonald Road, just a couple of minutes from the bus stand.. The **bus stand** is on Warners Road, south of McDonald Road and the **Trichy Junction Railway Station** is on Junction Road, on the east side of its big roundabout junction with Madurai Road.

The Old Town

The towering **Rock Fort Temple** and its adjacent tank are the focus of the old town. The entrance to the 250 feet climb up to the Shiva temple on top of the rock, is on Chinna Bazaar Street. Just inside, you come to the ticket office (camera fee Rs10), next to which is a safe place to leave your shoes for under a rupee. From there, it's a stiff climb up 344 steps, past several shrines which are off limits to non-Hindus, onto a rock plateau from where there are stunning views over the city and the coconut-palm and paddy-field patchwork of the Cauvery River plains. Another long set of steps then leads up to the tiny citadel shrine to Shiva that crowns the Rock Fort Temple. Again, the main attraction here is the view, although you will also find yourself the centre of much scrutiny from crowds of black-lungied pilgrims. These pilgrims are all on their way to Kerala via as many Tamil Nadu temples as they can fit in. They are almost all male—women are regarded as too 'unclean' for the pilrimage, although pre-pubescent and thus 'pure' females are sometimes among the crowds. The pilgrims seem almost universally happy, laughing and singing as they climb the rocky stairway to the sacred citadel.

Once you have climbed back down the endless steps to ground level, it is worth exploring the streets of the **old town**. Surprisingly clean, the narrow, 18th-century streets are lined with tiny craft workshops and small textile shops. Walk for 10 minutes down Big Bazaar Road—the main street running south from the temple entrance—and you come to the **Gandhi Bazaar**, a fruit and vegetable market bursting with life—the colours of the fruits, vendors touting for customers and yelling at stray cows, piles of chillis filling the air with throat-tickling spice dust.

Srirangam

About six miles north of town (take a bus from the bus stand half a mile north of the Rock Fort Temple's Teppakulam tank), is the large island of **Srirangam**, which divides the Cauvery River from its local tributary, the Kollidam. In the middle of the closely populated island is the huge **Sri Rangathaswamy Temple Complex**, one of the largest in India. A Vaishnavite temple of 21 *gopurams* (towers) linked by courtyards and separate shrines, Sri Rangathaswamy was built during the 13th and 14th centuries by a succession of different rulers, among them the Cholas, Hoysalas and Vijayanagars. However, the temple complex has been added to at odd times ever since. For example, the towering painted *gopuram* you pass underneath in order to reach the main complex was only completed in 1980. Just to the right of the entrance to this *gopuram* is the shoes deposit (you can choose between a shelf and a locker) and ticket office (camera fees are Rs10). Once inside the main complex, you will be besieged by local guides, most of whom have official IDs, wanting to take you around. It is a good idea to hire one, as the temple's many sets of carvings are better enjoyed when explained (for example, some depict Portuguese soldiers battling the locals) and the labyrinthine interior is bewildering without someone to lead you. Most of the guides are trainee priests but this will not stop them from trying to charge as much as they can. Do not pay more than Rs150 for your tour if in a group, or Rs75 on your own. A tour lasts about 2 hours.

If you are visiting in mid December, try to see the spectacular **Temple Car Festival**, when the massive temple chariots are drawn out for public veneration. These great, unwieldly carriages rise to several stories of ornately carved gods and deities and the near hysteria of the devoted who proceed behind them is thrilling to witness. The local guides will tell you the exact date of this year's festival.

The New Town

There are no sights or monuments in the scrubby, semi-industrial new part of Trichy, which lies south of the Wodakondam Channel, the river that divides the old town from the new. But as both the bus stand and the main train station are here, as well as most of the town's accommodation, it is worth knowing your way around

Trichy © (0431–)   ***Where to Stay***

expensive

The only expensive hotel worth the money is **Jenney's Residency**, on McDonald Road, © 461301, ⊕ 461451. Although the rooms are slightly gloomy, it has a pool (open to non guests for a Rs60 fee), a bar, a reasonable vegetarian restaurant, a slightly better Chinese restaurant and a discotheque where the town's small yuppie population comes to dance. Other hotels within the expensive category are no more luxurious than the town's moderate hotels but you could try the **Hotel Sangam** on Collector's Office Road, © 464700/1, ⊕ 461779 and the **Femina**, on Williams Road, © 32551, ⊕ 468158, which have recently undergone minor refurbishment.

moderate

The **Hotel Tamil Nadu** on McDonald Road, © 25383, offers the usual clean and comfortable state-run fare, with a choice of air-conditioned or non air-conditioned. The hotel's restaurant and bar are convenient after a day's sightseeing. More popular among travellers is the **Ashby Hotel**, on Junction Road, © 23652/23653, which still has a slightly colonial feel in its large, high-ceilinged rooms. Bathrooms are en suite and there is a restaurant and bar. Less nostalgic but slightly cheaper is the **Hotel Anand**, © 26545, on Racquet Court Road, which has bathrooms attached to all rooms and good food.

inexpensive

For good value, try the **Hotel Aristo**, a cheapish modern block on Dindigul Road, © 26565, the **Hotel Ramyas**, on Warners Road, just north of the bus stand and the **Ashok Bhavan** on Rockins Road, © 25783. All the above have vegetarian restaurants and a choice of air-conditioned and non air-conditioned rooms.

cheap

Trichy has plenty of good, cheap accommodation, mostly clustered around the bus stand. Many travellers go to the **Hotel Guru**, on Royal Road, ✆ 33881, the **Hotel Lakshmi**, on Alexandria Road, ✆ 25298 and the **Ajantha**, ✆ 24501, on Junction Road. All have a reasonable guarantee of cleanliness, though the rooms are pokey.

Eating Out

Trichy has few outstanding restaurants. An exception is **The Peaks of Kunlun** Chinese restaurant in Jenney's Residency Hotel, which offers a fairly expensive but good quality Chinese menu (avoid the Continental dishes, which are bland as cardboard). Apart from eating at your hotel, you could also try **Kanchanaa** on Williams Road, which caters for both vegetarians and non-vegetarians.

Traditional vegetarian restaurants proliferate in Trichy and most offer the usual cheap south Indian menu: *thalis* at under Rs20. Some of the cheaper hotels have particularly good restaurants, among them the **Anand** on Racquet Court Road and the Hotel **Ashby** on Junction Road.

Around Trichy

If you tire of the hot city and want to spend a day somewhere quieter, it is worth taking a hired taxi (approx Rs4 per mile) 40 miles to the rock-cut Jain cave temples of **Sittanavasal** (4th–5th century). Those who make the trip will be rewarded with frescoes similar to, though smaller than, those at Ajantha in Maharashtra. The animal and plant bas-reliefs and paintings make a nice change from the more usual Hindu temple art of gods and celestials. About 2 miles away is a much earlier Jain cave called Ezhadipattam, where there is a set of vast steps cut from the rock sometime in the early centuries AD. If you have time, Sittanavasal also has a few scattered **neolithic megalithic sites**, including some small stone circles. Unfortunately there is no accommodation but being only 40 miles away from Trichy, the sites make a feasible day trip.

Closer to Trichy (15 miles) is Grand Anicut, also known as Kallanai, a mighty stone flood barrage across the Cauvery built by the Chola king Karikala in the 2nd century AD. This ancient feat of engineering is all there is to see but it is an impressive sight and makes a good excuse to get out of the hot town and spend a cool afternoon under the palm trees by the river bank.

Madurai

Mad, mad Madurai: the largest, busiest and most aggressive of Tamil Nadu's temple towns comes as something of a shock to the traveller used to the more mellow pace elsewhere in the state. However, even if you don't visit any other temple town, to miss Madurai's temples is to miss one of the India's architectural wonders. The town's atmosphere is that of a medieval fair: un-put-offable touts will drag you into their shops and hotels, music blares from every corner and you will be kept awake by the thumps and giggles that come through the walls of the cheap hotels, many of which double as brothels. You will also have to contend with fierce heat, pugnacious rickshaw drivers and teeming crowds.

For all this godlessness, Madurai is a sacred site, the special abode of the goddess Meenakshi, 'the one with eyes like fish'. The vast temple complex built here in her honour is perhaps the finest achievement of the Dravidian architects and still remarkably intact. The nine soaring *gopurams* of Madurai are the first thing most visitors see, whether coming in by air, rail or road.

Over 2500 years old, Madurai takes its name from *mathuram*, the nectar which Shiva let fall from his flowing locks after Kulaskera, a Pandyan ruler, began praying for a new capital. The Pandyas, great patrons of Tamil art, architecture and learning, ruled 'Nectar City' from as early as the 6th century BC, right through to the 13th century AD, apart from a short period of Chola rule during the 11th and 12th centuries. After the Pandyas came the Delhi Sultans and the Vijayanagar kings but it was left to the enlightened Nayak rulers, who governed Madurai from AD 1559 to 1781, to build the city in its present form. It was laid out in the shape of a lotus flower, with the impressive Meenakshi temple at the centre, in accordance with the Shilpa Shastras (ancient laws of architectural science). In 1781 the British ousted the Nayaks, razed the old fort and converted the surrounding ditches into broad avenues known as *veli* (outer) streets. From then on, the growth of the modern town outside the temple walls was rapid.

Climate and When to Go

Full of colourful bazaars, itinerant street tailors, thronging pilgrims, academics and joyful religious processions, Madurai today is a small, bustling town which attracts up to 10,000 visitors each day. For fun and spectacle, come for the month-long **Chithrai Festival** in **April** and **May**. People have been known to pass out in the heat and crowds but it really is a glorious pageant. Otherwise, there's the cooler **Teppam** (Float) **Festival** of **January** and **February**. Madurai is popular all year round but the climate is most pleasant from **October to January**.

Getting There

by air

Indian Airlines flies Madras–Madurai daily, Trichy–Madurai daily and to Bangalore a couple of times a week. **EastWest Airlines** make daily flights to Bombay. From Madurai airport it's a 4 mile ride into the city centre by airport bus or taxi (Rs30–40).

by train

The fast *Vaigai Express* from Madras gets to Madurai in just 8 hours, stopping at Trichy on the way. The morning Madras–Quilon Mail takes 8 hours to reach Quilon in Kerala and crosses the scenic Western Ghats. You're not supposed to be able to book seats in advance for either train but they're often half empty. If you don't fancy just turning up on the off-chance, contact the TTDC information counter inside the station and see what they can do.

Daily train services also run to Trivandrum in Kerala, Tirupati in Andhra Pradesh and Tuticorin in far southern Tamil Nadu.

by bus

Madurai has two main bus stands, adjoining each other off West Veli Street. The PRC stand is for Kodaikanal and for local city buses. The TDC stand is for Kanyakumari, Madras, Trichy, Trivandrum and Kottayam. With TDC buses, you must buy your tickets in advance.

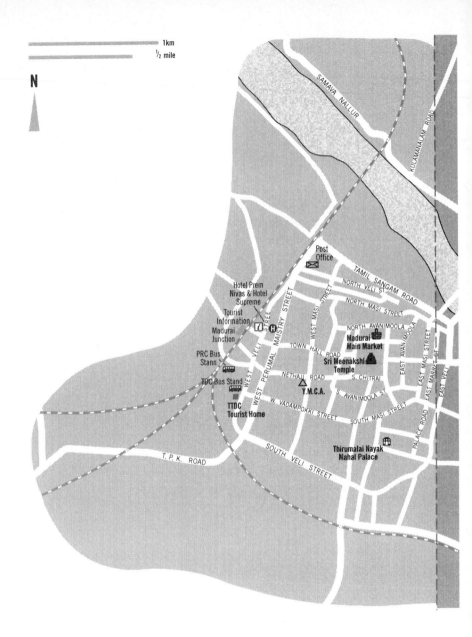

Madurai

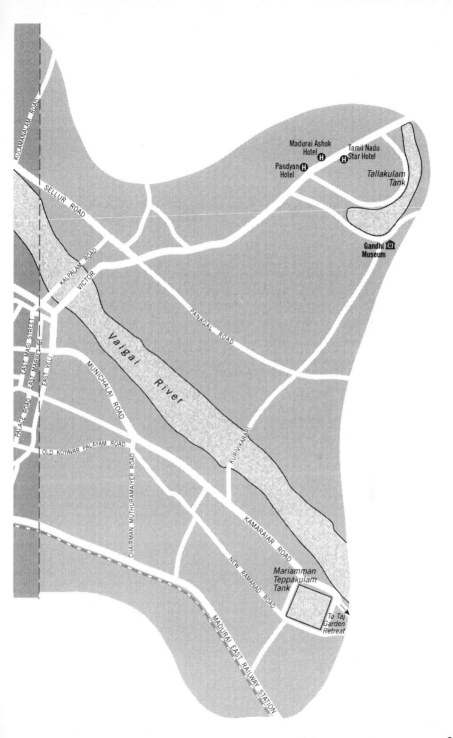

TTDC, West Veli Street, ✆ 22957, has good information and is very helpful. There are also tourist information counters at the rail station (though this one is notoriously *un*helpful) and at the airport.

The **post office** is in Scott Road, near the railway station. **Indian Airlines**, ✆ 22795, is at Pandyan Building, West Veli Street. For **foreign exchange**, the **State Bank of India** is also in West Veli Street. **Higginbotham's bookshop**, selling a useful city guide and map, is in the railway station.

The Town

Two small cities in one, Madurai is easily negotiable by foot or by cycle. The central Meenakshi Temple, aptly named a 'city within a city', is enclosed by the old town, which is itself enclosed by the four Veli Streets. The newer town, a mile north over the river Vaigai, is of little interest but has the better hotels. All the budget lodges, restaurants and tourist office are in the old town and so is all the action. Whenever possible sightseeing is best done on foot. But don't jaywalk round the temple area unless you want to be mown down by crazed cyclists. You can hire auto- or cycle-rickshaws for around Rs10–15 for short hops but most people only use them for out-of-town trips. Allow at least 2 days to see the sights.

City Tour

by foot or by rickshaw/taxi, full day

Sri Meenakshi Temple–Thirumalai Nayak Palace

From either the bus or rail station, it's a 15-minute walk up Town Hall Road to the **Sri Meenakshi Temple** (*open daily, 5am–12.30pm, 4–10pm, avoid Friday when hordes of pilgrims pour in*). This is one of the biggest temple complexes in India—846 feet long by 790 feet broad (258 by 241 metres). Most of it was built in the reign of Thirumalai Nayak (1623–55), though it was substantially added to by later rulers. It is a rectangular twin shrine: the

Temple elephant

southern temple dedicated to Meenakshi (a Pandyan princess who lost her embarrassing third breast when she met Shiva up on Mount Kailash), the other dedicated to Sundareswarar (Shiva himself). Dominated by four enormous outer *gopurams*, the usual entrance point is the Ashta Sakthi Mandapam on the east side. Within, are five smaller *gopurams*, enclosing the two small golden *vimanas* or central shrines.

Meenakshi temple is a constant buzz of noise and activity, especially around the East Tower Bazaar, full of exotic stalls selling bright clothes, jewellery, incense and spices. Enter the temple by the official gate, at the end of Town Hall Road where you must deposit your shoes outside. Just inside the entrance, bearing right, there's usually a row of fortune-tellers. Just past these are a couple of 'classrooms' where, in the early evening, you can hear tuneful songs and prayers being practised. Turning left, you'll find the **South Tower**. It used to be possible to climb to the top of this soaring *gopuram* and to enjoy spectacular views over the whole temple complex. But then came a bomb scare and the tower was temporarily closed to the public. It is worth asking if it is again open.

Continuing anti-clockwise, you'll come across the **Golden Lily Tank**, used by pious Hindus for sacred dips. The legend goes that any book thrown into it will sink if worthless (this guide is a rare exception!). Surrounding the tank is a pillared portico, its walls decorated with paintings from Hindu mythology and verses from the Tamil classic, *Tirrukkural.*

Beyond the nearby mural of Meenakshi's wedding to Shiva are the two single-stone sculptures of the temple's 12th-century founder and his chief minister. Behind the tank is the gate-facing shrine of **Sri Meenakshi Sannath**, guarded by two huge *dwarabhalagas* (doorkeepers). Through the entrance gate of **Sundareswarar Sannathi**, you'll find the beautiful hall of **Kambathadi Mandapam**, notable for its excellent sculptures of Shiva. Next, wander over to the nearby **Thousand Pillar Hall**, which actually has only 985 superbly carved pillars. Two small temples stand on the space intended for the other fifteen. Much of the rest of the hall has been given over to the extensive **Art Gallery**—a fascinating, if poorly lit, exhibition of Tamil temple art and architecture. Outside again, take directions for the **Puthu Mandapam**, opposite the Eastern Tower. Built by Thirumalai Nayak in honour of Sundareswarar, this is noted for its sculptures and for its imposing pillars, on which are carved representations of the four Nayak rulers. Just east of this is the **Rajagopuram**, a massive 170 feet (53.5 metres) tower base which, had it been completed, would have been the tallest tower in south India.

Don't feel obliged to follow this route to the letter, people often enjoy just wandering round Sri Meenakshi at random. The most enjoyable time of day to visit is the early evening, when it's relatively quiet and cool. There's normally some musical entertainment going on (informal and inspired) at the Golden Tank from 6.15 to 7.30pm and from 9 to 10pm. If you're at the South Tower around 9.15pm, you can see Shiva being 'put to bed'. Photographs are only allowed inside the temple from 1 to 4pm daily (camera fee Rs5) but you can pick up some good black and white prints in the bazaar, very cheaply.

In the afternoon, take an auto-rickshaw (it's complicated on foot) down to **Thirumalai Nayak Palace** (*open daily, 9–1 and 2–5*). This palace, built by Thirumalai Nayak in 1636, fell into ruins and was partially restored by Lord Napier, Governor of Madras from 1866 to 1872. The original palace was four times larger than the existing building, though enough remains to make a visit worthwhile. There's an excellent sound-and-light show in English here, commencing 6.30pm daily. Tickets are Rs5 or Rs7. The cheaper tickets are best—you see far more.

Enter via the magnificent granite portico into the rectangular courtyard, flanked by huge, tall colonnades. Walk up to the northwest of the building, to see the splendid Main Hall. Originally Thirumalai Nayak's bedroom, it measures 130 feet long by 65 feet wide (41.5 by 20.9 metres). It was also used as a theatre, where dancers, musicians and court magicians used to entertain the king and his guests. On the west side of the courtyard, visit the Celestial Pavilion (Swarg Vilasa). The large central dome is supported by 12 columns but appears to lack any support whatsoever. The fine decorative stucco *chunnam* (shell-lime work) on both the dome and its arches are a characteristic of Tamil ornamentation. The Celestial Pavilion is approached by a flight of steps guarded by a group of damaged carved mounted horsemen.

Sights Round-up

by local bus, full day

Thirupparankundram–Mariamman Teppakulam Tank–
Gandhi Museum–Government Museum

From the PRC bus stand, catch a no.5 bus (they leave every 10 minutes) for the remarkable rock-cut temple of **Thirupparankundram** (*open daily 5am–12.30pm, 4–10pm, adm free*), 5 miles out of town. This temple, carved into the side of a mountain, is one of the six sacred abodes of Subramanya, second son of Shiva and celebrates his marriage to Deviyani, daughter of the rain god Indra.

Entrance to the innermost shrine cut from solid rock is denied to non-Hindus but there's lots to see in the preceding series of *mandapas* or halls. These are generally packed to capacity with devotees preparing to go into worship. The head of each family distributes small lamp-lit bowls of coconut, fruit, rice and incense to his group and marks their foreheads with the lines of Shiva in red or grey powder. You can follow them on their way into devotions, as far as the door leading to the inner chamber. Just beyond the door is a small courtyard, containing 'Shiva's Postbox', where incinerated prayers drift up to the god through the soaring wicker-tower roof. In the centre of the courtyard is a brightly painted triumvirate of Nandi (Shiva's bull), a peacock and a rat fashioned out of black granite. The surrounding pillars are surmounted by fierce stone lions and the ceiling decorated with beautiful murals. Following the pilgrims out of the shrine, you'll see them making offerings of boiled rice to the schools of leaping fish in the temple ghat. Out in the street again, sit awhile over a cup of *chai* and enjoy the colourful flow of people: pilgrims, priests, holy men and Indian families on their way to prayer.

Back at PRC bus stand, catch bus no.4 or hire a rickshaw to **Mariamman Teppakulam Tank** 3 miles east of the city. Measuring about 365 square yards, this tank is almost as large as the Meenakshi Temple. Built by Thirumalai Nayak in 1646, it is the site of the big **Float Festival** held on the night of the January/February full moon. The central pavilion, **Mayya Mandapam**, houses a small temple and can be reached by boat, for a rupee or two. The tank is connected to the nearby Vaigai river by underground channels.

From here, take bus no.6 to the **Gandhi Museum** (*open daily 10–1pm and 2–6pm, closed Wed*), 3 miles north. It's a 5 minute walk from the Collector's Office in the new town. The museum contains various relics, photos and material relating to Mahatma Gandhi, a crafts exhibition of Khadi and Village industries and a south Indian handicrafts display. Also here is a relatively new, if rather scruffy **Government Museum** (1981). (*open daily 10am–1pm and 2–6pm, closed Fri*). To return to the old town, you'll need a bus no.3 or 4.

Shopping

Madurai is a living bazaar—there are shops, stalls and markets everywhere. Cotton and silk clothing are the best buys, followed by cheap costume jewellery. There is no problem finding good clothes here. The streets are alive with salesmen carrying armloads of clothes and silver trinkets around, pestering tourists with irresistible sales patter.

All the best tailors hang out opposite the East Tower of Meenakshi temple. Check out a man called 'Paramount' in Shop 100—several travellers have found him of great help. Both here and down by the South Gate, you can get clothes made up at very reasonable prices in under 4 hours. Bargain towards half what they quote you and you may end up with something approaching a fair price.

Poompuhar, the new government emporium opposite the train station, has a good selection of fabrics, wood- and stone-carvings, brass trays and cotton lanterns at fixed prices.

Madurai © (0452–)   ### Where to Stay

luxury

Madurai's most interesting hotel is the **Taj Garden Retreat**, Pasumalai Hill, © 88256 ✆ 88601, found on a hill 4 miles from the town. The house once belonged to the British manager/director of a large plantation and the steps to the upper level are still adorned with the antlers of the *sambar* deer he shot in the nearby mountains. The Taj Garden's grounds are extensively wooded and have superb birdlife and a circular walk is being planned through the woodland connecting the main accommodation area with the swimming pool. There are also well-maintained formal gardens and tennis courts.

Many of the other hotels are located in the new town, about 2½ miles from bus and railway stations.

expensive

The air-conditioned **Pandyan** in Racecourse Road, © 42470/1, ✆ 42020, has a good restaurant and fine temple views from its rooms. The **Hotel Madurai Ashok** in Alagarkoil Road, © 42531, ✆ 42530, is rather more impersonal and expensive but its travel desk is very helpful. Also at the top of this price range is the **Hotel Supreme** on West Perumal Maistry Street, © 36331, ✆ 36637.

moderate

For a really good deal, TTDC's **Tamil Nadu Star Hotel**, Alagarkoil Road, © 42461, has spacious double rooms priced well within this category and a couple of large comfortable suites for less than the Rs700 maximum. The vegetarian restaurant is also good and you can get reliable travel information here.

inexpensive

TTDC's **Hotel Tamil Nadu**, West Veli Street, © 37470, is rather a disappointment with uncomfortable, overpriced rooms. You can stay in better comfort in the 'cheap' price range listed below.

Madurai attracts a good crowd of budget travellers and there are many cheap lodges. Be warned however—Madurai is a money-making town, so don't be shocked if you find that some rooms in your lodge are being used by prostitutes. A few favourite back-packer hotels, with rooms around Rs75 single, Rs120 double, are **Hotel College House**, on West Perumal Street, near the Meenakshi Temple, **Hotel Prem Nivas**, at 102 West Perumal Street, ✆ 37531; **Ganga Guest House** opposite it; **Abinaya Lodge**, 198 West Masi Street; **P.S.B. Lodge**, West Veli Street; and **Aftab Lodge**, 12 Kakka Thopu Street.

Eating Out

Pandyan Hotel's **Jasmine** restaurant offers a superb Rs150 buffet lunch between 12 noon and 3pm daily. The *à la carte* is good too—a fine range of Indian, continental and (after 7pm) Chinese dishes at between Rs50 and Rs75. Helpings are huge. Three popular restaurants, all close together in Town Hall Road, are the **Taj**, the **Mahal** and the **Akbar**. They all serve Western-style food in addition to standard Indian fare but the Akbar has an air-conditioned lounge upstairs and gets the best mentions.

Old favourites like the **Indo-Ceylon** and the **Amudham**, also in Town Hall Road, are fairly drab now. More fun is the rooftop **Surya Restaurant** at the Hotel Supreme on West Perumal Maistry Street or the **Ruby Restaurant** on the same street, which has a pleasant outdoor terrace, set back from the temple crowds, yet close enough to take in the action. Prices here are between Rs20 and Rs35 per item.

The **New College House** continues to turn out the cheapest and best south Indian *thalis* in town. Similar fare can be had at the **Ashok Bhavan** opposite the tourist office, which serves 'special' lunches for Rs25–35 from 12noon to 2.30pm daily.

Entertainment and Nightlife

Lakshmi Sundaram Hall, Gokali Road, Tallakulam, ✆ 25858 and **Raja Sir Muthiah Mandram**, opposite the district court, hold regular dance and music programmes. Near Gandhi Museum, there's a yoga centre and a swimming pool. Ladies' hours are 2 to 4pm.

Thanjavur (Tanjore)

Tanjore is the last of the Tamil Nadu temple towns on most travellers' itineraries. Yet this city, more handsome than Trichy and calmer than manic Madurai, was the region's foremost between the 10th and 14th centuries under the later Chola kings, who made it their capital. The greatest of these kings, the unmistakeably named Raja Raja (985–1014) built most of the present city's remaining monuments, including the vast Bridashwara Temple Fort, modern Tanjore's main tourist draw. Although not as large as the Srirangam temple complex near Tiruchipalli (another Chola-sponsored structure), Bridhashwara is more regal in its architecture, reflecting its dual status as the centre of spiritual and temporal government, as well as the enormous wealth of the late Chola rulers.

Like Trichy, Tanjore can be divided between the old town around the Bridhashwara Temple and the new town around Gandhiji Road, where most of the accommodation and tourist information, restaurants and banks can be found.

Getting Around

by bus

Tanjore's bus stand is on Hospital Road at the southern end of the old city. The town has direct services to Madras (200 miles), Madurai (100 miles) and Tiruchipalli (30 miles).

by train

Direct train services run to Tiruchipalli (Trichy) (2 hours), Madurai (5 hours) and Madras (9 hours)—with several trains running to each city every day. The railway station is on Railway Station Road (the southern continuation of Gandhiji Road) in the new city, south of the Grand Anicut Canal which divides the old city from the new.

Tourist Information

Tanjore's **Tamil Nadu tourist information centre** is in the Tamil Nadu Hotel on Gandhiji Road, the main north–south drag that connects the old and new towns. The **G.P.O.** is 5 minutes further south, just off Gandhiji Road (also known as Railway Station Road for this stretch, just to confuse you), on the main road east to Nagapattinam. For **foreign exchange**, head down to the main **State Bank of India** on Hospital Road, or the **Canara Bank** on South Main Street.

The Old Town

Tanjore's **Bridhashwara Temple**, which translates roughly (and pragmatically) to 'the Big Temple of God', was Raja Raja's greatest achievement as a patron of temple architecture. Built at the turn of the 10th and 11th centuries, the central *gopuram* tower rises to almost 200 feet of tiered carvings. The top of the tower consists of a massive, single block of stone, weighing over 83 tonnes, according to the official literature. Getting this into place was a feat of engineering unusual for the early medieval world. Apparently a ramp was constructed with a gradient so gradual that it ended up being almost 4 miles long! The same engineers managed to manoeuvre a massive piece of granite into place before the portals of the inner shrine. Once there a team of sculptors fashioned it into the second-largest Nandi Bull in India. It is a mystery how the vast stone itself was transported to Bridhashwara, for there is no such rock anywhere on the Tamil Nadu plains and the thing must have been dragged in from the Deccan Plateau by boats, bullocks and men.

Once inside the main temple complex (*closed between 12noon and 4pm*), it is worth exploring all 15 chambers open to the public for their Chola frescoes—faded but still magnificent in their swirling, sensuous depictions of gods and celestials. There is also an **Archaeological Museum** (*open daily, 9–12noon and 4–8*) within the temple, which features a history of the Chola kings, as well as the restoration of the interior chambers.

About a mile from the temple is Tanjore's **Palace**, built by the Nayak and Maratha conquerers of the region who invaded between the mid 16th and mid 17th centuries. It's more a complex of buildings than a single residence, with two main towers and a massive armoury rising to several storeys, which can be seen from most parts of the city. Most of what has been left intact by time now houses government offices but the courtyards and cathedral-sized corridors give a fair idea of the grandeur of Tamil Nadu's early rulers. Tourists can also visit some small museums within the palace. The **Raja Raja Museum** (*open daily, 9.30–1.30 and 2.30–5.30 except public holidays*), has a collection of Chola bronze sculpture reckoned by many to have finer pieces than even the Sculpture Gallery in Madras Museum, as well as some stone carvings from the same era. Also open to the public is the **Sangeetha Mahal**, or hall of music, built by Raja Serjofi (late 18th century) for concerts. The hall is, apparently, acoustically perfect, though there is no explanation as to how the architects achieved this and the traveller must take the information on trust. Also within the palace grounds is the **Saraswati Mahal** (*open daily, 10–1 and 2–5*), an 18th-century library of antique texts, both Indian and European but the real treasure here is a collection of 30,000 palm-leaf manuscripts.

The same Raja Serjoi who commissioned the Sangeetha Mahal also had the **Schwartz Church** built near to the palace. Although the Raja was no Christian, he had the church built in 1779 to commemorate his tutor, the Danish missionary, Father Schwartz, who lived at the court during the the early 18th century.

The New Town

As with nearby Trichy, the new part of Tanjore (south of the Grand Anicut Canal) comprises the usual mix of heat, dust and semi-industrial ugliness that seems to afflict all of India's newer urban areas. But, again like Trichy, almost all the tourist accommodation is concentrated here, as are most of the restaurants and other amenities (*see* 'Tourist Information' above). The best place to visit is the **State Arts and Crafts Emporium** on Gandhiji Road, which has good local copper work on sale.

Tanjore ✆ (04362–)

Where to Stay

expensive

The **Hotel Parisutham**, ✆ 21466, on Grand Anicut Canal Road is Tanjore's best hotel. By no means of 5-star standard, the Parisutham nonetheless has excellent facilities including bright green lawns—a joy to the eye after the hard light of the dusty streets. The two restaurants are both above average and there is a bar. The only thing lacking is a swimming pool.

moderate

Go first to the state-run **Hotel Tamil Nadu** on Gandhiji Road, ✆ 21024/21325/21421. Built round a tree-lined courtyard, this is one of the most comfortable and attractive hotels in Tamil Nadu and more akin to an 'expensive' than a 'moderate' hotel. The restaurant serves better than average vegetarian meals. Otherwise, try the **Hotel Karthick**, ✆ 22116/22117/221152 or the **Hotel Valli** on M.K.M. Road near the main post office, ✆ 21584.

inexpensive

The **Ajantha Lodge**, on South Rampart Road and the **Ashoka Lodge** on Abaraham Panditar Road are clean and basic. Both are in the new town, south of the Grand Anicut Canal and convenient to the Railway Station.

Popular among backpackers and closer to the old town are **Rajarajan Lodge** on Gandhiji Road just south of the bridge over the canal, ✆ 2130, and the **Raja Rest House**, also on Gandhiji Road behind the Hotel Tamil Nadu and its Tourist Information Centre.

Eating Out

As is generally the case in the temple towns, Tanjore's restaurants are mostly good, cheap, *thali*-houses, the majority of which can be found along Gandhiji Road or clustered around the bus stand and train station. However, the **Parisutham Hotel** has two good, if pricey restaurants: one called **Le Repas** which despite its name does not serve French food but Chinese and north Indian. The hotel's vegetarian restaurant, the **Geetham**, offers the same fare as the cheap *thali*-houses in town but at twice the price. Better value is the south Indian **Golden Restaurant** on Hospital Road, at the southern fringe of the old town. Not only are the prices good at about Rs25 per head but the restaurant has rooftop tables that make it a great place to sit and have a beer after a hard day's temple-bashing.

Point Calimere (Koddikkaral)

On the coast some 50 miles east of Tanjore is a superb wetland wilderness now run by the Tamil Nadu Wildlife Department: Point Calimere Bird Sanctuary. Also known as Koddikkaral, the sanctuary has tourist bungalows and can be easily reached from Tanjore by bus in 3 to 4 hours, and then by auto-rickshaw. Each year Point Calimere sees the arrival of vast flocks of flamingos (the second-largest concentration in Asia, according to the official guidebooks), which turn the surface of the tidal swamps into a shifting, squawking carpet of pink from November to February. In spring, a variety of inland migrants appear, filling the swamp's woodlands with whistling, squeaking, cooing song. Birds to admire include green pigeons, rosy pastors, barbets, koels, orioles and mynahs. In winter, another wave of inland birds arrives, among them paradise flycatchers, pittas, swallows, drongos and woodpeckers.

Point Calimere is also a good place to view wildlife; the endangered blackbuck still thrives here, as do wild boar and *chital* (spotted deer).

Birdwatching and wildlife viewing is easy to arrange, whether in the Sanctuary's jeeps, or on foot with a guide. Both these can be booked at the reception desk when you get there.

chital

Accommodation within the sanctuary is in two Wildlife Department cabins; the **Poonarai Rest House** and the **Point Calimere Rest House**. Either make advance reservations through the District Forest Officer in Tanjore, or just turn up and argue until you get a place, unless you are visiting during November and December when the sanctuary is usually booked up.

Tiruneveli

Used mainly by travellers as a stopping point on the railway south towards Kanyakumari at India's southernmost tip, or across to Trivandrum in Kerala, Tiruneveli's official literature describes it as a town of 'hoary tradition'. In fact, the present settlement of over 200,000 people is only about 2000 years old. Tiruneveli served briefly as a capital for the Pandyan kings but today it is very much a provincial town.

Despite being one of the south's oldest Christian sites—St Francis Xavier began his evangelical mission here in the 16th century—the town's main attraction is the 1000 pillared **Kanthimathi Nellaiyappar Temple**, dedicated mainly to Parvathi, though there are shrines to her illustrious husband Siva as well. Like the great temple at Madurai, this one has a golden lily tank, sacred sculptures and a hall with musical pillars. A collection of jewels is also housed here but it is unlikely that the brahmins will let you see them.

If you have seen too many temples in the Tamil Nadu plains, take a bus out to the quiet coastal village of **Trichendur**, which has a beautiful shore temple and a cave of sacred carvings and the Hotel Tamil Nadu ('inexpensive'), ✆ 268. **Manapad**, 12½ miles further on was once a Catholic Mission and is now a tranquil fishing settlement still dominated by a large 16th-century church. Another option is to trip 40 miles from Tiruneveli up into the foothills of the Western Ghats to **Courtallam** and its nine waterfalls. The local waters are thought to have medicinal properties and there are forest walks. Not far from the town's main Siva temple is a small Nataraja temple with good frescoes. The temple's site is supposed to be on one of the five on which Lord Nataraja performed his cosmic dance of creation (these sites are called *sabhas*).

Where to Stay

inexpensive

Tiruneveli has a **Hotel Tamil Nadu** near the railway station, ✆ 24268, with clean singles and doubles. You could also try the **Barani** on Madurai Street, ✆ 23234, the **Sri Janakiram**, ✆ 24451, on the same street, or the **Sakuntala** on Trivandrum High Street, ✆ 71760.

cheap

For around Rs100, you can find accommodation at the **Narayan Tourist Lodge** on Trivandrum High Street and the **Blue Star** on Madurai Road.

Courtallam has Township Bungalows and a Forest Department resthouse bookable through the Tamil Nadu tourist Office at Courtallam bus stand. Tariffs are between Rs75 and Rs125.

Kanyakumari (Cape Comorin)

Kanyakumari is the Land's End of India, a staggering 2000 miles south of Jammu. It is named after the Kumari (Virgin) goddess whom the gods tricked out of a marriage with Shiva because they needed a virgin to defeat the powerful demon Banasura. It's just the kind of poignant, tragic love story that devout Hindus adore and they turn up here in their thousands to console the dejected goddess in her temple and to seek her help. They also come because

Kanyakumari is the meeting point of three great seas: the Indian Ocean, the Arabian Sea and the Bay of Bengal and bathing in the waters is believed to wash away all sins. Local tourists and foreign travellers come for the unique sunrises and sunsets which are most spectacular at full moon, when sunset and moonrise take place simultaneously.

Away from its temple and its beach, Kanyakumari is an unremarkable place which has somehow developed in the short space of a few years from a modest fishing village into a full blown Indian-style resort. And of all Indian resorts, this one is the most full of cheap tourist junk. It sells grass hats, funny masks, plastic whistles, plastic tropical plants and bags of coloured Kanyakumari sand. It even has a drive-in restaurant chicken corner. Noisy, well-to-do families clamber over the rocks, take invigorating beach promenades and wade into the shallows dressed in their best suits and saris. The high season months are from November to January and from April to June. For peace, quiet and a chance of a decent room visit between February and March. It's fairly cool then and you can enjoy the full moon.

Getting Around

Kanyakumari has a swish new bus station, with rest rooms, a restaurant and a shopping complex. Unfortunately, it's inconveniently situated; a long ¾ mile walk up the hill from Vivekananda pier. From here, **buses** go 4 times daily to Trivandrum, Kovalam and Madras (each a 16 hour ride), 3 times daily to Madurai and Trichy (an 8 hour journey) and at least twice a day to Coimbatore (about 10 hours) for connections with the Tamil Nadu mountains beyond.

Tourist Information

TTDC tourist office is near Gandhi Mandapam, ✆ 276, open 10am to 5.30pm except weekends. Staff regard Western visitors with undisguised shock and are generally too flustered to be really helpful. The **post office** and **State Bank of India** are both near the old bus stand.

The Town

This is a tiny seaside town, with one main street. Sights are few but walks are interesting. Stay for at least one sunrise and one sunset and during the day try the following jaunt.

Beach Tour

on foot, 3–4 hours

Sunrise Point–Kumari Amman Temple–Gandhi Mandap–Fishing Village–Vivekananda Memorial

Try to be up around 5am for the sunrise. This is best seen either from **Sunrise Point** down on the beach, or from your hotel roof. Every hotel near the shoreline has a roof and each one will be choc-a-bloc with jostling tourists. The sunrise itself takes place against an atmospheric background of Muslim muezzin-calls, Catholic prayers and picturesque fishing boats putting out to sea. Afterwards, you can go straight back to bed.

Later, take a walk down to the beach. Here you'll find **Kumari Amman Temple** (*open daily, 4.30–11.30am and 5.30–8.30pm; the sanctum is closed to non-Hindus*), dedicated to the virgin goddess who is now the nation's protective mother-figure. The deity sits in a small dark pavilion, flanked by four attendants. She used to look out to sea but her glittering nose-diamond lured so many sailors to their deaths (including the British vessel which purloined the original jewelled nose-ring) that the temple door was closed in her face.

Just west of the temple is **Gandhi Mandap**, the rather bizarre monument erected to commemorate the spot where the Mahatma's ashes were kept before being immersed in the sea. It's worth a visit (have 10 *paisa* handy, or you'll never get in), if only for the coastline views from the top-storey balconies.

A total contrast to the touristy new town is the quaint little **fishing village** just down the beach. Here you'll find a warm and friendly community of fisherfolk living in the same way they have for centuries. Give them a hand with a fishing line, or help push out a dugout to sea and you'll be their friend. For around Rs20, they run parties of 3–4 people out to sea for 'fishing trips'. You don't get to do a lot of fishing but you do get stunning views of mainland India and Sri Lanka from a mile or so out. Sitting for 2 hours in a primitive five-plank cata-maran leaves you very damp, so take a spare pair of trousers.

Beyond the village are lovely palm-fringed beaches: great for sunbathing, fatal for swimming. The coastal currents are generally dangerous. To swim in safety, use either the sheltered bathing ghat back in town, or the new pool on the shore built for visitors.

Above the village is the clean, white **Catholic Church**, established by St Francis Xavier in the 16th century. It's massive. So is the Disneyesque image of the Virgin Mary inside. She is the patron saint of the fishing community, afforded just the same reverence as is given the Kumari deity by the Hindu pilgrims across the bay. Since the congregation prefer to squat in the church, there are no pews.

Returning to the bathing ghat, take a boat (*daily departures from 7–11am, 2–5pm, except Tues, about Rs20 return*) out to **Vivekananda Memorial**, which lies on the two rocky islands 220 yards offshore. Dedicated to the philosopher-saint Swami Vivekananda, who came here and meditated in 1892 before setting out to become one of India's leading religious crusaders. It is a relatively recent structure (1970) which attempts to blend all the architec-tural styles of India. The security is over-strict, in part to highlight the sanctity of the site. Smoking and eating are prohibited and shoes must be removed. The views of the mainland from it are excellent. Pilgrims visit the rock to view the Kumari goddess' footsteps.

Try to be back at the ghat around 6pm for sunset. This is often low tide and best views can be obtained by wading over to the small observation rock opposite. Take care coming back though, as the rising tide has a nasty habit of leaving unwary tourists stranded. At the April full moon the setting sun and rising moon appear side by side on the same horizon.

Sports and Activities

There is sea-fishing (bring your own tackle); also one cinema. At sunset, pop over to **Suchindram Temple**, a 10-minute auto-rickshaw ride away for the evening *arti.*

Shopping

Apart from seashells, plywood toy racing-cars and 'precious sand of three seas', there's nothing local that is worth buying.

inexpensive

TTDC Hotel Tamil Nadu is just below the new bus stand, ✆ 257. Clean and friendly, it has the prime beach situation, with some lovely rooms overlooking the sea. Food is good and so is the cheaper dormitory accommodation. **Hotel Cape**, ✆ 222, is also run by TTDC, or you could try the brand new **Hotel Saravana**, opposite Vivekananda pier.

cheap

TTDC also run a **youth hostel** next to Hotel Tamil Nadu but this is often booked up. The better budget lodges are located down by the old bus stand. **Manickam**, North Car Street and **Lekshmi**, East Car Street, have the best roofs for views of the sunrise and sunset and offer clean, basic rooms.

Eating Out

Again, you won't find anything exciting. **Hotel Saravana** has the best vegetarian restaurant in town. Hotels **Sangam**, ✆ 351 and **Manickam** offer reasonable food for carnivores. Otherwise, it's back to *thalis*.

Tamil Nadu's Mountains

In Tamil Nadu, the Western Ghats rise steeply and suddenly from the plain, their sides covered in hanging forest, their tops a rolling upland of wild mountain pasture and densely wooded ravines (locally known as *shola* forests). The trekking and wildlife viewing possibilities are among the best in India and in some places it is possible to stay with mountain tribes whose cultures are far removed from mainstream Hindu.

On the eastern slopes grow deciduous forests that see rain only between August and February and lose their leaves in the dry season (between March and July). Wildlife viewing here is best in the winter, when the forests are green. In the dry season the game tends to migrate over to the wetter western slopes of Kerala state.

In winter you can see elephant, *gaur* (bison), tiger, leopard, sloth bear, *sambar*, *chital*, muntjac deer, striped hyena, *dhole* (hunting dog), jackal and a host of smaller species.

The best **wildlife sanctuaries** to visit are Anamalai (a high upland area known for large elephant herds), the dry forest of Chinnar (which has a wildlife viewing tower and arranges guided treks), Avalanchi, in the high Nilgiris, where trekkers stand a good chance of seeing Nilgiri *tahr* (a species of ibex unique to the region) and **Moyar Wildlife Area** of reserved forest around the small town of Masinagudi, where several small private game lodges have been set up. By far the

muntjac deer

best is Jungle Trails, which takes only a few guests at a time and from whose verandah elephant, *gaur* and even rare creatures such as sloth bear are often spotted.

The mountains have several **hill stations**. Smallest and quietest is Yercaud, in the centre of the province. Kodaikanal is popular with backpackers and used to be very tranquil. Recent development has sadly spoiled the old town but superb trekking can still be arranged in the surrounding hills. The largest hill station is Ooty, which used to be called Ootacamund and is now officially named Udhagamandalam, although no one ever uses this name. Ooty has lost almost all the rural charm that made it the most fashionable southern hill station during

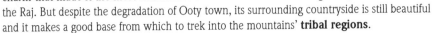

slow loris

the Raj. But despite the degradation of Ooty town, its surrounding countryside is still beautiful and it makes a good base from which to trek into the mountains' **tribal regions**.

Three tribes are accessible to trekkers, provided they have a guide known to the community; the **Todas**, who keep water buffalo, live in wattle and daub longhouses and worship a buffalo goddess; the **Kotas**, whose culture is based almost entirely around devotional music and the making of instruments and the **Kurumbas**, forest dwellers who have a reputation as magic-makers and diviners. More detailed breakdowns of the tribal cultures and information on how to trek into their areas can be found in the Nilgiris section of this chapter.

Mudanthurai Wildlife Sanctuary

This is the southernmost accessible point in Tamil Nadu's Western Ghats, where a Project Tiger Reserve has been established in the dry forest zone of the eastern slopes. With a large reservoir at the centre of its 84 square miles, Mudanthurai can be visited either by government jeeps, which leave from the reception office at around 7.30am and 5pm daily, or on foot with a guide. To take a guided trek involves some bureaucratic hassle (as it does in every wildlife refuge everywhere in the country) and you are supposed to apply in advance at the Wildlife office in Tiruneveli. However, just turning up and asking to speak with the chief conservator at Mudanthurai is more effective, providing you can convince him that your interest in the wild is genuine. The treks are by the day, returning each night to the (very basic) forest rest house near the reception area.

Mudanthurai's wildlife includes tiger, leopard, sloth bear, wild boar, *sambar* and *chital*, *nilgiri* and common *langur*, bonnet and lion-tailed macaque.

The easiest access is from Tiruneveli, 30 miles away: by bus to the closest small town of Ambasamudram and then by local auto-rickshaw or taxi to the sanctuary.

Kodaikanal (Kodai)

Until a few years ago, Kodai was a quiet, charming hill station, visited only by a few day-trippers from nearby Coimbatore and travellers wanting to cool off from hot, dusty travels down in the plains of Tamil Nadu. Situated 1½ miles up in the scenic Palani Hills, Kodai's temperate climate has remained but not, alas, its tranquility. In recent years the town has been developed as a major day-trippers' and honeymooners' resort, with attendant road and hotel development, tacky souvenir stalls, noise and increased traffic. The part of town immediately around the lake is still worth seeing for its nostalgic colonial feel but nowadays it has to be said that unless you plan to use it as a base from which to trek into the wild and beautiful Palani Hills, 3 miles from town, you would be better advised to avoid Kodai and head straight for one of the smaller hill stations or wildlife sanctuaries.

If you do decide to visit, the bus trip up from Coimbatore across rugged mountains, plummeting valleys and terraced coffee plantations is spectacular. The countryside around Kodai is famous for hill-fruits and plums and its pride is the rare Kurunji flower, which blooms just once every 12 years. Unfortunately, it last flowered in 1992. The two tourist seasons, when the place is rampant with groups of drunken Indian men, are mid-November to mid-January and mid-April to the end of June. For better weather and 20–30 per cent discounts at larger hotels come in February and March or August and September. If visiting between November and February, bring warm clothing as it gets very cold at night.

Getting There

From Kodai there are regular buses to Madurai; one bus daily to Coimbatore (4.30pm); one bus daily to Ooty (8am) and one bus daily to Bangalore (6pm). It's wise to book seats in advance.

Tourist Information

TTDC **tourist office** is near the bus stand, open daily from 10am to 5pm. The **post office** is between the market square and the lake. The **State Bank of India** is just above the bus stand.

The Town

The emphasis in town is on light exercise and recreation: walking, pony-riding and paddle-boating on the lake. Central Kodai overlooks the lake and is easily negotiated on foot. You can hire ponies and cycles by the hour or day down by the boat club on the lakeshore below the Carlton Hotel. There are also taxis but few people take them. Kodai is really just a place for long, invigorating rambles but in the hills away from the traffic and noise of the main roads. Allow 2 full days for the best walks and have a decent map handy (try Higginbotham's bookshop in Madurai).

Walk One

full day

Coaker's Walk–Sacred Heart Church–Kodai Lake–Bryant Park–
Golf Club–Green Valley View–Pillar Rocks

Rise at 5.30am, dress warmly and take a blanket for the sunrise over the mountains, Kodai's main attraction. A 15-minute walk up **Coaker's Walk** from the market-place brings you out on a plateau running along the steep southern face of the Kodai basin. The early morning scenery is glorious (though the crowds of holiday-makers are not) but latecomers be warned: the views are often lost in cloud by 9am.

After breakfast, proceed east from the market place down to the lake. On the way, divert right for a brief visit to **Sacred Heart Church**. It has a touch of Surrey with stained-glass windows, Gothic arches, a mock-Tudor tower and a small English cemetery. If not for the Tamil hymn books and alarming fresco of Christ rescuing a flock of anxious Indian villagers from a watery grave, you wouldn't know you were in India at all. Kodai's famous star-shaped **Lake** was formed in 1863 by Sir Vere Levenge and nestles in a wide range of dense wooded slopes. Covering 60 acres, it is the focal point of all life on the hill station. Clean, tranquil and scenic on its waters, if not its shore (which is the general promenade for the visiting holiday-makers), the lake feels very 'English'. Its small Boat House, to the left, coming down from the Church, *✆* 315, hires out four-seater rowing boats from Rs50 per hour. For a choice of boats and no crowds, turn up early. Nearby, you can hire out one of the underfed ponies for about Rs60 per hour, looked after by ostlers who accept no responsibility for 'any accident those who riding themselves without horse man'. From the pony rank, it's a 10-minute walk to the east of the lake, (look out for the signs prohibiting 'eve-teasing'—the Indian expression for male-female sexual harrassment) where you can enjoy a picnic lunch in pleasant **Bryant Park**, noted for both its hybrid and grafted flowers. There's a popular horticultural show here each May.

Even if you are not a golfer, the 4-mile walk up to the **Golf Club**, *✆* 323, is one of the best in the station. Take the road leading off the northern end of Bryant Park, ascend to the top of the ridge from where there are fine views down over the lake and whenever you hit a major fork, keep to your left. The walk is a continuous joy. Young boys may turn up to suggest 'short cuts' and they are reliable. You'll reach the golf club in around an hour. The course itself is beautifully kept and spans a succession of undulating meadows and hills. Cows are employed to keep the grass down. It's hardly ever used, except in May, when the 300 club members turn up for the annual tournament and for a small green fee of Rs120 you get clubs, balls, temporary membership and the course practically to yourself. An extra Rs45 will hire you a good caddy and for another Rs20 you get a spare set of balls.

Alternatively, take directions at the club for adjoining **Green Valley View**, which commands a beautiful view of the entire Vaigai Dam or walk further on past the golf course for **Pillar Rocks**, three massive boulders standing shoulder to shoulder, measuring 350 feet and providing a plummeting view down into the valley plains. There's a pretty waterfall here too.

Walk Two

full day

Observatory–Bear Shola Falls–Museum–Telescope House

For day two, try a pleasant 40-minute stroll up to the **Solar Physical Observatory** (*normally open April–June daily, 10am–12noon and 7–9pm; check at the tourist office before visiting*) 2 miles from town, approached via Observatory Road, 5 minutes north of the Boat House. Founded in 1898 at the topmost point of Kodai at a height of 7700 feet (2347 metres), it gives panoramic views of the town, lake and surrounding Palani Hills. On the return walk, take the rugged, picturesque path left for **Bear Shola Falls** a mile from the lake, another popular view point and picnic spot (though now sadly defaced by graffiti).

In the afternoon, stroll back up Coaker's Walk for the **Shenbaganur Museum** (*open daily, 10–11.30am and 3.30–5pm*) near the top of the rise, on the left. This is famous for its collections of flora and fauna including 300 varieties of orchid and is well maintained by the Sacred Heart College. The **Telescope House** at the nearby observatory is a good place to be at sunset. If it isn't free and it often isn't, enjoy the sun going down from the small knoll below which is a sheer drop of 2200 feet, with privacy guaranteed.

There are several other nice walks, notably **Prospect Point** (4 miles), **Fairy Falls** (3 miles) and **Silver Cascade** (¾ mile), behind the Sacred Heart Church.

Trekking in the Palani Hills

Although the area immediately around town has been deforested, it is worth arranging treks into the wilder, forested Palanis, which begin about half an hour's walk from the edge of town. Although unprotected, the Palani forests are still home to elephant, *gaur*, leopard, wild boar, the occasional itinerant tiger and a host of smaller game and birds. It is essential to have a guide, as the area has no maps.

Short treks around the Kodai hills for about Rs100 per day are offered by **A School in Nature Education**, c/o Greenlands Lodge, Coaker's Walk. These are easy-going nature rambles, geared to students and youth hostellers, which take place between May and June, September and November.

Longer treks of several days can be arranged through **Vijay Kumar's Nature Walks**, at Shop No.5, Bhuwaneswari Compound, behind the Telephone Exchange building on Observatory Road. These also cost around Rs100 per day but are well worth it as Vijay, the founder and guide, knows the area's flora and fauna intimately. He, along with several other prominent members of Kodai's ex-hippy community and International School staff (an unlikely mix but this is India), have formed the **Palani Hills** Conservation Council, aimed at getting the local eco-system the official protection it needs from the rabid developers of commercial Kodai. With funding now coming from Sweden's overseas conservation fund, it looks as though Vijay and his friends may well succeed in saving the area from an otherwise inevitable rape. A portion of your trekking fee will go to the council.

Sport and Activities

Apart from **golf**, **boating** and **pony-riding**, Kodai is a good area for **fishing**. Licences are issued from the Fisheries Officer (enquire at the tourist office) and charges are Rs5 per day for carp, Rs25 per day for trout-fishing in local hill streams.

Shopping

There's a reasonable selection of weavings and local crafts at the **Cottage Craft Shop** near the bus stand. It's open from 9am to 12.30pm and from 2 until 6pm, Monday to Saturday. You'll find attractive Tibetan produce and local *coir* mats for sale on the road leading down to the lake.

Where to Stay

expensive

There's elegance and lake-view rooms at **Carlton Hotel** on Lake Road, ✆ 40056/40071, 📠 41170. At the top end of this price range, the room rate includes meals and during the low season of mid-January to March and July to mid-October discounts of 25% or more are given. This 'warm-hearted luxury hotel you and your family deserve', has good food and good facilities which include a health club with jacuzzi, sauna and massages, billiards and tennis. But it's often full.

moderate

Slightly less expensive properties include **Hotel Kodai International**, ✆ 400649, which offers a choice between comfortable rooms and cottages. **Sterling Resorts** at 44 Gymkhana Road, ✆ 406760, has cottages only. However, the best place to stay is undoubtably the **Trattoria Venice Guest House**, about 2 miles out of town along the Fairy Falls Road (reached via Observatory Road), ✆ 40775, 📠 41288/40206. Owned by Ganesh, a local coffee-planter and conservationist and his Italian wife, the place is an old planter's bungalow with homely, old-fashioned rooms and superb Italian food. Tariff includes full board.

inexpensive

Among the budget hotels is the **Hotel Jai** in Lloyds Road, which has the rather alarming advertisement: 'Be our cosy guest tonight—wake up Gay in the morning'. If that sounds too much of a risk try **Hotel Clifton** in Bear Shola Road, **Hotel Anjay** near the bus stand, the **Holiday Home**, Golf Links Road or the **Hotel Tamil Nadu**, Fernhill Road. All offer clean, comfortable bases in the town centre.

cheap

Backpackers favour the excellent **Greenlands Youth Hostel** right at the top of Coaker's Walk with views out over the plains. Treks into the Palanis can be arranged from here: beautiful situation, lovely gardens, pleasant rooms. The other budget lodges up on Coaker's Walk are generally squalid, though the **Yagappa Lodge** has a few adequate rooms as does the **Taj Lodge**.

Eating Out

The best food in Kodai is not its most expensive. Head straight for the **Venice Trattoria**, 2 miles from town, first up Observatory Road, then left onto Fairy Falls Road, where the owner, Ganesh and his Italian wife prepare home-made pastas with fresh herbs that are as good as anything in Europe. A full meal is about Rs75–100. Also very good, though in basic surroundings—a tin shack on Bear Shola Falls Road, 5 minutes' walk from the lake—is the **Manna Bakery**, run by the bearded, charismatic Israel Bhooshi. His home-made breads, pizzas, soups and apple crumbles make up possibly the best Continental-style cuisine. Three courses here cost around Rs45.

Otherwise, there is a good range of Indian food at either the snooty **Carlton Hotel** or the **Hotel Tamil Nadu** for about Rs150 and Rs100 respectively—though only the brave can stand the Carlton restaurant's evening vibraphone player with his instrumental interpretations of old Beatles songs. The **Hotel Jai** does reputable non-vegetarian cuisine. The **Boat Club** restaurant is okay for snacks. Just below the market square are three good places: **Lala Ka Dhaba**, a *proper* Indian restaurant offering delicious Punjabi food in tasteful setting; **J.J.'s Fast Food**, a busy pizza and burger joint run by jolly Vincent; and **Tibetan Brothers** with delicious vegetable *momos* (deep-fried dumplings), fair Chinese food and homely service. Prices are cheap—about Rs40 for a meal.

Anamalai and Parambikulam Wildlife Sanctuaries

To reach either of these sanctuaries, you have to go back down to the plains (Coimbatore) and get a bus to Pollachi, from where local buses will take you to the sanctuaries' entrances.

Anamalai is known for large herds of elephant which divide their time between the thick forests of the lower slopes and the high grasslands and *sholas* of the peaks and ridges. Trekking is possible here with a guide, (*insist* at reception) and there is a good chance of seeing sloth bear or leopard if you are willing to spend several days in the mountains. There are also *gaur*, a few visiting tiger, many wild boar and good birdlife, including hornbills and black-headed orioles. Crocodiles swim in the sanctuary's reservoir.

A local beauty spot and look-out point called **Topslip** lies inside Anamalai and attracts hundreds of day-trippers in the December holiday season. Avoid it then but pay it a visit in the drier months, as elephants are often spotted near here. If no wild ones show up you can ride on a tame beast into the nearby forest, for the sanctuary keeps an elephant training camp here.

By contrast, almost nobody visits **Parambikulam** where denser forests make game viewing difficult. This is real rainforest, however and worth taking the trouble to get into. Beware of leeches in November and December. Parambikulam harbours the same game species as Anamalai. Trekking can be arranged at the reception office. Ask to speak to the chief conservator.

Where to Stay

Accommodation in **Anamalai** is provided in several comfortable resthouses: at Topslip (often full), Varagaliar, Sethumadai and Amarathinagar. You are supposed to reserve these in advance via the District Forest Officer in Pollachi, © 2508. If you do not have time, try your luck at reception. They may say they are full but are probably lying. Make a scene and you'll get a bed.

Accommodation at **Parambikulam** is more problematic. Unless you have arranged a forest trek—in which case you must put your sleeping bag down in the forest wherever the guide decides—you have to stay at one of the Anamalai resthouses and travel over to Parambikulam by bus or jeep in the early morning.

Coimbatore

You have to change buses in Coimbatore when travelling north to south in the Tamil Nadu ghats between Kodaikanal or Anamalai and Ootacamund (Ooty). Changing buses is all you should do here—Coimbatore is a large industrial hole of over a million people, sticky with heat and polluted air. However, if you get stuck here for a day, you can escape the city's heat and crowds in the **Botanical Gardens** at the far western end Bashyagarlu Road. About 600 acres of gardens laid out at the foot of the mountains, its formal lawns and flower beds soon give way to a gentle parkland of widely spaced mature trees that seem a world away from the desperate bustle of the town centre. Coimbatore also has two museums: the **Gass Forest Museum** (*open Mon–Sat, 9–1 and 2–4.30*) on Cowley Broan Street, which is not about gassing forests but has displays regarding aspects of commercial forestry in the Nilgiris; and the **College Museum** (*open Mon–Sat, 9–12noon and 2–5*), at the Agricultural College near the Botanical Gardens. Basically a local agricultural and natural history museum, its montages explain such riveting delights as fungal diseases in crops.

Getting Around
by train

Coimbatore is the point from where the little mountain train up to Ooty leaves at 6.30 every morning (about a 3 hour journey). There are also daily trains leaving for Madras, Bangalore, Cochin, Madurai and Mysore.

by bus

Coimbatore is a major centre of bus routes from all over southern India. Buses leave about every half hour for Ooty (5 hours), Kodaikanal, Pollachi (for Anamalai), Munnar and Cochin in Kerala. Several services run each day to Mysore, Madurai and Madras. The main bus stand is on Cross Cut Street (P. Gounder Street).

Tourist Information

The **TTDC Office** is on the railway station concourse, Patel Road, and is open daily.

For **foreign exchange**, the **State Bank of India** and **Canara Bank** are on Oppankara Street.

Coimbatore ⓒ (0422–)

Where to Stay
expensive

The **Surya International** on Racecourse Road, ⓒ 37751, is the best hotel in town. Most of the rooms are air-conditioned and the hotel is set in gardens.

moderate

The **City Towers** on Dr Nanjappa Road, ℭ 37681, has a pleasant rooftop restaurant. Try also the state-run **Tamil Nadu Star** on Arkiasamy Road, ℭ 33053.

inexpensive

The **Janaranjani** on Janaranjani Cross, ℭ 34101, the **Shree Shakti** on Shahstri Road, ℭ 34225, and the **Blue Star** on Nehru Street, ℭ 26395, are all clean and comfortable and convenient for the bus stand.

cheap

Try the **Guru Traveller's Lodge** near the railway station on Patel Road, ℭ 30341, has a good vegetarian reataurant. Failiing this, the **Shri Thewar** on Avanashi Road, ℭ 23341, has reasonably clean. On the same street is the **YMCA**, near the big flyover.

Ootacamund (Udhagamandalam)

Former summer capital of the Madras Presidency (now Tamil Nadu), Ootacamund, often known by its shorterned name of Ooty, is popularly known as the 'Queen of Hill Stations',

though the quiet charm it once had has been somewhat eroded over the past decades by its expansion into a small city with attendant crowds and dirt. Ooty now sprawls over several hills and into a wide valley of the Nilgiris (Blue Hills) near the junction of Karnataka, Tamil Nadu and Kerala, at an altitude of 7570 feet (2308 metres). Famous for being an eccentric place (snooker was invented here, the local army headquarters still keeps a pack of foxhounds and herds of wild ponies sometimes force you off the pavement), Ooty is within reach of some of India's most spectacular scenery and offers access to some of the Western Ghats most interesting tribal regions.

Ootacamund derives its name from a Toda term *Othakamanthu*, meaning 'village of huts'. The Todas, original settlers here before the British, are an aboriginal tribe who still own much of the wild grasslands of the countryside immediately north of Ooty. They still live in curved, wattle longhuts and worship a buffalo goddess, tending large herds of the beasts on the natural downlands. It is possible to trek into and sometimes to stay, in their settlements, as well as to other tribes of the area (*see* below).

The site for Ooty was discovered by the then Collector of Coimbatore, John Sullivan, who built first a residence (1819) and then created the lake (1823). The British quickly moved in, erecting stone cottages with flower

The train to Ooty

gardens, laying the beautiful Botanical Gardens (1840) and developing facilities for golf, horse-racing, polo and tennis. In 1869, the hill station became the summer headquarters of the government in Madras, with a rigidly stratified social life centred on the exclusive Ooty Club. Today, 'Snooty Ooty' is a rather rundown resort and retirement home for the rich. But it remains a popular watering hole for travellers, with a definite air of elegance and refinement still clinging to parts of it. There are Raj reminders everywhere, notably in the terraced Botanical Gardens, the English public schools, the churches and, above the town, the tea-gardens and eucalyptus plantations. At the centre of town is the huge (if scruffy) racecourse and in summer the stables here are still full of horses in training and racing meetings are held once a fortnight.

Climate and When to Go

Even the climate is British; cool and drizzly, even frosty, in the winter and one of the few places in India you'll need to bring warm clothing. Though most popular in **September/October** and **April/May**, it's far cheaper (low-season hotel discounts) and far less crowded in **February** and **March**. Ooty has its big **Summer Festival** throughout the month of **May** with tribal dances, live music and drama shows, held every evening at Anna Stadium. There's even a ballroom dancing competition when they can find enough people to participate!

Getting There

by air

Indian Airlines has daily flights between Coimbatore (3 hours by bus from Ooty) and Bangalore, Bombay and Madras.

by rail

The steam train up and down the spectacular escarpment between Ooty and Coimbatore on the plains leaves for Mettupalaiyam/Coimbatore at 2.50pm daily. From Coimbatore, there are regular mainline trains for Madras, Madurai, Cochin and other major destinations. To reach Mettupalaiyam directly from Madras take the *Nilgiri Express* which leaves Madras Central at 9pm and arrives at 7.20am in time to connect with the waiting *Nilgiri Passenger* to Ooty via stations with names such as Hill Grove, Coonoor, Ketti and Lovedale.

by bus

Ooty's smart, efficient bus stand has a handy reservation desk for buses to Mysore (8am, 9am, 11.30am, 1.30pm, 3.30pm; 4½ hours) and for Bangalore (6.30am, 10.30am, 12.30pm and 8pm; 8 hours). There are also hourly buses to Mettupalaiyam (2 hours) and Coimbatore (3 hours).

Tourist Information

The **tourist office** at the Super Market building, Charing Cross, ℂ 396, organizes tours. There's far better information (and good sightseeing tours) at **King Travels** across the road, ℂ 3137, and **Blue Mountain Tours**, Nahar Shopping Centre, Charing Cross.

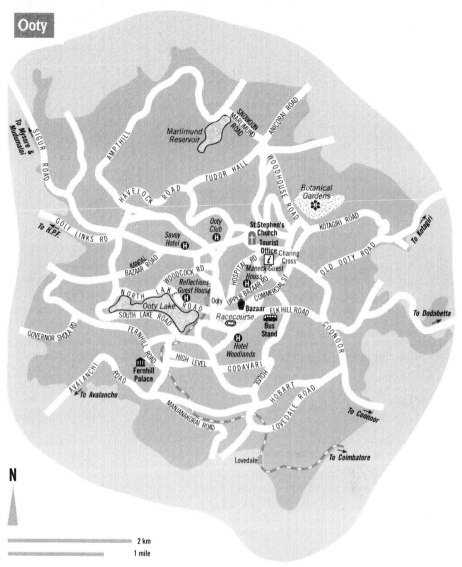

N

2 km
1 mile

The **post office** is near the Collectorate and the **State Bank of India** overlooks Commercial Street. **Higginbotham's bookshop** has two branches: the main one is opposite Chellaram's department store in the Charing Cross area, while the other one is opposite the main entrance to the post office.

The Town

Ooty is more a place to use as a jumping-off point for the Nilgiri wildlife and tribal areas, than a destination in its own right. However, the tens of thousands of Indian holiday-makers who come up here every year would say otherwise and the town is definitely geared for tourism.

If you decide to stay for a few days, there are still some lovely walks in the hils on the fringes of the town and the bazaar is worth exploring for its medieval feel. Many of the available walks climb to viewpoints over the town and surrounding country and, owing to the spread-out nature of these viewpoints, you'll need some sort of plan. The walking routes suggested below cover the main points of interest but there are several other mini-treks available. In town, get around on foot, by cycle (hire bicycles in the market) or by auto-rickshaw (Rs10 for short trips). The focal point of the small town is Commercial Street and the Upper and Lower Bazaars, which run parallel with it. The tourist office and banks are on Commercial Street, while the jewellers, bakers and craftsmen are in the bazaars.

Walk One

on foot, full-day

Botanical Gardens–St Stephen's Church–Ooty Club–Lake–
Golf Course–Wenlock Downs

From either bus or railway station on the east edge of the lake, it's a winding 1¼ mile walk northwest (via the racecourse, up busy, traffic-cursed Commercial Street) to the **Botanical Gardens**. Created by the Marquis of Tweeddale in 1847, these are 51 acres of terraced gardens and extensive lawns housing 650 varieties of plants. There's a big **Flower Show** here each May and visitors can buy flowers and seedlings from the Curator's office. Just below the mini-lake, check out the intriguing 20 million-year-old fossil tree. Ascending through gardens of ornamental plants, orchids, ferns, conifers and rockplants keep an eye out for the local Toda community (*see* 'The Nilgiri Hills') on the top levels—the closest tribal community to Ooty town. About 2000 of them live here, almost exclusively engaged in the cultivation of potatoes and weaving, having left behind their more traditional practise of buffalo-herding to trade with the townspeople and tourists. However, the women at least have kept to their traditional look, boasting tattooed skins, wearing bright handwoven clothes, keeping their hair in distinctive plaited loops and running their families with an iron rod. Toda women, unlike Tamil, are very feminist. They used to practise polyandry, having up to four husbands apiece, all of them henpecked. Near the village, you'll see the **Raj Bhavan** (Government House), still used by the Tamil Nadu Governor as a summer residence.

Out of the gardens, turn right at the end of Garden Road, then make a hairpin turn left into Higgins Road to **St Stephen's Church**; a 20-minute ascent. The creation of a Captain John Underwood (1829), it is a typically English parish church, with Gothic exterior and Tuscan interior. Just below it is the select **Ooty Club**, well worth a visit for its amazing collection of Raj memorabilia (contact manager for permission to view) and famous as the place where snooker was invented in 1875. From here, it's a straight walk down to **Ooty Lake**: small, picturesque, with good boating and fishing facilities but crowded with raucous holiday-makers in season and flanked by syces, or horse-copers, desperate to get you up onto one of their underfed, overworked ponies for a short, expensive (Rs60–100/hour) ride. Still, get out onto the water on a hot day and you'll find it the perfect place to spend an afternoon messing about in boats. The **Boat House** here (*open 8–6*) hires out rowing boats at Rs60 per hour (with a Rs35 deposit).

In the afternoon, try a lovely 3¾ miles walk (3 hours return) up to the **Golf Club**, bear right at the top of the Lake, then left at Finger Post into Golf Links Road. The scenery is very varied and picturesque and if you turn up at 9am sharp, you can usually get a game of golf (Rs150 green fee including hire of clubs and balls) on the expansive 18-hole course. A mile further on, you'll come to **Wenlock Downs**, offering spectacular views down over the local Bodega villages, the Coimbatore plains, Ketti Valley, the Mysore plateau and the tea estates. The more adventurous among you will notice that there are many unmarked paths snaking away into the plantation forestry around here. These are used by the local Bodega villagers for their fire-wood forages and make for lovely forest walking if you have a good sense of direction. In some of the glades you may surpise *sambar* deer or even *gaur* if you are out at either dawn or dusk and in some of the natural *shola* forest in the herat of these plantations, Nilgiri *langurs* still live among the evergreen trees.

Walk Two

by bus, then on foot, 5–6 hours

Dodabetta Heights

This is a very pleasant excursion, best done in the afternoon. Take a bus (20-minute journey, regular service from Ooty bus stand) up to **Dodabetta Heights**, the highest peak (nearly 9750 feet, 3000 metres) in the Nilgiris. There's an observation point with telescope at the top and on a clear day the views down over the hill ranges, plateaux and plains are superb. But the walk back down's a 3–4 hour, 6-mile descent through tea-gardens, terraced fields, wooded glades and pretty valleys. If you get tired, you can always hitch a bus for a quick lift back to town.

Other good viewpoints in the area include **Snowdon Peak** (panoramic view of Mysore), **Cairn Hill** (overlooking Avalanche River) and **Elk Hill**, which is just an hour's walk from Ooty. Further information, plus details of the many local treks available from the Trek Director, Department of Tourism, Government of Tamil Nadu, Madras (© 849803).

For real **trekking**, the Nilgiri Hills offer some of the most spectaculalr routes in India. A selection of these and their wildlife and tribal possibilities is included in the Nilgiri section on p.310.

If walking, pony-riding, boating and golfing are not enough, there's good **fishing** to be had (carp and trout) at Emerald and Parson's Valley and in Ooty Lake itself (contact the Assistant Director of Fisheries near the bus stand, ✆ 2232, for a licence). For **indoor games**: badminton, table tennis, visit Anna Stadium, below the Botanical Gardens. Of the several cinemas in town, the Liberty in Commercial Road is most popular.

Shopping

Tribal Toda jewellery, embroidered shawls and silver can be found at **Suraaj** in Main Bazaar, or **Suraaj Paradise** in Commercial Road. Prices are not cheap, so bargain hard. **Vimal Gems and Jewellery**, next to Nahar Hotel in Charing Cross, has a good selection of silver jewellery, semi-precious stones and Nilgiri spices and honey. Two government emporia nearby, **Poompuhar** and **Chellarams**, sell the full range of Ooty handicrafts at fixed prices. Buy tea and eucalyptus oil, the two most famous local products, at **Idco Tea** next to the tourist office. Home-made chocolate is another Ooty speciality. There are shops all over town but the **Sugar Daddy** outdoor ice cream parlour on Commercial Street stands out, about three blocks towards the bus stand from the tourist office.

Ooty ✆ *(0423–)*   *Where to Stay*

NB: In Ooty's hotels, rates are heavily discounted in the low season but charge 25% more during the Christmas–New Year period and in the May–June holidays.

luxury

There is a choice of deluxe rooms or cottages with verandah at Taj Group's reputable **Hotel Savoy**, 77 Sylks Road, ✆ 44142/3/4, ✆ 443318, the town's most famous Raj-era hotel. Good golf and poor quality horse-riding can be arranged here.

The Taj group have also recently taken over the **Fernhill Palace**, ✆ 43910, tlx 08504 built in 1842 by the Maharajahs of Mysore and set in a large estate. Although less well renovated than the Savoy, Fernhill is much more attractive, with its own woods and extensive gardens and a fantastic view out over the hills. For about US$60 you can have the Maharajah's own suite. If you ask, log fires are lit in the bedrooms and there is more Raj memorabilia than you can shake a stick at—animal heads, framed photos of the Ooty hunt in its heyday, an antique, professional-sized billiard table and a great hall. A word of warning though—stick to Indian items in the restaurant, despite the tempting French dishes on offer. They sound better than they taste.

In the same grounds as Fernhill is the **Regency Villa**, ✆ 43910, an attached shooting lodge and a smaller more intimate version of the palace. Prices are also a little lower and the food is good.

expensive

The most atmospheric hotel in this range is the **Nilgiri Woodlands**, ✆ 4643001, which overlooks the racecourse on Ettines Road. This is a late-Victorian set-piece, a

little run down but still handsome. Its lawns and verandahs
are a blessed relief from the
bustle of the main town and it
has a decent restaurant.
Choose between standard
double rooms, self-contained
cottages and old four-poster deluxe
rooms. **Quality Inn Southern Star**
Havelock Road, ✆ 43601, tlx 08504213, is
in better nick but is a bland modern building.

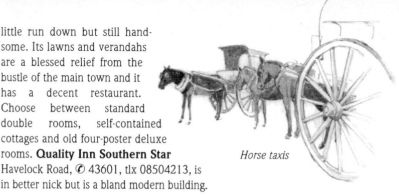

Horse taxis

moderate

Hotel Lake View, West Lake Road, ✆ 43904/43580, has a nice location overlooking the wide lake and clean, comfortable double rooms.

inexpensive

Reflections Guest House on North Lake Road, about half a mile north of the bus
stand, ✆ 43834, overlooking the lake. Reflections has double rooms and cheaper
dorms. The restaurant is good—both for Indian and Western food and you can eat on
an outdoor terrace. Ask Douglas, the owner, to play guitar for you—he's a virtuoso.

cheap

Ooty has some very good budget lodges. First choice goes to the Jain-run **Maneck
Tourist Home**, on the Main Bazaar, ✆ 43138/43494, which has clean, double
rooms overlooking the racecourse with small en suite bathrooms (Indian style) and a
decent vegetarian restaurant downstairs. Also good value is the **Nahar Hotel**, Charing
Cross, ✆ 42173, run by jolly Babuji. It's well run, well located and has a bakery, vegetarian restaurant and cosy rooms.

The **YWCA** on Anandagiri Ettines Road near the bus stand, ✆ 42218, caters for both
men and women and has a few charming cottage rooms. **Vishu Lodge** in the bazaar
has nice clean rooms, with bath.

Eating Out

For a real taste of the Raj, try to get invited to lunch or dine at the
Ooty Club. If this is not possible dine out at **Fernhill Palace**.
The palatial 'restaurant' features elegant but painfully slow
service, romantic lighting and well-priced Mughlai/continental
cuisine. Eat well for around Rs150 a head and have a chuckle over
the menu.

Punjabi food is good at **Paradise Restaurant** in Commercial Road and the nearby
Tandoor is reliable for non-vegetarian fare. Both cost from Rs60 per head. **Nahar
Tourist Home** has a cheap vegetarian restaurant, popular with *thali*-lovers. **Shinkows**
in Commissioner's Road (near the Collectorate) is best for Chinese food, while town
residents favour **Kurungi** (near the tourist office) for local-style Indian meals. Of Ooty's
many bakeries, **V.K. Bakery**, 148 Commercial Road, still makes just about the best
piping-hot fresh bread, mutton puffs, coconut balls, pies and cakes in India!

For cheap but good value, the **Maneck Restaurant** serves very good, if rather limited *jain* vegetarian food in the downstairs restaurant of the Maneck Tourist Home on the Main Bazaar. At **Reflections Guest Lodge**, on the road overlooking the lake, about half a mile north of the bus stand, there is a decent, cheap continental menu. Otherwise, buy your supper from one of the many street-side bakeries at the bus stand.

The Nilgiri Hills

Trekking into wildlife and tribal regions can be done more easily in the Nilgiris than in any other part of the Western Ghats. At an average elevation of around 7000 feet, with some much higher peaks, the Nilgiris themselves also offer some of the country's most spectacular scenery. Their high downlands (properly referred to as Watershed Grassland) are reminiscent of British uplands, while in some places reservoirs and huge pine plantations give the landscape a North American feel.

The area has several tribal groups: the Bodegas, who farm the land around Ooty; the buffalo-rearing, feminist Todas, who use the downs for grazing and still live in longhuts; the Kotas, known for making musical instruments and the forest-dwelling Kurumbas of the north slopes of the Nilgiris, who have a reputation for making magic and who still, in some places, live by shifting forest agriculture and hunting.

Trekking into the Tribal Regions

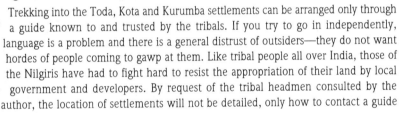 Trekking into the Toda, Kota and Kurumba settlements can be arranged only through a guide known to and trusted by the tribals. If you try to go in independently, language is a problem and there is a general distrust of outsiders—they do not want hordes of people coming to gawp at them. Like tribal people all over India, those of the Nilgiris have had to fight hard to resist the appropriation of their land by local government and developers. By request of the tribal headmen consulted by the author, the location of settlements will not be detailed, only how to contact a guide known to them.

To organize a trek into the Toda, Kota or Kurumba settlements, this guide can confidently recommend one (rather eccentric) guide, who accompanied the author and is known personally to the villagers. His name is R. Seniappan (or 'Sini') and he can be contacted through his home on 137 Upper Bazaar, in Ooty. Be warned though—these can be hard treks and accommodation in tribal villages is necessarily basic. You will also be expected to eat any food offered—including buffalo curd and butter-milk (not to everyone's taste).

Other specialist treks, for botanic, tribal and wildlife interest can be arranged locally through R. Ranjeet, of 'Meghdoot', Bokkapuram, Masinagudi (south of Ooty towards Mysore), ✆ 216; or in advance through Ranjan Abraham at Clipper Holidays, Suite 406, Regency Enclave, 4 Magrath Road, Bangalore 560 025, ✆/✉ (080) 5599032/34/5599833. Ranjan, a conservationist himself, offers one of the only reliable services for eco-tourism in India.

The Tribes

Most accessible (even as a daytrip from Ooty) are the **Todas**, who own most of the grasslands north of town and have protected them against the creeping settlement that is ruining the southern Nilgiris. With the protection of their buffalo goddess and the wealth of their buffalo herds, the 1500 Todas who still live traditionally, look set to stay in their economically strong position. Not only do they differ from the Tamils in religion, they also do in custom, as the women more or less run things and the men tend to hover in the background, often being told to shut up when they interject. For India—a man's society if ever there was one, this makes a refreshing change. Marriages are simple but beautiful, the couple going off to a tree in one of the *sholas* and dedicating themselves to the spirit there, before returning, hand-in-hand, to the village. Although the Todas will allow their youngfolk to marry outsiders, those who do may never return to the village.

The Todas also look physically different from both the Tamils and the other Nilgiri tribespeople, having more Caucasian features and a way of wearing both their embroidered cloths—almost like togas—and their hair (the women hang theirs in ringlets) that differs greatly from anything else in south India. Tradition states that their ancestors were soldiers of Alexander the Great, who migrated down from the conquered territories of the Indus Valley sometime in the 3rd or 2nd centuries BC. Whether this is true or not, they certainly look more northern Indian/Middle Eastern than Dravidian.

Toda tribesman

By contrast, the Kotas and Kurumbas are much darker and more delicately featured. Also unlike the Todas, both tribes speak dialects of Tamil and their religions are loosely based around Hinduism. The **Kotas** cultivate a philosophy of peace—towards both animals and men and regard blood-letting of any kind as sacrilegious. In fact, their religion has many parallels with Jainism and it has even been suggested that other similar tribal ideologies of non-violence may have been the wellspring from which Jainism developed. More 'modern' than the Todas (meaning that they cultivate crops and sell them at local markets), the Kotas are nonetheless regarded less as farmers than as a distinct society of craftsmen: skills in musical instrument-making, metal-working, woodcarving and pottery are passed from father to son and the Kotas are in great demand for their musicianship at religious festivals throughout the region. There are about 2000 Kotas currently living in the Nilgiris.

The **Kurumbas** (the name means 'forest-dweller') were traditionally the shamen, or medicine-men, for the other Nilgiri tribespeople and were held in some fear. Their hunter-gatherer culture changed only recently—though it persists in some deep parts of the northern Nilgiri jungles—to working for the local forestry and agricultural companies and certain Toda and Badega groups still seek out Kurumba diviners to make contact with the spirit world. Like the Kotas, today there are around 2000 Kurumbas in the region.

Two other tribes inhabit the southern and eastern sections of the Nilgiris: the Irulas and Kasavas. The **Irulas** have a tradition of herbal medicine and also fulfil certain religious functions for the rest of the Nilgiri peoples, including officiating at a great outdoor festival to the spirits of virility (Rangasamy) on Rangasamy peak, in the Kota territory. Like the Kurumbas, the forest-dwelling **Kasavas** were hunter-gatherers until recently. Nowadays they are mainly plantain cultivators, though certain groups have gone back to the forest.

Far more primitive are the Chodaikanal or **Sholanaikan** tribe; semi-nomadic cave-dwellers and hunters who live in the jungles of the southwestern end of the Nilgiris, where they spill over into Kerala. However, access to this area is completely restricted and the tribespeople themselves have deliberately resisted western influences and wish for no contact with travellers. The Sholanaikan men gather wild honey and use fire-hardened bamboo spears to take small forest game, while the women provide the bulk of the food—roots and forest fruits.

Trekking into the Mountains and Wildlife Sanctuaries

More mainstream trekking in the Nilgiris is also very rewarding. The following is a list of routes and where to stay in Forestry and Wildlife Department resthouses. Bear in mind that you have to apply for permission to stay in these places and that this can be incredibly hard to obtain. Your best bet is to put it into the hands of either Sini or Ranjan (*see* 'Trekking into the Tribal Regions' above), or somebody recommended by them and to give them at least two weeks' notice to get the paperwork in order.

Otherwise take a tent and make do for yourself but be ready to be cold at night and remember that you are not allowed to make fires in the Nilgiris.

Mukurthi Peak and Mukurthi National Park

This involves an overnight trek. Take a bus from Ooty to Anumupruram, near Pykara (about 25 miles) and hike the last 7 miles to the National Park. Accommodation is in a Wildlife Association hut but you take your own food and sleeping bag. Mukurthi Peak is a jagged, conical *arrête*, that the Todas refer to as the 'gateway to the world of the dead'. Rather, it is an idyllic landscape of high pasture, grazed by Nilgiri *tahr* and a pathway for roving bands of elephant migrating between Kerala and Tamil Nadu. The hidden rainforest of Silent Valley lies on the southwest part of the park but to get here you need to set aside at least three days.

Avalanchi

This is another high upland trek, with good possibilties of spotting Nilgiri *tahr*. Again, you should allow for at least an overnight stay; take a bus from Ooty to the Trout Hatchery, about 20 miles south of the town and hike the remaining 3 miles into the trekking region along the lake called Avalanche. Once in the wilderness area, you will travel though extensive areas of *shola* forest, where you stand a good chance of seeing Nilgiri *langurs*. Accommodation is in a beautiful Forest Department guest house near the Trout Hatchery. Built in the 1850s, its sound wooden walls still sport the trophy antlers of huge *sambar* deer. A guide for this trip is imperative, as there are no maps and the forest areas are too dense to risk getting lost in.

Upper Bhavani

You can trek into this region from Avalanchi or take a bus 37 miles from Ooty to Korakundah and hike the last 6 miles. Accomodation is in your own tent, or, if guided, in local tribal settlements. Like Avalanchi, Upper Bhavani has some huge tracts of *shola* forest, harbouring leopard, jackal and *langur*, between upland downs grazed by wild buffalo and Nilgiri *tahr*. There is a route into the Silent Valley rainforest from here but a good guide is essential.

The Moyar Wildlife Area

On the Mysore plateau to the north of Ooty and the Nilgiris is a vast area of dry deciduous forest divided into various areas of reserved forest and official wildlife sanctuaries. In the

30-mile stretch of wild country between the Nilgiris and the town of Masinagudi (itself on the edge of the huge Mudumalai and Bandipur Wildlife Sanctuaries) a number of wildlife lodges have sprung up in the reserve forest on either side the Moyar River. This is an area known for game density—particularly elephants, some of which have killed people, so don't walk off into the bush alone.

Offering a more intimate contact with the forest than the official sanctuaries, most of the lodges in the area offer guided wildlife and bird treks and sometime riding. It is rewarding to spend a week or so drifting between the different lodges: the scenery is spectacular, with the Nilgiris towering to the south and west, the forest alive with birds and insects and the game-viewing is better than anywhere else in the south.

By far the best of the lodges for seeing game is **Jungle Trails**, ☎ Masinagudi 56, which has a few double rooms at around Rs350 per night and a dormitory with viewing platform at Rs100. Meals and drinks are extra. To get there, take the bus from Ooty to Masinagudi (a 1½ hour journey which negotiates 36 hairpin bends on its way down to the Moyar River area) and ask to be set down at the driveway. From there it's a ¾ mile walk to the lodge. Be *sure* to do this before dusk, as elephant are very active in the area at night. From the verandah at Jungle Trails, you stand a good chance of seeing all the large and small south Indian game: sloth bear, bison and leopard as well as elephant among the regular visitors. There are also *machans* (bamboo viewing platforms) built into the trees on the Moyar's banks which allow great photo opportunities.

A few miles further along the road to Masinagudi is **Jungle Hut**, ☎ Masinagudi 40. Although the game is not so plentiful in this immediate area as at Jungle Trails, Jungle Hut also has regular visits from wild elephants. As part of the package, guests are taken to the nearby Mudumalai Wildife Sanctuary for the official Wildlife Department game drives there at morning and evening. Jungle Hut also gives guided treks up into the montane forest between the Mysore Plateau and the upper Nilgiris. Guests have been known to meet elephants on these treks...

Jungle Hut's accommodation is basic but comfortable but the food—both Western and Indian—is superb and the tariff of Rs500 per person per day includes meals. To get to Jungle Hut, take the bus to Masinagudi from Ooty or Mysore, then share a jeep taxi from the bus stand (about Rs25).

About 3 miles from Jungle Hut is the **Monarch Safari Park**, (access as for Jungle Hut). Not a safari park at all but a collection of cottages built on stilts as protection against snakes, centred around a central, open air restaurant, at the foot of the Nilgiris, it's not cheap (around Rs750 per person per night, meals extra) but it has some unique delights. Treks into the forest bordering on Mudumalai Wildlife Sanctuary are particularly rewarding for birdlife but Monarch's real attractions are its horses. The place has two stallions, a gelding and a mare of the Rajasthani breed. Similar to Arabians these crescent-eared, fiery horses are trained to dance—a system of movements evolved by the Rajasthani cavalrymen of the late Middle Ages, to make the horse completely obedient and manoeuvreable in battle. Being so well schooled, Monarch's horses are pure joy to ride. Because the game is less shy of horses than humans, you also have a good chance of seeing wildife while riding—especially the large herds of *chital* that live in the surrounding bush. For beginners, there are some good, steady ponies on offer and all rides are accompanied by a syce. Rides cost Rs150 per hour but are worth it for the quality of horse on offer. By night it is worth talking to Mahesh, the manager, who knows the area and its wildlife well and can arrange trips into Mudumalai Wildife Sanctuary.

The closest lodge to the sanctuary itself is **Bamboo Banks**, ✆ Masinagudi 222/211, Rs700 per night for a double, meals extra. Within sight of Masinagudi town, this place offers the best accommodation in the area and also serves excellent Western and Indian food. The proprietor Mr Kothavala is a brilliant raconteur and used to be Master of the Ooty Hunt. He still breeds Rajasthani horses and, like Monarch, Bamboo Banks offers good riding. Around the cottages are heavenly gardens, laid out by Zerena, Mr Kothavala's wife. The trees and flower beds are densely colonized by birds—black-headed orioles, tree pies, bee-eaters, brilliantly coloured woodpeckers and paradise flycatchers are all common.

Trips into Mudumalai are offered morning and evening and Bamboo Banks can arrange elephant rides there even when the staff there have assured you that there is 'no vacancy'. The rooms are pleasantly old-fashioned and you are given great privacy—something that is rather at a premium in India.

Mudumalai Wildlife Sanctuary

About 4 miles beyond Masinagudi town the sanctuary begins. You can reach it by bus or by taxi or hired jeep from the town and there is basic dormitory accommodation for about Rs100 per night. Trips into the forest—mostly teak—are offered at 7.30am and 5pm in Wildlife Department minibuses and trucks. This costs about Rs35 per person but limits your chances of good game viewing, as the vehicles stick to the same routes and make a lot of noise. However, during the dry season from February to August, large herds of elephant appear in the sanctuary and these will approach quite close. At any time of year you should see *gaur*, *chital* and *langurs* and giant squirrels in the tree-tops. If you are very lucky, you may see tiger or leopard, both of which are well represented here but they tend to stick to the core area of the reserve, where no tourists are allowed.

At the southern end of the sanctuary is an **elephant training camp**, where Rs50 elephant rides are offered on a short trail into the forest at the same time as the vehicle rides. These are very hard to get onto, however and the game viewing is limited as the trail stays close to the camp. You are better advised to visit in the evening when you can watch the inmates being fed and the trained youngsters doing *puja* at a small temple attached to the camp.

Every Wednesday at about 5.30pm, the elephant handlers put on an hour-long show for the tourists (Rs25) which includes an elephant football match and various acrobatic displays. While the show is going on, look out on the left for a big male wild boar who takes advantage of the elephant show to come and forage around the empty stalls. Sometimes he brings his family with him. They root about happily while the show is going on, then run off into the forest with alarmed squeals when the crowd disperses and wanders over to the elephant stalls

A rare sighting in Mudumalai

to pat the giant performers. If you have a good lens, the wild boar visit during the show offers an excellent chance for a bit of wildlife photography.

Mudumalai is about as far north as it is possible to go in the mountain and wildlife area of Tamil Nadu. A few miles on from the sanctuary's office, you cross into the state of Karnataka at Bandipur, another great protected wilderness.

Yercaud and the Shevaroy Hills

An increasing number of travellers are visiting this quiet, little-known hill station and its narrow range of mountains, the Shevaroys, which lie to the east of the main Western Ghat chain and connect them with the drier Eastern Ghats that stretch from northeast Tamil Nadu up into Andhra Pradesh and Orissa.

Yercaud is much smaller than both Ooty and Kodaikanal and therefore lacks their rather over-whelming tourist facilities. This makes it a pleasant place to be, as long as you avoid the crowded bazaar and bus stand at the centre of Hospital Road, the main drag. It can be reached by bus (1–2 hours) from the plains town of **Salem**, a textile weaving centre. Yercaud may be a scruffy little place but it has access to beautiful walking through citrus groves and forests and trekking into some little-known tribal areas.

The Town

About 1½ miles from the bus stand is a viewpoint called **Lady's Seat**, which overlooks the vast Tamil Nadu Plain and another mile from here is a small artificial lake, with wooded gardens and boats for hire. From here begin a whole series of walks. Pick up a local map from the tourist office. Try the 2 mile hike out to the **Kiliyur Falls**, a 300 foot waterfall that plunges through a wild, forested valley, into the tamer citrus groves of the lower hills. The 3½ mile walk up to **Cauvery Peak** is also worth doing but it's a stiff climb and takes all day there and back.

Also just out of town on the Shevaroy Temple road is the bat-infested **Bear's Cave**, which you can scramble inside and the **Horticultural Research Station**, which has a nursery of the Shevaroy Hills' many unique plant species. It is worth talking to the botanists who work here for more detailed information on **trekking** out into the wilder Shevaroys and the possibilities of access to **tribal villages** in the forests.

If you arrive in April or May, try to join the crowds travelling on foot to the annual Shiva festival at the **Shevaroyan Temple** 2 miles from town, which sits atop the small mountain of the Bear's Cave (*see* above) and attracts tribals from all over the range.

Getting Around
by bus

Services run up the mountain to Yercaud from Salem's bus stand on Omalur Road every 40 minutes. The journey takes between 1 and 2 hours. Salem is about 100 miles east of Coimbatore and 200 miles southwest of Madras. Bus services run to and from both cities about 4 times per day.

by train

You can reach Salem by train, then take a bus up to Yercaud. Daily trains go to Madras (6 hours), Coimbatore (3–4 hours) and Cochin (6–7 hours). The train station is near the bus stand on Omalur Road.

Tourist Information

The **tourist office** is on Rajaram Nagar, ✆ 66449, the **post office** is on Main Road and **foreign exchange** can be found at the **Canara Bank** and the **State Bank of India**, both on Main Road.

Where to Stay

Yercaud ✆ (04281–)

Yercaud doesn't have the luxurious top-range hotels available in Ooty or Kodaikanal. The best place to stay is the moderately priced **Shevaroys Hotel** on the Hospital Road near the lake, ✆ 288. Clean, comfortable singles and double cost around Rs275 and Rs320 respectively. Similarly priced is the state-run **Hotel Tamil Nadu**, ✆ 273.

There are a few cheap hotels too. Near the bus stand, the **Select Lodge**, ✆ 296 and the **Township Rest House**, ✆ 234, offer reasonably clean, basic rooms for under Rs100.

Salem ✆ (0427–)

If you arrive in Salem late and have to stay the night before going up to Yercaud, try the moderately priced **National Hotel** on Omalur Road near the bus stand and train station, ✆ 54100. The National has good, clean doubles and singles or self-contained cottages at about Rs300–700 per room per night. In the inexpensive range are the **Woodlands** on Five Roads (about 2 miles by auto-rickshaw from the town centre), ✆ 7272, the **Apsara** on Car Street in the centre of town, ✆ 63075, and which has foriegn exchange facilities and the **Gokulam** on Mayyanur Road, ✆ 7071. Unfortunately the cheap category is confined to the bug-ridden guest lodges on Omalur Road by the bus stand.

Hyderabad's Charminar Arch

Andhra Pradesh

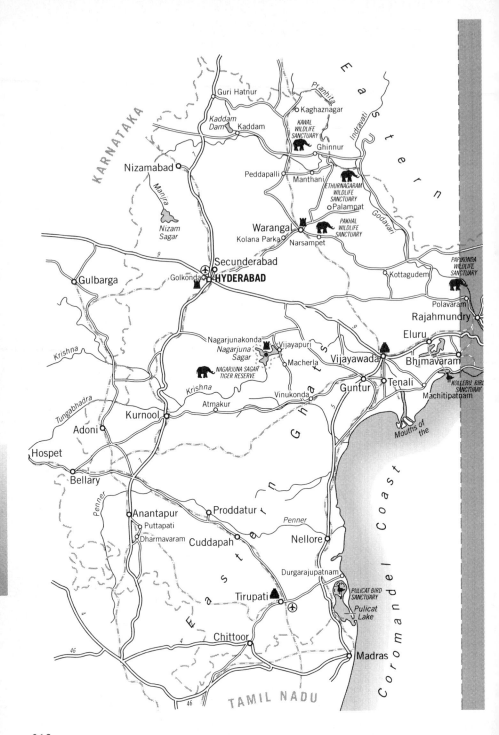

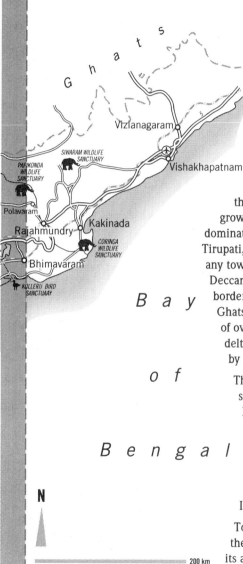

*I dreamed of
legendary kingdoms
guarded by hooded
cobras.*

Gita Mehta, *A River Sutra*

At the crossroads of southern and central India, this large Telegu-speaking state occupies a territory a little bigger than France, with a population of 66 million. From the arid Deccan Plateau in the centre and west, the land falls southward to a greener, rice-growing plain fed by large rivers and dominated by ancient temple towns, such as Tirupati, which claims to see the most pilgrims of any town in the south. At the far east of the Deccan Plateau and along the state's northern border run the forested ranges of the Eastern Ghats. At the eastern border is a long coastline of over 750 miles, broken by the great river deltas of Krishna and Godavari and battered by summer cyclones.

The state's main sights are historical. Be sure to visit the ruined cities of Nagarjunakonda, 1st–4th century, centre of an ancient Hindo-Buddhist empire; Warangal, early medieval capital of the Hindu Kakatiyas; and 16th-century Golconda, stronghold of the Muslim Qu'tb Shahs, who ruled Andhra until Independence in 1947.

Today, few travellers venture further than the state capital Hyderabad, which despite its atmospheric medieval centre, has become a hellhole with terrible overcrowding and raw construction sites. Consequently, these travellers tend to flee back to the other south

319

Indian states, without ever exploring the superb ruined cities of the deeply rural countryside, or the many wildlife sanctuaries of the mountains and river deltas, some of which have great possibilites for trekking. Andhra has India's largest Project Tiger Reserve, surrounding the ruins at Nagarjunakonda, a mere 100 miles southeast of Hyderabad at Nagarjunasagar; and the state has both central and south Indian wildlife, with wolf, the giant *nilgai* antelope and Indian gazelle among the forest mammals, saltwater crocodiles in the deltas, and rare birdlife such as the great Indian bustard on the plains.

The Plains of Andhra Pradesh

The road runs straight through near desert. The rare villages we pass through are composed largely of grey stone huts built of slabs prised from sedimentary outcroppings. There is little topsoil, but no shortage of rock. In the Muslim villages, the mosque is merely a wall facing Mecca.

Robin Brown, *Deccan Tamasha*

Central and western Andhra are part of the great Deccan Plateau—a seemingly endless rolling downland of bare brown hills, lone trees, poor villages often overlooked by abandoned Mughal fortresses and ancient Hindu temples. Occasionally the landscape is incised by great rivers, such as the Krishna and the Tungabhadra, their banks greened by irrigated fields and tall mango trees, but in general this rural hinterland is dry, dusty and poor.

The peasant population is supported by its incredible fertility: the rains come once a year, in June, after which the Deccan glows green and the fields are feverish with activity. However, once the harvest is in, the land returns to its parched state, and the inhabitants patiently wait for the next rains, eking out the produce of the previous harvest.

Occasionally the rains fail, causing huge famines and prompting a drift of rural families to the cities. Andhra's plains have only two real urban areas: Hyderabad and its satellite Secunderabad, which have grown out of all proportion, springing from the dry Deccan Plateau, their teeming crowds and pollution contrasting abruptly with the silent spaces of the surrounding countryside.

The southern end of Andhra's plains present a different picture. Here, the lower-lying country is better watered than the Deccan Plateau. A rice- and sugar cane-growing countryside, it is more populated, wooded and prosperous than the north. Great temple towns similar to those of Tamil Nadu have flourished on the local wealth since the 7th century. The biggest of these is the **Sri Venkatesvara temple** near Tirupati, which probably attracts more pilgrims than any other in the south.

Brahmins wearing the sacred thread

We emerged every morning from a house that in many ways was like a citadel. It had high white walls, courtyards that were never without flowers and stone terraces above which the sky stretched. The outside always beckoned.

Anees Jung, *India Unveiled*

Now capital of Andhra Pradesh, Hyderabad is a once-beautiful inland city set in a landscape of randomly strewn boulders the size of houses and bordered by great calm lakes, and is itself sometimes known as 'The Lake'. Now something of a boom-town, with the dust of a thousand construction sites blowing into the eyes of its inhabitants, it was founded in the late-16th century by the Qu'tb Shahi dynasty, Muslim rulers famed for their magnificent monuments and mosques. The city was laid out in 1591 by Mohammed Quli when Golconda, the fortress city from which the Muslim rulers had governed their Hindu subjects since 1512, fell prey to epidemics of plague and cholera, caused by poor water supplies.

Hyderabad was planned out on the grid system, and comprised two broad intersecting streets with the famous central Charminar Arch (described as the outstanding architectural monument of the Qu'tb Shahi period) at the crossing, and space for some 14,000 shops, schools, mosques and baths.

Successful trading in diamonds, pearls, printed fabrics and steel rapidly made Hyderabad one of the richest cities in India. Then, in 1650, the Mughal emperor Aurangzeb captured Golconda, and Hyderabad's short period of prosperity came to an abrupt end. Its importance as an administrative and financial centre declined, and the city fell into partial ruin. In the 18th century, with the disintegration of the Mughal empire, the Nizam (former Mughal Viceroy) of Golconda seized power and moved his court to nearby Hyderabad in 1763. Commerce and construction rapidly resumed, and the city once more became a major business concern. The Nizams soon became some of the wealthiest individuals in the world, a position they maintained up to, and for a decade beyond, Independence in 1947.

Today, while Hyderabad and its neighbouring city of Secunderabad comprise the fastest-growing city in Asia (though Bangalore also claims this distinction), it has yet to find itself as a tourist centre. The obvious attractions of its beautiful sights, its huge botanical gardens, good shopping (textiles and jewellery are the best buys here), and unique cuisine are largely offset by its remote location, slightly aggressive atmosphere, and its intense overcrowding and poverty. The beggars here are far more high-profile than in other cities in the south. You can feel the ancient Hindu/Muslim tension crackle over the chugging traffic and incessant judderings of jackhammers from the myriad of building sites.

But expect big changes in the near future. Hyderabad is rapidly equipping itself with tourist facilities, luxury hotels, better transport, shopping complexes, even a Rs100 *crore* Disneyland project around the Hussain Sagar lake. It is now patiently awaiting the expected boom.

Climate and When to Go

Situated 2000 feet above sea level, Hyderabad is clement through much of the year. The coolest (best) time to visit is from **October to February**. But from **March**

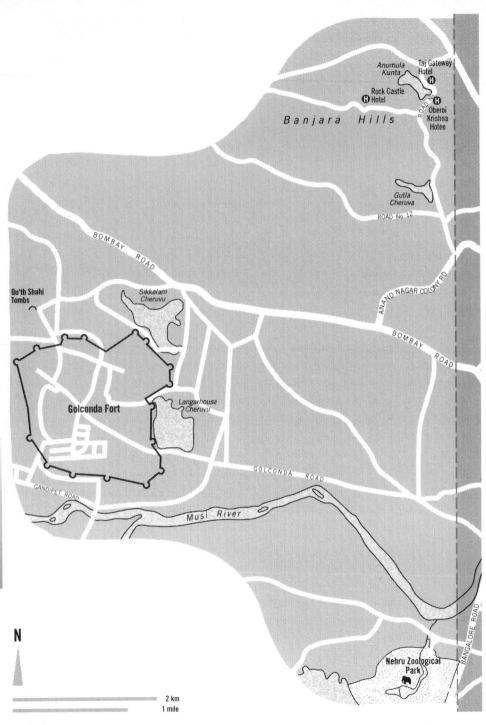

Taj Gateway
Hotel
Anumula
Kunta

Rock Castle
Hotel

B a n j a r a   H i l l s

Oberoi
Krishna
Hotel

*Gutla
Cheruva*

ROAD No. 12

B O M B A Y   R O A D

Qu'tb Shahi
Tombs

*Sikkalam
Cheruvu*

ANAND NAGAR COLONY RD

B O M B A Y   R O A D

Golconda Fort

*Langarhouse
Cheruvu*

GOLCONDA   ROAD

GANDIPET ROAD

Musi River

BANGALORE   ROAD

Nehru Zoological
Park

N

2 km
1 mile

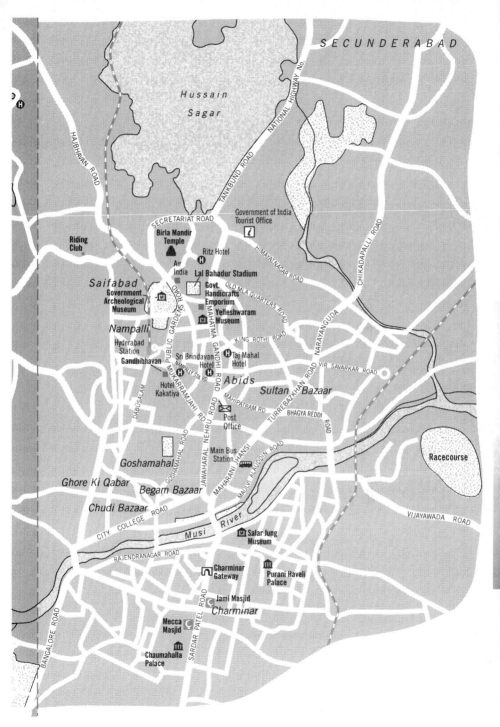

SECUNDERABAD

Hussain
Sagar

NATIONAL HIGHWAY NO.

HAIBHAVAN ROAD

TANKBUND ROAD

CHIKADAPALLI ROAD

SECRETARIAT ROAD

Government of India
Tourist Office

Birla Mandir
Temple

Riding
Club

Ritz Hotel

HIMAYATNAGAR ROAD

Air
India

Lal Bahadur Stadium

Saifabad

Govt.
Handicrafts
Emporium

OLD MLA QUARTERS ROAD

Government
Archeological
Museum

Yelleshwaram
Museum

PUBLIC GARDENS ROAD

MAHATMA GANDHI

Nampalli

KING ROTHI ROAD

NARAYANGUDA

Hyderabad
Station

Gandhibhavan

Sri Brindavan
Hotel

NAMPALLY STA. RD.

Taj Mahal
Hotel

VIR SAVARKAR ROAD

Abids

MUKARRAMJAHI RD.

Hotel
Kakatiya

Sultan Bazaar

DABUSALAM

JAWAHARAL NEHRU ROAD

MAHIPATRAM RD.

TURREBAZKHAN ROAD

BHAGYA REDDI ROAD

Post
Office

Main Bus
Station

GOSHAMAHAL ROAD

MAHARANI JHANSI ROAD

MAULV ALAUDDIN ROAD

Racecourse

Goshamahal

Ghore Ki Qabar

Begam Bazaar

Chudi Bazaar

CITY COLLEGE ROAD

River

Musi

VIJAYAWADA ROAD

RAJENDRANAGAR ROAD

Safar Jung
Museum

BANGALORE ROAD

Charminar
Gateway

Purani Haveli
Palace

Jami Masjid

SARDAR PATEL ROAD

Charminar

Mecca
Masjid

Chaumahalla
Palace

onwards you should avoid the place—it is not so much the actual heat as the very dry air that sets the pavements ablaze and has visitors reaching for the water bottle.

Getting There

by air

Indian Airlines offers daily flights between Hyderabad and Bangalore, Bombay, Calcutta, Delhi and Madras; less frequent connections with Bhubaneshwar, Nagpur, Trivandrum and Visakhapatnam. **Vayudoot** connects Hyderabad with Pune. Hyderabad's airport is some 6 miles from the city centre; a Rs40 auto-rickshaw ride *if* you persuade your driver to set his meter to zero before setting off!

by train

Trains to and from the south use **Hyderabad Station** while those from the north, the west and east use **Secunderabad Station**. This is where you will arrive if you come from Madras, 319 miles away. For southern-bound trains to Bangalore (the 3pm *Hyderabad–Bangalore Express*, arriving at 7.30am, is best) you can board at Hyderabad rail station in Abids area. It is essential to book seats in advance for all long journeys.

by bus

From Hyderabad's central bus depot, Gowliguda Road, there's one state bus daily to Madras (440 miles; 15 hours) and to Bombay (462 miles; 17 hours); plus 3–4 buses daily to Bangalore (350 miles). The above destinations, together with places like Aurangabad (375 miles) and Hospet, are also handled by private bus companies. You can, and should, pre-book seats.

Getting Around

 Hyderabad has overcrowded city buses, crazed auto-rickshaws which stop for absolutely nothing (Rs2.50 per mile), and a few maniacal taxis (Rs5 per mile, metered). The traffic is suicidal. In the city centre, you need nerves of steel to get around on foot. 'Daydreaming is dangerous', cautions one traffic sign. For worry-free travel, use the tourist taxi service offered by A.P. Travel and Tourism Dev. Corp., Gagan Vihar, Mukhram Jahi Road, © 557531, 556303, or your hotel. For out-of-town trips, cycling is pleasurable and cycles can be hired for Rs10–15 per day from several places; your hotel can advise). If biking around in town, make sure you have some decent insurance. City conducted tours are far too hurried, but they are a useful introduction and orientation. Then you should tour Hyderabad independently, allowing a minimum of 2 days for sightseeing and shopping. The traffic in the old city is often chaotic, and downright dangerous; ride wherever possible, and avoid walking across main roads. If you need a badge-carrying guide, contact A.P. Dept of Tourism, Gagan Vihar, 5th Floor, M.G. Road, © 557531 (you can also book them from the tourist information desks at Hyderabad and Secunderabad railway stations).

Tourist Information

The **Andhra Pradesh (A.P.) Tourist Office**, 1st floor, Gagan Vihar, M.G. Road, © 557531, is extremely helpful and well organized. Its city sightseeing tours run from 8am to 6pm daily, and cost about Rs60.

Outside the big hotels, the **State Bank of India** on Bank Street, or the main bank branches on M.G. Road above Abid Circle all exchange traveller's cheques and hard currency. **Thomas Cook** is out in Saifabad, ✆ 222 689.

The **post office** is on the south side of Abid Circle.

Reliable **travel agents** are M.N. Tours and Travels, 6-3-855, 10/A Sodat Mansil, Ameerpet, Hyderabad 500016, ✆ 213223, Sita World Travels, Hyderguda and Chapel Road, ✆ 233638/235549, and Sheriff Travels, Basheer Bagh, ✆ 237914.

Indian Airlines, ✆ 236902 and **Air India**, ✆ 232858, are both in Saifabad near the Secretariat building. **Vayudoot** is located on the 2nd floor, Samrat Complex, Saifabad, ✆ 234717/842855.

The City

The sides of the road are thick with crowds that take up all but the very centre, through which thrust and weave trucks and buses and all sorts of wheeled vehicles, right down to bicycles and a legless beggar, paddling a platform mounted on squeaky roller bearings.

Robin Brown, *Deccan Tamasha*

Hyderabad is effectively two cities in one, though the new city of Secunderabad to the north is of minimal tourist interest. All the sights, the hotels, the action and the bazaars are concentrated in the Abids area of Hyderabad town, directly south of Hussain Sagar, and north of the Musi River.

The city itself is a busy, bustling and sprawling complex where new multi-storeyed buildings and wide modern streets contrast strongly with the narrow medieval lanes and backstreets of the old town around the Charminar arch, and where the smoke of modern industrial factories meets the dust of busy roadside cottage workers, turning out some of India's finest handmade crafts.

Old City Tour

by auto-rickshaw/taxi, 4–6 hours

Golconda–Mecca Masjid–Charminar–Salar Jung Museum–
Birla Mandir Temple–Birla Planetarium

Set out for **Golconda Fort** early in the morning before the heat of the day. It lies 7 miles west of Hyderabad, and takes about 40 minutes by rickshaw (Rs60–70 return, plus a waiting charge of Rs10 per hour while you sightsee). Going by taxi takes slightly less time but doubles the cost. The fort lies in a very dry, exposed situation, so wear a hat/scarf and long-sleeved shirts. There are about a dozen good English-speaking guides at the fort entrance. It's not a bad idea to establish their fee in writing before you set out; you can pay them more if they're worth it, which they usually are. The inner fort of Golconda is 16 miles around, and you can tour its various palaces, audience rooms, baths, armoury and mosques comfortably in 1½ hours. If you wish to wander round on your own, buy the good little Golconda guide book with map, printed by Commercial Book Depot, Charminar, and available in many Hyderabad bookshops.

Golconda Fort

Golconda is the biggest fort in south India. Constructed from solid limestone, it took several thousand labourers, working day and night, 62 years to build. Founded in the 13th century by the Kakatiyas of Warangal, it was originally just a small hilltop fort with mud walls. Its name derived from the words *golla* meaning 'shepherd' and *konda* meaning 'hill'. In 1512 it became the capital of the Persian Qu'tb Shahi kings, who expanded the original structure into a massive fort with battlements and crenellated walls of granite some 3 miles in circumference. The 8 sets of gates were studded with iron spikes as protection against war elephants, and it boasted its own freshwater supply.

Like so many Indian forts, Golconda finally fell to treachery rather than to arms, a treacherous Qu'tb Shahi general letting the Mughal emperor Aurangzeb in the front ('victory') gate in 1687 following an 8-month siege. Thereafter the legendary fort and its famous diamond market went into decline, and power passed to the new capital of Hyderabad.

Though partly in ruins today, this monumental fortress, erected on a picturesque granite hill some 400 feet (123 metres) high and surrounded by three tiers of loopholed and battlemented ramparts, remains the major tourist attraction of the Hyderabad area. Of its eight original gates, four are still in use. The fort also has 87 semi-circular bastions, each 36 feet (15.4 metres) high, and each built of huge blocks of masonry weighing several tons apiece.

Start your tour at the **Grand Portico** (entry gate). Here you'll come across its unique system of acoustics, one of the fortress's most interesting features. A clapping of hands in the centre porch can be heard at the fort's highest point, the Bala Hissar, 380 steep steps above. This device was contrived, it is believed, to convey any message regarding visitors to the topmost guards. Behind this echo chamber is a purple-blossomed tree, popular with local people who use its hard-wood bark for cleaning their teeth.

Your guide will take you up into the fort via the 'common passage', leading past the armoury on your left; the mortuary bath where dead royals had a ceremonial dip before being buried, to your right; and the bodyguard barracks, with adjoining two-storeyed building used by the court ministers Akkanna and Madanna, also to your left. An ascent of 360 steps now begins, leading up to the **Bara Dar** (General Assembly Hall). On the ascent you'll see various deep wells, water reservoirs and watering canals.

Halfway up, you reach the **Ramdas Kotha**, an old storehouse which became the 12-year prison of Abdul Hasan Tanah Shah's chief cashier, Ramdas. He was interred for dipping into official revenue to renovate a nearby temple. It's a dark, gloomy place, full of the handmade deities (Ram, Lakshman, Hanuman) and faded carvings/paintings of animals and plants which the bored Ramdas made to fill in his time.

Past the jail, and just above the **Barood Kotha** (gunpowder store), there's a charming little Hindu temple cut into a large natural boulder the shape of a Nandi bull. A little further up is the simple, elegant **Mosque** of the royal family, built by the third king of the dynasty, Ibrahim Quli Qu'tb Shah in 1550. In those days, the king prayed in the mosque and his Hindu chief minister in the small rock-cut temple below; it was an age of practical religious tolerance. From the eastern side of the mosque, there's a beautiful view down over Golconda and across to Hyderabad city. From the northern side, you can see the Qu'tb Shahi Tombs, fully reflecting the glory and pomp of the rich sultans of Golconda, whose last resting-place these are.

Finally, you'll reach the **Baradari** or Durbar Hall at the summit of Golconda. This is a 12-arched, three-storey pavilion, with a top terrace giving panoramic views of the surrounding fort, and an open-air stone throne called Shah Nashin. Here, the Qu'tb kings used to sit out on the open terraces, or hold meetings with the royal family or court ministers. The Durbar Hall also has a 5 mile long secret underground passage which was used in times of emergency or danger. It is here, from the topmost point of the fort, that your guide will show the effectiveness of the 'clapping' technique, signalling down to the entrance gate for a demonstration.

You'll probably return down via the **King's Way**, which leads to the royal palaces and harem area. In olden days, the king was transported down this path by *palanquin*. You won't be, but the descent on foot is a pleasant one. On the way, look out for the fort's unique water-supply system. Huge tanks filled with water diverted from the Banjara hills 4 miles away, and ingeniously raised to the fort by a system of laminated clay pipes and Persian wheels, which moved it all the way up to the gardens, waterfalls and hanging gardens near the fort's summit.

Below, in the beautiful **Rani (Zanana) Mahals**, the first thing you're likely to be shown are the royal bathrooms. Only then will your guide point out the other attractions of the site. This series of crumbling, complex ruins used to be full of painted, jewelled palaces, arcades, Turkish baths, flower gardens and bubbling fountains. Little remains either of the lovely harem palaces nearby, though the royal kitchen, on the site of the old Camel Stable, is still in good condition. While here, you may well smell a strong scent not unlike buttered popcorn, emanating from the darker recesses. Follow it, and the smell is reinforced by a high chittering sound. Go further and you find yourself standing under one of the largest colonies of bats in southern India. The popcorn smell is in fact their guano. Squadrons of the nervous, flapping creatures fly about continuously amid the din. For fun (if you have a flash on your camera), go as far into the darkness as your creeping skin will allow, point your camera roofwards and take a couple of shots. You'll be surprised at how many bats are illuminated in the prints when you finally get the prints back. Return via the armoury to the entry gate.

The Qu'tb Shahi Tombs

The grand domes of the Qu'tb Shahi tombs (*open daily 9–4.30 except Fridays, camera fee extra*) rise about a mile to the north of Golconda fort. To reach them, walk through the Banjara gate and head across the great maidan to where the ten tombs rise from their surrounding formal garden. Richly ornamented with religious inscriptions and the remains of mosaics of glazed tiles, the tombs were restored and the present gardens planted at the turn of the century. The monarchs that lie here are: Sultan Quli Qu'tb Shah, who murdered his own father and founded the dynasty (1518–43), Jamshid Quli Qu'tb Shah (1543–50), Ibrahim Qu'tb Shah (1550–80), Muhammed Quli Qu'tb Shah, founder of Hyderabad, (1581–1612), Muhammed Qu'tb Shah (1612–26), Abdullah Qu'tb Shah (1626–72) and Abdul Hasan Tana Qu'tb Shah (1672–87). The Princess Kulsum Begum (d. 1608), Princess Hayat Baksh Begum (d. 1677) and Pammati, favourite mistress of Muhammed Qu'tb Shah (d. 1664) also have tombs here.

Golconda Town

Before returning to Hyderabad, take some time to explore the old town of Golconda, situated within the outer fort walls. In times past, this small bazaar town was a splendid fortress city, famed for its cutting, polishing and marketing of diamonds. The unique *Koh-i-noor* gem, now part of the British crown jewels, is said to have come from here. Today, the town is small, yet well-populated, and there are lots of cheap knick-knacks and trinkets being sold.

Old Hyderabad, the Charminar and the Mecca Masjid

From Golconda, return to Hyderabad city centre for the impressive Mecca Masjid. This huge white mosque is the finest in south India, and the seventh largest in the world. Begun in 1614 by Mohammed Quli Qu'tb Shah, it was completed in 1687 by Aurangzeb, the Mughal invader. It derives its name from the few bricks brought from Mecca (and the stone apparently brought from Mohammed's birthplace) which are embedded in its walls.

Entering the mosque, beware of unsolicited guides. Most are difficult to understand but if you take one on, he should charge about Rs5–10. Just inside the wide courtyard you'll see a long enclosure full of small marble tombs to your left. This is where many of Hyderabad's wealthy Nizams are interred. The mosque itself is a marvellous structure. Its huge entrance façade is built of a single block of stone, richly inscribed with sayings from the Koran. Inside are Portuguese chandeliers, an antique French clock, and inlaid marble flooring. This mosque is the principal place of Muslim worship in the city, and every Friday up to 50,000 people gather for prayers. The huge 70 feet (21.5 metre) high interior can accommodate 3000 worshippers, the grounds a further 7000. On important religious days and festivals even the streets outside are filled with kneeling devotees.

Just across the road from the mosque you'll find the **Charminar** (Four Tower Arch) (*open daily 9–4.30; illuminated 7–9pm*), Hyderabad's definitive landmark. This imposing arch, deriving its name from its four 180 feet high slender minarets, was built in 1591 by Mohammed Quli Qu'tb Shah, reputedly to commemorate the end of a plague epidemic. It stands a watchful guardian over the old city, serenely overlooking the surrounding chaos of anarchic traffic and crowded thoroughfares. A climb of 149 steps up a winding staircase brings you out near the top of the arch, at the tiny second-floor mosque. The high terraced balconies, notable for their profuse stucco decorations, balustrades and noble arches, offer superb bird's-eye views over the heart of Hyderabad city—busy, bustling scenes of battling rickshaws, thronging pavements, teeming mosques, and colourful bazaars of silversmiths, bangle makers, embroidery shops, perfume merchants and antique dealers.

Buffalo dairy

The Salar Jung Museum

Continuing on by rickshaw or taxi, visit the Salar Jung Museum (*open daily 10–5 except Friday; free guide service; photographs not allowed*) on the south bank of the Musi River, whose green, cultivated banks make a pleasant, if incongruous relief from Hyderabad's grim urban feel.

The rather ugly museum building houses the superb private collections of three Nawabs Salar Jung, successive *wazirs* or prime ministers of the Nizam of Hyderabad. Salar Jung III died in 1949 without an heir, and the collection was handed over to the Government of India in 1956. The 35,000 exhibits, gathered from all over the world, now fill 35 large rooms. The ornate entrance hall, with its beautiful chandeliers, leads into the ground-floor collection of textiles, Mughal glass, ivory, miniatures and a fascinating bell clock. On the first floor are Kashmir, Burmese, Chinese, Japanese and Western art, as well as a good selection of bronzes. The prize pieces of the museum are the ivory chairs and the turban of Tipu Sultan, and the swords and daggers of the Mughal emperors. Also of special interest are the small collection of Indian miniature paintings and the fine exhibition of jade. The Japanese ivory sculptures in the ivory gallery are humourous and exquisite—especially the miniature ones of demons and sages.

However, the fine art and textiles are overshadowed by the high kitsch of most of the other exhibits. Indian rulers were known as much for their great love of expensive tack as for quality stuff, and the museum has no shortage of expensive, tasteless, but fascinating bric-à-brac. Highlights are the plaster of Paris tableau of Snow White and the Seven Dwarfs, a huge doll's house complete with a girl wearing a negligé posing provocatively on one of the beds, the fake suits of European armour, the hundreds of lead soldiers and toy animals and a half-dozen terrible, sentimental Classical-style alabaster sculptures of large-breasted women and little girls.

If you still have the energy, finish off with a sunset visit to **Birla Mandir Temple** (*open Mon–Fri, 4–9pm, weekends, 7–11am and 3–9pm*). Set atop a rocky hill overlooking the southern end of Hussain Sagar, this modern Hindu temple, constructed from pure white marble, offers memorable views over the city at sunset. Nearby is the **Birla Planetarium** (English programmes at 3.30 and 6.50pm daily, plus an extra 11.30am show at weekends), arguably the best in India with its 'Japanese Technology Sky Theatre'. Pleasantly air-conditioned, it's the perfect place to cool off after a steamy day's sightseeing.

Nehru Zoological Park

Allow a full day to visit the Nehru Zoological Park (*open daily 9–6, except Mon*), thought by many to be the best zoo in India. It lies in a huge 300 acre expanse of undulating, semi-tropical landscape, and is the home of some 1600 animals. Famous for its Lion Safari Park and for its many birds (over 240 species), its extensive grounds vary from attractive landscaped gardens to peaceful picnic bowers, from lush jungle forests to still, serene inland lakes. A Rs45 rickshaw ride from the town centre, the Nehru Zoological Park is located just outside the old city walls on the Bangalore Road, quite near to Charminar.

Visit early in the morning, when all the big cats are still fairly alert (by noon, they're comatose), and spend all day wandering around. There's enough here to justify it. Inside the entrance, you'll find a useful map. Straight ahead, there's the small toy-train track that runs right round the inner park perimeter, and the Rs1 ride is a good way of orienting yourself quickly within the large grounds.

Back at the park entrance, head left on foot. This takes you via the tiger, cheetah and camel compounds, and over to the ever-popular elephants and white rhinos. You'll note that all the animals are very well kept, and live in near-natural surroundings separated from their human visitors only by the most unobtrusive of barriers.

At the top of the park, a 20-minute walk from the entrance, you'll come to the **Lion Safari Park**. Crowded but cosy minibuses speed off in search of lions every 15 minutes or so, from 9.30am to 12.15pm, and from 2 to 4.30pm daily. When the bus finds some lions, it generally screeches to a halt for photographs, sometimes it breaks down, and the lions wander over to stare at the tourists instead.

Out of the Lion Park, strike left down the outer perimeter path to find deer, bison, gnu and monkeys. Just past the waterbuck compound, head into the centre of the park for *sambar*, crane, *nilgai*, bear, water-birds and more lions. There's a couple of snack restaurants here, and a pleasant picnic area where you can enjoy a relaxing lunch. During the hottest part of the day (1–4pm), visit the **Natural History Museum and Aquarium** (*open 9am–1pm, 2–5pm daily*), both by the entrance ticket-gate while the animals rest. Then see the **Prehistoric Animals Park** and nearby **Ancient Life Museum**, both a short walk from the entrance. Otherwise, visit the monkeys who never go to sleep.

Sports and Activities

Hyderabad has an **Amateur Rider's Club** in the Siafabad suburb (about 3 miles from the city centre on the road out to Golconda). A few years ago, the club had immediate access to the countryside, but the city has grown so rapidly that it is now completely hemmed in by buildings. However, the horses are well looked after, and if you can be content with riding in the ring, the facilities should suit. Amazingly, the horses are still hacked out on exercise (with the grooms riding one and leading one) through the thick traffic of the main Golconda road that runs past the club's entrance.

Shopping

Not for nothing is Hyderabad known as the 'City of Pearls'. In olden days, the Nizams would settle for nothing less than the best of Gulf pearls. Today, while connoisseurs are content with beads from China and Japan, Hyderabad remains the only centre for their trade in India.

At a reputable pearl dealer like **Mangatrai**, Bashir Bagh or **Mangatrai Ramkumar**, Pathergatti or the Gateway Hotel, you can pick up old pearls from the Persian Gulf (known as Basra pearls) for as little as 20 per cent of current London prices. The cost of pearls varies depending on type and shape. Both the above dealers offer rice pearls, seed pearls, round pearls and drop pearls. A medium-sized string of pearls weighs about an ounce. But don't have pearls strung and set in Hyderabad—have them done in Bombay where it is far cheaper.

If you can't afford pearls, shop around for the famous, sparkling Hyderabadi bangles, *nagans*—the main street selling them is the Chudi Bazaar, which leads west from the Charminar. Often embedded with semi-precious stones, they are made from pure lac, a resin secreted by beetles, and are extremely lustrous and durable—nip off down the side-streets and watch the artisans making them with a small coal fire to melt the resin. Prices range from Rs15–500 per pair.

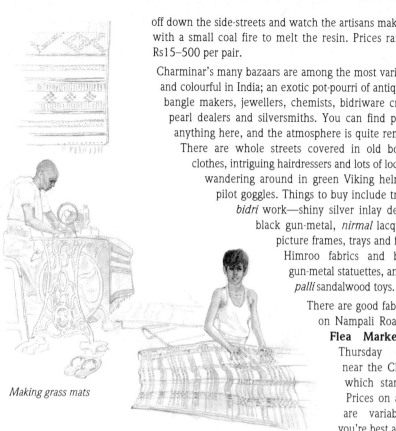

Making grass mats

Charminar's many bazaars are among the most varied, lively and colourful in India; an exotic pot-pourri of antique shops, bangle makers, jewellers, chemists, bidriware craftsmen, pearl dealers and silversmiths. You can find practically anything here, and the atmosphere is quite remarkable. There are whole streets covered in old books and clothes, intriguing hairdressers and lots of local people wandering around in green Viking helmets and pilot goggles. Things to buy include traditional *bidri* work—shiny silver inlay designs on black gun-metal, *nirmal* lacquer toys, picture frames, trays and furniture, Himroo fabrics and brocades, gun-metal statuettes, and *konda-palli* sandalwood toys.

There are good fabric shops on Nampali Road, and a **Flea Market** every Thursday morning near the Charminar which starts early. Prices on all goods are variable, and you're best advised to get a idea on what is fair at a reliable government emporium. Good ones are **Lepakshi Handicrafts Emporium** at Gun Foundry (top of Abid Road), **APCO Handloom House**, Sundar Estate (also Abids) and **Handloom House**, Mukharam Jahi Road.

There are good opportunities in Hyderabad to see traditional craft processes. The ancient process of *bidri* ware may be seen at **Mumtaz Bidri Works Coop Society**, 22-1-1042 Darush Shifa or **Yaqoob Brothers**, 995 Habeeb Nagar. To see *nirmal* ware being made, visit the factory and showroom of **Nirmal Industries**, Raj Bhavan Road; left off the main road between Panjagutta and downtown Hyderabad in Khairatabad. When at the factory, ask for directions to the nearby *Himroo* weaving centre.

bookshops

Try the **A.A. Hussain Bookshop**, Abid Road, which stocks Avion Escort's good city map/guide (Rs10). The tourist office sells M.A. Mahmood's excellent *Glimpses of Hyderabad*. *City of Legends* by Ian Austen (Viking, Penguin India 1992) is a popular history of the city. Another excellent book is *The Days of the Beloved* an oral history of life in Hyderabad under the last Nizam collected by Harriet Lynton and Mohini

Rajan; originally published by California University Press (1974), a local reprint by Orient Longman is available. The small pocket guide and map published by Sangam Books (Rs50) is locally available.

Hyderabad ✆ (0842–)

Where to Stay

In Hyderabad, you have the choice of staying either in isolated splendour up in the Banjara Hills 4 miles from the railway station, or in the seedier, but atmospheric Abids/Nampally Road area of the town centre.

luxury

The **Krishna Oberoi**, Road No.1, Banjara Hills, ✆ 222121, ✆ 223079, is set in 9 acres of beautifully landscaped gardens, with many rooms overlooking the Hussain Sagar lake. Its palatial-style architecture is perhaps over-emphasised by the presidential suites that have their own swimming pools.

The Taj's **Gateway Hotel** on Banjara Hill, ✆ 222222, ✆ 222218, just down the road from the Oberoi, has been completely renovated, has good food, and a choice of rooms overlooking the lake or Golconda fort. Most rooms have balconies. **Bhaskar Palace**, Road No.1, Banjara Hill, ✆ 226141 ✆ 222712, has all the facilities you would expect from a top-end hotel.

expensive

Excellent value (you can get a whole suite for Rs1500) is the fine old **Ritz Hotel**, ✆ 233571. Built as a summer residence for one of the younger sons of the last Nizam but one, it sits in its own gated enclave at the far end of Hill Fort Road, just north of the Lal Bahadur Stadium. It is an ex-palace with Raj-style charm, lovely views, attentive service, tennis courts and a massive pool. Ask for a room with individually controlled air-conditioning. A little more expensive are the **Quality Inn Green Park**, 7-1-26 Ameerpet, ✆ 224455, and the **Holiday Inn Krishna**, ✆ 223 467, ✆ 222684 have well-maintained rooms, but are a little bland. Both are up in the Banjani Hills, north of the Ritz.

moderate

The **Rock Castle**, on Road No.6, Banjara Hills, ✆ 33541, is a small family hotel with pleasant rooms and cottages (some air-conditioned) set in a large garden. The **Sampurna International**, ✆ 40165, on Mukranjahi Road is more central and has two restaurants, a good travel desk and most rooms are air-conditioned. **Hotel Jaya International**, Nehru Road, Abids, ✆ 232929, is very central, as is the **Hotel Taj Mahal**, King Kothi Road, ✆ 237988—an old favourite with a rooftop restaurant, but recent travellers report slovenly service and ill-kept rooms.

inexpensive

Head for the **Hotel Kakatiya**, ✆ 590200, ✆ 515713, on Nampally Station Road, just 5 minutes' walk eastwards from the railway station. More basic, but clean and well-run is the **Amakrishna**, ✆ 201551, down a lane almost opposite the Kakatiya and next to the Kamat. Further up towards Abid Circle is the slightly overpriced **Sri Brindavan Hotel**, ✆ 203970 with large, breezy singles and doubles.

The **Hotel Imperial**, ✆ 202220/202436, offers a good deal with basic but airy rooms, on Nampally Station Road. Closer to the station are a cluster of cheap lodges: the **Hotel Sri Durga**, ✆ 202227/202286—still half under construction but with quite nice rooms; the **Royal Lodge**—opposite the Sri Durga—a well-run place but with no frills. Next door, and offering similar basic fare is the **Gee Lodge**.

Eating Out

Hyderabad does fine southern Indian cuisine: *chat*, a delicious series of savoury/sweet hot snacks, tray-meal *thalis*, pancake-like *dosas*, rice and *dal idlis*, and flour-wafer *pappadams*. But the speciality dishes are *baghara baigan* (small eggplants stuffed with spices, cooked in tamarind juice and sesame oil) and *mirchi ka salan* (stuffed green chillies). Both are a bit hot for Western palates, so you may care to try the city's famous *birianis* or *tikka kababs* instead. Particularly recommended is *haleem*, a mildly spiced mutton and wheat preparation, followed by *khobani* (dried apricots cooked to a purée). Finish off with a pot of good rich south Indian coffee.

The city centre has a rich culinary heritage, and the **Dakhni** in the Gateway hotel has an excellent menu with meals from Rs300 per head. The menu at the Oberoi's **Firdaus** restaurant includes dishes culled from the personal collection of the city's most renowned gourmet, Salar Jung. Eat well à la carte at around Rs350–400 per head, or sample the good-value Rs200 lunchtime buffet served between 12.30 and 3pm.

Cheaper is the Gateway's **Kabab-E-Bahar** is a lake-side open-air barbecue open each evening. The **Abhiruchi** on Sarojini Devi Road serves non-vegetarian Andhra food and a meal costs from Rs100 per person.

In town, two good restaurants are **Palace Height**, 8th floor, Triveni Building, Abid Road, a stylish place, with great continental, Mughlai and Chinese cuisine at around Rs100 per head; and **Peacock Restaurant**, Basheer Bagh (similar quality, less expensive).

In the Abids area, you'll find cheap and tasty vegetarian fare at Emerald Hotel's **Sapphire Restaurant**, Royal Hotel's **Laxmi Restaurant**, and **Annapurna Hotel**'s air-conditioned restaurant. The Annapurna is particularly well known for its ice cream.

For good cheap eating try the **Brijvasi Chat Bhandar**, a strange little place down an alley (signposted) called Chirag Ali Lane, off M.G. Road a few blocks north of Abid Circle. The *chat* here is really good, and you can follow it up with soft ice cream, all for under Rs50. Below this price range are the usual south Indian *thali* houses, found on every street. Try the one at the Sri Brindhavan on Nampally Station Road (Abids end).

Entertainment and Nightlife

Dance, drama and musical concerts featuring both Indian and foreign performers take place nightly at **Rabindra Bharathi**, a beautiful air-conditioned auditorium. Good painting and sculpture exhibitions are held at the **A.P. Lalit Kala Academy**, Kala Bhavan, Saifabad, ✆ 34794. Full details of current events are given in the *Deccan Chronicle* newspaper.

As for **nightlife**, there isn't any. Andhra Pradesh is a 'dry' state and beer can only be bought by foreigners at big hotels, upon the filling-out of a tedious 'alcohol licence' form. The banning of alcohol in this Muslim-influenced state was only implemented in 1995. Since then the use of marijuana in Hyderabad has apparently increased dramatically.

Around Hyderabad

If you are stuck in Hyderabad for a few days, take a train 30 miles to the small rural station of Ramachandrpuram, and then a bus or taxi out to the little village of Sangareddy, 5 miles further on. This is a half-wild/half rural section of the Deccan, now protected by the **Manjira Wildlife Sanctuary**. A low lying marsh set between dry hills, Manjira was founded to protect an assortment of wildfowl, from herons, ducks, various raptors and kingfishers to associated woodland birds such as tree pies and paradise flycatchers. Crocodiles sun themselves on the marshy banks, and there are wild pig and deer in the surrounding woods. Manjira has a rest-house which you should book through A.P. Tourism in Hyderabad, ✆ 557 531.

If you are prepared to travel further into the Deccan, **Rollapadu Wildlife Sanctuary**, about 160 miles from Hyderabad, protects one of the few remaining nesting places of the endangered great Indian bustard, a huge, ground-nesting game bird that resembles something between a crane and a turkey. Although the reserve itself is only 3 square miles in size, the rolling grasslands surrounding Rollapadu harbour wolf, jackal and some small blackbuck herds. To reach Rollapadu, take the train south from Hyderabad to Kurnool. From there you have to travel the remaining 30 miles by bus or taxi. The reserve has a small hut, but backpackers will find it easier to camp. Take your own food and a stove, as fires would soon destroy the sanctuary and the ground-nesting sites that it protects.

bustard

Warangal

About 100 miles north of Hyderabad towards the mountains bordering Madhya Pradesh, the old fortified temple town of Warangal serves as a good gateway to the northern wildlife sanctuaries (*see* p.345), and is worth spending a couple of days in. Its main sight is the **fort**, 3 miles from the main town.

Getting Around
by train

Several daily services leave from Hyderabad and Secunderabad and take about 4 hours to cover 100 miles.

by bus

Services leave almost every hour from Hyderabad's main bus station. Journey time is 3–3½ hours.

The Fort

Set within three huge curtain walls (about 30 miles in circumference), Warangal's 'fort' was once a fair-sized town in its own right—so rich that it impressed Marco Polo as one of the principal cities of India. Capital of the Hindu Kakatiyas during the 12th and 13th centuries,

Warangal fell to the Mughals of Dlji in 1323, and was later taken over by the Bahmanis of Bijapur in Karnataka in the early 15th century.

As in so many of the Deccan towns, Warangal's rulers and people practised different religions from the 14th century onwards, with the Muslim rulers largely tolerating the Hindu hoi polloi and leaving their temples intact. However, Warangal fort's great **Siva Temple** was sacked and desecrated during the first ferocious onslaught of the Mughals and was never rebuilt—even though several smaller temples adjoining the site have remained in use to this day.

Make time for the **Kush Mahal**, a great audience chamber built in the 16th century, standing inside the fort's walls. Seven miles to the north of Warangal is the **Hagarkonda 1000 Pillared Temple**. Built by the Chalukyans (the dynasty that followed the Kakatiyas and were destroyed by the Mughals) in 1162, the dark granite temple is known for its impressive

Saddhu

carved elephants. A further 40-mile bus ride to **Palampet** takes you to the **Ghanpeshwaralayam** and **Ramappa** temples built by the Kakatiyas in the early 13th century. Palampet itself sits on the edge of a 10-mile wide reservoir built by the Kakatiyas, a testament to their engineering prowess. The temples' exteriors were built from a particularly attractive warm, pink sandstone and the interior carvings are superb—particularly the near life-size semi-erotic dancing maidens, their long, lithe forms offset by prominently carved labia.

Where to Stay
inexpensive

Warangal has no fancy accommodation, but some of its lodges are clean and comfortable. Try the state-run **Tourist Guest House**, while in the 'cheap' bracket are the **Vijya Lodge** and **Shanthi Krishna Lodge** (both backpackers' favourites) near the bus station.

South of Hyderabad: Vijayawada and Tirupati

Vijayawada

About 130 miles southeast of Hyderabad, on the vast, low-lying floodplain of the Krishna River is Vijayawada, a small city that you have to travel through on the way either to the great Hindo-Buddhist ruins of Nagarjunakonda or the wildlife sanctuaries of the Eastern Ghats.

Getting Around
by train

Vijayawada is on the main east/west railway between Hyderabad and the coast. Regular services leave several times a day for Hyderabad, Eluru, Rajamundry and Visahkapatnam. Daily services also run down the coast—change at Nellore for Tirupati. Daily express trains also go on to Madras and Calcutta. The railway station is on Bandar Road, near the river.

by bus

Direct daily services connect Vijayawada with all the main towns of Andhra Pradesh, and most of the other southern state capitals. The bus station is on Bandar Road, and has a 24-hour reservation office.

Tourist Information

The main **tourist office** is on Gopal Reddy Road, in the Governorpet suburb, ✆ 75382.

The Town

In the 1st and 2nd centuries AD, Vijayawada was a regional capital of the great Ikshavaku dynasty of Nagarjunakonda (*see* pp.342–4). From the 6th century it became the capital of the far northeastern Pallava Empire and through the high point of the Middle Ages it changed hands between the Hindu Vijayanagars and Muslim sultans of the Deccan, all of whom profited from the town's commercial wealth. Still a prosperous centre of just under a million people, modern Vijayawada is a classic textbook example of an Indian hellhole and should be avoided, especially in the blistering summer heat. However, if you find yourself stuck here for a night en route to Nagarjunakonda or the northeast, visit the **Victoria Jubilee Museum** (*open daily, 10.30–5, except Fridays*), whose surrounding gardens comprise just about the only greenery in the seething, sweaty metropolis. The museum's highlights are a very early Sculpture of Siva and the Nandi bull carved from white stone, and a tall, 2nd-century granite Buddha. Stone Age and Roman artefacts from Nagarjunakonda are also displayed.

Outside town are the 9th-century Hindu **Mogalrajapuram Cave Temples** and the **Ondavalli Caves**, dating from the 6th–8th centuries. Set in beautiful gardens, the Ondavalli caves have been fashioned into a four-storeyed temple. The interiors are decorated with fluid, sensual carvings of Vishnu and various sacred animals, with a set of strange-looking guardian spirits seated in the lotus position like huge chess pawns in front of the third gallery. Ondavalli's carvings are generally regarded as being of the same sculptural style and period as the cave and shore temple at Mammallapuram in Tamil Nadu. Ondavalli is about three miles south of Vijayawada, easily reached by bus or auto-rickshaw (don't pay more than Rs40–45 round trip).

Vijayawada ✆ (0866–) — Where to Stay

expensive

Top of the line is the **Kandhari**, ✆ 471311, on M.G. Road, with the standard facilties, such as air-conditioning two restaurants, travel desk and foreign exchange.

moderate

Try the **Mamata Hotel**, ✆ 61251 on Eluru Road, just across the road from the bus stand; or the **Swarna Palace**, ✆ 67222, also on Eluru Road, which offers a good deal as most of its rooms are air-conditioned. The state-run **Krishnaveni**, ✆ 75382 is also good—clean and well-run with a tourist information desk at reception.

Out on Besant Road, in the suburb of Governorpet, is **Shri Laxshmi Villas**, ✆ 62525, a large place with some air-conditioned rooms and a good Andhra restaurant.

Around the bus stand on Bunder Road, try the **Zila Parishad Guest Lodge** or the **Canal Guest Home**—both of which offer very basic comfort, but are at least clean.

Tirupati

About 380 miles south of Hyderabad, in the low-lying greener plains by the border with Tamil Nadu is the seething little city of Tirupati, set under the wooded Tirumalai hills. One of the busiest pilgrimage centres, Tirupati has grown rich on the never-ending stream of devout pilgrims come to ask special favour from the god Vankatesvara, an incarnation of Vishnu, at the huge **Tirumala Temple**, 15 miles up into the hills.

Getting Around
by train

 The railway station is at the south end of town (about 100 yards south of the junction of Ghandi and Tilaka Streets). There are several trains daily to Madras (5 hours), Hyderabad (22 hours), Bangalore (12 hours) and Mysore (14 hours).

by bus

From the bus stand opposite the railway station (*see* above) buses leave almost hourly for Madras, and about four times a day for Hyderabad, Mysore and Bangalore. Although there are daily direct services from Hyderabad, the journey takes close to 20 hours. Madras, about four hours away, is an easier bet, with several direct daily services. Bangalore and Mysore are about 10 and 12 hours away respectively, with daily services.

The Temple

While travelling in the south, you might well have noticed a blindfolded deity in shops, hotels and taxis. This is Vankatesvara 'the benign', whose gaze is so bright that it would blind anyone looking directly at him. You might also have noticed many people travelling with shaven heads, even women and children. These are almost always Vaishnavite pilgrims who, having grown their hair with the express purpose of sacrificing it to the god, have it all shaved off as an offering when they come to ask their favour. The barbers of Tirumala do a roaring trade of up to 50,000 heads a day and sell most of their thick, black harvest to the USA.

The temple is similar in style to the Chola and Pallava temples of the Tamil Nadu plains. Built in the 10th century, its architecture is typically Dravidian, with tall *gopurams* giving onto a square, walled compound. Unusually, the *sanctum sanctorum* is open to non-Hindus, but only if you pay a 'special *darshan*' fee of about Rs35 for the privilege. Console yourself with the thought that the money goes to help pay the temples estimated 6000 employees and innumerable dependent charity cases.

The temple bazaar is also unusual in that it stays open all day, year-round. The resulting atmosphere is festive, rather than reverent, and there is a general air of happiness about the pilgrims who, having mostly come with special requests to ask of the god, tend to go away full of hope. If you can, visit during September, when the **Brahmotsavam Temple Car Festival** is on.

The **temple museum** (*open daily, 8–8*), also known as the Hall of Antiquities is opposite the temple entrance on East Mada Street and mainly exhibits sacred sculpture.

Around Tirupati

If the crowds at Tirupati get too much, it is worth heading for the tranquility of the coastal wildlife sanctuary of **Pulicat Lagoon** (*see* p.351), or up into the mountains to the nearby **Shri Venkataswara Wildlife Sanctuary**. However, if you plan to go to the latter, you will need permisssion in advance, *see* p.345.

Tirupati ℡ (08574–)

Where to Stay

moderate

The Karnataka state-run **Mayura Hotel**, ℡ 7285, on Pravasi Mandir, in the south of Tirupati is near both the railway and bus stations, and is a traveller's favourite. Nearby is the **Vishnu Driyas**, ℡ 20300, with good air-conditioned rooms, a reliable travel desk and foreign exchange.

inexpensive

Head for the **Bhimas**, which welcomes backpackers and offers clean comfort. Situated on G. Car Street, it has a roof terrace and a few air-conditioned rooms.

cheap

Vast numbers of pilgrims stay in dormitory hostels in Tirumala, hundreds of which fill the buildings on the streets surrounding the big temple. If this kind of public living is not to your taste (although it is dirt, dirt cheap), try the cheaper rooms at the **Bhimas** (*see* above) or the **Gopi Krishna** which you can see immediately on leaving the railway station, though both these lodges are often full. Otherwise it's the lodges around the bus station, with only the most basic (and often bug-ridden) accommodation.

Puttapati

Also in the south but back up on the Deccan is Puttapati, a hot, dusty village, now grown into a town and home of **Sai Baba's** huge *ashram*, which attracts hundreds of thousands of devotees from around the world every year. Bangalore, 100 miles to the south (in Karnataka) is the easiest access point, with several direct bus services daily.

Getting Around

by train

This can be inconvenient. The nearest stations are Dharmavaram or Anantapur, both a good hour's bus ride away. The best direct access is by bus (*see* below).

Regular, direct services connect Puttapati with Bangalore (4 hours), with daily several services.

Tourist Information

Foreign Exchange is offered at the **State Bank** opposite the bus stand, uphill from the *ashram*'s main gates. Expect to queue.

Anyone travelling in south India will have noticed pictures of an orange-clad, smiling guru with an outrageously huge afro hair do, his image often gracing hotel lobbies, auto-rickshaw driver's mirrors or the cover of books. That's Sai Baba, who claims, and is believed by millions of devotees, to be a steadily progressing series of incarnations of the Hindu god Siva, appearing in a

different form every three or four human generations. Among his past incarnations have been Sikh Muslim holy men—Sai Baba being able to cross the frontiers of orthodox religion at will. The next incarnation will be as Siva/Shakti—that is, the full male and female union of all aspects of the supreme godhead, and mankind will enter a new era. However, our own generation must be content with following the teachings of Sai Baba's present incarnation, which seem in general to be simple exhortations to live morally.

Sai Baba is accused by many of being a fraud. Among the scores of books singing his praises are a number claiming to expose him. One author even goes so far as to accuse him of homosexuality and of making advances to those close to him.

The vast numbers of Sai Baba devotees have, of course, provided the *crores* of rupees necessary to buld the vast *ashram* complex, which covers a small hill. But if the guru has grown incredibly wealthy, he also uses much of the money for good works—in particular, a number of schools and hospitals in Karnataka and Andhra Pradesh have been subsidized by his *ashram*.

Whatever you belive about Sai Baba, Puttapati is certainly an interesting phenomenon: the once tiny Deccan village has become a compact, cosmopolitan centre, incongruous against the Deccan landscape of brown fields and bare, rocky hills. A huge number of little shops and stalls sell (at inflated prices) the white Punjabi suits favoured by Sai Baba's devotees and sell Sai Baba memorabilia—key rings, tapes, T-shirts, books, pens, and the like. Whether their profits are connected in any way with the *ashram* is difficult to ascertain.

Temple Car Festival, Tirupati

Visitors stay in comfortable dormitories at the *ashram* (for a mere Rs5 per night), or at lodges in the village, and assemble at dawn for the *darshan*, or public appearance, of Sai Baba himself. These *darshans* are reminiscent of school assemblies, though on a much larger scale. Squadrons of officious *ashram* 'security' workers brusquely order the crowd into queues and make them sit in neat rows—women on one side of the vast hall (their shoulders must be covered with a scarf) and men on the other. The security people can be rude and the temptation to be rude back is very strong. However, when Sai Baba appears, the atmosphere is electric and the audience hushed. The guru strews the crowd with small tokens—some say they are flower petals, others sweets and still others sacred ash. There is further confusion as to where he gets these tokens from; some say that he takes them from a tray, others claim that he manifests them from the air.

Most of Sai Baba's followers credit him with the ability to manifest various kinds of objects—notably gold rings and a sacred ash—that bring good fortune to the recipient, and many claim to have received these gifts after watching the guru materialize them from thin air. Even when you have witnessed a *darshan*, it is difficult to say exactly what you have seen, such is the atmosphere of mystique.

After the *darshan* comes a period of chanting—an emotionally charged sort of camp-fire sing-song rising from the huge crowd—comes breakfast. The *ashram* has several refectories (separate for men and women), where Indian food is served for a very fair Rs15 per meal. Through the rest of the morning, which quickly gets very hot, you can wander round the *ashram*, occasionally being shunted hither and thither by the security workers. There's a reading room of Sai Baba teachings and laudatory biographies and a small museum explaining the various incarnations of the guru—both uphill from the *darshan* hall. Although you will be made to take off your shoes before entering any of the buildings, beware of leaving them outside—the *ashram* is not free from petty pilfering.

It is also worth wandering downhill (outside the *ashram*) to the lower end of the village, where Deccan rural life goes on unaffected by the crowds. The countryside around here is very fertile, and a wander into the irrigated fields will soon attract a cluster of children anxious to show you around, albeit in Telegu. Their company may cost you a few rupees.

Where to Stay
moderate

Directly opposite the gates of the *ashram* is the recently built **Sai Towers**, a building several storeys high that looks incongruous up here on the dry Deccan Plateau, but can put you up in Western-style comfort.

inexpensive

There are several lodges dotted along the village main street below, downhill from the *ashram*. Try the **Sai Ram Lodge**, which is basic, but has clean double rooms at the cheaper end of the scale. Mosquitoes are always a problem in these lodges though, and you will need a net and/or coils to ensure a good night's sleep.

cheap

The *ashram* offers one of the best deals in India—clean, single sex dormitories with beds for Rs5 and shared rooms (much harder to get, but worth asking for) for about Rs20.

Lepakshi

Also up on the Deccan, 10 miles east of Hindupur (125 miles north of Bangalore) is the great Veerabhadra temple at **Lepakshi**, whose interior has some of the most beautiful frescoes in India. The painted ceilings are worth travelling several hours to see, especially the flowing series representing the incarnations of Vishnu and the royal hunting scenes, which include pictures of wild pig and cheetah being hunted to hounds. A late Vijayanagar building, built around 1530, Lepakshi's frescoes are almost all painted on a red background, showing that they have been influenced by the Jains, whose philosophical movement overtook the later Vijayanagar rulers before their final overthrow by the Deccan Sultans in the late 16th-century.

Also worth seeng are the finely carved pillars outside the temple, and the great Nandi bull chiselled from solid granite. The local tourist literature claims that it is the largest in India, but several other *nandis* share this claim too, and as yet nobody seems to have made a final decision.

There is no tourist accommodation at Lepakshi. Your best bet are the cheap and cheerful lodges near the bus stand at Hindupur, which will offer very basic but reasonably clean rooms, and good Andhra cooking.

Andhra's Mountains

Beyond a hillock in the direction of the forest there was a very old Banyan tree. Its top, like a green, round hat, could be seen from my window. Chogan Baba was an old man who had lived and died under the tree. He was considered a savant by the tribals. He had once told me that a swarm of invisible little imps lived in the tree. He saw them and spoke with them.

Manoj Das, *A Tiger at Twilight*

Andhra Pradesh has two sets of mountains: the Eastern Ghats which run from north to south and divide the dry Deccan from the wet, storm-battered coast; and the northern hill ranges, an extreme western spur of the Eastern Ghats, which divide Andhra from Madhya Pradesh and Orissa. Despite the dry country south and west of these ranges, all are well-covered by dry deciduous forest and support healthy game populations. India's largest tiger reserve, **Nagarjunasagar**, lies in the foothills of the Eastern Ghats, its reserved forests surrounding a huge reservoir at the centre of which is an island (once a hill) where sit the 4th–10th-century ruins of a once great Hindo-Buddhist empire. Here there are elephant, sloth bear, leopard, *gaur* (bison), *dhole* (wild dog), wolf, blackbuck antelope and *chinkara* (Indian gazelle), various deer species and a host of smaller game.

Various **tribal communities** still thrive up in the mountains, particularly those bordering Madhya Pradesh and Orissa. In some places, militant separatist

dhole

movements have become active—notably the Naxalite terrorists of the far north, whose ways of raising money via cannabis and abducting police officers seem to have more in common with central India's ancient *dacoit* (bandit) tradition, than with any real attempt at a political statement. Their activities can limit the chances of travellers wanting to get to the remote wildlife sanctuaries north of Warangal, and it is worh checking which sanctuaries are currently open with A.P. Tourism in Hyderabad or Warangal, before making the trip north.

Nagarjunakonda Ruins

The Indus Valley and Mesopotamia are generally regarded as the twin birthplaces of civilization, of settled agricultural communities and the first towns. However there were several other parts of Asia where the same forms of settlement were evolving, if somewhat out on a limb. Andhra Pradesh's **Nagarjunakonda** was one such site. For the last 400 years, Nagarjunakonda has not been inhabited, but archaeologists estimate that this stretch of the Krishna River has been settled for an estimated 200,000 years, and as recently as 6000 years ago, settled farming and village life had begun.

Getting There

by bus

To get to the dam, you can either take a tour bus from Hyderabad, booking through A.P. Tourism (*see* p.324), or go independently: several daily services ply the 110 mile, 8-hour route to and from Hyderabad, with a change at Vijayapuri (6 miles from the dam).

by boat

A boat service takes tourists across the lake from the dam at mid-morning and mid-afternoon (about Rs30 per person).

Tourist Information

The **A.P. Tourist Office** is in the state-run Project House, ✆ 2133, near the ferry.

History

Nagarjunakonda was 'discovered' in 1926 by the eminent Indian archaeologist A.R. Saraswathi. At first, great excitement was caused by his revelations that a 3rd-century Hindo-Buddhist empire once had its capital here. Then, further excavations revealed tools from the early Stone Age, closely followed by Neolithic cemeteries, stone circles and megaliths, evidence of early farming and metal working and finally of early towns—all in one continuous line of settlement. The greater part of the most ancient remains were submerged in the 1950s beneath the vast Nagarjuna dam. Only an island, what was the hilltop fort, remains, but fortunately many key finds were saved and relocated to the Nagarjunakonda hilltop and museum before the valley was flooded.

Thus the site was already ancient when the Ikshavakus, an early Hindu dynasty, established a fort on the hilltop, and began to lay out their own walled town around the existing mud and thatch settlements in the valley. The Ikshavakus were unique in south Indian history by actively encouraging both Hinduism and Buddhism in their kingdom, with direct patronage for both religions from the royal family.

The Ikshavaku hilltop city was called Vijayapur, or 'City of Victory'. There is some controversy over the origin of the city's present name: some believe that it refers to the 2nd-century Buddhist monk Nagarjuna, whose teachings were quoted in contemporary Buddhist texts from distant China. Others believe that the name simply means 'snake hill'. Whatever the origins of its present name, old Vijaypur was as prosperous as anything in contemporary Europe, and was known as far afield as Rome: Pliny wrote of a Roman trading post on the coast from which merchants came to Vijayapur to buy manufactured muslin cloth; the Roman coins and artefacts found on the site and now exhibited in the museum seem to bear this out. Before the valley was flooded, the archaeologists found an amphitheatre, laid out in the Roman style (and the only one of its kind in India).

Religious and secular building thrived under the Ikshavakus, who are credited by architectural historians with having developed one of the earliest, or 'archaic' forms of Dravidian architecture. Several Buddhist monasteries, Hindu temples, theological colleges, and even schools of sculpture and painting for both religions were found on the hillside and valley floor. Nine monuments were rescued before the flooding, and moved to the hilltop island where they have since been restored to something close to their original appearance.

It is possible the dynasty prospered too well and became a soft target—because the Ikshavakus were suddenly overrun in the 6th century by the Pallava armies of Tamil Nadu, and the town was sacked and abandoned—its distance from Tamil Nadu making it unfeasible for the Pallavans to garrison, but the ferocity of its fall being sufficiently great to cripple and ultimately kill the urban culture that had thrived there.

But Nagarjunakonda was too good a defensive site to remain unused for long. In the mid 7th century the Chalukyans took it over and at once began to build temples in their own heavily ornamented style next to the ruins of the starker Ikshavaku buildings. The Chalukyans held on to Nagarjunakonda until the gradual contracting of their great empire in the 12th century. From then, the town became a Vijayanagar outpost against the kings of Orissa, then against the Deccan sultans—first the Bahmanis, then the armies from Delhi. The hilltop fort continually changed hands between Hindu and Muslim warlords between the 14th and 16th centuries, but was again abandoned after the Vijayanagars were finally smashed by Golconda in the late 16th century.

Despite its strategic position and great cultural heritage, the site was never reoccupied, its ruins standing forgotten except by the local farmers who cultivated between the tumbled masonry of the valley and shunned the hilltop for fear of ghosts.

The Island

Now a World Heritage site, the island in the middle of Nagarjunakonda's vast dam (apparently the third-largest man-made lake in the world), can be visited by tourists. The restored buildings and ruins are not as spectacular as Hampi or Aihole in Karnataka (*see* pp.180–90) but the feeling of sheer antiquity has not been marred by the development of the dam; it rather increases the sense of eeriness and isolation. Few foreign tourists make it here, and you may well have the place to yourself if you visit on a weekday.

Among the restored buildings inside the late medieval Vijayanagar curtain walls of the old fort are a 2nd-century Vishnu temple, and several to Siva, whose different architectural styles show the progression of Dravidian forms from the ascetic Ikshavaku beginnings to the

Chalukyans' 12th-century high ornamentalism. There are fascinating sculptures too, including one that appears to be depicting the act of *suttee* (a widow throwing herself on her dead husband's funeral pyre); and some memorial pillars celebrating long-gone military heroes, with intricate depictions of their successful battles. Various Buddhist *stupas* from the early period have also survived, but there are few images of the Buddha, for the *Hinayana* form of Buddhism practised at the height of the Ikshavaku period always referred to the Buddha via symbols such as a swastika, a wheel or feet. The later form of *Mahayana* Buddhism did not have long to produce its art before the city fell to the Hindu Pallavas.

At the eastern end of the fort is the **museum** (*open daily, 9–4, except Fridays*), housing some of the more precious sculptures, including a huge 10 feet (3 metre) high standing Buddha. Many of the early Stone Age and Megalithic artefacts found on the site are also displayed here.

Where to Stay
inexpensive

 Andhra Pradesh tourism runs several lodges near the ferry. There's the **Vijay Vihar Complex**, which is very good value with air-conditioned rooms and some self-contained cottages. Try also the nearby **Soundarya Tourist Annexe** which has the same facilities, but is a little more expensive, and the **Project House**, © 2133, which has two floors of cheap rooms and a tourist office.

Nagarjunasagar Srisailam Tiger Reserve

The forested hills called the Malamallai, or 'Black Hills', surrounding the Krishna River Dam now harbour a vast wildlife sanctuary—at about 1150 square miles it's the largest tiger reserve in India.

Unlike most of Andhra's other sanctuaries, Nagarjunasagar has good tourist facilites. You can arrange game-spotting drives or guided treks to and from *machans*, (bamboo viewing platforms) built into the trees at various watering sites where the game comes to drink. Although there are no elephant here, visitors stand a reasonable chance of seing tiger, leopard, sloth bear, *dhole* (wild dog), wolf, striped hyena, jackal, *gaur* (bison), *nilgai* (Indian giant antelope), *chital* (spotted deer), *sambar* and muntjac deer, *chinkara* (Indian gazelle), blackbuck antelope, *chousingha* (the tiny, four-horned antelope) and a variety of langur and macaque apes.

However, because the forest is dense and there is a vast 'core' area where no human disturbance is allowed, visitors should aim to spend several days here if they intend to see game. There is accommodation in three resthouses by a set of ancient temples.

Getting Around
by train

Slow, infrequent services do run from Hyderabad to Machelsa, about 10 miles away, but it is more direct to go by bus.

Travel as for Nagarjunakonda (*see* p.342). From there, local buses run from the dam to the tiger reserve entance.

Other Wildlife Enclaves in Central and Southern Andhra

South of Nagarjunasagar, in the Deccan country bordering the Nallamallai foothills near Kurnool, a new national park has recently been declared to protect a population of tigers that has gradually moved into the area from the north over the last 10 years or so. Their prey species of wild pig, *chital*, *nilgai* (bluebuck antelope), *chinkara* (Indian gazelle), and blackbuck also have a foothold in the area, and there are small populations of *gaur*, wolf and sloth bear. As yet, tourism is not allowed, but there are plans to open the park up for wildlife viewing. Ask at A.P. Tourism in Hyderabad for information as to when facilities will be ready.

In the extreme southeast, the forests of the hills east of Tirupati have now received protection after a steady decline caused by uncontrolled felling for cattle grazing and sandalwood smuggling. The **Shri Venkataswara Wildlife Sanctuary** now conserves about 150 square miles of dry deciduous forest. Resident populations of leopard, *dhole* (wild dog), *chital* (spotted dear), wild pig and *gaur* (bison) have now stabilized after a long history of persecution. It can be difficult to get permission for access to the sanctuary, as the local Wildife Department is understandably nervous of the huge numbers of tourists who show up as pilgrims in nearby Tirupati, then stay in the area for a few days or weeks. However, if you can convince the authorities that your interest is genuine, they may let you in to trek. Apply via **M.N. Tours and Travels** in Hyderabad, ✆ 213223.

The Northern Wildlife Sanctuaries

Up in the hills north of Warangal that mark the border between Andhra, Madhya Pradesh and Maharashtra, there are several large wildlife sanctuaries with sizeable game populations. These can sometimes be off-limits to foreigners because of trouble with Naxalite insurgents, but in general access is granted. Check first with A.P. Tourism in Warangal (*see* p.334) before going all the way in.

If you go and see the District Forest Officer (Wildlife Division) in Warangal, you may also be able to organize **trekking** in these sanctuaries; possibly into some of the Banjara tribal villages that still dot the deeper forests. To avoid a flat 'no', you should first be armed with permission to enter the area. This needs to be granted from Delhi, and you should apply for it (via an Indian agent) a good month before setting off. Try **Clipper Holidays** in Bangalore, at Suite 406, Regency Enclave, 4 Magrath Road, Bangalore 560 025, ✆/🖷 (080) 5599032/34/ 5599833, tlx 0845-3095. They are used to arranging remote-area trekking.

Those not wanting to trek should also visit the D.F.O. in Warangal to book accommodation before going in. If you are really intrepid, however, you can always take a tent. There are no elephants in the area and there is no history of man-eating among the big cats. Do not light any fires though, as this is dry deciduous forest and can go up like a candle (with you in it) with little encouragement. Take a camping stove for cooking.

The easiest sanctuary to visit is **Ethurnagaram Wildlife Sanctuary**, where two forest rest houses are open to visitors without need for prior permission. You can generally arrange a guide to take you into the forest (*insist* on your right to access if the Forest Department people at the entrance refuse you). You should keep the windows of the resthouses shut against monkeys when you are out. Ethurnagaram's 250 square miles has the full range of south Indian willdife with the exception of elephant. (The sanctuaries are 60 miles north of Warangal. Direct services leave several times a day to Ethurnagaram, a 2–3 hour journey, from where you have to arrange jeep transport for the last 10 miles—approximately Rs75.)

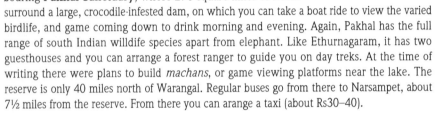

nilgai

If the accommodation at Ethurnagaram is full, try the neighbouring **Pakhal Sanctuary**, whose 270 square miles of forest surround a large, crocodile-infested dam, on which you can take a boat ride to view the varied birdlife, and game coming down to drink morning and evening. Again, Pakhal has the full range of south Indian willdife species apart from elephant. Like Ethurnagaram, it has two guesthouses and you can arrange a forest ranger to guide you on day treks. At the time of writing there were plans to build *machans*, or game viewing platforms near the lake. The reserve is only 40 miles north of Warangal. Regular buses go from there to Narsampet, about 7½ miles from the reserve. From there you can arange a taxi (about Rs30–40).

Just 100 miles into the hills from Hyderabad is **Pocharam Sanctuary**, surrounding Pocharam Lake. Sloth bears, wolf and leopard make up the big species, while *nilgai*, blackbuck and *chinkara* comprise the antelope. There are plentiful wild boar and a few small herds of *gaur*, and *chital*. The lake is known for its flocks of flamingos. As with Ethurnagaram and Pakhal, you can arrange trekking here via A.P. Tourism in Hyderabad (*see* p.324). The sanctuary has two forest resthouses for visitors. There are regular bus services from Hyderabad to Medak (approximately 3½ hours journey time), 5 miles from the sanctuary. A taxi can take you the rest of the way (about Rs25–30).

The Wild Northeast: Along the Orissan Border

About 30 miles north of Mancherial, a small railway station 60 miles north of Waranagal, is **Kawal Wildlife Sanctuary**. With two forest resthouses, this 275 square mile sanctuary covers mostly dry deciduous forest and harbours most of the big species, apart from elephant. Tigers are said to be common, though you will need to be in the forest for at least a week to have a chance of seeing one. Permission for accommodation and trekking is through the D.F.O. at Jannaram, about 37 miles north of Mancherial by bus, just before the entrance to the sanctuary.

Getting Around

Regular **bus** serices run from Warangal to Mancherial (3–4 hours) and the connection from here to Jannaram takes a further three hours.

Rajahmundry

Further along Andhra's northeast border with Orissa—back in the high ranges of the Eastern Ghats proper, are several remote reserves—Papikonda, Siwaram and Pranahita—all accessible from the small city of Rajahmundry on the River Godavari. The sanctuaries are in the wild country upriver from here.

Getting Around

Regular **bus** services run to the entrances of all the wildlife sanctuaries about 3 times a day from Rajahmundry, itself accessible by bus from Hyderabad (a full day's journey), with a change at Vijayanagar.

Rajahmundry is worth a brief stop before you head for the hills. The far eastern capital of the Hindu Chalukyan and Vengi Empires during the early Middle Ages, the city was taken by various Deccan sultans and Hindu kings of Orissa over the 15th–18th centuries before being taken over by the French in the 1750s. Unlike Pondicherry, down on the coast of Tamil Nadu, the French influence had disappeared long before Indian independence in 1947. Today it is a good place to buy underpriced sandalwood products—few tourists ever make it here, so prices have not gone up as they have in Mysore, another sandalwood centre. Carpets and Orissa-style printed handwoven cotton cloth are also very reasonably priced here compared with the cities of the south Indian tourist trail.

Papikonda Wildlife Sanctuary covers about 200 square mies of forest near the Godavari River as it cuts through the Eastern Ghats north of Rajahmundry. Tiger, leopard and wolf hunt through the mixed dry and moist deciduous forest. There are two forest resthouses and trekking/accommodation can be arranged through the District Forest Office (Wildlife Division) in Rajamundry. Alternatively, get an agent to arrange it; ask Monisha at M.N. Tours and Travels at 6-3-85 10/A Sadat Mansil, Ameerpet, Hyderabad, ✆ 213223.

In the same district as Papikonda are two other big sanctuaries: **Siwaram Wildlife Sanctuary**, also on the Godavari River, and **Pranahita Wildlife Sanctuary** on the Pranahita River, a tributary of the Godavari. Neither of these have seen any Western tourists for years (although the odd zoologist comes through), so anyone using this guide to go up there will be breaking new ground. Siwaram has three resthouses and Pranahita has two in its teak forests. Permission is given through the D.F.O., Rajamundry.

The far northeastern mountains have wildlife sanctuaries open to the general public. But plans are afoot to open several national parks in the mountains due north the small coastal town of Srikakulam. These include a 350 square mile area of forest to be known as **Donubhari National Park**, which aims to protect a large herd of wild elephant that have moved back into Andhra from the forests of neighbouring Madhya Pradesh. Elephant had previously been absent from Andhra for over 20 years, so the Wildlife Department is anxious to conserve the new arrivals. Ask at A.P. Tourism in Hyderabad (Gagan Vihar, M.G. Road, ✆ 500001), or Visakhapatnam (*see* below), whether the park is now open to tourists.

palm squirrel

Andhra's Coast

Low-lying, storm-swept and lushly tropical, the long coastline of Andhra Pradesh has never been developed for tourism. Its distance from India's major urban centres, combined with a reputation for summer cyclones, has preserved this stretch of the Coromandel coast for the fishermen. Unless you speak Telegu and are prepared to live at village level, most of Andhra's beaches are effectively off-limits.

The exception to this is the coastline around the port city of **Visakhapatnam**, a short distance from which are a collection of clean beaches where budget travellers can find a slice of coastal life well off the regular backpackers' trail.

Away from Visakhapatnam, it is best to visit Andhra's coast for its vast **river deltas**, some of the largest in Asia and most of which have been preserved as huge **wildlife sanctuaries**. Two of these, Kolleru and Coringa Wildlife Sanctuaries, protect the Godavari River delta in northeast Andhra, just south of Rajamundry. A third, the massive Pulicat Wildlife Sanctuary, protects the great freshwater lagoon system of the far southeast coast, just above the border with Tamil Nadu.

Finally, the Andhra coast has a connection with the West that few people would ever guess: it is the place where chintz was invented. Although regarded as a most English tradition, chintz in fact comes from the small industrial town of Masamalapattnam, and was first brought to Europe by Dutch and French traders in the late 17th century. The town still makes and exports chintz fabrics, more accurately known as *Kalamkari* textiles, hand printing the cottons with traditional vegetable dyes, but now sells almost exclusively within India.

Visakhapatnam

India's fourth largest port and a city of just over one million and rising, Visakhapatnam is built around one of India's few natural harbours. In the far northeast of the state and almost 425 miles from Hyderabad, it is only likely to be visited by those travelling on to Orissa, or heading up into the wild ranges of the Eastern Ghats that rise abruptly from the flat coastal farmland, 25 miles north of the city.

Getting Around
by air

 About 10 miles from the city centre, this small airport is connected by thrice-weekly **Indian Airlines** flights with Hyderabad and Calcutta. There is no bus connecting the airport with the city and taxis and auto-rickshaws are expensive. Expect to pay about Rs100–150.

by train

Direct trains connect Visakhapatnam with Hyderabad (daily, via Rajamundry and Vijayawada), Tirupati (daily), Madras (daily), Calcutta (daily), Konark (daily) and Bangalore (weekly). Connections to Bombay and Delhi can be made at Hyderabad.

by bus

Daily services connect Visakhapatnam with all the major towns in Andhra Pradesh, as well as with Konark in Orissa.

For those who make it to this obscure corner of south India, Visakhapatnam has some rewards. Avoid the crowded, filthy harbour, with its dockyards, Indian Navy wharfs, petrol refinery and steel mill and head straight out for the beach-side suburb of **Waltair**, about 6 miles north of the city centre. There are regular buses from the local bus stand on Station Road at the west end of town.

Waltair is clustered around three high, rocky hills, each one topped with a different religious building—a Hindu temple, mosque and Catholic church. The church has the highest vantage point, but you can climb to each centre of worship for views out over the town. Waltair's warm, breezy seafront has a number of good beaches, the most popular being **Ramakrishna Beach**, a stretch of sand dominated by a lighthouse standing on a rocky headland known as the Dolphin's Nose. This is the beach where most of the region's few tourists congregate. Head east along the strand and you soon come to the quieter **Lawson's Bay** and **Mission Beach**, which have good swimming and fishing villages where tourists are almost unheard of. Language can be a real problem here, and there is no accommodation. You will have to stay in Waltair, where there is a variety of places for all budgets.

Waltair also has the campus of the **Andhra University** (on University Road, south of and parallel to Waltair Main Road), and a large **Zoological Park**—one of the few in India to have broken from the Victorian tradition of iron-barred cages and sickly animals sleeping away their confinement. The big cat's cages have been landscaped and there are plans to open up the rest of the zoo, which lies just north of the main town.

To get out to the more remote coastline, take a bus about 20 miles out to the beach at **Bhimunipatnam**, a fishing village built on the ruins of a 17th-century Dutch trading post and cemetery at the palm-fringed mouth of the Goshthani River. You can swim safely here, but beware of places elsewhere on the coast away from Waltair, as Andhra's coast is known for dangerous currents. A longer trip is out to the limestone **Borra Caves**, in the foothills of the Eastern Ghats, about 50 miles north of the city. There are no cave temples here, but fabulous

stalactite and stalagmite formations. Guides can be hired at the cave entrance. Bargain as close to half of their asking price as you can, and withhold payment until the tour is over. The countryside around the caves is beautiful: wooded slopes leading down to the flat paddy country of the coastal hinterland, the higher, forested ranges rising behind. A series of new national parks have been planned for these further uplands —especially as wild elephant have recolonized the area, the first time Andhra has seen the species for over 20 years.

Visakhapatnam ✆ (0891–)

Where to Stay

luxury

Beach Road, on the Waltair seafront, has all the upmarket accommodation. The **Taj Residency**, ✆ 474849, is the city's smartest hotel and has two very good restaurants serving traditional Andhra dishes and fresh seafood. Right on the beach, all rooms have an ocean view and you can walk out of the hotel to the water, but it is more pleasant to take a taxi up to Ramakrishna beach several miles to the east.

expensive

The **Hotel Park**, ✆ 58461/554488, ✉ 554181, is also on Beach Road and is more attractive than the Taj, set in formal gardens with a good swimming pool. Otherwise try the **Dolphin**, ✆ 68411/64811, ✉ 63737, uphill from the beach on Dabagardens in the west end of Waltair. The Dolphin is cheaper than the Park but equally pleasant, with a rooftop restaurant serving good Andhra food, a pool and a more efficient travel desk than the other smart hotels.

moderate

The **Palm Beach Hotel**, ✆ 54206 is on Beach Road, next to the Hotel Park. Much cheaper than its neighbour, it also boasts a pool, outdoor restaurant and air-conditioned rooms for a fraction of the price. Mind you, it's not half so well-run and some of the rooms are very scruffy. Further east along Beach Road, where it curves north along the foot of the largest of Waltair's rocky hills, is the **Ocean View**, ✆ 54828, which offers straightforward air-conditioned comfort. In the town centre is the **Apsara Hotel**, ✆ 64861, on Waltair Main Road, a large hotel with good restaurants. The staff here are anxious to please, as they are in direct competition with the Beach Road hotels, so it's a reliable place to seek travel information.

Unfortunately, Waltair's budget accommodation is set away from the beach. Try the **Saga Lodge**, off Hospital Road in the hills just north of the town centre, where you might at least get a sea view. You can't get a meal here but the restaurant at the **Hotel Lakshmi**, a small place with some air-conditioned rooms, is recommended for Andhra dishes.

cheap

If you can, try to get in to the well-run, clean **Retiring Rooms** at the railway station. If these are full, head for Waltair's Main Road; although unfortunately there is a lack of dirt cheap accommodation here as an increasing amount of well-paid business travellers have forced the local prices up. However, try the **Hotel Poornam**, which is basic, but clean and comfortable, and should still have rooms within the price range.

The Coastal Wildlife Sanctuaries

The northeast Andhra coastline has two superb sanctuaries, due south of Rajamundry (west of Visakhapatnam) on the delta of the mighty Godavari River. The larger sanctuary is **Kolleru**, covering a staggering 350 square miles of lagoons, wetlands and jungle in the wild country between the Godavari and Krishna river mouths. Pelicans congregate here in huge numbers from November to March, bringing with them thousands of other migrants, including terns, flamingos, a host of different waders, ospreys, fish eagles and herons. Otters and fishing cats, large lynx-like felids, share the hunting rights with river, and a few itinerant saltwater crocodiles. Wild pig and deer graze in the marshland meadows. Accommodation is in five huts,

mugger crocodile

booked through the District Conservator of Forests in Rajamundry. To get to Kolleru, take the **train** to Eluru (west of Rajamundry) and then a bus the last 10 miles to the rangers' office.

Smaller than Kolleru is **Coringa Widlife Sanctuary**, a 75 square mile reserve at the eastern end of the Godavari Delta. Coringa has the same wildlife and habitat as Kolleru, but there is only one resthouse, also bookable through the D.C.F. at Rajamundry. It is possible to take boats out into the marshes, but you should be careful of walking around too freely: saltwater crocodiles are very common here and are known to be man-eaters.

In the far southeast of Andhra Pradesh is the vast **Pulicat Wildlife Sanctuary**. Like Kolleru in the north, this reserve protects a coastal lagoon habitat but where Kolleru is known for pelicans, Pulicat is famous for the thousands of flamingos that overwinter on the lakes. Pulicat has only one forest resthouse, bookable through the Wildlife Department Office in the nearby town of Sulurpetta. You can hire Wildlife Department guides to take you out onto the lagoons by boat. As at Coringa, there is a risk from crocodiles, and you stand a good chance of seeing wild pig, *chital* and, if very lucky, fishing cat or otter.

The sanctuary's southern boundary is the state-line between Andhra Pradesh and Tamil Nadu. Sulurpetta, the little town nearest the sanctuary entrance, is most easily reached by **bus** from Madras, 65 miles south of the mouth of the lagoon.

In south India the official language changes every time you cross a state border. There are five main state languages: **Tamil** in Tamil Nadu, **Kannada** in Karnataka, **Mallayallam** in Karala, **Telegu** in Andhra Pradesh and **Konkani** in Goa.

All these languages have a different kind of script, and all are very ancient and almost impossible to learn. For example, the Tamil alphabet has 126 letters and Mallayallam is reckoned by many linguists to be the world's fastest-spoken language (though quite how they work this out is unclear). Impressively, many south Indians speak two or more languages, but the *lingua franca* is **English**, and the English-speaking traveller will have an easy time here—which is just as well when the indigenous languages are so complex.

This marks a major difference between north and south India, for although north Indians also have English as their common language, the use of Hindi is widespread and travellers have to learn a little in order to communicate effectively. Not so in the south, where you can be lazy and all-but ignore the local tongue. Indeed, south Indians actually prefer you to use English; you will occasionally see a Tamil or Keralan impatiently shifting from foot to foot while a European tries to lumber through one or two local phrases, full of wrong pronounciations and in a strange accent, when English would have done perfectly well.

Basic Pleasantaries

Having said all this, what south Indian's *do* appreciated (as do we all), is being greeted and thanked in their own language, though you should come to terms with the fact that however you pronounce these words, you're going to be wrong. Subtle variations in intonation and dialect from state to state (and even from one town to the next) mean that you can expect a high failure rate till you've adjusted to each local tongue. But it's worth persisting. Indians may find your *faux pas* humorous at first, but they'll always respect the effort you're making and will help you pronounce things right. One hint, which will reduce local chuckles by about half, is that the letter 'h' is nearly always (except when the first letter of a word) silent. Listed below are the basic pleasantaries you will need:

Hindi (spoken in northern and central India)

Shubh prabhat	Good morning
Shubh ratri	Good night
Dhanyavad	Thank you

Mallayalam	**Telegu**	
Namaskaram	*Namaskar*	Good morning/night
Nandi	*Tamara Krutagntha*	Thank you

Language

Tamil	**Kannada**	
Vanakkam	*Namaskara*	Good morning/night
Nandri	*Vandane*	Thank you

Useful Indianisms

Some Hindi and English words have become universal in India and the traveller should know these:

Hindi

Namaste	Hello/goodbye—this is good for everywhere in India
Nahi	No (very useful for putting off touts)
Pani	Water
Dhobi	Laundry

High numbers are measured in Hindi by the *lakh* (10,000) and by the *crore* (10 million). There are no Hindi words for million or billion, just multiples of *lakhs* or *crores.*

English

'Only'—Indians love this word and will use it as often as possible. You can often make yourself better understood if you adopt the habit too. For example, if you put 'only' after something you want, as in 'One masala dosa *only*', or 'I want one double room *only*', it seems to make things run more smoothly and will spare you the barrage of qualifying questions that even the most simple requests can prompt.

'Coming from?' or 'Native place?' Indians will often fire these seemingly inane phrases at you out of the blue, particularly when sitting on buses or trains. However, in most kinds of Indian society, the desire to place people in their proper category is expected and not considered rude—indeed, it is often considered the most polite way to open a conversation. It is polite to respond with the country that you come from.

Head Waggling

As a final note on communication, we must consider the head-waggle. Most travellers realize within a few days that Indians do not nod when they mean 'yes', but waggle their heads from side to side in a motion that is dangerously similar to the head-shake for 'no'—which *is* used in India.

Like the word 'only', if you pick up the head-waggling habit you will often find yourself much better understood. This is not hard to do, as the waggle is definitely contagious and most travellers to India find themselves doing it on their return to the 'native place', to the consternation of friends and family.

There are different kinds of head-waggle, however. The brisk, business-like head-waggle, with the head slightly bouncing at the end of each side-waggle denotes a definite 'yes', or 'I understand'. If you want to be more ambiguous, slow the waggle down and put in a slightly longer bounce at the end of each side-waggle—this denotes that you are affirmatively disposed but not necessarily fully committed. Lastly, there is a high-speed head-waggle accompanied by a cheeky grin which serves both as an admission of having done wrong, but also of having got away with it. If a rickshaw driver uses it when you ask about a fare, you know he's cheating you. Similarly, if you stick to your price and use the same head-waggle, your adversary will know that you know that he's cheating you and are good-humouredly holding your ground, and will probably yield to a lower price with less argument and bad-feeling.

The following is not a definitive list of south Indian literature, but a selection
of books that best capture the feel of the place, at least in the author's opinion.

The *Puranas*: Hindu Mythology and Sacred Texts

The *Mahabarata*. One of India's most ancient texts, this epic tells the story of Krishna and the
Pandava brothers who fought against an apparently overwhelming cast of baddies headed by
the dastardly and numerous Kaurava brothers, who wanted to usurp the Pandavas' rightful
claim to the land of Bharat, or India.

The *Ramayana*. The origins of Valmiki, author of these stories of the great warrior Rama (an
avatar of Vishnu), are as murky as Homer's. But historians estimate that he wrote this book in
about 1000 BC. The laws of caste are laid down in its papers, and the concept of *karma*
explained. Hanuman, the monkey god, also makes his first appearence here. The actual story
centres around a hero, Rama, and his fight with the demon Ravana.

The *Bhagavad Gita*. During one moment of an episode in the *Mahabarata*, the god Krishna, for
Rama before one of the great battles betweeen the Pandavas and the Kauravas, utters the divine
ballad that makes up this great book. Written some centuries after the *Mahabharata*, the
Bhagavad Gita is thought to be the precursor of the more detailed *Upanishads* (*see* below).

The *Upanishads*. A later ancient text thought to be contemporary with the Athenian *Age of
Greece*, this is a book of moral teachings and spiritual disciplines, rather than an epic
mythology. The *Upanishads* cover every aspect of spirituality, from the power of speech—for
example, vowels represent the spirit of consciousness (Indra), while consonants represent
physical matter or death—to *karma* and rebirth. The vedic sciences such as massage, medicine
and yoga are explained, along with Tantra and other paths to enlightenment.

Frawley, David, *From the River of Heaven* (Moyilal Barnasidass Publishers, Delhi, 1992). It's
bit cheeky to put this modern book alongside the ancient texts, but this handbook covers it
all—explaining concisely the meaning of the *vedas* as well as the various systems of yoga,
ayurveda, tantra and the other mystical paths to enlightenment.

History and Culture

Jung, Anees, *Unveiling India* (Penguin, 1987). A short book, this deals exclusively with
Indian women and their response to the changing world around them. Anees Jung was born
into a traditional Muslim family in Hyderabad, yet became a successful businesswoman.
Marriage, widowhood, grinding labour, sexual servitude are balanced against examples of
women in marriages, both traditional and 'progressive', that work. One of the few texts that
gives any real idea of what it means to be a woman in India.

Ley, C. D. (ed.), *Portuguese Voyages* (Everyman Library, 1960). Contains the journal of
Vasco de Gama who rounded South Africa's Cape of Good Hope and 'discovered' the coast
of Kerala in 1498. The Portugueses' misunderstandings and wranglings with the rulers of

Further Reading

Calicut, and their wars against the Bahmani Sultans in Goa make for stirring, sometimes
humorous reading.

Malgonkar, Manohar, *The Devil's Wind* (Penguin 1989). Beautifully written, this historical novel tells the story of Nana Sahib, the reluctant leader of the rebel armies during the Indian Mutiny of 1857.

Nehru, Jawarhalal, *The Discovery of India* (Oxford Press, 1989). Written by India's first prime minister and originally published in 1946, this book is a historical classic. In the words of the publisher, it 'unfolds the panorama of India's past and seeks to analyse the sources of India's national personality and how she fits into the modern world'. The book covers 5000 years of history, from the Indus Valley civilization through the major dynasties—Hindu, Buddhist and Muslim, then from the time of the British Raj to the post-War period.

Tindall, Gillian, *City of Gold,* (Penguin, 1992). An excellent history of Bombay.

Venkatesa Iyangar, Masti, *Chikaveera Rajendra,* (Penguin, 1992). This historical novel is set in Coorg, a small kingdom in modern Karnataka, during the early 1830s. Having been tyrannized by an abusive rajah for too long, the Coorgis decide to invite the British in to settle matters and an intricate web of intrigue follows. Iyangar was a prolific writer in Kannada, the Karnatic language, and this book, his last, was published six years after his death.

Travel

Brown, Robin, *Deccan Tamasha,* (Wander World, 1993). Independently published by the eccentric author, this can be difficult to get hold of—at present only the Travel Bookshop in Blenheim Crescent, London W11 stocks it. But get hold of a copy if you can. The short book describes the author's journey across the dry Deccan Plateau of inland southern India on an old motorbike. The word *tamasha* means 'show' and the author treats both himself and the people he meets as characters in a show put on for their mutual enjoyment. Yet the writing is humble rather than patronizing, and in parts very funny.

Murphy, Dervla, *On a Shoestring to Coorg* (Flamingo, 1995). Murphy took her five-year-old daughter to this remote mountain corner of southwest Karnataka and dicovered one of the loveliest rural landscapes in all India. Travelling through the region's forests and coffee plantations, the Tibetan refugee settlements, racehorse studs, experimental farms, market towns, the book comes to no conclusions about India, but provides a well-written objective picture of the rural south and a Westerner's reactions to it.

Fiction

Banerji, B., *Pather Panchali, The Song of the Road,* (Lokamaya Press, 1987). Told through the eyes of Opu, a boy born into a high-caste but impoverished family in southern Bengal, this book provides an insight into Indian village life and the intricacies of caste and family bonding. There are few other books that understand and express the child mind so well.

Kipling, Rudyard, *The Jungle Book* (Everyman, 1994). No book better describes India's wild forests, nor deals so intimately with their natural history. Read it while you visit the wildlife sanctuaries of the Western Ghats.

Kipling, Rudyard, *Plain Tales from the Hills* (Penguin, 1990). Though most of these stories are set in northern or central India, it would be hard to find a book that comes close in terms of describing the European experience in India.

Markandaya, Kamala, *Nectar in a Sieve* (Jaico, Bombay, 1993). Set in rural south India, this novel charts the life of a poor village woman as she and her family try to adapt to the rapid industrialization of their old way of life. Powerful and beautifully written, the book gives an idea of how hard life is for poor Indians, yet reveals how rich is their culture, which sustains them even in times of famine and destitution.

Markandaya, Kamala, *Possession* (Jaico, Bombay, 1984). A wealthy English woman discovers a boy artist in a village in Tamil Nadu and forces her Indian friend to help her take the boy to England for training. Set in London, Madras and the plains of the Coromandel, *Posession* deals with the mutual fascination of European and Asian culture.

Mukundan, M. (ed.), *The Namaste Book of Indian Short Stories* Vol I and II, (UBSPD, Delhi, 1994). Many of these stories are set in the south. Of particular note are three stories from Vol II: *A Day with Charulata,* by Anupama Niranjana, which tells the story of a woman novelist of low birth trapped in a Karnataka village; *The Bison,* by Kunal Verma, which recounts an adolescent boy's hunting trip into the jungles of the lower Nilgiri Hills; and *Old Fateh,* by Subhadra Sangupta, a story of quiet rebellion told by a eunech at the court of Aurangzeb, the last great Mughal emperor.

Roa, Ranga, *Fowl Filcher* (Penguin, 1987). An often hilarious novel of India's slow decline into chaos in the decades following the Raj, seen through the eyes of an ineffectual, easily led country boy who gets caught up in other peoples' adventures. The mood of the book becomes increasingly sombre but there are some truly funny scenes and the book gives a Western reader a glimpse of the Indian way of looking at things—confusing though this may be.

Chapter headings and main references are in **bold** type; page numbers of maps are in *italics.*

Index